DATE DUE

DEMCO 38-296

THE OTHER JAPAN

Japan in the Modern World

Series Editor: Mark Selden

The calligraphy that graces the title page and section title pages is by Kyoko Selden. Most of the other graphics and their captions were provided by Nancy and Bill Doub of the *Bulletin of Concerned Asian Scholars.*

THE OTHER

JAPAN

Conflict, Compromise,
and Resistance
Since 1945

New Edition

Edited with an introduction by
Joe Moore for the **Bulletin of
Concerned Asian Scholars**

An East Gate Book

M.E. Sharpe
Armonk, New York
London, England

The other Japan

Gate Book

The Other Japan: Conflict, Compromise, and Resistance since 1945 is a substantially rewritten and expanded version
of *The Other Japan: Postwar Realities* edited in 1988 by E. Patricia Tsurumi for the *Bulletin of Concerned Asian
Scholars* from articles published in that journal. Six of the original fifteen articles have been retained (chapters 1, 3–6,
and 10). Eight more recently published articles from the *Bulletin* have been selected for inclusion (chapters 2, 8–9, and
11–15). Two articles (chapters 7 and 16) are published here for the first time.

The two articles published here for the first time are Muto Ichiyo's (chapter 7) and Joe Moore's conclusion (chapter
16). Of the fourteen articles previously published in the *Bulletin of Concerned Asian Scholars*, three have been
substantially revised or updated: Ohno Kazuoki's 1992 article (chapter 8), Rob Steven's 1988 article (chapter 9), and
Kenneth J. Ruoff's 1993 article (chapter 14). The remaining articles are listed below with their year of publication in
the *Bulletin:* Joe Moore's (chapter 1), 1985; John Price's (chapter 2), 1991; Brett de Bary's (chapter 3), 1974; Tamae
K. Prindle's (chapter 4), 1985; Brian (Daizen) Victoria's (chapter 5), 1980; Christopher Stevens's (chapter 6), 1985;
Yuki Tanaka's (chapter 10), 1986; Atsumi Reiko's (chapter 11), 1988; John Lie's (chapter 12), 1994; Watanabe
Kazuko's (chapter 13), 1994; and Richard H. Minear's (chapter 15), 1991.

Library of Congress Cataloging-in-Publication Data

The other Japan : conflict, compromise, and resistance since 1945 /
edited with an introduction by Joe B. Moore for the
Bulletin of concerned Asian scholars.—New ed.
p. cm.
"An East Gate Book."
Includes bibliographical references and index.
ISBN 1-56324-867-0 (alk. paper).—ISBN 1-56324-868-9 (pbk. : alk. paper)
1. Japan—Social conditions—1945–   .
2. Japan—Economic conditions—1945–   .
I. Moore, Joe, 1939–   .
II. Bulletin of concerned Asian scholars.
HN723.5.O76   1996
306′.0952—dc20
96-35872
CIP

Printed in the United States of America

The paper used in this publication meets the minimum requirements of the
American National Standard for Information Sciences—
Permanence of Paper for Printed Library Materials,
ANSI Z 39.48-1984.

BM (c)   10   9   8   7   6   5   4   3   2   1
BM (p)   10   9   8   7   6   5   4   3   2   1

Contents

Introduction

Japan in the nineties appears to the world to be tarnished, perhaps badly flawed. For a decade or more the treatment of Japan in news spots, articles, and books has become more critical, even harsh, with pundits, politicians, management gurus, and academics switching from urging upon the West wholesale borrowing of Japanese ways to pointing with alarm at the unfairness of Japanese capitalism's way of doing business abroad and at home. The reevaluation of Japan has been driven by changes in the global economic and political situation since the mid 1970s, the most obvious of which have been Japan's rise to global economic power in counterpoint to U.S. economic decline, the emergence of China as the coming capitalist miracle, the breakup of the U.S.S.R. and ending of the Cold War, and, most recently, Japanese economic stagnation in the nineties.

The Japan establishment in the United States has gone from patronizing Japan as an imitator, through acclaiming it as an economic and social miracle to be copied, to attacking it as an adversarial trader with an enigmatic culture alien to liberal values, to bemusement if not sly amusement over Japan's stagnation after the bursting of the "bubble economy" of the 1980s. One thread seems to run through most such broad characterizations—Japan is the "other." Politics, labor relations, the family, relations between the sexes, education, foreign policy—you name it and there is a prominent cultural interpretation of Japanese behavior that sets it apart from the rest of the world as the other, especially from the presumed universality of the "West." A parallel thread is that the "other" within Japan is seen as amounting to a few unfortunates left outside of the embrace of middle-class culture by race or circumstance.

For the writers of the chapters collected here, the "other" is far more concrete than the sweeping and all-inclusive cultural otherness so often used to explain Japan; and far more vital than the developmentalist view that there are always a few victims of progress. The other Japan of this volume stands for the really existing people who make up the majority, not merely a lower-class or deviant fringe alienated from an all-encompassing massive middle class. These are people who lead lives of difficulty, who must struggle to get by and achieve a measure of dignity. The other Japan is neither a class, nor the "people." It is not a coherent social group in the conventional sense, and may best be defined, perhaps, as those men and women who have borne the heaviest costs of the postwar alliance of patriarchy with growth-at-all-costs capitalist development—and who have resisted frontally and indirectly being made victims of a capitalist society careening toward total commodification of human existence.

The women and men of the other Japan stand against a system and an elite that would deny them control over their own circumstances and destinies for the greater good of family, firm, or country. It is made up of a tremendous variety of people and groups who have alternately resisted and been submerged by the tide of commercialization and creeping incorporation of all spheres of life into the sphere of patriarchal corporate capitalism. These are the people who see their farms and villages becoming housing tracts or airports as at Sanrizuka, their fishing villages and coastal waters turned into industrial complexes that poison the environment as at Minamata, and their neighborhoods and shops becoming "mansions" and chain stores. They know the reality of a kind of development that does not reckon human costs in human terms. The other Japan is difficult to define because it is constantly being formed and reformed in a complex interplay of changing elite strategies for achieving economic growth and social control and of recurring efforts from below to regain control of personal lives.

The first fifteen years until 1960 were critical for the survival of Japan's post–World War II democratization. The chapters by Joe Moore and John Price focus on the labor movement, which was both the core of the democratic movement of that time and a bastion against restoration of authoritarian rule. Moore discusses the implications of the spontaneous uprisings from below that challenged capitalist control at its most vulnerable point, the workplace. When the workers' movement of 1945–46 began to link up with other disaffected groups in Japanese society and move toward social revolution, the U.S. occupation authorities threatened to use military force and gave their blessing to a conservative Japanese government determined to contain the democratic revolution within the narrowest possible confines.

The labor movement nevertheless continued to grow at a phenomenal pace, centered in the 1950s in the left-of-center unions in Sohyo (the General Council of Trade Unions), which in cooperation with the Socialist and Communist parties spearheaded the broader social movement fighting to realize the democratic revolution against the conservative counterattack that began in earnest in 1948, with U.S. blessing. The subject of John Price's chapter is the coal-miners' union at the Mitsui Miike Mine that was a pillar of Sohyo. The miners' militance and their ability in a strike to choke off fuel for industry and transport drew the enduring hostility of business and government. Mitsui, the central government, and big business joined hands to crush the Miike union in 1960 with overwhelming force. But the greater casualty was Sohyo, and more generally the democratic movement. As Price sees it, this was the watershed that saw Japanese labor relations shift from militance and class struggle towards compromise and collaboration. The cooperative enterprise unionism that resulted would later be praised as "typically Japanese" and a key component in the economic "miracle."

High-speed economic growth in the 1960s brought higher living standards to Japan, but also carried costs that, because they were primarily to be borne by the other Japan, were initially ignored. One example is the construction industry, which was central to the scrap-and-build policies of the 1960s. Brett de Bary's chapter on day laborers spells out the way a corrupt alliance of big construction companies and labor contractors, in collusion with criminal gangs and the police, created an intricate network of exploitation through subcontractors that still exists today. Periodic attempts to organize against the terrible working conditions and misery of daily life have welled up in Sanya, Kamagasaki, and other day-laborer ghettos scattered around Japan—and have just as regularly been put down with police help, leaving no means for resistance beyond recurrent "riots." Far from sharing in Japan's prosperity, the day laborers have been stigmatized for their misfortune in a postwar culture that values the sanitized salaryman ideal of success above all else.

In contrast to the outcaste badge of "otherness" that the day laborers are compelled to wear as a condition of their ghetto life, the young women who were entering the office to work in large numbers in the 1960s were culturally defined as insiders by virtue of their assignment to the family as wives, mothers, and care givers. Their insider status in the office was strictly limited to service, however, and terminated decisively upon marriage. "Silver Sanctuary," Tamae Prindle's translation of Shimizu Ikkō's 1969 story about the tensions in a branch bank, reveals how tightly women have been hedged with cultural expectations that are nominally "traditional," but selectively reinforced by business to serve narrow profit interests. Prindle remarks that the name of Shimizu's tragic heroine is Yoko, which suggests the meaning of one who serves. In the end, the service of a woman like Yoko to her enterprise family was to be both fleeting and subordinate to her primary social role in a salaryman's family as wife and mother, thereby freeing her husband for total dedication to his company family.

The salaryman/husband, too, did not arrive fully fledged on the wings of the economic miracle. His self- and family-sacrificing dedication to the enterprise family had to be carefully nurtured. The recent past of bitter strikes lasting months, of reprisals and mass sackings, of fighting with company thugs and the police had touched office workers as well as workers on the factory floor. Brian (Daizen) Victoria's chapter lays out with exceptional clarity one variant of the cultural strategy that business has followed of carefully selecting certain fragments of Japanese "tradition" to cultivate extraordinary commitment to the capitalist enterprise. In this case it is Zen training for new employees that is used as a means of bending the individual to the group. Victoria draws a parallel between Zen training and military basic training (also used by some corporations), the common object of both being the breaking down of individual differences and the merging of employee/soldier/monk in the transcendent "enterprise" of which he is to be a part. Fads come and go, but the image of the wholly dedicated "corporate warrior" is one of the most common cliches of postwar Japan precisely because it approximates reality.

The efforts of the day laborers, office women, salarymen, and others who were building the economy were at least visible to anyone who looked, if only in the crass economic calculation commonly used to measure worker productivity and corporate profits. Those who bore the cruelest burdens of high-speed economic growth in the mercury, cadmium, and other poisons wracking their bodies did not even register on the consciousness of Japan's elite. The chapter translated by Christopher Stevens from Ishimure Michiko's book, *Bitter Sea, Pure Land,* puts before the reader the boy Yamanaka Kuhei in his pain and suffering—and asks the question of the social costs of all-out, unregulated capitalist development by examining the case of the Chisso Corporation, which polluted the seas around Minamata with mercury. Business and government officials conspired with university researchers in a cynical attempt to suppress that knowledge and evade pinpointing responsibility for as long as possible. Though the extract here does not address these issues directly, it is possible to see in the narrative how complete the ascendance of the ideology of high-speed economic growth and enterprise familism was. Members of the community found it easier to blame the Minamata victims for their plight than the company. If the disease could be blamed on unsanitary conditions or inferior family stock, there would be no need to confront Chisso and run the risk of economic hurt to the community from closure of the plant.

By the end of the 1960s, the elite's strategy of growth was under attack from several directions. Social protest reached new heights in the antiwar and student movements at the end of the 1960s. Women began to examine their position and formulate radical interpretations of the female role in Japanese society, as Muto Ichiyo's chapter[*] in Part III on the women's movement shows. Tanaka Mitsu's writings laid bare the intertwined connections between capitalist developmentalism and the patriarchal social relations at the center of the division of labor that fostered high-speed economic growth. She brought into the open the fundamental split between male and female roles so crucial to the regime of high-speed growth that requires men to efface themselves for the corporate cause and demands that women efface themselves in support of corporate men as mothers and as sexual beings. Growth and development came under harsh attack as well for the social and environmental destruction that came in their wake. Underneath the storm of protest, Japanese society was being transformed by pressure from the

---

[*]This chapter by Muto Ichiyo is part of a book-length manuscript on Japanese social movements that the author is preparing for publication. The editor would like to thank the author for permission to use this extract.

changing international division of labor in the 1970s, as is apparent in the chapters on agriculture and the move of business into Southeast Asia in Part IV.

Ohno Kazuoki documents the process whereby agriculture and rural communities were sacrificed to high-speed economic growth in order to free rural labor to move into industry, on the one hand, and to provide a market for U.S. agricultural products, on the other. It would be hard to overestimate the effect of the mass exodus of young men and women to jobs and crowded apartments in the booming industrial cities, where they would be increasingly fed by food brought into the country from the United States and more recently Australia. While business managers and government officials were extolling the traditional values of rural Japan to urban workers, their policies were in fact destroying that older way of life. It can be debated whether Japan should have aimed at self-sufficiency in food and should have in some way protected that rural way of life and made it easier. But, as Ohno makes clear, there was no public, democratic debate, any more than there was a debate about giving business carte blanche to dump its wastes on the public.

Japan's entry into the new international division of labor that was coming into being in the 1970s is the subject of Rob Steven's chapter. Steven's focus is Southeast Asia, but the same dynamic that stimulated the export of capital and industry to Southeast Asia in search of profitable investments and sources of cheap labor led to a global strategy of development based on gigantic multinational corporations. This trend foretold a further transformation of Japanese society from one organized around industrial production toward one based on a so-called postindustrial service economy. As Steven shows, a substantial part of Japan's smokestack industries and labor-intensive operations went to the ASEAN countries, in step with a decline in the industrial labor force that had been a large part of the core of the union movement. Reflecting on these changes, academics, business managers, and government figures began to put forth a tendentious vision of Japan as a "middle-class" or "middle-mass" consensual society sharing a common way of life and a common culture. That vision would become the cliché of the 1980s, one that concealed more than it revealed about the restructuring of Japanese society for capitalist efficiency. The driving force behind the restructuring was the turn of the economy in the late 1970s toward exports as the engine of growth. Simultaneously, business became intent on reducing labor costs in order to make massive exporting possible in ever more competitive world markets, methodically reducing the proportion of the regular lifetime employees.

Yuki Tanaka's chapter on nuclear power plant gypsies focuses on one strategy employers used to replace expensive regular workers, the hiring of male day laborers to do the difficult, dirty, and dangerous work that most Japanese would no longer undertake for low wages. The gypsies face a grim prospect for the future, cancer due to deliberate overexposure to radiation while doing maintenance and repairs on reactors. The resemblance to the day laborers of Sanya is hardly accidental, for the means were the same: recruitment through gang-dominated labor contractors, complex subcontracting arrangements that allowed prime contractors to evade responsibility, and mobilization of unskilled and comparatively old workers, especially from vulnerable groups like *burakumin* (outcasts), ex-miners, and retirees in need of income. Tanaka's chapter reminds us that the most "traditional" labor practices may coexist with the most modern of industries, all but invisible owing to the dominance of ideological constructions like enterprise familism and middle-mass society.

The influx of millions of new women workers in the 1980s certainly qualified the dominant image of the 1960s of young women working in office jobs until marriage led to a permanent commitment to homemaking and child rearing. Reiko Atsumi's chapter shows that the great bulk of the increase in women's employment came from married women in their late thirties or early 1940s returning to work in low-paid, part-time positions lacking job security or benefits. Women's continued acceptance of such jobs is in part due to financial necessity and in part due to the constant reinforcement of the idea that the wife's primary responsibility is to care for her children, her husband, and his parents so that the salaryman/husband can give his all to the enterprise family as it engages in economic war with Japan's competitors. Atsumi explains how business, in a self-interested interpretation of women's primary role as wife and mother, characterizes women's work as merely supplemental to the family income and acceptable only insofar as it does not interfere with the woman's proper role as wife and mother. That is, women's work is naturally part-time work because it can be scheduled around family responsibilities.

A primary reason that business sought out married women for part-time factory and service jobs from the mid-1970s onward was that the rural communities had mostly been drained of young people, leaving no other obvious pool of cheap labor within Japan. Cheap labor from overseas was another matter. Although it soon became tempting, it was rejected at first as incompatible with Japan's presumed homogeneous society and as likely to bring the same sorts of problems as the "guest" workers of Europe. John Lie's chapter makes the point that foreign workers began entering Japan in substantial numbers in the 1980s, the vast majority at first being women brought in by gang-controlled international labor contractors, often under false pretenses, to work as bar hostesses and prostitutes. By the 1990s the number of immigrants had increased substantially and become overwhelmingly men in search of work. Their poverty made them willing to endure miserable wages and working conditions in order to send money back home. Yet in 1990 their total number was still small, around half a million, a mere fraction of a percent of Japan's population. Lie distinguishes two dimensions to what by this time was being termed the foreign worker "problem." One was exploitation by the criminal gangs that recruited them and by the sweatshop operators who profited from them. The other was the challenge that the presence of foreign workers presented to the dominant ideology that routinely explained

Japan's "unique" customs in terms of racial and cultural homogeneity. Foreign workers, male or female, thus carry a double vulnerability that makes them all the more useful as a marginal workforce easily used and easily cast aside.

The elite restructuring of Japanese society for efficiency in the 1980s carried the day, but did not go unopposed. Resistance came from many quarters, such as locally based and oriented groups in opposition to nuclear power and to destructive "development" projects. Networks in support of cooperative production and distribution of natural foods sprang up. At the national level there was a push for equality of employment opportunity for women and vocal opposition to sexist and patriarchal treatment of women in the media. The chapters in Part VI address two important issues of the 1980s and 1990s with wider implications for resistance. Watanabe Kazuko discusses the 1990s movement for redress for the "comfort women" forced into sexual slavery for the Japanese military in World War II. The story is horrifying to relate, but forces attention to the all-too-many practices of the present—such as sex tourism—that spring from similar roots. One of the most distinctive features of the movement for redress for the comfort women is that it is organized across national borders to bring together women activists from many parts of Asia. She points hopefully toward an emerging global women's movement that is encouraging women to cooperate in putting a stop to trafficking in women. Watanabe directs attention to the necessity for taking action to change social structures today in order to end the commodification of women's bodies and violence against women, not only in Japan but in other countries as well.

The citizens' movement in Zushi City that Kenneth Ruoff discusses operated at a very different level and on a smaller scale. Its original goal was saving the Ikego Forest (about 700 acres of bushland) from development as housing for U.S. Navy personnel from the Yokosuka Naval Base. Although the lightning rod for the eleven-year struggle was the mayor of Zushi City, the social force behind him was a dedicated local grass-roots movement that soon went beyond the Ikego Forest battle (which they lost) to larger issues of environmental protection, elimination of racial discrimination, and governmental reform. Ruoff points to the relatively young supporters of the Zushi citizens' movement. He sees their actions as springing from a genuine commitment to the principles of democracy that animated the democratic revolution following World War II, a view in sharp contrast to the gloomy forecasts of those who say material prosperity has sapped the democratic vision in Japan.

It is fitting that this section should end with the poetry of Kurihara Sadako. In these translations by Richard Minear, there can be no mistaking the power of Kurihara's poems, a central theme of which is the hypocrisy of power, ultimately symbolized by the emperor. She carries a message of hope for the future, even as she speaks of the horrors of the past and the dangers of failing to overcome the dead hand of "traditions" selected as means for enhancing authority.

The tremendous diversity of social and political movements in postwar Japan should not be allowed to divert the eye from the central problem that runs through them all—the fundamental need and desire of those who constitute the "other Japan" to make the crucial decisions that determine the circumstances of their own lives at home, at work, and in the community at large. That need and desire can be seen in the miners' struggle at Miike, in the resistance of the day laborers of Sanya, in the women's movement, and at the grass roots in Zushi City. It is the striving for realization of these ends that holds out hope for constructing a society that respects otherness, that will no longer tolerate the manipulation of otherness as a weapon for creating divisiveness and inequity.

I

New Day—Old Conflict

John Price's "The 1960 Miike Coal Mine Dispute" describes the turning point for adversarial unionism in Japan, when tens of thousands of miners at the Miike Coal Mine fought for their jobs and their union's survival in battles over possession of the mine facilities. When Mitsui mailed discharge notices to 1,492 Miike workers on 5 January 1960, the strikers decided to return the notices and used the above helicopter to drop them into the heavily guarded company headquarters. After the Miike battles Japanese labor relations shifted from militance and class struggle toward the compromise and cooperation that became key components of Japan's economic "miracle." This photo is from a Miike union publication, *Miike toso no kiroku* (A record of the Miike struggle) (Omuta, Miike Tanko Rodo Kumiai, 1985), and it is reprinted here courtesy of John Price.

On the opposite page, newspaper and communications workers demonstrate in front of the Yomiuri headquarters in Tokyo on 24 June 1946 to show their support of the Yomiuri employees' successful takeover of this large newspaper. Joe Moore's "Production Control: Workers' Control in Early Postwar Japan" discusses the significance of the Yomiuri uprising and other early postwar protests from below that challenged capitalist control at its most vulnerable point, the workplace. This photo is from *Senryo to minshu undo* (The Occupation and people's movements) (Tokyo: Sanseido, 1975), vol. 10 of *Nihon minshu no rekishi* (The history of the Japanese people), p. 90.

1

Production Control: Workers' Control in Early Postwar Japan

*Joe Moore**

Introduction

When the Allied Occupation of Japan began in September 1945 neither the Japanese nor the Americans knew for certain what the eventual outcome would be for Japanese society. It might seem in retrospect that the only real possibility was the type of liberal reform of Japanese society that actually took place. Yet at that time there were many in both countries who feared an early return to fascist repression, while others were equally alarmed about a communist revolution.

The American scholars who have long dominated the study of the Occupation in the West have not taken such concerns seriously. Virtually transfixed by the Japanese "economic miracle," they have concentrated singlemindedly on finding the secret ingredients in the modernization of Japanese capitalism that took place during the decade and a half following World War II. Indeed, they scoff at the suggestion that there might have been some other outcome. Others, following the lead of Edwin O. Reischauer, have carefully constructed a chain of causality linking the democratic trends of the twenties with the supposed postwar political and economic democratization of Japan under American tutelage, all but ignoring the legacy of the period of fascism and the postwar reaction of the Japanese people to the long years of oppression. The natural consequence of this selective approach has been the loss of the sensitivity the scholar ought to have to paths not taken and possibilities unfulfilled. Instead, what eventually did happen in Japan has come to be regarded as what had to happen, a way of looking at things that is both convenient and satisfying for the American purveyors of this brand of establishment orthodoxy.

*I would like to gratefully acknowledge the help of a number of people who read this chapter in its various forms—Helen Chauncey, Bill Doub, John Dower, Ben Kerkvliet, Bob Marks, and Rob Steven—but I bear the sole responsibility for its faults.

The charge of writing history without people has been made in other contexts, but has truly been the case here. The flesh and blood of mass firings and joblessness, destitution and hunger, bitter strikes and union busting, political struggle and government repression has been submerged in dry statistics and abstract theory. The revolutionary ferment of the times has not come through, and the depth of the postwar crisis of capitalism in Japan has not yet been appreciated.

It takes only the briefest consideration of the vast differences separating Japanese society as it was before the war from what it came to be after the Occupation to see what a wrench was needed to "modernize" the country. The liberal reform of Japanese capitalism was in no sense automatic and only became possible at all through the combination of a catastrophic war and a foreign occupation. There was no preordained course toward liberal capitalism before Japan in late 1945, but a number of alternatives, the likely realization of which changed in response to changes in the strength and immediate interests of the three major participants in the battle to control the course of Japan's reconstruction: the Supreme Command for the Allied Powers (SCAP), the conservative economic and political establishment, and the working class.

Insofar as war and occupation had created a situation of flux by breaking the hold of the established elites in the economy and politics of Japan, thereby granting the working class increased freedom of action, it became an open question which road to reconstruction Japan would eventually follow. As the Japanese recognized at the time, the confrontation of labor and capital did indeed admit a number of different resolutions, ranging from a straightforward restoration of the prewar economic and political order to the establishment of a democratic people's republic.

Labor and capital fought it out, socialism versus capitalism, during the first nine months of reconstruction. The most outstanding characteristic of this period from August 1945 through May 1946 was that the working class went on the offensive while capital lost its nerve and sought refuge in a wait-and-see policy of economic retrenchment and political passive resistance. By May 1946 SCAP felt compelled to make common cause with the Japanese government in turning back the working-class challenge.

The impulse toward change from below was expressed most clearly in the early postwar attempts of wage workers to gain control over the workplace and to realize security and dignity in their personal lives through production control (*seisan kanri*)—the seizure and operation of a workplace by its employees for their own interests. This became both symbol and means for the broader social movement in 1945–1946, just as unionization assumed the central place for the working class thereafter. The society toward which Japanese workers were moving in the spring of 1946, when production control was spreading rapidly, cannot be fully known, however, for the simple reason that this drive for radical change was turned back. The workers' movement developed within a capitalist, occupied Japan and thus can give only a partial indication of what promised to become an alternative form of social organization. Nevertheless, such an indication can be seen.

The orthodox interpretation ignores this first phase in the postwar history of the working class, concentrating instead on the 1 February 1947 General Strike. Here Western scholars often have depicted the General Strike as the peak of a narrowly based revolutionary movement, the frustration of which by SCAP turned the tide back toward the essential moderation and conservatism of both the Japanese populace and their leaders. This shift has been viewed as marking the beginning of a policy transition within SCAP from democratization to economic reconstruction. In 1947–1948 conservatism and retrenchment became by-words following the initial period of quasi-revolutionary reforms inspired by the New Deal legacy in America. In this interpretation, the U.S. government and SCAP were clearly the active elements, defining not only the conditions for the conservative resurgence but also the conditions for the leftist challenge by extending to the Japanese an unaccustomed freedom of action which was used irresponsibly. Accordingly, the SCAP ban on the 1 February General Strike has been treated by many establishment authors as a legitimate action against leftist excesses.

It should be noted that the shift toward reconstruction has not been viewed as a rolling back of democratic reforms already implemented. Rather, it has been argued that the reforms had already provided the essential preconditions for the orderly development of American-style political and economic pluralism in Japan. In effect, all that remained to do from 1947 to ensure the institutionalization of the reforms was to put the economy back on its feet, as was supposedly done over the next few years.

One does not have to be Japanese to wonder if the Japanese people were truly as passive or malleable as this interpretation implies. That Japanese appear to come on stage and retreat to the wings in response to SCAP initiatives says less about Japanese "docility" than it does about the inadequacies of a problem consciousness and periodization that consistently place SCAP's activities and U.S. interests center stage. To mention but two groups, both the corporate giants *(zaibatsu)* leaders and the workers showed themselves to be determined from the outset to gain the upper hand in defining the course reconstruction would take. They engaged in a long series of bitter conflicts outside of SCAP control, though not immune to SCAP interference. Needless to say, this ill accords with the prevailing American interpretation of Occupation history.

The usual two-stage, America-centric interpretation that has dominated the field distorts the meaning of events even during the first phase of the Occupation, when the majority of the reforms were enacted. Accordingly, it will be abandoned here, and the following periodization used, one focusing on the working class as it experienced the broad economic and social changes taking place within Japanese society. Although this chapter deals with only the first of the three periods, it may be helpful to present an overview in order to give a sense of the general context within which the argument is posed.

Workers' Control

The early months after surrender (August 1945–May 1946) brought widespread popular revolutionary challenge to the old order by industrial workers, peasants, and impoverished city people. This period extended from surrender through the mass demonstrations in May against Premier-to-be Yoshida Shigeru. The first half of the period (August through January) began quietly but saw increasingly open expression of popular discontent practically everywhere and the first faltering steps toward organization. Workers on the shop floor sounded the keynote by spontaneously turning from ineffective strikes to production control (*seisan kanri*). A major part of their intent was to carve out a substantial degree of workers' control within the enterprises, but within the bounds of legality as defined by the liberal reforms being implemented by SCAP.

The second half of the period (February through May) was characterized by explosive growth in workers' organizations and the imminent transformation of production control into a revolutionary movement acting in disregard of capitalist legality. The situation was the more volatile because of the tentative coalescence of a broad popular movement around the industrial workers. By May 1946 the wider movement was gathering momentum. Goaded beyond endurance, urban and rural people were taking direct action at the point of production and distribution. Their immediate aims were worker control over industry in order to bring about the resumption of production in the face of a capitalist sit-down, peasant control over the compulsory delivery of staple foods to the state for rationing, and popular control over the rationing system itself.

The popular challenge to a capitalist reconstruction reached its peak in the mass actions of April and May, but it was burdened by a vacillating and foot-dragging national leadership which fell to pieces when confronted by SCAP opposition on 20 May. On that day, General MacArthur publicly threatened the suppression of the popular movement in a strong statement on mass demonstrations. The reinvigorated Japanese business and government elite, now assured of SCAP support for its continuation in power, went on the counterattack. With SCAP's backing they turned back the movement for workers' control. Thus the real beginnings of what has come to be called the "reverse course"—the halting or rolling back of democratic reforms proclaimed at the outset of the occupation—occurred in May 1946 and not February 1947.

Industrial Unionism

From spring 1946 to spring 1947 the working class and small farmers, foregoing their previous anti-capitalist demands for popular control over vital areas of the economy, turned toward defending and extending their own particular interests within the capitalist economic reconstruction that was now seen as inescapable. A decent job, an adequate food ration, and a share in the distribution of land became central concerns. Workers turned toward the union as the means for securing their rights and their livelihood within the capitalist order. But not all wage workers succeeded in unionizing, and not all unions were militant. The turn to trade unionism, therefore, meant a narrowing of the inclusive scope of the working-class movement of the spring. Organized labor hereafter avoided anti-capitalist direct action such as had typified production control and instead pressed conventional economic demands for union contracts, better wages, and job security, using the strike as the prime means of persuasion.

Big business and government leaders had already shown their determination not to knuckle under to the national federations of the unions, but to make the enterprise the fundamental unit for bargaining with organized labor. In order to counter this effort the leftist majority in the labor movement consolidated behind Sambetsu (Zen Nihon Sangyōbetsu Rōdō Kumiai Kaigi, Congress of Industrial Unions), and mounted an offensive in the second half of 1946 to establish the power of national union federations built upon a federation of subordinate enterprise locals. When the struggle escalated into an attempt to topple the vehemently anti-labor Yoshida government, SCAP once again stepped in. SCAP's prohibition of the 1 February 1947 General Strike was a major defeat that destroyed the chance for a unification of Sambetsu and Sōdōmei (Nihon Rōdō Kumiai Sōdōmei, Japan Federation of Labor) into one national organization for labor—a unification that had seemed within reach in midwinter. By preventing the unification of the unions, the SCAP doomed as well the fight to make industrial unions the basic means for worker organization in Japan. Although the national federations affiliated with Sambetsu held their own for a time after the failure of the General Strike, no doubt because a socialist premier had succeeded Yoshida, big business had in fact regained the initiative. This would become clear in early 1948.

Enterprise Unionism

Finally, during the period from spring 1947 to summer 1950, Sambetsu was broken and the enterprise union, Japan's contribution to industrial relations, was created. From 1947, the leftist labor unions had come under attack from within by so-called democratization leagues which claimed to represent rank-and-file discontent with the policies of left-wing leaders. There undoubtedly was dissatisfaction with the left, and resentment over communist influence, but the splits and bitterness resulting from the democratization movement served the employers' interests far more than the interests of any other group, except, perhaps, labor's right wing. These internal difficulties were compounded in 1948 by anti-labor legislation designed to cripple the strong public-employee unions that were the mainstay of the left and to permit big business and government employers to make mass dismissals as part of a program of economic retrenchment considered to be essential before recovery could begin.

The leftist labor federations proved unable to overcome internal disunity and fend off the damaging changes in labor laws and mass firings of union members that followed. The disarray the big business and government attack produced in the labor movement abetted the splitting of leftist unions by the democratization leagues working in close cooperation with management. This frequently resulted in the setting up of rival, "second" unions at the enterprise level to which management at once granted sole recognition. This period closed with an open red purge that put out of action those leftist party and labor leaders who had been putting up the greatest resistance to the reverse course in labor reform. Thus the attempt to establish industrial unionism went to defeat, and Japanese workers were driven back into the framework of weak and isolated enterprise unions.

The Old Order in Disarray

Yoshida Shigeru, who became prime minister in May 1946, characterized the period in which he came to power as revolutionary. In so doing, he had several things in mind—among them the resurgent Communist Party and the massive street demonstrations—but the main object of his concern was the phenomenon of worker seizure and operation of mines, factories, and offices, and production control. This situation was not at all unique to postsurrender Japan. Rather, those developments were of much the same nature as the factory occupations in Leningrad, Berlin, and Turin of some twenty-five years before. As European workers had done after World War I in Europe, large numbers of Japanese workers after World War II stood up to protest their situation, to make the radical demand for workers' control, and to take over and run their enterprises through their own system of councils.

The crisis of the old order was played out in circumstances of seemingly bewildering complexity. Big business was internally divided into conflicting liberal and conservative camps, and the governing bureaucracy was similarly split. Communists and socialists fought among themselves while battling the resurrected conservative parties for control of the government. The U.S. occupation headquarters loosed a flood of directives for democratizing Japanese society. Workers, farmers, and city people sought their own answers to the desperate times, organizing in unions and councils, and groping toward a new, populist order. Yet, one question cut through the complexity and provided a shared point of reference for coalitions forming on left and right: how to deal with economic chaos.

Foremost in actual power at the time was the old elite of big businessmen and government officials (from which military elements were now excluded) who were seeking through often contradictory policies a revival of the capitalist economy. Their rivals were party and union leaders advocating competing versions of socialist reconstruction, and a popular movement at the grass roots that the left hoped to lead. The nexus of their conflict was what form economic revival would take—socialist or capitalist. No one could avoid taking sides for long, and because the stakes over whose vision of economic reconstruction was to prevail were high, the fight was bitter.

When the Occupation began in August 1945, the labor front was peaceful. Measures for control of labor dating back to the Meiji period, and periodically extended as new crises called forth sterner measures, were still in effect in the immediate postsurrender weeks. The fact that surrender took place before war had destroyed the basis of the established social order had far-reaching effects. Until the fall of the Higashikuni Cabinet in early October, the old elite, even without the military, retained its grip on power and saw to it that the police continued to be active in enforcing repressive political and economic controls. With few exceptions the surrender did not bring early actions by workers, for the long decades of oppression had succeeded in uprooting workers' organizations and in undermining the will to resist.[1] Surrender had not brought home to the working class that a new dispensation was at hand. That understanding dawned only in the closing months of 1945, after workers realized just how vulnerable the old political and business leaders were and how greatly the old social order had been undermined by the disastrous war. In October 1945 SCAP made its contribution to kicking the props out from under the old regime by abolishing many repressive laws and organizations,[2] thereby clearing the way for the long-pending confrontation between capital and labor.

It has become a truism that business circles during the early occupation were demoralized, "lost the will to produce," and were unable to act in overcoming Japan's economic problems in the face of shattering defeat and uncertainty over Allied policy for Japan. Big business began a general retrenchment as a hedge against the troubled days ahead. They shut down production and dismissed many workers, while simultaneously trying to corner the remaining supply of essential commodities. These efforts went hand in hand with a looting of the government treasury and the wartime stockpiles of crucial materials, ranging all the way from food and medicine to machinery and precious metals.[3] The refusal by big businesses to produce and invest during the first few years of the occupation was directly related to their having amassed the wherewithal to wait out an extended period of inactivity and uncertainty. Statistics for the period are poor, but industrial activity in the winter of 1945–1946 may have amounted to as little as 10 percent of the 1935–1937 average (see table 1.1). The stoppage caused severe shortages of all kinds, giving rise to a major inflation that cut deeply into wages which were for the most part already below subsistence.

Conditions for blue- and white-collar workers alike were desperate at the time of surrender and steadily worsened with the onset of the first winter of occupation. Wholesale closures of factories resulted in mass dismissals, the effects of which were compounded by the return of several million servicemen and overseas residents. Unemployment soared to a staggering 10–12 million during the winter of 1945–1946, this at a time when Japan's non-agricultural labor force

Table 1.1

Index of Economic Indicators, 1945–46

Year	Month	Bank of Japan Note Issue (million Y)[a]	Tokyo Black Market Price (Consumer Goods) Index (9/45=100)[b]	Average Multiple of Official Price Level	Industrial Production (1935–37=100)[c]	Wage Index	Cost of Living Index (1937=100)[d]	Real Wage Index
1945	June	26,181	—	—	18.1	—	—	—
	Jul	28,456	—	—	12.8	—	—	—
	Aug	42,300	100	—	8.5	—	—	9
	Sep	41,426	92	28.7	9.0	229	2,540	9
	Oct	43,188	112	31.8	13.0	218	2,330	8
	Nov	47,749	128	29.7	13.6	231	2,740	10
	Dec	55,441	170	40.1	13.4	313	3,080	11
1946	Jan	58,566	200	39.8	13.4	452	4,000	14
	Feb	54,342	196	23.7	15.6	606	4,470	15
	Mar	23,323[e]	187	21.3	18.8	740	4,790	18
	Apr	28,173	191	15.1	21.8	827	4,510	18
	May	36,316	201	20.6	25.2	888	4,820	19
	Jun	42,759	200	14.7	25.7	986	5,310	20
	Jul	49,731	—	—	27.6	1,060	5,330	—

[a]Japan Prime Minister's Office, Cabinet Bureau of Statistics, *Japan Statistical Yearbook* (Tokyo: Cabinet Bureau of Statistics, 1949), p. 528.
[b]Bank of Japan, Statistics Department, *Economic Statistics of Japan (Annual)*, 1948 (Tokyo: Bank of Japan), p. 134.
[c]Japan Ministry of Finance and Bank of Japan, *Statistical Yearbook of Finance and Economy of Japan*, 1948 (Tokyo: Ministry of Finance Printing Office), p. 558.
[d]Ohara Shakai Mondai Kenkyūjo, *Saitei Chinginsei no Igi* (Tokyo: Daiichi Pub., 1949), p. 37.
[e]Currency conversion.

was approximately 18 million out of a total work force of roughly 32 million. Unemployment and shortages made the cities all but uninhabitable, and those who could returned to their family villages. The population of Tokyo alone had declined some 4 million by November 1945 to 2.8 million people. Even so, mass starvation loomed in Japan's urban areas as the first winter ended, and was narrowly averted by America's grudging importation of foodstuffs in the spring and summer.[4]

In midwinter all wage workers were driven to protect their jobs against the wave of dismissals and to increase production, but neither could be done by tactics like strikes or slowdowns when there was widespread retrenchment and mass unemployment. Employers were more than ready to meet the workers' challenge in that case simply by locking out strikers or closing down altogether. A strike could hurt only in the most essential industries and services like fuel or transportation, but here the real victims would not be the employers, but the public. Striking could only worsen the general economic situation and earn public hostility. Outside of big-business and government circles the need for production suffused the very atmosphere, and workers knew their personal survival was intimately tied to economic revival. In sum the sit-down by the *zaibatsu* had created conditions which required worker occupation and operation of factories if their twin demands for jobs and production were to be met. Japan's workers did not arrive at their solution of production control overnight; instead they began their efforts in the more orthodox vein of trade unionism.[5]

Business Unionism and Workers' Control

The response of workers and labor organizers to the new conditions began in October when the first postwar unions were formed and disputes began to break out widely (see Tables 1.2 and 1.3). From the outset workers displayed various and often contradictory tendencies regarding the structure of worker organizations and the nature of demands. Postwar worker organizations originated in one of two ways: from spontaneous, shop-floor efforts, and from the efforts of outside organizers representing one of the three basic camps of the prewar union movement.[6]

The second category, unions set up by outside organizers, included on the one extreme an orthodox "business-union" approach epitomized by right-wing social democrats like Matsuoka Komakichi and Nishio Suehiro, who in most cases sought to reimpose prewar-style hierarchical and conservative unions in close coordination with the old elites.[7] On the other extreme, such JCP (Japan Communist Party) leaders as Tokuda Kyūichi and Shiga Yoshio were constructing "red" unions which would take an active political and economic role, if not always a revolutionary one.[8] In between (and largely ineffectual) were those sympathetic with the position of the left wing of the JSP (Japan Socialist Party), who worked to erect a progressive union movement dedicated to a political and

Table 1.2

Rate of Unionization
(cumulative end-of-month totals)[a]

Year	Month	Unions	Membership
1945	Aug.	—	—
	Sept.	2	1,177
	Oct.	9	5,072
	Nov.	75	68,530
	Dec.	509	380,677
1946	Jan.	1,517	902,751
	Feb.	3,243	1,537,606
	Mar.	6,538	2,568,513
	Apr.	8,531	3,023,979
	May	10,541	3,414,699
	June	12,007	3,681,017
	July	12,923	3,814,711
	Aug.	13,341	3,875,272
	Sep.	14,697	4,122,209
	Oct.	15,172	4,168,305
	Nov.	16,171	4,296,589
	Dec.	17,265	4,849,329
1947	Jan.	17,972	4,922,918
	Feb.	18,929	5,030,574[b]

[a]Japan Prime Minister's Office, Cabinet Bureau of Statistics, *Japan Statistical Yearbook,* (Tokyo: Cabinet Bureau of Statistics, 1949)
[b]Membership only exceeds 6 million in December 1947.

economic transformation of Japan within the framework of parliamentary democracy.[9]

An examination of the initial demands of the unions organized from below shows a basic congruence with the immediate (i.e., non-revolutionary) goals set forth by the socialist left as a whole, which may be summed up in the catch phrases of industrial democracy in the workplace and political democracy for the nation. The workers' organizations originating on the shop floor made demands which usually came strikingly close to those already set forth by SCAP, including the right to organize, strike, and negotiate a union contract.[10]

In essence, these were demands for the extension to Japanese workers of basic economic rights possessed by labor in the democratic West. Broad support existed for a minimalist catch-up program for reforming Japan's labor relation establishing the basic conditions for the growth of unions. Indeed, the need was universally recognized in Japan except among conservatives.

Preeminent among conservative elite interests had been *zaibatsu* owners and top executives who pursued a corporate version of laissez faire through powerful

Table 1.3

Types of Dispute Actions and Workers Involved[a]

Year Month	Total		Strikes		Slowdowns		Production Control		Production Control as % of Total	
	A[c]	W[c]	A	W	A	W	A	W	A	W
1945 Aug.	—	b	—		—		—		—	
Sept.	2		2		—		—		—	
Oct.	20		16		3		1		5%	
Nov.	27		21		2		4		15	
Dec.	39		33		3		3		9	
1946 Jan.	49	37,720	27	6,142	9	2,549	13	29,029	26	77%
Feb.	53	29,176	23	6,532	10	6,847	20	15,806	38	54
Mar.	80	79,950	32	48,527	9	10,722	39	20,651	50	26
Apr.	89	50,417	30	14,726	6	840	53	34,815	60	69
May	106	51,295	42	9,047	8	3,401	56	38,847	53	76
June	80	26,707	29	6,735	7	1,916	44	18,056	55	70
July	90	27,346	48	14,721	17	10,147	25	2,478	28	9
Aug.	107	52,282	61	24,054	18	4,983	28	23,245	26	44
Sep.	124	118,242	59	81,368	28	14,484	37	22,390	30	19
Oct.	156	200,729	104	188,958	17	2,633	35	9,138	22	5
Nov.	127	87,488	89	76,563	14	3,262	24	7,663	19	9
Dec.	108	93,496	65	61,361	17	23,569	26	8,566	24	9
1947 Jan.	65	26,050	30	17,491	9	2,316	26	6,243	40	24
Feb.	90	34,600	52	28,101	14	1,462	24	5,037	27	14

[a]Japan Prime Minister's Office, Cabinet Bureau of Statistics, *Japan Statistical Yearbook* (Tokyo: Cabinet Bureau of Statistics, 1949), pp. 730–731; SCAP, ASS, Advisory Committee on Labor, *Final Report: Labor Policies and Programs in Japan* (Tokyo: 1946), p. 35; Miriam S. Farley, *Aspects of Japan's Labor Problems* (New York: The John Day Company, 1950), pp. 83–84.
[b]Figures not available for 1945.
[c]A = Actions. W = Workers.

big-business associations. Instinctively hostile to labor, but hostile also to any government interference in economic planning and to bureaucratic controls over business activity, these groups advocated self-regulation through a structure of monopolies and cartels. Their viewpoint dominated Japanese policy throughout most of the period considered here.[11]

The conservative mainstream was therefore responsible for the earliest and most reactionary approach to economic reconstruction. They sought to recreate the prewar laissez faire era, when *zaibatsu* activity was unfettered by government regulations, and labor was docile, hard working, and cheap. As before, cheap labor was considered a prerequisite for the Japanese economy for two interrelated reasons. Externally, resource-poor Japan desperately needed commodities for export to finance necessary imports of raw materials and technology, and in the past cheap labor had provided the margin for successful competition as an exporter of textiles. Internally, cheap labor had permitted the rapid accumulation of capital necessary to finance industrial expansion and would be even more important to rehabilitate war-devastated industries.[12] To the controlling elite that meant strong labor organizations could not be tolerated, not even business unions.

This attempt by conservatives to recreate prewar labor relations was likely to fail since the political conditions for keeping labor as cheap and docile as it had been in the past no longer existed. SCAP directives ordering the dismantling of the old curbs on civil rights had undermined the legal structure and police apparatus that had served in the past to keep labor under control in the face of harsh exploitation. Furthermore, the United States was actively pursuing its stated policy of encouraging a strong labor movement. Insofar as formation of strong unions guaranteed future demands for higher wages, a rethinking of the overall problem of economic reconstruction was in order, but that was yet to come. When it did it would be undertaken by the more progressive stratum of managers who felt the old-line conservatives were leading Japan to ruin by seeking a confrontation with labor. It would be better to recognize business unionism as a fact of postwar life and plan accordingly.

The Emergence of Production Control

The Japanese workers' advance bears witness to a tremendous desire and capacity to organize. Examples abound of workers spontaneously organizing unions far more quickly than SCAP had intended and striving to end the employers' "divine right" to rule the work force. One of the most original and effective of the tactics workers used to obtain their rights and their demands was production control, a form of struggle that the employees of the *Yomiuri* newspaper originated in late 1945 as part of their fight to democratize their paper.

The link between the official ideology of the state and the point of view of the leading newspapers had drawn closer than ever once war broke out in China. The defense of Japan's national interest soon seemed to require omission of certain kinds of news and eventually the printing of outright falsehoods about Japan's situation at home and abroad. The *Yomiuri* stood in the forefront of the controlled press, under the enthusiastic lead of its president, Shōriki Matsutarō.[13]

In the early 1920s Shōriki had been Director of the Secretariat of the Metropolitan Police Board of Tokyo and a key figure in the surveillance and suppression not only of the activities of the Communist Party in particular, but also of other leftist groups, labor, and Koreans. In 1924 he used contact with influential people in business, government, and politics to buy control of the faltering *Yomiuri*. By tightening control over employees to cut labor costs and raise productivity, and by adopting a policy of sensational yellow journalism, Shōriki made the *Yomiuri* into one of the three largest newspapers in Japan by the late 1930s. He was an ultranationalist who showed a preference for former police or intelligence figures who were staunch anti-communists like himself.[14]

During the war, newspapermen were among the few to have both the intellectual training and the access to hard news that would enable them to pass judgement on the company's activities. The newspaper employees bitterly resented Shōriki's policies for two reasons in particular: the reactionary editorial policy that subordinated news reporting to state propaganda, and the highly authoritarian system of personnel management which was designed to extract maximum work from each employee for minimum pay. When the war ended, both aspects of Shōriki's leadership came under sharp attack, and the *Yomiuri* employees put forward demands for pursuit of war responsibility and internal democratization of the paper, regarding them as at least as important as economic demands for better pay and benefits.[15]

The *Yomiuri* dispute broke out in mid-October 1945 when a group of employees presented Shōriki with demands for the democratization of the company's organization, a shakeup of personnel, acceptance of war responsibility by company officials, and better pay for employees. Shōriki angrily rejected the demands and on the next day called together all officials from the assistant department chiefs up to say:

> I will not permit employees selfseekingly to set up an organization within the company. If you set one up against my will, I will compel your resignations. It is outrageous that some wrong-headed employees are using democracy as an excuse for conspiring something else. This company is mine, and I am utterly determined to stop you.[16]

A few days later, in response, over 1,000 out of a total of 1,875 *Yomiuri* employees turned out en masse to demand the formation of an employees' union, a thoroughgoing democratization of the company's organization, better pay, respect for the employees as human beings, and the collective resignation of all bureau chiefs and higher executives (including Shōriki) on the grounds of war responsibility.[17] Shōriki had no intention of giving in and was determined to break through and establish a pattern at the *Yomiuri* for the settlement of future disputes throughout Japan. For him the *Yomiuri* was in the front line battling against a communist conspiracy to take over Japanese industry.[18]

Shōriki typified the conservative majority among business leaders who detested unions almost as much as they did communists and had feared the resurgence of both after the end of the war. Their ideal of proper labor relations was that of prewar Japan when government oppression kept labor fragmented and weak, and therefore cheap. Such men were unwilling or unable to distinguish militant unionism from communism, and insisted that any erosion of the rights of private property would contribute to the communist goal of destroying the whole capitalist system. Thus Shōriki insisted that his authority must be absolute within the *Yomiuri*, and that the workers' organization being set up was nothing but a front for a communist conspiracy.[19] Shōriki notwithstanding, the Communist party had nothing to do with the origins of the *Yomiuri* dispute, which arose out of the unique situation of the Japanese press during the early occupation.

In the fall of 1945 SCAP was promoting the democratization of the press at the same time that it was insisting that production of newspapers must continue because they were an essential vehicle for Allied policy in general.[20] When SCAP on the one hand said workers must not strike, especially newspaper workers, and Shōriki on the other categorically rejected all demands for reform, the *Yomiuri* workers were placed in a difficult spot. To strike invited trouble, since both the government and SCAP would oppose it, but far worse, a strike could end in the closure of the paper entirely, which Shōriki considered more desirable than handing the company over to the employees.[21]

What could be done? The answer came out of an informal gathering of *Yomiuri* workers at a restaurant on the evening of that day in late October when the mass meeting of employees had served far-reaching demands on Shōriki. One of those present proposed that if it was no good to strike, then:

> . . . why don't we put out the paper ourselves? If we do that we don't have to worry about bankrupting the company. And if we gain the support of the readers by putting out an excellent newspaper, then we can reconstruct the *Yomiuri* as a democratic paper . . .[22]

At that a lively discussion ensued that touched on such things as the prewar Italian and French examples of factory occupation and control. The result was that the editorial staff resolved, if need be, to take control over the editing, printing, shipping, and distribution of the *Yomiuri*.

The next day, Shōriki summarily rejected the demands and ordered the resignation of Suzuki and four others whom he considered to be ringleaders.[23] Suzuki and the others went back to the editorial office to report to the workers. On the spot a second employees' meeting was convened. Suzuki reported and ended by saying, "We are entering a state of dispute in order to achieve our demands. And from the newspaper for the 25th, we are going to put out the paper independently by ourselves." In order to carry this out, the meeting elected a supreme struggle committee with Suzuki as chairman, and decided that supporting struggle committees would be elected in every department. When the meeting ended, the workers, raising shouts of victory, occupied the editorial office and evicted the bureau chiefs. With this the *Yomiuri* newspaper production-control struggle began, the first in postwar Japan.[24]

The day after production control began, 25 October, a meeting of workers set up the *Yomiuri* Newspaper Employees' Union and elected Suzuki chairman, but in the struggle that followed the union did not play an active role. From the outset, real authority lay in the system of struggle committees through which production control was being carried out. The union members and executive committee acted merely as one of the constituent parts of the struggle committee, and the union chairman and standing executive committee had no function. As the production-control struggle progressed, decision-making and executive functions in the struggle-committee system were merged. Whenever a problem came up requiring some kind of action, the struggle committee would call together as many of the workers concerned as it could to discuss the matter. The mass meeting would make a collective decision, and collectively carry it out. In short, the struggle-committee system operated on the basis of direct, participatory democracy.[25]

Under production control the *Yomiuri* took a progressive editorial stance and overnight became the most left-leaning and outspoken of Japan's major newspapers. The new policy gained public approval, and circulation shot up to nearly 1,700,000 copies.[26] Many outside organizations, such as the other newspaper unions, the JSP, and the JCP, rallied to the side of the *Yomiuri* workers.

At first Shōriki was not to be moved, but in December he was finally forced into arbitration. The agreement arrived at on 11 December provided (1) Shōriki would resign and sell all shares he owned in excess of 30 percent of the total stock of the *Yomiuri*; (2) the company would be reorganized as a corporation, allowing a wider distribution of shares; (3) Baba Tsunego (a right-wing socialist and the former editor of the *Yomiuri* Sunday Review Section) was to be the new manager as Shōriki had urged; (4) a management council (*keiei kyōgikai*) on which management and employees were represented equally would be set up to consult on important matters concerning editing and business operations. Other items dealt with such specifics as further consideration of pay raises, withdrawal of dismissals for being active in the struggle, union recognition, collective bargaining, and conclusion of a contract.[27]

An editorial in the *Yomiuri* on 12 December 1945—the day after Shōriki had signed the arbitration agreement—celebrated the "settlement of the *Yomiuri* dispute" and proclaimed a new policy:

> Heretofore the newspaper has been the organ of capitalists, it has oppressed the people, it has published articles that deceived and has suffocated the voice of the people. Now the Yomiuri Shimbun has been freed from this yoke of capital. ... We proclaim that from this day the Yomiuri Shimbun will become truly a friend to the people and an organ of the people for eternity.[28]

The editorial argued that political democratization was meaningless in the absence of economic reform. An economic liberation from below, given impetus by the struggles of the people to stabilize their livelihood, was essential for the realization of a true democratic revolution. The *Yomiuri* now stood ready to support the people in their fight for economic sovereignty. The editorial cited the success of the *Yomiuri* workers in running the paper on their own, despite having to overcome "sabotage" by the company.

After the arbitrated settlement, the members of the supreme struggle committee disbanded the production-control committees and in their place established a similar system based on the management councils the agreement had provided for. The company was democratized and the employees gained unprecedented rights over what was to go into the paper and how the actual process of production was to be conducted. In effect, the reporters and writers were turned loose to dig up their own stories, regardless of how derogatory they were to the government and big business. Typesetters and printers threw out the oppressive system of top-down labor control that Shōriki had introduced in the twenties and took direct control over the printing of the paper. Thus, workers' control became a practical reality at the *Yomiuri*, with the enthusiastic participation of the mass of the employees,[29] who used the "democratic" *Yomiuri* to champion the radical, populist reconstruction of Japan.

The first *Yomiuri* struggle is significant in two ways. First, it shows the importance of the workers' fight in postwar Japan for greater control over the work process at the point of production. The *Yomiuri* employees had asked for the right to participate in management, but their own actions belied those moderate-sounding words both during and after production control. Spearheaded by the editorial bureau, their struggle committees had simply taken over production and distribution at the outset, and after the settlement the employees continued to dominate the paper, this time through the union and the management council.

Second, the widespread societal influence of production control was extraordinary. Even while the dispute was going on, workers and organizers streamed to the Tokyo *Yomiuri* headquarters from all parts of Japan to learn at first hand how to organize themselves and take action. And of course the *Yomiuri* newspaper, with its wide national circulation, carried the message to uncounted others unable to make the pilgrimage to Tokyo. The *Yomiuri* employees had won their dispute, without going out on strike and without interrupting production, by the novel step of dispossessing the owners and managers. The lesson seemed clear. Production was critically needed but so was radical social and economic change. If employers resisted worker demands, victory could still be had by seizing and operating the enterprise.

The Lines of Confrontation

The spread of production control throughout all sectors of Japanese industry contributed greatly to a sharpening of the lines of confrontation between the workers' movement and big business, and between the political extremes of left and right. On the one side was the conservative mainstream of business supported by established politicians and bureaucrats, on the other the radical shop-floor workers' organizations supported by the JCP taking up production control as their primary means of struggle. By midwinter all parts of Japanese society were coming to realize that what was being called into question by the growing economic and political crisis was capitalism itself; the government seemed unable to act even though the economy continued its plunge and threatened to bring on a collapse of tremendous proportions. Reconstruction had to begin but who was to do it and how? Under what conditions and limits? To many Japanese there seemed only two alternatives: a capitalist reconstruction by the holdover conservative establishment, seeking what was in essence a return to the laissez faire twenties, or a socialist reconstruction with the JCP playing a leading part.[30] The polarization was symbolized by two important events in early 1946: the production control and people's court incident of January and February at the Mitsubishi Bibai Coal Mine, and the government's Four Ministry Declaration issued on 1 February denying the legality of production control.

The Mitsubishi Bibai situation was relatively straightforward.[31] The coal miners had set up a union in early November covering all of the 5,000 or so workers of the Mitsubishi mines. Within a week the union sent the company a package of largely economic demands that the company replied to unsatisfactorily. In mid-November the miners struck and gained a very substantial increase in total pay, in the form of a basic wage plus allowances. Then in mid-December, when the government published its new, upwardly revised standards for total pay per worker recommended by the coal industry, the company discovered that it had been paying the miners a rate higher than the new standard, whereupon the company unilaterally deducted the "overpayment" from the workers' December pay and on the same grounds also abolished the special allowance for daily attendance at the mines.

Since the company's action threatened the miners' livelihood, the union hardened its position and submitted a list of eight demands in early January. The most important of these were (1) maintenance of the wage standard previously negotiated; (2) abolition of the contract system (a type of piecework, under which the productivity requirement was high); (3) continuation of the attendance allowance separately from the standard wage; and (4) opposition to the transfer to Tokyo of the refining-section head, who had been popular among the production and staff workers and had aided their efforts to organize unions.

A compromise agreement, negotiated in Sapporo by Assistant General Manager Noda Tōichi and union chairman Mizutani Takashi, conceded a great deal to the company. When the news reached the union, the miners' union repudiated the agreement on the grounds that Mizutani had conducted the negotiations on his own and did not have the authority to make an agreement in the first place. The company took an unbending stand on the wage issue, arguing that the matter had been settled and that in any case it could not exceed the new standard for coal-mine wages since this would cause difficulties at its other mines. Union members then not only reaffirmed their demands but added three more, including one about participation in management. No progress was made and a confrontation became unavoidable.

The union called an extraordinary meeting for 7 February at which the miners voted a list of three key demands: (1) abolition of the contract system for surface and pit workers; (2) inclusion of all existing allowances in the basic wage; and (3) continuation of the attendance allowance in goods "to the bitter end." After the company categorically rejected these demands, union members reconvened and voted to begin production control on the eighth if their demands were not met. The company in turn dismissed that decision as illegal and vowed to defend its management rights "to the bitter end."

The miners next set up a dispute organ (*sōgi dan*), and the four union executives who had been acting as the miners' negotiating committee became the leaders of the dispute organ. They were, by occupation, an outside-the-pit railway worker, a clerk-in-charge in the labor section, a construction-section assistant, and a coal miner. On the eighth the union entered production control at 7:00 AM and dispatched a control committee to the offices and to every workplace. For about ten days all went on much as before, with the staff still accepting instructions from the company and the workers digging coal under the supervision of the staff. Labor productivity and total output increased dramatically.

Due to the company's intransigence, negotiations had been discontinued completely since the workers' takeover, so on 17 February the union called a meeting to discuss the situation. The meeting ended with a resolution to push onward to victory. Afterwards a group of several hundred union members sought out and forcibly seized both General Manager Gōtō Tarō and Assistant General Manager Noda at an executives' clubhouse where the two were in conference with other high officials of Mitsubishi's enterprises in Hokkaidō. The union members forcibly marched the two through the snow to a meeting hall nearly two kilometers away, where the miners sat them down on the stage across the table from the union officials. The workers and their families jammed into the hall and with that began thirty-six hours of nonstop mass negotiations, the famous "people's court" incident.

Soon after the mass negotiations began, the union officials persistently questioned the managers, asking why the company could not pay the workers' wage demands. Noda was backed into a corner from which he tried to extricate himself by an evasive and flippant, "Anyhow, we can't pay it," provoking a torrent of abuse from the workers' assembly. This account of the beginning stages of the people's court by one of the main participants, Nishimura Takeo, catches some of the flavor of the anger of the miners and their families:

> "What's this, you can't pay [the demanded wages]?"
> "We workers are never going to be silenced!"
> "Hey! You managers, you came here to cheat us, didn't you? What about it? Answer!"
> General Manager: "That is not the case."
> "Liar! What about today's tempura?"

"You feed your dogs on white rice; where did you get that rice?"

"You are always cheating us of our sake and drinking it, aren't you? Just look at those red noses!"

In the midst of this twenty-some police poured into the hall with their boots on.

"What's this? Get those cops out of here. They're the capitalists' watchdogs!"

"What kind of thing is this, coming into our hall with your shoes on? Take them off!"

"Take off your hats!"

The crowd of people knew the ugly side of the police, who were in collusion with the capitalists.[32]

SCAP took a hands-off attitude even during the people's court, and the Japanese authorities were unable to take action on their own. Nearly thirty police had come out to the mine at the outset of the incident, but were uncertain what to do and asked their superiors for instructions. They were simply told to "take appropriate measures." The continuing abuse was too much for the police in the hall to take for long, and they left in pairs without doing anything. The company's appeal to SCAP was equally fruitless since the local occupation authorities who came to see what was going on were not inclined to intervene, merely giving the company the indifferent reply: "Should it lead to acts of violence inform us immediately."

The company officials were forced to listen to the bitter personal attacks of the miners and their wives for treating the workers brutally in the mines, and for callously feeding pet animals good food from their own excess stocks while the workers and their families ate scraps little better than garbage in order to survive at all. At one point, according to Nishimura's account:

A lone woman stood and rushed up onto the stage. Composing her white face, she took a handful of something from her pocket. Wanting to say something, lip quivering, boiling with agitation, she began to cry in mortification.

"Managers, please look at this. It's the guts of a pumpkin. While you were eating rice every day and drinking sake, there was no rice ration for us. We were told it was in order to win the war. The sweet potatoes ran out, and we came to the point of eating this, every day, every day (choking sob). Our family was patient with this, even though I couldn't even give my husband something to take when he went to work (cries). And what of the feelings of a mother when her child says again and again, 'Rice, I want to eat rice' (voice rising and crying). If you are human, you ought to understand a parent's feelings. And recently, when we thought that thanks to the union, wages had been raised a little, now they say that you will take back the sardines that we have been living on. After all that, are you human? If that were all, it might be endured, but what kind of a thing is it that you are snatching away the things we eat, that you are raising pet horses and dogs and letting them eat white rice? The coal-mine pitworkers are leading more miserable lives than dogs. We worry about something to eat every day, every day, and it feels like we will go crazy over getting something to eat. While I'm standing here right now I'm thinking about what we will eat this evening."

Unable to go on she broke down in tears. Her heaving shoulders touched the hearts of those present. It was probably the first time in her life she had spoken in front of people. Deeply moved by her own words, she finally broke down completely on the stage. The women in the hall raised their voices in a wail at the sad memories she had called up.[33]

The attitude of the gathered workers and their families was menacing as the pent-up hatreds bred of years, even decades, burst out in words such as these.

The Mitsubishi Bibai miners were, nonetheless, several steps away from conscious, anti-capitalist solidarity. A large step closer would be taken by subsequent production-control struggles when, in complete disregard of legality, the struggle committees would reach out to other organizations to make a breakthrough into a more self-sustaining form of production control. The Mitsubishi workers foreshadowed this when their struggle committee made an unsuccessful appeal to the Hokkaidō farmers' unions for a joint struggle to secure food for the miners, but the conscious intent to break with the capitalist order was yet to come.[34] When the company officials finally broke under the pressure and gave in to the union demands, the result was the same type of settlement that had come at the conclusion of most previous production-control struggles: large pay hikes, democratic reforms of the enterprise, recognition of labor rights, and formation of a management council.

Even before the people's court incident, the violence attending the main-office demonstration that had ended the production-control struggle at Japan Steel Tube had made Japan's leaders disturbingly aware of the social consequences of a continuing stagnation of production.[35] The workers' defiance of authority and the connections being forged with the JCP shocked them into action against what they saw as a communist-directed attack against the rights of private property.[36] The government responded on 1 February 1946 when the Home, Justice, Commerce and Industry, and Welfare Ministries in response to a request from the president of Japan Steel Tube[37] issued a joint policy declaration which branded production control an illegal act in violation of property rights.[38]

The intent of the Declaration could not have been clearer. Henceforth the government would regard production control as an illegal act to be dealt with summarily by the police. The government in principle acknowledged labor's right to engage in acts of struggle like strikes, but in reality the Declaration was a fundamental negation of that right, for it prohibited the sole effective means of dispute available at the time—production control—as "illegal and excessive actions," a phrase flexible enough to permit application of the Declaration much more broadly should the necessity arise.[39]

The increased resistance by business and government did not prevail for the time being, however, since SCAP would not countenance the Shidehara

Cabinet's unilateral proscription of production control and the projected use of the police to combat it, maintaining instead that the issue must be resolved through legislation or the courts.[40] Without the SCAP support and faced by a storm of protest, the government backtracked a week later and the question of legality remained unresolved.[41] But in effect, since the practice spread ever more widely over the next months (see table 1.3) in spite of concerted government and business opposition, the radical workers' organizations on the shop floor carried the day.

The workers' careful attention to keeping production control legal as a dispute tactic eroded as the employers dug in their heels and labor disputes became increasingly bitter. At this juncture, the anti-capitalist implications of production control surfaced in two ways: the workers' committees began to assume sweeping rights to use company assets and facilities during the dispute for whatever purposes they deemed fit, and demands for permanent extension of workers' control to matters of policy-making and organization began to displace strictly economic demands as the crucial issue. Stiffening government and business resistance was being countered by a growing worker radicalization in practice, and the smell of revolt in the factories began to permeate the air.

The JCP and Production Control

One of the more difficult theoretical questions for the Japan Communist Party after the war was the proper characterization of Japan's postwar stage of development. If Japan was still to a significant degree feudal, then the proper policy would be completion of the bourgeois-democratic revolution. If Japan was now on balance a mature capitalist society—not to mention monopoly capitalist— then a socialist revolution was the objective.

Some fifteen years earlier, the 1932 Theses of the JCP had resolved this debate by positing a rapid transformation of the bourgeois-democratic revolution into a socialist one through a two-stage revolution to be carried out by a soviet government of workers, peasants, and soldiers under the hegemony of the proletariat. The early formation of soviets and the rapid transition from the bourgeois-democratic to the socialist revolution could take place because "objective conditions for socialism exist and the necessity for the destruction of the capitalist system of exploitation has become fully developed."[42] In fact, the two-stage revolution in the 1932 Theses was telescoped to the extreme, coming down to a rapid and violent seizure of power by soviets under the leadership of the JCP.[43]

The thirteen years since 1932 had seen great economic and social change. The war had forced the pace of industrialization, and heavy industry displaced light to become the overwhelmingly dominant sector of the economy. By 1945 the now numerically larger non-agricultural work force could justifiably be characterized by its largest component as an industrial working class. Although "feudal remnants" did still exist, like the landlord and labor-boss systems, in Marxist terms Japan was indisputably a thoroughly capitalist society at the war's end[44] giving Tokuda and the other JCP leaders all the more reason for building upon the revolutionary positions in the 1932 Theses. Yet, even while tacitly acknowledging Japan's capitalist maturity in Party policies and pronouncements, the Party leaders also pointed to the facts of defeat and foreign occupation as preventing the use of tactics appropriate to normal times. That is, they did not believe it possible to take the theoretically logical next step of dedicating the Party to leading the socialist revolution openly and at once. Now at a point when capitalist maturity had largely been reached, the JCP still felt it necessary to fall back on a variant of the old two-stage line.

The two-stage line created a series of contradictions that would plague the JCP for some time to come, and were to prove especially costly during the first nine months when the revolutionary tide was rising. This compromise formulation avoided the necessity of a direct confrontation with SCAP, but it created an ambiguity in Party policies and formulations that led to confusion among party ranks and softened the Party's Leninist resolve to mobilize the working class for the cause of the revolution.

A prime example of the ambiguous analysis was the concept of the "people's republic" *(jinmin kyōwa seifu)*.[45] The 1932 Theses had not used this term, but had spoken of a soviet government to be followed by the dictatorship of the proletariat. Party policy called for the establishment of a people's republic, but this was not to be one composed of workers' and peasants' soviets. Rather, the term signified a parliamentary form of government in which a broad united front of democratic forces would hold power,[46] a progressive bourgeois democracy in which the unions and parties of the workers and peasants would not only sharply circumscribe the powers of the big bourgeoisie and their feudalistic allies, but would also outweigh and increasingly dominate other bourgeois elements that SCAP favored.[47]

It is clear that the strategic line of establishing a people's republic and completing the bourgeois-democratic revolution was an exceedingly elastic concept which could be used equally well to justify either an early drive onward to socialism or an extended democratic transition. The people's republic was an uneasy way station between the liberal capitalist order and socialism. Intentionally or not, these early Tokuda-Shiga formulations masked considerable theoretical vacillation about the speed with which the JCP could proceed to the main task of social revolution. It was one thing to talk about the character of the present revolution being bourgeois-democratic with a strong tendency towards progression into the socialist one—as did the 1932 Theses and postwar Party policy less precisely—but it was quite another to put practical content into that ambiguous phrase. A people's republic worthy of the program enunciated in the 1932 Theses would have to be built on soviets, not parties and unions, the very existence of which would compromise the viability of Japanese capitalism and arouse the wrath of SCAP.

The JCP did not have a well-worked-out policy on production control, however, nor was it promoting it solely to hasten the socialist revolution. This can be seen in JCP documents and publications from the period, but more convincingly in the actions of JCP organizers in mines and factories. In both writings and behavior, party theorists and organizers like Tokuda Kyūichi lumped together reform tactics with revolutionary strategy, just as had been done in the 1932 Theses.

The documents issued at the Fourth Party Congress in December 1945 (written under Tokuda's direction), for example, set out a policy of promoting unions and workers' control simultaneously. This was to be done by having the unions undertake two tasks: (1) bargaining with employers over narrow economic issues like wages and hours; and (2) taking basic *control over production* (this phase would be downgraded at the 5th Congress in February to *participation in management*) in order first, to overcome the economic breakdown, and second, to pave the way for socialist revolution.[48] Production control was facilely regarded as a workers' action appropriate for either end. In retrospect this was a blunder. Based as it was on worker direct action, posing a fundamental challenge to the rights of private property, production control pointed toward a worker-soviet or council type of factory organization, not the union. And in fact production control was usually carried out by production-control struggle committees, organizationally distinct from and superior to the usual union structure.[49]

Tokuda for one seemed to think that production control could coexist in the interim with unions using the more conventional labor tactics of strikes and collective bargaining, perhaps thereby preserving within the capitalist order the germ of the revolutionary factory society, much as was argued in the 1932 Theses of the JCP.[50] He apparently believed the progression from bourgeois democracy to socialism would be relatively rapid and peaceful, arising out of Japan's new democratic society in a matter of a few years or even months. This rapid progression would presumably make it possible for the nucleus of the production-control struggles to evolve into permanent soviet-style workplace councils.[51] However, at least this much is clear in retrospect: production control contradicted not only the capitalist organization of Japanese industry and society, but also the authority of conventional unions within the enterprise. Ultimately production control could no more coexist with business unions bent upon exercising maximum authority over labor's rank-and-file than it could with owners and managers determined to safeguard property rights.[52]

The councils in such a conception would not so much coexist with unions as gradually usurp their functions and engulf them. The continuing enlargement of the revolutionary role of the councils at the union's expense would presumably solve the theoretical and practical problems resulting from the confusion of production control as a dispute tactic with production control as a revolutionary act. To the extent that the progression from bourgeois democracy to socialism proved long and difficult, however, business and government resistance to the councils was bound to increase in intensity and effectiveness, thus making the survival of production control increasingly difficult. Tokuda did not face this problem squarely, and by and large it seems the enemies of production control saw the fundamental contradiction of preserving it under a revivified capitalism more clearly than its supporters did. Production control—just as conservative business and government leaders, right-wing socialists, and labor leaders realized—even when carried out strictly as a dispute tactic, amounted to using revolutionary means for non-revolutionary ends. Moreover, it threatened to become the central strategy in a popular movement developing in a revolutionary direction.

The JCP Changes Its Policy

The ambivalence with which the JCP had approached production control, simultaneously as dispute tactic and revolutionary strategy, ended abruptly when Nosaka returned to take over an important role in Party leadership and institute the so-called "loveable JCP" line of revolution through the ballot box.[53] If Japan was expected to follow the parliamentary road to socialism, rather than see the early establishment of a people's republic, then neither extra-legal revolutionary bodies like soviets nor illegal workers' takeovers of enterprises through production control could have a role.[54]

At the Fifth Party Congress of the JCP from 24–26 February, the policy on labor was rewritten to emphasize unions and their role as the proper vehicle for worker participation in management, and to delete earlier demands for worker control over essential enterprises as a basic precondition for Japan's reconstruction.[55] Tokuda, too, endorsed the policy change, though unwillingly. Consequently production-control struggles on the shop floor aiming at a radical rearrangement of authority in the enterprise were on their own, essentially without any national political organization interested in or capable of coordinating their individual struggles nationwide.[56]

This is not to say that the JCP had rejected what is sometimes ambiguously referred to as political unionism. That was hardly the case considering the unions' later political confrontations with the Yoshida Cabinet, culminating in the 1 February 1947 General Strike movement. What was being rejected in theory and practice was that part of the strategy laid down in the 1932 Theses calling for the organization of powerful workers', soldiers', and peasants' soviets for the purpose of enforcing the "transformation of the bourgeois-democratic revolution into a socialist revolution."[57]

Under Nosaka's lead the Party defined the postwar changes Japan was undergoing as completion of the bourgeois-democratic revolution. It was argued that an immediate and possibly violent socialist revolution to establish a people's republic could not succeed since Japan was occupied, but that a gradual and peaceful socialist revolution through the ballot box could.[58] The question of whether Nosaka's appraisal was correct is important, for if correct, then Tokuda's projected development of production control from dispute tactic to revolutionary soviet was doomed to failure. No categorical answer is possible, but Tokuda at least had been prepared to take the gamble and try to bring on the socialist revolution through adapting to Japanese conditions the Leninist program of all power to the soviets, and seizing upon the production-control struggle organization as the Japanese equivalent of the Russian soviet. Certainly Nosaka was wrong in thinking that the United States would ever stand by and watch even a loveable JCP be voted into power, as would become increasingly clear after the SCAP suppression of the 1 February 1947 General Strike which had been called to force the replacement of the Yoshida government with a leftist coalition cabinet.

At any rate, the economic corollary of the political recognition of parliamentary democracy by the JCP was acceptance of a capitalist reconstruction and by extension recognition of the rights of private ownership of the means of production. Workers' councils, such as those struggle committees engaged in production control, challenged property rights and were accordingly downgraded, while unions which eschewed such challenges were emphasized as the correct workers' organizations under existing conditions. From there it was but a short step to call, as the Declaration of the Fifth Party Congress (24–26 February 1946) did, for joint labor-management bodies whose role was to put the economy back on its feet, but, it must be noted, on capitalist feet. The JCP now conceived the role of production control to be solely that of a dispute tactic of industrial unions and a means of bringing about labor participation in management concurrently with continuing production for reconstruction.[59]

The relegation of production control to the role of a dispute tactic of labor unions or labor-capital cooperation in the form of the enterprise-level council blinded the Party to the meaning of the quickening of the workers' movement in the spring of 1946. Just when the production-control struggles were moving in a militantly anti-capitalist direction and beginning to reach out and forge alliances with the city's poor and needy farmers, the JCP fell behind the popular movement. As the Party became ever more deeply involved in parliamentary politics and the formation of popular electoral fronts, a gap opened between the JCP national leadership and the workers' movement.[60]

Business and Government Leaders Try Co-optation

The Shidehara Cabinet quickly took steps toward formulating a new, more moderate strategy after the failure of its outright proscription of production control in the Four Ministry Declaration of February 1946. These government efforts were complemented by conciliatory measures within that part of the business world that was dissatisfied with the confrontationist tactics of the advocates of laissez faire.[61]

Aware of their weakness vis-à-vis the popular movement and the organized left, the more progressive members of the elite began to seek grounds for accommodation. The leaders of Keizai Dōyūkai (the Japan Committee for Economic Development), which was formed in April 1946, were representative of this tendency, which they proposed to implement through imposition of economic controls and planning by a stratum of enlightened managers and technocrats freed from the domination of enterprise owners and government bureaucrats alike.[62]

The immediate object of these progressives was an increase in the supply of consumer goods in order to remove one of the basic causes of social unrest. Over the longer term they could envision a significant upgrading in technical skill and standard of living for the hitherto submerged workers and farmers. By treating labor less as an enemy and more as a junior partner, so to speak, they hoped labor could be brought closer to management, and cooperation, not conflict, could become the new keynote for labor relations. The cost would be unions strong enough to gain real benefits for their members. Hence, big business had to try to upgrade labor skills and productivity, because the financial impact of the increased wage bill could only be ameliorated by encouraging increased productivity from these workers.[63] There was also some willingness to extend limited recognition to production control as a dispute tactic of labor unions, insofar as it was carried out on a "production" basis, meaning continuation of production by the employees in strict adherence with the pre-existing plans of the rightful owners and managers.[64]

In early February the Shidehara Cabinet had already put together a new policy for reconstruction on the basis of light industry. The key aspects of the policy were (1) economic controls and priority planning stressing coal—coal because it was a crucial raw material for the chemical industry, rail transportation, and power generation—and chemical fertilizers as the essential ingredients for increasing the supply of consumer goods and foodstuffs; and (2) a plan to mobilize labor behind this end by encouraging healthy business unions and setting up joint labor-management factory councils in priority industries. These two items stand in sharp contrast to the government's prior laissez faire approach to the economic crisis.[65]

Although SCAP had provided the basis for unionization, and had begun to press the Shidehara government to devise a plan for taking effective steps towards economic reconstruction, this attempt to formulate a new and more progressive economic policy in early 1946 was primarily in reaction to the workers' movement. The rapid spread of worker organization and radicalization of production control seemingly gave substance to the fears of social revolution haunting every faction of the political and business elites in the winter of 1945–1946, however liberal or conservative.[66] The new policies were intended to neutralize the anti-capitalist inspiration behind production control in two important ways: on the one hand by drawing organized labor into the system, and thereby splitting the working class, and on the other by overcoming the deepening food crisis and general economic collapse that were generating serious social unrest. The enterprise-council structure of the production control struggle committee was vulnerable to cooptation by the kind of labor-management councils envisaged by both the Shidehara Cabinet and the more liberal representatives of the business world, the more so since the left parties also endorsed participation in the councils.

The outcome of the above shifts in policy, understandably, was eventually to be a convergence in the direction of accepting and institutionalizing a denatured form of production control within a reconstructed capitalist order through extending to legally recognized organizations of labor certain narrow rights to participate in management, but with no rights of control over management.[67] It could hardly have been otherwise, given the mutual acceptance by the JCP and the progressive elite of the necessity for an immediate capitalist reconstruction of Japan.

Radicalization of Production Control

Meanwhile, since February 1946 the production control struggles had been rapidly moving to the left, toward illegal factory seizure and operation, regardless of the various grand strategies for bringing them into line with one policy or another. On top of this, they also greatly increased in number, becoming the major form of labor dispute in April and May, with 110 production control struggles recorded and nearly 75,000 workers involved (see table 1.3). A pair of examples may help to show the strength of the workers' movement centering around production control.

At the Takahagi coal mines north of Tokyo, a dispute broke out in March which resulted in the implementation of production control from 6 April to 14 June. Once the dispute began, the issue boiled down to the question of whether payment for coal produced and sold by the miners should be made to the Takahagi union or the mine owners. Coordinated worker demonstrations, mass negotiations in Tokyo, and threats by the national union federation, to which the Takahagi union belonged, to institute production control at coal mines all over Japan soon forced the government to back down from its position that the payments must be made to the mineowners. It now took a hands-off position, declaring that until the legality of production control was decided the parties involved would be allowed to settle the dispute among themselves. Thereupon the national allocation and distribution agency for all coal, the Japan Coal Company, directed that payment be made to the mine owners. At this time employees' union of the Japan Coal Company itself instituted production control and arranged for payment to be made to the Takahagi union, and that settled the matter for the time being.[68]

The union and miners had won a clear victory over the government and the mine owners, but the payment of the fee to the union did not mean a return to routine operations pending settlement of the miners' demands. Instead the Takahagi workers went on to extend their support to the series of popular demonstrations against the Shidehara Cabinet in April and May that led up to Food May Day and General MacArthur's subsequent "Warning against Mob Disorder or Violence." Other gains were made besides the highly significant victory over the payment of the coal fee: first, extension of the scope of the production-control struggle beyond enterprise lines; second, attainment of coordinated broad support through the national union federation; and third, projection of workers' participation in production control onto the national political scene.

These gains pointed toward the acquisition by workers of the ability to conduct production control on a more or less long-term basis despite government and business opposition. A second struggle illustrates this theme even better, and also demonstrates the effective cooperation of workers and peasants with a common interest in increasing production of coal, fertilizer, and food. It shows in striking fashion that workers and peasants were capable of responding to the economic crisis by working out their own practical solutions independently of both government and business.

What the Takahagi workers had the consciousness and will, but not the means, to accomplish (i.e., establishment of nation-wide production control of their own industry), the chemical workers, coal miners, and farmers in the Tōyō Gōsei production-control struggle from 13 March to 27 August did accomplish. Tōyō Gōsei was a small chemical factory in Niigata City that was part of the Mitsui combine. Mitsui ordered the factory to be closed around the end of January, but the employees defied the order, publicly declaring: "Despite the closure order of the authorities, we will not close." Mitsui caused production to be suspended anyway on 19 February by cutting off materials. The next day the employees gathered to organize a union of 190 members. Besides presenting the usual demands for union rights, the employees expressed their total opposition to dismissals and demanded a guarantee of a reasonable minimum wage as well as the setting up of a labor-management council. The union also denounced and called for the ejection of the two top officials at the factory.[69]

In reply the company called in all the white-collar staff workers separately from the more radical production workers and put pressure on them. One company official said he was determined to either dismiss the union executives and close the factory or resign himself. The union held a third mass meeting on 27 February at which the production workers, over the objections of the staff, rejected the company's stand. Thirty-one staff workers reacted by withdrawing from the union. The company dealt the union another blow two days later when the two company officials put out a directive which said that the factory would be closed no later than the 28th, 108 people would be retained as interim employees for winding up business, and there would be a 10:00 A.M. deadline on the 28th for those who wanted to accept a dismissal allowance. Fifty-three workers immediately left the union to accept the offer of temporary employment.

On the day set for closure, the remaining union members convened a meeting which demanded that those who had left the union for temporary employment be discharged, that the factory not be closed, and that all union members be retained as employees. The company agreed to the discharges, but rejected the rest. The situation remained in limbo until 13 March when a company official visited the factory and declared that it was closed and that the company would not retract the dismissal of all employees.

Once again the union convened a general meeting, at which the workers decided to reopen the factory that very day by instituting production control. The workers at Tōyō Gōsei completely severed contact with the Mitsui combine leaders and unhesitatingly took whatever steps they deemed necessary to keep the factory in operation. They abolished the old hierarchy of managers and department and section chiefs and shouldered the burdens of management collectively, since most of the white-collar staff had already deserted the struggle.

The production workers took a long-range view and methodically set about reconverting the plant to the production of chemical fertilizer with the aim of attaining full operations on 16 June. The biggest hurdle was capital, and the first attempts to secure working funds failed. Then the Tōyō Gōsei workers learned about a Tokyo chemical factory, Edogawa Manufacturing, that was in the midst of implementing production control and had solved its cash problem by selling formalin (a 40 percent solution of formaldehyde in water) in the union's name. The Tōyō Gōsei union decided to sell methanol (used in the manufacture of formaldehyde) to Edogawa and thereby obtained ¥300,000 in cash.

In a related step, the Tōyō Gōsei workers worked out a mutually beneficial barter arrangement with the 15,000-member Niigata farmers' association whereby the factory got the coal and coke, and the farmers the fertilizer. The farmers' association organized among its members a special cooperative to which the farmers subscribed for ¥100 apiece. The association used the proceeds to buy coal and coke from coal mine workers, and bartered this in turn to Tōyō Gōsei for the fertilizer ammonium sulphate.

The hardheaded realism of this arrangement, by means of which production of industrial goods and foodstuffs both rose, illustrates the capacity of ordinary working-class people to manage their own interests. The Tōyō Gōsei workers acquitted themselves well. They installed complicated equipment, changed over from one product to another, expanded the work force, increased wages, and raised production using machinery that the company said was so antiquated and out of repair as to be nearly useless. They did all this in cool disregard for property rights and capitalist managerial prerogatives. What is more, the company and the government seemed powerless to resist.

Equally significant was the struggle at Edogawa Manufacturing, a small Mitsubishi company of about 500 employees. The employees had organized a union in January encompassing both the staff and production workers. They simultaneously set up a three-tiered system of elective worker's councils organized functionally according to the company's operating structure. The main decision-making body was the employees' general meeting, but there were also an elected central executive committee of twelve members, a small number of workshop committees, and a larger number of departmental committees staffed by workers which took over the formulation and implementation of a production plan.[70]

The Edogawa union presented demands on 12 February, but company officials arrogantly rejected them, the business manager going so far as to say, "I don't care if you employees die; I don't have to guarantee your right to live."[71] Until 1 March, when the workers instituted production control, the company and the union fought over which side was to receive payment for a large order of formalin that the national agricultural association had placed much earlier. The business manager, who controlled official allocations through his power over the chemical control association, had been quietly sabotaging the formalin shipment by obstructing the arrival of railroad cars. This he did because the price of methanol was rising at a dizzy rate, from ¥1,800 per ton in January, to ¥8,600 in February, and ¥13,500 in March, and he hoped to reap a speculator's profit. Now he suddenly rushed to complete the transaction with the national agricultural association in order to cripple the workers' position before production control commenced.

The Edogawa union frustrated his plans by itself negotiating with the agricultural association and obtaining a promise to pay the union. The shortage of formalin needed in the manufacture of fertilizers for use in the fields of Tōhoku and Hokkaidō was becoming critical at this time, and each day that passed without delivery would result in lower yields. The Edogawa workers' success was directly related to their ability to make early delivery, which it could do because of the support of the railroad workers' unions.

At this juncture the Edogawa workers received another hard-line rejection of their demands and decided in a general meeting on 1 March to begin production control. The employees organized for this by tight coordination of the union central executive committee vested with the highest authority and a production-control committee to administer operations. Overall they made few changes and ran the plant much as before, though entirely without the old managers.

The Edogawa workers immediately sent off the available railroad cars for Tōhoku and Hokkaidō loaded with formalin and, in spite of opposition from the Ministry of Transportation, managed within nine days to transport the whole amount that had been on order for two months. The cooperation of the transportation workers and their unions was important, as was the dispatching of two of their own union members to Hokkaidō for liaison work. Mitsubishi and the government tried to obstruct payment, too, by tying up funds through litigation. But the employees' union of the national agricultural association made common cause with the Edogawa workers and saw to it that payment was made.

Acquiring the raw materials for production posed a greater problem, one not entirely solved. To a small extent the Edogawa workers were able to circumvent the monopoly control of the *zaibatsu* and the government over coal supplies by establishing a tight liaison with the employees' union of the Japan Coal Board. Absolute shortages of coal and coke brought about the suspension of production of methanol in April, but, as related above, they managed to get it from Tōyō Gōsei. In this instance, the Edogawa and Tōyō Gōsei workers, by maintaining their internal solidarity and uniting in joint struggles with sympathetic outside organizations, overcame the limitations of workers' control conducted in a hostile, capitalist environment. The relationships they developed are presented schematically in chart 1.1.

Chart 1.1. **Expanded Production Control at Tōyō Gōsei and Edogawa Manufacturing**

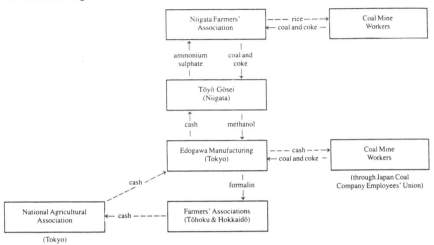

Source: Yamamoto Kiyoshi, *Sengo Kiki ni okeru Rōdō Undō,* vol. 1 of *Sengo Rōdō Shi Ron* (Tokyo: O-Cha no Mizu Shobo, 1977), pp. 147–150.

Workers might have embarked on production control in these coal mines and chemical companies and elsewhere at the outset in order to achieve a set of concrete and not very radical goals having to do with wages and job security. But as their struggles lengthened and became more difficult, they tended to escalate to a new phase. This new phase was marked by a more or less conscious decision to seek outside cooperation in producing essential commodities in critically short supply, commodities that were vital to improving the living conditions of the people. Altruism was a factor, but what counted most was that during the economic revival different sectors of the working class were able to advance their mutual interests outside capitalist relations of production. In short, profits and wages ceased to be the sole object of operations, and social needs assumed first place.

Several things are especially noteworthy about this struggle. The union took over and operated the company in its own name, completely excluding the company executives. They installed equipment, changed over from making one product to another, expanded the work force, increased wages, and took whatever steps they saw fit without concern for property rights or employer prerogatives. In addition to this, very large numbers of workers and farmers were drawn into the expanded struggle, the farmers' association alone having 15,000 members.

The taking of control over enterprise operations for the long term by a production-control struggle committee, as had happened at Tōyō Gōsei, assumed even greater significance in the light of the upswelling of popular protest move-

Chart 1.2. **Evolution of Production Control**

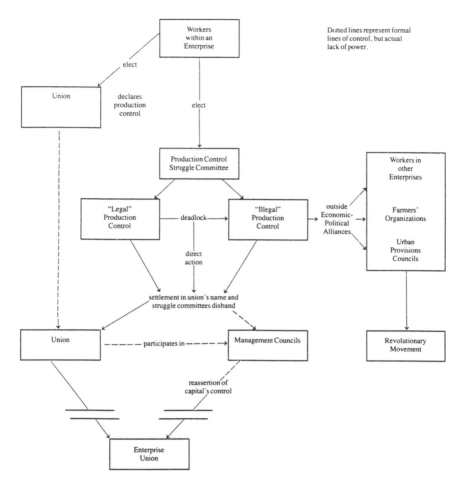

ments—notably the Tokyo city dwellers' efforts to assert control over food supplies through provisions councils and peasant efforts to assert their interests through leftist tenant unions.[72] The potential for an alliance between these movements and industrial workers carrying out production control certainly existed during the first half of 1946 (see chart 1.2). The goals of all three were complementary in much the same way the various participants' goals in the Tōyō Gōsei were. For example, as at Tōyō Gōsei, chemical fertilizer or agricultural implements could have been exchanged for food, thereby breaking through the "scissors crisis"—low official prices for foodstuffs in conjunction with soaring prices for manufactured goods, causing the withholding of food in the countryside for increased personal consumption, black-market sale, or speculation—that had led to a government policy of forced requisitions of food from the countryside.

Production Control and Parliamentary Politics

All of the above suggests that the time was ripe for a national movement prepared to challenge the conservatives for control of the government and the economy. The Democratic People's League (DPL) which was organized in March 1946 by Yamakawa Hitoshi, was intended to do just that. The League's activities, however, were somewhat removed from the popular currents which were gathering strength. The DPL sought to act as an umbrella organization for those who wished to topple the Shidehara Cabinet and install a center-left coalition cabinet under a socialist premier. As such, the League reflected the interests of reform-minded leaders of formal organizations like trade and tenant unions and the left-wing parties much more than it did the attempts by shop-floor workers to implement workers' control. Its main reason for existence was to take part in the parliamentary struggle for power attendant upon the April elections to the Diet, not to encourage and lead radical popular actions.[73]

The leftist national leadership associated with the League was eager to mobilize the already existing popular movement behind its electioneering efforts to bring a center-left coalition cabinet to power. Despite the moderation of the national political movement against Shidehara and then Yoshida in spring 1946, more than once the mass political demonstrations and rallies called to exert extraparliamentary pressure on the government exhibited a spontaneous radicalism alarming to SCAP and the U.S. government.[74] Strong public denunciations soon came from George Atcheson, the American Chairman of the Allied Council, and from General MacArthur who made a threatening speech on 20 May in reaction to the mass demonstrations on 19 May, Food May Day, which had been called to prevent Yoshida from forming a cabinet as well as to demand an immediate solution of the food crisis by putting the mechanism of distribution under popular control.[75]

MacArthur's speech had the immediate result of propelling Yoshida into power even though he had just given up the attempt to form a right-wing cabinet because of the widespread and vehement popular opposition to the kind of business-as-usual approach that he symbolized.[76] SCAP's blasts against communists and mob violence also served to reinforce the right-wing socialists' hold over the JSP and the conservative labor unions. Seeing SCAP openly repudiate the left and give open support for a most conservative cabinet—indeed reactionary in respect to labor—produced consternation among the left-wing socialists and the JCP. Divisions on the left were thus intensified, and the effort to form a parliamentary socialist opposition that would be nationally organized and unified quickly faded with the disintegration of the Democratic People's League.

The grass-roots mass movements which had rallied to the call on May Day, Food May Day, and other occasions and had shown themselves prepared to stand up against the old order were now set completely adrift without any organizational focus capable of helping them transcend their own individual interests—be it land distribution, food distribution, or factory control—in a comprehensive, nationwide solution of Japan's political and economic crisis. Thrust back upon their own resources it was hardly surprising that peasants, city dwellers, and workers alike turned to particular solutions to the urgent problems confronting them. For employed workers, obviously the best vehicle for overcoming the economic problems at hand was a strong union capable of gaining recognition, wage increases, job security, and so forth. Unfortunately, this kind of solution did nothing for the unemployed, the female worker, or those in small and medium businesses, and thus did not address the most pressing problem, that of resuming production on a new and more equitable basis for all working people.

SCAP had already been moving with its own solution to the demands for food distribution and land reform and had preempted both of these as issues for popular mobilization well before the next upsurge in the workers' movement in the winter of 1946–1947. Large-scale distribution of food imported from the United States began almost immediately after the May upheavals. The land reform program was passed by the Diet in October 1946. With both of these issues defused and the Japanese government moving against production control with SCAP backing, there was little likelihood of another opportunity of the kind that had surfaced in the spring of 1946. If Tokuda's program of Leninist revolutionary action had ever had a chance, that chance was now past.[77]

Conclusion

In brief, the period under review here witnessed the following progression in the deepening of Japan's postwar crisis. Economic breakdown attendant upon the lost war and a business sit-down combined to make production control the most effective dispute action for desperate blue- and white-collar workers. The severity of the economic crisis and the stubborn but not very effective resistance of business and government to workers engaging in production control stimulated a radicalization that was leading in the spring of 1946 to illegal anti-capitalist takeovers of enterprises by workers' councils.

By the time of the one-month socialist cabinet interregnum (April–May 1946) it had become apparent that despite the moderate parliamentarism adopted by the leftist party and union leaders, the possibility of a socialist reconstruction for Japan was being raised anyway by a popular movement attempting to solve the economic crisis by taking matters into its own hands at the point of production. It is problematical whether a further development of the radical production control struggles of the time in intimate cooperation with the popular movement could have succeeded in pushing a reluctant JCP leadership into the revolutionary vanguard role it claimed for itself. JCP reluctance was matched by a pragmatic readiness on the part of many conservative political and economic leaders to make tactical concessions and resume production on the basis of a reformed capitalism.

In any event SCAP's intervention stiffened the resolve of the conservatives, who counterattacked against the left. The disarray within the leftist leadership ensured that the popular movement would be left to its own devices. The participants in the struggles in the villages, on factory floors, and in local neighborhoods drew the conclusion that operating under continued conservative control required caution. Whether caution was dictated by a fear of retaliation or by the necessity of simply surviving while the old order still controlled the distribution of food and other necessities of life, there was a general turn away from radical answers toward making the best accommodation possible within the existing order. This rejection of radicalism became increasingly evident among the blue- and white-collar workers, who eventually abandoned their production control committees for a more orthodox trade-union movement.

Production control as an anti-capitalist act or as a dispute tactic was on the wane by June when SCAP sanctioned a government crackdown on its use, and strikes reemerged as the major form of dispute action. A minimal resumption of economic activity at about this time also had enhanced the effectiveness of strikes as a means to gain concessions for industrial workers, at least in key sectors of the economy like transportation, power, and coal. And from that point on it was the unions which became the main arena for the conflict with big business since the right to organize and to bargain collectively over wages and working conditions had become the central issue.

Since the advent of Taylorism[78] and scientific techniques of production and personnel management, capitalists have striven to extend their control over the processes of production down to the most minute level. They have pursued their quest for maximizing labor productivity by an ever-increasing curtailment of worker autonomy in organizing the actual work to be done. They have withdrawn matters of choice or of decision-making from the work process and made them the exclusive property of management. Harry Braverman has described how the consequent degradation of work has built the problem of overcoming worker resistance into the very tissue of modern capitalism.

> The apparent acclimatization of the worker to the new modes of production grows out of the destruction of all other ways of living, the striking of wage bargains that permit a certain enlargement of the customary bounds of subsistence for the working class, the weaving of the net of modern capitalist life that finally makes all other modes of living impossible. But beneath this apparent habituation, the hostility of workers to the degenerated forms of work which are forced upon them continues as a subterranean stream that makes its way to the surface when employment conditions permit, or when the capitalist drive for a greater intensity of labor overstrips the bounds of physical and mental capacity.[79]

Japan has not escaped the inevitable destruction of worker autonomy which Braverman cites as being characteristic of capitalist development. The subterranean drive for workers' control—understood here in the common-sense meaning of control over policy-making as well as the processes of production—surfaced after the war in the form of demands for the democratization of the enterprise and for participation in management. It gained added strength from the workers' pressing need to revive production in the face of capitalist sabotage. Workers did not arrive at their solution of production control overnight; instead they set out in the more orthodox vein of trade unionism.[80] As they organized, workers put forth three basic types of demands: for recognition of their economic interest, for democratization of personal relationships in the work place, and for democratization of the processes of production.[81]

The economic demands usually constituted a package calling for recognition of the workers' right to organize, strike, and bargain collectively over wages, hours, and working conditions. Goals like those pointed at particular solutions, at an attempt to overcome personal catastrophe by collective action within the framework given by the capitalist enterprise. Even if granted in full, they could not provide a means for surmounting the economic crisis, nor did they pose a radical challenge to employers.

Demands for democratization within the workplace focused primarily on putting an end to cruel and dictatorial treatment by employers and supervisors, and the abolition of the status system in the plant, which discriminated sharply between white-collar staff and production workers. They also encompassed attacks on those employers and managers who had been supporters of Japan's imperialist policies. Important as they were, such demands were not in themselves much more radical than economic demands centered on wages; they could be met by more employer attention to human relations in industry.

Workers' demands for democratization of the processes of production were most often summed up in the general demand for participation in management.[82] This could not be satisfied so easily. Whether it concerned the setting of company goals, organizing production or personnel policies, demands of this type impinged on the rights of private property, and no employer was ready to concede more than symbolic worker participation in management.

These demands, which correspond to those of workers in all industrialized societies, took on a heightened meaning in a country on the edge of economic chaos. Japan's working class somehow had to protect itself against a wave of dismissals and to increase production of essentials, but neither could be achieved by tactics like strikes or slowdowns during the immediate postwar period when there was widespread business retrenchment and mass unemployment. Employers could defeat a strike simply by locking out strikers, hiring strike breakers, or closing down altogether. A strike could hurt employers only in certain essential industries and services like fuel and transportation where employers had some stake in continued operation, but even here striking could only worsen the economic situation, victimize the public, and earn SCAP's displeasure. Thus capitalist sabotage had created conditions under which worker occupation of enterprises was the sole means available for attaining the mutually supportive goals of jobs and production.

Had economic goals, even the key ones of saving jobs and resuming production, been all that there was to production control, it might well be dismissed as nothing more than a dispute tactic of unions, one suited to exceptional times when strikes did not work. Many have argued in this way, discounting the seizure and operation of factories as the excesses of an immature union movement. Once production resumed, according to this view, there was no further use for such tactics and they faded away, to be replaced by collective bargaining as unions assumed their rightful place as the protectors of the economic interests of the working class.

As for this assumption that the basic demands of workers after the war were economic in detail and reformist in intent, the evolution of production control presents quite the contrary picture. Indeed, the congruence in early 1946 of a seemingly unresolvable economic crisis, the desperate needs of workers and their families, and a fundamental drive towards workers' control guaranteed that production control would not remain a mere dispute tactic of unions aiming at a better contractual bargain for labor.

The business union and its leaders ultimately recognize only the workers' right to withdraw labor, to strike; they seldom support the workers' right to seize control over and operate the enterprise in their own best interest. Union leaders pursue their ends through a process of collective bargaining which takes as given the legitimacy of the division between mental and physical labor, between managers and workers. Accordingly, they restrict themselves to but one aspect of the total organization of production within the capitalist enterprise, labor supply, and see their first order of business as the striking of the best economic bargain for the membership. The business union, dedicated to securing the privileged economic position of a relatively small aristocracy of labor, is opposed to mass organization and sees little to gain in acting as the spearhead of broader working-class interests. In this respect, it is the vehicle of a co-opted labor movement.

C. Wright Mills has described the leader of the American business union as a jobber and dealer who bargains and sells labor to the employer, who controls conflict and keeps worker discontent from erupting and spoiling the bargain once made. Even so, the labor leader must in part be a rebel against the capitalist system, for his power does not derive from property. His is an accumulation of power deriving from the organizational solidarity of discontented workers, themselves opposed to the undisputed dominion of capital. Paradoxically, the labor leader strives to gain acceptance into the existing capitalist system by mobilizing discontent against it.[83] Nevertheless, the labor leader's rebellion must always be partial, aimed at maximizing the union's power within the existing order:

> Yet even as the labor leader rebels, he holds back rebellion. He organizes discontent and then he sits on it, exploiting it in order to maintain a continuous

organization; the labor leader is a manager of discontent. He makes regular what might otherwise be disruptive, both within the industrial routine and within the union which he seeks to establish and maintain . . . the labor union is a regulator of disgruntlement and ebullience, and the labor leader, an agent in the institutional channeling of animosity.[84]

Unions are drawn into a defense of capitalist institutions as part of the bargain for economic concessions, but as pointed out by Braverman, conflict does not arise from economic deprivation alone. More is at stake—the loss of control over the work process. Herein lies the root problem of unions as organizations of the working class. The union must deny the workers' attempts to regain control at the point of production, or lose its legitimacy in the eyes of the employer and the state and its ability to secure economic concessions through collective bargaining.

Placed in the difficult position of having to cooperate with the employer even while standing up for the membership, the union leader must minimize rank-and-file participation in union affairs. The independence of the union leadership is vital to the union's ability to enforce its side of the contract because in addition to the guarantees of the workers' economic rights, the contract commits the union to enforcing unpopular prohibitions on the workers' rights in most other areas such as discipline on the job. That is the trade-off that the employer demands for extending recognition.

In the end, unions are not particularly democratic organizations, much less revolutionary bodies. They are an integral part of the system of industrial relations of advanced capitalism and cannot advocate radical goals like workers' control without undermining their own legitimacy and existence as unions. This applies with equal force to socialist or communist unions, which succeed in a capitalist society only to the extent that they in reality give up goals that cannot be achieved and are in contradiction with the capitalist system of production. Nor can a union long tolerate the existence of a rival body in the enterprise having workers' control as its aim, for dual organization in the workplace undermines the only power base that the union has, worker solidarity.

In times of chaos or revolutionary flux, however, the union may suddenly find it must respond to demands for workers' control. Two possibilities then face the union: either being remade internally in the image of the workers' council structured for operating the enterprise, or being thrust aside by the workers' own council arising from the struggle on the shop floor.

At the beginning the Japanese workers did view production control as an effective if unorthodox dispute tactic of labor unions, not as a revolutionary act. Participants in the early production-control struggles took care to stay within the law by keeping the locked-out management informed and by adhering to the existing production plan, often allowing company officials to continue making policy and operating decisions subject to worker review. Since they conceded the fundamental legitimacy of managerial prerogatives based on the rights of private property and kept accurate records in anticipation of turning things back over to the employer, the settling of a dispute made it easy for the temporarily dispossessed managers to resume control over the enterprise.

Even legal production-control struggle of this sort was indisputably an anticapitalist act, because the workers, against the will of owners and managers, in fact were denying the rights of private property in the means of production. They had to. Once embarked on production control, the workers in the enterprise found it immediately necessary to set up machinery accountable to themselves in order to continue production. This commonly took the form of the struggle committee (*tōsō iinkai*).

The struggle-committee system echoed the enterprise organization, but differed in that at the workshop, section, or department level the workers elected committees which became the building blocks for a three- or four-tiered pyramid culminating in an executive committee at the top. The committees might assume control over production by taking on the tasks of management directly, by election of responsible supervisors, or by holding existing supervisors accountable. The highest authority resided in the general enterprise conference (*taikai*) which often played an extraordinarily active role, making decisions as the need arose and implementing them at once through collective action. There was, consequently, no sharp organizational separation of policy-making and execution. The workers ran their own enterprise through the production-control struggle committee. Furthermore, the struggle committee either hollowed out or displaced the union, because it provided a more effective means for realizing the workers' interests than the union with its narrow bureaucratic channels designed for gaining economic rewards for its members.

Without doubt, big business and government opposition to production control from January 1946 onward can be accounted one of the major factors conducive to its radicalization. Unable to prohibit production control by law and suppress it with the police due to SCAP opposition, Japan's leaders sought to confine the duration and scope of production control by denying the participants access to funds, supplies, and markets, hoping thus to bring the workers to terms. This policy of containment generated intense pressures on workers engaged in production control as they ran out of money and materials, operations ground to a halt, and the possibility of achieving concessions of their demands steadily receded. Such stonewalling by management did not necessarily force the workers to a settlement. Instead it often precipitated rapid radicalization of the workers' struggle and their repudiation of the framework of legalism that had constrained the workers heretofore. (See Chart 1.2 for a schematic presentation.)

Two characteristics distinguished "illegal" from "legal" production control: a conscious denial of the legitimacy of capitalist legal limitations and other obligations that the workers had previously accepted in disputes between capital and labor, and the workers' impelling need to reach outside the enterprise for allies and resources to continue the fight. Once having taken the step into illegality, it was but a short step further to the position that the enterprise need not ever be returned to the control of the owners. Workers who crossed this line were tying their own fate to the fate of their collectively operated enterprise. The cost of failure would be high, certainly the loss of their livelihood and perhaps worse, and men with families did not undertake such an effort lightly. Behind their decision lay a basic confidence that they as workers could not only run an enterprise successfully, but also do it better than the capitalist owners.

Workers came by that confidence both by the example of others and by their own experience. For example, the workers at the *Yomiuri* newspaper gained tremendously in self-confidence as their struggle developed. Furthermore, their successful operation of the paper provided daily proof for all to see of the ability of employees to operate a business. Nonetheless, production control was bound to fail if confined by business and government opposition within the narrow legal bounds of a dispute tactic of labor within the capitalist order. Not the least of these restrictions was the workers' inability to secure supplies of raw materials for production at the same time that they found it difficult to sell the finished commodities.

In sum, the central issue of the workers' movement in Japan at the outset of the Occupation, when two central demands were for democratization and participation, was not unionization. Rather it was workers' control which involved mounting an attack on the prerogatives of employers, prerogatives which had long been virtually absolute. Production control called into question the most fundamental aspect of the capitalist system, private property. It pointed toward a sweeping reorganization of the internal order of business enterprise and a rapid erosion of the rights of management in hiring and firing, in supervision of the work force, even in making policy decisions on what to produce, to whom to sell, and where to allocate the firm's resources.

Production control was a manifestation of the disintegration, not the amelioration, of capitalist production in Japan, and business and government leaders could not afford to tolerate it any longer than they had to. In constant contradiction of the imperative of modern capitalism to appropriate all decision making as the exclusive preserve of management, production control could end in only two ways: in soviets and an unremitting revolutionary struggle for power, or in the total defeat of workers' control and the aggressive reimposition of unquestioned employer authority over the process of production.

Notes

1. Jerome B. Cohen, *Japan's Economy in War and Reconstruction* (Minneapolis: University of Minnesota Press, 1949), pp. 59f, 75f, 272–293, 318; Suehiro Izutarō, *Japanese Trade Unionism: Past and Present* (Tokyo: Mimeographed, 1950), chapter 3, section 5; Tōyama Shigeki, "Sengo Nijū Nen no Gaikan," *Shiryō Sengo Nijū Nen Shi*, Vol. 6, *Nempyō*, ed. Tōyama Shigeki (Tokyo: Nihon Hyōronsha, 1967), p. 3; U.S. Department of State, Interim Foreign Economic and Liquidation Service, *Labor Developments in Japan Since Surrender: August 15–November 15, 1945* (Record Group No. 226, Office of Stra-

tegic Services, XL 37772, Nov. 30, 1945), pp. 8–10; Yamamoto Kiyoshi, "Sengo Kiki no Tenkai Katei," *Sengo Kaikaku,* vol. 5; *Rōdō Kaikaku* (Tokyo: Tōkyō Daigaku Shakai Kagaku Kenkyū-jo, 1974), p. 84.

2. Supreme Commander for the Allied Powers (SCAP), General Headquarters, *History of the Non-military Activities of the Occupation of Japan,* Monograph 28, *Development of the Trade Union Movement: 1945 through June 1951,* pp. 10–14, appendix pp. 16–19.

3. Japan, House of Representatives Special Committee for the Investigation of Concealed and Hoarded Goods, *Supplementary Report* (Tokyo: December, 1947), in SCAP, GHQ, *Summation: Non-Military Activities in Japan,* no. 27, pp. 25–29; SCAP, Government Section, *Political Reorientation of Japan: September 1945 to September 1948* (Washington, D.C.: U.S. Government Printing Office, 1949), pp. 307–313; Ōuchi Hyōe, "Keizai," *Sengo Nihon Shōshi,* vol. 1, ed. Yanaihara Tadao (Tokyo: Tōkyō Daigaku Shuppan-kai, 1958), p. 82; Thomas A. Bisson, *Prospects for Democracy in Japan* (New York: The Macmillan Co., 1949), pp. 14, 98, 117.

4. Cohen, *Japan's Economy,* pp. 407–408; Japan Ministry of Finance and Bank of Japan, *Statistical Year-Book of Finance and Economy of Japan, 1948* (Tokyo: Ministry of Finance Printing Office, 1948), p. 670; Keizai Dōyūkai, *Keizai Dōyūkai Jūnen Shi* (Tokyo Keizai Dōyūkai, 1956), p. 14; Ōkōchi Kazuo and Matsuo Hiroshi, *Nihon Rōdō Kumiai Monogatari,* vol. 1: *Sengo* (Chikuma Shobō, 1969), p. 63.

5. SCAP, Economic and Scientific Section (ESS), Advisory Committee on Labor, *Final Report: Labor Policies and Programs in Japan* (Tokyo: 1946), p. 36; Rōdō Sōgi Chōsa Kai, *Tekkō Sōgi,* vol. 7: *Sengo Rōdō Sōgi Jittai Chōsa* (Tokyo: Chūō Kōron Sha, 1958), pp. 89–90.

6. Nihon Tankō Rōdō Kumai, *Tanrō Jūnen Shi* (Tokyo: Rōdō Jumpō Sha, 1964), pp. 43–60; Rōdō Sōgi Chōsa Kai, *Sekitan Sōgi,* vol. 1: *Sengo Rōdō Sōgi Jittai Chōsa* (Tokyo: Chūō Kōron Sha, 1957), pp. 49–59; Ōkōchi and Matsuo, *Nihon rōdō,* p. 98.

7. Takano Minoru, *Nihon no Rōdō Undo* (Tokyo: Iwanami Shoten, 1958), p. 11; Shioda Shōbei, "Zen Sen'i Sangyō Rōdō Kumiai Dōmei," *Nihon Rōdō Kumiai Ron,* ed. Ōkōchi Kazuo (Tokyo: Yūhikaku, 1954), pp. 288–289; Watanabe Tōru, *Gendai Rōnō Undōshi Nempyō* (Tokyo: San'ichi Shobō, 1961), p. 157; Ōkōchi and Matsuo, *Nihon Rōdō,* p. 82.

8. Nihōn Kyōsantō Chūō Iinkai, ed. *Nihon Kyōsantō Kōryōshū* (Tokyo: Nihon Kyōsantō Chūō Iinkai Shuppan Kyoku, 1962), pp. 100–104; Shakai Undō Shiryō Kankōkai, ed., *Nihon Kyōsantō Shiryō Taisei* (Tokyo: Ōdosha Shoten, 1951), pp. 23–25.

9. Arahata Kanson, *Kanson Jiden* (Tokyo: Ronsōsha, 1960), p. 530; Shinobu Seizaburō, *Sengo Nihon Seiji Shi* (Tokyo: Keisō Shobō, 1965), vol. 1, pp. 178–179; Tagawa Kazuo, *Sengo Kakumei no Haiboku,* vol. 1: *Sengo Nihon Kakumei Undō Shi* (Tokyo: Gendai Shichōsha, 1970), p. 3.

10. SCAP, ESS. Advisory Committee on Labor, Appendix A.

11. Horikoshi Teizō, ed. *Keizai Dantai Rengōkai Jūnen Shi* (Tokyo: Keizai Dantai Rengōkai, 1962), vol. 1, pp. 4–10, 25–26; vol. 2, pp. 490–496; vol. 3, pp. 304–307, 547–548.

12. Ibid.; Miwa Yoshikazu, "Keizai Dantai Ron," *Dokusen Keitai,* ed. Imai Noriyoshi, vol. 1: *Gendai Nihon no Dokusen Shihon,* (Tokyo: Shiseidō, 1964), pp. 215–216; Noda Kazuo, ed. *Sengo Keiei Shi,* Vol. 1: *Nihon Keiei Shi,* Nihon Seisansei Honbu (Tokyo: Nihon Seisansei Honbu, 1965), p. 51.

13. U.S. Department of State, Division of Research for Far East, Office of Intelligence Research, "The Yomiuri Shimbun Case: A Significant Development in the Post-surrender Japanese Press" (OIR Report No. 4247, March 19, 1947), pp. 5–6, (RG 331, box 8499, folder: Labor Rels: Disputes —Newspapers, Yomiuri Case [Confidential]).

14. Tōkyō Daigaku Shakai Kaguku Kenkyū-jo, ed., *Sengo Kiki ni okeru Rōdō Sōgi: Yomiuri Shimbun Sōgi (1945–1946),* part 1, vol. 6 of *Shiryō* (Tokyo: Tōkyō Daigaku

Shakai Kagaku Kenkyū-jo, 1973), pp. 9–11, 26–27, 75; Edward Uhlan and Dana L. Thomas, *Shoriki, Miracle Man of Japan: A Biography* (New York: Exposition Press, 1957), pp. 61–67; Tōkyō Daigaku Shakai kagaku Kenkyū-jo, ed., *Sengo Kiki ni okeru Rōdō Sōgi: Yomiuri Shimbun Sōgi (1945–1946)*, part 2, vol. 7 of *Shiryō* (Tokyo: Tōkyō Daigaku Shakai Kagaku Kenkyū-jo, 1974), pp. 18–20.

15. Tōkyō Daigaku, *Yomiuri Shimbun Sōgi*, part 1, pp. 19, 23–25; Takano, *Nihon no rōdō*, pp. 30–31.

16. Masuyama Tasuke, "Dai Ichiji Yomiuri *sōgi Sōgi Shi,*" Rōdō Undō Shi Kenkyū Kai, ed., *Sambetsu Kaigi: Sono Seiritsu to Undō no Tendai,* Vol. 53 of Rōdō Undō Shi Kenkyū (Tokyo: Rōdō Jumpō Sha, 1970), p. 22; Rōdō Sōgi Chōsa Kai, ed., *Rōdō Sōgi ni okeru Tokushu Kēsu,* vol. 6: *Sengo Rōdō Sōgi Jittai Chōsa* (Tokyo: Chūō Kōron Sha, 1957), pp. 13–14; Uhlan, *Shoriki,* p. 169.

17. Tōkyō Daigaku, *Yomiuri Shimbun Sōgi*, part 1, pp. 9–10, 22.

18. Rōdō Sōgi Chōsa Kai, *Tokushu Kēsu,* p. 16; Tōkyō Daigaku, *Yomiuri Shimbun Sōgi*, part 1, pp. 9–10.

19. Rōdō Sōgi Chōsa Kai, *Tokushu Kēsu,* p. 27; Uhlan, *Shoriki,* pp. 170, 172; Tōkyō Daigaku, *Yomiuri Shimbun Sōgi*, part 1, pp. 9–10.

20. Tōkyō Daigaku, *Yomiuri Shimbun Sōgi*, part 1, pp. 5–6.

21. Masuyama, "Dai Ichiji Yomiuri Sōgi," p. 28.

22. Ibid., p. 29.

23. Rōdō Sōgi Chosa Kai, *Tokushu Kēsu,* pp. 15–16.

24. Ibid., pp. 21–22; Masuyama, "Dai Ichiji Yomiuri Sōgi," pp. 27, 29; U.S. Department of State, "The Yomiuri Shimbun Case," pp. 73–78.

25. Tōkyō Daigaku, *Yomiuri Shimbun Sōgi*, part 1, pp. 33–35, 38–39; Yamamoto Kiyoshi, *Sengo Kiki ni okeru Rōdō Undō,* vol. 1: *Sengo Rōdō Undō Shi Ron* (Tokyo: O-Cha no Mizu Shobō, 1977), pp. 262–265.

26. Mark Gayn, *Japan Diary* (New York: William Sloane Associates, Inc., 1948), p. 23.

27. Rōdōshō, pp. 7–8; Rōdō Sōgi Chōsa Kai, *Tokushu Kēsu,* pp. 29–33; U.S. Department of State, "The Yomiuri Shimbun Case," pp. 17–18.

28. Tōkyō Daigaku, *Yomiuri Shimbun Sōgi*, part 1, p. 80.

29. Ibid., p. 81.

30. Sumiya Mikio, "Mitsubishi Bibai Sōgi," Tōkyō Daigaku Kagaku Kenkyō-jo, ed. *Sengo Shoki Rōdō Sōgi Chōsa,* vol. 13 of Chōsa Hōkoku (Tokyo: Tōkyō Daigaku Kagaku Kenkyū-jo, 1971), p. 25; William J. Sebald, memorandum of conversation with leading Japanese businessmen (February 12, 1946), pp. 1, 3, enclosure to Dispatch No. 258, Max Bishop, Office of the Political Adviser (Record Group 59: 740.00119/2–1546).

31. The following discussion is based on: Rōdōshō, *Shiryō 20–21-nen,* pp. 44–58; Sumiya, "Mitsubishi Bibai," pp. 22–30; Nihon Tanko Rōdō Kumiai, *Tanrō jūnen shi,* pp. 68–69; Rōdō Sōgi Chōsa Kai, *Sekitan* pp. 66–69.

32. Nishimura Takeo, *Jinmin Saiban no Shinsō,* (April 15, 1946), p. 33. I am very much indebted to Professor Yamamoto Kiyoshi for making this document available to me.

33. Ibid., pp. 43–44.

34. Sengo Kakumei Shiryō Hensan Iinkai, ed. *Seisan Kanri Tōsō: Shiryō Sengo Kakumei* Rinji Zōkan: Jōkyō (Tokyo: Jōkyō Shuppan, October 1, 1974), p. 184.

35. Nikkeiren Sōritsu Shūnen Kinen Jigyō Iinkai, ed. *Jūnen no Ayumi* (Tokyo: Nikkeiren Sōritsu Shūnen Kinen Jigyō Iinkai, 1958), pp. 100–102; Horikoshi, *Keizai dantai,* vol. 1, p. 38; vol. 2, pp. 498–499; vol. 3, p. 689; Keizai Dōyūkai, *Jūnen Shi,* pp. 34–36.

36. Asahi Shimbun Sha, ed., *Shōdo ni Kizuku Minshushugi,* vol. 1: *Asahi Shimbun ni Miru Nihon no Ayumi* (Tokyo: Asahi Shimbun Sha, 1973), p. 153; Noda, *Sengo keiei shi,* p. 243; Horikoshi, *Keizai dantai,* vol. 3, p. 689.

37. Yamamoto, *Sengo Kiki,* p. 168.

38. Ōkōchi, ed., *Rōdō*, Vol. 4: *Shiryō Sengo Nijū Nen Shi* (Tokyo: Nihon Hyōronsha, 1966), p. 8.

39. Chūō Rōdō Gakuen, ed., *Rōdō Nenkan: Shōwa 22* (Tokyo: Chūō Rōdō Gakuen, 1947), pp. 292–293; Max Bishop, Office of the Political Adviser to the Supreme Commander for the Allied Powers, Despatch No. 250: "Political Parties in Japan: Developments During the Week Ending February 9, 1946," (R.G. 59: 740.00119/2–1346), pp. 3–4. Noda, pp. 242–243; Horikoshi, *Kezai dantai*, vol. 1, appendix, p. 136.

40. Theodore Cohen, Chief, Labor Division, ESS, SCAP, conference with Mr. Iguchi, Chief, General Affairs Bureau, Central Liaison Office, in regard to issuance of government statement on legality of production control (Record Group 331, box 8481, folder: Production Control); Rōdōshō, pp. 33–34; Keizai Dōyūkai, *Jūnen Shi,* p. 32.

41. SCAP, GHQ, *Summation,* no. 5, p. 194.

42. George M. Beckmann and Genji Okūbo, *The Japanese Communist Party: 1922– 1945* (Stanford: Stanford University Press, 1969), p. 341.

43. Ibid., pp. 336–41, 343, 346.

44. Sumiya Mikio, *Social Impact of Industrialization in Japan* (Japan: Government Printing Bureau, Ministry of Finance, 1963), chaps. 4 and 5 passim; Shinobu, *Sengo Nihon seiji shi,* p. 188.

45. Shakai Undō Shiryō Kankōkai, *Nihon kyōsantō,* pp. 3–4; Tokuda Kyūichi, Shiga Yoshio, et al., "An Appeal to the People," appendix 2, Despatch No. 31 of October 27, 1945 from George Atcheson, Acting Political Adviser to the Supreme Commander for Allied Powers, "Periodic Report: Developments of Political Parties and Movements for the Week Ending October 26, 1945" (General Records of the Department of State, National Archives, R.G. 59; 894.00/10–2745).

46. Nihon Kyōsantō Chūō Iinkai, ed., *Nihon Kyōsantō no Gojū Nen, Zenei,* Rinji Zōkan, no. 342 (August, 1972), p. 114–116.

47. Tokuda Kyuichi, E. Herbert Norman, John K. Emmerson, "Communist Party Policy and Current Japanese Problems," Memorandum of Conversation, Despatch No. 51 of November 13, 1945 from Atcheson to the Secretary of State, "Political and Economic Policies of the Japanese Communist Party," (R.G. 59: 894.00/11–1345). Saitō Ichirō, *Sengo Rōdō Undō Shi,* (Tokyo: Shakai Hyōron Sha, 1974), p. 31.

48. Nihon Kyōsantō Chūō Iinkai, ed. *Kōryōshu,* pp. 99–111.

49. Tōkyō Daigaku, *Yomiuri Shimbun Sōgi,* part 1, pp. 33–39.

50. Beckmann and Okubo, *Japanese Communist Party,* pp. 341–346.

51. Shakai Shiryō Undō Kankōkai, *Sengo Nihon seiji shi,* pp. 3–7, 23–25, 36–37; Nihon Kyōsantō Chūō Iinkai, ed. *Kōryōshū,* pp. 100–104; Tsukahira Toshio, *The Postwar Evolution of Communist Strategy in Japan* (Cambridge: Center for International Studies, Massachusetts Institute of Technology, 1954), pp. 8–9.

52. Yamamoto Kiyoshi, " 'Sangyō Saiken' to Shoseiji Shutai," *Sengo Kaikaku,* Vol. 5: *Rōdō Kaikaku* (Tokyo: Tōkyō Daigaku Shakai Kagaku Kenkyū-jo, 1974), pp. 208–209.

53. Shakai Undō Shiryō Kankōkai, *Sengo Nihon seiji shi,* p. 53.

54. Yamamoto, " 'Sangyō Saiken,' " pp. 212–215.

55. Nihon Kyōsantō Chūō Iinkai, *Kōryōshū,* pp. 105–107.

56. SCAP, Gov. Sec., Harry E. Wildes, et al., report of interview with Nosaka Sanzō, (February 19, 1946), pp. 2–3 enclosure to Dispatch No. 265, Max Bishop, Office of the Political Adviser (Record Group 59: 740.00119/2–1946).

57. Beckmann and Okubo, *Japanese Communist Party,* p. 338.

58. Shakai Undō Shiryō Kankōkai, *Sengo Nihon seiji shi,* pp. 53–56; U.S. Army Forces, Pacific, GHQ, Office of the Chief of Counter-Intelligence Research and Analysis,

"Strategy of the KYOSANTO (Community Party)," memorandum of interrogation of Nosaka Sanzō, (January 31, 1946), p. 2, enclosure to Dispatch No. 243, Max Bishop, Office of the Political Adviser, (Record Group 59: 740.00119/2–1946).

59. Nihon Kyōsantō Chūō Iinkai, *Kōryōshū*, pp. 106–107.

60. Yamamoto, " 'Sangyō Saiken,' " pp. 215, 219–220.

61. Horikoshi, *Keizai dantai*, vol. 3, p. 309.

62. Arisawa Hiromi and Inaba Hidezo, eds. *Keizai*, vol. 2: *Shiryō Sengo Nijū-nen Shi* (Tokyo: Nihon Hyōronsha, 1966), p. 116; Miwa, "Keizai dantai ron," p. 223; Horikoshi, *Keizai dantai*, vol. 3, pp. 309–310; Keizai Dōyūkai, *Jūnen Shi*, pp. 3, 32–36.

63. Keizai Dōyūkai, *Jūnen Shi*, pp. 3, 32–36.

64. Gōshi Kōhei, "Seisan Kanri no Keizaiteki Seiyaku," *Keiei Hyōron.* vol. 1, no. 2 (May, 1946), pp. 6–9; Takano, *Nihon no rōdō undō*, p. 32; Keizai Dōyūkai, *Jūnen Shi.* pp. 3, 32–36.

65. Keizai Kikaku Chō, Sengo Keizai Shi Hensanshitsu, ed. *Sengo Keizai Shi: Keizai Seisaku Hen* (Tokyo: Ōkurashō Insatsukyoku, 1955), pp. 66–68; Ouchi Hyoe, *Finance and Monetary Situation in Postwar Japan* (Tokyo: Japan Institute of Pacific Studies, International Publishing Co. Ltd., 1948), pp. 22–24; SCAP, *GHQ, Summation*, no. 5, pp. 203–223, 225–226.

66. Keizai Dōyūkai, *Keizai Dōyūkai Gonen Shi* (Tokyo: Keizai Dōyūkai, 1951), p. 2; Keizai Dōyūkai, *Jūnen Shi*, p. 27.

67. Yamamoto, " 'Sangyō Saiken,' " pp. 229f.

68. Rōdōshō, pp. 90–99; Nihon Tankō Rōdō Kumiai, *Tanrō jūnen shi*, pp. 63–66; Rōdō Sōgi Chōsa Kai, *Sekitan*, pp. 71–75; Sengo Kakumei Shiryō Hensan Iinkai, pp. 184–186.

69. The following discussion is based on: Rōdōshō, pp. 83–84; Yamamoto, *Sengo Kiki*, pp. 147–150.

70. Nihon Sangyō Rōdō Chōsa-kyoku, "Sōgi Shudan Toshite no Seisan Kanri," Tokyo Daigaku Kagaku Kenkyu-jo, ed., *Sengo Shoki Rōdō Sōgi Chōsa*, vol. 13 of *Chōsa Hōkoku* (Tokyo Daigaku Kagaku Kenyu-jo, 1971), pp. 286–287; Yamamoto, *Sengo Kiki*, pp. 147–150.

71. Nihon Sangyō Rōdō Chōsa-kyoku, "Sōgi shudan," p. 287; The following discussion is based on: ibid., pp. 286–291; Yamamoto, *Sengo Kiki*, pp. 147–150.

72. Rōdōshō, pp. 920–921; Unno Yukitaka, Kobayashi Hideo, Shiba Kiyoshi, eds. *Sengo Nihon Rōdō Undō Shi*, Vol. 1 (Tokyo: San'ichi Shobō, 1961), p. 92; Yamamoto, *Sengo Kiki*, pp. 154–190 *passim*.

73. Ōkōchi Kazuo and Ōtomo Fukuo, "Sengo Rōdō Undō Shi," *Rōdōsha to Nōmin*, Vol. 7 of *Nihon Shihonshugi Kōza: Sengo Nihon no Seiji to Keizai* (Tokyo: Iwanami Shoten, 1954), pp. 36–37; Bishop, Dispatch No. 250, p. 2; Bishop, Dispatch No. 314: "Political Parties in Japan: Developments During the Week Ending March 16, 1946," (Record Group 59: 740.00119/3–1946), p. 2.

74. Gayn, *Japan Diary*, pp. 164–171.

75. SCAP, Gov. Sec., "Counter-Measures Against the Subversive Potential in Japan—1946 to 1951 Inclusive," Tabs A and B, (Record Group 331, box 8497, folder: Communism: Miscellaneous Data on Communist Counter-Measures Committee); Allied Council for Japan, Meeting 4, Verbatim Minutes, (May 15, 1946, Afternoon session), pp. 10–12, (Far Eastern Commission, National Archives, Record Group 43, Allied Council Japan, Box 70), pp. 13–16.

76. George Atcheson, U.S. Political Adviser to the Supreme Commander for the Allied Powers, Dispatch No. 453: "Demonstrations and Growing Tendency towards Violence in Japan," Enclosure 4: "Summaries of 20 incidents in Japan involving violence or threatened violence (September 12, 1945 to May 19, 1946)," (Record Group 59: 740.00119/6–1946). Ōkōchi and Matsuo, pp. 144–147.

77. SCAP, GHQ, *Summation,* No. 10, pp. 183–190; No. 11, pp. 181–186; SCAP, Gov. Sec., "Counter-Measures," Tabs A, B, and C; Ronald P. Dore, *Land Reform in Japan* (London: Oxford University Press, 1959), Chap. VI, passim; Andrew J. Grad, *Land and Peasant in Japan: An Introductory Survey* (New York: Institute of Pacific Relations, 1952), Chap. 4, passim; Ōkōchi, *Rōdō,* pp. 8–9.

78. Taylorism is a system of scientific management aimed at raising production through rationalization of the means of production and the installation of piecework and incentive systems for workers. See F.W. Taylor, *Scientific Management* (New York: Harper and Bros., 1947).

79. Harry Braverman, *Labor and Monopoly Capital: The Degradation of Work in the Twentieth Century* (New York: Monthly Review Press, 1974), p. 151.

80. SCAP, ESS, LAC, *Final Report,* p. 36; Rōdō Sōgi Chōse Kai, Tekkō Sōgi, vol. 7: *Sengo Rōdō Sōgi Jittai Chōsa* (Tokyo: Chūō Kōron Sha, 1958), pp. 89–90.

81. Japan Prime Minister's Office, Cabinet Bureau of Statistics, *Japan Statistical Yearbook* (Tokyo: Cabinet Bureau of Statistics, 1949), pp. 734–735; for examples see Rōdōshō, pp. 7, 14, 23, 44, 82–83.

82. Suehiro Izutarō, "The State's Policy in Respect to Production Management [Control]," *Mainichi,* April 15, 1946, translation in Supreme Commander for the Allied Powers, Economic and Scientific Section, Labor Division, National Archives, Suitland Record Center, (R.G. 331, box 8481, folder: Production Control).

83. C. Wright Mills, *The New Men of Power: America's Labor Leaders* (New York: Harcourt, Brace and Co., 1948), pp. 6–7.

84. Ibid., pp. 8–9.

2

The 1960 Miike Coal Mine Dispute: Turning Point for Adversarial Unionism in Japan?

John Price*

Thirty years ago, workers and employers in Japan confronted each other in the most intense labor-management conflict in postwar Japan—the 1960 coal mine dispute. This bitter struggle began ostensibly as a conflict over layoffs. The coal miners' union, representing 15,000 miners at Mitsui Mining's Miike collieries in Kyushu, refused to go along with a company proposal to reduce the work force. As the conflict escalated, however, it soon became apparent that Mitsui Mining and Nikkeiren (Nihon Keieisha Dantai Renmei, or Japan Federation of Employers' Organizations) had conspired to crush the Miike union because it had become too powerful. Not only was the union's independent, adversarial stance setting a militant example for other unions, but its opposition to rationalization of the coal mines also threatened to upset Japanese employers' plans to replace coal with imported oil—the energy revolution that would power Japan's industrial revolution up to the 1973–74 oil crisis. Thus, much more was at stake in the 1960 confrontation than simply miners' jobs at Miike, and the intensity and scope of the struggle reflected serious class antagonism.

One miner was killed and hundreds seriously injured in bloody clashes that erupted when the company attempted to reopen the collieries two months into the strike. The labor movement mobilized thousands of supporters who traveled the length of the country to bolster Miike picket lines. Traveling to Miike became both a pilgrimage and an adventure in combat. At one point over 10,000 police stood cheek-by-jowl with 20,000 picketers. As commentators and participants repeatedly remarked at the time, the Miike dispute became an all-out struggle between labor and capital.

It is little wonder, then, that the Miike struggle occupies a prominent spot in Japanese historical accounts of the evolution of postwar labor-management rela-

*I would like to thank Donald Burton, Joe Moore, E. Patricia Tsurumi, and William D. Wray for their help and encouragement in writing this article. A revised version of this article will be in John Price's *Japan Works: Power and Paradox in Postwar Industrial Relations* (forthcoming).

tions. In its official history even Nikkeiren concluded that: "1960 was an epoch-making time for the postwar labour movement with the 1960 anti-security treaty battle and the Miike struggle at the center."[1] More than thirty years have since elapsed, and yet outside of Japan almost nothing has been written about Miike. Instances of class aggression, it seems, are not easily reconciled with the contemporary image of Japanese-style management as being "human-oriented." In this context, the telling of the Miike story is indeed long overdue.

The Background

The Mitsui name has been synonymous with coal mining in Japan since 1888, when the Mitsui trading company bought Japan's largest mining deposit, Miike, in western Kyushu. Ever since that time Miike has remained Japan's single largest coal producer. Mitsui first used convict labor to dig Miike coal, later supplementing the work force with impoverished farmers, *burakumin* (outcasts), indentured laborers from Korea, and, during World War II, prisoners of war. Until the 1920s, women constituted nearly 25 percent of the work force, but mechanization, mining legislation, and male prejudice conspired to reduce their numbers to less than 5 percent by 1930.

Immediately after World War II, many miners quit, abandoning the mines that had become virtual prisons of slave labor. Occupation officials immediately helped repatriate Caucasian prisoners of war from the mines but attempted to force Korean and Chinese miners to dig coal for the Occupation. This led to riots and rebellion at Miike and other mines, and the Occupation forces were obliged to repatriate most indentured laborers and prisoners by the end of 1945. But because coal was Japan's major energy source, the Occupation and the Japanese government subsidized coal production, and the Miike work force quickly grew to 28,960 by 1948, surpassing the wartime high of 23,700 miners.[2]

Miike miners unionized in 1946, and in May of that year they joined miners from other Mitsui mines in Kyushu to form a regional federation. Through this federation, Miike miners affiliated with the national coal miners' federation, Tanro (Nihon Tando Rodo Kumiai Rengokai), itself established in 1947. In 1949 a national federation of Mitsui coal miners brought locals in Kyushu and Hokkaido under one umbrella federation, Sankoren (Zen Mitsui Tanko Rodo Kumiai Rengokai).

It was from about this period that many miners in the Miike local became politically active in the left wing of the Socialist Party. At the same time, labor-management confrontation increased in the coal mines as operators attempted to reduce the work force and impose a limit on wage increases. These events culminated in a sixty-three-day general strike by 282,000 coal miners in 1952. Although the strike was broken by government legislation, coal miners came out of the strike united and with a heightened consciousness of their strength as a union.

Miike miners faced a new challenge in 1953—a Mitsui Mining proposal to

Table 2.1

Mitsui Mining Production, Employees, and Assets
(By Division)

Division	Production*	Employees	Assets
Miike	1,644.4	15,140	4,428.3
Tagawa	1,019.9	9,791	1,918.2
Yamano	571.2	4,895	1,193.5
Sunagawa	704.2	5,468	2,288.3
Ashibetsu	773.0	4,714	2,727.5
Bibai	587.1	4,205	1,070.2
Miike Machine Works	—	1,823	603.8
Miike Harbor Works	—	1,480	365.6
Others	—	1,083	695.6
Totals	5,299.8	48,599	15,291.1

*Production figures are for fiscal 1953. Others are as of March 1954.

Source: This table is from the Mitsubishi Economic Research Institute, *Mitsui-Mitsubishi-Sumitomo* (Tokyo, 1955), p. 37.

lay off 5,738 workers, including 1,722 at Miike. When Mitsui officially announced the layoffs, Miike miners began a forty-eight-hour sit-in. Huge demonstrations in front of company offices followed, and on 9 August 25,000 miners and their supporters held rallies at thirty-one sites outside company-owned housing for workers.[3] These actions were followed by work-to-rule campaigns, rotating work stoppages, and other demonstrations. Production stalled. In the end, the company was forced to give in, and 1,815 miners designated for layoff followed by dismissal were reinstated. The 1953 landmark victory brought the Miike miners and Sankoren nationwide attention and this "113-day battle without heroes," as the union called it, made Sankoren a pillar of militant trade unionism within Tanro and Sohyo (Nihon Rodo Kumiai Sohyogikai, the national labor federation Tanro was affiliated with).

After the 1953 victory, the Miike local gained further strength and won other battles. In 1954 it managed to abolish the *sewagata seido*, a system of company control in the housing for workers. With the cooperation of labor credit unions it was able to renegotiate miners' debts amounting to over 200 million yen and thereby reduce heavy interest payments. Throughout the 1955–58 period the Miike local continued to do battle with Mitsui Mining. It introduced shop-floor struggle tactics whereby worker grievances were no longer sent up through the labor-relations bureaucracy but were resolved in the mines on a daily basis through negotiations with foremen and, when necessary, through local work stoppages. Independent adversarial unionism had become a fact of life for Miike miners. The shop-floor struggle tactics were also being taken up at other work sites and were being integrated into a new organizational strategy being debated within Sohyo.[4]

Figure 2.1. **Mitsui mining divisions**

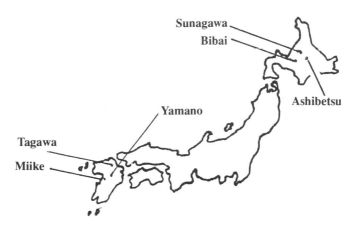

In 1888 Mitsui bought Japan's largest mining deposit, Miike, in western Kyushu. Ever since that time Miike has remained Japan's single largest coal producer. In 1946 Miike miners unionized and later joined miners from other Mitsui mines to form a regional federation, which in turn affiliated with the national coal miners' federation, Tanro, when it was formed in 1947. This map and the table and figures accompanying this article are courtesy of John Price.

This resurgence of adversarial unionism within the labor movement in the late 1950s constituted a new challenge for Japan's major employers. Immediately after the war, employers had been put on the defensive by liberal Occupation labor policy and a powerful union movement. Indeed, for a brief period, employers' control of the means of production slipped and the specter of revolution sent shudders through executives everywhere.[5] But as Occupation policy shifted from liberalism and economic aid immediately after the war to anti-communism and restraint after 1947, employers began to reorganize. The formation of Nikkeiren in 1948 marks the beginning of an employer offensive to reestablish their hegemony in the factories. Nikkeiren was obliged to acknowledge the fact that contrary to the situation in prewar Japan, unions were legal and would remain so. But employers hoped to limit their influence to bargaining over wages and to reduce them, essentially, to consultative bodies not unlike the company unions that existed prior to the war. Employers would not brook an active union presence on the shop floor, militant shop steward structures, or a confrontational grievance procedure. This hybrid corporatist-business-unionist vision of labor-management relations was to guide Nikkeiren's activities over the next decade. It was a vision, however, not accepted by most unions immediately after the war. Thus to achieve the labor–management "harmony" of the corporatist model, employers resorted to coercion. From 1948 on, Nikkeiren was intimately, if at times surreptitiously, involved in a systematic campaign to break independent unions. Nikkeiren intervened in the 1949 Toshiba dispute, in the 1953 lockout/strike at Nissan, and in the Nihon Steel conflict at Muroran in 1954.[6] In each case, Nikkeiren encouraged the respective employers to attempt to break the militant union and establish a procompany union in its place. Often these disputes had broad repercussions. The defeat of the Nissan union, for example, led to the eventual dissolution of the national automobile workers' federation. In this context, the resurgence of adversarial unionism that Miike so powerfully symbolized in the late 1950s flew in the face of Nikkeiren's decade-long campaign to housebreak labor. A new showdown was in the works.

Prelude to Confrontation

An economic recession and a decline in the price of imported crude oil in 1958 were two important factors that precipitated the events leading up to the 1960 Miike lockout. The coal industry had been protected from competing oil imports since 1955 when the government imposed oil tariffs and restricted construction of oil converters. Through these measures and rationalization measures (that is, modern methods of efficiency) also enacted in 1955, the government hoped to give the coal industry a period to modernize, to concentrate production in large, efficient mines, and become competitive with oil. The opposite occurred, how-ever, as mines proliferated, prices increased, and coal companies pocketed sub-stantial profits. Between 1955 and 1957 the price of regular thermal coal (Tokyo, CIF) jumped from 5,537 to 6,436 yen per ton, nearly a 20 percent increase. Profits for eighteen major coal companies climbed from an aggregate 4.5 billion in 1955 to 12.4 billion yen in 1957.[7] When the Japanese economy went into a short recession in late 1957, coal stockpiles began to rise but coal companies attempted to keep prices high, sparking an outcry from major coal consumers. The consumers, including representatives from the steel, electric power, ship-ping, and rail industries, gathered in August to form the Federation to Oppose Crude and Heavy Oil Tariffs (Genjuyu Kanzei Hantai Domei) in a bid to obtain cheap imported oil. This action put them on a collision course with the coal industry, which wanted continued protection against oil imports. Keidanren (Keizai Dantai Rengokai or Federation of Economic Organization) then inter-vened to mediate this clash between industrial sectors, forming a *kondankai* (discussion group) that fall. Industrial consumers eventually won this battle in 1959, forcing the government to reverse its energy policy and make oil Japan's principal industrial fuel. Even by the fall of 1958, however, the coal companies had begun to come under heavy pressure for price reductions, provoking them to consider serious rationalization measures, including large-scale layoffs.

Coal operators, particularly Mitsui and Mitsubishi, also came under intense pressure from other quarters just as the economic squeeze intensified. Nikkeiren had been displeased with concessions that the two coal giants had been making with their respective unions since 1953, and in late 1958 it began to openly criticize them through the *Nikkeiren Times*.[8] Sakisaka Itsuro, a noted Kyushu scholar and radical socialist who advised the Miike union, dates the initiation of management's offensive against the Miike union from the publication of an unprecedented full-page feature article in the *Japan Times* by Benjamin Martin, a U.S. union representative on leave to study in Japan. Published on 1 September 1958, the article accuses the local union at Miike of ultraleftism and using the negotiating process for political gain.[9] Similar criticisms were voiced at Nikkeiren's October semiannual convention by Maeda Hajime, a Nikkeiren executive director, in his report on the labor situation.

After two profitable years in 1956–57, Mitsui Mining announced losses of nearly 2 billion yen for the first half of 1958, and in September took the extraordinary measures of cutting executive and staff salaries and then refusing to pay its workers full year-end bonuses that had been negotiated as part of the master agreement with Tanro that fall (the bonus had been cut from 22,000 to 14,000 yen). By this time reporters had caught the scent of the coal crisis, and in early October 1958 the *Asahi Shimbun* newspaper published a major article outlining Mitsui's plans to meet the crisis. This in turn provoked the Miike local union to assess the situation, and on 17 October it published a report warning its members: "The company, from its experiences in previous struggles, will no doubt come up with new tactics. Recent labor battles have been plagued by organizational splits due to the formation of second unions so we believe the company's main strategy will be to split our organization and split the fight."[10] Mitsui Mining officially proposed its "first company reconstruction proposal" *(daiichiji kigyo saikenan)* on 19 January 1959. The Mitsui proposal called for:

- increasing productivity by strengthening managerial controls and discipline at the work sites;
- halting the recruitment of miners stipulated by previous collective agreements;
- reducing expenditures by postponing or canceling construction projects for housing, a hospital, baths, daycare centers, sewers, and roads;
- implementing reductions in labor-related expenses by cutting overtime; and,
- if necessary, reducing the work force by 6,000 through "voluntary retirement" *(kibo taishokusha boshu)*.[11]

These proposals were made to the two Mitsui union federations, Sankoren (mine workers) and Sansharen (staff union), but both unions rejected the proposals (see Figure 2.2 for union structures). They resolved instead to struggle together against any deterioration in working conditions, defend democratization of the

Figure 2.2. **Union Structures**

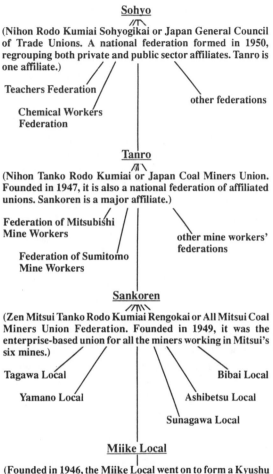

Sohyo

(Nihon Rodo Kumiai Sohyogikai or Japan General Council of Trade Unions. A national federation formed in 1950, regrouping both private and public sector affiliates. Tanro is one affiliate.)

Teachers Federation

Chemical Workers Federation

other federations

Tanro

(Nihon Tanko Rodo Kumiai or Japan Coal Miners Union. Founded in 1947, it is also a national federation of affiliated unions. Sankoren is a major affiliate.)

Federation of Mitsubishi Mine Workers

Federation of Sumitomo Mine Workers

other mine workers' federations

Sankoren

(Zen Mitsui Tanko Rodo Kumiai Rengokai or All Mitsui Coal Miners Union Federation. Founded in 1949, it was the enterprise-based union for all the miners working in Mitsui's six mines.)

Tagawa Local

Yamano Local

Bibai Local

Ashibetsu Local

Sunagawa Local

Miike Local

(Founded in 1946, the Miike Local went on to form a Kyushu federation with Mitsui mine workers at Yamano and Tagawa and later joined with the Hokkaido Mitsui miners to form Sankoren. The Miike local split during the 1960 lockout.)

split

Shinro

(Miike Tanko Shin Rodo Kumiai or New Miike Miners Union. Split during the 1960 lockout and took over one-third of members. Used as strikebreakers by Mitsui Mining.)

workplace and company housing sites, maintain full employment, and resist any firings. A "joint struggle committee" was set up by the two unions in mid-February with the express purpose of avoiding any splits in the face of the Mitsui proposals. The response of the national mine workers' federation, Tanro, which the two unions were affiliated with, was to draw a direct link between Mitsui's proposed rationalization measures and that spring's wage negotiations: "The 1959 spring wage offensive is integrally related with resolving the fight against Mitsui's rationalization measures. These are not separate struggles and must be fought as one."[12]

After a series of short work stoppages during March, Tanro launched an all-out strike over the two issues on 23 March. At this time, the Central Labor Relations Board (CLRB) intervened with a proposal to mediate in the wage negotiations. Tanro accepted mediation under the stipulation that no agreement would be reached until the Mitsui negotiations were completed. The CLRB brought forward its mediation proposal on 31 March, and negotiations then moved to high-level talks between Mitsui representatives on the one hand and Sankoren, Sansharen, and Tanro on the other. On 4 April, an agreement was worked out whereby the union would go along with "voluntary retirement" and reductions in welfare expenditures. In exchange, the company withdrew its proposals to tighten workplace control and to cut back overtime. This compromise in fact constituted an important concession on Tanro's part, one that would reverberate throughout the coal fields. By accepting the "voluntary retirement" at Mitsui, Tanro had opened the floodgates through which other major companies soon poured. One month after the 6 April agreement, Mitsubishi, Sumitomo, Furukawa, and Yubetsu submitted layoff proposals to their respective unions. Mitsui had been a testing ground for gaining concessions, and Tanro leaders had indeed backed down on their own policy, which since its adoption at Tanro's Twenty-first Annual Convention in 1958 had been to refuse to bargain any layoffs including "voluntary retirements."

Mitsui recruited voluntary retirees at its six mines through May and June, but the 1,324 miners who stepped forward fell far short of the company's goal of 6,000. Staff, however, came forward in droves with 586 ready to retire, 26 more than the original objective. As a result, the company estimated that its savings from lower personnel costs and cutbacks in welfare would only reach 862 million yen over a six-month period, substantially lower than the 2.3 billion it had projected.

Tensions mounted in the summer of 1959. On the one hand, Mitsui had been unable to implement its layoff proposals and it claimed its deficit continued to mount. Furthermore, as stockpiles of coal increased in late 1958, the government moved to cut back production, imposing a 20 percent reduction with specific quotas for the major mining companies beginning 1 May and continuing for six months. At the same time, oil prices continued to drop, putting further pressure on the industry. In early April, Keidanren's Discussion Group on General Energy

Policy met and announced that while a thorough review of energy policy was necessary, it expected the coal industry to begin to rationalize immediately. The mounting pressure led to dissension within both the company and the union.

In Mitsui Mining, for example, contradictions emerged between the then president Kuriki Kan and head of personnel Yamamoto Sengo. As previously mentioned, Nikkeiren had, as early as 1958, single out the Miike miners' local as a hot spot that had to be dealt with. This position was reiterated at Nikkeiren's two regular conventions in April and October 1959, with Maeda Hajime sounding a strong warning in his speech on the labor situation at the October meeting: "There are some mines where women and youth groups are extremely strong and in these places we can't guarantee major incidents will not occur which could quickly escalate into social unrest if things are not handled properly."[13] Working closely with Maeda was Sato Kiichiro, president of Mitsui Bank and Nikkeiren's chief international liaison. Both Maeda and Sato held Yamamoto responsible for letting the Miike union gain unwarranted strength. They wanted to resolve the problem quickly by firing a large number of union activists as part of the Mitsui rationalization plan.[14] Mitsui's financial position deteriorated during the summer of 1959, and in July Sato had Mitsui Bank cut off further loans to the mining corporation. Summer bonuses went unpaid, and Mitsui attempted to convince its unions to accept an installment plan on unpaid wages. This was refused, but Mitsui implemented the plan anyway.[15]

Mitsui mine managers were not the only ones under increased pressure. The coal unions at the local, company, and national levels were confronted with both an immediate attack at Mitsui, impending cutbacks at other mines, and an uncertain future as the industry faced the oil challenge. At Tanro's twenty-second annual convention in June, the cutbacks facing Sankoren were characterized as a special attack against Tanro's most militant component. This characterization contained, according to later accounts, the implicit issue of whether or not Sankoren had "gone too far" and thus invited the retaliation. This same debate carried over into Sankoren's convention in late July when the Sankoren executive submitted a two-stage battle plan. Basically, the executive did not think Mitsui would resort to designated layoffs or firings and based its first plan on this assumption. This plan was to draw the line at designated layoffs (*shime kaiko*) and to compromise on "voluntary retirements" while cooperating in production. The Miike local of Sankoren disputed this approach, regarded layoffs as imminent, and interpreted the rationalization as largely a political struggle, with itself and Tanro as the targets. These divisions in the union would prove decisive later. The final compromise was to fight the company and if the central struggle committee judged it feasible, to defeat the layoffs.

Mitsui proposed its second reconstruction proposal in late August. Essentially, the proposal was tougher than the first and called for 4,580 layoffs with set criteria for deciding who should be laid off. The criteria, particularly article 3, clearly put union activists at risk:

1. those whose job was not essential to support the family
2. those unsuitable for work
3. those unable to adapt to collective life
4. those in extremely poor health
5. those over fifty-two
6. those under twenty-five
7. those with less than five years continuous service.[16]

Each mine was assigned a quota (Miike, for example, was expected to lay off 2,210), and those who fit the criteria would be "advised to retire" *(taishoku kankoku)*. Although such "advice" did not constitute a formal layoff or discharge, it amounted to basically the same thing. The proposal also contained further provisions to cut back social benefits, overtime, and safety expenditures, as well as containing provisions to regulate all outstanding local issues for each mine. Furthermore, the proposal called for separating the machine shop from the rest of the Miike operations and taking the skilled tradesmen out of the Miike union.

Collective bargaining over the second proposal broke down on 10 September, and the various union levels prepared for battle. Tanro's central struggle committee called for rotating strikes beginning 16 September at Miike and at two other mines where layoffs were also expected, and for escalating limited strikes at fourteen major coal companies beginning 1 October. Sankoren, in the face of anticipated "designated discharges," took the position that its members would refuse to recognize any discharges, that Sankoren would guarantee the livelihood of those who refused, and that the union had to get prepared for a company-inspired attempt to create a second union.

By this time it became increasingly evident that coal-consuming industries, demanding a complete overhaul of the coal industry and drastic price reductions to bring coal prices in line with those of oil, had gained the upper hand. Coal operators met with labor representatives on 7 and 18 September and announced that they expected to lay off up to 100,000 out of 180,000 miners then employed by the eighteen largest coal companies. The bottom line for industrial coal consumers at this point was that their energy sources be cost competitive and that coal be forced to compete with oil. While Keidanren had always maintained the position that coal should not be protected, policy direction at this stage was not to lift oil tariffs or controls on oil converters but rather to force coal operators to reduce their prices through massive layoffs. Nikkeiren endorsed this policy, convinced that as a labor-relations organ it could obtain its own objective of cutting out what it considered a cancerous threat—the Miike union—in the process of the layoffs. Thus employers displayed a high degree of unity in their support for Mitsui in its attempt to rationalize and to take on Sankoren and, in particular, the Miike local.

Economic motives on the part of coal consumers and producers converged with political motives on the part of Nikkeiren to create a united capitalist class aimed at reducing the influence of Miike miners, Sankoren, and ultimately, Tanro and Sohyo. This was much in evidence at Nikkeiren's semi-annual convention in October 1959 when the chairman of the Federation of Automobile Employers rose to present an emergency resolution on the crisis in coal to the convention that concluded: "To us this [the coal crisis] is not an issue which can be resolved by the coal industry alone. It will have important repercussions on every industrial sector, and we believe Nikkeiren must go all out and extend a helping hand and through concrete measures work to bring about a fundamental resolution."[17]

The presidents of seventeen major coal companies met on 17 September to work out policies to support Mitsui's reconstruction proposals. As early as 4 February that year, the other coal operators had resolved to cover any shortfall in Mitsui coal shipments that might arise from a strike and, furthermore, to cover the costs of such shipments.[18] At their September meeting the presidents resolved not to take advantage of a probable Miike lockout to steal Mitsui customers and reaffirmed their earlier decision to supply the coal necessary to cover Mitsui shortfalls.

On 5 October Tanro held its twenty-third special convention, where the coal crisis and impending layoffs at Miike were the main topic. It had become apparent to delegates that 100,000 jobs were on the line in the industry, and this resulted in a direct link being established between the escalating Miike confrontation and coal miners everywhere. Tanro resolved at least on paper to reinforce shop-floor actions, establish self-reliant organizations, prepare for a general strike, reinforce unity with Sohyo and workers in other industries, and strengthen regional and district joint struggles.

Discussions between Mitsui and Sankoren over the second reconstruction proposal broke off on 7 October. Mitsui then began the process of garnering its "voluntary retirees" at all of its mines, but the methods differed at the various locations. At Miike the strength of the union made it difficult for the company to recruit potential retirees directly, and it therefore resorted to using airplanes to distribute leaflets calling on miners who met the retirement criteria to come forward. In the other mines the company was able to "shoulder tap" *(kata-tataki)* those who fit the criteria. Sankoren, however, had issued directives on 10 October advising its members to refuse to comply with retirement advice, and it backed up the directive with notice that those who accepted would be internally disciplined for disobeying union policy. Thus, Mitsui reached its layoff objectives at only two of its mines (Tagawa and Yamano) while at the others it fell far short, recruiting less than one-third of its target.[19] At Miike it recruited only 142 of the 2,210 volunteer retirees it had hoped for.

In the meantime, Mitsui successfully pushed forward with its plan to separate the Miike machine shop, and the workers there agreed, breaking away from the Miike local. The staff union, Sansharen, also applied to Tanro to conclude an agreement with Mitsui. On 28 October collective bargaining resumed, at which time Mitsui Coal president Kuriki asserted that Mitsui would not rest until it had reached the 2,210 layoffs necessary at Miike, including 300 "production obstructionists." The obstructionists were, from the union's point of view, its shop-floor organizers and stewards who constituted the very heart of the union. Union representatives from Miike, Sankoren, and Tanro rushed to Tokyo on 7 October to work out, if possible, a joint response to Kuriki's latest pitch. The three union levels agreed to oppose Kuriki's plan, but after top-level negotiations a compromise was agreed upon: "(1) absolute opposition to designated discharges; (2) the union would cooperate in production; and (3) if the first two items were agreed to then the union would not try to discipline members who decided to retire of their own free will."[20]

This position is basically similar to the 6 April agreement worked out with the Central Labor Relations Board. The Miike local had previously rejected the proposal of layoffs through early retirement, but probably agreed to this new compromise because it realized that its life as a union was now at stake and that Tanro was not able or willing to take a firm stand against layoffs in the industry. Kuriki, however, was no longer willing to take such a proposal at its face value and had by this time resolved to purge the Miike union of its militant members.

Negotiations resumed briefly on 10 November but broke off again on 12 November, at which point the CLRB again attempted to mediate. CLRB chairman Nakayama Ichiro made a seven-point proposal on 21 November that called for labor-management cooperation in raising production, "voluntary retirements" without company pressure or union interference, and further discussions if the retirement quotas were not met. These proposals provoked an intense debate among Mitsui managers (one presumes principally between Kuriki and Yamamoto), but the mediation proposal was rejected because, the company said, it would not resolve its problem with the Miike union.[21] Sankoren was willing to discuss the mediation proposal with Mitsui, but Mitsui refused, insisting that it had to discipline the Miike union. Sohyo held its thirteenth special convention during the mediation period, and the coal miners' struggle and opposition to the proposed renewal of the Japan-U.S. Mutual Security Treaty (Ampo) were the issues of the day. The convention resolved to back Tanro financially to the tune of 300 yen per member up to April 1960. On 2 December, Sohyo leaders including Ota Kaoru and Iwai Akira visited Miike to meet with local members and pledged 1 billion yen to support the local. This was followed by a visit by 32 leaders of Japan's largest unions who carried with them 75 million yen in contributions and assurance of a further 1.8 billion in loans. The same day, Mitsui mailed redundancy notices to 1,492 workers at its Miike operations.

Over the next few days, the Miike union responded with general meetings in the regional assemblies *(chiiki bunkai)* and at the workplace *(shokuba bunkai)*, culminating in a twenty-four-hour general strike (the seventeenth since the start of the rotating strikes) and a huge demonstration in which, even according to

company documents, 30,000 miners and their families and supporters participated. Of the 1,492 workers given notice, 214 decided to accept the notices,
while the remaining 1,278 declined and were subsequently mailed registered
letters on 10 December informing them that if they did not accept the layoffs by
15 December they would be fired. On 15 December, 1,202 workers were fired.
These included over 600 union activists as well as 120 Socialist Party members
and 31 members of the Japan Communist Party.[22] The Miike union continued its
tactics of rotating strikes, and on 7 January 1960 the union ordered its members
to begin a disobedience campaign that led the company to retaliate with a full-
scale lockout on 25 January at all its Miike facilities except the port. The union
retaliated the same day with an all-out strike, shutting down the port as well.

Three Hundred Twelve Days

The Mitsui lockout was not a spontaneous decision but a carefully planned
strategy that had been worked out, in a general sense, after Mitsui lost a 1953
dispute where union-organized slowdowns and partial strikes had paralyzed production and forced Mitsui to withdraw a layoff proposal. At that time Mitsui had
been unable to retaliate with a general lockout for a variety of reasons.[23] Since
then the company had taken measures to insure it was in a position to implement
a general lockout. As mentioned earlier, Mitsui had come to an agreement with
the other major coal companies that Mitsui's market share would be preserved in
the event of a strike and the other operators would cover any shortages in Mitsui
coal shipments due to the strike and absorb any extra costs. Furthermore, Mitsui
had the full support, and even exhortation, of Nikkeiren to purge the Miike local.
Finally, Mitsui had lined up financing to undertake the lockout. The Mitsui
Bank, under Sato Kiichiro, had cut off further financing to Mitsui Mining in July
1959 both for economic reasons and, one might reasonably suppose, to pressure
Mitsui Mining into disciplining the Miike local union. Once the battle was joined
Sato was more than happy to turn on the financial tap once again. Under his
leadership, a cartel of eight banks including Mitsui Bank and Mitsui Trust was
established to finance the fight. Over the course of the dispute these eight banks
provided Mitsui Mining with 6.9 billion yen in loans, with the first installment of
3.3 billion handed over at the end of 1959.[24]

Mitsui also adopted a strategy of intervening in the Miike union directly in an
attempt to split it. Internal union opposition to the militant tactics of the local had
existed ever since the 1953 strike, and the company now counted on that opposition
to form the nucleus of a "second union." To avoid the appearance of direct involvement that might result in legal action against itself, Mitsui called on the services of
professional union-busters such as Mitamura Shiro. According to union documents,
on at least three separate occasions dissident elements in the Miike local attended
"lectures" and "schools" sponsored by Mitamura and his cohorts, with 280 attending
a "Labor University Short Course" in Fukuoka on 12–13 March.[25] Union claims

that such activities were sponsored by Mitsui seem reasonable since Mitsui itself admits organizing similar "lectures" in the early 1950s.[26]

In the initial phases of the lockout and strike, Mitsui was clearly on the offensive, while the unions, including the Miike local, Sankoren, and Tanro, were forced on the defensive as splits occurred. Tanro apparently was not fully aware of its precarious position. At its convention on 14 February, delegates resolved to provide further financial backing of 600 yen per affiliated member (1,000 for workers in the Mitsui union federation). On 26 February Tanro's Central Struggle Committee even came to the conclusion that the situation was increasingly favorable for the miners due to a decrease in coal stockpiles, a growing anti-Kishi sentiment related to the Security Treaty dispute, and increasing momentum in Shunto (Spring Wage Struggle) activities. It decided to call an all-out coal miners' strike for 5 April with Sankoren going out some days earlier.[27] In the meantime the staff union, Sansharen, having made its peace with Mitsui, communicated its refusal to pay the 600-yen-per-member Miike support assessment to the Tanro Central Struggle Committee on 3 March.

Breakaway Union Splits Miners

This fissure in union solidarity cracked wide open a week later when the opposition in the Miike local presented the union's executive committee with a petition signed by 96 out of 254 members of the central committee calling for a special general meeting of the entire central committee to consider ways of ending the dispute quickly. The executive of the union acceded to the request, and a special meeting was held on 15 March with thousands of workers and supporters from both sides demonstrating outside the meeting hall. The dissident faction submitted a four-point proposal calling for (1) an end to the strike and reopening negotiations; (2) acceptance of "voluntary retirement" for those dismissed, with the company to help find new jobs and cover interim living expenses; (3) legal redress for those who refused to be dismissed; and (4) their proposal to be put before the general membership in a secret ballot. The central committee rejected the proposal and the opposition then left the hall.

On 17 March the opposition held a special meeting that became the founding convention of the New Miike Mine Workers Union (Miike Tanko Shin Rodo Kumiai, or Shinro for short), and in their report to the company they cited an initial membership of 3,076 members or about 20 percent of the work force. Mitsui immediately recognized the new union, and negotiations between the two parties led to a 24 March agreement to start up production with the new union. All of the issues in dispute were left to future deliberations, the old contract was resumed, and the lockout was lifted.

During this period Tanro and Sohyo responded to the situation first by sending in 2,000 reinforcements *(orugu dan)* with, in the case of Sohyo, union activists spending five nights and six days in each shift backing up the picket lines at the mine. On 18 March Tanro implemented Directive 203 calling for a general strike in coal on 5 April and an earlier walkout by Sankoren. A week later, however, it became evident that the other Mitsui local unions were unwilling to strike, and union leaders in the other mines warned of further splits within the union if Tanro pressed ahead with their strike strategy. On 27 March the Tanro Central Struggle Committee admitted defeat, called off the planned strike, and initiated a mediation application to the CLRB to resolve both the Miike dispute and that year's wage increase. But having successfully isolated the Miike local and with the momentum in its favor, Mitsui declined to enter into the union-initiated mediation process, informing the CLRB chairman of its decision on 28 March. Despite Mitsui intransigence, the new CLRB chairman, Kobayashi, decided to proceed with mediation, announcing his intentions that evening. The wage issue, however, would be dealt with separately, a process that the other major coal companies agreed to.

Mitsui had made important progress in its attempt to purge the Miike union by skillfully utilizing divide-and-rule tactics. For example, at Mitsui's Bibai colliery in Hokkaido miners had not come forward to "voluntarily retire" in the numbers desired, but Mitsui did not attempt to lock out the workers. Instead it proceeded with an ongoing campaign to find voluntary retirees, but this strategy was expressly dismissed for the Miike union. As Mitsui president Kuriki expressed it, it was not just a question of quantity but also one of quality; in other words, Mitsui was determined to fire 300 union activists at Miike, come what may. Mitsui Mining's labor-relations director, Yamamoto Sengo, recounted in his recollections of the strike how he had opposed the Nikkeiren-Kuriki view that it was necessary to openly purge the Miike local.[28] By soft-pedaling the layoffs in the initial stages, Mitsui had been able to cajole Sankoren and Tanro into accepting voluntary layoffs, thereby eliminating the issue as the basis for a common struggle by the Miike local, Sankoren, or Tanro as a whole. Once Sankoren, the most militant component in Tanro, accepted the 6 April agreement, layoffs (in the form of "voluntary retirement") were inevitable in the other coal mines given the economic rationale of the industry and government at the time. A second factor that allowed the company to divide Sankoren and Tanro was its campaign to malign the Miike local, which, as Sakisaka Itsuro pointed out, began in 1958. This campaign became crucial when Mitsui let it be known in late 1959 that it was determined to purge the local union. By branding the Miike local as troublemakers, Mitsui had been able to sow certain seeds of doubt about the Miike union—perhaps they had indeed gone too far in their militant tactics.

Picketer Killed

While Tanro was reeling from the divisions within, the Miike local continued to stand firm despite the formation of the breakaway union. Mitsui's determination to break the Miike local and restart production using the new union as strike-breakers led to vicious clashes on the picket lines. In the early morning of

28 March, 1,500 members of the breakaway union charged the picket lines at the Mikawa colliery and the clash turned bloody, with over 100 workers injured. The evening headlines of the *Asahi Shimbun* screamed "Unions Clash at Mitsui Miike."[29] That evening Mitsui applied for, and received, a restraining order from the Fukuoka District Court, prohibiting the first union from entering the mine and barring them from preventing breakaway union members from entering. The Miike local took the position that the formation of the breakaway union itself, not to mention the negotiations with the company and the lifting of the lockout, all constituted unfair labor practices. The picket lines remained, and in the late afternoon of 29 March, Kubo Kiyoshi, a picketer from the original union, was stabbed during a clash with one of the procompany goon squads and died soon after. Miike once again received national headlines, and the picketer's tragic death both engendered widespread sympathy for the Miike original union and raised the battle at Miike to a new plane—that of national politics. As the *Asahi Shimbun*'s 31 March editorial pointed out, the incident had endangered the company's position, and it was inevitable that criticism of the company for provoking things to the point of murder should surface: "Even in the Diet criticism is being raised and the question asked why the company insisted on restarting production when blood was surely going to be spilled. Even the bloody incident between the two unions on March 28 could have been avoided if the company had not attempted to start up again."[30] In the following days, thousands of mourners gathered in memorial services for the murdered striker, but despite the adverse publicity, Mitsui refused to enter into mediation.

Nevertheless, CLRB chairman Kobayashi released his mediation proposals in early April. His first proposal, made on 5 April, called for a 395-yen-per-month wage increase for miners, a proposal that both the coal operators (except Mitsui) and Tanro agreed to. The second proposal, made the following day, dealt with the Miike situation and called for (1) Mitsui to rescind the 10 December designated dismissals; (2) those named by the above to voluntarily retire; (3) an additional 10,000 yen severance allowance to be paid; and (4) the company to help find them new jobs to the extent possible and consider rehiring them once the company was back on its feet.[31] The proposal was a clear-cut endorsement of Mitsui's position and a blow not only to the Miike union but to Tanro and Sohyo in particular. Sohyo general secretary Ota Kaoru, realizing the serious implications of the Miike striker's death, clearly stated his position to CLRB chairman Kobayashi in a 30 March interview:

1. By setting up a second union and employing goon squads the company is trying to destroy the first union. We won't yield and will fight to the end. The death of Kubo has reinforced the unity of workers there. Sohyo also intends to step up the fight at Miike and will send in further reinforcements.
2. The company shows no remorse regarding the recent incidents. If it insists on reopening the mine, bloodletting can't be avoided. In order to avoid this

worst-case scenario we expect a mediation proposal based on an impartial CLRB analysis.

3. To condone the firing of the 1,200 workers is to legitimize future firings due to technological change. Moreover, it is a complete denial of workers' rights and tantamount to submission to the current policy of making the union movement a hand-maiden to capitalists.[32]

Taking such a position with Kobayashi was one thing, but to convince Sankoren and Tanro to reject the mediation proposal was another—a lot of water had gone under the bridge before Ota decided to get his feet wet. Tanro's Twenty-fifth Convention was slated to begin on 8 April, but because the Central Struggle Committee was deadlocked over whether or not to accept the Kobayashi proposal, the convention opening was delayed a day. Even when it did open on the ninth, it almost immediately went into recess. Sankoren threatened to walk out if the mediation proposal were not accepted, despite Ota's pleas to reject the proposal in his speech opening the Tanro convention. Two emergency meetings of Sohyo's general council were called just prior to and during the Tanro convention where new support policies were adopted, including a further 150 million yen in financial aid.[33] The Miike local also sent delegates who pleaded for Tanro to continue the fight. The Miike local's central committee had unanimously rejected the Kobayashi report. On 17 April, the Tanro convention voted to reject the Kobayashi report. Sankoren, having walked out of the convention a number of times, washed its hands of the struggle, and on 18 March the Miike local left Sankoren. Tanro was in tatters, but the fight continued. As the Miike local's own history summarized: "The period from the formation of the breakaway union and the failure of Tanro Directive 203 to the rejection of the Kobayashi report transformed a Tanro dispute into a Sohyo battle and brought about a new phase in the struggle."[34]

Sohyo had committed itself to a nationwide campaign of support for the Miike miners. Its strategy was to try and link the Miike struggle with the anti–Security Treaty struggle. At the Miike mine itself the confrontation centered on control of the Mikawa colliery hopper, which was a bottleneck in the production process. The Miike union, backed by thousands of Sohyo activists, concentrated its picketing at the Mikawa hopper. Clashes erupted between the Miike strikers and breakaway union members who, with police support, were trying to get into the hopper. In a 20 April incident, a number of people were injured, and on 12 May violence flared up again as police charged 2,000 picketers at the hopper, injuring 180. The town of Omuta was in a state of siege. In an extraordinary measure, Sohyo decided to hold its fourteenth convention in Omuta from 8 to 9 June, the first time it had been held outside of Tokyo. This was followed by Tanro's twenty-sixth convention held in Fukuoka on 13–14 June. While somewhat symbolic, the convening of the general assemblies near the scene of the Miike confrontation served notice that Miike was not simply a regional struggle but was intimately linked to the national political situation, in particular to the anti–Security Treaty struggle.

The Miike battle escalated to a fever pitch during July as heated battles were fought at sea when Mitsui tried to bring in replacement miners and supplies to its island collieries. On 5 July the Fukuoka District Court, responding to a Mitsui appeal, placed the area around the Mikawa hopper under the direct legal control of a court officer. With this extraordinary writ, Mitsui prepared to completely eject the Miike strikers and their supporters with the backing of the courts and the direct intervention of the police. A bloody showdown was in the offing. Sohyo in the meantime prepared for battle, dispatching 10,000 union activists to defend the Mikawa hopper picket line while it also called for a mass demonstration on 17 July. Tensions reached boiling point on that day as 20,000 unionists picketing the Mikawa hopper stood face to face with 10,000 police in full riot gear. Nearby, 100,000 Miike union supporters gathered in a huge rally. The mobilization of union support led to a standoff, but Mitsui was determined to have the Mikawa hopper cleared of picketers before its interim injunction expired on 21 July. Tensions increased.

Ikeda Intervenes

The fall of the Kishi cabinet on 15 July and the ascent to power of Ikeda Hayato as leader of the Liberal Democratic Party (LDP) represented, if not a fundamental break with the conservatism and anticommunism of Kishi Nobusuke, at least a determination to defuse the explosive situation at Miike. Ikeda formed his cabinet on 19 July and appointed Ishida Hirohide as labor minister with the mandate to intervene immediately in the Miike confrontation. Ishida called on the CLRB to mediate, and the CLRB initiated discussions with the two sides. The CLRB, with the government's backing, demanded that the two sides commit themselves to accept the CLRB's final recommendation, with the two previous mediation proposals serving as a basis for the final decision. On this basis, the imminent clash at the Mikawa hopper would be averted, with pickets remaining at the Mikawa hopper.

This proposal was accepted by the Miike local, Tanro, and Sohyo, and indeed the picketers at the Mikawa hopper were exuberant about the government intervention, feeling that their perseverance had brought the fight to a standstill and that the government could not use force to rout the workers, given their numbers and determination. The government's decision to avert a showdown also caused consternation among certain sectors of the ruling class. Mitsui was unhappy with the proposal and wanted the government to first give a lesson in law and order by enforcing the court order to clear the hopper of pickets. In what must have been an extraordinary session, Ishida personally went to Mitsui headquarters on 20 July to meet the top leaders of the business world, including Sato Kiichiro, president of Mitsui Bank, Uemura Kogoro, vice president of Keidanren, the chairman of the Japan Chamber of Commerce, four top Nikkeiren officials, as well as Kuriki to persuade them to go along with mediation.[35] In the end Ishida

Figure 2.3. **Mitsui Mining's Miike Facilities**

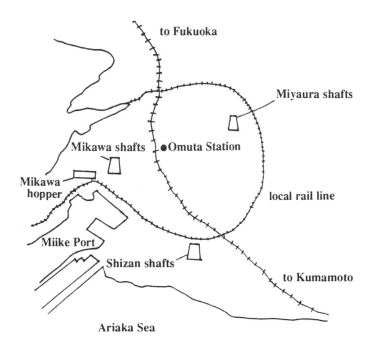

This map is from Miike Tanko Rodo Kumiai. *Miike 20-nenshi.* p. 248.

and the government won out, Mitsui's court order expired without being enforced, and both parties acceded to the mediation process. Calm gradually returned to Omuta.

On 10 August the CLRB came down with its ruling, which included the following points:

- the designated layoffs appeared unavoidable, and it was impossible at that stage to deal with each individual case to establish whether the layoff was justifiable;
- workshop struggles had been excessive, and blame was attached to both the company and the union;
- violence had gotten out of hand, and was unacceptable;
- the company should rescind its designated layoffs, but those named should voluntarily retire;
- those retiring and those named would receive 20 and 50 thousand yen respectively;

- those laid off could appeal their cases to the labor board or the courts;
- the government and company would work to find new jobs for those laid off;
- the company and unions would form a committee to work out details to restart production, and the company would not discriminate between the new and old unions.

The company immediately accepted the mediation proposal, but the Miike local rejected it. Once again Tanro faced an impossible decision. The issues were thrashed out at Tanro's Twenty-seventh Convention in Tokyo beginning on 18 August, but again the delegates found themselves deadlocked and the convention was adjourned for further reflection. Finally, after nearly twenty agonizing days, the convention ratified the proposal despite the objections of the Miike local. Almost all agreed that the proposal was unjust and antilabor, but the view that the union movement was unable to continue the struggle given the forces against it eventually won out. The emotional moment was recorded by an *Asahi* journalist:

> When the CLRB mediation proposal was adopted, the 60 people from the Miike local who were crammed into the back of the Tanro Convention remained silent, neither clapping nor speaking. They appeared stupefied. Among the miners' wives with their white headbands, a few women cried. A number of motorcycle riders who had come up to the convention in khaki suits and white helmets struggled to take off white jerseys inscribed in bold letters "Reject the Mediation Proposal." Most of the Miike wives were in tears or were wiping their faces with handkerchiefs. It wasn't unexpected, but as one terminus in a long, bitter struggle—and having to swallow 1,200 dismissals— the disappointment went deep. Looking at those faces even I felt tears on the way. Later in the hallway wives hugged each other, crying. "Stop crying now, it's not a time for tears," Sakisaka Itsuro softly chided them, his own eyes red with emotion. At that the wives burst out, tears rolling down their cheeks. The CLRB proposal was adopted amid Miike's tears of grief.[36]

Following the Tanro decision, the Miike local had no choice but to follow, and on 1 December 1960, 312 days after the lockout began at the mine, the Miike miners returned to work. The original union survived, scarred but resolute, and continued the struggle to preserve its autonomy. More than thirty years later, it remains active and defiant but no longer represents the majority of Miike miners.

Repercussions

The Miike confrontation and eventual defeat of the independent, militant miners' union had significant implications for our understanding of industrial relations in Japan.

First, from a historical perspective, Miike obliges us to reappraise our understanding of the stages and dynamics in the postwar evolution of industrial relations in Japan. For example, some historians have stated that by the mid-1950s labor-management relations had stabilized and were marked by close coopera-tion between unions and managers. [37] If this is true, how can we explain the class-against-class nature of the Miike dispute in 1960, five years after the sys-tem was supposedly stable?

The fact is that sharp class struggle continued in Japan right into the 1960s. To be sure, by 1955 major employers, abetted by the right wing of the labor movement, had made significant inroads against adversarial unionism in strate-gic industrial sectors. But it is a mistake to conclude that employers had gained overall hegemony in labor-management relations at this time. In fact, labor rela-tions remained volatile for a number of reasons. Some workers, such as the Miike miners, did not succumb to employers' attempts to regain hegemony in the workplace. As well, other workers in hitherto unorganized sectors became more active. Maeda Hajime recalled how, just when managers thought they had things under control, disputes in new sectors broke out: "Around 1955 labor battles had changed quite a bit. In places where you wouldn't think struggles would occur, such as in banks, investment dealers, hospitals, and schools, struggles began to break out."[38] Class conflict actually became more generalized as indicated by a steady increase between 1946 and 1965 in the number of labor disputes and the number of workers involved.[39] At the same time, public-sector workers contin-ued to fight for the right to collective bargaining and the right to strike, teachers fought against an efficiency rating system, and many industrial workers contin-ued to defend their unions against management encroachment as during the Oji Paper Mill strike in 1958. These struggles were not isolated events but often involved support activities by Sohyo, regional labor councils, and community groups. The ongoing employers' offensive had provoked Sohyo, in fact, to trans-form itself from a U.S.-sponsored, anticommunist, collaborationist union central in 1950 into a relatively militant, anti-U.S. imperialist labor federation by 1955. In that year, Sohyo affiliates initiated the Shunto, the coordinated spring wage offensive, to counteract the growing influence of enterprise unionism.

The continuous turmoil throughout the decade and resultant class polarization were requisite conditions for the confrontation that erupted at Miike in 1960. Even Japan's managers cite the Miike struggle as the apex in an epoch of industrial relations strife: "At the same time, this [the Miike battle] was the climax in a lineage of long struggles beginning with the Tanro and Densan unlimited general strikes right after the peace treaty, continuing through the Nissan and Nihon Steel/Muroran disputes and up to the Oji Paper battle."[40]

The fact that the Miike union and Sohyo lost the 1960 battle, however, did represent a severe setback for adversarial unionism in Japan. This is the second significant aspect of the Miike experience. Prior to the Miike defeat, Tanro and other militant unions were pressing for Sohyo to adopt a plan for affiliated unions to strengthen their roots in the factories through a plan of workshop struggle whereby workers in each plant would exercise direct control over bargaining and strike action. The Miike local's success in implementing this type of action in the late 1950s caused more than a little consternation on the part of Nikkeiren. In fact, it was one of the primary factors leading to Nikkeiren's direct involvement in the strike. As Maeda Hajime recalled:

> There were two kinds of poisons that were eating at the roots of Mitsui Mining. One was the power of the union in the mines—they were so strong they could defy foremen's orders. The other was the influence the union had in the company residences—they were strong enough to eliminate company influence. Labor relations at Miike generally were unstable due to syndicalist ideas and action, and it was hopeless to expect a return to sound management without resolving this problem.[41]

Defeat at Miike in 1960 undermined the campaign for workshop struggle within Sohyo and also weakened Sohyo's organizational base in the private sector. As a result, those few major private-sector unions that remained within Sohyo (such as the Federation of Iron and Steel Workers' Unions) increasingly abandoned local dispute tactics and began to restrict their activities to joint consultation and collective bargaining over wages. In many ways these limited activities were not dissimilar to those of private-sector unions affiliated with the right wing of the labor union represented by Zenro Kaigi (which later became Domei Kaigi in 1962 and Domei in 1964). This similarity in function among private-sector unions—regardless of central affiliation—created the requisite conditions for bringing private-sector unions together. The most important initiatives in this direction were the creation of the International Metalworkers Federation–Japan Committee, established in 1962, and Zenmin Rokyo (National Council of Private Enterprise Workers' Unions), established in 1982. Both of these organizations were sponsored by the right wing of the labor movement and brought together by private-sector unions with different central affiliations for the express purpose of developing a unified labor front around issues of mutual concern. This consolidation of enterprise unionism in the private sector began to eat away at Sohyo's base in the private sector.

Although numerically the largest nationally centralized labor organization, Sohyo's main basis of support became public-sector unions, which were more political and militant as they strived to regain the right to strike lost in 1948 under the Occupation. Despite valiant efforts, including an eight-day work stoppage in 1975, Sohyo has been unable to regain the right to strike in the public sector. In the meantime, Sohyo's two largest public-sector affiliates, the railway union and the teachers' federation, have basically fallen apart—the former because of privatization moves on the part of the government, and the latter because of internal dissension. These trends in the private and public sector are the historical background that led Sohyo to decide to dissolve in 1989 and join the private-sector-sponsored labor federation Rengo. While it would be gross oversimplification to attribute these later developments to the Miike struggle, the defeat in 1960 was in many respects a watershed in that it marked the beginning of decline for adversarial unionism within Sohyo, particularly among private-sector affiliates.

The third arena where Miike had a dramatic impact was in the conflict that accompanied Japan's conversion from coal to oil as the country's major fuel source. The defeat of the Miike union and the subsequent layoffs at Mitsui and at other companies marked the opening salvo in the "energy revolution."[42] I have attempted to show that the Miike conflict was largely political in nature, that is, Mitsui was determined to break the militant, independent Miike local by firing union activists. Having said this, however, economic factors should not be underestimated. Under pressure from industrial consumers (the steel industry, among others) for lower coal prices, coal companies hoped to rationalize their operations by laying off thousands of workers and by closing less efficient mines. Mitsui's successful attempt to disembowel the Miike union was a signal that full-scale rationalization could be carried out. Thus, in the 1960–70 period alone, the number of operating mines dropped from 682 to 102. In this same period, mine employment declined precipitously from 244 to 52 thousand as miners were thrown out of work on a scale as large as autoworker layoffs in the United States in the 1980s. Tanro continued to oppose the rationalization program and layoffs after 1960, but the defeat of the Miike union robbed the federation of its strongest component, and the attempt to halt the layoffs was largely ineffective.

In an ironic twist of fate, the mining industry faced a labor shortage in the 1963–65 period. Miners began to abandon the coal shafts as working conditions and wages deteriorated. Life in the mines became precarious. While the accident rate was declining in every other industry in Japan during the 1959–69 period, in the coal industry the accident rate actually increased by 50 percent. Mine disasters became endemic. Tragically, Miike miners, who had suffered so much during the 1960 conflict, were not spared this new affliction. On 13 November 1963, barely three years after miners had returned to work, a huge explosion ripped through the Mikawa colliery at Miike, killing 458 miners and injuring 800 others in one of the worst mining disasters in world history. Mitsui cutbacks in the mine were cited as a contributing factor in the disaster. Even mainstream sources were obliged to recognize the link between the rationalization program and the numerous mine disasters. As one Labor Ministry official obliquely put it: "One can hardly say that the rapid increase in productivity had nothing to do with the mine disasters."[43] Faced with thousands of unemployed miners in the streets and recurring mine disasters, the government had little choice but to begin relief efforts. It spent about 59 billion yen during a twelve-year period for unemployment insurance and job retraining schemes. Over the same period, the government put 260 billion yen directly into the pockets of coal operators as subsidies during the phasing out of coal production. The economics of accelerated growth that characterized the 1960s were thus inextricably bound to the politics of breaking independent adversarial unionism.

Notes

1. Nikkeiren Sanjunenshi Kankokai, *Nikkeiren sanjunenshi* (Tokyo: Nihon Keieisha Dantai Renmei, 1981), p. 348.

2. Mitsui Tanko Kabushiki Kaisha, ed., *Shiryo: Miike sogi* (Tokyo: Nihon Keieisha Dantai Renmei Kohobu, 1963), p. 22.

3. Miike Tando Rodo Kumiai, *Miike 20-nenshi* (Tokyo: Rodo Junposha, 1961), p. 85.

4. For the debate on strategy, see Rodo Kyoiku Senta, ed., *Sohyo soshiki koryo to gendai rodo undo* (Tokyo, 1979).

5. For a solid account of the early postwar upheaval, see Joe Moore, *Japanese Workers and the Struggle for Power, 1945–47* (Madison, WI: University of Wisconsin Press, 1985).

6. No systematic account has been done of Nikkeiren's involvement in these and other labor disputes. One primary source is a two-part autobiographical series by Maeda Hajime, a managing director of Nikkeiren during the turbulent 1950s. See Maeda Hajime, "Tosho ichidai" (A fighting life); and "Nikkeiren ni ikita nijunen" (Twenty years with Nikkeiren), in *Bessatsu chuo koron, keiei mondai*, vol. 8, nos. 2 and 3, p. 364. The Mitsui role is outlined in Hoshino Yasunosuke, *Mitsui hyakunen* (Tokyo: Kagoshima Kenkyujo Kenkyukai, 1978). For an English-language account of the struggle at Nissan, see chapter 3, "The Human Drama: Management and Labour," in Michael Cusumano's *The Japanese Automobile Industry* (Cambridge, MA: Harvard University Press, 1985), pp. 137–85.

7. Figures for prices and profits are from Mitsui Tanko Kaisha, ed., *Shiryo: Miike sogi*, pp. 434, 436.

8. Cited in Sakisaka Itsuro, *Miike nikki* (Tokyo: Shiseido, 1961), p. 83.

9. Martin's article is an open attack on the union. Interestingly enough, articles by Martin similar to this one were reproduced in *Far Eastern Survey* and in *Postwar Japan* (New York: Random House, 1973). Martin's role in this whole affair and his own status are somewhat suspect, to say the least. It appears that Martin joined the United States Information Agency in 1961 as a field officer in Chile and then went on to become senior State Department labor analyst. Moreover, Sakisaka indicates that Martin met with Mitsui officials but not with any Miike union representatives—somewhat strange given that Martin was supposedly a union man himself. Sato Kiichiro, a prominent anti-union executive with Mitsui Bank, was also Nikkeiren liaison for international affairs at this time, and although the evidence is circumstantial, it is possible that Martin was in contact with Sato and Nikkeiren.

10. Mitsui Tanko Kaisha, ed., *Shiryo: Miike sogi*, p. 439.

11. For the complete proposal, see ibid., pp. 442–48.

12. Tanro Directive no. 44, 21 Feb. 1959, cited in Miike Tanko Rodo Kumiai, *Miike 20-Nen*, p. 252.

13. Nikkeiren, *Nikkeiren jigyo hokoku, 1959* (Tokyo), p. 61.

14. For Yamamoto's perceptions of the situation, see *Nikkeiren sanjunenshi*, pp. 744–45.

15. Mitsui Tanko Kaisha, ed., *Shiryo: Miike sogi*, p. 482.

16. Ibid., p. 484.

17. Nikkeiren, *Nikkeiren jigyo hokoku, 1959*, p. 100.

18. Mitsui Tanko Kaisha, ed., *Shiryo: Miike sogi*, p. 552.

19. Ibid., p. 518.

20. Miike Tanko Rodo Kumiai, *Miike 20-nenshi*, p. 301.

21. Mitsui Tanko Kaisha, ed., *Shiryo: Miike sogi*, p. 529.

22. Sakisaka, *Miike nikki*, p. 117.

23. Mitsui Tanko Kaisha, ed., *Shiryo: Miike sogi*, p. 175.

24. Nikkeiren, *Nikkeiren sanjunenshi*, p. 357.

25. Miike Tanko Rodo Kumiai, *Miike 20-nenshi*, p. 330.

26. Mitsui admits organizing a series of lectures at Enoshima by the same right-wing leaders in 1952 as part of a special anticommunist "factory defense movement" initiated by Nikkeiren. It was found guilty of unfair labor practices by the Central Labor Relations Board at the time. For details of Mitsui's previous involvement with the Mitamura school, see Mitsui Tanko Kaisha, ed., *Shiryo: Miike sogi*, pp. 113–18.

27. Miike Tanko Rodo Kumiai, *Miike 20-nenshi*, p. 327.

28. Nikkeiren, *Nikkeiren sanjunenshi*, pp. 744–747.

29. *Asahi Shimbun*, 28 March 1960.

30. *Asahi Shimbun*, 31 March 1960, p. 2 editorial.

31. Cited in Mitsui Tanko Kaisha, ed., *Shiryo: Miike sogi*, p. 613.

32. Miike Tanko Rodo Kumiai, *Miike 20-nenshi*, pp. 368–369.

33. Nihon Rodo Kumiai Sohyogikai, ed., *Sohyo junenshi* (Tokyo: Rodo Junposha, 1964), p. 719.

34. Miike Tanko Rodo Kumiai, *Miike 20-nenshi*, p. 345.

35. Miike Tanko Kaisha, ed., *Shiryo: Miike sogi*, p. 696.

36. *Asahi Shimbun*, 6 Sept. 1960, p. 3.

37. This view is commonplace. Even one of the best books on Japan's labor history takes this position. See Andrew Gordon, *The Evolution of Labor Relations in Japan: Heavy Industry, 1853–1955* (Cambridge: Harvard University Press, 1985), p. 367.

38. Maeda, "Nikkeiren ni ikita nijunen," p. 363.

39. See statistical analysis in Okochi et al., eds., *Workers and Employers in Japan* (Tokyo: University of Tokyo Press, 1973), pp. 309–26.

40. Nikkeiren, *Nikkeiren sanjunenshi*, p. 355.

41. Maeda, "Nikkeiren ni ikita nijunen," p. 364.

42. Unless otherwise stated, information on the decline of the coal industry and the impact on miners is taken from my M.A. thesis, "Labour Relations in Japan's Postwar Coal Industry: The 1960 Miike Lockout," University of British Columbia, 1986.

43. Rodosho Shokugyo Antei Kyoku Shitsugyo Taisakubu, ed., *Tanko rishokusha taisaku junenshi* (Tokyo: Nikkan Rodo Tsushinsha, 1971), p. 338.

II

Paying the Bill: Costs of the "Miraculous" Growth of the 1960s

The day laborers of Sanya, Tokyo, presented in Brett de Bary's 1974 "Sanya: Japan's Internal Colony" have not disappeared with time. Japanese capitalism constantly replenishes their ranks. More than ever they have no alternative but to live on the streets, with only pieces of cardboard, sleeping bags, blankets, plastic sheets, and umbrellas to protect them from the elements. The places where these people sleep are now dispersed throughout the city. This photo of a stroller stacked with a Sanya laborer's meager possessions is by Miyashita Tadako and appears in her book *Yama mandara* (Sanya mandala) (Tokyo: Taishukan Shoten, 1995), p. 46; the photo is reprinted here courtesy of Miyashita Tadako and Taishukan Shoten.

Japanese employees eating in a company cafeteria. The large number of young women who became office workers in Japan during the sixties were expected to remain in the workplace only until they married, and even within their companies they were usually limited to traditional roles of service to the family, although in this case to the enterprise "family." Tamae Prindle's translation of Shimizu Ikko's short story "Silver Sanctuary" (Gin no seiiki) illustrates this situation in the case of a young bank employee who goes to great lengths to have some of her own needs met while maintaining her subservient role within the bank structure.

Brian (Daizen) Victoria's "Japanese Corporate Zen" explores the way Japanese business has used Zen training for new employees to bend them to the group and cultivate extraordinary commitment to the capitalist enterprise. The resulting "corporate warriors" are expected to selflessly sacrifice their personal lives for the profit of their corporations. This 1968 photo of the Zen temple Nan-zen-ji in Kyoto is by and courtesy of David Paulson.

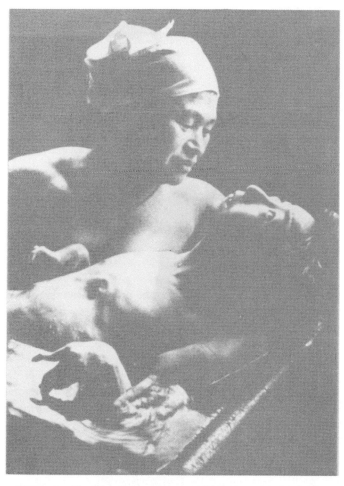

Christopher Stevens's translation of Ishimure Michiko's "The Boy Yamanaka Kuhei" brings home the social costs of unregulated capitalist development as she shows us the suffering of people with mercury poisoning from the Chisso Corporation's pollution of the seas around the town of Minamata in Kyushu, Japan, during the fifties. By 1995 there were 3,000 officially recognized victims, and 10,000 who had applied for but not yet received government recognition. "Minamata disease" affects the central nervous system and to varying degrees causes convulsions, tremors, and impaired vision, hearing, and ability to speak or move. One of those so afflicted was Uemura Tomoko, shown above in her mother's arms; Tomoko first showed symptoms of Minamata disease as a baby and died from it at the age of twenty-one. This photo is by W. Eugene Smith, © Aileen Mioko Smith, and reprinted here with permission.

3

Sanya: Japan's Internal Colony*

Brett de Bary

Day Laborers in Japan

You have to get up early to know Tokyo. Take Baba as a case in point. By day, it is an ordinary, slightly run-down park beside the tracks of the city's central commuting loop, halfway between Shinjuku and Ikebukuro stations. Go at dawn and a thousand men populate the park—young men in shirts and sneakers; carpenters in their belling, knicker-like pants; the muscular *dokata*, construction workers, duffel bags thrown over their shoulders and heavy black cloth shoes on their feet; a handful of men in office suits and leather shoes; old men, hobos—the park is a different world. At six, the action begins. Vans pull up and encircle the square, the contractors dismount, enter the crowd, and wait as clusters of men gather around them to negotiate the sale of their day's labor. Small eating carts dot the park, and along the cement paths second-hand-clothes vendors peddle pants and jackets piled on squares of open cloth. The bargaining reaches a climax at seven, when wages are highest, and goes on for another hour as weaker, less aggressive men take what is left. Then, one by one, the vans with their cargoes of workers drive off, the cart owners lock up, the clothes vendors bundle their goods back into their squares of cloth, and by eight Baba is once more a drab, empty park.

But in the world of Tokyo day laborers, Baba is only a way station. The number of men who work out of the park, about a thousand, is comparatively small: the proportion among them of student dropouts or temporarily unemployed who will eventually work their way back into the white-collar strata is large. Those for whom the daily morning auction and day-labor have become a way of life usually drift, instead, to the *doyagai* (flop-house town) that is Tokyo's largest community of day laborers, Sanya.

---

*A slightly different version of this paper appeared in *Ampo: Japan-Asia Quarterly Review,* vol. 6, nos. 3–4 (summer–autumn 1974).

Sanya, too, is a carefully camouflaged part of the city. When tourists from all over the world gathered in Tokyo for the 1964 Olympic Games, the city government launched a "clean-up campaign" of the possibly embarrassing eyesore, despite the fact that Sanya's human population was increasing through massive labor recruitment for the construction of superhighways, superexpress railway lines, and Yoyogi Stadium. Since, needless to say, hunting for Tokyo's slums was hardly a high-priority item on the schedules of Olympic tourists, the campaign—largely replastering on the flop-house street front entrances—achieved modest success. More recently, the Japan Socialist Party (JSP) administration of Minobe Ryokichi again made Sanya the subject of beautification efforts, as part of its "modernization" program for Tokyo. As a result, garbage collection services in the area improved, a few more "modern" flophouses were built, and the notorious word "Sanya" was removed from the city map. Today, only the more poetic of the area's ancient titles remain, contrasting oddly with the reality they identify: "Street of Pure Waters," "Bridge of Tears," "Jewel Princess Park."

More difficult for the zealots of cleanliness to sweep away has been the social structure of Sanya: the labor contractors and the invisible corporations which employ them, the gangster organizations which control them, the 15,000 or so men who rely on this work for their daily existence. Here, behind the garbageless streets and face-lifted entrances, the human Sanya lives on, in conditions of misery which belie current myths of prosperous Japan. Step inside a *doya*, for example. "Sanya is a place where you can live with nothing more than one *tenugui* (the small towels Japanese laborers wrap around their heads to absorb sweat) to your name," one resident said. Inside a typical Sanya flop-house, where one rents a bed by the night, the average living space is estimated at one *tatami* mat (about 3' x 6') per man. A typical *doya* room has 8 mats, and 8 men. To leave as much open space as possible in the room, two beds are placed, one on top of the other, like bunks, on each of the four walls. Set on the floor beside each bunk will be two duffel bags containing tools and work shoes, the sum of the worldly possessions of the occupants. At night, or when there is no work, men gather together on the open space left in the middle of the room, talking, gambling, drinking. The crowded dark rooms, compounded by the general dampness of the Japanese climate, make them an easy breeding place for tuberculosis. This year, when statistics revealed Sanya's TB rate to be two times that of the rest of Tokyo, squeamish public officials in the local welfare office demanded ultraviolet lights over their desks to disinfect the day-laborer applicants! Alcoholism, which to an advanced degree is said to afflict over 70 percent of the *doya* population, is an even more serious problem than TB.

But a bed in a *doya* is not the only accommodation Sanya has to offer. This January, when a series of riots in the district made newspaper headlines, middle-class Tokyoites shuddered guiltily as their TV screens flashed shots of day laborers in the bitter 5:00 A.M. cold, fistfighting, crawling over each others' shoulders, even forcing their way through the windows of one of Sanya's dingy employment centers in a desperate struggle to line up for jobs. Hit first and hardest by the economic slowdown brought on by the oil "crisis," many of these men had been jobless for weeks, destitute, and facing the prospect of a night (perhaps not their first) in the cold if they went jobless that day. In fact, spending a night outdoors has always been a familiar feature of life in Sanya: in the unique slang of the slum there is even a special word for it—to "blue-can," stand under the open sky around a fire of whatever can be foraged from the street. What the TV news reports did not mention was that an average of 40 men die each year in Sanya "blue-canning." During this year's long New Year holiday, as businesses around the nation shut down to celebrate and save on fuel bills, three people froze to death in Sanya's "Jewel Princess Park."

Where Do Day Laborers Come From?

Outcroppings of Sanya dot the city of Tokyo. The street crews, with their picks and pneumatic drills, already hard at work when the commuters step from their doors on winter mornings, the groups of men squatting around scrap wood fires and smoke-blackened kettles, taking a noontime break at roadside construction sites, the *tobi*, or "hawks," specklike figures on the frames of skyscrapers that soar above downtown streets, the flimsy prefab dormitories, appearing overnight in the midst of residential areas when there is building to be done, vanishing as suddenly when the project is finished . . . all these are as familiar as trains and buses on the surface of Tokyo life. But to the average citizen they are no more than disconnected fragments. He does not follow the *tobi* and the street crews home at night, does not know where the residents of the prefab dormitories retreat when their work is finished and the temporary shelters dismantled. A wall of prejudice prevents him from tracing them to their source in Sanya.

To inquire about Sanya among Tokyo residents at large is to discover Japanese stereotypes of the day laborer strikingly similar to those of minority races held by dominant groups in more racially heterogeneous societies. Most prevalent is the myth of the "dangerousness" of Sanya. The majority of "respectable citizens" of Tokyo claim to know "nothing at all" about the area: "I wouldn't dare set foot in it." On the heels of this comes a refusal to admit that the plight of day-laborers is worthy of attention, no less sympathy. Sanya's residents, the citizen staunchly maintains, have "chosen to live there of their own free will." What is more, "they could leave any time they wanted to." In a logic which closely parallels that of white racism toward ghetto blacks, the entire responsibility for the existence of Sanya and the day-labor system itself is traced to the moral weakness of its victims, the individuals who live there.

Often the most heart-rending glimpses of Sanya life appear in such conversations, used as illustrations of the moral degeneracy of the residents of the slum. "You have to see it to believe it," a man who had worked briefly in an employment agency declares. "Sanya is a place where you can sell anything. You can eat rice for breakfast in the morning and sell the chopsticks and the bowl you ate out of when you're done." A prosperous doctor, who recalls with distaste doing part-time work in a blood bank near Sanya in his student days, offers his own recollections as proof of the "good-for-nothing" character of day laborers. "Whenever they get desperate for money, they come in and sell their blood. Most of them do it far too often. You know there are weight requirements for blood donors. Well, we'd be putting these guys on a scale and the next thing we know we'd find they'd put rocks in their pockets to get them up to standard weight." The doctor complained that collecting blood in Sanya was bad business because of the frequency with which the donors fainted and had to receive transfusions of the same amount of blood.

Who, then, becomes a day laborer? How "freely" is the way of life chosen, and how freely can it be escaped? Sanya must first be understood in the context of the historical events and social conditions which led to its formation.

Hidden History of the *Yoseba*

To anyone familiar with the ghettos of Europe and America, the slums of Djakarta and Hong Kong, Tokyo's Sanya will seem small and tidy by comparison. In Japan itself, conditions in Sanya are slightly better than in Osaka's day-laborer area, Kamagasaki, which has a population of 40,000. But both Sanya and Kamagasaki are only points on an extensive network of day-laborer hiring sites which runs up and down the Japanese archipelago from Sapporo to Koza, Okinawa. Every major Japanese city and port has its *yoseba*, auction site where labor is hired by the day, and surrounding slum. Supplementing these, at construction sites all over urban and rural Japan, are thousands of *hanba*, temporary dormitories for men working on a daily wage basis, although they have contracted their work for the duration of a particular project. Historically, two processes—peasant migration during the declining period of Tokugawa feudalism and Japan's postwar industrial transformation—were decisive in the formation of the system as it exists today.

The *yoseba* first appears as a word and an institution in late eighteenth century Japan, where its roots overlap with a more ancient system of caste-like discrimination existing since pre-Nara times. In the mid-1700s, a series of famines and floods coupled with soaring rice prices had sent desperate peasants streaming into cities in search of food and work. A number of edicts forbidding peasant migration after 1777 failed to stem the tide, and while women were absorbed into flourishing pleasure quarters as prostitutes, men, frustrated in their search for employment, became part of a swelling, potentially explosive population of drifters. Jails and stockades filled to overflowing, and in 1790 the *bakufu* set up its first labor camps, known as *yoseba*, in the cities of Edo (present-day Tokyo), Nagasaki, and Osaka. The site of the Edo *yoseba* was an island called Ishikawajima, to which homeless men, rounded up at periodic intervals, were sent to perform forced labor. Initially men sent to the *yoseba* were classified as "non-criminal homeless" people, but the island gradually became a depot for criminal offenders as well. After the breakup of Tokugawa feudalism, the area survived into the Meiji period as the Ishikawajima Prison.

While ordinary peasants were sent to the Ishikawajima labor camp, a separate *yoseba* was set up in 1848 for classes of people who had traditionally been kept separate from the rest of society. It was this *yoseba* which existed on the site of the present-day Sanya, amidst a cluster of communities of *eta* (those working the polluting leather trades) and *hinin* (an even lower caste of "non-humans") and the Yoshiwara pleasure quarters. Forced labor for *hinin* consisted of leading prisoners to the famous Kozukahara execution site, carrying out punishments and executions, and disposing of the dead bodies.

In prewar militarist Japan and during World War II, *yoseba* persisted in camps for forced-draft Korean laborers known as "octopus rooms" because, like the octopus traps used by Japanese fishermen, there was no getting out once one had gotten in. The camps were presided over by criminal gangs which used violence to coerce labor on military projects and to prevent the escape of the Korean inmates. The Kajima Gang, forerunner of today's giant Kajima Construction Company, was one of these groups.

Despite its origins in feudal Japan, the proliferation and institutionalization of the *yoseba* system has been a unique product of the postwar era. It may seem ironic that Japan's population of poverty-ridden, unskilled day laborers was spawned and grew in numbers precisely during those decades when the nation's GNP was growing by leaps and bounds. Beneath the seeming paradox lies the stark reality of Japan's "economic miracle," with its underpinnings in a vast domestic force of subcontract laborers of various types: day-laborers, seasonal laborers, temporary laborers, elderly and married women working in their homes, and tiny, non-union factories with five or six employees.

An increasing pace of rationalization in industry and the dramatic decline of Japan's postwar economic program have been driving forces in creating the pool of unemployed tapped by the day-labor system. In the case of Sanya, the steps in the conversion of the prewar redlight, *buraku* (outcast) areas into full-blown *yoseba* have paralleled almost exactly the accelerating phases in the nation's postwar industrialization. The initial influx of unemployed men to Sanya, for example, coincided with the implementation of the "Dodge Line" Occupation policy—reviving the *zaibatsu*, snuffing out small businesses, neglecting agriculture—in 1949. Between September 1949 and March 1950 the number of independent businesses in Japan dropped by 30–40 percent, there was widespread abandonment of small (one hectare or less) farms, and over one million people were unemployed. The establishment of the first private employment agency operating out of Sanya followed soon after, as the Korean War boom led to heavy demand for labor in teeming shipyards and construction sites.

Throughout the fifties bankrupt farmers, handicapped war veterans, and coal miners thrown out of work by the shift to oil energy drifted into Sanya and were fed through its employment agencies into these two industries. The decade of the sixties, famous as the era of Japan's "high-speed economic growth," witnessed a further dramatic increase in the ranks of day laborers. Mammoth construction projects such as the Shinkansen superexpress railway, the Tokyo Olympics, and the Osaka Expo coincided with such rationalization programs as the Agricultural Structural Reform, aimed at diverting farmland to industrial use. This policy brought the effective dissolution of what remained of Japan's small farmer class. Between 1962 and 1963 alone an estimated 90,000 farmers abandoned their land. The portion of the national population involved in agriculture, 32 percent in 1955, had fallen to 19 percent by 1967. Sanya's population doubled in roughly the same period (6,000 in 1953, over 15,000 by the mid-sixties), as did that of other *yoseba* throughout the country.

While a growing pool of unemployed labor has been one half of the *yoseba* equation, the perfection and perpetuation of the system have been the work of certain sectors of big industry with close cooperation from the Japanese underworld. Prime movers in the process have been shipyard owners and the construction industry. Although a certain portion of day-labor contracts is for miscellaneous distasteful or dangerous jobs (garbage collection, morgue work, hazardous aspects of steel production), the overwhelming majority of contracts come from shipyards and construction firms. At the root of the demand has been the desire of the two industries to cover their relative vulnerability to fluctuations in supply and demand by reliance on a "disposable" labor force. This has been particularly true of the construction industry, which in Japan is virtually 100 percent dependent on subcontract labor. The fluid nature of construction work, in which not only the amount and type of labor used but building materials and machinery vary vastly from project to project; its vulnerability to daily weather changes; and a high accident rate caused by the prevalence of superspeed projects all make construction capitalists loath to assume responsibility for the wage and insurance costs of a permanent labor force. The result has been the evolution of the *yoseba* system as it exists today: giant construction companies pass on the responsibility for hiring labor through a complex network of smaller and smaller companies terminating in the individual labor contractor (the often feared *tehaishi*) on the daily auction site. The *tehaishi* guarantees the firm a certain number of workers per day and receives as his salary a cut out of the wage paid to each worker. Since conditions of work are frequently illegal or involve deception in making oral contracts, the ultimate linchpin in the system is the use or threat of physical force by the contractor on the work site. Accordingly, a majority of contractors and the small companies they represent are part of underworld organizations. (The National Police Report on Organized Crime for 1973 estimated that 2,500 construction companies were controlled by criminal gangs. Since collusion between police and underworld gangs is common, this should be seen as a low estimate.)

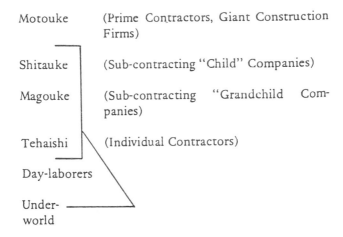

Motouke — (Prime Contractors, Giant Construction Firms)

Shitauke — (Sub-contracting "Child" Companies)

Magouke — (Sub-contracting "Grandchild" Companies)

Tehaishi — (Individual Contractors)

Day-laborers

Under-world

The *yoseba* system has sometimes been compared to an intricate network of nodular roots extending from the giant construction companies through the mass of day-laborers. According to conditions of the market, lengths of roots may be disconnected at any place along the nodes (the subcontracting companies and *tehaishi*), beginning with those furthest from the parent firm. The day laborer is thus rendered supple and pliant in the hands of capital, which passes all the brutality of the vicious cycle of supply and demand on to the *yoseba*, pitting young against old, strong against weak, in the daily struggle for survival.

Octopus Rooms in 1974?

February 1974 ... the story of 30-year-old Mr. I., who appeared unexpectedly this February at a Soka Gakkai gathering this reporter was observing in a quiet residential area of Tokyo, illustrates vividly the forces which converge in the making of a contemporary Japanese day-laborer. Mr. I. responded to the group's questions about how he had become a "believer."

Mr. I. was one of five children born into a farming family on Sado Island off the northern coastal city of Niigata. His father, a tenant farmer at the time of the Occupation land reform, received a plot of land barely large enough to support his family. Income from raising rice was so slim that the children in the family had to gather wood and make charcoal to earn the meager amount of spending money they needed at school. I.'s only thought when he graduated from high school was to leave the difficult life on the farm and find a well-paying job in Tokyo. But with minimal social connections and no technical skills, I. was only able to land a job as a milk delivery man, rising at 3:00 every morning with a starting salary of 3,000 yen a month (1956). After fourteen years at this job, I. earned a modest salary of 100,000 yen per month, but in 1970 the small company where he worked fell victim to that other phenomenon of the era of "high-speed economic growth," the insolvency of small businesses. Left with no other alternatives after the milk company went bankrupt, I. kept himself alive for four years at a number of jobs which he found through newspaper ads and employment agencies—all of them extremely low paid and requiring 24-hour work shifts twice a week. In August 1974, I. was approached at an employment agency by a man claiming to be a representative of the Ota Steel Company, with what seemed an attractive job offer. For driving a truck transporting steel girders from the Ota factory to different construction sites, I. would receive a wage of 2,800 yen per day. The wage, the Ota man assured him, would be sheer savings, because the company would provide him with a room—bath attached!—and all his living necessities at their dormitory *(hamba)* in Saitama-ken, just beyond the northern boundaries of Tokyo. I. made an oral contract for one month's work on the spot, and left for Saitama-ken the following day.

"As soon as I got inside the dormitory I realized I was in an octopus room." I. found himself in a structure made of the thinnest plywood. Although he arrived during the last October warm spell, temperatures soon dipped, but there were no heating facilities in the building. "From the beginning of November, the tap water was frozen every day. We couldn't even get water to try to warm ourselves with tea." The "bath attached" which I. was promised turned out to be "attached" to the outside of the building: a converted oil drum heated from beneath. Far more devastating, however, was I.'s discovery that the dormitory, and all the truck drivers in the area, were controlled by an underworld organization known as the Morimoto Gang.

At the end of his first month, I. found himself with only 24,000 yen of the 84,000 yen he had been promised to clear. Two thousand yen of his daily 2,800-yen salary had been subtracted for meals, rent, and bath fee! More, he confessed frankly, was lost in nightly gambling sponsored by the gang in the dormitory. "By December I was desperate to quit. It wasn't only the loss of money and the cold, but the work itself was extremely dangerous. A little slip loading or unloading these steel girders and you're crushed. I knew there had been many accidents." But when I. announced his decision to leave, the Morimoto Gang threatened retaliation on his family and effectively forced him to work on. Finally, with the help of a boyhood friend from Sado, I. managed to escape from the dormitory during his three-day New Year's holiday, forfeiting fifteen days' wages. He had temporarily found work as a painter in Tokyo and had come to the Soka Gakkai meeting because "I should practice my religion from now on. That other life must have been a punishment for my sins."

I.'s story is atypical only in its still tentative conclusion, his escape from the world of day labor. Its basic elements are the classic ingredients in the experience of Japanese day laborers, except that for most there is no way out. Of Sanya's peak (wintertime) population, for example, one-third are seasonal rural migrant workers who will return to their farms, one-third are permanent day-laborers who wander from yoseba to yoseba, while one-third are permanent residents of Sanya.

No Escape: Life Cycle of a Day Laborer

A dissection of Sanya's social structure reveals the day laborer trapped in a vicious cycle of economic relationships, while social prejudice bears down with equal force from outside. Caught between the two, the alienation of the day-laborer is an extreme within Japanese society. "After you live here for awhile," says Nakamori Kishin, a pastor in the ghetto for 20 years, "you realize there is absolutely no basis for community in Sanya. I can think of only two things that really bring these men together: the drinking stand and the park bench." According to Nakamori's observation, the competition of the *yoseba*, unsteady supplies of cash which force men to drift from one inn to another; the infiltration of the *doya* by plainclothes men hunting for fugitive criminals, all debilitate potential bonds of unity between the men. Sexual alienation reinforces their isolation. Mistrust and contempt on the part of "ordinary society" make it extremely difficult for men in Sanya to marry. At present only 200 men, about 1.5 percent of the population, have wives.

Underlying the day laborer's existence in Sanya is a predatory economic network including *tehaishi*, inn owners, restaurant-owners, underworld-controlled recreational facilities, and police, which over time renders him economically, physically, and psychologically unable to leave the ghetto.

Conditions of Life in Sanya

1. Tehaishi, Wages, and Work

Daily contracts are made between 5:00 and 7:00 A.M. Seventy percent of men in Sanya seek jobs from approximately 150 blackmarket *tehaishi*, either with introductions from private employment agencies, innkeepers, or by going directly. Current black market wages for day labor range from 4,500 yen to 5,000 yen per day. While this at first glance appears high (assuming full employment, the monthly 110,000-yen income would equal that of a middle-aged male company or government worker), the impression is deceptive, for the wages are offered under conditions which in fact leave the day laborer in the most economically weak and vulnerable position in Japanese society.

Lack of job security: Contracts negotiated on illegal terms with *tehaishi* or small subcontracting firms offer day laborers none of the fringe benefits and bonuses which beef up the income of ordinary salaried workers. Most damaging to the day-laborer is the failure to guarantee steady work. Completely at the mercy of supply and demand fluctuations, no day laborer is in a position to find employment on every working day of the month. On a typical day at the Sanya *yoseba*, there is a 30 percent unemployment rate. Even in peak working seasons, the average day laborer is employed only about 20 days per month.

The winter season: A city employment office set up in Sanya in the early sixties does offer a minimal dole of 1,200 yen per day to unemployed day laborers. To qualify, however, an applicant must produce a stamped card proving that he has worked 28 days out of the preceding 60-day period. The effect of this system is to disqualify most laborers from unemployment compensation at precisely the time when they need it most. This is during the winter season, when Sanya fills to overflowing with workers from the countryside. By increasing the labor supply and accepting work at lower rates, incoming farmers drive wages down and sharply intensify competition for jobs. Since the number of jobs drops drastically after November, by late January large numbers of men in Sanya lack the qualifications even for the unemployment dole. This year, with the added impact of the oil crisis, the number of workers qualified for the dole was effectively zero—sparking the riots mentioned above. Dread of the winter season is a major factor driving men to sign up for 3- or 4-month stints at *hamba* such as the one I. went to.

Lack of accident insurance: Day labor is by definition the most physically strenuous, distasteful, and dangerous work available. This is especially so in the construction industry, which achieves high productivity by building at the fastest speed and lowest cost possible. The hiring of inexperienced workers for hazardous work, introduction of new machinery without training sessions, failure to block traffic around work sites in congested streets, the use of flimsy scaffolding which all too frequently collapses—these and other features give the construction industry one of the highest accident rates in Japan. Despite this, firms offer virtually no accident insurance to day laborers. While formally the giant companies sometimes provide their employees with a policy, the red-tape process involved in this all but nullifies its effect for the day laborers.

City Employment Agencies: In the 1960s the city established two employment centers in Sanya, offering contracts on legal terms, unemployment and health insurance included. Daily wages for these jobs, however, are only one-half to one-third of the black market rates for the same work. Accordingly, only about 30 percent of Sanya workers, usually those whose age precludes them from effective competition on the *yoseba*, rely on these agencies.

2. Lodging, Food, Recreation

In step with Japan's spiralling inflation, inn rates in Sanya have risen exorbitantly in the last three years. The fee for one night in a bunk-bed—50 to 80 yen in the fifties—now ranges from 300 to 500 yen. Since this equals a monthly sum roughly equivalent to that paid by many Tokyo office workers and students for small rooms in residential areas of the city, outsiders often ask "why don't they just move out of the slum?" The obstacle is the parasitic structure in which the day laborer is caught, one which makes it literally impossible for him to lease an apartment in Tokyo. Once having entered Sanya "with only one *tenugui* to his name," the day laborer finds himself dependent for every aspect of his existence on those whose profit, in turn, derives from his daily cash wage. "Extras" like cigarettes, soap, toothpowder, which his innkeeper handily produces for a slight service charge, substantially inflate the cost of a night's lodging. To restaurant owners and drinking-stand operators go payments for food and for alcohol, the fastest source of relief after an exhausting day's work. Houses of prostitution take a further cut of his daily wage. What is left sooner or later filters into the gangster-dominated gambling networks, which are perhaps the cruelest form of economic and psychological oppression of the day-laborer. Race-track betting, which thrives on his pathetic hopes of the lucky break which will bring wealth, respect, and a ticket back to normal society, is so prevalent in Sanya that the *yoseba* is literally depopulated on the last day of a series of races.

No wonder that Sanya is sometimes referred to by its residents as a "great, big octopus room." A day laborer who tries to defy these conditions of his existence finds himself confronting three tightly knit walls of resistance: the underworld gangs, the Sanya Innkeepers' Union, and the police. Sanya's twenty-odd years as a *yoseba* have been marked by an increasing degree of internal organization and cooperation between these three groups, while during most of this period day laborers have remained a weak and divided mass.

As the first employment agency was being set up in Sanya, for example, landlord Kiyama Kinjiro allied himself with the demands of industry and the *tehaishi* by devising the "bunk-bed system" for converting the welfare barracks in the area (set up under SCAP for homeless wanderers right after the war) into lodging houses for day laborers. The first campaign of the Sanya Innkeepers' Union, founded soon after, was to drive prostitutes out of Sanya into neighboring Asakusa, a major step in the area's conversion to a full-fledged *yoseba*. In the decade of the sixties, the Innkeepers' Union has been a driving force behind the gradual expansion of police control in the area. After the First Sanya Incident in 1959, when workers attacked the small local police box, the Innkeepers' Union backed construction of a new and greatly enlarged station in its stead, contributing chairs and funds for the building. Innkeepers and merchants, jealous guardians of the law and order which guarantee their incomes, have been firm supporters of the "candy and whip policy" (welfare measures accompanied by police repression) which the government has evolved in recent years to cope with increasing outbreaks of violence in Sanya.

Health Conditions: "A day laborer is always shifting between three modes of life: worker, unemployed man, and sick man," says a young worker organizer in Sanya. "Usually he ends his life in the last category." The large majority of workers in Sanya, a backwater of Japanese society as far as health conditions are concerned, suffer from some kind of physical ailment. Almost all suffer from stomach, liver, and kidney diseases associated with alcoholism. Lacking health insurance policies which most Japanese receive from their companies, day laborers are forced to rely on city hospitals, where conditions are deplorable and which are unbearably lonely for men with no family. As a result, many workers in

Sanya shy away from medical treatment and put up with their ailments while they continue to work. A prevalent pattern in Sanya is for the condition to gradually worsen until a man passes out, is taken by ambulance to the hospital where he dies, perhaps never having realized to that point the extent of his illness.

There is another dimension to the problem of health in Sanya, for illness of the day laborer provides yet another vulnerability which may be manipulated to keep him supple and pliant within the system. City hospitals and mental institutions in this sense may be seen as extensions, in slightly more subtle form, of the repressive network which maintains law and order in Sanya. This is most clearly suggested by the pattern of close cooperation between city hospitals and the police force. Sweep arrests of drunks in the Sanya area are common, particularly during economic slumps and other periods of potential unrest. Police records show the astonishingly high yearly average of 10,000 arrests for drunkenness—just short of one arrest per head of the population. Slightly over 1,200 of these arrestees, often workers who stand out for their rebellious and defiant attitudes toward authority, are turned over by police for periods of confinement in city mental institutions, a striking commentary on the double function of these institutions. An estimated two-thirds of the patients in Tokyo's public mental hospitals are day laborers.

Resistance and Repression

The history of organized resistance to conditions of oppression in Sanya has been a bleak one. A first labor union, formed in the early fifties by day laborers, Koreans, and Communists released from prison under early SCAP policy, was crushed by the arrest of its leaders after the "Bloody May Day" of 1952. Sanya workers spent the rest of the decade of the fifties without any form of union organization, totally at the mercy of subcontractors, and excluded from even the minimal welfare programs of the state.

Sanya's first outbreak of rebellion came on 22 October 1959, against the background of the escalating national struggle against the renewal of the U.S. Security Treaty. Sanya's local police box, long an object of resentment for its role in enforcing the order of exploitation imposed by subcontractors and merchants, was attacked by 300 men and one patrol car was set ablaze. The action provoked a wave of alarm which spread from the local power structure to the National Diet, and in the following summer the government authorized the construction of what workers have ever since referred to as "Sanya's mammoth police box," base for a 55-man force, in Sanya. The Tamahime "Consultation Center" (its name aptly circumscribing the limits of its services) was opened in the fall, the first government welfare office to be established in Sanya. The all-too-obvious "candy-whip" nature of the government's policy, however, only fanned rebellion in the ghetto: the mammoth police box was attacked a few weeks after its opening, and summer 1961 brought a chain-reaction outburst of riots in Kamagasaki. In the following year the government responded by drawing up a "Consolidated Welfare Policy" for the two ghettos. A welfare center was opened in Sanya in July 1962 and relocated and expanded in 1965. But so far government welfare programs, which carefully leave intact the fundamental contradictions of the *yoseba* system, have proved utterly useless in defusing worker discontent. Riots have continued to occur with yearly regularity, gradually exposing the teeth in the policy of the government, which has simply escalated its application of police force to suppress them. Since 1970, this has included dispatching *Kidōtai*, special riot police, to quell ghetto disturbances.

The decade of the sixties brought renewed efforts by left groups to channel spontaneous worker rebellion into an organized movement, but this ended in failure, due both to the increasing severity of police repression and the lack of a viable ideology for the day-laborer struggle. Between 1964 and 1969, seven different struggle groups coalesced in Sanya, including one organized by the JCP; all but two of these collapsed within a year of their organization. Of those which have survived into the seventies, one, the Sanya Independent Consolidated Labor Union, now confines its activities largely to the operation of a small cooperative restaurant. The second, the Tokyo Day Laborers' Union, which had a substantial base among day laborers into the early seventies, was disbanded this winter after a scandal involving misuse of funds collected from members at New Year's.

In spring 1972 the successful action of a small band of militant workers in smashing one of Kamagasaki's notorious subcontracting groups, the Suzuki Gang, sparked the birth of a radical new form of struggle among Japanese day-laborers. Dramatically rejecting the passive, negotiating stance adopted by organizers of the sixties in favor of pitting struggle directly against the immediate agents of oppression, the subcontractors on the worksite, a small group of day-laborers, disillusioned unionists, and New Left activists came together in Sanya and Kamagasaki in autumn 1972 to form two fraternal organizations—the Work Site Struggle Group (Genba Tōsōiinkai) in Sanya, and the Joint Struggle Group (Kamakyōtō) in Kamagasaki. According to the bold vision to which these two groups have committed themselves, negotiating, which focuses on making "demands" while continuing to work within an exploitative system, is an implicit acceptance of that system, and a denial of the basic right of the worker, not the capitalist, to determine the conditions under which he will work. The guiding vision of "struggle on the work site" is a recognition of worker sovereignty, a positive endorsement of the worker's most potent weapon, spontaneous rebellion, and of necessity, when no other means avail, of using physical force to directly counter the physical force which is the linchpin of day-to-day oppression. The aim is to develop a dynamic, ongoing struggle against each case of oppression, when and where it occurs: when men discover they have been deceived by contractors, made to perform excessively dangerous or dirty work, are forced to work overtime, and so forth. But since individual efforts are sure to be crushed, as they have been so many times in the past, the key to "struggle on the work site" is collective action: "When you come up against a problem, don't brood by yourself," advises *Notes For Workers*, a "little red book" written by and distributed among struggling Sanya workers, "call your friends and get them to help you."

The formation of the Work Site Struggle Group in Sanya was followed by a rapid series of offensive actions in fall and winter 1972–1973 which gradually elicited the support of growing numbers of day laborers. Whenever a case of oppression was encountered in the course of a day's work, it would be reported to the group, and on the following day a workers' collective would be dispatched to the same work site to protest. Although in many cases the *tehaishi*, numerically overwhelmed, would yield after a brief verbal debate, tactics of physical intimidation and refusal to hire were gradually adopted by Sanya gangs as they became aware of the Work Site Struggle Group and its aims. By winter a state of "near-war"—including flare-ups of violence, police interference, and worker arrests—had broken out between the struggle group and a number of Sanya's hard-core contracting companies. In July 1973 these culminated in an all-out confrontation between workers and the Arai Construction Co. (Arai, a subcontractor for giant firms such as Mitsubishi, Kajima, and Shimizu, is notorious in *yoseba* throughout Japan for its *takobeya*—reliance on physical coercion to enforce illegal working conditions—and its affiliation with the nationwide underworld organization Kyokutō.) On 19 July, a Sanya worker who had protested against working conditions on the construction site of the Mitsui Building Skyscraper in Shinjuku was threatened into submission by *tehaishi* wielding iron bars. On the following day, 50 workers filed into the Arai office on the construction site demanding an apology for the incident and redressing of the worker's complaint. Arai summoned twenty police to forcibly eject the workers from its office, but a campaign to oust Arai from all *yoseba* in Tokyo gradually gained momentum. Arai quickly found itself alienated from the majority of other subcontracting companies in Sanya and forced to rely increasingly on bodyguards provided by the Kyokutō organization. The climax of the struggle came on 11 September, when an attack by a small group of workers on a band of Arai's bodyguards flared into a small-scale riot as growing numbers of resentful workers joined in the fray. Special riot troops were brought in to suppress the riot, and 13 workers were arrested. These workers are currently involved in a court battle with Arai, but general worker resistance to the company has by now become so effective that Arai has had to completely abandon its hiring in Sanya.

Simultaneous to the development of militant struggle against subcontractors, the Work Site Struggle Group launched a wide variety of programs designed to develop among Sanya workers the capacity to deal autonomously with their own most vital needs. Health being one of the foremost of these, worker medical cells were formed where techniques of preventive medicine, particularly acupuncture, were studied, and where procedures for receiving health and accident insurance (of which many workers were ignorant because of the bureaucratic jargon in which they are usually explained) are studied and discussed. "People's patrols" were also formed: bands of workers to patrol the streets and help men fallen through illness, hunger, or alcohol, before they are arrested. The most dramatic development on this second front-line, however, has been the yearly "Struggle to Survive the Winter," carried out during the national New Year's holiday, the most dangerous period of the year for day laborers, since employment openings drop to zero while dwindling supplies of cash force large numbers of men to "blue-can" in the bitter cold. In 1973–74, the Work Site Struggle Group erected huge tents in Jewel Princess Park, where food (supplied by Sanrizuka peasants), fires, and free medical attention were provided. This winter, 1974, when the heavy toll taken by the "oil crisis" in unemployment among day-laborers made the situation particularly severe, the Winter Struggle developed into a complex political struggle to demand greater attention from the city welfare structure to the acute problems of day-laborers' existence. The struggle continued into late January, when the city, attempting to avoid the high cost of paying a daily dole to the huge numbers of unemployed workers, announced a termination of the dole and herded workers into an institution where they could literally do nothing but sit on their hands all day, waiting for three substandard meals. On 20 January, when worker anger over their humiliating situation welled up into a riot within the center, *kidōtai* (riot police) were again called in, 20 workers were arrested and the protest severely repressed. Two days later the center was closed and all workers sent back to Sanya. In the following month 50 other workers known to have participated in the protest movement were arrested on various charges.

While the growth of the Work Site Struggle in Sanya clearly symbolizes a giant step in the revolutionary consciousness of Japanese day laborers, it has also made clearer than ever before the tenacious roots of the *yoseba* system in Japan and its vital importance to the Japanese economy. According to the struggle group members' own analysis of their experience, escalating attacks on the subcontracting system have consistently evoked greater and greater police and government intervention to unabashedly support and rescue those under attack. (Preparations for the 1974 Winter Struggle, for example, had to be carried out under surveillance of a 300-man Special Riot Force detachment.) Since May 1972, 160 members of the Work Site Struggle Group have been arrested and indicted on various charges (the figure for Kamakyōtō during the same period is 250). With the exception of the long-continuing and fierce struggle of Sanrizuka peasants to oppose the construction of an international airport at Narita, no other Japanese protest movement at the present time faces such intense state repression as the day laborer movement.

The campaign continues to heighten at the present time. In the past few months, for example, a concentrated police campaign to label Work Site Struggle members as former Red Army members has been launched, accompanied by a wave of arrests and indictments on preposterous bombing charges which are clearly frame-ups. In the face of this repression, many members in the Tokyo and Osaka areas have been forced to disperse to *yoseba* all over the country, while those remaining in these two central cities are concentrating their energies on expanding such aspects of the movement as the medical program (which are legal and not so easily subject to repression) and waiting, as one member put it, "while the seeds of the struggle are sown in *yoseba* all over Japan."

4

Shimizu Ikkō's "Silver Sanctuary" (Gin no seiiki): A Japanese Business Novel

Translated and introduced by Tamae K. Prindle

Translator's Introduction

"I want to describe the many people who are directly involved in business," says Ikkō Shimizu, pioneer of the industry novel (*kigyō shōsetsu*), a sub-genre of the Japanese business novel (*keizai shōsetsu*). As the name suggests, industry novels pertain more specifically to industries than do business novels, which cover a broader spectrum of socioeconomic issues.

Born in Tokyo in 1931, Shimizu attended Waseda University. As a freelance writer, he contributed to stock-market journals before bursting onto the literary landscape in 1966 with his novel *The Stock Market: Fiction* (Shōsetsu Shima), an instant best seller. He has since published some 100 novels and almost as many short stories. His *Artery Archipelago* (Dōmyaku rettō, 1975) was awarded the twenty-eighth Japanese Mystery Writers Association Prize. A good two dozen of his works have been turned into films and television dramas. Today, he is one of Japan's most prolific and popular novelists.

As Shimizu notes, Japanese industry novels are "young," dating only to the mid-1960s. The distinctive feature of these novels is their "immediacy to the business world." The stories expose the internal mechanisms of business transactions and the mentality of the people involved, making technical information accessible to a lay audience and convincing even to economists.

"Silver Sanctuary" begins with the discovery of a breach of confidentiality in the administration of three confidential long-term savings accounts. A type of account unfamiliar to most Westerners, it is opened under a pseudonym and utilized primarily for tax purposes. The customer's real name and address are known only to a very limited number of bank employees. Transactions on the account are carried out by means of a registered stamp (*inkan*) bearing the customer's pseudonym. Shimizu has taken a special interest in this peculiar system.

"Silver Sanctuary" unravels the tenuous interpersonal and inter-institutional relationships to be found in the banking world. At the personal level, there are two career paths: vertical and horizontal. Only executives-in-training have the privilege of promotion beyond the level of division head. Hence, personnel rotation brings about psychological tension among employees, who are like cogs in a wheel turned by the institution. The cogs are subject to the basic principle that "a banker must be trustworthy and almost impartially serious, and at the same time have no idiosyncrasies." Women are expected to play a secondary role.

The dramatic present of "Silver Sanctuary" is the early 1960s, almost twenty years after women's suffrage was recognized in Japan (1945) but more than twenty years before the Equal Employment Law passed the Diet (1986). The M-shaped demographic curve of the women's labor force—with women in their early twenties forming the first peak and those in their mid-forties a second but less prominent peak—is already in place. That is, women typically leave their jobs to bear and rear children and subsequently return as part-timers. Misako in "Silver Sanctuary," who marries Tagawa and stays home, lives a more idealized woman's life than does Yōko, the tragic protagonist of the story. The name Yōko, meaning a person who serves, who is constant, even stupid, symbolizes an old maid's social status. And in fact Yōko becomes persona non grata, and even a criminal, after offering everything a woman can to Tagawa, Saeki, her father, and a number of other men. We, along with Tagawa, the elitist banker, get to glimpse the interior of her aching heart. From a more practical standpoint, the rapid turnover among women workers makes the female labor force cost-effective and elastic. All told, "Silver Sanctuary" is a skillful blend of literature and expository reporting.

"Silver Sanctuary" (*Gin no seiiki*) was first published in the Japanese monthly *All Reading* (Ōru yomimono), January 1969, and was later included in *Nine Consecutive Hits* (Chūren Pōton) (Tokyo: Kadokawa Bunko, 1984).

1

A strange thing happened exactly three months after Junji Tagawa became manager of the N branch of Nittō Bank. Although the youngest branch manager in the bank, Tagawa found himself settling into the job.

"Something's fishy here," Assistant Manager Kenji Nishiyama said to Tagawa after a business meeting. He looked puzzled. "I got a call from Mr. Ikuno of the fifth ward. You know him, don't you? He's the one who installs greenhouse heating systems. He was asking why a representative from Daidō Bank across the street called on him."

Tagawa parroted the question. "You mean . . . why he visited?" Shortly after his recent promotion, he had paid a courtesy visit to Ikuno's house with

Nishiyama. If he remembered correctly, Ikuno lived in a rusty prefabricated hovel to which a brick shed had been added. Obviously, the owner of this drab building with no business signboard had been cutting quite a few corners. Yet in the N branch alone, Ikuno had a confidential long-term savings account of 25 million yen. Tagawa had trouble putting two and two together.

"In other words, Mr. Ikuno doesn't believe he was picked at random. He says we're the only institution with any knowledge of his twenty-five-million-yen savings. You remember that miserable shanty of his, don't you? The reason he lives there, he says, is to avoid unnecessary taxes. So, how did Daidō Bank catch on? He's in a panic. Now that Daidō's found out, he thinks the tax bureau's close behind, ready to sniff out his actual income."

Tagawa smiled disapprovingly. He was not all that critical of Ikuno's penny-pinching mentality, but it didn't make sense for Ikuno to tie the Daidō man's visit to the tax issue and let it frighten him.

"Daidō didn't ask him to transfer his twenty-five million yen, did they?"

"Heaven forbid!"

"Why worry, then?"

"The thing is—maybe it's just a coincidence, but Mr. Norisaka on K Street, whom I dropped in on yesterday, has also been tapped by Daidō."

Norisaka owned a small grocery store. Small, yes, but its owner was once the largest landlord in the area, and he was a steady client at the Nittō N branch. His long-term savings account contained nearly 30 million yen.

"Wonder what's up over at Daidō—a memorial savings campaign, something of that sort?"

"Nothing that I know of," answered Nishiyama.

Tagawa peered through the thin lace curtains at the white, two-story Daidō bank kitty-corner across the narrow intersection in front of N Station. Next door to it was a mutual bank. Altogether, six financial institutions had branches in the neighborhood.

"Well, then, did they decide to spirit away our good customers?"

If it were a matter of one customer, Tagawa could reasonably ignore the case as a coincidence. But when two customers with confidential accounts were approached in such short order, he had to be solicitous.

N Station belonged to a private railroad company. It was only thirty minutes from Ikebukuro Station on the heavily traveled Yamate Line. The daily flow of commuters through this station totaled some 20,000. The district enjoyed growing popularity as a newly developed residential area, and new banks had mushroomed as fast as the regional development itself. Now that the area was completely built up, as many as six bank branch offices stood side by side. They vied bitterly with one another for customers. But on top of the usual business competition, the new banks had another evil to combat: new homeowners had no money to save. Energetic representatives in search of customers had only other banks' territories to explore.

Located in one of the most competitive zones in Tokyo, the office managed by thirty-seven-year-old newcomer Junji Tagawa was no exception. Bank management always demanded a steady growth of clientele, and sales representatives' concerns were pretty much centered in this matter. Banks, then, were understandably edgy about the movements of large depositors.

"Just to be on the safe side, I'll go talk with our two clients," said Tagawa.

"That might help."

Tagawa knew he had to safeguard his bank before he could counterattack. The first thing to do was procure a clear picture of what his opponents knew and what they wanted.

Ikuno and Norisaka, the two clients Tagawa visited that day, gave him a piece of their mind, saying that a person's financial secrets shouldn't be used as a weapon to fight the competition. They demanded an assurance of confidentiality.

"I don't understand it. Somehow the list of confidential deposits must have gotten out of Nittō Bank." Ikuno kept after Tagawa, frowning nervously. It was an odd sight, this placid, chubby man fidgeting.

"I swear, sir, that there was no oversight."

"I'm not convinced of that."

"It's our responsibility to guard the confidentiality of our clients," Tagawa said crisply, putting a stern expression on his handsome face. "May I ask the name of the Daidō man?"

"I think it was Saeki, something like that."

The name corresponded to the one on the calling card Tagawa had seen at Norisaka's house just a while ago. According to Norisaka, the man had a flat, pale face.

Tagawa made up his mind to check on Saeki before long. But he was prompted to act sooner when he found Tatsuo Aoki, another large deposit holder, waiting in his office.

"What the hell's going on, Manager?" The bald-headed visitor tossed a calling card on a side table. "This fellow came to see me. I hope you have a good explanation."

Stooping over to peer at the card, Tagawa saw Saeki's name again and almost let slip, "Oh, he went to your house, too." Instead, he sat down opposite Aoki and spoke calmly. "I see, Daidō Bank. Is this the first time?"

"He asked me to put some money in his bank." Aoki's voice mirrored his disappointment in failing to rouse Tagawa. But his belligerence returned in no time. "First I tried to get rid of him. Told him I had no money to save. Then, guess what? This fellow with the silly-looking glasses had the nerve to say, 'We know you do.' He had a big grin on his face!" Aoki's voice grew louder.

"My God, he *is* forward!"

"But he knew what he was doing. Listen. The man said, 'For starters, you have fifty million yen at Nittō Bank in a confidential account. It happens to be maturing next month, and we were wondering if you'd be kind enough to take advantage of our services and deposit just half of it with us.' Imagine—can you think of anything more preposterous?"

Tagawa, deflated, tried to catch his breath. Aoki's self-confidence rekindled when he noticed this reaction. He grew coarse and pressed his advantage. "I just can't get over this. Is someone at Nittō giving away information to Daidō?"

"Nothing of the sort, I can assure you."

"But don't you see that things are getting out of hand?"

Tagawa feared that this mix-up might turn into a fatal blow to his career. Only an insider could have leaked information about the confidential long-term savings accounts.

"Say what you want!" roared Aoki. "All I know is that I can't trust your bank—I feel stupid leaving my money with you. I want it all back!" Aoki banged on the armrest of the sofa. The arteries of his boarlike neck bulged grotesquely.

A 50 million yen withdrawal—it might very well cripple the achievement record of the N office. Feeling cornered, Tagawa edged forward on the sofa and did his best to win Aoki's heart. "You know the old saying 'a hundred devils marching at night'? Well, you're probably aware of this, but that's the situation with banks now. The competition is horrendous. At the moment, it's impossible to tell what kind of trap Daidō has set for us. But it's very unlikely there's been a leak from here. In any event, I'll investigate right away. Please be kind enough to give us time to figure things out."

Suddenly, a strange anxiety welled up in Tagawa. Or rather a queer gut feeling, a presentiment, struck him. An image loomed momentarily in the back of his brain, like a shadow floating between dark waves. It disappeared only to resurface, again and again and again.

"Please give me a week. That should do. I can rectify matters as soon as the cause comes to light."

"And then what?

"I'll see to it that you won't be inconvenienced." Tagawa bowed low.

"When the manager is young, the management is bound to be remiss," Aoki huffed. He left after making it clear he would not wait more than a week.

Tagawa pondered the anxiety he had just felt, and reexamined the shadow that had wafted through the back of his mind. He felt he'd been unfair to the woman he suspected, but judging from her position in the bank, there was good reason to suspect her. Also, if her personal resentment against Tagawa was still there, she could have done this intentionally as a way of revenge.

Tagawa lifted the intercom. "Does the name Kikuo Saeki ring a bell?"

"Which company, sir?"

"What I mean is, does either of you remember anybody from our bank calling a person named Saeki, or Saeki calling somebody here?"

Tagawa heard the two switchboard operators whispering to each other. Holding the receiver, he tasted an acrid premonition that the young women would name the person whose image had just passed through his mind.

"If we remember correctly, sir, Miss Yōko Takigami used to call him. But she stopped about two months ago."

Tagawa winced. It was exactly as he had feared. He heaved an audible sigh.

2

How ironic! There was no other way to describe Tagawa's reencounter with Yōko at the N branch office.

Tagawa had graduated from the Department of Economics of A University. After entering Nittō Bank, he worked for five years as an executive-in-training. Initially, he belonged to the first section of the General Affairs Office in the main building. Subsequently, he was sent to the Ikebukuro branch office, in Jōhoku District, as a trainee in branch-office management. It was here that he was introduced to Yōko Takigami. She was a teller at the front counter in charge of day-to-day transactions.

Yōko had graduated from high school three years earlier and had worked at the branch office ever since. She was twenty-one, but more experienced than Tagawa both as a teller and also with respect to the general ins and outs of life at this regional office. With the quick wits of a city woman, she covered up Tagawa's blunders. For his part, Tagawa had a difficult time adjusting to the monotony and boredom of life in a regional office, having known only the vibrant life of the main office.

He also learned that employees in peripheral branch offices had few outlets for their frustrations. Tagawa's supervisor in charge of day-to-day transactions, Junichi Konno, was a good example. He had graduated from a provincial university and been sent to a branch office as his first assignment. He had never been included in the high-level executive track as Tagawa had. Never in the future would Konno have an opportunity to work in the main office. It was evident that Tagawa and other future executives would outrank him before long, and he would be placed under their supervision. At times, Konno bickered with the inexperienced Tagawa as would a mother-in-law. Then he would suddenly soften up and take Tagawa to a bar to cajole him under the influence of alcohol: "Please help me out in the future."

Such frustrations tested the forbearance of these underlings and trained them to mold their personalities gradually into a solid "banker type."

Tagawa's first year-end party at the Ikebukuro office came about shortly after he was transferred there. It turned out to be a nightmare.

"Too bad the manager is going to miss the party again," Yōko remarked. She was resting her hands from the bookkeeping that followed the closing of the tellers' windows.

"Isn't he sending funds for the party? We may have a better time without him."

"Only if nothing happens. . . ."

At the time, Tagawa had failed to catch the delicate nuance contained in this comment.

The party took place in a neighborhood restaurant. It was a merry affair at first, but then the fun and games got out of control. Suddenly the lights were off, the women were shrieking in abandon, and shadows were swooping down on the deputy manager, who sat across from Tagawa. Taking this to be part of the frolic, Tagawa had no suspicions. But then the deputy's pathetic protests pierced the darkness, tables were kicked over, dishes and bowls were smashed. The whole thing was ominous and bizarre. Startled, Tagawa tried to stand up. Somebody grabbed his hand and pulled him back down. In the murky gloom, he couldn't make heads or tails of the melee, couldn't even tell who had pulled him down. And then he heard something thud down the stairs.

"Don't move. Don't look. Just sit still!" It was Yōko, ordering him in whispers.

The lights came back on to a cheer from the party. But the deputy manager was no longer there. Only the distraught screams of the restaurant workers made Tagawa finally realize that Yamazaki, the forty-five-year-old deputy manager, was groaning at the bottom of the stairs he had been thrown down.

The victim took nearly a week off from work to recover. It was an atrocious, incredible incident, a sinister rebellion by the employees against an institution that had forced them into a uniformity in which one must not stand out, must not be praised or berated, must avoid the spotlight. One must strive in every way possible to commit neither virtue nor vice.

The day after the party, the bank was again the smiling, classy workplace it had always been. No mention was made of Deputy Manager Yamazaki's injury. Those who had beaten him in the darkness out of pent-up resentment received customers as politely as always. Employees threw themselves into their work as diligently as a congregation of saints.

"Did you know what was cooking?" Tagawa asked Yōko a couple of days later when they ran into each other on their way home.

Yōko forced a cheerless smile and shook her head.

"It's not your concern, Mr. Tagawa. You see, you're here just temporarily. Someday you'll go back to the main office and be a section head or an executive. The sooner you forget about that business, the faster you can finish up here. I wouldn't get involved if I were you."

Tagawa momentarily felt that Yōko was more mature than he.

Something else happened precisely a week after the party. Waiting on customers as usual, Yōko matter-of-factly attached a short note to a check and sent it to Tagawa, who craned his neck to look at it.

"This check has been altered."

Tagawa had to read it twice to be convinced. He glanced at Yōko.

"Please have a seat." Yōko was calmly addressing a sallow-faced fellow in his forties who looked like the kind of man that would own a small factory. Tagawa's head throbbed. He lost his composure, but Yōko, as if to divert the sallow-faced man's attention, took on another customer.

Tagawa put the check and Yōko's note among some other documents and walked over to Chief Clerk Konno. His knees trembled, making it difficult for him to stand up straight in front of his supervisor.

The check had been altered all right, but in a very amateurish way. The Chinese ideograph for "6" had been altered to the ideograph for "9"; 61,000 yen had become 91,000. It was the kind of tampering somebody would have noticed eventually, even if a teller didn't. Seen from another angle, it showed how hard pressed the forger was. The man was arrested on the spot.

Assuming that the ideal image of a banker is not to be praised, not to be criticized, nor even to be talked about, Yōko Takigawa's difficulties, it may be said, started at this point. Mostly because it happened to be the end of the year, and at the height of a crime-prevention campaign, the incident caught the attention of reporters. Most newspapers praised the exemplary way in which Yōko had handled the situation: "An Ingenious Banker," "Skillfully Detects Forger," and the like. Tagawa appeared in the newspapers as well, standing next to Yōko in a photo.

Tagawa learned from these articles that the criminal's name was Ichirō Hirayama. Hirayama manufactured plastic bags with a machine set up in the vestibule of his small house. This small-scale manufacturer and his wife undertook every level of work, from operating the machine to delivering the products to wholesalers. The couple labored from before dawn until deep into the night, but couldn't make ends meet at the close of the year. After many qualms, Ichirō resorted to forgery.

The incident precipitated an intimacy between Tagawa and Yōko. Yōko practically made Tagawa join a company ski trip to the Jōetsu Highlands during the three-day New Year's vacation. They spent the entire vacation as very close friends. Yōko was in high spirits, more buoyant than youth itself. She captivated Tagawa with her laughter and agility.

It was mid-January when Yōko asked politely, "Would you like to have tea with me on our way home?"

Tagawa met her by the west exit, which was on the other side of the station from their bank. The young couple walked past the unabashedly cluttered honky-tonk district in front of the station and came to a Western-style delicatessen/coffee shop near North Ikebukuro.

"There's something I'd like to ask your advice about, Mr. Tagawa," Yōko began after ordering their beverages. She told Tagawa that her father was a security officer at the Nippori branch of Nittō Bank. It was he who had arranged her employment at the Ikebukuro office. "The deputy manager asked me yesterday if I would be interested in moving to the General Affairs Department in the main office," Yōko announced with hardly a sign of jubilation.

"Sounds great!"

"I have a feeling that the forgery incident has something to do with this transfer."

"Whatever the reason may be, it's an exceptional break for you. No matter how you look at it, the main office is the best—you really feel like you're working for a bank."

Apparently, the bank had been obliged to make a gesture of appreciation for Yōko's feat now that the incident of the forged check had received so much publicity.

"But . . ." Yōko glanced downward pensively. Then she abruptly looked straight into Tagawa's handsome face. "When can you go back to the main office, Mr. Tagawa?" Her tone was urgent.

"I wish I knew. It's only been four months since I came to Ikebukuro. I doubt I could go back for another two or three years," Tagawa equivocated, flinching at Yōko's abnormally intense stare. "What does your father say? That's more important."

"He wants me to accept the offer because it's a great honor."

"I thought so. Also, the main office has a lot of good-looking men. They'll come after you as soon as you get there," Tagawa bantered. The chain of events starting with the forged check and the New Year's ski trip, which had developed into three dates, had made Tagawa a bit flippant with her.

Instantly, though, Yōko's large eyes clouded and her head drooped.

"That's why I'm reluctant to go. If you talk like that, I'm going to turn down the offer," she said in a trembling voice.

"What do you mean?" Tagawa was caught off guard by this sudden change in mood. Had he been nasty to her? All he had said was that the main office was better than a branch office. Anyone would agree with that. Yet, Yōko shook her bowed head. And presently she shook it again, more violently, as if to brush aside Tagawa's question.

"Did I say something wrong?"

"You said that the handsome men there would come after me."

"Well, it's true. Something like that might really happen."

"Please, don't talk like that—you make me feel uneasy," Yōko interrupted, baring her virginal innocence. She had no interest in strangers' proposals. "I like our Ikebukuro office better."

"Oh? Even if you never came across another chance to go to the main office?" Tagawa suspected that if she turned down this offer, Yōko would most certainly be transferred elsewhere during the next personnel rotation. Now that she had detected the altered check, been written up in the papers, and drawn media attention, Yōko had ceased to be an invisible teller like all the rest. Visibility could be deadly for a career in banking.

A bank simply had to be a place where nothing unusual happened, where people could leave their money with no hint of anxiety. Even if things were going well, the very fact that something had happened—even the smallest thing—would slow down the canvassing activities. Yōko's presence at the front window of the Ikebukuro office was undesirable because it would keep triggering clients' memories of an unpleasant incident. A bank usually hastens to wipe out any trace of such memories. This was where personnel rotations came in handy. Tagawa meant to explain that it would be far better for her to be sent to the main office than to another dead-end place, but Yōko's raised eyes tried to block out his words.

"If I go to the main office, I won't be able to work with you."

"Work with me?" asked Tagawa, thrusting his face forward. Yōko gave a big nod. Tagawa looked back at her, alarmed. Yōko's eyes, ardently set on his, were filled with burning desire. He sensed her desperate affection. The sparks of her eyes were ready to ignite. She was tacitly but frantically soliciting him for love.

"Shall we go now?"

"No, please, not yet." Yōko shook her head wildly. And in a yet more precipitous tone she pleaded, "I want to work with you. Please tell me point blank if it bothers you."

"Oh, no, not if you don't mind." Tagawa cast his eyes downward.

"Thank you." Yōko spoke as if clinging to his words with her entire body.

Tagawa looked up, smiling, to see rapturous exultation spread over Yōko's blushing cheeks. Her youthful glamour captured his heart. At that very instant, he wished to satisfy his flaring passion by attaining deeper and more concrete proof.

"Let's have a drink." Tagawa took the initiative, being cautious at the same time not to let her see that he had a man's desire to get down to business at once.

Yōko nodded gently with a somewhat hesitant smile.

Outside the coffee shop, a chilly wind swirled and wrapped itself around them. Yōko accepted the arm Tagawa casually thrust out. That night, Yōko's fair skin was stained by fresh blood, and Tagawa became engaged to her.

3

It didn't take long for talk of their relationship to spread among the Ikebukuro office employees. Yōko was in constant rapture over the idea of marriage to Tagawa. When her colleagues teased her, she blushed happily, even appreciatively. Such scenes made Tagawa feel he should conclude the marriage without delay.

"Let's talk to your father first."

No matter how quickly he wanted to proceed, there were certain preparations to make, and a certain order in which to go about them. He worked at them steadily, bolstered by the euphoria of having Yōko's moral support.

Yūkichi Takigami, Yōko's father, a security officer at the Nippori office, received Tagawa very congenially in his Takinogawa apartment.

"I've heard much about you from my daughter. Please don't worry about me. I'll manage by myself after she gets married. I only have this six-mat room to keep up." Speaking calmly and courteously, Yūkichi expressed his sincere concern that Tagawa not worry about disrupting the father-daughter bond.

"I'd like to have the wedding this spring. If I wait until fall, I'll be twenty-nine years old."

Lowering his gray-haired head, Yūkichi humbly thanked Tagawa for suggesting that the wedding be made simple so that the financial burden on the bride's father would be minimal. Tagawa then made a plan to introduce Yōko in early February to his parents, who lived by themselves in Yamanashi Prefecture.

Very early that February, Ichirō Hirayama, the check forger, and his wife committed suicide.

It was shortly before the five o'clock closing hour, and Chief Clerk Konno, who had completed his work for the day, was glancing at the evening paper. "Look! That son of a gun has committed suicide!" he called out to Tagawa in a disturbed voice.

Tagawa twisted around toward Konno. "That son of a gun?"

"Yeah, that forger."

"What! You mean Hirayama?"

Tagawa kicked back his chair and rushed to Konno's desk. "Small Businessman Commits Suicide." The large headline leaped out at him. Tagawa bent over a photo of Hirayama's suicide note. "Once convicted of forgery, it's impossible to make a living . . ." read the caption.

"A family of five," Konno reported to the other staff members, whose eyes were fixed on him

"A family suicide!" someone shouted.

Two or three people rushed over for a look at the newspaper. "With gas," one of them groaned.

"I never got to see him up close, but who would have guessed that he had such cute children. What a nightmare!" Konno desperately shook his head.

It was thought that Hirayama and his wife had waited until their children fell asleep, then had taken sleeping pills and turned on the gas.

Everyone remembered that the check forgery was only a matter of thirty thousand yen. Because there was no real loss, the bank chose not to have Hirayama prosecuted, and he was released that day.

Finishing the article, Tagawa swung his head toward Yōko. She had turned pale.

"It was only thirty thousand yen. Why did he have to die?" another teller commented.

Yōko dropped her head, put her hand over her mouth, and ran out to the locker room. Tagawa followed and found her standing motionless at the end of a row of lockers. At the sight of Tagawa, she hid her face in her hands and melted in tears.

"Let's not worry about this." Tagawa took Yōko's shoulders and pulled her toward him. "It wasn't our fault, was it?"

"But it's all because I spotted the forgery. Yes, I'm the one who drove them to suicide." Yōko lifted her wet eyes pleadingly.

"You're being too sensitive."

"But I can't forget that man's exhausted face." Yōko buried her face in Tagawa's chest and sobbed. "It was my fault, absolutely. I get to marry Junji-*san* because of that incident. Meanwhile, someone else is driven to suicide. . . . Does that make sense?"

"That's enough. Don't let it get you down."

No words were needed to explain how the Hirayama family must have suffered after the forgery was written up in the papers. But were Yōko and Tagawa the ones to bear the blame?

"Oh, I hate it. I can't stand it! He must have died cursing us. Don't you think so?" Yōko lamented.

More important than whether or not he cursed us is what kind of image Yōko and I presented to him. Did we look like merciless prosecutors? Stuck-up money mongers? Tagawa wondered. He felt as wretched as Yōko.

"What else could we do? Bankers can't simply ignore forgery. And that means we're not accountable. Even if the outcome is a family suicide. Who's guilty, then? Money! Yes, money is the evil force."

Tagawa drew Yōko tightly against his tall frame, as if to leave no room for confusion.

"I'd like you to wait awhile before you take me to your parents," said Yōko the next day.

Tagawa agreed to wait until she had recovered from the trauma of the Hirayama suicide. But this wait led to a permanent breakup of their engagement. For, exactly a week later, just when Yōko was coming out of shock and regaining her mental equilibrium, her father became embroiled in a scandal. That morning, Tagawa was awakened by his apartment manager. "Telephone!"

"My father is in trouble." It was Yōko, sobbing helplessly.

Rubbing his sleepy eyes and gathering together the collar of his robe, Tagawa asked clumsily, "What's going on?"

"I was right. The man who committed suicide was cursing us." Yōko's words made little sense. Finally, she got a grip on herself and began to explain in a choked voice: "My father is in critical condition." Patching her choppy phrases together, Tagawa grasped that there'd been a carbon monoxide poisoning from a gas burner at her father's Nippori office. Two young bankers who happened to be staying overnight in the night-duty room had died. Yūkichi had barely survived.

"I'm calling from the hospital. My father is in the emergency room, and . . ." Upset and distraught, Yōko lost track of her thoughts.

"Where is the hospital? . . . Do you hear me? Which hospital are you in?"

"Nippori Hospital, near Nippori Station."

"I'll be right over. Your father's holding out all right, isn't he?"

"They're giving him oxygen."

"There's no such thing as Ichirō Hirayama's curse, so calm down. Understand? Take it easy."

Tagawa rushed back to his room, changed, and ran out. It was difficult to find a taxi. The one that finally stopped for him moved steadily but cautiously. In frustration, Tagawa heard Yōko's desperate voice calling from the other shore of the river Styx. *Why did that gentle man have to . . . ?* Tagawa brooded over the nature of the accident. When at long last he arrived at the hospital, he found Yōko doubled up on a chair. A chilly breeze blew down the corridor.

He ran up to her. "How did it go?"

Yōko looked up vacantly and directed her empty gaze toward the emergency room. She was drained of the energy to shed tears.

"Does it seem like he's going to make it?" Tagawa asked.

"I have no idea."

"I wonder if it's really serious."

"He may not make it."

"Don't be silly." Tagawa squeezed Yōko's hand firmly.

Presently, the deputy manager of the Nippori office came running in, and the police who had inspected the site arrived to check on Yūkichi's condition.

The deputy manager explained what might have happened: Yūkichi had been on duty the night before. The two bank clerks had gotten drunk in the Nippori area and had missed the last train, and Yūkichi had allowed them to stay overnight. The two younger men, it seemed, had brought more alcohol with them and continued drinking. Yūkichi had joined them. He had fallen asleep drunk on the floor without shutting off the gas burner. Incomplete combustion had released the carbon monoxide.

"Wait," Tagawa interrupted, "Mr. Takigami doesn't drink."

"There's such a thing as being obliged to drink."

The Nippori deputy manager insisted that Takigami couldn't have fallen asleep on the floor unless he was under the influence. But how was it possible, Tagawa asked, that the two young men had died and the oldest, Yōko's father, had survived, if they had been drinking together? The deputy turned deaf ears to this question. Tagawa grasped that the finger of accusation would be pointed at Yūkichi regardless of the truth.

Yōko's father barely pulled through and was brought to his Takinogawa apartment after a week and a half in the hospital. By then, muscular paralysis and brain damage had transformed him into a human vegetable. As if this weren't enough, the Nippori office fired him on the grounds that his fingerprints were found on a teacup—their proof that Takigami had been drinking on duty.

4

Personnel rotation at Nittō Bank usually takes place in May and November. Because the bank judged that Tagawa was indirectly involved in the forgery incident as well as the gas-leak accident, it included Tagawa among those to be transferred in May. He was sent back to the main office earlier than planned. In the administration's eyes, Tagawa and Yōko stood out too conspicuously in the Ikebukuro office.

"We'd have been been married by now if nothing had happened," Tagawa said pensively to Yōko after reporting his transfer. He knew that she needed him more than ever, but one's personal circumstances could not countermand the periodic rotation.

"My father may get better by fall. Also, Junji-*san* will still be in Tokyo, even after you move to the main office."

We can see each other anytime we want. Yōko wished to say this, but it wasn't true. All her free time was spent on her father, who was no longer able to control his bowel movements. The couple had already gone three months without a date, not to mention physical contact. Yōko's financial burden also piled up. Out of a twenty-one-year-old woman's salary, she had to scrape together money for her father's medical expenses as well as their room and board. Yūkichi had no income. Tagawa was well aware of the magnitude of the problem and offered to help, but Yōko would not accept.

Yōko's last shred of hope to restore the helpless invalid was mercilessly snatched away that autumn, the very autumn she had once looked forward to. Yūkichi's condition worsened. Yōko started missing work to look after him. The news traveled through the Ikebukuro office that Yōko had been absent more than ten days. Tagawa dropped by the Takinogawa apartment for the first time in a long while.

Yōko was sitting next to her father's pillow, gazing distractedly into space. A sad smile appeared on her pale, lifeless face when she saw Tagawa.

"The doctor gave him a shot about an hour ago."

Yūkichi was asleep, his mouth agape like a child's. Yōko suggested a walk. "He just fell asleep, so he'll be all right until morning."

The round, red, early October moon was almost brutally bright for the couple, who found themselves walking side by side for the first time in months. In silence, each craved for a place where they could embrace. In a narrow alley leading to Asukayama Park, Tagawa saw the poky little signboard of an inn. He turned back to Yōko, who nodded, pressing her body against his.

The walls and ceiling of the dark room were filthy. The comforter, lacking the usual white coverlet, looked unsympathetically cold.

Yōko faced Tagawa. "I've wronged Tagawa-*san*," she said formally without her typical "Junji-*san*."

"You haven't done anything wrong," Tagawa consoled her. He took Yōko's thin, limp hand and embraced her.

Yōko lay back on the comforter and sought his lips, trembling. Not just her body, but the very marrow of her soul had been longing for gentle affection. At his first embrace, her body and soul flared up. She kept repeating, almost deliriously, "I've done something awful to Tagawa-*san.*"

That night, for the first time, Yōko reached climax. Engulfed by her frenzied and violent reaction, Tagawa felt intoxicated.

It was shortly thereafter that Yōko called off the wedding. They couldn't marry as long as she was taking care of her invalid father, she proclaimed, and there was little hope for his recovery. She pleaded desperately with Tagawa not to let her become an obstacle to him.

"I'm no longer worthy of your love. I can't even offer my body when you need it." Yōko dissolved into tears, remonstrating with Tagawa—and finally shouting at him—to forget her, because there was no hope for them.

Never again did Yōko telephone Tagawa. When he visited her Takinogawa apartment, using Yūkichi's illness as an excuse, she received him with empty formality, as if he were a stranger.

A new marriage offer came Tagawa's way early in November.

Business Department Manager Yūzō Koyanagi had invited Tagawa to his Shiba-Takanawa home on a holiday. "You're asking for trouble by staying a bachelor for such a long time."

The name of the woman Koyanagi brought to Tagawa's attention was Misako Oribe. She was the second daughter of Nittō Bank's leading customer. She had a B.A. in French literature from A University.

"She's not young by any means, but she's good-looking, as you can tell from this photograph. She has the perfect background for a banker's wife." Koyanagi hammered away at Tagawa. "You know what kind of place a bank is. It's different from ordinary companies. A person can't marry just anyone."

"I appreciate your concern."

Tagawa was on the verge of telling Koyanagi that he was engaged to Yōko Takigami when Koyanagi continued knowingly, "For example, one must not marry the daughter of a guard who, out of carelessness, got drunk and fell asleep and as a result took the lives of two promising young men."

"But that accident was—"

"I know. I talked with the manager of the Ikebukuro office. And you probably want to add that the woman is the one who spotted the forged check. But that, in itself, is a problem to us now."

"A problem?"

"Don't you see? Suppose you marry her; every time you're up for promotion, someone's bound to say, 'Well, Tagawa's outstanding, but his wife isn't the ideal type.' Think about it. And that business with her father, and then the forged check. Both will affect your future adversely—they'll make you a good conversation piece. You see, these things are detrimental to the image of an ideal banker. They add nothing to your future. That's why I transferred you out of the

Ikebukuro office. Once you're tainted, it's too late. A person in charge of personnel—whoever he may be—if he had to choose between you and someone else, he'd pick the less-tainted one."

"Tainted?"

A strange word, Tagawa mused. While it has virtually no meaning in and of itself, its connotations are boundless. In the extremely limited context of bank parlance, moreover, the word had the power to define people's characters.

"I want you to do some good thinking," continued Koyanagi, "about the expression we hear all the time—'a typical banker.' "

A banker must be trustworthy and almost impartially serious, and at the same time have no idiosyncrasies. Koyanagi was asking Tagawa to fit himself into the assigned mold. One could not stay in the narrowly defined orbit of an executive without agreeing to conform to this standard.

Tagawa asked Koyanagi to give him some time to make up his mind. Koyanagi patiently kept after him through the end of the year, going so far as to warn him, "This is your last chance to wipe out the stain you got at the Ikebukuro office."

In January of the following year, Yōko was transferred to the Sugamo office as part of an irregular rotation. The spurious reason given by the bank was that it would be easier for her to look after her father if she worked closer to her home. But in reality, it took more time for her to commute to the Sugamo office. There was no telling where she might be sent next.

Tagawa finally made up his mind and wrote Yōko that he would probably be married in the near future.

His marriage to Misako Oribe took place just as he was offered a promotion to chief clerk of the Business Department, First Section. The letter of promotion was dated May 1. Upon returning from his honeymoon, Tagawa heard that Yūkichi had died. It was truly ironic. He had been ill for over a year. The brain damage had made him as frightened of death as a child during the last hours of his life. So the report said.

A son was born to Tagawa, and two years later a second son. In the fourth year after his marriage to Misako, Tagawa was appointed deputy section chief of the Business Department. This gave Tagawa a clear sense of future success: he was definitely on the high-level executive track. The turn of events could very well be interpreted as a reward for marrying someone recommended by Business Department Manager Koyanagi.

About a year before he was appointed manager of N office—that is, seven years after he moved from the Ikebukuro office back to the main office—Tagawa heard about Yōko, the woman he had nearly forgotten. The occasion was Kōichi Aizawa's transfer from the Sugamo branch office to Tagawa's section. Tagawa sponsored a small welcome party for him

"Sir, do you know of a woman named Yōko Takigami?" Aizawa asked as an afterthought when the conversation drifted to the topic of personnel.

"Yōko Takigami!" repeated Tagawa, taken aback. It was a name he had put out of his mind quite a while ago.

"I hear she worked with you at the Ikebukuro office," Aizawa went on, smiling the easy smile of an ignorant bystander.

"We used to sit next to each other at the customer window. But that was when I was twenty-eight—seven years ago, I guess. How do you know her?"

"She's in the Sugamo office."

"In Sugamo? Is she still single?"

"Of course. Didn't you know?"

Oh, she hasn't married yet. Tagawa recalled his affectionate relationship with Yōko, which had never borne fruit.

"And how is she doing these days?"

"They say she'll be transferred. There's a problem."

"A problem?"

"Nothing serious, but we call her Miss Nymphomania in the Sugamo office."

"Miss Nymphomania?"

Aizawa nodded with an eloquent smile.

"To make a long story short, I think she wants to get married."

"That's understandable. She must be getting on in years. But what exactly do you mean by Miss Nymphomania?" The expression was new to Tagawa.

Two or three young clerks looked at each other and chuckled.

"Haven't you heard, sir? It's a type you often see among old maids. She'll be the first to approach a new entrant. It's because nobody who knows her will go out with her. From what I hear, women like her will even date someone they meet at the teller's window, or who calls sight unseen over the telephone. At least so they say."

Yōko!

Every year around April or May, Tagawa would notice the couples—experienced office women and newly employed company men, it would seem. They were seen in such popular dating places as Chidorigafuchi and Yoyogi Olympic Park. It was disturbing to think that Yōko, now twenty-eight, had become expert in this role, worrying one minute over flaking face powder and acting quite sophisticated the next. Worse, in Tagawa's eyes, it showed moral depravity.

"I wonder why she doesn't get married. She's a smart, polished woman."

"I'm not sure. She does strike you as a nice person when you talk with her. She's kind to everyone and particularly considerate to men. It's just that she occasionally acts licentious. Maybe people are turned off by something soiled about her."

"Soiled?"

"Betrayed, trampled on by many men, that kind of impression. . . ."

Soiled—Tagawa found it distasteful, but apparently this was the very word to describe the history of Yōko's relationships with men following her separation from him. He felt guilty.

Of all places, Tagawa found Yōko in the N office, to which he had moved with so much ambition. It was there that she had been transferred from Sugamo.

"How are your children?" Yōko would ask casually when they passed in the hall. But that was all. Tagawa invited her out once; she smiled slightly but turned away.

<h2 style="text-align:center">5</h2>

It was Yōko Takigami who had disclosed the confidential information that could determine the fate of the bank! . . . Tagawa fought the idea. But Yōko had been in charge of the long-term savings accounts and was familiar with the confidential large-account holders. Now that it was evident that she'd had contact with Kikuo Saeki from Daidō Bank, there was no need for further scrutiny.

Tagawa thought first of calling Yōko to his office, but in the end, he couldn't bring himself to make the interrogation quite so official. So he told Yōko over the telephone, "I have something to ask you about Kikuo Saeki. I think you know him."

Yōko's reaction was difficult to gauge, but after a moment's hesitation, she replied, "I see." Tagawa told her that he wanted to meet her in front of the department store by the west exit of Ikebukuro Station.

At 7:00, the appointed time, Yōko was standing in front of the iron grille of the closed department store. She wore bright lipstick.

"Shall we take a walk?" asked Tagawa.

Yōko nodded. Her face, once round and chubby, had become angular, and her cheekbones protruded. Her skin looked strikingly rough in the neon light at dusk.

"It's been eight years since we walked like this." Tagawa spoke warmly, turning toward Yōko.

Yōko lowered her gaze. "Mr. Tagawa, won't you be in trouble if someone sees you walking with a woman like me?"

"Let's not talk that way. How about some food?"

"I'd rather drink."

"You drink?" Tagawa could only throw back the question. That evening eight years ago, when she so passionately propositioned him, Yōko had turned crimson after a single glass of gin.

"Yes, that's the only way to . . ." Her tone was petulant.

The honky-tonk shacks had been cleared from the area in front of the west exit of the station, replaced by a sprawling thoroughfare. Tagawa led them to the bar district near north Ikebukuro and walked down a flight of steps to a basement Suntory Bar. Yōko ordered whiskey on the rocks. As he observed her, Tagawa realized he would have to proceed carefully. Perhaps to avoid Tagawa's eyes, Yōko impatiently reached for the first glass that arrived.

"Do you hate me?" Tagawa started slowly. This, in fact, was the worst imaginable. Suppose it was proved that Yōko had leaked the confidential information out of personal animosity toward him; if she had intended to ruin his career, there was nothing he could report to the main office.

"If you're disgusted with me," Tagawa repeated, "I won't ask more."

Yōko burst into wild laughter.

"What's the matter?"

"Don't worry. I don't hate you, and I don't have a grudge against you. I was the one to break off the engagement."

"Am I right in believing that this is not revenge against me?" Tagawa asked cautiously.

Yōko took a king-size cigarette from her pocketbook, held it in the corner of her mouth, and lit it.

Tagawa's life had changed greatly in so many ways since he had married Misako. For one thing, he had taken his first step on the executive track. But he understood now that Yōko had changed even more, much more than he could imagine.

"Mr. Saeki," Yōko began with a grin and a slight shrug of her shoulders, "reminds me of you."

"Me?"

"Especially in the way he's built. He's tall and thin and slightly hunch-backed."

"Are you going to marry him?"

"Why?"

"Aren't you?"

"I can't—he has a wife." Yōko blew a puff of smoke at the blue lights overhead.

Why does she wear such heavy makeup? Tagawa's eyes were fastened on Yōko.

Yōko looked up, challenging Tagawa's sympathetic gaze.

"You'll never understand why a woman goes out with a married man. But just don't look at me as if you feel sorry for me."

Yōko abruptly placed her pocketbook on the table. "Let me show you the things I always carry with me." She opened the metal clasp with a dull click.

"Four handkerchiefs. Can you guess what they're for? Men often forget their handkerchiefs, so I let them borrow these. I ask that they bring them back unwashed. . . . Here are needles and thread. See? Not just black and white—I have navy blue, brown, and every kind from cotton to nylon. . . . Three kinds of spare buttons. I replace all the men's lost buttons and mend the rips in their clothes. I even keep an iron in my desk at the office."

Poking in her pocketbook the way a child searches her toy box, Yōko started lining up all sorts of paraphernalia on the table. Then she produced a dozen thousand-yen notes from her red leather wallet.

"Since young men spend a lot, their salaries don't always tide them over till the next payday. I can at least help out with a little. But I never lend more than two thousand to one person. Because they'll stop coming to me if the debt gets too big to pay back."

It was a strange scene. Yōko would put down her cigarette, pick up the glass, put the cigarette back in her mouth, and ransack her pocketbook.

"Shall I tell you something else? You know Mr. Kaneko, who's getting married this fall? I used to go out with him until quite recently. I introduced his fiancée to him—can you guess why?"

"You've told me enough. Don't torture yourself anymore."

"It doesn't bother me. I'm used to it. It was like this when I worked in Sugamo. When I'm going out with a young man, I'm always afraid he'll refuse to go out again, or he'll call off a date on short notice. You'll never understand, but I feel desperate. So, just before I'm thrown out, I introduce the man to a young woman who's a good match for him. This way, I'll never be totally thrown out. I can do without the pain of being abandoned. And they might even go on seeing me once in a while."

Yōko's words were strangely emotionless. After a while, she carefully put back the thread, needles, handkerchiefs, and wallet.

"Laugh at me if you want. But so much has happened. And I'm already twenty-nine. Nothing can change that. Mr. Saeki has been really nice to me. But, you see, I couldn't think of anything to do for him—until he asked me for the list of confidential clients."

A turbulent anger churned up through Tagawa's chest, a feeling diametrically opposed to the nonchalance with which Yōko told her tale. Did she have to go to that extreme just because Saeki was nice to her? Did she have to make a mess of her life, letting herself be toyed with by a middle-aged married man? *Bastard! Our enemy has taken advantage of a woman who covets men, hungers for marriage, a woman full of weaknesses, naked and defenseless.* That Saeki resembled him annoyed Tagawa.

"Are you going to keep on seeing Saeki?" Tagawa asked, barely suppressing his boiling anger. He made up his mind to march into Daidō Bank early tomorrow. He would reveal Saeki's cowardice and bring back Yōko's list. Saeki would suffer the fate of a disgraced banker when it became known that he had used a woman—even if he had done so for the benefit of his bank. Banks try to stay out of trouble. This case was truly scandalous.

Instead of answering Tagawa, Yōko called a nearby waiter and ordered another drink. Her sigh of despair coincided with Tagawa's.

"I suppose it's not going to work," Yōko said in a low voice. "A banker's career ends when people start talking about him. It's the same in any bank, isn't it? No matter how hard I try to keep him, Mr. Saeki will start running away from me, like all the others."

My situation was different; I didn't run away from you. Tagawa choked back these words, realizing that a man who had chosen to project the image of a model banker had no right to defend himself in front of a woman like Yōko. He wasn't even confident enough to help Yōko, who had no prospects for the future. He found himself wondering if Saeki, who had taken advantage of her, was far more humane than he.

"I'll get the list back. Please don't make an issue of it. I'm sure Mr. Saeki will understand that a scandal would make a mess of his career," Yōko said, her head drooping.

Yōko was absent from work for two days. On the third day, an envelope from her arrived by special delivery in Tagawa's office. The contents were a letter of resignation and the list of the confidential long-term savings account holders. A single line had been scribbled in the corner: "Mr. Saeki went along with my request."

"What shall we do, sir? Mail Miss Takigami her retirement benefits?" asked Deputy Manager Nishiyama. Yōko was probably still living in the Takinogawa apartment.

"Yes, of course."

"The electric iron in her drawer—shall we send that back, too?"

"An iron?"

"Yes, she used to press young men's shirts and things."

"We'd better not. That would be too heartless."

"Oh?"

"I'll keep it."

At Nishiyama's direction, one of the office girls brought Tagawa a rusty iron. Tagawa's hands responded to the feel of the cold iron and the peculiar weight of the lead inside. He carefully buried it deep in his bottom desk drawer.

Artwork by and courtesy of Kazan Prindle, 1996

5

Japanese Corporate Zen

Brian (Daizen) Victoria

In the popular Western mind, contemporary Japanese Zen is characterized by austere yet beautiful Zen gardens, and monks with shaven heads seated serenely in meditation. Various television programs have also popularized the idea that monks spend a good deal of their time studying either karate or another form of the martial arts. However, contemporary Japanese Zen is also characterized by the growing number of Zen temples in the countryside which, due to a decrease in rural population, either have no permanent resident priest or only a *nichiyō-bōzu*, a priest who holds a secular job as a school teacher or clerical worker during the week and only functions as a priest on Sundays. Moreover, many urban Zen priests have utilized their temple lands to build highly profitable condominiums, supermarkets, parking lots, kindergartens, and the like.

In spite of the increasing secularization of Zen (and, for that matter, traditional Buddhism as a whole) in Japan, the close observer would notice another interesting phenomenon at those relatively few Zen temples where meditation is still practiced with some regularity. The phenomenon referred to is the increasing number of both lay men and women who are coming to Zen temples for short periods of time to participate in meditation and other forms of Zen training.

This increased lay interest might seem to indicate a revitalization of contemporary Japanese Zen. Indeed, during the past few years the popular media in Japan have often referred to a so-called *Zen-būmu* (boom). Interestingly enough, one cause given for this *Zen-būmu* is that the Japanese, particularly young people, have come to regard Zen more highly because of the attention it has received in the West. While that may be partially correct, it cannot be the complete answer. Careful investigation of these lay trainees reveals that many of them are not participating by choice. That is to say, many of these trainees have been sent to Zen temples by the companies in which they are employed. Usually these employees have just entered the company, and their Zen training is considered part of their orientation program.

Zen training is not limited to freshman employees alone, however; middle management, even top management, groups are also numerous. There are, in fact, management consultants in Japan who specialize in arranging Zen training sessions for the various strata of company employees. It is also not unknown for members of top management themselves to conduct, or at least partially conduct, these training sessions for their employees.

Unfortunately, no hard statistical data exist on the numbers of employees involved in these training programs. Observation at upwards of a dozen major Zen temples, belonging to both the Rinzai and Sōtō traditions, however, has convinced me that a significant number of individuals are involved. In the Tokyo area, for example, the Rinzai Zen-affiliated temple of Engaku-ji in Kamakura has become one of the centers of this kind of training. On any given morning, and especially on weekends, one can see anywhere from ten to over one hundred company employees filing in and out of the meditation hall. These employees are easily distinguishable from the other lay trainees because of their uniform dress, often with the company's crest emblazoned on their jackets and baseball caps. At the Sōtō Zen temple of Jōkūin in Saitama Prefecture, where I trained for some time, there were approximately 5,000 lay trainees a year, between 60 and 70 percent of whom were in company-related groups.

What benefits do these employees, or more properly, the companies which send them, hope to derive from Zen training? Could it be that these companies wish to have a group of "enlightened beings" on their payroll? Would such enlightened beings insure greater corporate profits? As compassionate and self-sacrificing Bodhisattvas, would they perhaps be able to eliminate the cut-throat competition of the marketplace? It is to the "why" of corporate Zen training that this article will address itself. At the outset, I would like to suggest that the companies involved have some very pragmatic and immediate reasons for wishing their employees, new and old, to undergo Zen training. This proposition is borne out by the fact that corporate Zen training is often conducted in tandem with, or in place of, so-called "temporary enlistment" *(Kari-nyūtai)* in the Japanese Self-Defense Forces. It seems unlikely that employees would be made to undergo military training if the company's goal were truly their enlightenment!

What, then, are these "very pragmatic and immediate reasons?" The answer to this question is closely related to what it was that made Zen training attractive to Japan's ruling elites in the past. To demonstrate the validity of this statement, however, it is necessary to investigate some relevant aspects of Zen's traditional sociopolitical role in Japanese society.

The Traditional Sociopolitical Role of Zen

Although Buddhism was first introduced to Japan in the sixth century, it was not until the Kamakura period (1185–1382) that Zen took root in Japan as an independent school.[1] The two monks primarily responsible for this were Eisai (1141–

1215) and Dōgen (1200–1253), founders of the Rinzai and Sōtō Zen sects respectively. Although contemporaries, these two men had many differences. For example, the esoteric rituals of the then-predominant Shingon school played a much greater role in Eisai's Zen than they did in Dōgen's. Furthermore, Eisai taught that the goal of Zen training was the attainment of enlightenment. Dōgen, on the other hand, maintained that such training, particularly the practice of the Zen form of meditation known as *zazen*, was itself the manifestation of enlightenment.

There were, of course, many similarities as well. Both men had studied Zen in China and both reacted strongly against the scholastic doctrinalism and degeneracy of the Buddhist prelates of their day. In terms of this article, the most important similarity is that, to varying degrees, they both identified Zen with the welfare of the state. In his famous treatise, *Kōzen-gokoku-ron* (The Spread of Zen for the Protection of the Country), Eisai argued that it was through the universal adoption of the teachings of Zen that the nation could be protected. Dōgen also wrote a similar treatise entitled *Gokoku-shōbō-gi* (The Method of Protecting the Country by the True Dharma).

Although the contents of this latter treatise are no longer extant, its title, as well as Dōgen's other writings on the same subject, suggest a similar position to that of Eisai. In the *Bendōwa* section of Dōgen's masterwork, the *Shōbōgenzō* (lit., True Dharma Eye Treasury), for example, he states:

> When the true Way is widely practiced in the nation, the various buddhas and heavenly deities will continuously protect it, and the virtue of the emperor will exert a good influence on the people, thereby bringing peace.

Eisai and Dōgen were not, of course, the first Japanese priests to identify Buddhism with the welfare of the state. Both Kūkai (774–835), the founder of the Shingon school, and Saichō (767–822), the founder of the Tendai school, had previously written tracts similar to theirs. In fact, it can be argued that this element is found in Japanese Buddhism from the very beginning. Prof. Anesaki Masaharu, for example, points this out in his book, *History of Japanese Religion*. In discussing the introduction of Buddhism in the sixth century, he writes that "A close alliance was established between the throne and the [Buddhist] religion, since the consolidation of the nation under the sovereignty of the ruler was greatly supported by the fidelity of the imported religion to the government."

Still, it cannot be denied that by their actions Eisai and Dōgen set the stage for the later close relationship between the interests of the state and Zen. This is particularly true in the case of Eisai, who, unlike Dōgen, closely aligned himself with the feudal military government in Kamakura. It was this alignment with the Kamakura Shogunate, and its associated samurai class, that was, in the following years, to produce a uniquely Japanese development of Zen, the belief in the efficacy of Zen training in warfare.

The origin of this belief may be traced back to Shogun Hōjō Tokimune (1251–1284) and those Zen priests who surrounded him. Like his father, Hōjō Tokiyori (1227–1263), Tokimune was deeply interested in Zen. Unlike his father, however, he was faced with the first serious threat of foreign invasion in recorded Japanese history. In his book, *Zen and Japanese Culture*, the noted Zen scholar, D.T. Suzuki, describes how Tokimune sought strength from Zen to deal with this threat.[2] According to Suzuki, he went for guidance to his spiritual mentor, a Chinese Zen master by the name of Tsu-Yüan Wu-Hsüeh (Sogen Mugaku, 1226–1286), shortly before the expected invasion.

When Tokimune said: "The greatest event of my life is here at last," the master asked: "How will you face it?" Tokimune replied by merely shouting the exclamatory word: *"Katsu!"* as though he were frightening all of his enemies into submission. Pleased with this show of courage, Tsu-Yüan indicated his approval of Tokimune's answer by saying: "Truly, a lion's child roars like a lion." Subsequently, with the assistance of a "divine wind" *(Kamikaze)*, which was, most likely, merely a timely typhoon, Tokimune was successful in repelling Mongol invaders.

It should be noted that the shouting of *"katsu,"* a teaching method first advocated by the Chinese monk Lin-chi I-hsüan (Rinzai Gigen, d. 867), originally had nothing to do with making one fearless in the face of an enemy. Rather it, together with the use of sharp blows, was a method of forcing the trainee to transcend discursive dualistic thinking and grasp reality immediately and directly. The purpose was to comprehend the true form of things, not to subdue an opponent who, in reality, was nothing but another manifestation of oneself.

Although dating several centuries after the preceding incident, there is a letter written by the famous Zen master, Takuan (1573–1645), which clearly shows how the mind which has transcended discursive thought, technically known in Zen as "no-mind" *(mushin)*, came to be identified with martial prowess, particularly in the use of the sword. Addressing the famous swordsman, Yagyū Tajima no kami Muncnori (1571–1646), Takuan writes:

> "No mind" applies to all activities we may perform, such as dancing, as it does to swordplay. The dancer takes up the fan and begins to stamp his feet. If he has any idea at all of displaying his art well, he ceases to be a good dancer, for his mind "stops" with every movement he goes through. In all things, it is important to forget your "mind" and become one with the work at hand.
>
> When we tie a cat, being afraid of its catching a bird, it keeps on struggling for freedom. But train the cat so that it would not mind the presence of a bird. The animal is now free and can go anywhere it likes. In a similar way, when the mind is tied up, it feels inhibited in every move it makes, and nothing will be accomplished with any sense of spontaneity. Not only that, the work itself will be of poor quality, or it may not be finished at all.
>
> Therefore, do not get your mind "stopped" with the sword you raise; forget what you are doing, and strike the enemy.[3]

It was during the Ashikaga Shogunate (1392–1568), when the political center of Japan was once more in Kyoto, that Zen exerted its strongest influence on almost all fields of Japanese life and culture. Zen monks were to be found in such diverse occupations as trade representatives in negotiations with China and teachers of young people in the small schools attached to temples in the country-side. Some of them also served as the spiritual and political advisers and confi-dants of the Ashikaga Shoguns, often, it is said, with salutary effect. Zen monk Gidō, for example, close confidant of Shogun Yoshimitsu (1358–1408), encour-aged the latter to pursue religious and literary studies, with the result that Yoshimitsu became one of the greatest patrons of Zen and the arts in Japan's history.

It was, however, in the field of social philosophy that Zen, or rather Zen monks, were to have what was in many ways their most profound influence on the future development of Japanese society. It was they who had first introduced the Neo-Confucian teachings of the Song dynasty (960–1279) into Japan. While the new Buddhist-influenced metaphysics of Neo-Confucianism had only a lim-ited appeal to the military rulers, its social philosophy was very attractive. The latter taught the need for a social order characterized by a strict hierarchical structuring of the classes. It further required the conformity of all people to the obligations imposed by the five primary human relationships: that is, the rela-tionships between father and son, ruler and subject, husband and wife, older and younger brother, and two friends.

In medieval Japan, the obligation of a subject to his ruler came to mean, at least among the samurai class, complete devotion or loyalty to one's feudal lord. The emphasis that Japanese Zen came to place on such devotion can be clearly seen in the following statement of Zen monk Suzuki Shōsan (1579–1655). In a classic work on Buchidō (the feudal warrior code) entitled *Hagakure*, he said: "What is there in the world purer than renouncing one's own life for the sake of one's lord?"[4] What Shōsan, and Zen Buddhism in general, did was to equate the self-renunciation of Zen, based on the Buddhist teaching of the non-substantiality of the self *(muga)*, with absolute loyalty to one's lord.

Nakamura Hajime has pointed out in his book, *Ways of Thinking of Eastern Peoples*: "The ultimate aim of Zen practice became, among the warriors, devo-tion to the lord."[5] How at variance this aim was with the original teachings of Buddhism can be seen in the fact that little or no esteem for the sovereign, be he/she feudal lord or king, is to be found in the early Buddhist writings of India.[6] This is not surprising, for it was Buddha Sākyamuni himself who taught the equality of all members of the Buddhist monastic community (Sanskrit, *samgha*) regardless of their prior caste affiliation. This equality was practiced in the early *samgha* by making monks' rankings dependent upon their years of service and by putting all important questions to a majority vote.

Be that as it may, Japanese Zen continued through the succeeding centuries to place heavy emphasis among the samurai class on loyal and faithful service to the lord. At the same time, its temple schools instilled in the common people respect for the Confucian ideal of a hierarchically structured society in which everyone had a rigidly defined place and function. In terms of social morality, at least, Confucianism, or more accurately, Neo-Confucianism, had become Zen dogma.

With the coming of the Meiji Restoration in 1868 and the elimination of the feudal system, however, devotion to one's lord became an anachronism. The temple school system, too, was abolished by the new government, and in its place a state-supported public school system was established. As a result, Zen, and the other traditional Buddhist sects which had, in general, played a similar role vis-à-vis feudal authority, were thrown into confusion. The emergence of Shinto as a state religion and the repressive governmental measures directed towards Buddhism served to worsen the situation.

It did not, however, take traditional Japanese Buddhism, particularly Zen, long to adjust to the new environment. Although there were no longer lords, the new oligarchs of Japan needed the devotion of their subjects as much, if not more, than did the old feudal rulers. No longer was it sufficient for the military class alone to be instilled with absolute loyalty to their superiors. Now, the whole nation must be made to respond with the same unquestioning obedience, especially as Japan had embarked on a policy of foreign conquest and expansion.

It should be pointed out that not all Zen priests supported this new sociopolitical role for themselves. A few, influenced by newly introduced socialist and anarchist ideas, objected to it quite vigorously. One of them, a Sōtō Zen monk by the name of Uchiyama Gudō (1874–1911) even dared to oppose the revitalized emperor system itself. He did this in a pamphlet entitled *Nyūgoku kinen* (In commemoration of those imprisoned). The result of this publication, however, was not only his ouster from the Sōtō sect but also his own imprisonment. Subsequently, while still imprisoned, he was charged with earlier involvement in an anarchist plot to kill the emperor, and in 1911, together with eleven other alleged co-conspirators, he was executed.

In spite of exceptions like Uchiyama, most Zen priests became adept at promoting the cause of devotion and loyalty to the new central government and its military policies. At the time of the Russo-Japanese War (1904–1905), for example, Shaku Sōen (1859–1919), abbot of the Rinzai Zen-affiliated monasteries of Engaku-ji and Kenchō-ji in Kamakura, made an extended visit to the United States. During one of his lectures given at that time and recorded in his book, *Sermons of a Buddhist Abbot*, he said: "In the present hostilities into which Japan has entered with great reluctance, she pursues no egoistic purpose, but seeks the subjugation of evils hostile to civilization, peace, and enlightenment."[7] In describing the purpose of his visit to the battlefield during this conflict, he went on to say: "I also wished to inspire, if I could, our valiant soldiers with the ennobling thoughts of the Buddha, so as to enable them to die on the battlefield with the confidence that the task in which they are engaged is great and noble."[8]

Given the preceding sentiments, it is not surprising to learn that Shaku Sōen refused to sign a joint peace appeal with the famous Russian pacifist and author Leo Tolstoy. Tolstoy had appealed to the abbot on the basis of the Buddhist precept against the taking of life. Sōen replied, however, that as a loyal subject of the Japanese Empire he would never sign such a declaration. In this connection it is worthy of note that his pupil, D.T. Suzuki, was also a strong supporter of Japan's military actions on the Asian mainland. D.T. Suzuki is, as mentioned earlier, well known for his pioneer work in introducing Zen to the West. In one of his earlier writings entitled "A Treatise on New Religion" *(Shinshūkyō-ron)*, Suzuki also discussed the relationship of religion to the state. He said: "The first duty of religion is to seek to preserve the existence of the state."[9]

As Japanese militarism grew ever stronger in the 1920s and 30s, the emphasis on the efficacy of Zen training in actual combat also became more pronounced. Ichikawa Kakugen, himself a Rinzai Zen priest and professor emeritus of Kyoto's Hanazono University, has written about this development in a number of books and articles. Zen Master Iida Tōin, for example, is recorded as having said:

> We should be well aware of how much power Zen gave to Bushido. It is truly a cause for rejoicing that, of late, the Zen sect is popular among military men. No matter how much we may do *zazen*, if it is of no help to present events, then it would be better not to do it.[10]

Ichikawa also discussed one of the most famous exponents of what was to become known as *Kōdō-zen* (Imperial Way Zen), namely Rinzai Zen Master Yamazaki Ekishū, abbot of Buttsū-ji (temple). This master described the relationship of Zen to the emperor as follows:

> With awareness of our daily actions, we investigate the "self." In the great concentrated meditative state [i.e., *samādhi*] of Zen, we become united with the emperor. In each of our actions we live, moment to moment, with the greatest respect [for the emperor]. When we personify [this spirit] in our daily life, we become masters of every situation in accordance with our sacrificial duty. This is living Zen.[11]

It was in this spirit that Master Yamazaki taught the military men under his guidance. One of these, a young captain by the name of Matsumoto Goro (1900–1937), was destined to become immortalized as the very incarnation of the Japanese military spirit. It was claimed that though mortally wounded in combat in Manchuria in 1937, he not only turned toward the east and saluted in the direction of the Imperial Palace, but he actually died standing up, as if ready to give his next order.

Not only were Captain Matsumoto's utter devotion to the emperor and fearlessness in the face of death thought to be the results of his Zen training, but his ability to die while still standing was believed to be an expression of his deep spiritual attainment. This latter belief stemmed from the traditional Zen teaching that enlightened persons could choose their own posture at death.[12]

After his death Captain Matsumoto's heroism was written about and eulogized throughout Japan, particularly in the schools. His posthumous book, *Daigai* (Great Loyalty) became the object of intense study, and he became the ideal for all youth to emulate. At the same time, Zen masters occupied themselves more and more with giving military men Zen training. A large meditation hall was built in the heart of Tokyo and used exclusively to train military men to the very end of the war. What Japan lacked in material military power she hoped to make up for with spiritual military power.

Zen priests were not only busy on the home front. They served in the military itself as both soldiers and chaplains. Often they would tour the front lines to inspire the men. One of them, Zen Master Yamada Mumon, now president of Rinzai Zen-affiliated Hanazono University, is quoted by Ichikawa as having said the following during one such visit: "This is a sacred war to drive out the European and American aggressors from Asia. Please fight without any regard for your lives."[13]

In the same spirit were these words by the abbot of Hosshin-ji (temple), Harada Sogaku (1870–1961). Ichikawa quotes him as saying:

> Forgetting [the difference between] self and others in every situation, you should always become completely one with your work. [When ordered to] march—tramp, tramp; [when ordered to] fire—bang, bang; this is the clear expression of the highest Bodhi-wisdom, the unity of Zen and war . . . [14]

Needless to say, despite all the words of encouragement given by Zen masters, and the spiritual martial powers derived from Zen meditation and training, Japan lost the war. Misguided *samādhi*-power was, in the end, no match for the nationalist and revolutionary resistance of the Asian peoples combined with American technological might. Seemingly, with Japan's military bankruptcy, the unity of Zen and the martial skills had come to an end, after a history of some 700 years.

Postwar Economic Development and Zen

Japan's "miraculous" emergence as an economic power less than a generation after total defeat has been described exhaustively by both Japanese and Western writers. Hence, there is no need to repeat that description here. As Japan has emerged as an ever greater economic force, however, those factors which contributed to growth have become the subject of intense study and speculation by "Japanese experts" and business analysts of every type. Each of them has attempted to unlock the secrets of "Japan, Inc.," with particular focus on those elements which make the Japanese worker into the dedicated, loyal, diligent part of the corporate machine that he/she is. In his book on Japanese business entitled *Japan: The Fragile Superpower*, Frank Gibney, for example, notes four characteristics of the modern Japanese corporation: "(1) the dedication to the group goal, (2) the sense of hierarchy, (3) the dependence on superiors, and (4) the formalism."[15]

Gibney ascribes the origin of the preceding characteristics to the social values of the Japanese village. While he may be correct to some extent, it is also equally true that, as anyone even slightly acquainted with Japanese Zen monastic life will recognize, these are exactly the same characteristics which are to be found in Zen training. Furthermore, even if these characteristics have their origins in village society of the past, the vast majority of Japanese today are born and raised in an urban environment divorced from traditional village society. Where and how, then, do they acquire these values?

It would appear that this same question has also been of concern to Japanese business leaders. In the June 1977 issue of *Focus Japan*, an English-language magazine published by the semi-governmental Japan External Trade Organization (JETRO), there is a highly revealing article entitled "Marching to the Company Tune." In describing the history of training programs for new employees, the article states:

> [These programs] were developed in the late 1950's when companies realized that schools were no longer emphasizing the old virtues of obedience and conformity. Living and training together, sometimes for as long as a month, are designed to artificially recreate the old neglected virtues.

If "artificial recreation of the old neglected virtues" is the goal, what better place to accomplish it than in a Zen monastery where monk and lay trainees rise at 3:30 A.M. to meditate, eat rice gruel for breakfast, and endure the winter cold with only tiny charcoal braziers for heat! There can be no doubt that this spartan life style does increase the ability to withstand adversity, and, as Prof. George A. DeVos has pointed out, endurance has long been a highly desirable virtue in Japanese business organizations.[16] In this regard, it should also be mentioned that even for the experienced meditator, let alone the novice, extended periods of sitting in the traditional cross-legged "lotus posture" can be physically quite painful. If even the slightest movement is detected, the meditator will be "encouraged" to remain immobile by repeated blows of a long wooden stick known as a *kyosaku* wielded by a senior monk-monitor.

It is, however, in the social rather than the physical environment of a Zen monastery that the great emphasis on obedience and conformity is to be found. To be allowed to enter a monastery as a trainee, a monk is expected to prostrate himself in supplication before the entrance gate for hours if not days (depending on the monastery). When asked why he wishes to enter the monastery, the monk should reply: "I know nothing. Please accept my greetings!" This answer is thought to indicate that his mind is like a blank sheet of paper, ready to have his superiors inscribe on it whatever they may wish. If a monk fails to give the foregoing answer, he is struck repeatedly with the *kyosaku* until the desired state of mind is achieved.

Once given permission to enter the monastery, the monk, like his lay counterpart, finds that everyone is his superior to some degree. Even a fellow monk who was only admitted a few hours before him will automatically precede him on any formal or semiformal occasion, even at meals, and exercise some degree of authority over him. Those senior monks who have been in training for more than one or two years seem, to the new entrant, to be superior mortals; they not only wield the *kyosaku* but also determine whether or not the novice's work assignments are done satisfactorily. These senior monks wear nicer and more colorful robes than their juniors and live in more spacious quarters. They also have the official privilege of leaving the monastery for short periods of time and the unofficial privileges of surreptitiously eating meat, drinking alcohol and keeping petty monetary and in-kind gifts made to the monastery.

If the preceding description seems not unlike that of basic training in the military, I can attest, having experienced both, that the parallels are indeed striking. Senior monks act much like drill sergeants, and novice monks are their recruits. Although it is not generally well known, the Japanese military establishment prior to World War II modelled itself organizationally along the lines of a Zen monastery. Even the ordinary Japanese soldier's mess kit was adapted from the monk's set of rounded eating bowls. It is little wonder, then, that Japanese corporations continue to find the military-like discipline of a Zen monastery attractive. As one new salesman who had just completed his company's training program noted: "My work has much in common with that of a soldier."[17]

If senior monks are the drill sergeants, then it is the Zen master or masters who act as the generals (or, in the contemporary context, corporate heads). They enjoy the real authority in a Zen monastery and are ultimately responsible for directing the training programs for both monks and laypersons. In the talks they give to incoming trainees, one of their most recurrent themes revolves around the Zen phrase: *"Daishu ichinyo."*[18] This phrase means that all members of the monastic community should act as one. That is to say, when it is time to do *zazen*, everyone sits. When it is time to eat, work, sleep, and so on, everyone likewise does these activities together *as if they were one body*. To do otherwise is called *katte na kōdō*,[19] or *"self-willed"* action, and condemned as the very antithesis of the Zen life. Total conformity is thus by no means an old neglected virtue in a Zen monastery.

Discipline, obedience and conformity are not the only attractive features of monastic life for corporate Japan. The traditional Buddhist teaching of the nonsubstantiality of the self (that is to say, the lack of any eternal and unchangeable substance in the self) has also been given a unique corporate twist. This twist is well illustrated by Ozeki Shūen, the abbot of Daisen-in (temple) and one of the best known Zen priests conducting employee training courses. In a collection of his sermons delivered during such training courses, he states:

> Employing your vital life force, you should exert yourselves to the utmost, free of any conceptual thought. . . . This is what it means to be alive. That is to say, at every time and in every place, you should work selflessly.[20]

A further example is provided by Sakai Tokugen, another leading Zen master involved with employee training programs. Master Sakai is also a professor of Buddhist Studies at Sōtō Zen-affiliated Komazawa University in Tokyo. In the May 1974 issue of *Daihōrin*, a popular Buddhist magazine, he lamented the lack of sincerity in carrying out the orders of one's superiors on the part of postwar Japanese. He wrote:

> Sincerity [in carrying out orders] means having feelings and actions of absolute service, giving one's all [to the task at hand]. In doing this there can be no thought of personal loss or gain. . . . By carrying out our [assigned] tasks, we become part of the life of the entire universe; we realize our original True Self. . . . This is the most noble thing human beings can do.

In other words, for Master Sakai, selfless devotion to the accomplishment of one's assigned duties is none other than enlightenment itself. Little wonder that he is a popular leader of employee training courses. Here, certainly, the Protestant work ethic has met its match.

Conclusion

At the beginning of this chapter it was suggested that the companies which arranged for their employees to participate in Zen training programs had some very pragmatic and immediate reasons for doing so. At this point the truth of this proposition should be quite apparent. The discipline, the emphasis on group rather than individual action, the ability to endure hardship, the heightened sense of "selfless" loyalty and subordination both to one's group and to one's superiors are all aspects of Zen training which have immediate relevance to corporate life.

It should also be clear that, in essence, the same spirit pervades Suzuki Shōsan's words about "renouncing one's own life for the sake of one's lord" and Sakai Tokugen's lamentation quoted above, or for that matter, the exhortations of Harada Sogaku and the other Zen supporters of Japanese militarism. The only difference between them is on the question of to whom, or to what, one should be loyal and devoted. Originally, it was the feudal lord; later it became the central government and its policies as embodied in the person of the emperor; and now, of course, it is the corporation and its interests. It should be noted, however, that to an even greater degree than in the United States,

Japanese corporate interests are closely connected with those of the state.

There is one other aspect of Zen training which is very attractive from the corporate standpoint. This is none other than the practice of *zazen* itself. As Zen Master Iida pointed out earlier, the *samurai* were indeed strengthened by the concentrated state of mind achieved through the practice of *zazen*. This *samādhi*-power was originally utilized in Zen training to give the practitioner a deeper insight into his or her nature and the nature of reality itself. Yet, it can be and, as already noted, has been applied to any work in which one may be engaged— everything from wielding a *samurai* sword with lightning swiftness, or fighting "selflessly" in battle, to assembling a color television set with flawless precision. What could be more attractive to a Japanese company than the utilization of *samādhi*-power, and thus *zazen*, for its own corporate ends?

This, however, brings up an extremely important question: "Is corporate Zen training a legitimate expression of Zen Buddhism?" The answer in the best Zen tradition must be both yes and no. On the affirmative side it must be admitted that if one looks at corporate Zen training in terms of its historical antecedents, this training is very much a part of the popular tradition of Japanese Zen. Although historical analogies can be misleading, there is a very real sense in terms of values in which the corporate leaders of present-day Japan are actually samurai disguised in Western clothing. Instead of the long and short swords of the samurai they wield the computer and pocket calculator.

On a deeper level, however, there is reason to ask whether corporate Zen is not as alien to the true spirit of Zen as were its historical antecedents—"feudal Zen" and "militarist Zen." Although a whole article could be devoted to this topic alone, let it suffice here to quote Zen Master Dōgen's most succinct expression of the goal of Zen training. In the *Genjō-Kōan* section of the *Shōbōgenzō*, he states:

> To study the Way is to study the self. To study the self is to forget the self. To forget the self is to be enlightened by all things. To be enlightened by all things is to remove the barriers between one's self and others.[21]

A true student of Zen, then, would use his *samādhi*-power, first and foremost, to break through those barriers of ignorance which separate him from his own True Self and from others. Having accomplished this, he would, in accordance with the Bodhisattva ideal, use that same power to aid others in their own search for release. To use that power for his or a particular group's selfish ends, at the expense of others, would be completely alien to him. To borrow Dōgen's words again: "[Only] the foolish believe that their own interests will suffer if they put the benefit of others first."[22]

This is the true spirit of Zen. Interestingly enough, even some Zen masters who are involved in corporate training programs admit to this. How, then, do they justify their involvement in such programs? Zen Master Murase Genmyō, leader of the lay training center at Obaku Zen-affiliated Mampuku-ji, has expressed the belief that out of any large group of employee trainees there will be at least a few who will "acquire a taste" for Zen in spite of the companies' goals. This will lead to their further practice of Zen and, eventually, to an understanding of its true spirit.

While one can certainly hope this will occur, it is my experience, based on ten years of training in Japan as a Zen monk, that few if any employee participants ever do reach an understanding of Zen's true spirit. Were employees to adopt the Bodhisattva ideal they would clearly become a liability, not an asset, to their corporate bosses. Statements like those made by Master Murase are nothing more than feeble attempts to rationalize the symbiotic relationship which presently exists between Zen and corporate Japan. This relationship, as has been shown, is based on more than 700 years of Zen cooperation with, and support for, the power structure of the day. Its reform will be no easy task.

Japanese Zen is not, however, completely without hope for progressive change. As has been noted, there were Zen priests like Uchiyama Gudō who recognized the basic incompatibility of Zen and capitalism as early as the late Meiji period. He gave the following explanation of why he had become a socialist:

> As a propagator of the Buddha's teachings, I believe that all sentient beings have Buddha-nature [i.e., the capacity to realize enlightenment]; that they are all equal, without any superiors or inferiors; and that they are all my children. These are the golden words which form the basis of my faith. I discovered that these golden words are identical with those spoken by socialists. It was for this reason that I finally became a believer in socialism.[23]

Although priests like Uchiyama almost completely disappeared (or more accurately, were removed) from the Zen tradition during the 1920s, 30s, and 40s, a few did reappear after World War II. These were priests like Ichikawa Hakugen who has already been mentioned. Included in his books condemning Zen's (and his own) collaboration with Japanese fascism are discussions of Zen's political, economic, and social thought. In *The War Responsibility of Buddhists (Bukkyō-sha no sensō sekinin)*, he devotes one full chapter to the direction of a possible "Buddhist socialism."[24] Rooted in the Buddhist concept of *sūnya* or "emptiness" (the absence of any permanent, changeless entity in the universe), he maintains that Buddhist socialism would be characterized by, among other things, a humble and open spirit cleansed of the will to power and the absolutism of self. It would, furthermore, work toward the ultimate demise of state power and the emergence of a communal society free of the capitalist mode of private property.

A generation of students of Zen at Hanazono University has grown to maturity under Ichikawa's guidance. One of them, Kashiwagi Ryūhō, has only recently written the most complete account of Uchiyama Gudō's life and thought yet available.[25] Together with a small group of Buddhist intellectuals and social activists, he has formed the "Gudō Society" *(Gudō no kai)*. It already counts as one of its members Setouchi Harumi, a Buddhist nun and one of Japan's leading woman writers.

It is, of course, still much too early to talk about the existence of a significant Zen (or Buddhist) socialist movement in Japan. The most that can be said is that the potential does exist. In the meantime, employee training programs will continue to be the main "social activity" of the majority of Japanese Zen Buddhist monasteries. In fact, in the short run these programs will undoubtedly be expanded. As the worldwide crisis of capitalism deepens, the Japanese corporate need for a disciplined *and subservient* work force will become greater than ever before. However, given the growing strength of both the external and internal forces opposed to "Japan, Inc." (and its American and European allies), there is no more reason to believe that contemporary Japanese Zen leaders will, ultimately, be any more successful in maintaining the corporate state than their predecessors were in maintaining the feudal and fascist regimes of the past.

Notes

1. The meditative aspect of Buddhism had been introduced into Japan at a relatively early date. The Japanese monk Dōshō (628–700), in fact, built the first meditation hall in the then-capital of Japan, Nara, in the latter part of the seventh century.
2. Although there are other more "Zen-like" interpretations of this exchange, another noted Zen scholar, Heinrich Dumoulin, agrees with Suzuki that the following exchange reveals the way in which Tokimune derived courage from his Zen training to face the Mongol invaders. Thus, this incident may well be said to mark the origin of the belief in Japan that Zen training was efficacious in warfare. See Heinrich Dumoulin, *A History of Zen Buddhism* (Boston: Beacon Press, 1963), p. 138, and D.T. Suzuki, *Zen and Japanese Culture* (Princeton: Princeton University Press, 1959), pp. 66–67.
3. D.T. Suzuki, *Essentials of Zen Buddhism* (Princeton: Princeton University Press, 1962), p. 458.
4. Charles A. Moore, ed., *The Japanese Mind* (Honolulu: University Press of Hawaii, 1967), p. 233.
5. Nakamura Hajime, *Ways of Thinking of Eastern Peoples*, ed. Philip P. Wiener (Honolulu: East-West Center Press, 1964), p. 430.
6. Ibid., p. 429.
7. Shaku Sōen, *Sermons of a Buddhist Abbot* (LaSalle, Illinois: Open Court Publishing Co., 1913), p. 202.
8. Ibid., p. 203.
9. Ichikawa Hakugen, *"Shūkyō-sha no sensō-sekinin o tou,"* in *Nihon no shūkyō*, vol. 1, no. 1 (Dec. 1974), p. 38.
10. Ichikawa Hakugen, *Zen to gendai shisō* (Tokyo: Tokuma Shoten, 1967), p. 206.
11. Op. cit., p. 45.
12. Toward the latter part of the *Fukan-zazengi* (A Universal Recommendation for the Practice of *Zazen*) Dōgen wrote: "By virtue of *zazen* it is possible to transcend the difference between 'common' and 'sacred' and attain the ability to die while doing *zazen* or while standing up."
13. Maruyama Teruo, *Nihonjin no kokoro o dame ni shita meisō, akusō, gusō* (Tokyo: Yamate Shobō, 1977), p. 49.
14. Ichikawa Hakugen, *Zen to gendai shisō*, p. 173.
15. Frank Gibney, *Japan: The Fragile Superpower* (New York: W.W. Norton and Co., 1975), p. 204.

16. George A. DeVos, "Apprenticeship and Paternalism," in *Modern Japanese Organization and Decision-Making*, ed. Ezra F. Vogel (Berkeley: University of California Press, 1975), pp. 221–23.

17. "Marching to the Company Tune," *Focus Japan*, June 1977, p. 36.

18. [Both notes 18 and 19 were omitted from the originally published article.]

19.

20. Maruyama Teruo, *Nihonjin no kokoro o dame ni shita meisō, akusō, gusō*, p. 194.

21. As quoted in Yokoi Yūhō's *Zen Master Dōgen* (Tokyo/New York: John Weatherhill, 1976), p. 5.

22. Ibid., p. 62.

23. As quoted in Kashiwagi Ryūhō's *Taigyaku jiken to Uchiyama Gudō* (Tokyo: JCA Shuppan-sha, 1979), p. 29.

24. Ichikawa Hakugen, *Bukkyō-sha no sensō sekinin* (Tokyo: Shunjū-sha, 1970), pp. 150–68.

25. Kashiwagi Ryūhō, *Taigyaku jiken to Uchiyama Gudō* (Tokyo: JCA Shuppan-sha, 1979).

6

Ishimure Michiko's
"The Boy Yamanaka Kuhei"

Translated by Christopher Stevens*

An abandoned boat adrift on an open sea—
this bitter sea of life and death unending

There is a village called Yudō that lines the shores of a small inlet on the Sea of Shiranui. The waves in the cove are never rough except once or twice a year when a typhoon strikes. Floating in the bay are small boats and sardine nets, riding the waves flecked with whitecaps that flutter like fretful eyelids. Children, completely naked, enjoy themselves leaping from boat to boat and plunging into the water.

In summer, the voices of these children rise up past the orange orchards and wooded groves, through the large, gnarled sumac bushes and the spaces in the stone walls, and can be heard in every house.

At the lowest spot in the village, at the foot of the first terrace from the boat mooring, is the old and large communal well and a place for washing clothes. In the shade of the moss that lines the stones of this large, square well, minnows and attractive red-colored crabs sport about. It must be that a spring bubbles up sweet-tasting water into this well that has crabs such as these living in it. In this area there are springs that bubble up even at the bottom of the sea.

Lying sunken at the bottom of the well water that no one draws anymore, the accumulated sediment assumes the forms of ship spikes and the flowers of camellias.

From the rocky slope above the well, aged camellia bushes whose years no one can determine hang in masses over the washing place and the terrace before it. Their darkened leaves and twisting branches embrace the boulders their own

---

*This translation is of the first chapter of *Ku gai jo do* (Bitter Sea, Pure Land) by Ishimure Michiko, who gave permission for its publication in the *Bulletin of Concerned Asian Scholars* in 1985.

roots have split apart, releasing the ancient spirit of these crags; and the shadows beneath are always cool and still.

Near the inlet on which the village of Yudō is situated there used to be landfall sentinel stations of the Higo clan and a sea entry station at the border of Satsuma. Beyond lies the Sea of Shiranui. The fishermen say things like "We stopped over at Go Sho no Ura last night and then zipped right back here while it was calm in the morning." From Yudō, Go Sho no Ura is in sight in the island group of Amakusa. Facing Amakusa, if you turn to the left, you can see both the land and sea routes that link up with Satsuma. Beyond the inlet is the hamlet of Modō. On the outskirts of this village runs a river where you can wash clothes. Like a moat, it is the prefectural boundary, "The River of the Gods" by name. If you wash rice standing on the pebbled river bank, the milky water will cross over the border towards the farther shore where they speak the dialect of Kagoshima.

Beyond Modō heading south in Kagoshima Prefecture are Izumi City and Kome no Tsu. On the Kumamoto Prefecture side traveling along Route Three from Modō, one arrives at Fukuro, Yudō, Detsuki, and then enters the harbor of Hyakuken. This is the region where outbreaks of Minamata disease are prevalent. From the harbor one enters the city streets of Minamata. In Hyakuken Harbor is the drainage pipe from the New Japan Chisso Factory at Minamata.

Standing on this plain dotted with wells is a public building—a young men's club—whose wooden rooms and walls are beginning to decay. This cabin, faded by the sea breezes, has long been vacant. It is as if the loneliness the older men have come to secretly feel has condensed in this building and blows about the air. This unused clubhouse has robbed the village of its vitality to a significant degree. The days when young men would settle down in Yudō as fishermen have long since passed. Especially since Minamata disease first appeared, things have never been the same. No matter how skillful the fisherman, he can no longer hand down his knowledge to his son. The older fishermen think about this grimly. Each one considers himself the expert at catching sea bream, or the best man at spear fishing, or the cleverest with mullet traps. It is just as they say; each man is an expert, the likes of whom exist nowhere else. Their pride supports their livelihood, the city fish market, the protein source for the citizens of Minamata, and one part of the fishing industry on the coast of the Sea of Shiranui.

An old man sits on the floor of the abandoned clubhouse, its door awry, with his grandchild he has brought with him. His ear, like a conch shell, is turned towards the Shiranui Sea. Like an overcast sky, his eyes are dim. Perhaps it is because he can no longer see well enough even to repair nets that his youngest grandchild has been given to him to baby-sit.

The floorboards of this young men's clubhouse, which continue to split apart day by day, should have held memories for him of the vitality he had when he was young, but all the old fisherman shows is an uneasy and vacant expression as he looks at the sea and his grandchild. The child is crawling around on the floor, and the old fisherman knows he cannot match his grandchild in bodily strength. The old man seems half asleep, and already in another world from his descendant, who has stopped crawling around and is sucking his thumb.

This old fisherman's face has a look similar to those of the old farmers from my village. Their sons and daughters no longer know when to draw water for their rice fields, and when to drain them, and where to cut the embankment between their neighbor's fields and their own on the appointed evening in order to drain their own fields, and how to repair the bank afterwards, and so forth. At rice planting time the old farmers would hang around the tiller brought in to turn up the soil. Staring steadily at it they would suddenly raise their voices—it was impossible to tell if they were sighing or cursing—saying, "Yeah, nowadays, people who own machines have it made. In the old days, if you worked your whole life maybe you could buy a cow or a horse. If you can buy a tractor, you're spoiled." With a sigh they would pull off the leeches stuck to their calves and crush them to death on the embankment.

Like those old farmers crushing leeches to death, the old fisherman uses the end of his walking stick to try to mash a boat worm that has crawled up between his legs, but the worm in its panic is more nimble than the end of the stick the old man lowers on it with a vague expression in his eyes. Its rear end is crushed, it rolls and falls through to the floor, leaving a smear on the planks.

The older people endure within themselves the uneasy feeling that this form-less inheritance, this secret knowledge that must be handed down to their descen-dants, will perish with themselves. Like the clubhouse that continues to decay, their living spirit and flesh continue to weather. Even in the summertime, no matter where one walks along the beach, this feeling lurks in the air.

I remember the afternoon of a day two years ago after summer had passed. It was the fall of 1963. The children had long since come back up to the village from their summer frolic in the sea. The autumn sun cast long shadows on the red earth of the hillside paths around Yudō. The flowers in the fields had already fallen and the smell of still-green oranges floated through the air. There was hardly a sound, either from the ocean or the houses. It was that time of day when a soothing silence visits this village of many fishermen's homes. Everyone must have gone down to the sea or into town, and even the chickens were napping in their roosts.

Breathing shallowly, I stood in the front yard of Kuhei's house, which stands halfway up the slope in the village facing the sea. Surprisingly enough, he was outdoors. He was repeating some kind of "practice" with complete determina-tion. It was apparently some kind of baseball practice, but his movements were so awesome that I felt deterred from calling out to him. Rooted to the spot, I started to breathe with the same rhythm as the boy. Whether he tried to stand up or squat down, he gave the impression of being a hunchback or a cripple. His posture was completely inappropriate for a boy his age. If you only glanced casually at the lower half of his body from behind, you could not help but think that he was an old man. This outward appearance belied his natural constitution and his inner will. If you looked closely, you would see that the back of his neck was smooth just like any other boy his age, and that if he had not contracted Minamata disease his physique would be that of a husky boy entering his early manhood who had grown up in a fishing village like Yudō. He had a battered pair of clogs on his feet. I knew that it required a lot of effort for him to put them on.

He stretched his legs. The strain was so great that faint tremors ran up and down both legs to his waist. He squatted down and drew an arc on the ground with the stick like a compass. He inched along, leaning his head with its closely cropped hair to one side. And now with one hand on the ground, he thrust the stick he held in the other hand along the dirt. He seemed to be searching for something with its tip. After a number of trials, it made a noise of hitting the rock he was searching for. Kuhei was blind. With great care he laid the stick on the ground and for a long time held the rock that he had been groping for in his left hand between his bent knees as though he were caressing it. He used his left hand because his right hand was half paralyzed. This rock was the size of a fist and protruded slightly from his hand. It was oval shaped rather than perfectly round and fitted the palm of his crippled left hand quite well. The moisture from the rock and the sweat from his hand mixed faintly together.

(I learned later that he had picked up this rock five years before at the time when a road was being constructed in front of his house. The boy had cherished it ever since. He would always squirrel it away in a hole he had dug in a corner of the dirt-floored room in the house so that it wouldn't roll away any great distance. With his eyes averted and half-closed in blindness he would creep forward, groping for the cavity he had dug, and would touch it with trembling fingers. The sight of this boy putting away his rock was painful to watch and I sensed a heaviness that the rock contained.)

After a while, Kuhei half rose, the way an extremely old man would get up, and with a serious expression faced the sky and threw the rock he had been grasping up in the air. Then, with the nimblest of all movements he had made so far, he flailed the stick sideways with both hands. His body buckled, but he didn't fall down. By the time he swung his stick, the stone had come down in the wrong direction and had hit the ground, so he missed it. He quietly tilted his head in the direction where the stone had fallen and once again started to probe the ground with his bat.

The noon meal was over and everyone had gone to the fields or to fish or to the town. The entire village had become a vacuum. Although on an autumn afternoon like this you can hear from amongst the stone walls and houses and the narrow winding paths on the hillside the sound of boats chugging in the inlet below and the voices of older people calling their grandchildren and the clucking of chickens as they peck at the earth, it was as though Kuhei alone was the single driving force of human will in this afternoon village, making this vacuum move with his strenuous actions as he played "baseball" by himself. Nothing else stirred.

My breathing was attuned: it mingled with the stones and plants and trees that release their breath from the earth. It merged with his movements. The back of his neck was sopping wet with sweat. I felt that a long time had passed. I drew closer to him, and called out his name.

He was extremely startled and dropped his stick with a thud. Somehow the harmony that had come into being between the soundless village and himself collapsed at that very moment. He was unable to move. He seemed to be trying to concentrate on where the door to his house was. And then, walking backwards, as if he were making a dash for it, he disappeared behind the door.

This was the first time that Kuhei and I had ever met in person. I have a son who is about the same age as Kuhei. I became upset, and maternal feelings writhed within me.

When I talked with employees from the Minamata City Health Department about Kuhei, they abruptly flashed broad smiles at me which mixed confusion with feelings of affection for the boy. They said things like, "Yamanaka Kuhei, yes . . . well . . . that Kuhei really is something else . . . "

The Health Department had made a big stir about the boy. Of those at the Department, Mr. Yomogi, in particular, would narrow his eyes when discussing Kuhei, as though he were even keeping a personal watch over the boy. It is the officials of the City Health Department who get in touch with the patients when the Kumamoto University Medical School gives the disease victims medical examinations and performs other research at the Minamata Municipal Hospital or in the local hamlets.

The Health Department owns a private bus to transport the patients to the examination facility. The driver of this private bus, a young man by the name of Ōtsuka, squeezes the bus into the narrow lanes of the village, getting as close as he can to each patient's house. He honks his horn when he pulls up. And then, from on the bus, there leisurely comes into view groups of three or five people assembled in the village lanes, and next to the rice fields, and the cliff sides, and the cryptomeria groves, and the road that runs along the ocean.

Held in the arms of their mothers or their grandparents, or else carried on their backs as their heads loll to and fro, the children are gathered together with the adult victims who hobble despondently along. This scene, as these people stand on the side of the road next to the rice fields or the seashore, is, to say the least, different from that of an ordinary bus stop.

People walking past draw back slightly and look at the groups of deformed children. Greetings are kept to a minimum, and one can perceive both kindness and its absence in the passers-by. The rice fields and the muddy roads and the glinting crests of the sea waves somehow seem to freeze, if only because the children are there with the adults who are standing around. The grown-ups look pathetically modest and bewildered. They show feelings welling up from hearts that have been very profoundly moved. Smiles of friendliness are constantly drifting across their faces.

Ōtsuka, the driver, calls out, "Tomoko, I see you made it!" in a vigorous voice.

And then, as soon as this young man uses his strength to shut the bus door with a big slam, I always sense a subtle change in mood that is different from the anxiety these people felt when they were outside. The conversations of the adults unwind smoothly against the background murmuring of the speech-impaired children. The children, who are ten years old or so, are held in the arms of their mothers or grandparents. They *feel* the passing scenery outside the bus as their heads droop backwards. These children are either completely blind, or else have an extremely restricted field of vision. Judging from the voices of these speech-defective children, and what they appear to be gazing at, it seems clear that these kids, who hold their stiffened, skinny, birdlike limbs drawn close to their chests, looking for all the world like some "four-legged human animal," are absolutely delighted at being given a ride on the bus. The adults compare the children with their eyes, smile at each other, and gradually slip into intimate conversation.

The situation on a bus such as this one tells us that these people have been getting through life since Minamata disease first occurred without ever completely fitting into life when they *aren't* on the bus, that is to say, into the life of their hometown, where they were born and grew up and are making a living for themselves. The moment Ōtsuka, the driver, shuts the door with a bang, and in a booming voice calls out "Well, here we go!" as he grasps the steering wheel, everyone feels relieved, and the atmosphere of congeniality revives. They are liberated from the frozen scene outside. Their awareness of the young driver fades away, and the interior of the bus dissolves into a kind of natural scene in itself.

The young man keeps his lips firmly sealed except when he calls out greetings, such as "Hi there" and "hello," to these children who can make him no reply. After he and the Health Department officials help the children to get their exhausted and unmanageable bodies into the seats, he returns to the driver's seat and erases the smile from around his eyes. He even looks angry. This shows that he will not waste a single word in unnecessary small talk.

His manner is always like this when he comes in contact with people who have Minamata disease. His goodwill gives the impression of being forced. The truth, however, is that he conceals it in the depths of an expression that is sullen, brusque, and yet somehow amiable all at once. Without him realizing it consciously, he has come to store a pool of anger within himself, and even seems irritated with the situation. This young man, who lives near the upper reaches of the Minamata River, and grew up exchanging visits with his friends from the seaside, surely has an instinctual bond with those kindred souls from the same hometown. There are any number of ways that the residents reveal their reactions to the Minamata disease situation; his attitude is pragmatic. Like water that circulates at a subterranean level, he gives indications of his feelings of communion.

When Minamata disease first appeared, he was a taxi driver in the city. In the midst of that uproar he drove all over the place, giving rides to people who poured into town from all over the country—reporters, officials from the Welfare Ministry or the Ministry of Such-and-Such, Congressional Representatives, and other unfamiliar and unusual people who were apparently academic types. The destinations of these personages, about whom he must have thought that they had come because of Minamata disease, were places like the Chisso factory, and the Yu no Ji Hot Springs Resort, and the Yamatoya Inn, and the Municipal Hospital, and City Hall, and so forth. Members of the Kumamoto Medical School visited their patients and the villages where they were from on a regular basis. Having gone through all of this, the young man must have had his own opinion about the whole Minamata disease situation, but he kept it to himself.

Now he is a driver for the City Health Department. When he gets on the bus and shuts the door, the disease-ridden children and the adults all feel relaxed, and they burst into gleeful laughter even at little things, even when little Miss Shinobu's flowered hat flies off her head with a puff of wind from the bus window.

The accuracy of certain statistics has been called into question. These statistics indicate a higher rate of concentration of congenital cerebral palsy among the children born in fishermen's households between 1954 and 1959 in those villages where Minamata disease had already appeared. However, in January of 1962 the Minamata disease Investigation Committee reported that seventeen children were afflicted with congenital Minamata disease. At the end of March of 1964 they reported the names of six or more children, bringing the total to twenty-three in all. These children were invaded with mercury poisoning while they were still in their mothers' wombs and came into this world enduring its affliction.

Congenital Minamata disease has cropped up in the same general region where other forms of the disease have appeared. This zone extends from the villages along the downreaches of the Kami no Kawa River, Izumi City and Kome no Tsu in Kagoshima Prefecture, past Minamata City in Kumamoto Prefecture, up to Ta no Ura in the Ashikita District.

Even when they were two years old, these children could not walk, let alone crawl, talk, or use chopsticks to eat. They were seized with spasms and convulsions from time to time; mothers never even suspected that those mild-suckling babies, who have never eaten fish, were suffering from Minamata disease. Until they heard that diagnosis, the parents walked around the hospital in town selling off their boats and fishing equipment in order to scrape together enough money to pay for the medical treatments.

Four or five years pass. The children have no choice but to be left lying around the house for the greater part of the day. Shuttered in houses along the village lanes, they spend their lives sensing with their entire being the activities of their parents working outdoors, and the cats and kittens and boat bugs that frisk about their bedside.

The ones who are able to crawl around and stand up weakly by themselves require more attention. In order to keep them from falling into the fireplace where the kettle and the warming blankets are, or from rolling off of the raised floor of the entrance hall, these kids are lashed onto a house pillar by means of a sash wrapped around their skinny stomachs that is long enough to permit them to stand up or crawl around with a certain amount of freedom. Even then, most of them have burns from falling into the hearth, or bruises from falling off the porches. Most of these children cannot call for help, even if they fall into the fireplace. Some of them have lost their fathers or their older brothers to Minamata disease. They are totally unaware that they are the victims of congenital Minamata disease, to say nothing of their ignorance of the fate that has befallen their families. At any rate, even if their brothers and sisters are still alive and off at school, and their parents are out fishing or in the fields, it is not their own idea to be forced to live lashed onto a pillar in an empty house. The gaze of these children left lying around for years at a time shows more than mere wonderment; it looks clairvoyant.

It is up to the age of about ten or so that children are the most sensitive to solitude and isolation in all the aspects of their emotional life. Therefore, it is hardly surprising that their faces light up when they look at the sky outside their house and then get on the bus. They start to realize that soon they will be on the bus and on their way, as soon as their diaper and kimono are changed and they are carried in the arms of one of their parents away from the house they have been isolated in.

Even though these children are ten years old, they invariably have a look of infantile innocence about them. They express with their entire bodies their anticipation (mingled, of course, with anxiety) of getting on the bus and going to the hospital—which is to say that they are looking forward to getting in touch with the life of the community that is so different from the situation they have been experiencing inside their own house.

It certainly must be wrenching for a parent to see her child in such a state of health as this. She cannot help but wonder what will happen to him or her after she is gone. But now that they are both alive and in each other's arms, the mutual sympathy that is closer than a hand's breadth must be a consolation to them both. The interior of the bus is filled with the sad affection of family members such as these. When little Miss Shinobu's flowered hat, which she is so proud of, is wafted off of her head by a breeze from the bus window and falls onto the floor between the seats, and the little girl (who can neither see nor hear very well) stares off in some other direction, not knowing that her hat has fallen off, the passengers find it hilarious. The bus sways from side to side as the scene dissolves in laughter, and even though little Master Kazumitsu and little Miss

Matsuko are getting their heads bumped around, the bus suddenly becomes a romper room.

Yamanaka Kuhei obstinately refuses to get on the bus and go to be examined. Yamanaka Kuhei is sixteen years old (born in July of 1949). His father and his ancestors were fishermen in Yudō in the City of Minamata, but his father died unexpectedly of a cold in 1950. His older sister Satsuki (born in 1927) contracted Minamata disease in July of 1956 and died that same year on 2 September. He got sick one year before his sister did, in May of 1955. He and his sister were both admitted to the Shirahama Contagious Diseases Hospital for a period of time, but since then until now he has been treated as an outpatient. He is patient number 16. He lives with his mother, Chiyo, who is getting along in years; she is fifty-seven.

From autumn, through winter and spring, the boy usually wears a black cotton school uniform, and in the wintertime he also wears a large quilted vest over it. This vest has vertical stripes and is padded with cotton. It is very thick and threadbare; it has thoroughly blended in with the life in a fisherman's household.

The Shiranui Sea where they used to go to fish looks as though it were spread out on the front yard of the Yamanaka house. In the yard, not a single one of those tools of the trade whereby fishermen earn their living is in evidence: nets, fish baskets, landing nets with handles, and so forth, which in other circumstances would be arranged and hanging up to dry. Somehow the yard looks too big. A breeze blows gently through the tall trunks of an old persimmon tree, as it embraces to itself the faint rustling of the leaves of corn planted beneath its branches.

However, this oversized and thickly padded vest that the boy wears has absorbed the long history of time spent soaking up the salt breezes. It could tell the story of how they used to live their lives up until ten years ago. His father wore it on the boat, and so did his sister. Now that both these workers are dead, the boy's mother has given this piece of hand-me-down work clothing to her youngest child to wear.

Interrupted during his "baseball" practice, the boy was now sitting in front of a radio placed on the wooden floor of a dimly lit room in the house. As usual, he was wearing his quilted vest. I had heard that when people showed up from other places at the Yamanaka house—people from the Municipal Hospital and Kumamoto University, and officials from City Hall, and people who came to observe, or should we say express sympathy for, a Minamata disease victim, and mysterious strangers like myself—Kuhei would sit in front of the radio and gruffly turn his back on them. So, I knew what to expect. He was sitting in front of the radio this time also, looking as though he had been in the same place since the beginning of time. His back was turned towards me, and his squared shoulders and his closely cropped hair gave an impression of real boyishness. He was stretching his neck and leaning forward from the waist as he clicked the radio on and off.

His bent back was arched and taut like a bow, held in a posture that was filled with an extraordinary tension. But it was bowed in such a way that it also gave the painful impression that he had not been able to release it swiftly and decisively at its target, even once. His left hand quivered irritably as it groped for the on-off switch and the tuning dial of the radio. He felt for the radio and then removed his hand, again and again, as his big, black, unseeing eyes stared up obliquely into space.

Mr. Yomogi of the City Health Department called out to him.

"Kuhei."

Kuhei didn't turn around. He twisted the radio dial, very agitated. Hashi Yukio was singing a song.

"Kuhei, the distinguished doctor from Kumamoto University has come. Why don't you come along with me to see him . . . "

Kuhei's mother glanced at her son who refused to speak and replied for him.

"I'm so sorry things are like this. You've come here so many times." She looked over in her son's direction. "Listening to the radio is the only thing he enjoys in this world . . . "

"Yes, I'm sure that's true. He can't even go to school."

Kuhei's mother started to plead with him.

"Kuhei, Kuhei, your friend from the City Health Department has come for you again . . . what are we going to do?"

The boy didn't turn around, and twisted the dial violently. A baseball game was on. Mr. Yomogi, who was used to the way the boy acted, turned nonchalantly towards his mother, and talked in a loud voice. Kuhei can hear very well.

"It's better to take the medical exam today. It looks like the condolence payments from the company might go up, even though they're next to nothing. As you know, the way they decide the amount is to divide the cases between adults and children, and between serious cases and light cases . . . It seems that they are going to raise the amount according to the severity of the damage."

Chiyo laughed vaguely and then looked at her son.

"I've heard that the condolence payments might go up." Dropping her voice, she said, "It's amazing that the doctor from Kumamoto University hasn't given up. Kuhei never makes a definite decision to go. He hates going to the hospital more than anything else. We used to go there all the time. If he felt better now, or if he could see better, or if he could even move the fingers of his right hand better, he'd be glad to go and get himself examined. For the first three years we went to the hospital every day. It was the Oda Hospital. The doctors from Kumamoto University took care of him very well. But no matter what they gave him—pills, injections—nothing worked. People tell me he has a rare disease and there is no doctor who can cure it. His sister died like this, too . . . "

There was a roar from the baseball game on the radio. Kuhei muttered something but I couldn't catch what he said.

His mother spoke again.

"It seems that there's this guy named Shibata who can run really fast. He gets all excited when Shibata runs. You know baseball is the only thing he enjoys."

Mr. Yomogi picked up the thread of her conversation.

"Oh yes, Shibata. He really runs fast. They say he runs just like a deer. Kuhei, what do you think of Nagashima*?"

There was a lot of static on the radio. The boy rocked back and forth, as though the radio were the only thing he could hear, and turned the dial violently. Another popular song. The program was a singing competition. Mr. Yomogi hung in there. The song was over. And then Mr. Yomogi, the official from the Health Department, suddenly stood up and said, "Kuhei, why don't you come along with me and get on the bus."

The boy faced the radio and kept fumbling with the dial without looking around. He got the baseball game again. There was no doubt that he was paying attention to the game. Every time he heard a roar from the stadium, he flapped his thin, trouser-clad legs up and down as he sat cross-legged on the floor. In the meantime, he kept touching the radio with his quivering right hand, and his left hand over which he had some control. He was ready to turn the dial again if he needed to. His back was obviously squared towards the intruders, and he leaned forward, like a bow that is bent with the utmost effort of the body. The dial was his answer. It was the indication of his will. The radio was his weapon, and he embraced it. It looked as though he had transformed himself into a sensitive and cautious instrument that could detect lies.

His aging mother glanced at him with a glazed eye. She gave him no rebuke. As though nodding to herself, as though talking to herself, she spoke calmly.

"We won't be able to make ends meet if the condolence payments don't go up. But our Kuhei—if things were normal he'd be an adult already. Around here, as soon as a kid goes to junior high school he's a full-fledged fisherman. When it comes to the condolence money, though, he's considered a child. It's only 30,000 yen a year. I'm sorry. He likes baseball, you know. He spends the whole time listening like this because he can't do it himself. Really, radio is the only thing he enjoys in this whole world. He'll probably go when the baseball game is over. Isn't that right, Kuhei?"

Mr. Yomogi had been getting ready to leave. Now he was thinking that his performance as an official of the Health Department was developing some cracks under the stress of this strange situation, and that he was going to have to face things more philosophically. He sat down again. Singing competitions, Shibata baseball players—he could keep Kuhei company with all of it.

Mr. Yomogi is a loyal public servant and a citizen of the City of Minamata. Like the young bus driver, Mr. Ōtsuka, he keeps his composure, but when he is with a Minamata disease victim he gives everything he has. The real reason for this philosophy is that the boy has pierced him to the bone. He even seems to feel as close to Kuhei as he does to his own blood relations.

---

*A famous baseball player.

He felt embarrassed at his own sensitivity. He said, "Well, Nagashima's the best one around, isn't he. Well, it's over. Let's go, Kuhei."

And so forth; he was crying out to the boy.

Kuhei covered the dial with his hand. He finally made his answer in a heavy, mumbling voice without turning around.

"No, I don't want to go. I'll be killed."

"Be killed? . . . no, there's no such thing. The distinguished doctors from Kumamoto University are here and they'll examine you. It'll be all right because I'll be with you."

"No. If I go I'll be killed."

For a while Mr. Yomogi couldn't remember what he had planned to say.

*   *   *

The Research Division of Kumamoto University has joined forces with the Rehabilitation Hospital of the City of Minamata to fight against Minamata disease, and the hospital would make a bed available to Kuhei if only he would agree to the arrangement. When one considers the accomplishments and authority of the Research Division of Kumamoto University, and the fact that the Rehabilitation Hospital, opened in April of 1985, uses sophisticated techniques, Kuhei's remark about being killed is utterly unjust and absurd.

Nevertheless, it is obvious that the boy has been completely cut off from what should have been a promising future for him. He rejects the officials of the Health Department, which has been dealing with Minamata disease for generation after generation, and refuses to be examined or hospitalized.

That day, he glued himself to the popular songs in the singing contest, and then gained some time listening to the pro baseball game, in the same way that he had been able to befuddle his visitors on a previous occasion with a sumo wrestling program. Shrinking away as though he were about to be captured, he spit out "No, I'll be killed" under the pressure of the situation.

The physical agent of Minamata disease has been invading his brain cells for the last ten years, during the period of his active growth from age six to sixteen. He has been living with this substance in his body and will clearly continue to do so until the end of his life. He has been fighting it—truly, every day he has fought it like a man thrown into a tiger's lair—but he has gone completely blind and can't move his hands, or his legs, or his mouth the way he wants to. People he has felt close to, such as his older sister, and his cousins who used to be his neighborhood playmates (a boy older than himself, and a girl who was younger), have been taken away to the hospital; that was where they all finally died.

The boy cannot help but think that he will be killed. What this signifies is that time is running out for Kuhei, and that he is completely trapped in the midst of this large-scale mercury poisoning scandal that goes along burying its strange and inhuman life-essence in graves as it erupts and continues to spread.

It is the trend of the times to feel that we should forget about Minamata disease, and that we should let it slip casually past that has never been fully explained. Kuhei has been left behind, alone, in this darkness that stealthfully continues to entomb him. It has already half succeeded.

*   *   *

"Yamanaka Kuhei is still alive. He doesn't know that I wrote about him in my book." Ishimure Michiko, from a December 1984 letter to Christopher Stevens.

III

Resistance and the Rise of New Movements for Social Change in the 1970s

As Muto Ichiyo explains in "The Birth of Japan's Women's Liberation Movement in the 1970s," the "Lib" movement that emerged in Japan in 1970 called for a fundamental remaking of male-dominated Japanese society through struggle by and in the name of women. Although this movement attacked internalized male values as well as a sexist society, it united with traditional-role-based women's movements in its first confrontation with the state—nationwide opposition to a government proposal to revise the 1940 Eugenic Protection Law. The proposal was to no longer allow abortion for economic reasons but allow it in the case of handicapped offspring. Although this proposal was defeated, in 1982 the government again proposed a revision, which the women in this photo are demonstrating against on 13 March 1983. This photo is from *AMPO:Japan-Asia Quarterly Review*, vol. 18, nos. 2–3 (1986), p. 99, and it is reprinted with permission.

7

The Birth of the Women's Liberation Movement in the 1970s

Muto Ichiyo *

In 1970, when the radical student movement known as the Zenkyoto movement[1] was retreating, a new women's movement sprang up amidst jeering by media and antipathy from all other quarters of the male-dominated Japanese society. It also startled and enraged most of the women's movement establishment with an iconoclastic appeal to which they had never been exposed—liberation of women's sexuality, suppression of which, it was contended, was the concealed, tabooed base of women's oppression, and in fact, of human oppression in general. The appeal, however, proved to be a moving message from women to women, reaching not only those in the movement but also women of no definite political persuasion, addressing the kernel of their never openly told issues, and liberating their minds, mouths, and senses. That was the women's liberation movement, dubbed "Woman Lib" or just "Lib," pronounced so in Japanese. Launched by spontaneous groups of young, anonymous activists, Lib marked the emergence of a radical feminist movement, in fact a reemergence after the first in the 1910s, the Seito (blue-stocking) movement, which pioneered radical feminism in Japan.

The explosion of the radical feminist movement in the United States in the 1960s and 1970s obviously provided a powerful stimulus. It was such a historic time that new movement initiatives in one country could easily traverse a large space to capture the imagination of people in other countries. Media coverage of the American women's movement was shredded and biased, focusing almost exclusively on sensational actions of American women such as throwing off brassieres and disrupting beauty contests. But even through such biased reports, women activists immediately grasped the significance of what was happening in the United States. Betty Friedan had been translated into Japanese already in 1964, but now pamphlets, declarations, and reports from American feminist

*This chapter is part of a book on Japanese social movements that Muto Ichiyo is currently preparing for publication.

movements were translated and shared. More major works by Shulamith Firestone, Kate Millett, and Juliet Mitchell were translated by women's groups in quick succession. Wilhelm Reich was also read and had a tremendous impact, particularly on new feminists in the Zenkyoto movement.

Matsui Yayori, a prominent feminist journalist who was a member of WOLF (Women's Liberation Front), one of numerous Lib groups that mushroomed around 1970, recalls that reading American feminist books and articles came as an eye-opener to the nature of sexist Japanese society, putting in a solid, coherent context what had been felt keenly in daily life but had not been conceptually crystallized. "It was like reading *Capital* and beginning to see capitalism in an entirely different light."[2]

However crucial the American impact, Japanese Lib was in no sense a transplanted American feminist movement. Of necessity, it welled forth from Japanese reality and found its own voice and expressions.

Coming close on the heels of the virtual collapse of the Zenkyoto movement, Lib was partly the successor to Zenkyoto, while at the same time vehemently negating it. In fact a number of initial Lib activists came from the Zenkyoto student movement. But the main thing was that the new dimension of political struggle opened by Zenkyoto provided the starting point for Lib—the understanding that the seat of power is everyday relationships.

"The campus struggle of 1968," recalls Funabashi Kuniko, a feminist scholar and activist, "began as a personal query by each individual."[3] She says:

> We asked ourselves what it meant to us to study here on this campus. The Zenkyoto movement was alien to the New Left [vanguardist] movement in that each and every student was to become the subject of the movement as an individual. Even though women's issues never surfaced at that time, at least as a way of thinking, that is, asking ourselves personal questions like what does all this mean to me personally, Women's Lib [could occur only] as a post-Zenkyoto movement.

In this context Zenkyoto's gut-level politics broke the ground for Women's Lib.

But the legacy ends there. For Lib came into being as women activists' rebellion against the male-dominated New Left, including the Zenkyoto movement. In this there was a close parallel between Japanese Lib and American radical feminism in the '70s. In spite of its pledge to revolutionize existing social relationships here and now, Zenkyoto was totally insensitive to male-female relations. Male culture was never questioned, despite the active participation of a large number of women students in the struggle. A glaring example: during a campus festival held by Kyoto University Zenkyoto, professional female dancers were hired to dance naked on the balcony of an occupied building for amusement. What would have happened if the Zenkyoto knife of revolution had been thrust home into this blatant demonstration of Zenkyoto sexism? But that did not occur.

Tanaka Mitsu, one of the most powerful pioneer Lib thinker-activists in the '70s, who with her colleagues founded the "Group: Tatakau Onna" (Group:

Fighting Women), tersely said that women existed merely as she-animals (*mesu*) even in the New Left movement.

> All the heavy work, invisible like the submerged mass of an iceberg—preparing stencils, printing handbills, working to earn a living to support 'revolutionaries,' cooking, rearing babies, washing and doing all the everyday chores—had been imposed on them in silent violence. Easily recognized violence is not the only violence. Women are haughtily told, "Hey, explain this passage of Trotsky, can't you?" Big words like 'proletarian consciousness' are hurled to intimidate them. Under such menace and threat, women have to silently do menial jobs. Ah, she-animals called women! Prostrate before men who brazenly declare they would prefer non-movement women as wives, they slave, preparing meals and cleaning the toilet even in the barricaded campus, doing so when it is all too clear that a revolution that would only add pain to women is after all a revolution for men. Female Uncle Toms supporting the male revolution headquarters with the mother's generosity and the prostitute's coquetry![4]

Lib came as a brusque rejection of this oppressive hypocrisy. From the beginning the movement was profoundly self-reflective, simultaneously a fight against internalized male values as well as against the external enemy, a sexist society.

When many Zenkyoto activists were dispersing on their pilgrimages to the peripheries in quest of encounters with hard social realities, women activists who formed Lib felt that the oppressive situation they themselves were involved in was itself the harsh social reality they sought to change. As Ueno Chizuko, one of the most popular feminist scholars in the '80s, put it in cool detachment:

> New Left men who went to Minamata and Sanrizuka . . . had to go somewhere else to discover issues because they had no issues of their own, but women stayed where they were as they were already in the midst of their issue.[5]

In June 1970, a mimeographed handbill was delivered to women participants in an anti-security-treaty rally attended by 70,000 people at Yoyogi Park in Tokyo. It was the first open appeal from Japanese Lib. Issued in the name of a preparatory committee for women's liberation, it called upon women to "launch a women's liberation movement in Japan." At this early stage Lib statements and declarations were still very much armored with New Left jargon. We will see that in a very short period the diverse groups that coalesced would create their own culture, logic, language, and style of organization clearly distinct from the male left culture. But even at this early stage, problems were clearly delineated. A declaration from the same preparatory committee group issued in August 1970 stated:

> We women are deprived of various human freedoms simply because we are women. Whatever eulogy bourgeois ideology may lavish on freedom of love,

we are after all the ones whose commodity value is appraised for the sake of marriage and who, after entering the family, are supposed to behave exactly like others and are recognized only as the wife of somebody. The family we know is not a creative place in organic interaction with society but a closed prison, which is also a haven from society. In that prison wives are constantly bombarded with TV messages and shaped into plastic monsters. Women are also oppressed as mothers. They have to manage to keep the household economy going by setting aside from a meager income the burgeoning education costs for children, take care of their husbands, and take care of the children. Mothers are forced to work 24 hours a day. What is the nature of this labor? It is labor expended to reproduce the husband as a worker and reproduce the children as future workers. For this labor wives and mothers are paid nothing. How many people understand that the family exists on this sacrifice of women called wives?

One of the earliest statements was titled "Declaration of Eros Liberation."[6] It declared, "Oppression of sexuality being the basic means to keep human beings subjugated, the liberation of us, women, will inevitably unfold as the liberation of sexuality." How the notion and practice of "Eros liberation" were developed by Lib will be explained later, but here it should be pointed out that this focus on sexuality marked the Lib movement's clear departure from the New Left, as well as from the preceding postwar women's movements. Put to the test from this vantage point were the myth of monogamous marriage, the notion of family, role division by sex, state control over abortion, myths about a woman's body, accepted notions of motherhood and a woman's life-cycle, as well as all forms of discrimination against women in the workplace and in public and private life.

Postwar Japan had women's movements addressing various issues facing women that were powerful in terms of size. Housewives had their national organization, and women's community associations were organized into a huge national body. Working women were organized into women's sections of trade unions. Major political parties had their women's wings, mobilizing their female constituency for campaigns under their respective party platforms. All these traditional women's organizations, however, conducted themselves within the female roles prescribed to them by society. The Federation of Housewives, a very powerful pressure group, would often demonstrate carrying large wooden rice spoons symbolizing the kitchen and cooking. But the question of whether the kitchen should be the natural place for women never surfaced in the consciousness of this movement. The Mothers' Conference, held every year since 1955, brought together thousands of progressive women who defined themselves as mothers aspiring for peace for the sake of their children. But motherhood itself was never questioned. In the Japanese historical context motherhood was a sanctified element of the prewar "*ie*" system, the mother assumed to readily sacrifice herself for her children and offering them to the state as soldiers. This understanding of motherhood, of course, disappeared under postwar democracy, but why motherhood was so conveniently utilized by the emperor state was never questioned when it was again eulogized as the natural base of the women's anti-war movement.

All these role-based movements left out one thing—the actual woman with her woman's body and desire to live in her wholeness as a woman before being a wife, mother, or worker. From the socially prescribed notions of wife and mother shared by the existing women's organizations, sexuality was singularly left out, as it was personal and the personal was not political. Lib reversed this common sense of the women's movement, reviving sexuality as the kernel of the movement.

The 1970s Lib had its predecessors. In 1911 Hiratsuka Raicho and her comrades launched a new magazine, *Seito* (blue stocking), articulating the deep-rooted aspirations of Japanese women to become full human beings. The famous poetic declaration by Hiratsuka printed in the first issue reads: "At the beginning woman was a sun, a real human being. Now woman is a moon, pale, like a sick person, given life by others and illuminated by others' light. We must take back our hidden sun, right now!"

Women in that period were suffering from the heavy yoke of the *ie* family system imposed by the authoritarian Meiji government. The *ie* is the institutionalized patriarchal system, imparting supreme power to the male head of the household and depriving women of rights as independent individuals. Marriage, as an affair between two households, was arranged by the two male household heads. Household properties were inherited by the eldest son. Adultery by women was punished as a crime, but there was no punishment for men for the same conduct. The law and state-imposed ethics totally subjugated women's sexuality to the *ie* and men's convenience, dooming women to be machines producing boy babies for the longevity of the *ie* and the state.

Hiratsuka and her "New Women" comrades boldly defied this whole system, directing their attack on the oppressive *ie* itself and declaring that women should be restored as "the sun." Free-love marriage had a revolutionary significance. Seeing women's subjugation being perpetuated through subjugation of their sex to the man who personified the *ie* system, liberation of women's sexuality and revolution in the female-male relationship were the cornerstone of the New Women's movement.

The reaction to this new movement was vehement, as it struck at the very fabric of the Japanese state and society then emerging as a late imperial power in dire need of internal order to support its external wars and conquests. The *ie* units as integrated with the emperor system were in fact the building blocks of this order. The new women were vilified as saboteurs of national morality and ethics, depicted as sexually degenerate freewheelers, and even slandered as drunkards. Caricatured, bruised and battered, Seito ended in 1916. The short-lived movement nevertheless opened up new horizons for the Japanese women's movement. In its wake came the socialist women's movement and a broad reformist movement for women's suffrage in the 1920–30s.

In the post-Seito prewar movements, however, the keen concern of Seito with sexuality, if not totally eradicated, receded to the background. Socialist theories made women's liberation contingent on proletarian revolution, promising that after the revolution women, too, would be automatically free and urging women to devote themselves to the cause of proletarian revolution. The women's suffrage movement focused on securing women's political participation. In neither did sexuality find its rightful place.

Now 60 years after Seito, the women's movement returned by a circuitous route to the centrality of sexuality. But it was not mere repetition. The enemy was not the same.

The postwar reform democratized the "feudal" systems of prewar Japan in many aspects of life. The new constitution declared men and women equal and marriage an affair between independent men and women. The new civil code basically destroyed the old *ie* system. Nuclear families quickly replaced the patriarchal *ie* households, as economic supergrowth attracted more and more young women and men from the countryside to Tokyo and other urban centers. Love marriages became commonplace. Women's labor-participation rate increased. In 1945 women at last won full voting rights and exercised these rights for the first time in 1946. Formal, legal equality was established between both sexes. In addition, in the early 1960s the widespread use of home electrical appliances, washing machines in particular, was said to have set housewives free from household chores. Women no longer had to confront the institutionalized *ie* patriarchy directly linked with the authoritarian state. But this did not bring women substantive equality with men. On the contrary, women were enmeshed in a more sophisticated and finely knit net, from which escape was extremely difficult.

The dominant force shaping the fate of women was the corporations, which became the real masters of postwar Japanese society. In the early 1960s, resurgent Japanese industry and the government, in close collaboration, set out to define the female life cycle from the point of view of optimal control of human resources. In other words, the government-business complex undertook to place the area of reproduction under its control to maximize efficiency in the area of production. The general prescription was that a woman who chooses to work after finishing school would go through four consecutive stages of life. She (1) works as an employee, (2) quits her job at marriage in her mid-20s and becomes a housewife/mother, (3) returns to work part time after child-rearing duties become lighter, and (4) quits her job and devotes herself to the care of the elderly in-laws and then her aged husband. The stubbornly persisting M-shape in the Japanese women's age-employment diagram indicates that this pattern has not changed up to this day (see figure 7.1).

Of course the designated life cycle cannot be imposed directly by decree or legislation. Rather, it is implemented through intracompany systems, induced by government policies such as tax and pension policies favoring part-time work,

Figure 7.1. **Percentage of Women Who Are Working, by Age Group**

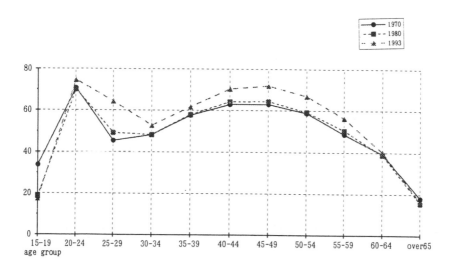

Source: Ministry of Labor

and cemented by a culture molded to internalize the values of corporate society.

What does it mean to follow this life cycle? An idealized model case might be as follows: A young woman fresh from school is hired on the assumption that she will work only for a few years and quit upon marriage to "enter the family." For this reason she is assigned to a job clearly defined as supplementary to men's jobs. She marries and quits the company. As the wife of a company man, she is expected to play a logistic role for the company by enabling her husband to devote himself fully to company work. As their children reach school age, family expenditures go up: most parents send children to private study courses to prepare for extremely competitive entrance exams to a good school, which will promise them a secure future in a big company. This is also the time when the family needs to buy a home with the aid of housing loans, repayments of which evaporate a large chunk of their monthly and bonus income. Thus, the wife begins to work to earn a supplementary income while doing all the housework and child care. As old-age pensions are far from enough to support the couple's post-retirement life, the family must save. And to save, the husband must work harder to be well regarded by management and promoted, as well as taking the short cut to a larger cash income by working longer to get overtime premiums. Japan's exceptionally high savings ratio largely results from this arrangement. A vicious circle thus sets in—the harder they work, the more tightly the whole family is caught in the trap set by corporate power.

Despite the vast number of women working in it, the Japanese company was (and still is) a veritable man's world, where male employees are pressured to devote themselves fully to the company cause, sacrificing their extra-company life, leaving child care and housework entirely to their wives, and internalizing company values. The trade union movement, composed overwhelmingly of regular male workers, is nothing but a movement of men who comfortably accept this gendered definition of the corporate world, assuming as a matter of course business-government control of women's life cycles. Thus, formally independent nuclear families were in practice integrated with this corporate system of production and reproduction resting on the sacrifice of women. As such, nuclear families became the building blocks of Japan's postwar corporate empire.

But that was concealed by ideological mystification. Kaji Etsuko characterized this mystification device as "my-home-ism," which came into vogue in the '60s. "My-home-ism," according to her, "projects an image of women's happiness in the nuclear family and petit bourgeois life style. . . . "It has a double function."

> On the one hand, it converts alienation from social labor into the illusion of happiness in a home life supposedly free of the drudgery of monotonous and exhausting work in order to stimulate the flow of young women from the workplace to home. (This serves as an invitation to early retirement.) On the other hand, since a primary function of the nuclear family is consumption, women are forced to earn money to add to the family's disposable income; but in this case, they are taught to think of themselves not as workers but as housewives trying to earn "just a little extra."[7]

With this sweetener, corporate values easily penetrated family life and influenced the pattern of conjugal life—the wife helping the company-man husband to work more efficiently for the company and herself devoted to educating her son to make of him a good, high-incomed, salaried man of a prestigious company.

However idealized, this stereotype was oppressive to women. And women were tied to this role because they were women and not because they chose it. Since they were tied to this role through marriage, this meant that women's sexuality was conveniently subjected to exogenous values that were unabashedly company- and male-centered. The resurgence of sexuality as the central theme of the women's movement is contexualized by this particular type of patriarchy, the societal patriarchy based on corporate-state management of a woman's life cycle that has characterized postwar Japanese society.

It was no longer the solidly institutional and ideologically monolithic *ie*-state system that women had to combat for their liberation. The new adversary was more elusive and permeating, and fighting it required that the Lib women anchor themselves deep in the bedrock, women's sexuality, and from there create and develop new gender relations for themselves. It was not enough to be anti–status quo. What was required was the creation of alternative, autonomous gender relations in the midst of everyday life. The status quo would show its full contours only when women began to assert their full womanhood and to fight for and live an alternative life.

But before we explain how Lib approached this issue, let us sketch the course of events.

Lib in Action

The first Lib action was a women-only demonstration staged on 21 October 1970, on Tokyo's Fifth Avenue, the Ginza. Two hundred women wearing red and black helmets, most of them young, held a rally and demonstrated for women's liberation. The organizers were The Group: Fighting Women, the Preparatory Committee for Women's Liberation, and a few other newly born women's liberation groups. October 21 was the so-called international anti-war action day (an "international action" observed in Japan alone since 1966), and all progressive forces mobilized in the streets, as did the riot police. Compared to half a million people who took to the street in 800 places throughout the country that day, the Lib demonstration was numerically microscopic. Kurata Kazunari's chronologically meticulous account of the New Left [8] does not even mention it. The organizers of the demonstration had also been severely criticized by New Left sects, including their female members, for not focusing on anti-war slogans.

But it was a new topic for the media. A host of reporters descended on the small park with cameras and TV lights in avaricious curiosity. Recognizing that the media were covering Lib only to disparage it, the demonstrators refused to cooperate. As anticipated, newspaper reports the next day were full of sexist ridicule. Women "yelled" and "shrieked," and Lib fighters "opened their handbags and preened" as soon as the demonstration dispersed.[9] The implication was that a novel species of animal appeared to have emerged but turned out to be just women after all—so take it easy, no need to worry too much. The media attitude toward Lib generally remained mean and vulgar throughout the early 1970s.

But the Lib appeal was not a lone voice. It was heard. It mobilized. Numerous small Lib groups cropped up mainly in urban environments. No central body authorized these spontaneous groups, nor was participation limited to those coming from the student movement background or to young women. Housewives, labor movement activists long suffering from the unions' gender-insensitive and often sexist attitudes, women journalists, TV announcers, and members of traditional women's organizations, feeling that something was lacking in or wrong with their movements, started to form groups and to act as Lib.

On 14 November 1970, 500 women from all walks of life overflowed a small auditorium in Shibuya Ward in Tokyo to attend "Women Lib Symposium: What Women's Liberation Means to Me," organized by progressive publisher Aki Shobo. The atmosphere was totally different from that of conventional political gatherings—no rituals, no speeches from the stage, participants sitting around the moderator and speaking freely. Joining this seven-hour meeting were a wide variety of women from all generations and diverse backgrounds. Besides new Lib people and activists from traditional women's movements, participants included working women, housewives, students, teachers, and career women from different professions. To guarantee a space allowing women to speak unobstructed, the hall was off limits to men and media reporters. Higuchi Keiko, a well-known writer, who was the moderator, reported:

> As the moderator I prepared four agenda items . . . but that did not work at all, for people spoke up so freely in their own way about problems they had. Therefore it is extremely difficult to summarize what was discussed. . . . But as discussion went on, certain phrases emerged as passwords that one woman after another began to favor to use—"let's say we hate it when we hate it" was one of them. Women from their teens to their 60s chimed in with this, making clear what was so hateful—"I am the breadwinner but management refuses to enter my husband as my dependent"; "women are supposed not to have sexual desire"; "my parents tell me that no one will marry me unless I behave"; "why should women alone bear the burden of child rearing?"[10]

The deeply felt experiences uninhibitedly related by women from so many different situations demonstrated that personal aversions toward the behavior of men who were injuring them were not just personal. This was a collective discovery that the personal is political. Higuchi pointed out in the same article,

> Women's grudges were shared as their common asset, and the common starting point for all of us was the painful awareness that women had been made to endure what was palpably unjust, and that precisely because they were women.

The other "password" according to Higuchi in this article was "women's logic":

> By women's liberation nobody meant that they wished to become like men or overtake and outrival men. People rather felt that women should be more loyal to women's senses. If women become "ferocious company persons" they would only be trapped by the logic of men. Instead of becoming a female elite, we want to be ourselves as women. . . . For women to be themselves, many repeated, they needed women's logic, and not the logic made by a male-chauvinist society.

This sharing of direct personal experience became the basic channel through which Lib spread from woman to woman. It was a process whereby women sought to acquire their own forms of expression. "That was a creation from chaos," as a Lib activist recalled. Ehara Yumiko, a feminist sociologist, pointed out in her succinct review of Japanese Lib that this process of "politicization of personal experience" was what American feminists had made into a method and educational program of consciousness raising. "Though in Japan consciousness transformation [in this manner] was not clearly identified as a means to produce activists, the early Lib meetings and live-ins certainly played the same role."[11]

The breakthrough in Lib history was a four-day *gasshuku* (live-in) held in August 1971 at a mountain resort at Iiyama in Nagano prefecture. A total of

1,200 women came from different parts of the country. The Group: Fighting Women issued an invitation written in cheerful, colloquial, but scathing personal language. Many participants in this live-in recall that it was a revolutionary and truly liberating experience. Kanai Yoshiko, now a prominent feminist philosopher, recalls that "scales fell off" her eyes by participating in it. Because Lib rejected ritualistic procedures, the organizers left no "official" records about this important event. Let us therefore have a glimpse of it through a buoyant report in the Women's Democratic Club's weekly paper by Nishimura Kiyomi:

> Women came all the way to Iiyama with something to speak about and luggage to carry, gathered together to avenge the wrongs they suffered. For four days beginning August 21 all sorts of women, in their 20s in the main but some in their 50s, including student libs, mother libs, and elderly libs, and from north and south, arrived. . . . The usually quiet country villa was filled with women's fever for the few days, perhaps astonishing the ripening ears of rice plants, reddening apples, and flocking dragonflies. . . . All the participants found it extremely significant that they were able to speak in their own personal language, attracted and subscribing to the Lib principle that there is no women's struggle without beginning with themselves. As Lib says, one can fight only on the basis of the pain one suffers and a woman can start only by facing and gazing at her misery. . . . Group discussion started in the hostel rooms and outdoors. Anybody could set up any session by inviting interested people. "Let's run away from home," "Divorce is wonderful," "Discussing 'bad women,' " "Bombard the male revolutionary headquarters," "Women's liberation in America," etc. Convinced that each of us has unlimited possibilities, we feel out in one another if there is anything in common, in our thinking and in our plans. A little flame burning within each of us women, who met for the first time, now unites us in horizontal solidarity. We are opening an entirely new field. "Let's start a Lib newspaper!" "Let's have a clear policy for unmarried mothers, comrades!" "Let's organize high school lib!" . . . "Let's talk about contraceptives!" Sharing common topics, energies explode and enthusiasm is generated to create new groups of women.[12]

The sense of emancipation and excitement generated by this encounter may be fathomed from the same reporter's description of the "happening" that occurred during the "live-in."

> The open space in the mountains of Kuroiwa. It is night and totally dark. The whole world exists only around this bonfire. Scores of young women around it are dancing, go-going, rocking. A white panty flies in the air, catches fire and burns off. A beautiful woman's body as naked as she was born is lit up. 'Yes, you've done it!" I shout. One after another, they strip and dance. Young hearts, young blood. They are nude both in body and mind!

The live-in in Nagano was the watershed, and from this time on Lib spread all over the country—small circles were created, sessions on women's bodies

held, contraceptives studied and devices displayed, solidarity actions with persecuted women conducted, battered wives' shelters set up, women's spaces
opened, women's communes organized, lib songs made and sung, women's
cultural festivals held, and numerous women's publications inaugurated. Lib
groups were created in Sapporo, Otaru, Hirosaki, Osaka, and Fukuoka, while
women's liberation study groups (Jokaiken) formed one after another on campuses all over the country. Asked how many Lib groups were born in the height
of the movement, Yonezu Tomoko, one of the core members of the Lib Shinjuku
Center, said that though no survey was made, the number was hundreds and not
thousands, counting students' Jokaiken groups. An explosion of feminist activ-
ism characterized the first four years of the 1970s.

Lib gathered momentum in 1972. On International Women's Day, 8 March,
women and children from all over the Kanto plain gathered in Tokyo and demonstrated in the evening carrying candles, appealing "Let's create a society
where women can live independently." On 30 April the First Lib Conference
was held in Tokyo, drawing 1,900 women. There the need for a Lib center was
strongly voiced. The Group: Fighting Women, together with other radical lib
groups, set up the Lib Shinjuku Center near Shinjuku, Tokyo's most bustling
quarter, in September. Earlier, in May, a large rally was held to "thoroughly
discuss all issues of Lib," where a new middle-aged Lib group, Red June, was
inaugurated. The Lib Shinjuku Center started its periodical, *Konomichi Hitosuji*
(*This Way Only*). In the same year *Onna Eros* (*Women Eros*), a 180–page Lib
quarterly magazine, was launched by another group. *Agora,* another national
feminist magazine inaugurated in the 1960s, also served as a forum to circulate
women's views. Women's mini-journals were started one after another, such as
Onnano Hangyaku (*Women's Rebellion*) and *Group Honoho* (*Flame*). Fifteen or
so women's journals were thus launched between 1971 and 1972.

International sisterhood also became one of Lib's concerns. In October 1972,
an international beauty contest was held at the Budokan Stadium, and Lib mobilized to protest. In December 1973, Lib activists staged actions inside Tokyo's
Haneda International Airport protesting against Japanese men's sex tourism in
South Korea. Tourist agencies were openly recruiting Japanese men for package
tours to South Korea having as their component a night with Kaeseng, Korean
entertainers. This was in response to protest actions against Japanese Kaeseng
tourism staged by students at Eihwa Women's College in Seoul.

This campaign had a tremendous social impact and developed into a movement protesting against Japanese men's rampant sex tourism, which was promoted openly by travel agencies, even prestigious ones. Under the pressure of
the women's campaign, the Lower House of the Diet had to take up the issue of
sex tourism to South Korea. Socialist representative Kobayashi Susumu grilled
the government on the mention of "night life" in a Japanese government report
on development of South Korea's Cheju Island, which apparently implied promotion of prostitution tourism. These actions forced travel agencies to refrain

from at least openly recruiting men for obvious group sex tours. The Asian Women's Association, an internationalist feminist group launched in 1977, persistently pressed this issue after other wings of Lib shifted attention to other issues and practically dropped it. In 1983, the government revised the Travel Agency Law and prohibited licensed travel agencies from promoting "unwholesome travel," meaning sex tourism.

Struggle for Control

Higuchi Keiko concluded her earlier-quoted *Asahi Shimbun* article on the 1970 first Lib meeting by saying, "What we need now most urgently is a simple, concrete goal of action to channel the energies of grass-roots Lib into a viable movement." Just as Lib was emerging, such a focus was given by the ruling Liberal Democratic Party (LDP). About the time the First Lib Conference was held, the LDP presented amendments to the Eugenic Protection Law to the Diet. This was another major attempt to strengthen state control over women's bodies. It provided the occasion for Women Lib's first confrontation with the state. This issue brought all Lib groups together in sustained nationwide struggle.

The LDP government proposed deletion of the clause in the law that makes economic reasons a ground for abortion and inclusion of a provision that legalizes abortion when the baby to be born is found physically or mentally "handicapped." Abortion was (and is) illegal under the criminal code, but is practically permitted under the Eugenic Protection Law. The law itself was unsavory in both its origin and its implications. The original law was enacted in 1940 in line with the Nazi's ideology of racial purity and to assure the reproduction of strong soldiers. The postwar law amended in 1948 declared as its purpose the prevention of "the birth of inferior posterity and to protect the life and health of mothers." From the beginning it was a law based on the ideology of state control of women's bodies and reproductive functions to suit the goals of the state. Because black-market abortion cases had become dangerously common the law was revised in 1949 and 1952, ultimately allowing abortion for economic reasons with a certified doctor's permission.

Conservative forces, religious and secular, were clamoring that Japan had become a "paradise of abortion," constituting a national disgrace. In the 1970s there were 2 to 3 million abortions a year. But the real intent of the right-wingers' and LDP's drive was elsewhere. Then Prime Minister Sato Eisaku viewed the issue from the angle of "destruction of the social order." He stated: "Respect for life is being ignored in these times—as symbolized by the confusion in sexual morality. . . . We must preserve the sense of nurturing the embryo as our own child, a gift from Heaven. Not for the labor supply, but to prevent social disorder, we should revise the Eugenic Protection Law. . . . "[13]

There was massive protest against this attempt to restrict abortion. The major trade union federation, Sohyo, opposed it on the grounds that low wages, bad housing conditions, and lack of adequate child-care facilities compelled women to have abortions. Such prestigious women's organizations as the Tokyo YWCA, the Japan Nurses' Association, the time-honored Women Voters' League, traditional progressive organizations like the Women's Democratic Club, and a score of others rose up. The Aoi-Shiba-no-Kai (Blue Lawn Association)—the most radical organization of the disabled, consisting of those with cerebral palsy—was furious with the proposed law revision from a different angle. It found in the proposed amendment a murderous attempt to denigrate the disabled as not being full human beings. If cerebral palsy patients were not supposed to be born, then they who had been born already were ones not supposed to live. They declared that the amendment "denies the right of the 'handicapped' to live."

Thus, a two-year struggle by women unfurled, including sit-ins at the Welfare Ministry, numerous public rallies, study meetings, and confrontations with the riot police. In the broad coalition of women's movements the Lib played a major role by enlarging the ranks of joint struggle, as well as in mobilization, confrontation, and theoretical underpinning. Women and organizations of the disabled fought against the legal revision in close collaboration, although serious contradictions appeared among them. The Lib opposed the government proposal with the slogan: "A woman decides whether she bears or not." It upheld the right of women's control of their bodies, or sovereignty over their own bodies. But the groups of disabled expressed strong objection to this, finding in it the same odd-man-out implication as in the proposed revision to the law. Controversies flared between Lib and the disabled, and also among women themselves. In the midst of debates and controversies, Enoki Misako, a WOLF member, launched a new move, Neo-Lib as she called it, calling for full legalization of the use of contraceptive pills. This triggered another round of debates among Lib groups.

Facing the criticism of the disabled, the women's movement adopted a slogan, "For a society where we can give birth! For a society where we want to give birth!" Later we will come back to discuss how Lib faced this difficult issue.

The campaign ended in victory in June 1974, when the revised bill was scrapped. Throughout the 1970s, the women's movement was the only movement that successfully thwarted LDP-planned legislation.

Style of Action

Though the abortion law was the focus of early Lib action, the campaign itself was not particularly new in style—mobilization, sit-ins, street demonstrations and petitioning. But this was the tip of the iceberg. Beneath the campaign surface, dynamic and imaginative processes of networking were taking place among women throughout this period. Numerous new encounters, initiatives and joint action over specific cases of women's sufferings fast created a world of sisterhood. Entrepreneurship was also remarkable. Women's spaces in the form of coffee shops, restaurants and bookstores or combinations of some of those were opened one after another. The major ones were Three Point in Ginza Street in Tokyo (1970), Women's House in Nagoya (1974), Hirahira in Sapporo (1974), Hokiboshi in Shinjuku, Tokyo (1975) and Shambara in Kyoto (1977).

"We planned many events based on Hokiboshi," recalled Iwatsuki Sumie, one of the chief organizers of the Witch Concert, which was first held in summer 1974. "We did them because they sounded exciting. None of them was done out of a sense of duty or obligation as women's lib. That was because we were Lib." She stated this at a round-table discussion in 1983 attended by early Lib activists.[14] Things developed this way:

> **Iwatsuki:** Three of us opened a women's communication floor in the Ginza called Three Point, a fairly large coffee house. We displayed movement publications, sold handicrafts and offered a space and facilities to change diapers. But that did not pay, so we took on contract research on menstrual products. We did door-to-door interviews with housewives in housing estates. The interviewees, first a little bit wary, tried to look smart, but finally began to speak from their hearts—I want to escape from this estate, I want to throw myself out of this window, do you believe I can only meet a man from society (her husband) at six o'clock in the evening, and that man only. . . . I shuddered at the life of wives in these urban nuclear families. . . . They asked us questions about contraceptives and women's bodies, and so we started lecturing on women's bodies at Three Point. High school girls came and complained about the lack of sex education, and we encouraged them to provide it themselves and they started, making pamphlets. . . . We held a rock concert every Friday, and we smuggled in discussion on menstruation between performances, which shocked the audience, but some women came back to attend our lectures on women's bodies. . . . At that time, the K-ko san case arose. She was an unmarried mother whose right to rear her baby was denied by the court, apparently a case of discrimination against unmarried mothers. A network of women to support K-ko san was organized, and people decided to raise money to help her in the court struggle. Some proposed a bazaar and other conventional ways, but others wanted a music festival. If we do that, why should we make it only for K-ko san? People agreed on the idea. And this was the beginning of the Witch Concert. . . . Discussion was exciting. Why should we use the term "unmarried woman" instead of a single woman with children? It was the time we began to choose words to express ourselves correctly. Some men did not like the idea of a concert because they wanted the movement to be rigid and moralistic, and so we agreed that everything would be done by women only as women felt comfortable. Men were allowed to help. All kinds of requests rushed to us. Some people wanted to talk about the use of soap instead of detergent, and others wanted to appeal for solidarity with women in other Asian countries. . . . Numerous women offered help, many women we had not known at all volunteered to have their names listed as sponsors. We were young and ran at full speed, and finally the staff swelled to 200. Men set up courses to train themselves in how to change diapers and let children play. During the concert 50 men were in charge of baby sitting. . . .

> **Moderator:** Why did you name it Witch Concert?
>
> **Iwatsuki:** Because K-ko san's trial was like a witch inquisition. . . .

The Witch Concert was very successful, extremely lively, drawing thousands. It was fun but it was also deadly serious. A second was held in 1975 and the third and last in 1977.

Iwatsuki's account of the development of the concert graphically illustrates Lib's style—leaping from one spot to another, from women to women, easily overcoming barriers set up by the establishment, and creating women's own expressions. The development was dynamic, haphazard if you like, compared with the traditional movement way of rigorously implementing an action plan prepared by the executive committee or the like. But it had an underpinning in K-ko san's case. K-ko san, who physically took back her baby, had to run away from the foster parents and police, go underground with the baby, hide and be protected by women's networks.

At its height in the early 1970s, Lib created a new style, a new movement culture.

Lib's Scalpel

As a social movement, Lib of course struggled to achieve political goals such as the abolition of pernicious laws. Its impact, however, lay in its effort to fundamentally challenge and transform the basic relationships of male-dominated society. "If I am to concisely summarize the path traversed by the '70s Lib movement," Ehara Yumiko wrote, "it was a path from a movement to oppose something to one building an alternative." She explained:

> The victims of oppression and discrimination are forced to begin by rejecting the negative identity imposed upon them. . . . Women are no exception. Why are women discriminated against in employment? Why are they not given responsible positions? Why are they paid less than men? Not because women are inferior in capacity. Women can do all that. . . . Lib thus had to start as an "anti" movement. But anti-something will never make you somebody. Through trial and error, and by negating itself as an "anti" movement, Lib searched for ways that women can live as women on the basis of their own personal choice.[15]

This was an extremely difficult task, and the Lib movement therefore had to inch ahead by trial and error. Ehara continued:

> But exactly those trials and errors can be seen as evidence that Lib was a movement of women themselves who drilled their way ahead, and not a movement constituted on the basis of one or another of the existing ideologies.

Reading Tanaka Mitsu, we are brought anew to the realization that early Lib's scalpel reached such a depth of Japanese society that it touched its elementary organism. The alternative that Lib sought, accordingly, had to involve fundamental remaking at this depth, and not at a surface, pragmatic level. Though Lib was a collective movement from which no personality should be singled out as "the mastermind," Japanese Lib thinking cannot be properly evaluated apart from Tanaka's originality, power of language and personality. She did not come from a student movement background. Growing up in a matter-of-fact urban family, she started to work after high school and was involved on the fringe of the anti–Vietnam War movement and then in the anti–Immigration Law campaign. She was in her late twenties when she took part in the early moves that led to the creation of Lib.

One of the earliest Lib pamphlets that had an electrifying effect on Lib thinking was written by Tanaka. Provocatively titled "Liberation from the Toilet," it circulated widely in August 1970. The argument was unrefined and still retained New Left discourse such as loyalty to the proletarian cause, but the main tenets of Lib are already unmistakably discernible. What does "toilet" mean? The pamphlet stated:[16]

> When we say that sexuality is used as a basic means to keep human beings subjugated, we mean a mechanism that oppresses women's sexuality through the medium of man's consciousness, a consciousness that in turn oppresses man's sexuality. Men's consciousness, which works as a medium of this dual oppression, is one that fails to find woman as a whole woman who has both tenderness and sexuality as the expression of her tenderness.
>
> For man, woman's image is divided—one image represents mother's tenderness (motherhood) and the other represents a mere tool to satisfy his sexual desire (toilet). Within this divided consciousness, man allocates his two separate feelings, one each to one of the two imagined aspects of woman, which are again abstractions created by man.
>
> Facing this disjointed consciousness of man—a consciousness formed to suit the convenience of the ruling classes—woman, in whom sexuality as tenderness and sexuality as sensuality are one, is dissected and she is forced to live as dissected parts. But the man who compels woman to live only as her parts, by the same token, must also live only as his parts, suppressing his own sexuality.
>
> Since men and women are mutually related, the misery of women's sexuality is the misery of men's sexuality, and all this is symbolic of the misery of modern society.

How can women free themselves from this man's-consciousness-bound being? By realizing that toilet and mother are two sides of a coin.

> When a woman becomes aware that it is essentially the same thing and that it makes no difference which category she is classified in, mother or toilet, then she stands up against man and against the powers that be.

This "stand up against" is a poor translation for the Japanese verb *inaoru*, a favorite Lib word. Literally it is closer to "sit down" than stand up, if you sit and refuse to move. You *inaoru* when you refuse to flatter or conform to dominant others as if to shout "What's wrong with me? I am I!"—you affirm yourself even when there is not yet full logical or moral justification. It is an audacious and risky way to stand up.

> A cute and lovely woman, shaped in that image by man and favored in that definition by state power, begins to establish herself as subject of her destiny when she stands up with her sexuality as the foothold. She then begins to confront the ruling power, which survives only by turning the woman into the toilet. Here she encounters her "security treaty system (*ampo taisei*)."

The "security treaty system" may sound abrupt, but since the abrogation of the Japan-U.S. Security Treaty was the accepted strategic goal of all progressive movements in that period, it simply meant big politics. This is Tanaka's way of saying that the personal is political. But it goes beyond that. It implies also that the political is personal.

But that is not so simple. Every woman has contradictory selves. Tanaka Mitsu later developed her peculiar term "derangement" as a dialectical development of the struggle between the two selves in every woman—"the self wishing to flatter the dominant values and the other that refuses to do so." If the two selves assert themselves, "derangement" is inescapable. But precisely in this derangement, Tanaka said, "our promising future is pregnant." Derangement is painful, and you fall into darkness. The notion of darkness and pain comes in. In another essay, Tanaka explained:

> Darkness, or pain, is absolute to the one who suffers from it. Of course we are not fated to darkness. Darkness is because we have ostracized ourselves from the dominant system's values. If so, by facing and questioning ourselves who feel it darkness, we can transform our existence and embrace new values, blasting phony values imposed by society.

"Our struggle does not start with a perfect revolutionary woman, who in fact exists nowhere," she said, "but with 'me, here,' with all contradictions, all that contradict reason." That is the actual woman. " 'Spite and grudge of woman,' as it is called, reflect irritation with, and unredeemed sorrow for, herself who is masochistically practicing what she thinks she should refuse."

> "Of course, you understand me, don't you?" Conversation among women often goes like this. Underlying this kind of exchange is women's shared grudge against man, society and herself, elusive substance that escapes your fingers even if you want to hold it. It is through hurling the grudges back to man and power holders that we can begin knitting our theory of women's liberation, our logic of liberation of women as women.

This understanding offers a methodology—one of grudge sharing. And the first Lib meetings succeeded by creating an arena for self-expression, grudge sharing, and through it self-affirmation.

Reiterating that Lib did not start from the socially recognized women's roles (mother, housewife, working woman), Ehara rejected the notion that Lib was an elitist women's extravagance because it refused to take such roles for granted.[17] There were quite a few traditional women activists who complained that Lib language was hard to understand and reproached Lib with holding common women in contempt and putting them off. "But that was not true," Ehara contended. "It was common women (housewives, students, part-timers) who showed the highest degree of sympathy with Lib." The recognition of the ambivalence of woman, her existence as a dissected being, ensured Lib access to, and readiness to involve itself in, the situations of common women. For Tanaka Mitsu, this contradictory self was a central theme.

But when Tanaka says woman is liberated as woman, what does she mean by woman? She argued in the "toilet" pamphlet:

> The absolute difference between men and women is that the former do not bear children and the latter do.... Thinking through this difference, we are brought to the stark fact that women, because of their biological function, are beings that can grasp themselves as diachronic, or historical, beings, and that men are beings fated to fade away in front of women and children. [Only the mother is in a position to ascertain her blood bond with her children.] Man needs logic in order to understand himself as a historical being, but woman is already historical in her existence. Man is more authoritarian than woman precisely because his existence is more precarious.... Woman, because her existence is already historical, can locate herself more easily in the social context and horizontally relate with, for instance, farm women at Sanrizuka and Shibokusa,[18] without whose strength these struggles would not be maintained. They are powerful because in the struggle they have situated themselves in vertical (historical) and horizontal (social) relationships.

The original "toilet pamphlet" was ten mimeographed regular-size sheets of newsprint casually stapled—too shabby to be called a pamphlet. No author was credited except The Group: Fighting Women, which few knew. The style was unique, even bizarre, to many used to conventional movement literary style. Nevertheless, it came like an electric shock to the post-Zenkyoto women activists. It was a moment of rare productive encounter between a statement and the needs of the times.

From the foothold of the "toilet" pamphlet, early Lib sank its scalpel into the body of Japanese postwar corporate society to gouge out its focal infection—a male-dominated culture that, according to Tanaka, was built on the logic of productivity. Despite Tanaka's generally essentialist characterization of man and woman, here, man, whose bones were made visible by Tanaka's X-ray, was no longer an abstract man. He is a socially concrete man molded by postwar Japanese corporate society who internalizes corporate values and has a specific ingrained pattern of behavior and perception. In the invitation to the Lib "live-in," Tanaka explained:[19]

A society that allows woman to live only as a she-animal also allows man to live only as a race horse. Nevertheless, we don't mitigate our accusation of male society and male culture. If woman as a she-animal directs her femininity toward man, man as a he-animal directs his masculinity toward society. When the logic of masculinity, now as well as before, is based on the assumption that man "should efface himself for the sake of a great cause," he is easily trapped by the corporate cause—profit making. Then, even if he may be frustrated, or in despair, at his inability to display this masculinity fully, he does not squarely face the kernel of his misery, that is, he is completely subjugated by the logic of corporate productivity.

The big cause, whether the state cause, the corporate cause, or the revolutionary cause, is essentially external to man and does not involve his personal pain. And he sacrifices himself for that cause. That is comfortable for the man, for as long as he is beefed up by his cause, he need not pay attention to the fact that this logic and attitude cuts off all who are useless to the cause. At that moment, man loses the ability to feel his own pain.

The man society expects him to be is a "strong man" who never betrays the logic of productivity. Man thus makes it his self-imposed obligation to become stronger and run faster. Man is allowed to exist only in the process of constantly making himself something, and that process is oriented toward the social cause, and so for the man creating himself is synonymous to losing himself. Even for a man who takes the side of an anti-systemic movement, this historicity incarnated in him allows him only to conduct a struggle not originating in his own pain. Hence man can easily sacrifice his own liberation for the sake of generally accepted slogans [*tatemae*].

Thus, "the animal called man" does not want to talk about problems as his personal problems.

Man has been made to speak such a language. The language of man who does not feel his own pain is one that is uttered to protect his "face" rather than talk about himself, a language of enlightening others, and for that matter a language of dominating others.

In the same vein, in male-dominated society, knowledge and perception also bypass one's real self. "Long ago, our ancestors must have faced a life-or-death choice when they found a new species of grass and had to decide whether or not to eat it," Tanaka said.

This seriousness of our ancestors is found even in our childhood experience. When we saw the ocean for the first time, we must have faced it with all our bodily and spiritual might—we tasted sea water and learned it was salty, heard the ocean roar and met the tenderness and horror of the sea with our eyes, nose, limbs and pores. . . . The ocean that impressed itself so strongly on the small child's mind degenerates gradually into a mere image of waves in monotonous motion. The sea does not degenerate, of course. [The image degenerates because] the "human being-controlling factory" justified in the name of education teaches us, with a patchwork of knowledge, how "nature" can be conquered. If you turn a page or two, you can know everything about the ocean, and that would suffice in order to pass the multiple-choice exam. Then you simply run to the bookstore if you want to know about the ocean. You have not tasted brine from all the seas of the world, yet it is taken for granted that brine is salty. It is on this premise that houses are built, cars run and factories constructed. The logic of productivity, a running mate of modern rationalism, has deprived human beings of nature. With "have knowledge about" becoming a substitute for "knowing," the leisure industry and polluting factories, for their own ulterior purposes, have unabashedly raped the sea.

Tanaka Mitsu's discourse, finely studded with parables and personal experience, was a distinctive, fundamental critique of modern industrial society, one with a strong ecological tone. From this vantage point, she singled out the negative commonality between the mainstream and the male-dominated opposition in productivity-oriented postwar Japanese society. Though the two have different political goals, they speak in the same male language that never touches themselves and therefore does not help to change themselves. Women are in a position to reverse this dominant man-made standard and to create an alternative society in which language, human relations, politics, nature, and sexuality are plowed back into the living totality of the human being. Fighting male domination means all that.

As the "toilet" pamphlet already suggested in rough outline, Tanaka Mitsu contended that woman has the immanent capability of creating such a society. Man separates language from his body, dismissing the fact that the body is doomed to pain. But woman cannot do so. Tanaka Mitsu "intuitively knows" that "woman, in her encounter with other human beings and nature, is capable of constantly refreshing and resurrecting herself." The source of this is "woman's womb, its nature, its horror and its life power."

It is noted in this connection that Japanese Lib did not go in fully for technological solutions concerning women's bodies, except for, perhaps, the above-mentioned group Chupiren (Alliance of Women's Liberation Opposing the Abortion-Prohibiting Laws and Demanding Liberalization of Contraceptive Pills). This group, headed by a flamboyant leader, Enoki Misako, called for full liberalization of the sale of contraceptive pills, a clear-cut assertion that the pill was the best means to minimize the burdens on a woman's body. The group also resorted to eye-catching street actions, such as demonstrations at the offices of particular male sexual abusers. The group's pink helmets and pink flag drew media attention and curiosity, and for some years Chupiren was presented by the media as the most typical example of Lib.

It might be fair to say that Chupiren did not represent the mainstream of '70s Lib thinking. Groups concerned about the body set up many educational sharing sessions, mobilizing all scientific knowledge available, but the idea of a test tube baby, for instance, never really attracted them. In the early '70s, establishment medical organizations were encouraging amniotic-fluid tests, telling women that this was the way "not to give birth to unhappy children." Lib strongly opposed this. The Lib Center was even very careful about the use of contraceptive pills. A special issue of *Konomichi Hitosuji* on this matter editorialized: "Don't mistake the pill for women's liberation. Isn't it important to relate our interest in the pill to our adherence to the way of life we choose?"[20]

Lib strongly warned against the monsters of biotechnology that had been developed as yet another more sophisticated device to control woman and her body. Rather, many Lib activists chose oriental medicine or other organic methods, without, of course, excluding Western medicine.

As mentioned before, during the anti–Eugenic Protection Law campaign in the '70s, women's assertion of their right to abortion met strong protest from organizations of disabled persons, which were also strongly opposed to the revision. If abortion was a woman's right, the disabled questioned, didn't it mean that in effect she had the right to negate the life of the disabled?

This was a trying moment for women's groups involved in this struggle. The debate did not come to a clear-cut conclusion. In the midst of this controversy, "the mainstream of the Lib movement developed its argument in favor of a positive appraisal of giving birth," Ehara observed. In this controversy "life" and "choice" were not considered simple alternatives. Listen to Ehara's interpretation of Lib's stance:[21]

> Haven't women who have sought abortion in an "easy-frame of mind" made themselves party to the logic of productivity that cuts off the weak? ... This reflection was the Lib movement's answer to the question asked by the disabled. Lib argued that abortion means stopping a life, killing a possibility, and so is a pain to the woman too, but even so, in the existing circumstances, we have to insist on our right to abortion.

The Lib position was in no way a compromise between "life" and "choice." It firmly and consistently stressed women's choice. Rather it was a position of existential dialectics, rejecting pragmatic instrumentality. Solidarity among oppressed groups could not be built on instrumentality. Listen to Tanaka Mitsu when she talks about solidarity with other oppressed peoples:

> When we recognize our darkness and take it upon ourselves, we encounter the origin of our liberation, namely, light. Our darkness is our darkness. We cannot share the darkness of the Buraku people, the darkness of Korean residents, the darkness of peasants. But in adhering to my darkness, I take upon myself this impossibility of sharing, the whole weight of this impossibility, that is what "I am I" means. By making our darkness jostle with others' darkness, that is, engaging our life way [*ikizama*] with that of others, "our [common] future" will conceive light. ... we can revolutionize ourselves through confronting our life way with others' life ways.

Pioneers

The Lib Shinjuku Center was a coordinating center, a beehive where activists from various women's groups would come and go day and night, hold meetings, plan actions, print pamphlets and debate. Although it is true that the Lib Center's thinking set the tone for the whole Lib movement in the 1970s, there were, of course, differences of views among the numerous Lib groups, and not all accepted Tanaka Mitsu's approach and rhetoric.

Though all shared radical Lib perspectives in one way or another, emphasis differed from group to group and from personality to personality. The social positions of Lib participants were also diverse. While the Lib Center group was based on young women not yet well anchored in society, other groups consisted of women with longer and richer experience in society, including front-line professional women and labor union women. They felt that the Lib Center people lacked concern about ways to change the establishment from within, as well as the power to do so. Women union activists, having adopted radical lib views, had to concentrate on painstaking everyday struggles to change the blatantly male-centered corporate union practice. They had to use a language understood in the male union culture.

There were also those who felt that the women's struggle should be oriented toward transforming the global structure of women's oppression, which involved not only Japanese women but women in other Asian countries and beyond. But this approach was not adopted by mainstream Lib activists. Internationalist feminist Matsui Yayori, then a member of WOLF, recalled that when she proposed at a Lib Conference in 1972 that solidarity and sisterhood with women in other Asian countries victimized by Japanese sex tourists should be discussed, a leading Lib activist frontally opposed her, saying, "If I have time to worry about women in foreign countries, I would rather teach a woman sitting by my side how to use tampons."[22] In 1977 Matsui and like-minded others established the Asian Woman's Association to carry out what she proposed in 1972. Similarly, Ozawa Ryoko, an articulate anti-war movement activist and one of the early Lib spokespersons, became critical of what she considered the mainstream Lib tendency—exclusive concentration on personal concerns, at the sacrifice of political action.[23]

Differences and ruptures notwithstanding, all these tendencies shared one thing in common—a sense of conversion into women's Lib and consensus that male-dominated Japanese society should be fundamentally remade through struggle by and in the name of women. In other words, each felt she was Lib. The base of the women's struggle was remade, and for those who acquired this Lib consciousness, there was no return to the pre-Lib role-defined women's movements. As Tanaka Mitsu said, "those who have seen, have seen." In this sense, early 1970s Lib as a whole constituted a profound cultural revolution in the women's movement.

Besides, government imposition of legislation controlling a woman's body broadened the women's front to involve even traditional role-based women's movements. Insofar as the campaign against this legislation, driven by Lib's cultural revolution, was successful, Lib became more than a cultural revolution. It temporarily became a viable sociopolitical movement whose voice the establishment had to take into account.

But in retrospect the 1970s Lib's fundamental critique of Japanese society went unheeded, let alone developed, by other movements, this in spite of the general discovery by movement activists that politics was in the midst of every-day life. The remaking of the basic movement culture through efforts to incorpo-rate Lib thinking, however painful, as happened to a considerable degree in the United States, did not occur in Japan. Lib was by and large considered a sectoral movement tackling "women's issues." The issue framework in which the move-ments were more or less comfortably couched impeded the natural development of interaction among them. There was little interaction between the Lib and other movements, particularly the labor movement.

In addition to this general reason, the Lib critique was so fundamental and demanding that many issue-oriented movements sought to evade it. Taking in Lib's message would have required a fundamental review of the premises and values on which movements securely rested.

The heat of Lib of the early '70s began to be lost after the first campaign against the revision of the abortion law secured a victory for women. The cul-tural revolution could not evolve into a process of fundamentally transforming Japanese society. As erstwhile Lib Center activists now recall, Lib burnt itself out. Lib became pent up within itself.

The early 1970s Lib mapped out a total alternative. But how was that alterna-tive to be put into practice? Precisely because the envisioned change was funda-mental, this question was not easy to answer. Building women's communes appeared to be the answer, and a number of groups tried it for a few years. But none could last. The Lib Shinjuku Center, itself a commune, closed in 1977, following Tanaka Mitsu's 1975 departure for Mexico. *Onna Eros* struggled on until 1986, when it, too, closed.

"While Lib began as a radical critique of everyday life," Ehara observed, "there emerged a conservative tendency to cut off as empty and abstract all problems and issues other than those directly related to everyday life." This was a paradox as "Lib's topics gradually became confined to children, sex, everyday life and family—the areas of concern traditionally considered a women's area."[24] The personal is political, but if so, there should be a new way of creating a new political dimension that goes beyond the "women's arena" and is not alienated from the personal level. Early Lib seems to have faltered in this reverse mediation.

The Lib scalpel was sharp. But overturning Japanese society from the depth the scalpel had reached required a tough lever. Nevertheless, as did other radical move-ments in the decade, Lib left an indelible trace in the Japanese women's movement.

Notes

1. In the late 1960s a stormy student revolt erupted in Japan. Though issues varied from tuition hikes and dormitory autonomy, through school managements' corruption to exploitative internship systems for medical students, the struggles came to share a com-

mon stance of confronting the power relationships and structures on the campuses them-selves. This entailed strongly moralistic dimensions—fundamentally questioning the en-trenched values of educational insitutions. The logic of the revolt thus bore a striking resemblance to French students' "contestation" during their May 1968 struggle. This movement was distinct from the previous student movement in that it found culpable the existing social relationships justified by conventional values and ideologies, while the earlier student movement had confronted only the external political power of the state. It was contended particularly at the prestigious Univeristy of Tokyo that since dominant "bourgeois" values had permeated the students themselves, the students should negate themselves as students. The fiercest confrontations occurred at the University of Tokyo and Nihon Univerisity in 1969. At the height of the movement in 1968–69, more than 70 university campuses were occupied and barricaded by students. These struggles were conducted by numerous spontaneous action committees, which coalesced on an all-cam-pus basis. "Zenkyoto" means the "all-campus joint struggle committee"—hence, the Zenkyoto movement. For details on the Zenkyoto movement, see Muto Ichiyo, "Beyond the New Left 2," *AMPO* (vol. 17, no. 4).

2. The author's interview with Matsui in 1992.

3. Nihon Joseigaku Kenkyukai (Japan Women's Studies Society), Feminist Kikaku Shudan, ed. *Feminism no Genzai to Mirai* (The Present and Future of Feminism). Kyoto: Women's Book Store, 1986, p. 222.

4. Tanaka Mitsu. *Inochi no onne Tachi-e* (To Women of Life). Tokyo: Tabata Shoten, 1975. Unless otherwise indicated, all quotations from Tanaka Mitsu in this chap-ter are from this anthology of Tanaka's works written in the 1970s.

5. Shudan, ed., *Feminism no Genzai to Mirai*, p. 213.

6. The original mimeographed text of the Eros Declaration.

7. Kaji Etsuko. "Herded into the Labor Market," *AMPO* (vol. 18, nos. 2–3).

8. Kurata Kazunari. *Shinsayoku Undo Zenshi* (The Complete History of the New Left Movement). Tokyo: Ryudo Shuppan, 1978.

9. *Asahi Shimbun,* Oct. 22, 1970 (Tokyo edition).

10. *Asahi Shimbun,* Nov. 17, 1970.

11. Ehara Yumiko. *Josei Kaiho to yu Shiso* (Women's Liberation as a Thought). Tokyo: Keiso Shobo, 1988, pp.121–122.

12. *Fujin Minshu Shimbun* (Women's Democratic News), Sept. 10, 1970.

13. Nagano Yoshiko. "Women for Control." *AMPO* (1973, no. 17).

14. *Shin-chihei*, Aug. 1983

15. Ehara, *Josei Kaiho to yu Shiso.*

16. The second mimeographed edition of *"Benjo karano Kaiho."*

17. Ehara, *Josei Kaiho to yu Shiso.*

18. "Sanrizuka" refers to the struggle of farming communities near Narita, Chiba Prefecture, against the construction of an international airport. Shibokusa is a farming community at Oshino village on the eastern slope of Mt. Fuji nearly all of which was confiscated and used as a U.S. and Japanese military exercise ground. The community as a whole was engaged in a protracted struggle against the shelling exercises by sending "guerillas" into the target areas. In both struggles, women were organized into their own action groups and played important roles.

19. Tanaka, *Inochi no onne Tachi-e.*

20. *Konomichi Hitosuji.*

21. Ehara, *Josei Kaiho to yu Shiso.*

22. From the interview with Matsui cited in note 2.

23. *Fujin Koron,* July 1972.

24. Ehara, *Josei Kaiho to yu Shiso.*

IV

Japan and the Changing International Division of Labor

In his "Japanese Agriculture Today: The Roots of Decay," Ohno Kazuoki documents how Japan's agriculture and rural communities have been sacrificed to high-speed growth in order to free rural labor to move into industry and to provide a market for U.S. agricultural products. Between 1960 and 1990 Japan's farm population dropped from close to twelve million to four million! Most of the remaining farmers have responded to their reduced incomes by holding full-time jobs off their farms during the week and farming only on weekends. They have done this by enlarging the sizes of individual paddy fields, using much larger doses of chemicals for a higher yield with less effort, and increasing mechanization, as is illustrated in the above photo, where a farmer is using an automatic rice planter instead of the traditional method of transplanting rice seedlings by hand. This photo is from and courtesy of Henebry Photography.

Rob Steven's "Japanese Foreign Direct Investment in Southeast Asia" examines Japan's entry into the international division of labor in the seventies and Japanese dominance in Southeast Asia by the nineties. Note the Technics billboard and the quantity of Nissan and Suzuki vehicles and billboards in this photo of a busy thoroughfare in Bangkok, Thailand, in 1992. This picture is by Sean Sprague, Impact Visuals, and it is reprinted here with permission.

8

Japanese Agriculture Today:
The Roots of Decay

*Ohno Kazuoki**

Internecine War

With its market at home withering and reproductive base decaying, Japanese agriculture is on the brink of total collapse. What is happening today to the nation's farms and farming population?

Though labels—"productive readjustment," "planned production," and so forth—vary, cutback policies are now applied to most of the country's major crops, including rice. Paddy rice cultivation, for centuries the backbone of Japanese agriculture, was first subjected to cutbacks in 1970, when 236,000 hectares of paddy field were set aside. The figure has steadily increased, and in 1990 as many as 830,000 hectares, or about 30 percent of the country's total paddy area, were taken out of cultivation. Some of this land just lies fallow, but much of it has been planted in other crops, mostly vegetables and fruit trees. The shift from rice production to other crops has occurred on such a vast scale that oversupply in these crops has resulted, making for extremely volatile prices.

Production of milk was subject to regulation beginning in 1979, and the late 1970s and early 1980s saw the implementation of similar readjustment schemes for a host of other products including eggs, pork, mandarin oranges, silk cocoons, and tobacco leaves. Thus, with the beginning of the 1980s, Japanese agriculture entered a process of overall reduced production.

The single most important factor in the cutback of rice production is the enormous amount of imported grains, amounting to approximately 28.2 million tons in 1987. This was more than twice the total domestic grain production in

---

*This is an updated and lightly edited version of an article, "Japanese Agriculture Today: Decaying at the Roots," originally published in *AMPO: Japan-Asia Quarterly Review,* vol. 20, nos. 1 and 2 (1988), pp. 14–27. Although the article as published here is the same as the version published in the *Bulletin of Concerned Asian Scholars* in 1972, it is followed by a four-page update written in 1996.

the same year, which stood at around 11.9 million tons, with rice accounting for 10.6 million tons. The increase in imported grains has given rise to a very strange phenomenon, the simultaneous presence of abundance and shortage. In 1985, for instance, Japan's self-sufficiency ratio in rice production was 100 percent, while in the production of grains it was a mere 30 percent. In the crop year 1986–87 a total of 175 million tons of grains other than rice was traded internationally, and Japan consumed as much as 16 percent of the total in 1985. Although a big chunk of the 27 million tons of imported grains is for use as animal feed, the amount allocated for direct human consumption is by no means small. Bread and other foodstuffs made of inexpensive imported flour are contributing to reduced rice consumption by the Japanese, and rice consumption is decreasing at a rate of 2 percent annually. Imported grains, then, are clearly one of the factors depriving Japanese paddy farmers of the domestic market and forcing them to curtail rice-production operations.

Much the same thing can be said about other crops. Mandarin oranges are now a major crop—often more important than rice—in many areas of western Japan, an area with a mild climate. Ehime Prefecture in Shikoku, the country's leading mandarin orange-producing prefecture, is a case in point. Farmers producing oranges there were hit hard by the huge drop in orange prices in 1987, when their average annual net income fell by 64 percent. Although the production readjustment scheme brought about a production drop from 3.6 million tons in 1979 to approximately 2.5 million tons in 1987, the pace of the cutbacks has not been fast enough to keep up with the decline in consumption. According to a survey of household finances by the prime minister's office, per capita consumption of mandarin oranges, which amounted to 20 kilograms in 1975, dropped to 14.5 kilograms in 1980, and to 9.6 kilograms, or less than half the 1975 figure, in 1985. Prices have consequently declined, often dropping precipitously.

In contrast, imported citrus has steadily increased—from 234,000 tons in 1975 to 308,000 tons in 1980, 347,000 tons in 1985, and 460,000 tons in 1987. Exotic fruits as well have been imported in ever growing amounts due to the high yen. This veritable flood of imported fruit is having a devastating effect on Japan's fruit growers.

As a result of Japan-U.S. bilateral talks, the Japanese orange and beef markets were liberalized starting in April 1991. Japanese citrus growers operate mostly on coastal hillsides in the western part of the country. They have neither the space, nor the impetus, to carry out rationalization and cost reduction. Disappointed by years of production cutbacks and constantly dropping prices, an increasing number of younger farmers are giving up orange production. With very few sons and daughters taking up orange farming, the average age of orange farmers is increasing rapidly, as is the total area of orchard being left to go to weed. The planned liberalization of orange imports will hasten the demise of orange growing in Japan.

The "Milk War"

As the market for domestically produced farm products has shrunk, competition for this decreasing market among various farming areas has intensified. Competition is so stiff among milk producers that it is referred to as an internal "war." The most harshly fought war is for the gigantic milk market in the Tokyo area, involving dairy farmers in Hokkaido and those in the hinterland of Tokyo, the traditional suppliers of dairy products to the capital.

Dairy farms in Hokkaido are fairly large in size, with the average number of dairy cattle around fifty. This is comparable to the number of cattle kept by an average dairy farm in European Community countries, and 2.5 times the number kept by an average Japanese dairy farmer outside of Hokkaido. Hokkaido accounts for no less than 36 percent of the total production of raw milk in Japan. Because it is so far from major consumption areas, as much as 82 percent of this raw milk has traditionally been processed into cheese, butter, cream, condensed milk, skim milk, and other dairy products. However, associations of dairy farmers in Hokkaido have been desperately trying to shift to milk for direct consumption.

The reason for this turnabout is the ruling in February 1988 by the General Agreement on Tariff and Trade (GATT) in favor of the U.S. claim that Japan should liberalize its imports of ten farm products, including dairy products. The Japanese government expressed its willingness to respect the ruling, even though it specifically stated at the same time that totally liberalizing the imports of two of the ten items, dairy products and starch, would be extremely difficult. Despite the reservations, the official international commitment that has been made will have to be enforced sooner or later, and in the case of dairy products, the date of enforcement will most likely be sometime in the early 1990s. But if and when the import restrictions are lifted, Japanese dairy products will have no chance of surviving the competition from imported products, because the prices of skim milk and butter produced in Japan are, respectively, around 4.5 times and more than 5 times the international prices. Most dairy farmers in Hokkaido have no chance of surviving if they continue to produce raw milk to be processed into dairy products—thus the desperate efforts to shift to supplying fresh milk to consumers in the Tokyo area and to improve transportation and other facilities necessary for that end.

Hokkaido dairy farmers cannot compete internationally, although they are very powerful domestically. At present they net around 70 yen per kilogram of raw milk, while their counterparts in the Kanto region, who supply fresh milk for consumption in the Tokyo area, net around 100 yen. (As of 1987, the national average producer's net selling price of raw milk was 80 yen per kilogram.) If dairy farmers of Hokkaido start shipping their raw milk to Tokyo for direct consumption, all but a few dairy farms in Tokyo's hinterland will be wiped out.

This does not mean that Hokkaido's dairy farmers have a secure future. One survey revealed that even assuming a producer's selling price of 90 yen per kilogram of raw milk, as many as 36 percent of Hokkaido's dairy farmers are actually unable to cover production costs. In fact, between 1981 and 1988 the number of dairy farming households in Hokkaido decreased by 22 percent, from 22,000 to 15,700. In the same period, the corresponding number for the entire country, which stood at 106,000 in 1981, decreased by 35 percent to 70,600 in 1988.

The emergence of the phenomenon of relative surplus due to the shrinkage of the market gives rise, by necessity, to falling prices. From the start of production readjustment of raw milk, the government support price for raw milk for process- ing was frozen. This continued for many years, and since 1986 it has actually been lowered. And the lowering of the government support price has produced downward pressure on the price of raw milk for drinking, which price is deter- mined through negotiations between dairy farmers and milk processing compa- nies. The decline in the number of dairy farmers is indeed the direct consequence of the declining producer's price. The escalation of the war between the dairy farmers of Hokkaido and those in Tokyo's hinterland will surely force many more farmers out of business. And the winners in this internecine war must then fight in an international war with imported products priced at one-quarter to one-fifth of their own products. How many Japanese dairy farmers will be able to survive?

Price Drops

The declining process of dairy products is typical of what is happening to almost all farm products. Government support prices for wheat, various dry-field prod- ucts, and stock farm products, including raw milk for processing, have been reduced consistently since 1986, while the government purchase price for rice began to go down beginning in 1987.

Obviously, the government's purpose in enforcing these price reductions has been to bring the domestic prices of farm products down artificially to a point as close as possible to international levels, and thus to pave the way for the overall opening of Japanese markets to imported farm products. These reductions signif- icantly affect the pricing of other farm products in the open, free markets. By carrying out these pricing policies and precipitating internal wars among various farming areas, the government is actively trying to weed out those sectors of Japanese agriculture deemed internationally uncompetitive, thereby bringing Japanese agriculture in line with a changing world market.

Part of the World Markets

Clearly, then, the single most important factor dragging the country's farmers into cutthroat competition is the curtailment of markets for domestically pro- duced farm products, a curtailment that was itself a reaction to increases in farm products imported from abroad. Within a matter of several decades since the end of World War II, Japanese markets for locally produced farm products have rapidly shrunk as its agriculture has been incorporated even more deeply into the world market for farm products.

Becoming Dependent

Broadly speaking, the incorporation of Japanese agriculture into the world market has proceeded in three stages. The first stage began with the signing in March 1954 of the Mutual Security Act (MSA), and also its appendage, an agreement on purchases of surplus agricultural products. Legislated by the Truman administration in 1951 in the wake of the escalation of the Cold War and the outbreak of the Korean War, this act was meant to facilitate U.S. military aid. It was subsequently revised several times under the Eisenhower administration into a law meant to serve three purposes: disposal of surplus agricultural products, overseas food aid, and military aid. The idea was to enable aid-receiving foreign governments to purchase U.S. surplus farm products by using part of their MSA dollar funds, sell the food domestically in the local currency, and save the proceeds in the local currency for financing military build-up.

Under this "aid" program, Japan made its first purchase of MSA surplus wheat, worth U.S. $50 million, in the spring of 1954. This sum was not paid directly to the U.S. Treasury; rather, U.S. $40 million was allotted for use by the U.S. forces stationed in Japan, with the balance earmarked for helping Japanese weapons manufacturers install weapons manufacturing equipment. This shipment of MSA wheat was meant to serve the double purpose of resolving the U.S. problem of surplus food and nurturing Japan into a front-line defense outpost facing the Soviet Union, and it brought about a drastic turnabout in Japanese agricultural policy.

Following its defeat in the war in 1945, Japan's agricultural policy placed priority on expanding food production to feed the malnourished population, and that part of the national budget allotted for agriculture and forestry grew by great margins each year. However, beginning with 1954, the year when the first purchase of MSA wheat was made, the state budget allotted for agriculture and forestry began to decrease swiftly, not only in proportion to the total sum, but also in absolute size.

Compared to the budget for agriculture and forestry in FY 1953, which amounted to 171 billion yen and comprised 16.6 percent of the total state budget, the figure for FY 1954 decreased by as much as 25 percent, accounting for a mere 11.2 percent of the total. Three years later, in FY 1956, the budget for agriculture dropped further, to 91.3 billion yen, or a little over one-half the 1953 figure. This was 8.4 percent of the total budget, also approximately half the 1953 ratio.

It should be noted that when the government took these budget-slashing measures the country's food production was still insufficient to meet domestic demand. Clearly, the government had opted to abandon its policy of encouraging food production at home and adopted instead a policy of dependence upon imported food. The government pushed up the defense-related budget for FY 1954 by 25 percent under strong U.S. pressure for Japanese military build-up, while mercilessly cutting the budget for agriculture and forestry. At the first stage, therefore, Japan made the choice to place itself under the U.S. military and food umbrellas.

The MSA aid program, however, being primarily for a military purpose, was not wholly appropriate for resolving the U.S. farm glut. The Agricultural Trade and Development Act, or PL480, was devised in July 1954 under the Eisenhower administration as a means of overcoming this drawback. It was aimed at simultaneously promoting overseas military aid, dumping costly and burdensome U.S. agricultural surplus, and opening up new overseas markets of U.S. farm products. In the period from the late 1950s to the 1960s, Japan purchased U.S. $445 million of U.S. surplus agricultural goods in PL480 aid.[1] A portion of the yen counterpart funds raised from the sales of these goods in Japan was spent to promote the sale of U.S. agricultural products. Typical of such sales-promotion efforts was a nationwide campaign to encourage Japanese to change their staple food from rice to bread. This campaign was staged in the latter half of the 1950s jointly by the Japanese and the U.S. governments and involved many nutritionists and medical doctors.

These sales efforts were successful, and imports of U.S. agricultural goods on a commercial basis soared phenomenally. In the aforementioned period, when Japan received U.S. $445 million in PL480 aid, its imports of U.S. farm products amounted to U.S. $10.8 billion.[2] Japan became a showcase for U.S. agricultural exports.

Higher Economic Growth and the Farmer

The Japanese policy of procuring food supplies primarily from without rather than from within, a policy that was established with the acceptance of surplus food from the United States, began to gather momentum in the early 1960s when the country's economy began to take off on a high-growth path. If one country wants to expand its food exports to another country, it must see to it that the eating habits of the latter's population are receptive to, or can be made receptive to, the foodstuffs to be exported. With respect to Japan, the United States had already made significant headway in this regard. Both the campaign that had been staged, as part of the PL480 "aid" program, to encourage the Japanese to eat more bread, as well as the school lunch program with its exclusive emphasis on bread and deep influence on the tastes of the country's elementary and junior high-school kids, had paved the way for a flood of U.S. agricultural goods to invade Japan.

After achieving economic revival thanks to the special war procurement boom in the wake of the Korean War, in 1960 Japan entered a period of high growth. In June of that year the Japan-U.S. Security Treaty was concluded, stipulating the countries' economic as well as military cooperation. At the same time the Japanese government laid down its "Fundamental Principles on the Liberalization of Trade and Foreign Exchange." These had the aim of raising the country's trade liberalization rate to 80 percent in three years. In December the government announced its ten-year "National Income-Doubling Plan." The year 1961 saw the establishment of the Fundamentals of Agriculture Law, which was meant to readjust the country's agriculture to the needs of the high economic-growth policy. This heralded the beginning of the second stage of the incorporation of Japanese agriculture into the international market for farm goods, and in accordance with the economic cooperation stipulated in the Japan-U.S. Security Treaty, paved the way for Japan's dependency on the United States for food. Under the U.S. military and food umbrella, Japan's economic development jumped into high gear.

In line with the "Fundamental Principles on Liberalization," a series of agricultural goods was designated for step-by-step import liberalization; coffee beans and cattle in 1960; fresh vegetables and soybeans in 1961; raw silk in 1962; bananas, raw sugar, coffee, and honey in 1963; and so on. A system of automatic granting of import permits had already been adopted with regard to feed corn, the item representing the largest share in Japan's total import of agricultural goods, and natural cheese. In February 1963 Japan became a GATT Article 11 member, and was thus barred from establishing or maintaining any trade prohibition or restriction except for tariff surcharges. In 1964 Japan became an International Monetary Fund Article 8 member and joined the Organization of European Community Development, creating an environment in which Japanese capitalism was able to fully enter the international market.

By the end of 1962, the import liberalization measures brought the number of agricultural, marine, and forestry product items subject to import restriction down to 103, and from 76 in 1963 to 74 in 1966. The figure continued to decrease thereafter until it was down to 22 by October 1974. These 22 items remained unchanged until the February 1988 GATT ruling mentioned earlier, the ruling that Japan was in violation of GATT regulations with regard to import restrictions on 10 of the 12 items about which the United States filed a claim. The Japanese government accepted these rulings except for those on dairy products and starch—they claimed that these should be exempted—and started to liberalize its domestic markets in these items during the October 1988–April 1990 period.

With trade restrictions considerably eased, foreign agricultural goods began to flood into Japan. For instance, import figures for the two major feed grains, feed corn and grain sorghum, totaling 1.4 million tons in 1960, scored a fifteenfold increase to 20.48 million tons by 1987. In the same period the volume of

Table 8.1

Increased Agricultural Imports and Declining Food Self-Sufficiency
(Self-sufficiency in Food, 1960–89)

	1960	1970	1980	1989
Rice	102	106	100	100
Wheat	39	9	10	16
Soybean	28	4	4	6
Vegetables	100	99	97	92
Fruits	100	84	81	67
Chicken	101	97	98	98
Dairy products	89	89	82	80
Beef	96	90	72	54
Pork	96	98	87	77
Sugar	18	22	27	35
Self-sufficiency ratio in calories	79	60	53	48
Self-sufficiency ratio in grains, including feed grains	82	46	33	30

Notes:

1. Overall self-sufficiency ratio in edible agricultural goods = (value of domestic production) ÷ (value of domestic consumption) × 100; where the values of domestic consumption and domestic production are based on 1975 wholesale prices, with adjustments made for the double calculation of those portions allotted for animal feed.

2. The self-sufficiency ratios in grains and individual items of agricultural goods are derived by dividing the "amount of the item concerned produced domestically" by the "amount of the same item destined for domestic consumption" and multiplied by 100, where (amount destined for domestic consumption) = (amount of domestic production) + (amount of net import) − (increase in stock).

3. The overall self-sufficiency ratio in edible agricultural goods and the self-sufficiency ratio in grains are premised upon the assumption that the demand for and supply of rice are in balance.

Source: Ministry of Agriculture, Forestry, and Fisheries, *Shokuryo jukuhyo* (Tables of foodstuffs supply and demand).

soybean imports rose from 1.13 million tons to 4.8 million tons; that of wheat from 2.68 million tons to 5.48 million tons; and that of meat from 30,000 tons to 820,000 tons, a twenty-sevenfold increase. Consequently, as shown in table 8.1, Japan's self-sufficiency in agricultural products in general precipitated rapidly, and self-sufficiency in grains in particular is now stagnating at a low of 30 percent. A glance at figure 8.1, which compares the changes in grain self-sufficiency ratios of advanced capitalist countries, shows that Japan alone is following an abnormal path.

The rapid increase in agricultural imports and rapid decline in the country's food self-sufficiency ratio forced a "rationalization" of agriculture at a correspondingly rapid pace. The Fundamentals of Agriculture Law, with its three

Figure 8.1. **Self-sufficiency of Selected Countries in Grains, 1960–82**

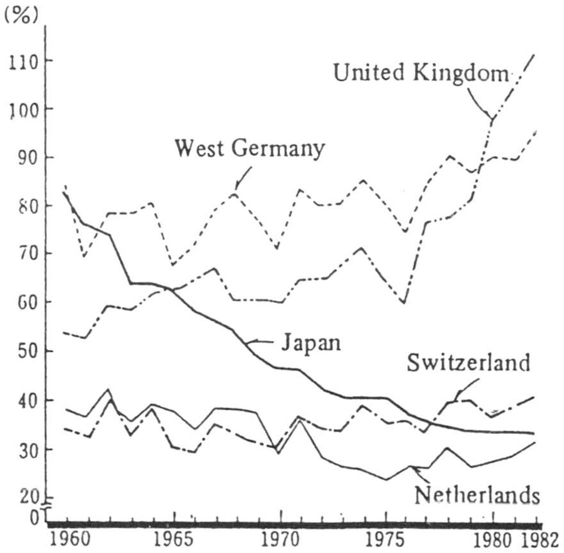

(%)

110

100

90   United Kingdom

80   West Germany

70

60

50   Japan

40   Switzerland

30

20   Netherlands

0

1960   1965   1970   1975   1980 1982

Source: Shokuryo jukyunhyo (Tables of foodstuffs supply and demand), by the Ministry of Agriculture, Forestry, and Fisheries. "Food Consumption Statistics," by the Organization for Economic Co-operation and Planning.

clear-cut objectives, was devised especially to enforce this rationalization. One objective was to do away with very small landownership and make Japanese agriculture internationally competitive by reducing the number of farming households, concentrating the plots of the squeezed-out farmers in the hands of the remaining elite farmers, and expanding these latter farmers' operations. The second objective was to shore up productivity through modernization and technical innovations like mechanization, upgrading of irrigation and other facilities, and improvement and readjustment of partitions of agricultural land. And the third objective was to reorient Japanese agriculture toward "selective expansion," that is to say, to make Japanese agriculture better adapted to the "improvement"—or Westernization—of the consumers' eating habits, by diversifying into cattle raising and fruit production.

One effect of the policies implemented under this law was a mass exodus of the farming population into other sectors. The rate of decrease in the farming family population, 3.5 percent in 1955, increased to 5.5 percent in 1960 and jumped further to 12.6 percent in 1970. The number of those aged fifteen or above who flowed out of farming households, not including those already holding outside jobs, was 796,000 in 1960 and 850,000 in 1965. These figures in themselves are staggering; but of particular significance is the fact that the majority of these people—63 percent in 1960 and 72 percent in 1965—were under twenty. One important factor that made Japan's high economic growth possible was that industrialists were able to count upon a continuous supply of young, docile, and low-paid workers from the countryside.

The exodus that first took the younger generation away from farming eventually began to involve even middle-class, middle-aged farmers, the very backbone of the country's agriculture. Many of these farmers, with families to support and therefore unable to simply make a fresh start as industrial workers, took outside jobs while continuing to till their land. This form of farming has become widespread. Contrary to what the Fundamentals of Agriculture Law prescribed, the number of farming households did not decrease much, and thus the average farm size did not increase much either. On the other hand, a small number of farmers faithfully followed the advice of the government, trying hard to expand their operations; but the harder they tried, the more elusive their goal became, until, as will be explained below, they finally reached a dead end. It was also in the second stage that, as mentioned already, various schemes for production cutbacks were instituted, beginning with paddy cultivation.

It should be kept in mind, however, that the country's major crops were still being protected, even if unsatisfactorily. The most serious problem Japanese agriculture was facing at this stage in relation to the world market was the rapid increase in grain imports, including feed grains. This increase in feed-grain imports was typical of Japanese agriculture's overall incorporation into the international market at that time. And the growth of agricultural imports was necessitated by the very characteristics of Japanese industrial capitalism that thrived in this period. The country's heavy and petrochemical industries grew competitive by absorbing inexpensive labor power from the countryside, and also by pursuing export-oriented strategies. In order for these industries to grow further, they had to export more, and this meant that more agricultural goods had to be imported in return. Put briefly, the country's agriculture and its farming villages were sacrificed doubly in the interest of high economic growth: on the one hand, they were forced to offer manpower, land, and water resources for the sake of industry; and on the other, they were forced to compete with the increasing amounts of agricultural imports.

Not surprisingly, this economic structure gave rise to cases of friction with the U.S. economy: in 1971–72 Japanese textile imports in the United States touched off a dispute; in 1977–78 steel became an issue, and since the early 1980s Japanese cars and high-tech products such as computers and semiconductors, as well as the limited access to the Japanese market of U.S. banking and service industries and construction and civil engineering industries, have been disputed. Throughout these disputes, the U.S. negotiators have persistently demanded that Japan import more U.S. farm products, and the Japanese negotiators have always pacified their counterparts by agreeing to increase import quotas bit by bit. Thus the question of opening up the Japanese market to foreign agricultural goods essentially originates from the problems inherent in the Japanese economic structure.

Japanese Agriculture Amidst the Readjustment of the World Markets for Farm Products

By the mideighties Japan's economic structure had grown even more export-oriented. It had amassed the world's largest trade surplus, and had increased its share in world production to 10 percent. It had become imperative for Japan to open up its economy still further, simply in order to sustain its growing economic empire. But what could the country import in greater quantity than it already did? The answer, obviously, was agricultural goods.

Meanwhile, international trade in agricultural goods was also facing the inevitability of readjustment. Many advanced capitalist countries other than Japan, with a glut of agricultural goods, had begun competing fiercely for international markets, and the agriculture of the United States, the largest exporter of farm products, had been seriously depressed. The advanced capitalist countries are also major exporters of agricultural goods and are spending unbearably large amounts of state funds to protect their respective agricultures and to promote the sales of their farm products. Competition between the United States and the European Community countries takes the form of dumping subsidized agricultural goods in international markets. In FY 1986 the U.S. government spent a total of U.S. $25.8 billion—ten times as much as in FY 1980, or 14 percent of the total federal deficit spending—in price-support programs for agricultural goods and in directly subsidizing U.S. farmers, while European Community governments in 1987 spent a total of 23.1 billion European Community Units— or approximately twice the amount they spent in 1980—to shore up their agricultures.

The impasse, the officials of these agricultural-exporting countries reasoned, could only be overcome by expanding the international markets, especially the lucrative Japanese market. These Western countries, led by the United States, cried louder than ever for total liberalization of the Japanese import market for farm products. If Japan had to commit itself on the ten items covered by the GATT ruling, as well as on beef and oranges, perhaps by the early 1990s rice, for centuries supposedly a "sacred" crop, would also one day be subjected to trade liberalization. If the domestic rice market was opened up too, the country's agriculture would be thrown totally at the mercy of the international food market. In this sense, the February 1988 GATT ruling announced the beginning of the third stage.

Thus the demand for the full opening of the Japanese domestic market for farm products comes not only from Japanese industrialists but also from the international agricultural interests of advanced capitalist countries that have embarked upon the realigning of world markets for agricultural goods. To make this possible, the advanced capitalist powers, including Japan, jointly implemented international currency realignment, forcing down the value of the U.S. dollar. The currency realignment caused the value of the yen vis-à-vis the dollar to appreciate rapidly, with the exchange rate, which was 240 yen to the dollar in 1985, rising to a little over 120 yen to the dollar in two years. To better adapt the Japanese economy to the era of the "strong yen," the Japanese government has carried out structural readjustment, forcing those industrial sectors whose international competitiveness has been eclipsed by the yen's appreciation either to move their production operations abroad or close down.

The net result of this rationalization policy is the phenomenon of deindustrialization. A large number of manufacturing firms, not only big ones but also small- and medium-sized parts manufacturers, have established offshore operations in Asia and elsewhere, while coal mining and many smokestack industries like steel and ship building have closed down or otherwise drastically streamlined their operations at home by mercilessly throwing out workers. The next victim would surely be agriculture.

In fact, a policy proposal compiled in April 1986 by the Study Committee for Readjustment of the Economic Structure, a private advisory body to then prime minister Nakasone—known as the Maekawa Report after the chairman of the study group—explicitly proposed that the uncompetitive sectors of coal mining and agriculture give way to imported products. Japanese capitalism has chosen to demolish agriculture to ensure its own survival, a choice that also satisfies the demands of other advanced capitalist powers, especially the United States. The GATT Uruguay Round, which started in 1986, served as the venue for these negotiations. These talks had to be finished by the end of 1990. Their focus was on the Japanese agricultural market liberalization as well as the U.S.-Europe dispute over agricultural protection and subsidies.

How is the government of Japan planning to procure food supplies for the population once the country's agriculture is at the mercy of foreign agriculture? The existing structure of Japan's food imports provides the answer. Table 8.2 shows the breakdown of major agricultural imports by supplying countries. The United States enjoys a dominant share of every single important food crop imported into Japan except barley. If the importing of rice is liberalized, Japan will have to rely entirely on the United States, because at present the United States alone has the capacity to produce in excess of domestic demand the japonica variety favored by the Japanese. Dependency on foreign food supplies essentially means dependency on the U.S. food umbrella.

This fact shows that the food problem is not simply an economic issue but also a political issue and inseparably related to the framework of the Japan-U.S. Security Treaty system. The policy that took shape under the MSA Treaty in the midfifties is still basically intact today. On the other hand, changes in Japanese agricultural imports have appeared. The rising yen has increased the gap between

Table 8.2

Major Agricultural Imports by Country of Origin
(Units: 1,000 tons and %)

	1985		1986		1987		1990	
Wheat	5,510	100.0	5,620	100.0	5,476	100.0	5,474	100.0
1. USA	3,232	58.7	3,241	57.7	3,103	56.6	3,055	55.8
2. Canada	1,234	22.4	1,377	24.5	1,373	25.1	1,412	25.8
3. Australia	1,044	18.9	1,002	17.8	1,000	18.3	1,007	18.4
Barley (including rye)	1,661	100.0	1,363	100.0	1,248	100.0	1,272	100.0
1. Canada	908	57.6	772	56.6	703	56.3	843	66.3
2. Australia	613	31.8	529	38.8	544	43.6	428	33.6
3. China	—	—	—	—	—	—	—	—
Corn	14,225	100.0	14,653	100.0	16,504	100.0	16,008	100.0
1. USA	10,970	77.1	9,244	63.1	12,816	77.7	14,013	87.5
2. South Africa	78	3.3	1,280	8.7	1,683	10.2	1,093	6.8
3. China	2,578	18.1	2,689	18.4	1,655	10.0	813	5.1
Sorghum	4,793	100.0	4,976	100.0	3,977	100.0	3,839*	100.0
1. USA	2,571	53.7	2,079	41.8	2,488	62.6	2,722	70.9
2. Argentina	1,266	26.4	1,578	31.7	796	20.0	365	9.5
3. Australia	793	16.5	748	15.0	525	13.2	346	9.0
Soybean	4,910	100.0	4,817	100.0	4,797	100.0	4,681	100.0
1. USA	4,345	88.5	4,332	89.9	4,100	85.5	3,456	73.8
2. Brazil	221	0.5	128	0.5	307	6.4	857	18.3
3. China	289	5.9	323	6.7	290	6.0	284	6.1
Beef†	150,579	100.0	179,104	100.0	220,032	100.0	376,000	100.0
1. Australia	95,222	63.2	105,167	58.7	121,127	55.0	196,000	52.1
2. USA	46,514	30.9	63,689	35.6	85,292	38.8	163,000	43.3
3. New Zealand	6,954	4.6	6,038	3.4	7,862	3.6	10,000	2.7

*This figure is for 1989.
†Beef is in tons (i.e., not thousands of tons) and does not include intestines.
Source: Ōkureshō (Ministry of Finance), *Nihon boeki tokei* (Japanese trade statistics).

domestic and international prices of agricultural products. This has brought an increase in Japanese imports of fresh agricultural products and semiprocessed products from Southeast Asia, pushed by the multinational food companies' drive to export to Japan agricultural products produced in countries where wages are low and cheap raw materials are available. Thus from 1985 to 1988 Japanese imports of agricultural products increased 138.4 percent, and Japan became the largest agricultural importer in the world.

Farms Disappearing

How is the Japanese farmer faring, faced with ever intensifying assaults from within and without? First, it can be said that both farmers and farmland are disappearing rapidly. Table 8.3 traces the changes in the major economic indices of farming households from 1960 to 1985. Over that quarter century the farming population in general decreased by 56 percent. The decrease in the population whose main occupation is farming was even greater: 68 percent. As of 1987, farming households exclusively engaged in farming accounted for a mere 15 percent of all farming households. Farming households earning larger incomes from sources other than farming constitute a whopping 70 percent. Most Japanese farmers till their farms only on weekends.

Aging of the farming population is another feature of Japanese agriculture. Agriculture is the largest employment sector for males over sixty, with a 46 percent share, followed by service at 12 percent, wholesale at 9 percent, manufacture at 8 percent, and construction at 8 percent. In the predominantly agricultural Tohoku region, the figure is 33 percent. Meanwhile, the number of young people leaving school who take up farming is only 4,000 per year, far fewer, for instance, than the number of medical doctors licensed each year. Male farmers of marriageable age have difficulty finding brides, a situation that has given rise to "bride importing" from the Third World countries of Asia. Some local governments have even gone into the international matchmaking business to stave off the depopulation of their farming communities.

Farmland area, too, is shrinking. Dry-field land decreased by 40 percent in the twenty-five-year period from 1960 to 1985, while paddy-field land decreased by more than 10 percent in the same period. Importing of dry-field crops is largely responsible for the abandonment of dry-field land, while the decrease in paddy-field land is due to a large extent to the rice-production cutback measures that went into effect in 1970.

Farmlands near cities have been gobbled up for housing plots and plant sites. Paddy fields on the slopes of mountains in sparsely populated areas have simply been abandoned. These fields rapidly turn into wild wastelands, making the irrigation systems and the feeder roads malfunctional, a situation that leads to the abandonment of even more farmland.

In the township of Matsunoyama in Niigata Prefecture only half of the 1,200 hectares of paddy fields that were worked twenty years ago are still being tilled. Throughout the Ioetsu area where Matsunoyama is located, noted for its heavy snowfall in winter, the population is decreasing at a rate of over 10 percent annually, and many of the departing farmers can find no one to buy their lands.

The problem is not confined to remote areas. In the town of Ogano, a mountain village in Saitama Prefecture not far from Tokyo, a 1984 survey revealed that of the total 553 hectares of agricultural land, 331 hectares, or 60 percent, lay

Table 8.3

Changing Features of Agriculture, 1960 and 1990

	1960	1990	(%) 1990/1960
Farming households	6,057,000	3,835,000	63
Full-time farm households (farming households specializing in farming)	2,078,000	447,000	22
Farming population (persons)	14,542,000	5,653,000	39
Core persons mainly engaged in family-operated farming (key family operators)	11,750,000	2,927,000	25
Graduates taking up farming (persons)	127,000	1,800	1.4
Cultivated acreage (hectares)	6,071,000	5,243,000	86
Paddy fields	3,381,000	2,846,000	84
Dry fields	2,165,000	1,275,000	59
Orchards	451,000	475,000	105
Pasture	81,000	647,000	799
Cumulative area under cultivation	8,129,000	5,340,000	66
Average annual income of farming household (yen)	410,000	6,602,000	1,610
Average annual income from farming (yen)	225,000	1,163,000	517
Costs of farming operation per farming household (yen)	134,000	1,839,000	1,372
Agricultural chemicals	5,000	119,000	2,380
Lighting, heating, and power	4,000	71,000	1,775
Agricultural machines	22,000	411,000	1,868
Feed	24,000	272,000	1,133
Annual living expenses per farming household (yen)	369,000	5,274,000	1,429
Share of farming income in a farming household's annual income (%)	55	18	
Farming income's contribution to a farming household's living expenses (%)	61	22	

Sources: Nogyo sensasa (Agricultural census), *Nogyo shugyo doko chosa* (Survey on employment trends in agriculture), *Kochimenseki chosa* (Survey on farmlands), *Nohka keizai chosa* (Survey on family economy of farming households).

idle, and of this idle land, 65 percent had turned into wasteland totally unfit for farming. The farmers were simply too old to withstand the hard farming work on the mountain slopes.

Even in the leading agricultural districts of Hokkaido, Tohoku, and Kyushu, the prices of paddy fields in the very productive plain or delta areas have recently begun to decline. In Hokkaido, where large-scale agriculture is common, paddy-field prices have declined steadily, dropping by 33 percent from 1985 to

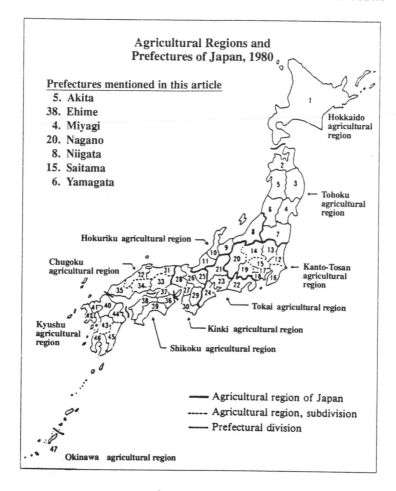

Agricultural Regions and
Prefectures of Japan, 1980

Prefectures mentioned in this article

5. Akita
38. Ehime
4. Miyagi
20. Nagano
8. Niigata
15. Saitama
6. Yamagata

Hokkaido agricultural region

Tohoku agricultural region

Hokuriku agricultural region

Chugoku agricultural region

Kanto-Tosan agricultural region

Tokai agricultural region

Kyushu agricultural region

Kinki agricultural region

Shikoku agricultural region

—— Agricultural region of Japan
----- Agricultural region, subdivision
—— Prefectural division

Okinawa agricultural region

This is a slightly modified version of a map of the agricultural regions and prefectures of Japan from Ogura Takekazu's *Can Japanese Agriculture Survive?* (Tokyo: Agricultural Policy Research Center, 1980). The map has been modified by BCAS to make it more compact and to identify the prefectures mentioned in this article.

1988. In the Tohoku region, famous for its rice production, these prices have continued to decline since 1987.

Contradictions

Farmers responded to the flood of imports in two different ways. The great majority chose to combine paddy cultivation with outside jobs. Various schemes for modernization and increasing productivity that were implemented under the

Fundamentals of Agriculture Law were phenomenally "successful." These measures, enlargement of the size of individual paddy fields, intensive mechanization, and the use of huge doses of chemicals enabled, for instance, a farmer who had spent a total of 171 hours of labor to raise paddy in 10 acres (1,000 square meters) of paddy field in 1960 to do the same job in 55 hours by 1985. A farmer can now easily tend one hectare or so of paddy field on weekends, and thus hold a full-time job off the farm during the week. This is exactly what a majority of farmers have done, cutting off almost all farming operations except paddy cultivation to manage it. The government's pricing policy, allowing dry-field crop prices to plummet under pressure from imported agricultural goods while maintaining a relatively high price for rice, has encouraged this result.

Another group of farmers, a small minority, chose to expand their operations by specializing in one specific crop, what the Fundamentals of Agriculture Law called "selective expansion." The two most typical specialty crops chosen were stock raising and fruit cultivation, but some farmers chose to specialize in paddy-rice cultivation while others took up one vegetable or another.

The case of stock raising illustrates well where this expansion-through-monoculturalization leads. Stock-breeding farms amount to "animal processing plants," fueled by assorted feed made almost entirely of feed grains imported from abroad. To attain maximum efficiency, these plants are rigorously managed, often with the aid of computers, to maintain as many animals as possible in the limited space, feed them with the most cost-efficient combination of feed, and maximize labor productivity.

Both of the above farming patterns—combining rice cultivation and an outside job, and expansion through monoculturalization, contain numerous contradictions. First is the waste of the land and other natural resources. Located in the northern tip of the Asian monsoon zone, Japan has developed an agriculture with very unique features. Blessed by a tropically humid summer and a dry winter similar to that in the European wheat-growing area, Japanese farmers can use the same plot of land for double cropping, growing rice in the summer and wheat in the winter. An exceptionally wide variety of crops can be planted in dry fields as well all year around. However, wheat, as one-half of the double-cropping operation, and many other important crops for dry fields have been wiped out by the flood of imports. As a result, the farmland utilization rate, which in 1960 still stood at 134 percent, decreased to 105 percent by 1985. The cumulative total area planted decreased by 30 percent over the same period.

The second contradiction is that agriculture, which is supposed to make use of natural cycles, now disrupts such cycles, exploits the soil, and pollutes the natural environment. A case in point is Japan's animal processing plants, which are detached from the soil and depend exclusively on imported feed. The animal waste is not recycled into the soil in the form of compost, but is dumped into the environment, hazardously increasing the concentration of nitric acid and ammonium in the country's rivers, lakes, coastal seas, and underground water. At the same time, Japanese farmland is rapidly becoming sterile due to the overdosage of chemicals, the exploitation of soil through monoculturalization, and the loss of the indigenous, land-based stock raising that used to supply manure.

The third contradiction is that monoculture has increased the fragility of Japanese agricultural operations. Producing only one crop means that the only way to cope with a drop in prices is by stepping up production, which in turn causes a greater glut, pushing prices down even further. Violently oscillating prices and a long-term downward trend have similarly afflicted stock raising, fruit cultivation, and other specialty crops. New floods of imported agricultural goods accelerate these trends still further.

The fourth contradiction lies in the costliness of Japanese agriculture. While farm income rose only 5 times in the twenty-five-year period from 1960 to 1985, the overall costs of farm operations increased 14 times, with the cost of chemicals increasing 24 times, lighting and power 22 times, and machinery 17 times. Paddy-rice farmers with outside jobs are operating their farms in ways that are apparently more energy-intensive and costly than rational calculations would permit. Their behavior can only be considered rational in view of the fact that they must get the farming work done as quickly and efficiently as possible to be able to report for their more lucrative outside jobs on time.

The farmers pursuing expansion through monoculture are in a far more serious situation. They constantly invest more and expand to survive the cutthroat competition with farmers in the same boat. These investments are financed almost totally by borrowing. A survey by the Ministry of Agriculture, Forestry, and Fisheries on the social accounting of agriculture and farming households revealed that as of 1985 the farmers of Japan were saddled with debts to the tune of 15 trillion yen, while their farming production for the year totaled only 13.4 trillion yen, and farming sales, 11 trillion yen. A decade earlier, the total debt amounted to 8 trillion yen, as against farming production worth 9.8 trillion yen and farming sales of 8 trillion yen.

A survey conducted in 1985 by the prefectural government of Hokkaido, where farming operations are far larger than elsewhere in Japan, revealed that on the average the Hokkaido farmer was 20 million yen in debt, with beef-cattle farmers most seriously indebted, followed by those in dairy farming, those in dry-field farming, and those in paddy-field farming. Only 33 percent of the debt-carrying beef-cattle raisers were consistently earning incomes large enough to pay the principal and interest. Even among the paddy-rice cultivating farmers, burdened with smaller debts, the proportion was only 61 percent. Farmers with less healthy operations were only barely managing to pay back interest or, unable to pay back even the interest, were helplessly watching their debts snowball.

The fifth contradiction is that farming operations in Japan are, to a greater and greater extent, at the mercy of capitalists. The operations of the farmers combining paddy-rice cultivation and outside jobs are indirectly subject to capitalist control through purchases of machines, energy, and various agricultural chemicals. Farmers pursuing expansion through monoculture, meanwhile, are under a more direct form of control by capital. Typically, many of the livestock-raising operations have exceeded the limits that would be suitable for direct control of the individual farmers concerned, and thus have been increasingly subject to the control of feed-supply firms, in turn closely linked with multinational agribusiness interests. Thus an increasing number of livestock-raising farmers of Japan, especially those with medium- and small-sized operations, are being integrated directly into the multinational agribusiness interests.

The sixth contradiction pertains to the safety of the products produced by these contradiction-ridden farming operations. The heavy doses of insecticides and herbicides sprayed on Japanese farmland are finding their way to the dining tables of the Japanese people, adversely affecting their health. So too are the antibiotics and other medicines injected in or fed to the animals in the country's animal processing plants. The last contradiction is perhaps the most serious of all, for an agricultural system incapable of providing food fit for human consumption can no longer even be called agriculture.

Sick System, Sick People

Given the above, it is not surprising that the agriculture system in Japan is having a debilitating effect on the minds and bodies of Japanese farmers and their families. Recently allergic diseases among farmers have been reported to be on the increase. Long hours of monocultural farming work inside greenhouses and overuse of agricultural chemicals are believed to be factors. Greenhouse farmers raising mushrooms are afflicted with allergic inflammation of the lungs. Strawberry growers develop allergies to pollen. Farmers growing beefsteak tomato plants or leeks on a large scale suffer from allergic skin diseases. Lettuce growers suffer from asthma caused by inhaling too much of the vapor of the lettuce leaf juice, and so on. Fruit growers are no better off. Overuse of insecticides in apple and pear orchards has given rise to many cases of pollinosis among farmers who, artificially pollinating the trees, literally do the work of bees. Cases of asthma caused by bactericides also occur.

The eruption of these new occupational diseases calls into question the very way in which farming is practiced in Japan and the way in which it forces farmers to compete harshly with one another to survive in the artificially created glut of farm products. The fact that the tillers are afflicted with these allergic diseases is symptomatic of how seriously sick Japan's agriculture is.

This sickness affects the minds of children in farming areas, too. A pediatrician in a rural area of Akita Prefecture reported a significant increase in cases of the children of farming families suffering from psychosomatic disorders. In 1977 the pediatrics department at the clinic there diagnosed a total of 62 children as suffering from psychosomatic disorders. Four years later, in 1981, the number increased 2.3 times to 140, although the total number of patients remained virtually unchanged. The doctor attributed this increase in pediatric cases of mental disorder to several factors, including rapid urbanization of agrarian areas, an increase in the degree of farming families' exposure to the market economy as a result of both parents earning wages away from the farm, and a growing tendency for the wage-earning parents to pursue a rationalistic and pleasure-seeking lifestyle at the expense of their children.

Agrarian communities and farming families in Japan have already suffered much from the realignment of Japanese agriculture amidst the glut of farm products. What more lies ahead when the Japanese agricultural markets are fully opened up?

UPDATE

Many changes have taken place in Japanese agriculture. The decay has gotten deeper. Japanese agriculture has lost productivity so dramatically that it is even said to be on the brink of total collapse. The situation can be explained briefly.

Farmers Decreasing and Aging

According to the statistics of the Ministry of Agriculture, Forestry and Fisheries, the percentage of "core farmers" (those described by the Ministry, Forestry and Fisheries as "core persons mainly engaged in family-operated farming") over 60 years of age was 50 percent in 1993. Three years before that, in 1990, it was 48 percent, while in 1985 it was 36 percent. By comparison, the percentage of young people—those under 30—was only 2 percent in 1993. The number of core farmers decreased over the same period; by 14 percent from 1990 to 1993, and by 15 percent from 1985 to 1990.

Abandoning Farmland

The result is that large farming areas are now left unused simply because there are no producers. "Abandoned farmland," ("land left unplanted for over one year and which will remain unplanted for several years") in 1985 amounted to about 130,000 hectares and in the 1990 survey accounted for 220,000 hectares, a nearly 70 percent increase in five years.

If we add "unplanted farmland" (fields where no crops were planted the previous year) to abandoned farmland, the total amounts to 380,000 hectares. Since four years have already passed since the investigation, it might safely be said that the day will soon come when the area of abandoned farmland will come to 500,000 hectares, one-tenth of all farmland in Japan.

Declining Food Self-Sufficiency

This deplorable situation for the land and for the people who support Japanese agriculture is clearly reflected in Japan's inability to supply food. In Japan, the

Figure 8.2. **Overseas Areas under Cultivation Required for the Main Imported Agricultural Products (1992)**

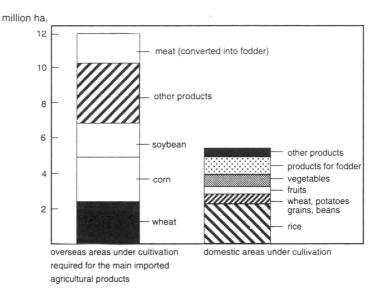

overseas areas under cultivation
required for the main imported
agricultural products

domestic areas under cultivation

Figure 8.3. **Self-Sufficiency Rate of Agricultural Staples**

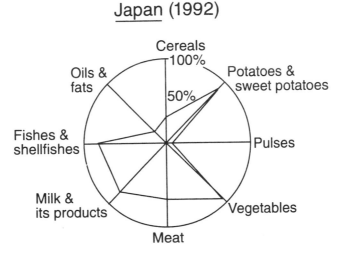

percentage of agricultural self-sufficiency in 1992 was 46 percent if calculated on a calorie basis, but only 29 percent in terms of grains. The insufficiency has to be made good by imports. If we think of these imported agricultural products in terms of the area required to produce them, it comes to 12 million hectares, about 2.3 times Japan's total area under cultivation (see figures 8.2 and 8.3 and table 8.4).

Table 8.4

Rate of Self-Sufficiency in Agricultural Products

	FY1975	FY1980	FY1985	FY1993 (rough estimate)
Self-sufficiency rate for essential agricultural products				
Rice	110	100	107	75
Wheat	4	10	14	10
Fruit	84	81	77	54
Milk and dairy products	82	82	85	80
Meat	77	81	81	64
Beef	81	72	72	44
Pork	86	87	86	69
Sugar	15	27	33	33
Overall self-sufficiency for agricultural commodity foods*	77	75	74	58
Rate of self-sufficiency in calorific supply*	54	53	52	37
Self-sufficiency rate for cereals (foodstuffs and fodder)*	40	33	31	22

Note: *Indicates that the computation is based on the premise of balanced supply and demand of rice. Looking at Japan's self-sufficiency rate (based on calorific value) for FY1993, the overall self-sufficiency rate for agricultural foods, the rate of calorific supply, and that for cereals (foodstuffs and fodder) all plunged from the previous year, from 65% to 58%, 46% to 37%, and 29% to 22%, respectively. The plunge was primarily due to poor harvests, especially of rice, caused by unusual weather in 1993.

Source: Ministry of Agriculture, Forestry, and Fisheries.

Now we are facing the collapse of Japanese agriculture itself. In the background is the broad opening of markets for agricultural products and a strong yen, both of which are results of Japan's prodigious export of industrial products. As a result of the GATT Uruguay Round Agreement, the markets for all agricultural products except rice were forced open. It was decided that the rice market should be partially opened for the time being, and the amount of imported rice is gradually increasing.

The strong yen expedites the increased import of agricultural products. Fresh vegetables, meat, and even such indigenous products as garlic, race, ginger, lotus root, and black mushrooms are threatened. Their imported equivalents are raised in various parts of Asia mainly by contract, with capital provided by Japanese supermarkets and trading companies. The initiative for setting the price of such domestic agricultural products has already been shifted to these low-cost producers of imports. This means that Japanese farmers are being forced to abandon agriculture because they have to pay much higher prices for land, wages, and materials than foreign producers.

If we compare the way the index for imports of agricultural products has grown (see table 8.5) at the same time that prices have been cut (see table 8.6), it becomes all too clear that Japanese farmers have been abandoned by government policies.

Table 8.5

Growth of Imports of Agricultural Products

	1985	1990	1994
Grains	100	105	141
Fruits	100	156	217
Vegetables	100	150	235
Meats	100	200	295
Total food	100	141	173

Table 8.6

Dropping Prices of Agricultural Products

	1985	1990	1994
Rice price	100	88	87
Wheat price	100	83	82
Milk price	100	86	84
Beef price	100	88	78
Pork price	100	67	67

Notes

1. Sekishita Minoru, *Nichibei boekimasatsu to shokuryo mondai* (Japan–U.S. trade friction and the food problem) (1987), p. 220.
   2. Ibid.

9

Japanese Investment in Thailand, Indonesia and Malaysia: A Decade of JASEAN

Rob Steven

Japan is currently wallowing in its worst recession ever. During the first six months of 1995 each day's fall in land and share prices brought closer the possibility of a 1930s-type financial collapse, because, as was widely agreed, the banking system's bad debts in relation to its shrinking asset base had long since reached enormous proportions. From a high of 38,916 at the end of 1990, the Nikkei stock average index plummeted to 14,390 in mid-1992, and although it subsequently clawed its way over the 20,000 level, the Kobe earthquake eroded the premature confidence and by July 1995 it was teetering on the brink of the 13,000 level. Even officialdom accepted that Japan's so-called recovery had come to a "standstill." A month later, in spite of a partial revival of share prices and a marginally cheaper yen, mining and manufacturing production continued its unabated fall, with few signs of any end to the slowdown.[1] The main reason why the country's problems have been so intractable is that the solutions which have so far been applied have actually constituted their most fundamental cause and have therefore tended to fan the flames of recession rather than extinguish them. Japan has been suffering from a classic case of underconsumptionism and its associated chronic deflation.

Through its awesome power both to raise the productivity of labor and to restrain the income of workers, Japanese capital has increasingly painted itself into a corner. Since low wages erode the domestic market for consumer goods, Japanese capital has found it difficult to locate customers for the growing output of its consumer goods industries. Its first and most obvious expedient was to export the surplus to the advanced countries, where wages were high, but Japan's increasingly protectionist rivals have been throwing up barriers against "excessive" exports and sending the problem back to where it came from. The financial markets dominated by the advanced powers have responded to Japan's trade surplus by lifting the value of the yen to levels which have made Japan into an unambiguously high-cost production place. At first, in the mid-1980s, Japanese capital's response was to use its power over labor to cut costs even further, but now after almost a decade of austerity there is not much left to squeeze on the cost side. And so the current "rush" to relocate the country's export industries in countries where both costs and markets can be combined more harmoniously has become the panacea for all Japan's ills. The purpose of this article is to examine only one aspect of this strategy, Japanese direct investment in the currently three most favored ASEAN countries: Thailand, Indonesia, and Malaysia. Space precludes discussion of the Philippines, into which the historic "rush" by Japanese capital followed the rise of Marcos and ended with his fall; Brunei, which is exceptional in any context; and Singapore, which is more appropriately examined in the context of the so-called NICs (newly industrialised countries). I do briefly look at the crisis in Japan to show the links between the two developments. I will argue that foreign direct investment (FDI) in ASEAN is the outcome of Japan's domestic crisis and expresses a growing alliance between Japanese capital and its counterparts in ASEAN, an alliance from which both sides benefit. I do not have the space to show how the ordinary people on both sides pay the price.

A new revolutionary force, which was born out of the ashes of World War II but which has been gaining momentum over the years, is increasingly transforming the entire Southeast Asian region. That force is capitalism, and the catalytic upsurge in its development has been coming from Japan, increasingly from the crisis of Japanese capitalism which was first sparked off by the oil shocks of the 1970s but which has continued in one form or another to the present day. To understand the dynamism of the current capitalist transformation of Southeast Asia therefore requires analysis of the social forces which the capitalist crisis in Japan is jettisoning into the outside world. It requires understanding the dynamics of present-day Japanese imperialism.

Capitalist imperialism, in the tradition within which I am writing,[2] is essentially an attempt by capital in an advanced country to displace its problems onto the peoples of less developed countries. This might involve assuming state power in the colony, as in the classical period before World War Two, or simply forming some kind of alliance with the overseas ruling class, with itself as the dominant partner, as happens currently under neo-colonialism, notwithstanding the end of the Cold War. Foreign investment, trade, aid, and foreign lending are all typical outward forms of what might be called this "new" imperialism. However, since the production place is the prime site of capitalist exploitation, where the surplus is created by labor and transferred to capital, foreign investment is the single most important concrete form assumed by the new imperialism.

Foreign investment, especially its most typical current form, the joint venture, expresses an alliance between two ruling classes. When both that of the investing and that of the recipient country are from the advanced capitalist world, the benefits are more or less equal and the "imperialistic effects" are not apparent. But when investment goes into less developed countries from the technologically advanced countries, the usual outcome is what I have elsewhere called "patterned underdevelopment"[3]; uneven development, the destruction of local industry, the replacement of lateral linkages among local firms with vertical import and export markets dominated by transnational corporations, balance of payment crises, escalating overseas debt, and persistent social and political crisis. The foreign investment is accepted by both sides and cements their alliance because it helps solve each side's most stubborn problem: technical backwardness in the case of the less developed countries and excessive labor costs in the case of the advanced countries. To understand the functioning of the new imperialism thus requires a concrete historical analysis of the crises on both sides, crises which led each to look to the other for assistance.

Crisis and Restructuring in Japan

The current crisis of Japanese capitalism can be briefly explained by focusing on what has in the past been its greatest source of strength: an ability to cut costs by exploiting divisions within the domestic working class and squeezing the lesser members of the capitalist class in the country's widespread system of subcontracting. But even though both of these were vigorously used during each of the main postwar recessions, they were on their own unable to restore prosperity, and foreign investment was boosted each time in an attempt to find overseas sites of even lower-cost production, especially in Asia.[4]

The first wave of FDI comprised the textile and electrical appliance investments of the 1960s, and it grew out of the rise in real wages in Japan following the revival of capital accumulation in the late 1950s. In spite of the priority the Meiji state had assigned to heavy industry, textiles remained the mainstay of Japanese capitalism right into the late 1930s and then again after the war well into the 1950s. The power of capital, revealed by its capacity to accumulate, rested heavily on the rigid division of the working class by both industry and gender. The men were concentrated in the rising heavy industrial sector, the women in the labor-intensive textile sector where wages were less than half the men's. The high rate of exploitation of these women was thus a major source of the total social surplus accumulated by Japanese capital in these years.

In addition to this industrial/gender division within the working class, there was a division which grew out of the subcontracting relationships between large and small firms, mainly in manufacturing. Particularly in labor-intensive processes where low wages and work discipline crucially affected profitability, workers in small subcontracted firms, isolated from one another and without trade unions, paid much of the price for accumulation in large firms. Wages and conditions in the smallest firms were typically only about half those in the core firms.

During the 1960s, however, the power of Japanese capital, which derived from its hold on low-paid workers in labor-intensive areas was, threatened by capital with an even stronger hold on low-paid workers, that is, capital in Southeast Asia. Japanese wages, even those of women, had risen sufficiently to give Southeast Asian capital an edge, and Japanese companies developed a three-pronged strategy, which they would repeatedly use in the years to come. First, they intensified the (uneven) exploitation of Japanese workers at home. Second, they consciously moved out of the lighter industries where they were losing their competitive advantage and they consolidated their strength in the heavy industrial sector. Finally, if they were to retain their lead in the old industries, then they needed access to workers who were more vulnerable than their own, that is, they had to ally themselves with the capitalists of Southeast Asia and embark on a program of FDI.[5]

All three prongs of the strategy were implemented simultaneously and Japanese capitalism boomed in the 1960s and early 1970s. But then the mounting world-wide recession, which first manifested itself in the ability of rentier capital (capital which owns raw materials) to claim for itself an extra share of the total available surplus, struck with unusual sharpness at the profitability of Japanese capital, which had restructured itself into the heavy chemical and raw material processing industries. Again the now proven three-pronged strategy was mobilized, but this time on a grander scale and with more far-reaching effects. However, increasingly the measures showed signs of failure, and unsolved problems from one period were carried over into the next, calling for more widespread industrial restructuring, a broader range of foreign investments, and more costly attacks on the domestic working class, but all with ever diminishing results.

The second wave of FDI, roughly spanning the years 1974–1981, continued the emphasis on lower wages for Japan's labor-intensive industries, which were again relocated primarily in Southeast Asia, but it also included a powerful new thrust into raw-material processing as well as the heavy polluting industries. Among the largest undertakings were the Asahan aluminium smelter in Indonesia, the Kawasaki steel sintering plant in the Philippines, and the Sumitomo petrochemical complex in Singapore. So although even as late as 1985 Japan's FDI was modest in comparison to that of the other advanced capitalist countries, in this second period the productive investments (chiefly manufacturing and mining) were overwhelmingly located in the underdeveloped countries, largely in Asia but also in Latin America.[6]

The onslaught on the domestic working class in this second period included an expansion of the part-time labor force (women, day laborers, contract workers, temporaries), a reduction in the number of regular jobs in government and in large companies, a rationalization of the labor process through new technologies, an extension of the system of subcontracting, and a freeze on the living standards of the less secure two-thirds of the working class. Finally, the restructuring involved moving out of the heavy and basic metals industries into motor vehicles and electronics, where Japanese capital's competitive edge was the sharpest.[7]

Again, the story is familiar, although its success has been exaggerated. The motor vehicle and electronics industries boomed, but they had to rely increasingly on demand outside Japan, especially in the developed countries of Europe and North America, and so they became more vulnerable to conditions overseas. The running down of the "structurally depressed industries" was slow, because this now meant closing down plants on which whole communities depended for their livelihood, that is, the sort of social dislocation Japanese executives had always claimed was impossible in Japan. And even in the booming industries, the move abroad and the widespread introduction of the new technology destroyed hundreds of thousands of jobs, so that the growing real rate of unemployment threatened to break through the facade of official statistics.[8]

If the first period ended with the oil shock of late 1973, the second had no clear cutoff point but merged into the third. Nevertheless, the two were distinguishable in terms of the main causes of crisis, the influences behind the waves of FDI as well as the main geographical locations of the investments. In 1974–1981, Japan's restructuring at home and abroad was designed to recover a competitive power that had been lost with the oil crisis. The emphasis was on reducing costs and raising productivity, which driving force sent FDI mainly into areas of lower costs, of raw materials and labor in Southeast Asia. FDI in Europe and America was concentrated in finance and commerce, since its purpose was more to sell the goods, which were competitively produced through a careful division of labor among low-paid workers in Japan and Southeast Asia, in countries where high wages provided buoyant markets.

However, the power of Japanese capital in transport and electrical machinery to conquer markets in Europe and America added intolerable dimensions to the recessions in those parts of the world. Rivalry among the major powers thus escalated, and the yen was pushed up from 238 to the dollar in September 1985 to 129 in December 1987. The United States even imposed sanctions on Japanese semiconductors and the EC tariffs on imports of unfinished goods.[9]

The distinctive feature of the third wave of FDI, which began in the mid-1980s and lasted until the onset of the current recession, lay in Southeast Asia's role in reviving the profits (eroded by the continually rising yen) of Japanese exporters and attenuating conflict with the United States and Europe. One part of the strategy involved component manufacture in Asia for use in Japan and in Japanese subsidiaries in the advanced countries, so that the parts the latter imported would come from countries other than Japan and not add to the latter's already "excessive" exports. Japanese capital would then have the best of both worlds. Via trade it would continue to reap the transfers of wealth resulting from the higher yen, but it would restore the volume of its overseas sales to pre-revaluation levels by cutting the costs of components, which would be made in low-cost Southeast Asian countries rather than by their relatively more expensive subcontractors in Japan.[10]

In Japan, the main victims of the mid-1980s high-yen crisis *(endaka fukyō)* were workers, whose money wages rose above those of U.S. workers, but whose real living standards remained no more than about 60 percent of the latter's.[11] By mid-1995, when the value of the yen fluctuated between 80 and 100 to the dollar, the gap between the two countries' living standards had widened even further. So while capital moved to America and Southeast Asia for lower wages, additional pressure was placed on the jobs and living standards of Japanese workers, large numbers of whom already endured conditions comparable to those in Southeast Asia.

In iron and steel alone, over a hundred thousand jobs were lost through the restructuring resulting from the high yen recession, and layoffs in other "sunset" industries, especially aluminium, were almost as devastating.[12] The scale of the layoffs in the machinery industries directly affected by the rising yen was not as great as was expected at the time, mainly because the cost-cutting and restructuring into higher value-added products, such as luxury cars, helped put a swift, although only temporary, end to the recession.

By 1988 Japanese capital was steaming ahead once again on the crest of an investment-led boom driven by domestic demand. But the big spending did not come from working-class buying power, even though some of it was for consumer goods. It was an upper-class splurge resulting from the need to find outlets for the massive profits that had accrued at home and abroad from Japan's rapidly escalating strength in the car and electronics industries. Its catalyst had been the rise of the yen, which forced cost-cutting investments in new plants and equipment and so further shifted the composition of domestic demand away from consumption expenditure and toward investment. The domestic demand that drove the boom was thus largely investment demand. But growing financial deregulation had also allowed a lot of the money, which would previously have been sent into productive investments, to try its luck in old and new forms of speculation: at home in land and shares, and abroad in almost everything from giant American corporations to Australian beaches.

The result was the "bubble economy" of the late 1980s. The greater the amount of upper-class wealth that went into buying assets, the more the increasingly inflated prices of those assets fed upper-class spending power. Although some of this went into consumer goods, many of them were luxuries and included products from the advanced countries that had forced the yen higher in order to gain access to the Japanese market. Investment, in productive capacity and speculation, absorbed most of the speculatively created wealth, leaving the increased capacity of the consumer goods industries with a potentially massive shortfall in demand. The stage was thus set for the plunge into the country's most serious recession ever and the most recent wave of investment in Southeast Asia.

The wider the gap between the real and the inflated values of Japanese land

and shares, the bigger would be the fall once capitalists recognized the need to close the gap and sell. Hence the current (fourth) wave of FDI, which is taking place in the midst of a deflationary recession in order to help rescue the system from its doldrums, is in many respects almost the opposite to the previous wave that immediately followed the high recession. At that time, surplus money poured into speculative activities in the advanced countries, whereas this time money is being withdrawn from overseas in order to prop up a teetering financial system. However, the two were similar in their quest for low-cost production sites in Asia to counteract the effects of the rising yen on Japan's cost structure. From ASEAN's point of view, therefore, the past decade can be seen as constituting a single wave of investment from Japan resulting from a continually rising yen.

The most recent bout of *endaka* stemmed mainly from the success of the measures which were used against the previous bout of the mid-1980s, namely, cost-down and restructuring into new products, such as luxury cars, to recapture the foreign markets lost by goods which had been priced out of the market. Japan's trade surplus thus increased, putting renewed pressure on the yen. To make matters worse, the prolonged recession and never-ending deflation of asset prices prevented the domestic market, not simply from compensating for the damage done to export markets by the rising yen, but from being able to attenuate that rising yen by sucking in the level of imports which it could in the late 1980s. And to top it all off, the excessive investment of the late 1980s so delayed the revival of investment that Japan's unit labor costs, for the first time in many years, have risen above those of the United States in some of the key industries in which the two sides compete. Things could hardly be worse for Japanese capital, which has now even lost much of the productive strength which drove it in quest of foreign markets in the first place, markets which are now under attack from both foreign protectionism and foreign productive strength. Since the latter can only be reversed by a revival of domestic investment, which remains remote because of the delayed revival of domestic consumption, Japanese capital has needed a foreign investment strategy to solve all its problems simultaneously: cut costs, secure markets, revive asset prices, and keep the United States quiet.

The answer it is devising is to relocate more and more of both its productive power and its markets into Asia, implying a relative withdrawal from the United States and Japan, where both the cost side and demand side have confronted such bottlenecks. American protectionism, which reached its most aggressive level to date in June 1995 with unilateral threats of sanctions and full-scale trade wars, now requires a rear-guard strategy of holding only past gains rather than extending them. And just as the high yen failed to provide Japanese workers with higher living standards or spending power on the demand side, so is it now making growing numbers of them redundant on the cost side and finally beginning to hollow-out *(kūdōka)* Japanese industry on a scale comparable to the United States and the United Kingdom.[13] All that is left is a full-fledged "Asia-zone strategy," which now consciously involves combining the quest for lower costs with the quest for secure and growing markets.[14]

However, not all Asian countries have been equally suited to the Japanese strategy. Although making sophisticated components requires a level of technology and infrastructure found mainly in the NICs (Singapore, South Korea, Taiwan, and Hong Kong), the latter's wages have risen intolerably over the past decade. And so it was not until massive Japanese aid and spending by ASEAN governments on infrastructure in the 1980s that the region's main assets, cheap labor and potentially enormous markets, were able to attract large-scale Japanese investments. The rise and fall of commodity prices had reduced ASEAN's bargaining power and left the region feeling high and dry during the early 1980s when the rush into the NICs took place. Tables 9.1 and 9.2, which summarize approved Japanese FDI to March 1995, show the two main changes that occurred over the past decade, spanning the two most recent waves of FDI into Asia. First, there has been a growing concentration on ASEAN and China for productive investments in mining and manufacturing, and a lessening of the weight of the United States, not just in productive industries, but even in the unproductive ones (commerce, finance, and real estate), which had for many years absorbed the bulk of Japanese money that went abroad. As the Asia-zone strategy takes shape, the importance of Latin America, even in the productive industries, has been falling, although that continent still provides important tax havens, such as the Bahamas and the Cayman Islands, or flag-of-convenience shipping, such as Panama (as does Liberia).[15]

The attraction of ASEAN and China is not just the opportunity their low wages offer Japanese capital to recapture the competitive power it lost with the rise of the yen, but also their growing actual and potential markets. If one looks at the numbers of investments in Table 9.2 rather than the amounts of money involved and remembers how much more can be bought in Asia than in the United States with the same amount of money, then the importance of Asia is especially marked. Even then, some changes are not revealed by the very general pictures covered in these tables. For example, for the first time in many years, the current recession is driving more manufacturing investment, however this is measured, into Asia than into North America. In fiscal 1994, Asia received $5.18 billion compared to North America's $4.76 billion. Asia also absorbed over half the money invested in electrical machinery, with the North American share falling to a third of the total.[16] Moreover, even many of the manufacturing investments in North America in the bubble years, such as Sony's takeover of CBS, were largely speculative.

To support the claim that ASEAN has been transformed into JASEAN, or that the catalytic force behind the awesome capitalist development in ASEAN lies in Japan, requires tracing the process by which capital in each ASEAN country found that some kind of alliance with Japanese capital was central to its power to accumulate. In this chapter I attempt to do so with respect to the manufacturing

Table 9.1

Approved Japanese FDI, by Country and Fiscal Year, 1951–1995

	1951–1986		1987–1991		1992–1994		1951–1994	
	$mil.	%	$mil.	%	$mil.	%	$mil	%
North America	37,406	35.3	117,602	47.7	46,885	42.2	202,690	43.7
Europe	14,471	13.7	54,165	22.0	21,231	19.1	89,867	19.4
Asia	21,790	20.6	31,665	12.8	22,761	20.5	76,216	16.4
Indonesia	8,673	8.2	4,060	1.6	4,248	3.8	16,981	3.7
Hong Kong	3,433	3.2	7,342	3.0	3,106	2.8	13,881	3.0
Singapore	2,571	2.4	4,596	1.9	2,368	2.1	9,535	2.1
South Korea	2,118	2.0	2,280	0.9	871	0.8	5,268	1.1
Malaysia	1,283	1.2	2,828	1.1	2,246	2.0	6,357	1.4
Taiwan	1,051	1.0	2,084	0.8	862	0.8	3,997	0.9
Philippines	913	0.9	869	0.4	1,035	0.9	2,817	0.6
Thailand	884	0.8	4,346	1.8	1,954	1.8	7,184	1.5
China	513	0.5	2,888	1.2	5,326	4.9	8,729	1.9
South America	20,373	19.2	23,447	9.5	11,327	10.2	55,148	11.9
Panama	8,841	8.3	8,960	3.6	3,983	3.6	21,784	4.7
Brazil	4,857	4.6	1,874	0.8	2,118	1.9	8,849	1.9
Mexico	1,556	1.5	512	0.2	726	0.7	2,793	0.6
Cayman Islands	1,279	1.2	6,210	2.5	1,760	1.6	9,249	2.0
Bahamas	1,247	1.2	2,315	0.9	183	0.2	3,744	0.8
Bermuda	617	0.6	1,193	0.5	1,747	1.6	3,557	0.8
Oceania	5,234	4.9	16,144	6.6	5,873	5.3	27,250	5.9
Australia	4,502	4.2	14,110	5.7	5,319	4.8	23,932	5.2
Africa	3,678	3.5	2,895	1.2	1,123	1.0	7,698	1.7
Liberia	2,743	2.6	2,796	1.1	1,075	1.0	6,614	1.4
Middle East	3,016	2.8	504	0.2	1,216	1.1	4,737	1.0
World Total	105,970	100.0	246,421	100.0	111,214	100.0	463,606	100.0

Source: Ōkurashō (Ministry of Finance), "Heisei 6 nendo no okeru taigai oyobi tainai chokusetsu tōshi jōkyō" [Internal and external foreign investments for the year 1986], 6 June 1995; Ōkurashō, *Zasei kinyu tōkei geppō: Tainaigai minkan tōshi tokushū* (Special issue on internal and external private investments), no. 476 (December 1991), pp. 30–35 and no. 500 (December 1993), pp. 28–33.

industries, the key sectors of which tend to be dominated by joint ventures with Japanese companies, in Thailand, Indonesia, and Malaysia.

The main conditions which "push" the ASEAN ruling classes into a willingness to work with the Japanese relate to their relative technological backwardness resulting from their colonization and late entry into full-fledged competition with the world's leading powers. Because capitalism is a system of production for profit or not at all, and because within all industries capitalists are in constant competition with one another, continually renewing their techniques in order to get ahead of rivals or at least to avoid falling behind them, survival in an industry depends on the degree to which the techniques of the leading producers can be

Table 9.2

Total Approved FDI, by Main Regions and Industries, to March 1995

	North America		Europe		Asia		South America		World Totals	
	Cases	$mil.	Cases	$mil.	Cases	$mil.	Cases	$mil.	Cases	$mil.
Manufacturing	5,972	59,277	2,625	21,227	13,149	33,531	1,164	8,436	23,310	128,896
Food	744	2,983	129	747	978	1,778	146	284	2,165	7,383
Textiles	255	1,144	395	1,370	2,197	3,108	172	497	3,091	6,181
Lumber/pulp	220	2,653	36	136	579	755	55	407	1,026	4,197
Chemicals	599	7,914	281	2,945	1,363	5,619	149	913	2,464	18,901
Metals	489	5,495	410	851	1,294	4,143	117	2,430	2,483	13,832
Gen. machinery	895	5,964	411	3,462	1,280	2,948	149	587	2,793	13,113
Elec. machinery	1,138	5,043	394	6,004	2,246	7,847	152	809	3,976	29,869
Trans. machinery	499	6,999	144	3,751	616	2,726	99	2,298	1,404	17,028
Other	1,133	11,082	425	1,961	2,596	4,606	125	211	4,408	18,391
Non-manufacturing	20,265	141,687	6,498	66,234	9,929	41,207	7,100	46,634	49,592	327,170
Agr./for./fish.	370	729	56	121	877	889	441	575	2,326	3,171
Mining	437	2,583	121	2,093	346	8,427	183	1,918	1,576	20,233
Construction	379	1,880	53	288	625	1,212	75	297	1,266	3,984
Commerce	8,033	24,354	3,212	12,783	3,389	6,570	747	3,681	16,586	49,755
Finance/ins.	629	27,271	977	32,207	672	7,537	641	18,352	3,091	87,770
Services	3,588	34,617	1,087	6,657	1,775	8,321	468	2,894	7,634	57,213
Transport	361	1,264	163	469	446	2,134	3,720	17,417	5,390	26,412
Real estate	5,509	46,755	594	10,558	967	4,481	70	299	8,574	71,088
Other	959	2,233	235	1,058	532	1,639	870	1,203	3,149	7,543
Total*	28,684	202,691	9,560	89,867	23,963	76,216	8,424	55,148	77,507	463,606

Source: Data Bank, *Kaigai shinshutsu kigyō sōran* (Japanese multinationals: Facts and figures), 1995, in the special issue (zōkan) *Shūkan Tōyō Keizai Rinji*, p. 1, 158; and Ōkurashō (Ministry of Finance), Heisei 6 nendo ni okeru taigai oyobi tainai chokusetsu tōshi jōkyō, 1995.

*For each industry world totals include the other regions of Oceania, Middle East, and Africa. For each region, the totals include monies in branches and real estate.

matched. It depends essentially on the level of what Marxists call "productive forces." The power of advanced countries thus always rests on their greater technological capacity to compete, to ruin rivals whose techniques are not on a par with their own, that is, whose productive forces are less advanced. To an extent success is a matter to timing, of having got into an industry first and then maintaining the leading position by continually reinvesting profits in the most efficient technologies. Leading corporations earn the largest profits which enable them to undertake the largest investments and thereby retain their leading position.

Sometimes the resources necessary to enter an industry and remain competitive within it can be hastily acquired by merging with already successful firms, or by receiving state assistance. Both of these strategies are attempted in underdeveloped countries, but each has its limitations. State assistance presupposes that the resources are available and can simply be switched to the required industries. However, in most underdeveloped countries this is not normally the case, and the only feasible road to capitalist development is to link up with already successful firms, which means foreign ones. But foreign capital will only be interested if it can make its customary profit, and that is the heart of the problem in underdeveloped countries: with generally backward productive forces, profit making is so much more difficult.

Normally in such countries there are only a few natural endowments which single out a limited number of industries for successful capitalist development. Because of special raw material deposits, water for power generation, climate for growing crops, and so on, money can be made in related industries, and foreign capital becomes willing to invest in them. Some industries never really get off the ground, because there are no natural endowments to prop them up, and capital elsewhere has such a long history of accumulation and technical advantage that late entry in effect means permanent exclusion. If foreign capital is to be enticed into such industries, capital in the underdeveloped countries has to offer some special enticement to give it a "comparative advantage," such as a cheap disciplined labor force. Development in countries with backward productive forces is at best uneven, concentrated as it is in industries favored by nature or by government policy.

In the context of the steady rise of the yen over the past decade, the cheap disciplined labor (to cut costs) offered by the ASEAN countries has proven more and more attractive to Japanese capital than the relatively advanced infrastructures of the NICs or the greater purchasing power of the advanced countries. Especially in manufacturing, Japanese capital's profits in ASEAN countries have regularly been higher than anywhere else in the world,[17] and the high yen has kept this consideration in the forefront of its overseas strategies.

While in the 1980s, especially before the yen began its long ascent, North America and Europe were the main outlets for Japanese FDI, a shift towards Japan's traditional emphasis on Asia began around 1986, was interrupted by the bubble economy, and then was powerfully reasserted again in the early 1990s. The move has not just been towards Asia, but especially towards ASEAN and other Asian countries that can match that region's potential for low-cost production and growing markets, such as Vietnam (which has now joined ASEAN), China, and India. It is time take a closer look at developments in the three selected countries.

Thailand

Thailand is the only ASEAN country whose ruling class has had a longstanding alliance with the Japanese. It held even during the Pacific War, although afterwards and well into the 1970s the Japanese did not have what their Thai counterparts most needed: military assistance. That came from the United States, and for some time even after the liberation of Vietnam the U.S. military presence remained a central feature of neo-colonialism in Thailand. However, substantial investments from Japan were welcomed in the early 1960s, mainly because they promised to advance productive forces in industries where local capital had hitherto achieved very little.

Although Thailand was never formally colonized, it had in effect been treated by the British as part of Malaya, and capital had poured into industries where profits depended more on natural endowments than on past accumulations: rice, tin, rubber, and teak. But since money could be made in industries like these without much reinvestment, little was undertaken and most of the profit left the country in the typical neo-colonial fashion. Not much capitalist development occurred.[18]

By the early 1960s the situation was so desperate that the military government was forced to initiate its First Development Plan and to provide the minimal infrastructure required by overseas investors: power, transport, and communications. The New Investment Promotion Act of 1962 envisaged development by means of import substitution (ISI) through protective tariffs and tax concessions, and it established the most liberal climate for foreign capital anywhere in Asia. Soon Japanese FDI began to pour into the country, mainly in the textile industry, which by the end of the decade had become the second most important branch of manufacturing in Thailand (behind food processing). Japan was the leading foreign investor, with Japanese companies accounting for over two-thirds of the country's production in textiles, nearly three-quarters in cars, and everything in motorcycles and sheet glass.[19]

Because import substitution and its accompanying subsidies favored capital which produced for the domestic market, it tended to favor local capital, which had some experience in doing just that. But local capital, and even foreign capital operating in Thailand, could not always produce goods for this market as cheaply as they could be imported, and so supporting tariffs and subsidies were often needed. However, throughout Southeast Asia, the logic of capitalist development, as repeatedly pointed out by the World Bank and the IMF, considered this wasteful. It might create a more *even* development, but "artificially" protecting relatively backward industries, rather than putting all resources into ones which can stand on their own, is contrary to the purpose of capitalist production, which is making profit, and hence contradicts "allocative efficiency." And so by the early 1970s the policy of Thai governments edged towards favoring export industries. The 1977 Investment Promotion Act signaled the final burial of import substitution, coming as it did just after the military coup that would deepen the Thai ruling class's alliance with foreign capital. The new export subsidies were intended to attract foreign investment and to prepare local producers to stand on their own.[20]

Thailand's export-oriented incentives greatly encouraged foreign capital to use the country's cheap labor, since the domestic market was limited by the poverty of peasants and low-paid workers. And by the early 1980s considerable export-led growth had occurred, with manufacturing as a whole growing by about 10 percent in the 1970s. But the growth concealed a massive unevenness, since most of it was in textiles, apparel, and transport equipment. In all industries foreign capital spearheaded the process, in varying degrees of cooperation with local capital. Table 9.3 shows the sales of Thailand's top 1,066 companies in 1980 in mining, manufacturing, and trading, and it indicates the shares of companies which were partly or wholly foreign owned. Although foreign capital from different countries predominated in different industries, for example the United States in mining and the European Community (EC) in pharmaceuticals, Japanese capital was strong in almost every sector.[21]

It would be wrong to conclude that Thai capital has simply been a puppet of old and new forms of imperialism. In a number of industries it remains a powerful force, and in finance, where the state has limited the entry of foreign capital, it is the dominant force spearheaded by four leading families: Sophonpanich (Bangkok Bank), Lamsam (Thai Farmers Bank), Tejapaibul (Bangkok Metropolitan Bank) and Ratanarak (Bank of Ayudhaya).[22] Elements of the local ruling class also have independent forms of organization, not least the military and some new bourgeois political parties, which at times enable it to function with considerable autonomy. What must be grasped, therefore, is the existence of an *alliance* between local and foreign capital, from which both benefit, although the balance of power within it varies.

For example, partly because of the Vietnam War, the struggle for democracy in Thailand escalated in the early 1970s, and the military rule to which the people had been subjected since 1932 was replaced by a brief liberal democratic interlude, in which the balance of power moved towards the local ruling class. But a bloody coup, with barely concealed U.S. complicity, restored military rule and with it much of the previous weight of American imperialism.[23] Not long afterwards, in the early 1980s, the collapse of commodity prices saw a further increase in foreign capital's leverage. The fall in rice, wheat, tin, and rubber

Table 9.3

Foreign Control in Thailand's Top 1,066 Companies (1980)

	Sales (Bmil)	Number of companies	Foreign share of sales (%)	Foreign share of companies (%)
Mining	1,889	20	50.3	45.0
Food, bev., tobacco	50,212	137	32.1	32.1
Textiles and apparel	22,836	93	71.6	54.8
Wood and wood products	1,515	15	11.6	26.7
Paper and printing	4,971	26	52.8	30.8
Chemicals, rubber	73,085	104	95.0	66.3
Ceramic and glass	18,304	32	28.6	40.6
Iron and steel, metals	20,277	22	84.1	40.9
Machinery	31,702	96	82.2	55.2
Other manufacturing	724	3	5.7	33.3
General trading	85,697	169	70.1	29.0
Agr. wholesaling	12,869	53	4.6	5.7
Food wholesaling	24,294	75	9.7	6.0
Other wholesaling	37,892	221	32.0	13.6
Total	386,267	1,066	59.3	32.7

Source: Somsak Tambunlertchai and Ian McGovern, "An Overview of the Role of MNCs in the Economic Development of Thailand," *Proceedings of the Conference on The Role of Multi-National Corporations in Thailand,* July 7–9, 1984, Thammasat University, Bangkok, ed. Nongyao Chaiseri and Chira Hongladarom, p. 81.

prices, which still provided the bulk of exports and a major area of local capital's strength, caused a sharp decline in business activity, including foreign investment. However, the partial recovery of commodity prices, the continued cheapness of oil (which Thailand imports), as well as Japanese capital's never-ending search for cheap labor, all helped to revive accumulation and produce a series of booms led by foreign (mainly Japanese) investment. Politically, the country has see-sawed between intense democratic struggles, the intervention of the military, and intermittent assertions of parliamentary authority by the country's bourgeois parties.

Data from the Board of Investment confirmed how the balance of influence between local and foreign capital in the mid-1980s shifted in response to these changes: whereas in 1984 and 1985 foreign capital comprised about 26 percent of the total registered capital of firms granted promotion certificates, in 1986 its share soared to 34.1 percent. The pattern has since continued: for example, of the total capital in firms granted promotion certificates by the Board of Investment (BOI) in the first half of 1992, 40 percent was foreign.[24] The revival of investment capital accumulation had to be led by stronger more technically advanced firms, which

Table 9.4

BOI Approved Investments with Foreign Participation

Main Investor	1983–1985		Total to 1986		Total to 1992	
	B mil.	%	B mil.	%	B mil.	%
Japan	10,311	27.8	48,884	20.5	309,446	25.6
United States	6,445	17.4	45,542	19.1	187,147	15.5
United Kingdom	1,705	4.6	12,759	5.3	80,244	6.6
Taiwan	2,810	7.6	14,742	6.2	74,344	6.2
Hong Kong	n/a		7,653		208,463	17.3
Total	37,055	100.0	238,694	100.0	1,208,058	100.0

Source: Board of Investment, Japan Unit; and Nihon Bōeki Shinkōkai (Japan External Trade Organization), *1994 Jietoro hakusho, tōshihen: sekai to Nohon to kaigai chokusetsu tōshi* (1994 Jetro White Paper, investment: The world and Japan's foreign direct investment) (Tokyo: Nihon bōeki shinkōkai, 1994), p. 189.

in today's world are overwhelmingly transnational. Table 9.4 shows the importance in Thailand of capital from different countries, confirming the leading position of Japan even before the rise of the yen, but especially afterwards. Japanese capital has managed over the years to forge a vast array of links with the leading elements of the Thai ruling class, both indigenous and Chinese, especially the foremost business groups and families listed in Table 9.5. I discuss only the first three.

By far the largest of these is the Bangkok bank group controlled by the Sophonpanich family. Bangkok Bank itself was set up in 1944 by Chin Sophonpanich out of wealth accumulated from exporting lumber and building materials, and it has since become the largest bank in Southeast Asia with Chin (until his death about a decade ago) as its largest shareholder and probably the richest individual in the region. Mutual stock holdings bind over 60 companies together, but because of the weak capital base of most Thai manufacturing firms, the bank's lending power raises the number of companies under its influence to over 140, including the Saha Union and Saha Patana groups, as well as the Charoen Pokhapand group (the largest agribusiness conglomerate in the country), and even the Siam Motors group.[25]

It is hardly accidental that Japan's top company, Toyota, should have linked up with the Bangkok Bank group and produced the single largest Japanese presence in Thailand, which is also the third largest foreign company (behind Shell and Esso) and the country's ninth largest corporation, namely, Toyota Motors Thailand. Set up in 1962 with two-thirds of the capital from the parent in Japan, the company had two factories producing 20,000 cars in 1986, but since then it has massively expanded its productive capacity, not just to increase its

Table 9.5

Leading Thai Business Groups and Families

Group	Family	Ethnicity	Main industries
Bangkok Bank	Sophonpanich	Chinese	Banking/insurance, trade, real estate
Siam Cement	Royal family	Thai	Cement, iron and steel, pulp and paper, machinery, chemicals, electronics
Siam Motor	Phornprapha	Chinese	Cars and parts, machinery, musical instruments, leisure
Saha Patana	Chokwatana	Chinese	Toiletries, cosmetics, pharmaceuticals, clothing, household electrical goods
Saha Union	Darakanand	Chinese	Textiles, plastics, clothing, chemicals
Charoen Pokhapand	Chiravanont	Chinese	Trade, fodder, livestock, commerce, food, chemicals, communications
Thai Farmers Bank	Lamsam	Chinese	Banking and finance
Bank of Ayudhya	Ratanarak	Chinese	Banking, finance, cement, flour
Metropolitan Bank	Tejapaibul	Chinese	Banking, liquor, sugar, chemicals
Sukree	Pothiratta-nangkun	Chinese	Textiles, synthetic textiles

Source: Inoue Ryuichirō, *Ajia no zaibatsu to kigyō* (Asia's Business Groups and Firms) (Tokyo: Nihon Keizai Shinbunsha, 1987), p. 154; 1994 edition, p. 176.

share of the Thai market, which remains totally dominated by Japanese cars, but to put Thailand at the center of its Southeast Asian and even its global strategy. By 1991 Toyota's most popular model alone sold 50,000 units and today the company retains about 30 percent of the market. Another joint venture, Siam Toyota Manufacturing Company, was set up in the mid-1980s in partnership with Siam Cement, Thailand's largest manufacturing firm, to produce diesel engines and components for export. This venture, together with Toyota's third major presence in the country, Toyota Auto Body Thailand, greatly extended Thailand's role in supplying parts to the Toyota group, especially metal moulds to Indonesia (since 1986), Taiwan (since 1987), and Malaysia (since 1988), all for use in the production of cheap pressed parts for markets such as Australia. Toyota carefully considered the alternatives before it finally selected Thailand as its base for producing metal moulds for export throughout the region. Because the company had also been involved since 1978 in a joint venture with Hino making Hino and Toyota engines, Thailand had a well-proven record of success.[26]

In October 1988 a Brand to Brand Complementation (BBC) agreement was concluded among ASEAN countries which did two very important things. It in effect allowed all components imported from within the region to be included in local content and it slashed import tariffs by 50 percent for participating companies, including Toyota, Nissan, and Mitsubishi. Toyota's BBC scheme came on stream in the second half of 1992, and it uses Thailand to make diesel engines, pressed parts, and electronic apparatus; Malaysia to make steering gears, shock absorbers, and radiators; the Philippines to make transmissions; and Indonesia to make gasoline engines and pressed materials.[27]

Toyota's partner in its diesel engine factory is the giant which towers over all others in Thailand's manufacturing industry and which absorbs the top elite from the nation's universities. With the royal family as its major shareholder, Siam Cement symbolizes the success of indigenous capital and is as close as one gets to a national bourgeoisie in Thailand. Siam Cement was founded in 1913 in an attempt to bolster self-sufficiency, and it has since received considerable equipment and technology from Denmark. Today it has 21 companies under its umbrella, including the country's top iron and steel firm (Siam Iron & Steel) as well as leaders in building materials (Siam Fibre-Cement, Concrete Products and Aggregate), machinery (Siam Toyota, Siam Kubota Diesel, Thai CRT, Siam Nawaloha Foundry), pulp and paper (Siam Pulp & Paper, Siam Kraft Paper), tires (Siam Tyre), trading (SCT, International Engineering), and plastics (Thai Polyethylene). The group's most recent areas of growth, motor vehicles and electronics, have been spearheaded by joint ventures with Japanese companies.

Apart from its agreement with Toyota, since 1980 Siam Cement has had a major joint venture with Kubota and Marubeni, Siam Kubota Diesel, which makes diesel engines for agricultural machinery. Also in line with government support for engine manufacturing is the agreement between Hino and Thai Engineering Products to make auto parts for the local as well as the Japanese and U.S. markets. Siam Cement's other links with Japanese capital include Siam Sanitary Ware, which is a joint venture with Toto operating since 1969, and a joint venture between Toto and group member Nawaloha to make sanitary porcelain. A major coup for the group was the establishment in the mid-1980s of Thai CRT, a joint venture between Siam Cement (40 percent), 17 local electrical companies (30 percent), and Mitsubishi Electric to manufacture braun tubes for colour TV sets from 1989, all under the protection of a government monopoly. Mitsubishi seized on the opportunity to further its strategy for the 1990s by establishing two more joint venture companies: Melco Consumer Products and Siam Compressor Industry. Today Mitsubishi Electric has nine joint venture companies in Thailand. Among the Japanese-linked Siam Cement affiliates which make and market TV sets are Conception Industry (51 percent NEC owned) and Home Electronics (48 percent NEC owned) respectively.[28]

Siam Motors is a third major Thai conglomerate which has extensive links with Japanese capital. Including 43 companies in 20 industries, the group is held together by Siam Motors, which deals in Nissan cars and owns 40 percent of group assets. Siam Motors was founded by Thawron Phornprapha, who, having visited Japan on numerous occasions, was an early Japanophile and began importing Nissan trucks in 1948. By 1962 he had concluded a licensing agreement with Nissan and set up a wholly Thai-owned assembly company for Nissan vehicles, Siam Motors, and Nissan, in which the Japanese parent now owns a quarter interest and which employs 1,500 locals. In 1973 another joint venture company was set up to make commercial vehicles, Siam Nissan Automobile Co., which now has about 1,100 workers. Since then Siam Motors has greatly expanded its activities in the vehicle industry, throughout relying heavily on joint ventures and licensing agreements with the Japanese majors: Nissan, Mitsubishi, Isuzu, Suzuki, and Yamaha. A third key (B350 million) joint venture with Nissan, Thai Automotive Industry, in which Siam Motors provided 70 percent of the capital, was set up in June 1988 to produce 2500 cc diesel engines and 1,500 cc petrol engines.

Of the 43 companies in the Siam Motors group, a full 19 are related to motor vehicles, and almost all are linked in one way or another to Japanese capital. Many of the other companies in the group also owe their existence to agreements with Japanese interests, for example, with Komatsu in construction machinery, with Hitachi in elevators, and with Daikin in compression engines. In all, 11 of them are in trading (notably Siam Motors International Trading), 12 are in manufacturing, four in finance and real estate, five in raw materials, and two in Thailand's most notorious industry, "leisure." Although the Siam Motors group has been dramatically affected by the higher prices of imported components due to the rise of the yen, it has been happy to take advantage of the government's encouragements for export industries as well as Japanese capital's search for cheap components. Nissan sees its tie-up with Siam Motors as having a major role in its global strategy to make Thailand one of its low-cost production bases, and in October 1986 it announced its key plan to supply the markets of Taiwan, Malaysia, Bangladesh, and Pakistan.[29]

There are clearly long-standing ties between Japanese and Thai capital, and these have contributed much to Thailand's current second-most-favored (to China) status among overseas low-cost production sites for Japanese capital. Japan's two largest trading companies, Mitsubishi Corp. and Mitsui & Co., also continue to siphon off Thailand's raw materials, with 27 and 36 joint ventures in the country respectively.[30] Investment from Japan in the late 1980s and early 1990s probably contributed more than one percentage point to Thailand's double-digit growth rate each year. Associated with the increasing amounts invested has been a continuing shift from import-substituting projects to export-oriented ones for the European, U.S., and Japanese markets, especially as a result of the higher yen. This has happily coincided with the encouragement given to export companies by the Thai government's Sixth Development Plan (1987–1991). The reason for the departure is clearly illustrated in the move by companies like Pioneer and Minebea from Singapore, where wages averaged $300 in 1986, to Thailand, where they were only $75, as their main production bases for export to Japan, the United States, and

Table 9.6

Some Export-Oriented Investments in Thailand in the Late 1980s

Company	Products	Market
Sharp	Electric stoves, refrigerators	United States, Europe
NEC	Color TVs	Nearby countries
Mitsubishi Electric	Compressors for air conditioners	Japan
ToyoSash	Aluminum sash window frames	Japan, China, Southeast Asia
Nippondenso	Metal molds	Southeast Asia
Jomatsukawa Plastic	Metal molds	Japan
Fuji Spinning	Outerwear	Europe, United States
Bandai	Toys	United States
Nihon Gakki	Skis	Japan, United States, Europe
Aderans	Wigs	United States
Nichiden Kagaku	Starch	Japan

Source: Nihon Keizai Shinbun (NKS), 25 September 1987, p. 23.

Southeast Asia. Some of the other export-oriented investments in Thailand reported during the high yen recession of 1986–1987 are listed in Table 9.6.

The venture by Toyo Sash was the company's first big overseas project which was expected to "dwarf the existing Thai aluminium building materials industry."[31] Since one hundred percent of its output was to be exported, it was one hundred percent Japanese owned and required little more from Thailand besides its 1,000 workers and the generous incentives offered by the Thai government. These included tax holidays of three to eight years, exemptions from business tax and tariffs on machinery imports and raw materials exports, and special incentives for factories located in the investment zones.[32]

The division of labor between the poorer ASEAN countries and the NICs in the 1980s was illustrated in the plans of the electronics majors, which concentrated chip manufacture in Singapore and Malaysia but household consumer goods in Thailand (and Indonesia): Hitachi expanded its production of refrigerators, colour TVs, and rice cookers, Toshiba relocated its production of rice cookers, while Sharp relocated its production of electric stoves and refrigerators, "in some cases moving whole factories out of Japan, or even Taiwan, as part of a global reorganisation" and bringing with it a whole range of component makers.[33] Most recent FDI has been closely related to Japanese capital's global strategy in the electronics and car industries, and Thailand has now become a favorite of the chip makers as well. Among the other firms to have set up major ventures in the country are Fujitsu (a 3,700-worker electronics component factory opened in 1990); Toshiba (a 1,500-worker refrigerator factory opened a year earlier); Osaki

Table 9.7

Rates of Growth of Main Thai Economic Indicators, 1985–1987

	1985	1986	1987 (estimate)
Real economic growth	3.2	3.5	5.5–7.1
Consumption	6.2	3.7	7.6
Investment	1.4	0.5	14.0
Private	−4.2	2.2	18.0
Government	11.5	−2.3	7.5
Foreign	18.5	−0.1	*821.4
Exports	10.3	19.6	15.0
Imports	2.5	−3.9	22.0

Source: *NKS*, 22 September 1987, p. 3.
*June 1986 to June 1987

Sogyo (wire harnesses); Minebea (ball bearings); Hoya (plastic lenses for eyeglasses); Fujikura Cable Works (cables for electronics equipment); Tokyu, Fuji, and Jusco (supermarkets).[34] The full list is endless.

Accumulation in Thailand rose rapidly in the second half of the 1980s, not least because of Japanese capital's growing interest in using cheap labor to produce goods for export which the rise of the yen made too costly to produce elsewhere. The resulting export-led boom in Thailand was thus both a symbol and an outcome of an ever more intimate alliance between the Japanese and Thai ruling classes. The Board of Investment even has a Japan Unit in Bangkok, and its Tokyo office is constantly engaged in public relations with government and private interests. Table 9.7 shows the weight of foreign investment in the revival of capital accumulation in 1987.

At the time, the *Far Eastern Economic Review*'s correspondent, Phillip Bowring, summed up Japan's importance to Thailand's manufacturing industry as follows:

> The icing on the cake is that Japanese businessmen have made it plain that Thailand is now their preferred spot in ASEAN for investment in manufacturing.
>
> At a time when Japanese companies are desperate for lower-cost production, this fact alone could be worth at least one percentage point on the growth rate for the next three years or so.
>
> Although most investments aimed at the local market are joint ventures, an export-oriented plant still offers an opportunity to put a toe into the local market. Companies now being granted export promotion privileges by the Board of Investments are being allowed to sell up to 20 percent of their production locally. This is upsetting existing domestic producers. ... [T]he surge of foreign investment, while bringing short-term gains, will swamp nascent local manufacturers which have been so important to the growth of self-sustaining industrial groups in South Korea and Taiwan.[35]

One example of this conflict centered on the promotional privileges granted by the Board of Investment to a Sumitomo joint venture with CH Autoparts (which makes bodies for Toyota) to produce rolled steel sheets. The 21-member Rolled Steel Sheets Club petitioned the Industry Ministry, arguing that the production of some 30 companies, none of which were promoted, already exceeded demand and that the 67 jobs created by Sumitomo would result in a loss of 1,400 existing jobs. Some voices even among top business leaders in Thailand also spoke of an "overpresence" of Japanese investment in the country.[36] Today, the same voices can still be heard in the same circles, in spite of, or perhaps because of, the increasing dependence of upper-class prosperity on Japanese FDI.

Indonesia

Although the Japanese gave some encouragement to Indonesian nationalism at the outset of the Pacific War, their subsequent actions dissipated the goodwill they might have won, and they faced massive demands for reparations. Eventually in 1957 after Japan whittled away the original claim to some $223 million, $400 million in aid and a cancellation of trade debt, diplomatic relations were restored.[37] However, it was only after the downfall of Sukarno (who had nationalized all foreign property) and the massacre of communists that followed, that the Japanese saw opportunities in Indonesia, anticipating that one day it would be the most important part of the region to them.

The new Suharto regime resolved to tackle the crisis of Indonesia's underdevelopment firmly within the constraints of capitalism. An alliance with the United States was its chief expedient, and massive injections of capital flooded in from the United States, the World Bank, and the International Monetary Fund (IMF) as well as all the military aid the new regime required. Liberal foreign investment laws were passed, and from 1968 Japanese capital entered, mainly in manufacturing.[38]

The free market policy and near subservience to World Bank and IMF orthodoxy, which persisted until 1974, was attenuated only by the central position which import substitution still held in the First Five Year Plan (1969–1974). But as in Thailand, import substitution did not deter Japanese investors, since their strategy rested on capturing market shares as a first step in their broader assault. Besides, they could enjoy the advantages the plan provided in such priority industries as fertilizers, chemicals, cement (all relating to agriculture), and textiles (basic needs).[39] Table 9.8 shows the total amounts of approved non-oil and non-gas investment by industry and by the law (foreign or domestic) of approval to December 1973.

If the "rush" into Thailand by Japanese companies was a recent phenomenon, resulting from the high yen and the quest for cheap labor, then the corresponding periods in Indonesia were firstly the 1970s, a result of the mounting resource crisis which reached its climax in 1973,[40] and secondly the current period, also a result of the higher yen. Although cheap wages were the main target in the textile investments of the 1970s as well as the recent ones in machinery (cars and

Table 9.8

Approved Non-Oil and Non-Gas Investments in Indonesia, 1973

	Foreign		Domestic	
	$mil.	%	$mil.	%
Forestry	495.5	58	356.8	42
Agriculture and fisheries	113.0	33	232.5	67
Mining	860.5	95	46.2	5
Manufacturing	1,045.1	38	1,740.9	62
of which textiles	436.9	37	749.0	63
Tourism, hotels, real estate	195.9	50	200.0	50
Other	118.3	37	207.0	63
Total approved	2,828.3	49	2,978.5	51
Total realised	1,131.2	56	876.0	44

Source: Richard Robinson, *Indonesia: The Rise of Capital* (Sydney: Allen and Unwin, 1986), p. 142.

electrical), Indonesia's resources have remained that country's most distinctive attraction. Table 9.9 shows the distribution, by date and by industry, of the projects undertaken in the years 1951–1992. Sukarno's nationalist regime had delayed the influx of the textiles FDI which rising Japanese wages had sent elsewhere into Asia in the 1960s, so that when the mounting oil crisis began to swell the resource investments of the 1970s, the two currents combined into a tidal wave. Immediately following the new Foreign Investment Law, both of the companies licensed in 1967 were in fisheries, while six of the nine licensed the next year were also in resource exploitation, as were seven out of 17 in 1969. Only in 1970 when the government revised the investment laws to set up 12 priority categories did the lure of Indonesian wages result in a flood of manufacturing FDI, including textiles: 27 companies (22 in manufacturing) were licensed, while in 1971 another 27 were, with 22 in 1972 and the peak of 45 coming in 1973.[41]

Japanese capital was involved at every level throughout the 1970s, principally in joint ventures in resource development, textiles, car assembly, and pharmaceuticals, but also in loans for major projects in petrochemicals and natural gas. By 1976 Japan's energy-related loans were twice its foreign investments, which themselves had already in 1974 replaced those from the United States as the single largest source of foreign capital.[42] Table 9.10 shows that Indonesia was then a close second only to South Korea as an outlet for Japanese textile investments (Thailand came third), but the top venue for synthetic fibres and rope. These investments were made by large textile companies and *sōgō shōsha* (general trading companies), typically in concert, with half of the latter's FDI in the industry concentrated in Indonesia.[43]

Japanese capitalists worked closely behind the scenes with leading generals

Table 9.9

Japanese FDI in Indonesia, by Date and Industry

	1951–1980		1981–1986		1987–1992		1951–1992	
	$mil.	No.	$mil.	No.	$mil.	No.	$mil.	No.
Manufacturing	1,528	566	835	254	**2,814**	362	5,177	1,182
Textiles	**345**	120	143	48	257	92	745	260
Wood/pulp	57	60	35	30	**217**	45	309	135
Chemicals	73	93	58	43	**1,409**	55	1,540	191
Metals	**753**	96	460	44	267	44	1,480	184
Elec. machinery	39	29	15	9	**174**	33	228	71
Trans. machinery	61	31	73	32	**252**	16	386	79
Non-manufacturing	**2,888**	365	3,414	197	2,922	354	9,224	916
Agr./for./fish.	**169**	168	31	69	63	71	263	308
Mining	**2,522**	35	3,247	24	1,288	77	7,057	136
Finance/insurance	65	19	9	10	**943**	41	1,017	70
Services	48	18	59	43	**382**	90	489	151
Total	4,424	976	4,249	451	5,736	716	14,409	2,143

Source: Ōkurashō (Ministry of Finance), *Zaisei kinyū tōkei geppō, Tainaigai minkan tōshi tokushū* (Special issue on internal and external private investments), no. 500 (December 1991), pp. 68–69 and 1993, pp. 60–61.

Bold figures indicate the periods in which each industry received the largest investments.

Table 9.10

Japanese Textile Investments in Asia, March 1974 ($1,000)

	Synthetic fiber	Spinning weaving	Knitting mill	Cordage and rope	Apparel	Other made up	Other	Total
Taiwan	11,938	7,536	998	167	1,322	215	603	22,779
South Korea	23,777	102,174	2,471	381	3,404	206	94	132,507
Hong Kong	—	16,047	1,147	16	3,451	—	—	20,661
Philippines	2,230	1,389	559	—	652	—	—	4,830
Indonesia	47,450	67,459	—	6,292	—	400	—	121,601
Thailand	8,048	36,631	135	1,745	508	610	—	47,677
Malaysia	6,098	18,068	383	—	827	67	—	25,443
Singapore	20	2,898	245	81	691	85	10	4,030
Total	99,561	252,202	5,938	8,682	10,855	1,583	707	379,528

Source: Kunjo Yoshihara, *Japanese Investment in Southeast Asia* (Honolulu: University of Hawaii Press, 1978), p. 110.

and proved themselves equal to the demands of graft and corruption that dealing with the Indonesian bureaucracy required. It was thus natural that they should be the target of the periodic outbursts of protest against foreign capital and corruption, as occurred with considerable rioting in 1974. The burning down of Toyota's joint venture company was the most conspicuous of the many signs that the "rush" into Indonesia had revived an anti-Japanese nationalism which would remain a permanent problem.

Together with the oil shock, which lifted Indonesia's finances into unheard-of surpluses, the political events of 1974 signaled a shift in the balance of power away from foreign capital towards the Indonesian ruling class. Foreigners were given strict limits within which to work, and then only when the scale and level of technology were too great for local capital to do the job. There were requirements to achieve 51 percent Indonesian ownership within ten years, to have all investments as joint ventures, to favor *pribumi* (indigenous Malays), and to exclude foreign capital from sectors where domestic capital might take over. Priority was given to major resource-processing projects, but in order to establish forward and backward linkages to promote a more even development across the whole range of industries.

All this was really only feasible because oil money allowed unprecedented independence from foreign capital, providing around 60 percent of government revenue and 70 percent of export earnings in this period. The result was rapid accumulation centering on a number of domestic conglomerates under the protection of the state, such as Salim, Astra, Rodamas, Bakrie, and Mercu Buana. Industry (manufacturing, mining, and construction) grew at a rate of 12.6 percent in 1972–1980, and realised domestic investment exceeded realized foreign investment, reversing the trend of the previous period.[44]

The industrial restructuring out of the heavy-chemical and resource-processing industries that the oil crisis had forced on Japanese capital was partly accompanied by their relocation abroad. So although the investment climate in Indonesia was cooler towards Japanese capital after 1974, there were forces in both countries which maintained the alliance. The Indonesian side needed the technology and finance which Japanese capital in the heavy resource and chemical industries commanded, while the latter was happy to find an overseas outlet for industries it was running down domestically. But with the rise of the yen, Japanese capital's interest in Indonesia shifted to its low wages for labor-intensive manufacturing.

Most of the leading Indonesian conglomerates which rose to prominence in the 1970s, especially those with some strength in manufacturing, developed on the basis of tie-ups with foreign capital, mainly Japanese, although not quite to the extent that they did in Thailand. In some cases, especially in resource-related industries, state patronage was more important in the group's early development than were connections with foreign capital. Table 9.11 ranks the main Indonesian business groups by their estimated turnover in 1993.

The most notorious of these is the Salim group, whose influence not only traverses the entire Indonesian economy, but extends worldwide.[45] At least 200 companies are bound to the group, whose power network is primarily held to-

Table 9.11

Ranking of Indonesian Business Groups, 1993

Group	Main industries	Bil.R
Salim	Cement, finance, motor vehicles	18,000
Astra International	Motor vehicles, plantations	6,000
Sinar Mas	Paper, pulp, fats and oils	4,200
Lippo	Finance, property	4,750
Gudang Garam	Cloves, tobacco	3,600
Bob Hasan	Timber, tea plantations	3,400
Barito Pacific	Timber, plywood	3,050
Bimantara	Commerce, property, chemicals	3,000
Argo Manunggai	Textiles	2,940
Djarum	Cloves, tobacco	2,360
Dharmala	Agricultural product processing, property	2,530
Ongko	Property, finance	2,100
Panion	Finance	2,081
Rodamas	Chemicals	2,000
Surya Raya	Property, plantations, commerce	1,975

Source: Inoue, *Ajia no zaibatsu to kigyō*, 1994 ed., p. 295.

gether by personal and institutional connections and comprises three main tentacles: the companies which are directly controlled by the Liem family, the Bank of Central Asia (BCA) group (which cooperates with the Suharto family), and the Lippo group, which is controlled by Liem's right-hand man, Mochtar Riady. Deep and complicated connections between the Liem family, Suharto's family, and leading members of the Chinese community are forged by interlocking directorships and the pattern of stock holding in the companies of the different subgroups. For example, the president and holder of 10 percent of the shares in Bogasali, the nationwide giant which monopolizes flour manufacturing, is Suharto's younger cousin. Moreover, according to Bogasali's articles of incorporation, 5 percent of profits go to a foundation set up for the wives of the president and the generals.

Starting out in his uncle's peanut oil business, Liem Sioe Liong (alias Sudono Salim) moved into trading and military supplies during the independence struggle of 1945–1949, when he built his crucial links with senior military officers, including Suharto. But his empire developed only after Suharto came to power and gave him lucrative government concessions, like the monopoly right to import cloves. In the 1960s Liem entered the textile business, obtaining bulk supplies of cloth from the military and having products made cheaply elsewhere, and in 1969 he founded Bogasali, receiving the monopoly right to manufacture flour in western Indonesia and later nationally. In 1975 he set up a cement factory, which grew rapidly in the boom of the 1970s, and in 1989 the group's core company, Indocement, was listed on the stock exchange. Toward the end of the 1970s, Liem branched into real estate, developing upper-class housing in cooperation with Marubeni. In 1975 Liem began to assemble Volvo knockdown sets, later adding Suzuki, Hino, Mazda, Ford, and Nissan as well as diesel engines. In 1983 he acquired a majority share in Suzuki's motorcycle assembly plant, and the three Japanese majors remain closely linked to Salim group members in the industry: National Motor, Unicor Prima, Indo Mobil Utama, and Indohero. In 1987 Liem opened a steel sheet factory for motor vehicles. Overseas, he has long had close ties with the top groups in Taiwan, Hong Kong, Singapore, and Thailand (particularly with the Sophonpanich family).

Although the Salim empire has achieved a degree of power and independence from foreign capital which is rare in Southeast Asia, it does not have the technical-industrial base which is vital to real independence. Cement and flour have been its central productive activities, but both remain heavily dependent on state concessions and government projects. It is significant that Salim's foreign investments have concentrated on commerce and finance, and not on any manufacturing line in which productive forces have advanced sufficiently to hold their own internationally. When Liem entered fields requiring a technical-industrial base, such as motor vehicles, he had to work closely with foreign capital. One of his most recent ventures in this industry is with Sumitomo Rubber in a $120 million tire (35 percent for export) and golfball plan (100 percent for export) which is to begin production in 1997.[46]

A similar conclusion could be drawn in relation to the second largest group in Indonesia, Astra, since although manufacturing in high-tech industries is relatively more important than in the Salim group, so too is the dependence on foreign capital and technology overwhelmingly Japanese. It was thus not accidental that Astra Motor (Toyota) was targeted in the anti-Japanese riots of 1974.[47]

The group's core company, Astra (later Astra International), was founded in 1957 by Tjia Kian Liong (alias William Suryadijaya), whose first business experience was in selling soft drinks and exporting agricultural products. But in 1962 he reconstituted GM's previously nationalized factory and established a car assembly company, Gaya Motor. When his plan to assemble GM cars failed, he turned to Toyota, beginning a very profitable series of ventures with Toyota, Daihatsu, and Honda. Encouraged by the government's ISI policy, the Astra group expanded into motor vehicle components, again in cooperation with Japanese companies such as Nippondenso, which is Toyota's chief components maker and a multinational in its own right. Thereafter it began to produce engines for cars (with Daihatsu and Toyota) and motorcycles (with Honda) as another step towards its goal, a national car. Since the Astra group was firmly locked into ISI, the collapse of the oil price in the 1980s, which slashed domestic demand, critically affected its fortunes, as did the rising cost of imported car parts following the higher yen. The group thus shifted into export production, including auto parts, a strategy which perfectly suited the interests of its Japanese partners.

During the late 1980s, of the 7 core companies (out of the total of 200, 180 of which were domestic) in the group, 6 were closely linked to Japanese capital: Astra Graphia (licensed Fuji Xerox dealer), Astra Motor Sales (Toyota dealer), Federal Motor (Honda motorcycle assembly and sales), Daihatsu Indonesia (Daihatsu car and parts maker), United Tractor (Komatsu dealer and partner in truck assembly) and Multi Astra (Toyota assembly). The seventh, Midas Oil, was an offshoot of the U.S. giant, Caltex. Other major joint ventures with Japanese interests included PT Kutai Timber Indonesia, which was set up in 1970 with Sumitomo Forestry. But in 1992 the group underwent a major reorganization when the founding family members (William Suryadijaya's four children) disposed of their share holdings, and ownership of Astra International, which at the end of 1994 boasted the largest turnover among the 220 companies quoted on the Jakarta stock exchange, was taken over by large private interests, government financial institutions, foreigners (largely Toyota-related), and individual shareholders, in that order. Hence what constitutes the Astra group today are the 78 companies directly and indirectly related to the parent Astra International. The companies owned by the Suryadijaya family now constitute the Surya Raya group.[48]

Since its separation from the control of its founding family, Astra International has become more amenable to the interests of Japanese capital. Although the share of group profits from motor vehicles fell from around 80 percent to 70 percent in the period 1987–1992, the shares of heavy machinery and of finance and services (mainly motor vehicle finance) almost tripled to 13.8 percent and 10 percent respectively, with electronics parts rising by half a percentage point to almost 4 percent. Joint ventures with Japanese capital dominate each of the group's main areas of specialization: PT Komatsu Indonesia in heavy machinery, PT Toyota-Astra Motor and PT Astra Daihatsu Motor in cars, PT Honda Astra Engine Manufacturing and PT Honda Federal Incorporated in motorcycles, and a whole range of Toyota-related companies in component manufacturing: PT Nippondenso Indonesia, PT Daikin Clutch Indonesia, PT Kayaba Indonesia, PT Kokusai Godo Denso, PT Showa Indonesia Manufacturing, PT GS Battery and PT Steel Centre Indonesia. It is thus no exaggeration to say that the Astra group functions as a local receptacle for and facilitator of the investments in Indonesia of a number of key Japanese companies. Japanese cars account for 90 percent of the Indonesia market, with those in the Astra group occupying half the Japanese share, and the Salim group affiliates (Suzuki, Mazda, and Nissan) and the others (Mitsubishi and Honda) making up the rest.[49]

A much smaller group, but one with an even greater dependence on Japanese capital is Rodamas (literally "gold exporter"), founded and still personally managed by Tan Siong Kie (alias Hanafi), who remains one of the wealthiest persons in the country. Tan made his fortune mainly in a joint venture with Asahi Glass set up in 1973, PT Asahimas Flat Glass (which has 2,745 workers today), and its offshoot in 1976, PT Asahimas Jaya Safety Glass (for cars), both of whose success derived from a combination of state concessions and the power of Japanese capital. Today he directly controls 29 companies, mainly in manufacturing but also in finance, insurance, and real estate. The most important of these, PT Asahimas Subentra Chemical, commenced production of plastics (PVC, EDC, VCM) in 1988. Capitalized at $420 million with Asahi Glass providing 45 percent and Rodamas and Subentra the remainder, the project represented the largest investment from Japan for eight years. Other core joint venture companies in the group included Summitmas Property, with Sumitomo & Co., PT Salompas Indonesia, with Hisamitsu Seiyaku, and P.T. Dai Nippon Printing, with the Japanese company of the same name. More so than any other in Indonesia, the Rodamas group owes its origin and continued strength mainly to Tan's tie-ups with Japanese capital.[50]

With the partial exception of Salim, which depended on both state concessions and foreign capital, *pribumi* groups have relied more on the former and *cukong* (Chinese) ones more on the latter, perhaps because *pribumi* groups, which command fewer financial and entrepreneurial resources than the Chinese groups, are relatively more involved in agricultural and raw-material-related industries and Chinese ones relatively more in finance and manufacturing. Bakrie, the second largest of the *pribumi* groups but still small compared to the Chinese ones, is typical of this tendency. Only one of its core companies, PT Bakrie Kasei Corporation, has Japanese (Mitsubishi Kasei) participation and was set up only in 1991, although Bakrie's core steel-pipe manufacturing firm is one of a growing number of cooperative ventures with U.S. capital. A major recent creation, PT Seamless Pipe Indonesia Jaya, was a $600 million joint venture with the Hong Kong–registered U.S. company, Asia Pacific Pipe Investments, and had been guaranteed a variety of subsidies and supports from the state. Although it was to commence production in 1990, the project was finally aborted. The Bakrie group's main growth strategy has thus tended to be cooperation with government and merger and takeover rather than reliance on advanced technology in cooperation with foreign capital. [51]

Another reason for this tendency is political and has been changing over the years. In the pre-Suharto period Indonesian nationalism distanced the *pribumi* somewhat from foreign capital, but an increasingly conservative post-Suharto nationalism has drawn them into growing cooperation with foreign firms. For example, a *pribumi* group which is even more dependent on Japanese capital than the Chinese Astra group is Gobel, which rose to prominence on Matsushita's coattails following Sukarno's fall and which today comprises mainly joint ventures with Matsushita.[52] These include PT National Gobel (1970), PT Met and Gobel (1974), PT Matsushita Gobel Battery Industry (1987), PT National Panasonic Gobel (1991), PT Matsushita Gobel Electric Mfg. (1992) and PT Matsushita Denko Gobel (1993).[53]

An important remaining area of cooperation between Japanese and *pribumi* capital takes place in state projects and government-owned industries, which

tend to be concentrated in large-scale labor-intensive or resource-related projects, of which the most outstanding is Asahad.[54] One of the offshoots of this
cooperation in the 1980s has been the largest *pribumi* group in the country, the
diversified conglomerate Bimantara, which comprises 82 companies held together by the core firm Bimantara Chitra and associated with Suharto's family
members, who have used it to secure their future for when the president finally
disappears from the scene and can no longer deliver his customary favors.[55]

While distinguishing *pribumi* from Chinese capital reflects a real fractional
difference within the Indonesian ruling class, the division only exists meaning-
fully within the upper class, and does not, as in Malaysia where the Chinese
population forms a substantial proportion of the working class, become an inter-
class division as well. From the point of view of the Indonesian masses, it
matters little whether capital is *pribumi* or non-*pribumi*. Apart from the state
enterprises, which are unambiguously *pribumi*, and the business groups, which
can be identified one way or the other, is often very difficult to tell whether or
not a company is *pribumi*. Many Chinese interests are so-called "Ali-Baba"
firms, which have *pribumi*, often important government officials and military
officers, as their representatives in order to secure favorable treatment from the
state. One study which tried to identify how far Japanese capital favors joint
ventures with *pribumi* or non-*pribumi* elements in the ruling class eventually
gave up in despair. Having discovered so many layered linkages among military
officers and Chinese and *pribumi* capitalists, it concluded that the class forces
which bind the different fractions of the Indonesian ruling class together vastly
overshadow the ethnic and institutional forces which divide them. [56]

There is no question that liberal government revenues following the oil price
hikes of the 1970s helped local capital extend its independence, even though
foreign capital remained an important ally and often found ways around the
regulations that limited its participation. For example, joint ventures operated
under increasingly high debt-equity ratios (up to 80:20), with foreign capital
holding the debt and thus the balance of power. A typical case was PT Toyota
Mobilindo (parts maker), in which the Astra group contributed $3.9 million,
which was 43.3 percent of total equity capital. However, a further $23.8 million
was borrowed, reducing Astra's share of the total investment to less than 12
percent. Similarly, the Indonesian government's share in the Asahan project fell
from 25 percent of equity capital to a mere 5 percent of the investment because
79 percent of it was financed by loans, from Japan.[57]

The collapse of oil prices in the early 1980s plunged Indonesian capitalism
into its deepest crisis since 1967. Growth came to an abrupt halt, and the
nation's debt soared, just to maintain government expenditure and cover the
trade deficit. Foreign capital's leverage, from the loans it provided and the fact
that it suddenly became the main source of investment, was reminiscent of the
immediate post-Sukarno years. FDI regulations were liberalized, export-oriented
industrialization was fully accepted, state projects were transferred to the private

sector, interest rates were decontrolled, and the currency was massively devalued. Almost all the recommendations in a 1981 World Bank report on Indonesia, which were ignored at the time, were implemented.

Japanese FDI in Indonesia slowed down as a result of this crisis, which was partly why the regulations were so extensively liberalized in August 1986. But even in the worst year, 1987, investment from Japan remained larger than from anywhere else, as did Japan's accumulated total. The devaluation of the rupee and the rise of the yen that year once again made Indonesian wages an irresistible lure for Japanese capital. In the first half of 1987, total FDI in Indonesia increased fourfold over the year before to $624 million, of which 55 percent was in new ventures. Much of the expansion by existing foreign firms came from Japan, as companies shifted into export-oriented projects, not just in textiles as before, but now also in car components, electrical machinery, and pharmaceuticals. Ajinomoto established a special large-scale factory for producing monosodium glutamate for export to China, Taiwan, and Africa. Inoue Rubber made its Indonesian subsidiary a base for export to the United States in place of South Korea and Taiwan. PT Asaminas Flat Glass massively increased its capacity, in order to commence worldwide exports and to make it the largest supplier in Southeast Asia. Other companies to expand or start up export activities in this period included Teijin (to increase apparel exports), Toto (to make high-quality bath sets for export throughout Europe and Asia, including Japan) and Hitachi Shipbuilding (its first venture in Indonesia, to make components for chemical plants for worldwide export). The Japan Pulp & Paper Company, which had been exporting paper to Indonesia but which had decided to close its Jakarta office due to falling demand, suddenly realized Indonesia's potential as a cheap production site and reversed the decision. In motor vehicles, falling domestic demand by 1987 also persuaded Federal Motor, which makes Honda motorcycles under license, to commence exports to China.[58]

The 1990s have seen a further extension of this trend, with the amounts of approved foreign investment exceeding approved domestic investment by almost two to one in most years. In 1989, the proportion was almost three to one. Although the excess of foreign over domestic fell in 1994, this was only because the surge in the former matched the massive 200 percent increase in the latter, largely because the so-called PP-20 deregulation package announced mid-year allowed a full 100 hundred percent foreign ownership and removed ten sectors from the "negative" list, including motor vehicles and tobacco. As was pointed out by a local business consultant: "foreigners no longer have to pay Indonesians to be involved with their business."[59] In the first six months of 1995 alone, the $21 billion worth of approved foreign investment almost equalled the previous year's massive total of $24 billion.[60] Table 9.12 indicates the breakdown by country of origin of approved projects since 1967, but it excludes investments in finance, oil, gas, and energy, all sectors of even greater dependence on Japan. The latter's predominance is thus unchallenged, and Indonesia has come to de-

Table 9.12

Total Approved Net FDI in Indonesia, by Country of Origin, to 1992

	1967–1986		1967–1992	
	Cases	$mil.	Cases	$mil.
Japan	221	5,251.4	517	13,068
Hong Kong	116	1,880.6	237	5,238
United States	91	1,215.8	144	2,716
Holland	52	685.2	97	2,256
United Kingdom	58	605.0	121	2,454
Germany	30	501.3	55	1,865
Singapore	34	313.7	190	2,059
Australia	32	292.9	125	1,275
Hong Kong	—	—	237	5,238
Taiwan	—	—	250	3,936
South Korea	—	—	276	2,965
Others*	171	5,062.9	414	25,184
Total	805	15,808.8	2,426	63,016

Source: Badan Koordinasi Penanaman Modal (Investment Coordinating Board) to 1986, thereafter Nihon bōeki shinkōkai, *1994 Jietoro hakusho*, 1994, p. 200.

*Before 1986 includes Taiwan and South Korea; after 1986 includes multinational.

pend more heavily on Japanese capital than ever before. To compensate for an excessive reliance on oil and gas rents, the Indonesian ruling class has tried to boost manufacturing exports, but this has in turn made it more vulnerable to the whims of Japanese capital, especially high-tech export firms in quest of lower wages to compensate for the higher yen.

Much of Indonesia's attraction in recent years has stemmed from the way it combines low wages to reduce costs with a market of almost limitless potential, especially in industries most critical to Japan's industrial structure, that is, electrical and transport machinery. Manufacturing absorbed a full 65 percent of Japanese investment in the country in 1992, with expansions by existing textile companies, such as Toray, and motor vehicle and electrical companies, such as Toyota and Sanyo, comprising especially significant increases. Also important were joint ventures, in public housing and golf courses, between Taisei Construction and the Salim group ($2.6 billion), and in hotels, by Mitsui and Japan Airlines. In 1993, the weight of manufacturing was even greater.[61] Japan's revolutionary role in Indonesian capitalism remains unchallenged.

Malaysia

The impetus Japan's occupation of Malaya gave to decolonization was more ambiguous than in Indonesia. On the one hand, the Japanese cruelly persecuted the Malayan Chinese upon taking over the country, massacring thousands of individuals in the *sook ching*, or "purification" program, but on the other they gave moderate encouragement to Malay and Indian nationalism. The latter strategy was intended as much to strike against Western imperialism in Indonesia and India as against the British in Malaya. They also cynically encouraged ethnic conflict among the peoples of Malaya, relying on the same means as the British to preserve their rule.

For their part, the British failed to see that they had been expelled in 1941 partly by nationalist forces which had gained momentum during the war, and they used every means at their disposal in an attempt to regain their position afterwards: an unprecedented use of military power (equalled only during the Vietnam War) during the "Emergency" period and as calculated a campaign of racist divide-and-rule as had ever been employed outside South Africa. But the best they could hope for was some sort of neo-colonial set-up, and they did everything possible to bolster a specifically conservative Malay nationalist movement under the leadership of the Sultans. To the present day, the United Malay Nationalist Organisation (UMNO) has maintained a close alliance with the leading foreign powers of the region, chiefly Japan.[62]

The only way to check postwar revolutionary nationalism, which was based on the mainly Chinese working class, was by mobilizing a right-wing anti-Chinese nationalism, and the Malay community was open to such manipulation. With the vast majority of its members in a peasantry which was even worse off than the working class, it provided a popular base on which the country's traditional elite could safely raise a nationalist banner. The interests of labor could be presented as somehow "foreign," while peasant interests could be sacrificed on the pretext that the state looked after Malay needs. By framing every policy in terms of the "race" of the people affected, rather than of the situations they were in, UMNO got away with furthering the interests of only the upper class, as well as with shifting members of the traditional elite from their old to their new positions of power.

Even though the largest ethnic group among today's working class is Malay rather than Chinese or Indian, UMNO continues to win support from poor Malay workers and peasants, because it promises to single them out for upward class mobility. Any political movement that attempts to tackle the circumstances confronting the poor, who comprise members of all ethnic groups, is branded as being opposed to the Malay nation.[63] The same tactic has been used by the traditional elite in a country to which the British bequeathed a tragically similar heritage, namely, Fiji.

The way class conflict has been communalized in Malaysia crucially affects the form in which foreign and local capital cooperate. Both sides know that their interests can only be protected so long as chauvinistic Malay nationalism is fed, not by policies which improve the lot of the poor, but ones which alter the ethnic composition of the rich. Both sides continue to accept the logic of the New

Economic Policy (NEP), which was never to transfer wealth from one class to another, but to ensure that Malay individuals (and institutions) would occupy jobs in proportion to their numbers in the total population and own 30 percent of capital, with foreigners owning a further 30 percent and other Malaysians the rest. Although the goal had been achieved on the employment front by the target date of 1990, Malays still owned only 20 percent of capital with other Malaysians owning 46 percent. The foreign share had been brought to 25 percent by relying heavily on such expedients as having foreign companies incorporate themselves in Malaysia.[64]

The Chinese and Indian members of the upper class, organized in the Malaysian Chinese Association (MCA) and the Malaysian Indian Congress, have gone along with the communal strategy for controlling the masses and play a comparable role within their communities to UMNO within the Malay community. If Malay workers and peasants vote UMNO because it supposedly helps them rise out of their classes, then many Chinese and Indian individuals vote along ethnic lines for similar reasons. The causes of poverty, rather than who will stay poor, remain firmly excluded from the political agenda.

Only when the rich cannot get from the Barisan national coalition (previously the National Front) what they want, as was the experience of the MCA over the government's decision some years ago to allow non-Mandarin speakers to assume senior positions in Chinese primary schools, does the coalition threaten to fall apart.[65] In that respect, the division between *bumiputra* (indigenous Malays) and Chinese is an intra-class one similar to the division in Indonesia, having salience only within the upper class. However, since a considerable proportion of Malaysian workers is also Chinese, the division exists within the working class as well and thus affects inter-class relations, whose broad limits are set by the structure of capital accumulation and the continued importance of foreign capital.

Neither *merdeka* (independence) nor the NEP brought any resolve to alter the structure of what was in ASEAN the most uneven development spearheaded by unequalled foreign ownership. Two commodities dominated production (for export), and European companies controlled most of it: 83 percent of rubber estates, 62 percent of tin output, and 60 percent of commerce. FDI was intended to remain the motor of growth, the 1968 Investment Incentives Act providing extremely attractive fiscal encouragement for firms in pioneer, export, and labor-intensive industries. The government also provided 21 industrial estates scattered all over the country as well as four free-trade zones, where foreign export companies could get tax-free use of local labor and land. Today Johor alone boasts 20 industrial estates with plans for another 12 before the end of the century, covering 2,700 hectares.[66]

However, although NEP was not conceived as a strategy of national against foreign capital, but one of comprador capital[67] against the peasantry and working class, it had effects along the former lines. Since too few Malay individuals had the money to buy shares, the government set up public companies to act in trust for the *bumiputra* community, eventually selling their shares to *bumiputra* individuals. During the rapid growth of the 1970s, these trust agencies, notably Perbadanan Nasional (PERNAS) and later the Permodalan Nasional Berhad (PNB), aggressively bought shares in, merged with, or totally took over established foreign companies. By 1982 the government had invested $2.4 billion for PNB to acquire companies.[68]

The result of NEP was not just a substantial shift in the proportions of *bumiputra*, other Malaysian and foreign-share ownership (to 21.9 percent, 48.4 percent, and 29.7 percent in 1985),[69] but the creation of institutionally based indigenous capitalists with their own vested interests. As in Indonesia, the state served as a base for the rise of a national bourgeoisie, high oil prices provided the funds for state spending, and then the collapse of commodity prices plunged the government into fiscal crisis and a dangerous level of international debt, thus shifting the balance of power back in foreign capital's favor.

It is important not to exaggerate the independence achieved before the bubble burst in 1985. The power of foreign capital is not limited to the share holdings of foreign residents, and even minority holdings in joint ventures can coincide with very high levels of actual foreign control. Moreover, government-appointed directors are often politicians with little understanding of the businesses concerned, whereas the foreign directors are normally experienced company people. The influence of Japanese capital in Malaysia has thus increased steadily, partly because of a relative decline in ownership of British firms, partly because Japan's extraordinary technological might lifts the power of Japanese firms well above the level of their actual shareholdings.

Since the British were still in Malaya when reparations agreements were concluded with Japan, they claimed the bulk of the indemnity. But when the mass graves of Chinese victims of the Japanese occupation were discovered in Singapore in 1962, the question of blood obligation was raised, although the Japanese refused to recognize it and matters dragged on until 1967 when they finally offered two ships. Even though a few investments had occurred before this, such as the large joint venture with Yawata Steel (Malayawata), most of the characteristic FDI in textiles and electrical components took place afterwards.[70]

From the outset NEP suited Japanese capital, which was content to set up joint ventures with *bumiputra* (and other) interests. Because the targets of the takeovers and mergers were British firms, the temptation to play the different foreign interests off against one another proved irresistible. At least this was how Mahatir's policy of "Look East" was interpreted in the 1980s, although when pressed he always insisted that he was addressing the labor movement: emulate the Japanese work ethic instead of the "English sickness" (class struggle). Whatever the intention, a clear consequence of NEP was a shift in the relative strengths of British and Japanese capital. Table 9.13 shows MIDA's (Malaysian Industrial Development Authority) record of accumulated FDI (fixed-asset basis) by country of origin to December 1992. Japan is prominently in the top position,

Table 9.13

Accumulated FDI in Malaysia by Country of Origin (Rmil.)*

	Accumulated total to:			Incremental amounts in:		
	1985	1986	1987	1988	1989–1990	1991–1992
Japan	1,642	4,657	4,335	561	2,843	6,390
Singapore	1,462	1,500	1,480	172	591	1,557
United Kingdom	2,196	2,188	2,188	95	—	1,850
United States	479	533	503	253	314	5,097
Holland	266	121	153	—	—	141
Hong Kong	379	511	653	130	249	—
Taiwan	—	55	84	384	3,266	5,107
Germany	139	172	170	26	—	—
France	—	—	—	—	—	4,093
Others	1,140	889	891	390	2,406	10,592
Total	7,666	10,626	10,457	2,010	9,629	34,827

Source: Nihon Bōeki Shinkōkai, *Jietoro hakusho, tōshihen: sekao to Nihon no kaigai chokusetsu tōshi,* 1990, p. 439, 1994, p. 194; Aoki Takeshi, "Nihon no chokusetsu tōshi to netowāku keisei'(Japan's foreign investment and network formation), in Kohama Hirohisa ed., *Chokusetsu tōshi to kōgyōka: Nihon, NIES, ASEAN* (Direct investment and industrialization: Japan, NIES and ASEAN) (Tokyo: Nihon Bōeki Shinkōkai, 1992), p. 65.

*Amounts exclude hotels and tourism after 1987; all amounts include the loans required by the investments; other investors include all countries for which specific amounts are not noted; and gaps indicate the absence from my sources of specific data, usually because the amounts in the relevant years were not large enough to be noted.

although the continued importance of Britain is understated by this purely book-value measure of foreign capital's presence.

Although substantial investments were also made in the 1970s and early 1980s, the most rapid "rush" by Japanese firms into Malaysia was after 1986 into the manufacturing industry, when the forces culminating in the high yen crisis most strongly expressed themselves. Each of the three main waves of FDI focused on a range of industries and was related to obstacles to accumulation in Japan, as revealed by Table 9.14. If the years 1981–1986 were ones of reduced Japanese investment with the exception of the metals branches of manufacturing, then the period since 1987 was one of all-around skyrocketing growth, with the 1970s having importance mainly in mining, textiles, and chemicals.

The first wave of investment was in the labor-intensive industries threatened by rising wages in Japan towards the mid-1960s, chiefly electrical goods and textiles. As in Indonesia, these could only get underway after the political climate had been cleared in 1967. However, within a decade Japanese capital was the leader in both industries: 10 out of 21 foreign-controlled electrical machinery companies were Japanese, as were 15 out of 22 foreign-controlled textile companies. In the forefront were the majors: Toray (two fully owned polyester

Table 9.14

Japanese FDI in Malaysia, by Date and Industry (reported basis)*

	1951–1980		1981–1986		1987–1992		1951–1992	
	$mil.	No.	$mil.	No.	$mil.	No.	$mil.	No.
Manufacturing	456	332	400	212	**2,625**	528	3,481	1,072
Textiles	**105**	38	32	11	20	15	157	64
Wood/pulp	45	62	7	10	76	51	128	123
Chemicals	**168**	41	21	13	251	41	440	95
Metals	29	32	**124**	25	264	67	417	124
Gen. machinery	8	10	6	15	**224**	34	238	59
Elec. machinery	52	55	75	61	**1,180**	169	1,307	285
Trans. machinery	7	9	88	23	**132**	16	227	48
Non-manufacturing	189	238	228	190	**905**	219	1,322	647
Mining	**120**	32	28	1	134	6	282	39
Construction	5	25	21	70	**102**	37	128	132
Commerce	12	69	**96**	59	86	40	194	168
Finance/insurance	6	15	42	9	**139**	19	187	43
Services	8	12	14	20	**188**	53	210	85
Real estate	—	—	8	7	**206**	42	215	49
Total	650	603	633	406	3,532	747	4,815	1,756

Source: Ōkurashō (Ministry of Finance), *Zaisei kinyū tōkei geppō: Tainaigai minkan tōshi tokushū*, no. 476 (December 1991), p. 7,273 and no. 500 (December 1993), pp. 64–65.
*Bold figures indicate the periods in which each industry received the largest investments.

factories in free trade zones), Toyobo, Kanebo, Matsushita (with its six projects, mainly in free trade zones), Sanyo, Toshiba, and NEC. In both industries the investments were in labor-intensive unskilled areas, such as assembly, and had as their overriding motive the use of Malaysia's highly disciplined and under-paid work force.[71]

About the same time a second wave began to build in order to exploit Malaysian resources. It gained momentum in the 1970s following the oil crisis and then gradually tapered off in the 1980s. The projects ranged from Malayawata Steel (1962) through a whole series of investments related to timber (Daishowa Pulp, many commercial investments in Sabah and Sarawak for importing logs, and a few ventures in furniture), food, mining, and Malaysia's richest resources, rubber and palm oil. A series of investments in chemicals, particularly polluting ones, accompanied the quest for raw materials, as Japanese capital relocated abroad much of the heavy industry which in the 1970s was being replaced by machinery as the hub of the industrial structure.[72]

The current tidal wave of investments in the machinery industries was drawn into Malaysia by its cheap labor, although a state-led building boom was an additional attraction for the many construction companies that entered in the 1980s. While falling commodity prices put a virtual end to the building boom, the merits of cheap labor increased with the higher yen. Component manufacture and assembly in the electronics and to a lesser extent car industries were the typical targets of the rush into Malaysia.

The crisis of falling incomes and negative GNP growth in the mid-1980s threw the Malaysian government at the mercy of foreign capital, and in September 1986 a new set of conditions was announced for FDI providing generous fiscal incentives and permitting 100 percent ownership for companies which exported over 50 percent of their output and employed 350 full-time workers in accordance with the country's ethnic composition.[73] Table 9.13 shows that throughout this recent period Japanese FDI again greatly exceeded that from other countries. Already in 1986, if the large Dutch petroleum-related chemical project is ignored, Japan was the clear leader, with 44 approved projects worth M$67.6 million and employing 7,907 workers.[74]

The rush into Malaysia extended the alliance between the Malaysian and Japanese ruling classes, because the rise of the yen, which forced Japanese capital abroad, fortuitously coincided with the collapse in the prices of commodities, which constituted Malaysian capital's traditional source of independence. The most remarkable response was in the electronics and motor vehicle industries, especially semiconductors, which became Malaysia's top export item already in 1986, even exceeding crude oil, and making Malaysia the world's third largest producer of semiconductor components. Plants in the free trade zones of Penang and Kuala Lumpur formed a version of Silicon Valley, but with a crucial difference. Of the two major production processes—writing patterns on wafers and attaching frames—only the latter, the more labor intensive, was significantly transferred to Malaysia. Until recently, the more technically advanced initial process had remained entirely in the home countries of the investing companies. But while America's National Semiconductor already in the 1980s opened in Penang the first wafer-fabrication plant in Southeast Asia outside Singapore and Intel the second,[75] Japanese capital revealed little willingness to transfer the higher technology. The resulting weakness of the Malaysian side in the alliance was noted by the *Japan Economic Journal*:

> As for the finishing process, wages or workers determine the competitiveness of the products. The wages of workers in Malaysia are relatively low, but still twice those of Thailand's and, if the investment climate in Thailand improves, Malaysia is likely to face a challenge from its northern neighbour.[76]

If cars and electronics attracted the chief interest in the 1980s, and semiconductors received their main boost from the rising yen, then the corresponding peak in motor vehicle investments was around 1984–1985, when component makers were pulled in behind Mitsubishi to capitalize on the national car, Proton Saga.

However, all car makers suffered from falling domestic demand due to the collapse of commodity prices, with Toyota and Mazda even suspending production in November 1986. As in Indonesia, Japanese capital therefore shifted its emphasis towards manufacturing cars for export.

The increasing number of small and medium firms moving to Malaysia, mainly to make parts for the electrical and motor car majors, has not meant the latter are any less active. They remain prominent among the many companies which the higher yen has been driving either into setting up operations in Malaysia or into expanding their existing operations. In consumer electronics, Matsushita continues to lead the way, more than doubling its commitment in the 1990s with seven new projects opening in 1990–1992 alone. The company now employs almost 20,000 Malaysians in its 15 subsidiaries, 12 of which are fully owned by Matsushita group members, and which jointly account for a full 4 percent of Malaysian exports.[77] The large investments in air conditioners included the establishment of an R & D center and transferred effective control of production from Japan to Malaysia, from where the products are now exported to Japan and the United States. Other electrical companies followed suit. Sharp rapidly expanded its color TV and printer base production for export to Europe and the United States, with the output of its third factory, opened in December 1986, representing a calculated shift of what had hitherto been produced in Japan. In June 1990 the company opened a new M$44 million VCR factory in Johor with 1,200 workers. Specifically to circumvent conflict with the United States over semiconductors, Hitachi and Toshiba made large investments to produce 256K DRAM chips, the former adding five projects in 1990–1991 alone to bring the group's total to 14. Like Sharp, Hitachi has transferred entire product lines from Japan to Johor, "which has become a centre for the manufacture of household appliances such as VCRs and televisions."[78] NEC, Fujitsu, and Sony were other electronics companies to climb on the Malaysian bandwagon over the past few years. Sony added five new ventures in 1988–1990 alone, one of them making CD players, radio cassettes, other stereo equipment, and color TVs, all for export. Today Sony employs over 7,000 Malaysians. Among the reasons for its move were "the strong political and economic climate of the country" and "the implementation of the new foreign equity guidelines" of September 1986 allowing 100 percent foreign ownership for exporting companies. If one adds the huge 1,300-worker factory set up in 1991 by Sony's subsidiary, Aiwa, the scale of Sony's move is even more remarkable.[79]

Japanese companies fleeing the high yen have also recently invested in plastic moulds, synthetic resin (Nippon Pigment), and even in raw material processing. In 1988 Fuji Oil and Itochu opened a fully owned palm-oil refinery, for export to Japan and Singapore. Apart from manufacturing, the main interest over the past few years has been in large-scale retailing by such giants as Jusco, Chujitsuya, and Yaohan. The total turnover of Japanese firms currently comprises 15 percent of Malaysia's GNP, confirming their "massive presence."[80]

The significance of the Japanese investment is apparent in the Malaysian partners selected, a growing number of which are state institutions, making the *bumiputra* bureaucratic-based fraction of the ruling class the most important Japanese ally. An early example was Malayawata Steel, which although it began as a private undertaking in 1961, by 1967 became the first industrial project in which the government had a stake. Later on Pernas Engineering acquired a controlling 46 percent of its shares. Today it is the ninth largest Japanese manufacturing company in Malaysia.[81]

The form in which the Malay bourgeoisie allies with Japanese capital is overwhelmingly through the state's NEP and its associated institutions: PNB (Permodalan Nasional Berhad), PERNAS (Pernodalan Nasional), and HICOM (Heavy Industries Corporation of Malaysia, which was recently privatized in a flurry of selling of public assets). Prestige state projects, such as in the costly heavy and resource-related industries, are thus the main ones in which this type of alliance is found, although the difficulties many of the projects have faced have strained the alliance on more than one occasion. I only mention a few examples.

Malaysia LNG is a joint venture between Mitsubishi Corporation, Petronas, and Shell, while Perwaja Trengganu, a large venture between a Nippon Steel consortium and HICOM which was formed in 1982 to make billets and briquetted iron, was a less fortunate product of Matahir's industrialization program of the 1980s. The plant was shut down soon after it opened in February 1987 for failing to produce the output specified in the contract.[82] The most important of the prime minister's industrialisation projects and the most successful from the point of view of Japanese capital was Perusahaan Otomobil Nasional, a joint venture between Mitsubishi and HICOM, which currently employs 3,700 workers making the first country's national car, Proton Saga. Among the Japanese component makers associated with the project was Nippondenso's venture with HICOM, which was also the Malay partner in a number of motorcycle projects, with Honda, Yamaha, and Suzuki.

Proton Saga has faced a mountain of problems. The recession of the mid-1980s coincided with the vehicle's first appearance, and according to sources in rival Japanese companies, each car had to be subsidized by as much as M$15,000. The same sources told me that Mitsubishi would not be updating the design of the car and that Proton would probably become a cheap source of components, especially body panels, for export to Mitsubishi plants elsewhere in Asia. However, the fortunes of operations were revived by a combination of continued government subsidies, the assumption of key top management positions by Mitsubishi appointments, and a revival of the domestic economy. Proton managed to increase its share of the Malaysian car market from 11 percent in 1984 to 73 percent in 1989 (but around 65 percent since then) and gradually even to commence sizable exports. These were not just to Japan's traditional dumping grounds for failed projects (Bangladesh, Sri Lanka, Brunei, Jamaica, and New Zealand), but more recently also to Britain, which now absorbs 85 percent of exported vehicles, which themselves comprise about 20 percent of total production. Following its float on the Kuala Lumpur Stock Exchange in 1992, Proton became Malaysia's ninth largest company and the largest of all with Japanese partners. Its privileged position between the buffers of state protection and Mitsubishi productive, marketing, and financial strength was further consolidated in the early 1990s when it commenced assembly of engines and gearboxes. In May 1993 Mitsubishi licensed technology for the development of a new model, the Wira, which on its appearance on the Australian market was described as having "few indications of . . . being much different to driving a Lancer . . . [or] com[ing] from anywhere other than a Japanese production line.[83] The government was sufficiently pleased with the venture to announce the country's second national car in autumn 1994, to be jointly produced by PNB, UMW (Toyota's ally in the country), and Daihatsu (a Toyota subsidiary in Japan).

But Japanese capital also has some important links with the country's leading Chinese business groups, the largest and most representative of which is Kuok, comprising 23 major companies in Kuala Lumpur alone but well over 100 worldwide. It main activities are in finance and services in Malaysia, Singapore, and Hong Kong, but it also has influence in Thailand, Indonesia, the Philippines, Fiji, Austrialia, and China.

The rise of the Kuok empire began in 1949 with the establishment of the trading company, Kuok Brothers, which dealt mainly in rice and sugar. In the 1950s the leading light of the Kuok family, Robert, formed a joint venture with Mitsui & Co. and Nisshin Sugar Manufacturing. Thus began an intimate relationship with Mitsui as well as the very profitable development of Malayan Sugar Manufacturing, which by the 1960s had given Robert Kuok the title of "Sugar King." Today he controls 80 percent of the Malaysian market and 10 percent of the world market. From its base in sugar, the Kuok group expanded into manufacturing (wheat, flour, synthetic woods, cement, chemicals), shipping, finance, real estate, and most recently hotels, notably Shangri-la hotels. Along the way it accumulated an impressive list of joint ventures with Mitsui (which today has over a dozen joint projects in Malaysia) such as Perlis Plantations, Malayan Adhesives, and Bulk Chemical Terminal; with other Japanese giants (e.g., with Sumitomo in Malaysia Shipyard & Engineering and with Tosco in Century Chemical Words, in Rasa Sayang Hotel and in Hong Kong's Shangri-la Hotel); as well as with other giant Malaysian companies, such as Malayawata Steel, Sime Darby, and Malaysian International Shipping.[84]

Other leading Chinese groups are also relatively well linked to Japanese capital, although they also have ties with other foreign firms as well as with *bumiputra* capital and, like the Kuok group, do not have the importance in the high-tech manufacturing sector which state-sponsored companies do. Chinese groups in Malaysia tend to specialise even more than their counterparts in Indonesia in the service and raw-material-related industries they were involved in during the colonial period. An important example is the Kwek family's Hong Leong group, whose main base is in Singapore but which also has an impressive network of companies in Malaysia and Hong Kong. Its specialty is finance and its main overseas linkages have been with British rather than Japanese capital, but it has entered a number of joint ventures with Japanese companies in manufacturing and trading. Examples include Steel Pipe Industry of Malaysia (with Itochu and Kawasaki Steel) and a few ventures in its main area of growth during the construction boom of the early 1980s: with Mitsubishi in construction machinery, with Takasago in tile manufacturing, with Marubeni in leasing and selling construction equipment, and most recently with Itochu in developing intelligent buildings. Hong Leong also has a number of ventures with Yamaha, making and selling motorcycles (including engines), as well as a joint venture with Mitsui making paper bags.[85] However, the group's chief emphasis has remained in finance, real estate, and construction, and its allies have been in Britain, Hong Kong, and with the Malaysian government rather than with technologically advanced Japanese or U.S. companies. In that sense, it resembles the many Chinese conglomerates throughout Southeast Asia that have continued their colonial emphasis on the industries that service, rather than those which create, the country's wealth.

On the opposite end of the spectrum is another of the big-four Chinese groups in Malaysia, United Motor Works Holdings, which assembles Toyota vehicles in a 1,200-worker joint-venture factory opened in 1982, UMW Toyota Motor, and makes steering parts for the Toyota group in another one opened in July 1992, T. & K. Autoparts. Nippondenso also makes Toyota parts in two joint ventures with HICOM. Apart from its core business in motor cars, UMW Holdings sells and leases construction machinery in a few ventures with Marubeni. One of UMW's main competitors, Tan Chong Motor Holdings, is Nissan's chosen partner in an enormous 3,300-worker factory, Tan Chong Motor Assembly. Of the other Japanese motor vehicle majors, Honda is well-linked to Chinese capital in a number of joint ventures with Oriental Holding, but also to the state in making motorcycle engines. The need for joint-venture partners in the car industry stemmed largely from the pivotal position Mahatir gave to this industry in his industrialisation plans.[86]

In electronics, however, the Malaysian government has allowed 100 percent foreign ownership, and few local partners have been necessary. Japan's main presence has been through Matsushita, Sanyo, Sharp, Sony, Toshiba, NEC, Mitsumi, Hitachi, Alps, and Fujitsu. Both of the recently opened factories by Alps are 100 percent owned, both of Fujitsu's factories are 100 percent owned (although its sales and its service companies are joint ventures), Toshiba's main IC factory is 100 percent owned (although its fax and phone factory opened in 1991 is a joint venture with Inventec Corp.), all three of Mitsumi's factories are also fully owned, Hitachi's massive presence has only a few local participants, and apart from the 52 percent of Matsushita Electric's shares which were sold to the public, the Matsushita group's massive presence is almost entirely Japanese owned, as is that of Sony. Both of the remaining companies, Sharp and Sanyo, which do have major local partners, are allied to Chinese capital, Sharp to the powerful Roxy group. All four of NEC's ventures in Malaysia have local partners, the most important of which is Pernas Engineering.[87]

Because of a phenomenon we found in Indonesia whereby Chinese interests often have Malay front persons in order to receive advantages from the state, it is harder to be certain of the degree to which capital which appears to be *bumiputra* is genuinely so. Even in the case of Sime Darby, the ex-British conglomerate which amassed its wealth in rubber and palm oil plantations but which the NEP managed to convert into a mainly indigenous empire, this is not unproblematic. The company's colonial past reveals strong ties with Chinese interests, and even today its chairperson is the prominent Chinese ex-Finance Minister, Tun Tan Siew Sin. So the threat to Malay control of Sime Darby, the country's top private firm which is second only to the state's petroleum company, Petronas, comes not simply from its British colonial past, but also from Chinese capital. With over 150 companies under its umbrella, including major ones in Singapore, Hong Kong, Thailand, Britain, and the Philippines, as well as an obsession to penetrate China, the conglomerate will never really be fully under Malay control. Nevertheless, because it has sought to expand high-tech manufacturing, it had to find appropriate foreign allies, but these have generally been British. Among its few joint ventures with Japanese companies are Sime Diamond Leasing (with Mitsubishi Bank and Diamond Lease) and Sime Inax, which makes satellite porcelain. The only genuine private *bumiputra* business group, Promet, went into liquidation in the mid-1980s.[88]

The alliance between Malaysian and Japanese capital continues to deepen, not because of any growing affinity, but because of the latter's productive, marketing, and financial power and the former's need to access these advantages if it is to survive in an increasingly competitive world. Occasionally, for all his "Look East" rhetoric, even Mahatir has publicly attacked Japan, "for continuing to perpetuate its unequal relationship with Malaysia."[89] But like it or not, Malaysia needs Japan more than vice versa, and for the same reasons as in Thailand and Indonesia, Japanese companies dominate the capitalist revolutions that continue to drive development in all three countries.

Conclusion

The alliance between the ASEAN and Japanese ruling classes has its basis in the sphere of production which generates the wealth from which both sides have benefited so massively over the past decade. While local business groups have been able to function independently of the Japanese so long as they limited their activities to the service industries which they first entered in the colonial period, the capitalist revolution that is sweeping Asia today is based on a unique combination of the region's low wages and Japan's advanced technology. However, it is not possible for Asia's business classes to appropriate the bounty resulting from that cutting edge unless they find some way to gain access to the advanced technology that their less developed status has historically denied them. Alliance with Japanese capital, either through their own state-sponsored institutions or through their existing business groups, has thus been essential. But even though the terms of the alliances have fluctuated with changing global and local political economic conditions, there is no question that the Japanese have throughout retained the upper hand and appropriated the lion's share of the benefits.

Although each of the three ASEAN countries examined has enjoyed either double-digit or near-double-digit-growth since the yen began its meteoric rise in the latter half of the 1980s, the key inputs into that growth, with the exception of labor, have come from Japan. These not only include the technology the latter brings in and controls so tightly, but also the worldwide marketing networks through which it distributes the outputs and the financial backing it provides even when its own banks raise money locally from within the ASEAN countries themselves. To grasp the full impact of the interlocking networks of power through which the Japanese dominate the accumulation processes within ASEAN requires examination of Japan's trading and financial activities as well as a fuller examination of its investment strategies than was possible in this limited study.[90] Only then is it possible to see how and why even the explosive accumulation ASEAN has recently enjoyed does not affect the basic problems of underdevelopment the region faces: low capacities to control or generate technology, heavy reliance on foreign investment in technology-intensive industries, the replacement of local market networks with the unregulated global networks of transnational corporations, balance of payments crises resulting from excessive imports (especially of plant, equipment, and components by foreign investors), spiraling international debt which further reinforces foreign capital's control over investment, and last but not least, widening gaps between the elites that benefit from the alliance with foreign capital and the masses of people whose wages are controlled as much by widespread unemployment and underemployment as by authoritarian political regimes.

One of the main differences between the new imperialism of the 1990s and its predecessors is the growing similarity of the class structures of the advanced and the less developed countries. Whereas in the 1960s one could have said that the overwhelming majority of people in the advanced countries benefited from, while the overwhelming majority of those in the less developed countries were harmed by, the neo-colonial system that emerged after the war, the social consequences of the new imperialism are much more geographically diffuse. The advanced countries themselves now contain growing numbers of victims, while the less-developed countries have generated sizeable middle classes. Nevertheless, a qualitative difference persists in spite of these changes, since the continued absolute and relative poverty of the great mass of peasants and factory workers, especially in the ASEAN countries and countries like them (China, India, and Vietnam), shows almost no sign of being alleviated in the foreseeable future. JASEAN might have improved the lives of the upper classes within the region, but lower-class existence remains at best unchanged, and it will remain unchanged until some way is found to combine the political organisations opposing Japan's new imperialism that exist in Japan with those in the Asia Pacific region.

Notes

1. *Nihon Keizai Shinbun* (hereafter *NKS*), 25 July 1995, p. 8; 29 July 1995, p. 1.

2. The best example of this tradition is Albert Szymanski, *The Logic of Imperialism* (New York: Praeger Publishers, 1981). For my own attempt to theorize the functioning of imperialism since the end of the Cold War, see Rob Steven, "The New World Order: A New Imperialism," *Journal of Contemporary Asia*, vol. 24, no. 3 (July 1994) and Rob Steven, *Japan and the New World Order: Global Investments, Trade and Finance* (London: Macmillan, 1995). See also Rob Steven, *Japan's New Imperialism* (London: Macmillan, 1990).

3. Steven, *Japan and the New World Order.*

4. For a fuller discussion of Japan's class structure, the crisis since 1974, and the resulting foreign investment, see Rob Steven, *Classes in Contemporary Japan* (London: Cambridge University Press, 1983), and "The High Yen Crisis in Japan," *Capital and Class*, no. 34 (1988).

5. On this first wave of FDI, see Kunio Yoshihara, *Japanese Investment in Southeast Asia* (Honolulu: University Press of Hawaii, 1978).

6. The best source on FDI in the 1970s is *AMPO.*

7. See Steven, *Classes in Contemporary Japan,* chs. 6 and 7.

8. See Steven, "The High Yen Crisis in Japan."

9. Ibid.

10. Ibid.

11. See Rōdōshō (Ministry of Labor), "Nihon-America oyobi Nihon-Nishi-Doitsu no shōhi kōnyūryoku heika (suikei)" (Consumer Purchasing Power Par Value between Japan and America and between Japan and West Germany [Estimates]), December 1986.

12. For contemporary analyses, see Kudō Akira, "Ijō endaka to sangyō kōzō no chōsei" (The Unusual Rise of the Yen and the Adjustment of the Industrial Structure), *Keizai*, February 1987, p. 50; Sasaki Noriaki, *Oshiyoseru daishitsugyō: zaikai no 21 seiki senryaku to sangyō kūdōka* (Mounting Unemployment: Deindustrialisation and Zaikai's Strategy for the 21st Century) (Tokyo: Shin Nihon Shuppansha, 1987).

13. See Kamata Satoshi, *Kūdō Nihon* [Hollow Japan] (Tokyo: Iwanami shoten, 1995).

14. See Steven, *Japan and the New World Order.*

15. Ōkurashō (Ministry of Finance), "Heisei 6 nendo ni okeru taigai oyobi tainai chokusetsu tōshi jōkyō" (Internal and External Foreign Investments for the Fiscal Year 1994), 6 June 1995.

16. Ibid.

17. Tsūshō sangyōshō sangyō seisakukyoku kokusai kigyōka (International Company Division of the Policy Bureau of the Ministry of International Trade and Industry), *Dai 22 kai wagakuni kigyō no kaigai jigyō katsudō* (Overseas Business Activities of Our Country's Firms, No. 22) (Tokyo: Ōkurashō insatsukyoku, 1993), p. 116.

18. David Elliot, *Thailand: Origins of Military Rule* (London: Zed Press, 1978).

19. Yoshihara, *Japanese Investment in Southeast Asia,* pp. 58–61, 74–83.

20. "Japanese Investment in Thailand," *Bangkok Bank Monthly Review,* May 1981.

21. See Motoyoshi Suzuki, "Theory and Some Empirical Evidence of Japanese Foreign Investment in Thailand," M.A. Thesis, English Language Program, Faculty of Economics, Thammasat University, Bangkok, April 1986; and Pasuk Phongpaichit and others, eds., *The Lion and the Mouse? Japan, Asia, and Thailand,* proceedings of an international conference on Thai-Japanese Relations organised by the Faculty of Economics, Chulalongkorn University, Bangkok, April 1986.

22. Suthy Prasartset, *Thai Business Leaders: Men and Careers in a Developing Economy* (Tokyo: Institute of Developing Economies, 1981).

23. Lek Kiat-Luecha, "Thailand: One Year after the October 6 Coup," *AMPO,* vol. 9, no. 3 (1977).

24. *Business Thailand,* November 1992, p. 82.

25. See Inoue Ryuichirō, *Ajia no zaibatsu to kigyō* (Asia's Business Groups and Firms) (Tokyo: Nihon Keizai Shinbunsha, 1987), pp. 33, 147–154; and revised edition (1994), pp. 178–79.

26. *NKS,* 9 October 1987, p. 8; *Japan Economic Journal* (hereafter *JEJ*), 17 October 1987, p. 6; *Business Thailand,* December 1992, pp. 48–49; Tōyō Keizai Shinposha, ed., *Nihon kigyō no Ajia Shinshutsu mappu* (A Map of Japanese Companies in Asia) (Tokyo: Toyo Keizai Shinposha, 1995), pp. 78–79.

27. Steven, *Japan and the New World Order,* ch. 4.

28. *The Nation,* 1 April 1987, p. 19; Inoue, *Ajia no zaibatsu to kigyō,* 1987 edition, pp. 241–246; revised 1994 edition, pp. 275–283; Shūkan Tōyō Keizai, *Kaigai shinshutsu kigyō sōran,* 1987; *JEJ* 25 September 1987, p. 12.

29. *NKS,* 17 July 1987, p. 9; *The Nation,* 30 March 1987, p. 1; Inoue, *op.cit.,* 1987 edition, pp. 155–161; *Far Eastern Economic Review* (hereafter *FEER,* 25 June 1987, p. 69); Shūkan Tōyō Keizai, *Kaigai shinshutsu kigyō sōran,* 1995; Tōyō Keizai Shinposha, *Nihon kigyō no Ajia shinshutsu mappu.*

30. Shūkan Tōyō Keizai, *Kaigai shinshutsu kigyō sōran,* 1995.

31. *FEER,* 18 June 1987, p. 66.

32. *JEJ,* 12 September 1987, p. 17.

33. *FEER,* 25 June 1987, p. 69; *NKS,* 16 October 1987, p. 9; *Asian Finance,* 15 August 1987, p. 67.

34. *NKS,* 17 May 1987, p. 4; 1 August 1987, p. 17; *Asian Finance,* 15 August 1987, p. 66; *FEER,* 25 December 1986, pp. 63–64; Nihon bōeki shinkōkai, *1987 Jietoro hakusho, tōshihen: sekai to Nihon no kaigai chokusetsu tōshi* (Tokyo: Nihon bōeki shinkōkai, 1987), pp. 127–128; Shūkan Tōyō Keizai, *Kaigai shinshutsu kigyō sōran,* 1995.

35. *FEER,* 25 June 1987, pp. 68, 70.

36. *NKS,* 17 May 1987, p. 4; 8 July 1987, p.12; *The Nation,* 31 March 1987, p. 17; 1 April 1987, p. 17.

37. Jon Halliday and Gavan McCormack, *Japanese Imperialism Today* (Penguin Books, 1973).

38. Malcolm Caldwell, ed., *Ten Years' Military Terror in Indonesia* (Nottingham: Spokesman Books, 1975).

39. Richard Robison, *Indonesia: The Rise of Capital* (Sydney: Allen and Unwin, 1986), ch. 5.

40. See Kitazawa Yoko, "Japan Indonesia Corruption," parts 1 and 2, *AMPO,* vol. 8, nos. 1 and 2 (1976); J. Panglaykim, *Japanese Direct Investment in Asean: The Indonesian Experience* (Singapore: Maruzen Asia, 1983).

41. *AMPO* (Special Issue Transnational Enterprises in Indonesia), vol. 12, no. 4

42. W. Robinson, "Imperialism, Dependency and Peripheral Industrialisation: The Case of Japan in Indonesia," in R. Robison and R. Higgot, eds., *Southeast Asia: Essays in the Political Economy of Structural Change* (London: Routledge, 1985).

43. Yoshihara, *Japanese Investment in Southeast Asia*, p. 123.

44. Robison, *Indonesia*, ch. 6.

45. For details on the Salim group, see Inoue, *Ajia no zaibatsu to kigyō*, 1987 edition, pp. 168–176; 1994 edition, pp. 196–205; Robison, pp. 296–315; and *FEER*, 7 April 1983, pp. 44–56. For links with Japanese capital, see Shūkan Tōyō Keizai, *Kaigai shinshutsu kigyō sōran*, 1987, 1995.

46. *The Australian*, 21 July 1995, p. 26.

47. For details on the Astra group, see Robison, pp. 277–296; Inoue, *Ajia no saibatsu to kigyō*, 1987 edition, pp. 177–184; Satō Yuri, "Indonesia ni okeru keiei kindaika no senkusha: Asutora gurupu no jirei kenkyū" (Pioneer of Modernization of Management in Indonesia: A Case Study of the Astra Group), *Ajia Keizai*, vol. 36, no. 3 (March 1995). Links with Japanese capital are listed in Shūkan Tōyō Keizai, *Kaigai shinshutsu kigyō sōran*, 1987 and 1995.

48. Sato, "Indonesia ni okeru keiei kindaika no senkusha."

49. Inoue, *Aija no zaibatsu to kigyō*, 1994 edition, p. 294, Satō, "Indonesia ni okeru keiei kindaika no senkusha," p. 13.

50. Inoue, *Aija no zaibatsu to kigyō*, 1987 edition, pp. 184–91; Shūkan Tōyō Keizai, *Kaigai shinshutsu kigyō sōran*, 1995.

51. Inoue, *Aija no zaibatsu to kigyō*, 1987 edition, pp. 247–255; 1994 edition, pp. 284–291.

52. For a general discussion on *pribumi* groups, see Robison, *op. cit.*, ch. 10.

53. Shūkan Tōyō Keizai, *Kaigai shinshutsu kigyō sōran*, 1995; Himpunan Usahawan Indonesia-Jepang (Indonesia-Japan Entrepreneurs Association), *A Decade of Himpunan Usahawan Indonesia-Jepang 1974–1984: The Role and Contribution of Indonesia-Japan Joint Venture Companies* (Jakarta, 1984).

54. See Robison, *Indonesia*, ch. 7; Shūkan Tōyō Keizai, *Kaigai shinshutsu kigyō sōran*, 1995; Himpunan Usahawan Indonesia-Jepang (Indonesia-Japan Entrepreneurs Association), *A Decade of Himpunan Usahawan Indonesia-Jepang 1974–1984: The Role and Contribution of Indonesia-Japan Joint Venture Companies* (Jakarta, 1984).

55. Inoue, *Aija no zaibatsu to kigyō*, 1994 edition, pp. 292–301.

56. *AMPO*, 1980, p. 37.

57. Himpunan Ushawan Indonesia-Jepang, *AMPO*, pp. 232, 293.

58. *NKS*, 19 July 1987, p. 9; 13 September 1987, p. 4; 25 September 1987, p. 23; 30 September 1987, p. 9; 9 October 1987, p. 8.

59. Robin Bromby, ed., *"The Australian* Special Survey: Indonesia," *The Australian*, 17 August 1995, p. 9.

60. Ibid. p. 1.

61. Nihon Bōeki Shinkōkai, *Sekai to Nihon no kaigai chokusetsu toshi: 1994 Jietoro hakusho, tōshihen*, p. 204.

62. See Mohamed Amin and Malcolm Caldwell, eds., *Malaya: The Making of a Neo-Colony* (Nottingham: Spokesman Books, 1977).

63. See Martin Brennan, "Class, Politics and Race in Modern Malaysia," *Journal of Contemporary Asia* (hereafter *JCA*), vol. 12 (1982); Michael Stenson, "Class and Race in West Malaysia," *BCAS*, vol. 8, no. 2 (1976); Lim Mah Hui, "Ethnic and Class Relations in Malaysia," *JCA*, vol. 10, no. 1/2 (1980); Fatimah Halim, "Rural labor Force and Industrial Conflict in West Malaysia," *JCA*, vol. 11, no. 3 (1981).

64. Khor Kok Peng, *The Malaysian Economy: Structures and Dependence* (Kuala Lumpur: Marican & Sons, 1983), pp. 73–74; Aoki Takeshi, *Yushutsu shikō kōgyōka senryaku:*

Marēshia ni miru sono hikari to kage (The Strategy of Export-led Industrialisation: Looking at the Bright and Dark Sides of Malaysia) (Tokyo: Nihon Bōeki Shinkōkai, 1993).

65. *FEER,* 12 November 1987, pp. 12 ff.

66. Khor, *The Malaysian Economy,* Robin Bromby, ed., *"The Australian* Special Survey: Malaysia," *The Australian,* 31 August, 1995, p. 34.

67. Comparador capital identifies totally with foreign capital. It is often contrasted with national capital, which puts the interests of local business first.

68. Khor, *The Malaysian Economy,* p. 75.

69. Khalid Ibrahim, "Corporate Restructuring: The PNB Experience," in K. S. Jomo and others, *Crisis and Response in the Malaysian Economy* (Kuala Lumpur, Malaysian Economic Association, 1987), p. 197.

70. See Chee Peng Lim and Lee Poh Ping, "The Role of Japanese Direct Investment Malaysia," Institute of Southeast Asian Studies, 1979.

71. Ibid, pp. 10–15; Shūkan Tōyō Keizai, *Kaigai shinshutsu kigyō sōran,* 1987.

72. Ibid.; Nihon Bōeki Shinkōkai, *1987 Jietoro hakusho, tōshihen: sekai to Nihon no kaigai chokusetsu tōshi,* pp. 135–136.

73. *Business Times,* 1 October 1986, p. 1.

74. *NKS,* 31 August, 1987, p. 9.

75. *FEER,* 26 November 1987, p. 69.

76. *JEJ,* 19 September 1987, p. 14.

77. Shūkan Tōyō Keizai, *Kaigai shinshutsu kigyō sōran,* 1995; James Abegglen, *Sea Change: Pacific Asia as the New World Industrial Center* (New York: The Free Press, 1994), p. 38.

78. Robin Bromby, ed., *"The Australian* Special Survey: Malaysia," *The Australian,* 31 August, 1995, p. 34.

79. *NKS,* 11 November, 1987, p. 9: *The Star,* business section, 25 March 1987, p. 1; *JEJ,* 19 September 1987, p. 11; Shūkan Tōyō Keizai, *Kaigai shinshutsu kigyō sōran,* 1995.

80. Tōyō Keizai Shinposha, *Nihon kigyō no Ajia shinshutsu mappu,* p. 60; *Industria,* July 1987, pp. 44–45; *JEJ,* 12 September 1987, p. 17; Nihon Bōeki Shinkōkai, *Jietoro hakusho, tōshihen,* 1987, pp. 132–136; Shūkan Tōyō Keizai, *Kaigai shinshutsu kigyō sōran,* 1995.

81. Chee and Lee, *The Role of Japanese Direct Investment in Malaysia,* pp. 46 ff.

82. Shūkan Tōyō Keizai, *Kaigai shinshutsu kigyō sōran,* 1987; Harian Perintis, *Malaysia: Commerce and Industry, 1986/87* (Kuala Lumpur: Harian Perintis, 1986), pp. 87–89; Jetro Kuala Lumpur Centre, *Japanese Related Companies in Malaysia* (1986); *JEJ,* 9 May 1987, p. 11; *FEER,* 23 April 1987, pp. 73–77.

83. *The Australian,* 10 August, 1995, p. 16. On the history of the project, see Inoue, *Aija no zaibatsu to kigyō,* 1994 edition, pp. 329–337.

84. Inoue, *Aija no zaibatsu to kigyō,* 1987 edition, pp. 199–205; 1994 edition, pp. 235–245; Shūkan Tōyō Keizai, *Kaigai shinshutsu kigyō sōran,* 1995; *FEER,* 30 October 1986.

85. Inoue, *Aija no zaibatsu to kigyō,* 1987 edition, pp. 206–212; 1994 edition, pp. 245–253; Shūkan Tōyō Keizai, *Kaigai shinshutsu kigyō sōran,* 1987, 1995; *NKS,* 31 July 1995, p. 1.

86. Shūkan Tōyō Keizai, *Kaigai shinshutsu kigyō sōran,* 1995.

87. Ibid.

88. Shūkan Tōyō Keizai, *Kaigai shinshutsu kigyō sōran,* 1995; Inoue, *Aija no zaibatsu to kigyō,* 1994 edition, pp. 321–328.

89. Harien Perintis, *Malaysia,* p. 38.

90. See Steven, *Japan and the New World Order.*

V

**Restructuring Society for
Capitalist "Efficiency" in the
International Division of Labor**

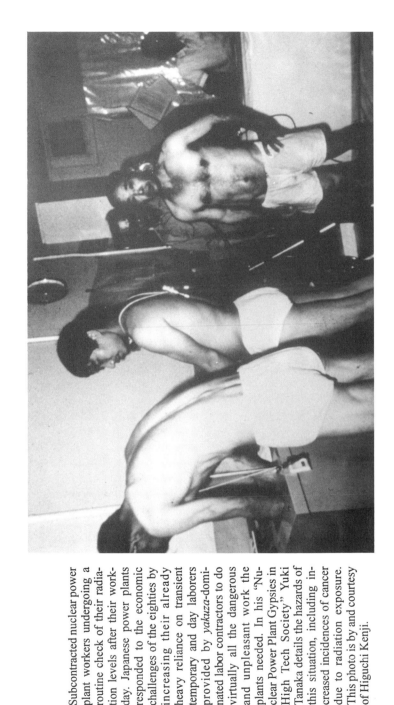

Subcontracted nuclear power plant workers undergoing a routine check of their radiation levels after their workday. Japanese power plants responded to the economic challenges of the eighties by increasing their already heavy reliance on transient temporary and day laborers provided by *yakuza*-dominated labor contractors to do virtually all the dangerous and unpleasant work the plants needed. In his "Nuclear Power Plant Gypsies in High Tech Society," Yuki Tanaka details the hazards of this situation, including increased incidences of cancer due to radiation exposure. This photo is by and courtesy of Higuchi Kenji.

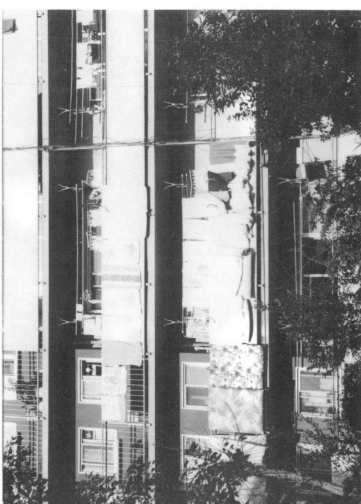

In the eighties millions more women joined Japan's work force, mostly married women in their late thirties or early forties returning to work in low-paid, part-time positions lacking job security or benefits. These women have typically been willing to accept low-level jobs since their primary work is still considered to be in the home. Many of the working women interviewed by Atsumi Reiko in her "Dilemmas and Accommodations of Married Japanese Women in White-Collar Employment" lamented that when they returned to work they could no longer air their family's bedding as is customary since this chore has to be done during sunny times of the day. This photo of the familiar Japanese scene of futon bedding being aired out is by and courtesy of Atsumi Reiko.

Filipino workers checking a job board in Manila for information about jobs abroad. Although cultural and political barriers are enormous, many Filipino workers have ended up in Japan. John Lie's "The 'Problem' of Foreign Workers in Contemporary Japan" identifies two main problems with having foreign workers in Japan: their being exploited by criminal gangs and sweat-shop operators, and their presence in Japan challenging the prevailing Japanese preconception of Japan's racial and cultural homogeneity. This photo is by and courtesy of Nagakura Norio and was taken in 1988.

10

Nuclear Power Plant Gypsies in High-Tech Society

*Yuki Tanaka**

Who permitted them to permit?
—Albert Schweitzer, in pointing out that it was scientists
who determined the "permissible dosage of irradiation."

Introduction

The severe overproduction crisis that struck Japan during 1974 and 1975, accompanied by sudden inflation, brought significant changes in employment policy throughout all sectors of Japanese industry. Hardest hit were the workers at the bottom of Japanese industry, the temporary and day laborers—in 1975 roughly 14.4 percent of the Japanese work force.[1] Most of these workers were and still are in the forty-five to sixty-five-year-old age group.[2]

In the grim economic atmosphere of structural depression, the rapidly growing Japanese nuclear power industry has provided these retrenched workers with significant new job opportunities. As of October 1986 there were thirty-six nuclear reactors operating in Japan, with eleven under construction, five more planned, and a gigantic complex known as the Mutsu Ogawara Development in the initial planning stages

*This article is based on a paper presented at the Japanese Studies Association of Australia Conference, La Trobe University, May 1985, and is an updated (1988) and shortened version of the article that was published in the *Bulletin of Concerned Asian Scholars*, vol. 18, no. 1 (January–March 1986), pp. 2–22. Another version of this article was published in *The Japanese Trajectory: Modernization and Beyond*, ed. Gavan McCormack and Yoshio Sugimoto. Much of the information was made available to me by S. Saito and T. Shibano (Cambridge and New York: Cambridge University Press, 1988). To them I extend my most sincere appreciation; however, I accept full responsibility for the contents. I also wish to thank Kenji Higuchi for providing the photographs. (Editor's note: In this article the Japanese names are in the Western order, with the given name first and the family name second.)

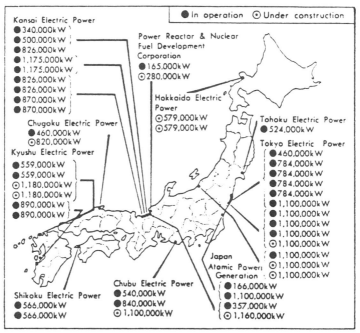

Nuclear reactors in Japan. (This map is from *Earth Island Journal* (San Francisco), vol. 2, no. 2 (Spring 1987), 15.)

for far northern Aomori Prefecture. Scheduled to begin operation in 1991, the Mutsu complex will include a spent-fuel reprocessing factory and two nuclear power plants. Many of the workers attracted to this growing industry have become known as *gempatsu jipushii* (nuclear power plant gypsies) because they wander from plant to plant seeking relatively highly paid jobs. They are often exploited, however, and their jobs are generally the most dangerous in the industry.

As will be explained in detail later, nuclear power companies must hire unusually large numbers of workers to keep their plants operating. The many temporary workers and day laborers needed for maintenance and repair of the plants are hired through an unusually complex recruitment system. A few big electric power companies, such as the Japan Atomic Power Company (JAPC), work closely with the five large nuclear power industry groups.[3] Each of the electric power companies makes a contract with several prime contractors to secure the work force needed by the power companies it is associated with. These prime contractors then require numerous subcontracting companies to recruit these workers for them. The subcontracting companies in turn employ sub-subcontracting companies to help with the recruiting, and these sub-subcontracting companies use labor suppliers who are often also workers (see chart A[4]). In this system, as many as seven subcontractors may be involved in the hiring of one worker!

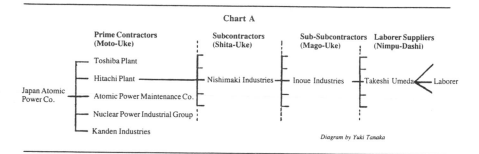

Chart A

Diagram by Yuki Tanaka

This recruitment system leads to the subcontracted workers being exploited in a number of ways. Each subcontracting company takes a percentage from the wages of the workers it has helped recruit, and workers' wages are typically reduced to one-quarter or less of what they would have been without these deductions.[5] In addition, prime contracting companies often exploit both their subcontracted and their full-time workers by withholding from them funds that have been provided for covering special expenses, such as overtime pay and housing allowances.[6] And when big businesses face bankruptcy, rather than meeting their obligations to their workers directly, they send their workers to nuclear power plants and have the subcontractors pay most of their wages.[7] *Yakuza* (Japanese Mafia) syndicates operate some of the subcontracting companies, and when this happens the subcontracted workers are even further exploited. Every hundred days or so nuclear power plants need thousands of extra workers for their regular inspections, and the *yakuza* are especially involved in recruiting these extra workers.[8] The *yakuza* syndicates sometimes use intimidation to get enough workers to fill the quotas,[9] and they finance themselves not only through the percentages they take from the workers' wages, but also through loans and drug sales to workers.

The number of subcontracted workers employed by nuclear power plants in Japan is increasing dramatically, from 1,675 in 1970 to more than 53,000 in 1986. Since 1971 subcontracted workers have made up over 80 percent of the work force of nuclear power plants in Japan, and in 1986 they made up over 90 percent of the work force. These workers are all unskilled and comparatively older, often ex-miners, day laborers, *buraku* (outcasts), farmers away from their homes during the slack season, and local retired workers. These *gempatsu jipushii* come to nuclear power plants seeking a good life for themselves through wages that are usually higher than those they can earn elsewhere, but they are being exploited in ways far more serious than the wage and benefit reductions already mentioned. They are endangering their health, and all too often risking their lives, exploited by an industry and technology that has hazards we are only beginning to understand. This article examines the difficulties and hazards these *gempatsu jipushii* face when they work at Japanese nuclear power plants, and explores the likely fate of these victims of high-tech society.[10]

Dosage of Irradiation

Why is it that nuclear power plants require such large numbers of temporary workers and day laborers? The answer is directly related to the high levels of radiation contamination inside the power plants. There is always a danger that workers will be exposed to high doses of radiation if they work beyond a certain length of time in areas of the plants where radiation levels are high. Thus electric power companies require as many laborers as possible so that jobs can be rotated in order to reduce the amount of radiation to which individual workers are exposed. The number of subcontracted workers has grown very rapidly not simply because of the increase in power plants, but also because radiation contamination at nuclear power plants worsens as time passes. Consequently it is necessary to increase both the number of subcontracted workers required during regular inspections and the number needed for everyday maintenance.

In order to understand the actual working conditions of nuclear power plant workers and the amount of radiation to which they are exposed, it is necessary to analyze the existing knowledge of radiation hazards to man. There are two units frequently used to gauge radiation levels, the rad and the rem, which are roughly equivalent. Japanese law regarding radiation hazards is based on the advice of the International Committee for Radiation Protection. The law states that the "maximum permissible level of radiation dosage" over a period of three months is 3,000 millirems (i.e., 3 rems) for workers at nuclear power plants, and the annual *average* (not maximum) permissible level is 5,000 millirems (i.e., 5 rems). For ordinary people not engaged in work with radiation, the law stipulates a maximum of 500 millirems per year. U.S. regulations stipulate a seemingly similar 5,000 millirems (5 rems) per year for workers involved with atomic energy, but this is a *maximum* dosage, not an average dosage as in Japan. For an individual in the population at large, the U.S. regulations state that the maximum permissible level per year is 500 millirems (.5 rems), which is the same as Japan's, but then the U.S. regulations go on to recommend a maximum average of 170 millirems per person per year in any identifiable segment of the population at large, such as a particular city. This stricter regulation provides a greater degree of protection for the group as a whole because radiation is more hazardous for some people (babies and children, for example) than others; the lower maximum for the whole group will presumably give even these more vulnerable members of the group the protection they need.

These officially approved radiation hazard levels have remained the same in the United States even though as early as 1969 two prominent American biophysicists who worked for the Atomic Energy Commission predicted that accepting such levels could have dire results. At a meeting at the Institute for Electrical and Electronic Engineers in San Francisco, John Gofman and Arthur Tamplin presented the results of a study they had made of the expected deaths from cancer and leukemia resulting from exposure to various amounts of radiation. They predicted that:

If the average exposure of the U.S. population were to reach the allowable 0.17 rads [170 millirems] per year average, there would, in time, be an excess of 32,000 cases of fatal cancer plus leukemia per year, and this would occur year after year.[11]

At the time these results were announced neither of these biophysicists was any longer a staff member of the U.S. Atomic Energy Commission, and they could thus be open in their criticism of the U.S. government and the nuclear industry as a whole. During the sixteen intervening years they haven't changed their views at all. In fact, both continue to claim that:

No one has ever produced evidence that any specific amount of radiation will be without harm. Indeed, quite the opposite appears to be the case. All the evidence, both from experimental animals and from humans, leads us to expect that even the *smallest* quantities of ionizing radiation produce harm, both to this generation of humans and future generations. Furthermore, it appears that progressively greater harm accrues in direct proportion to the amount of radiation received by the various body tissues and organs.[12]

They further suggest that the present permissible level should be reduced to a maximum of 1.7 millirems. Moreover, their belief that there is no such thing as a permissible level of radiation dosage is gaining increasing support among scientists working in this field.

To what extent are the Japanese subcontracted workers irradiated? According to my calculations, based upon official statistics published by the Bureau of Radiation Control, the annual average of 410 millirems per worker in 1978 is the highest on record. This is 241 times the permissible level that Gofman and Tamplin recommend. The annual average for the ten years between 1974 and 1986 is 292 millirems, over 170 times the level that Gofman and Tamplin suggest. Although these annual averages are very high when compared to the Gofman and Tamplin recommendations, they may seem surprisingly low when compared to the figures for irradiation dosages mentioned earlier, such as the average permissible level of 5,000 millirems per worker per year and the 300 millirems per week each worker may receive. The reason that the average annual dosages are relatively low is that they are *average* dosages for *all* the subcontracted workers at Japanese nuclear power plants, and these averages thus include many unexposed subcontracted workers who are employed to do odd jobs in Areas A and B and are not engaged in the dangerous work in Area C. Even security officers are considered subcontracted workers and are included in these figures. In addition, most of the subcontracted workers working in Area C move from one nuclear power plant to another, and this means that some subcontracted workers are counted two and even three times in this official figure. Thus, although the figures for annual averages may seem relatively low, the actual irradiation dosages to which workers in Area C are exposed are much higher,

Table 10.1

Number of Nuclear Power Plant Workers

Year	A. Company Employees	B. Subcontracted Workers	C. Total	B/C (%)
1970	823	1,675	2,498	67.1
1971	904	4,339	5,243	82.8
1972	1,056	4,753	5,809	81.8
1973	1,512	6,960	8,472	82.2
1974	2,076	10,282	12,348	83.2
1975	2,282	13,798	16,080	86.8
1976	2,555	17,241	19,796	87.1
1977	3,233	22,129	25,362	87.3
1978	3,578	30,577	34,155	89.5
1979	3,759	30,495	34,254	89
1980	3,976	31,978	35,954	88.9
1981	4,374	36,158	40,532	89.2
1982	4,688	35,941	40,629	88.5
1983	5,367	41,072	46,439	88.4
1984	5,784	45,726	51,510	88.8
1985	5,698	48,881	54,576	89.6
1986	5,735	53,131	58.866	90.3

Source: Tables 10.1, 10.2, and 10.3 were compiled by the author from information published in documents issued by the Bureau of Radiation Control, which is under the direction of the Ministry of Energy and Resources.

and these exposed workers often exceed the Gofman and Tamplin recommended permissible levels by much more than the annual averages indicate.

It is interesting to note that although the average dosage of radiation to which an electric power company employee is exposed has decreased considerably over the years, the dosage to which subcontracted workers are exposed has remained about the same. Another important fact that can be detected from these official statistics is that prior to the worst period of the oil shock depression in 1975, the average irradiation dosage to which a company employee was exposed was much higher than that to which a subcontracted worker was exposed. However, in 1975 these levels became equal, and thereafter the situation was reversed. In 1986 the average irradiation dosage to which the individual subcontracted worker was exposed was 2.38 times that of a company worker. If one considers the total irradiation dosage, it is clear that from the beginning subcontracted workers have been bearing well over 50 percent of the irradiation burden at nuclear power plants, and since 1977 well over 90 percent of the irradiation has been directed at these workers. (See tables 10.2 and 10.3, and graph 10.1.)

These facts indicate clearly that subcontracted workers are recruited specifically for work involving exposure to high levels of radiation, and that in such

Table 10.2

Total Irradiation Dosage (rems for all workers)

Year	A. Company Employees	B. Subcontracted Workers	C. Total	B/C(%)
1970	236	326	562	58
1971	370	896	1,266	70.7
1972	464	1,433	1,897	75.5
1973	596	2,098	2,694	77.9
1974	701	2,427	3,128	77.6
1975	716	4,283	4,999	85.7
1976	769	5,473	6,242	87.7
1977	726	7,399	8,125	91.1
1978	782	12,418	13,200	94
1979	858	10,872	11,730	92.7
1980	828	11,105	12,933	93.6
1981	785	11,933	12,718	93.8
1982	733	11,767	12,500	94.1
1983	661	11,206	11,867	94.4
1984	621	11,534	12,156	94.9
1985	572	11,933	12,505	95.4
1986	466	10,278	10,744	95.7

Table 10.3

Average Irradiation Dosage

Year	A. Company Employees	B. Subcontracted Workers	B/A (times)
1970	0.27	0.19	0.66
1971	0.41	0.21	0.51
1972	0.44	0.30	0.68
1973	0.39	0.30	0.77
1974	0.34	0.24	0.71
1975	0.31	0.31	1.0
1976	0.30	0.32	1.06
1977	0.22	0.33	1.5
1978	0.22	0.41	1.86
1979	0.23	0.36	1.57
1980	0.21	0.38	1.81
1981	0.18	0.33	1.83
1982	0.17	0.33	1.94
1983	0.12	0.27	2.25
1984	0.11	0.25	2.27
1985	0.10	0.24	2.40
1986	0.08	0.19	2.38

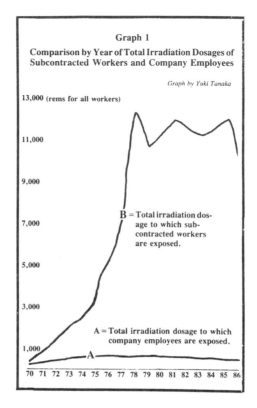

Graph 1

Comparison by Year of Total Irradiation Dosages of Subcontracted Workers and Company Employees

Graph by Yuki Tanaka

13,000 (rems for all workers)

11,000

9,000

7,000   B = Total irradiation dosage to which sub-contracted workers are exposed.

5,000

3,000

A = Total irradiation dosage to which company employees are exposed.

1,000

70 71 72 73 74 75 76 77 78 79 80 81 82 83 84 85 86

cases they act as substitutes for company employees, thereby lessening the health hazards for the latter. Thus these statistics reflect a deliberate decision by the electric power companies to foist the most dangerous jobs onto subcontracted workers and thereby avoid responsibility for problems that may arise from radio-active contamination. Because subcontracted workers constantly move from one plant to another, it would be very difficult to trace an overdose of radiation to a particular source, especially as the effects are rarely felt immediately. It should be emphasized further that when compared with first-hand information,[13] these official statistics do not appear to represent accurately the actual amount of radiation to which nuclear power plant workers are exposed.

Workers' Safety Education

Legislation requires that prior to commencing actual work at a nuclear power station, subcontracted workers receive "safety education" on the work they are about to undertake. During special sessions a radiation control worker provides some information on radioactive materials and the hazards of irradiation, although this amounts to nothing more than the most basic facts. Indeed, the major content of the lectures is irrelevant to radiation and deals with such common-sense matters as the need to wear an ordinary safety helmet, which offers no protection against radiation. At some plants, subcontracted workers are given pamphlets on safety information to study and then are tested on their understanding of this information. There is evidence, however, that during the examination the correct answers are often dictated by a radiation control worker.[14] This so-called safety education is therefore nothing but a formality to qualify subcontracted workers officially so that they can begin work as soon as possible.

The details workers are given on radiation during these sessions is as follows. First, they are informed that their standard level of radiation dosage will be 100 millirems per day and 300 millirems per week. Most Japanese power plants take these figures as the set norm in order to keep the amount of irradiation subcontracted workers receive to within the government regulations, that is, to within 3,000 millirems (3 rems) in three months. However, the way in which "one week" is defined differs from one company to another. For example, at the Fukushima plant of the Tokyo Electric Power Company workers are officially instructed that the amount of irradiation should not exceed 300 millirems during any seven-day period. If the amount exceeds 300 millirems the worker is not allowed to work in the so-called controlled area for the following four days. At the Tsuruga plant of the JAPC, on the other hand, four days of every month— i.e., the 1st, 9th, 17th, and 25th—are designated as checkup days. On each of these four days, the accumulated total irradiation of each worker is set back automatically to zero. Therefore, if, for example, a worker is exposed to 100 millirems of radiation every day for the three days between the sixth and the eighth of a particular month (i.e., a total of 300 millirems), he can still continue to work in the high radiation areas after the ninth because on that day his record reverts officially to zero.[15] Clearly, then, the safety regulations and associated education are somewhat haphazard and variable in regard to actual worker radiation exposures.

Workers' Garments and Equipment

The inside of a nuclear power plant is divided into two sections: the non-contaminated area (Area A), regarded as a radiation-free zone, and the contamination control area which is a highly irradiated zone. According to law, the so-called control areas are those registering a minimum of 30 millirems during any one week. The buildings in this category are the concrete shield building (i.e., the nuclear reactor building), the buildings attached to this shield building, such as the turbine building, and the radioactive waste storage area. This control area is further divided into two sections: Area B (the secondary control area) which has a low level of contamination, and Area C (the primary control area) with high radioactive contamination. The concrete shield building and the nuclear waste storage building are classified as Area C.

Illustration 1. **Passing Uniform**

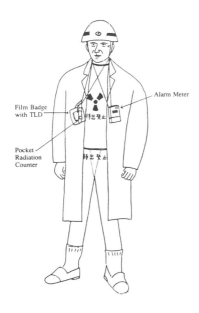

Illustrations 1–6 were drawn by the author based on illustrations in K. Horie, *Gempatsu Jipushii (Nuclear Power Plant Gypsies)* (Tokyo: Gendai Shokan, 1984) and in T. Shibano, *Gempatsu no Aru Fukei (A View of Nuclear Power Plants)* (Tokyo: Mirai-sha, 1983).

When workers pass from Area B to Area C they go through a checkpoint. Before passing this checkpoint they must first use a nearby toilet, as there are no toilets inside Area C. Building of toilet facilities is prohibited in this area because of the high levels of contamination. The workers then have to change into specially provided underwear (a long-sleeved singlet and long johns), put on the socks provided, white overalls, a helmet, and special rubber shoes with steel covering over the toe area. (See illustration 1.) Having changed into this "passing uniform," they pick up an alarm meter (which beeps when the radiation reaches a certain level), a pocket radiation counter (a simple measuring instrument in the shape of a fountain pen), and a film badge with a TLD (thermoluminescence dosimeter). Before entering Area C the worker inserts the TLD into a reading machine which automatically records the level of radiation. When the worker returns to the checkpoint, the TLD is again inserted so that the difference in the level of radiation before and after working in Area C may be ascertained.[16] However, this TLD record is not usually checked unless the pocket radiation counter registers above a certain level of irradiation, usually 200 millirems.[17]

Thus equipped, the workers pass through a wooden-hinged door and walk along a corridor about 200–300 meters long to a changing room where they change into an Area C uniform. First, they take off the white overalls and put on an Area C uniform. An alarm meter, a pocket radiation counter, and a film badge with a TLD are placed in the inner pocket of the uniform. (See illustration 2.) They then put on another pair of socks, cotton gloves, rubber gloves over these, and a hood over a cloth cap. Sometimes they wear a garment made of paper called a "tie-back" over the uniform. They then put on another pair of rubber gloves and seal these tightly at the cuffs with gum tape. With the exception of the rubber gloves, none of the garments are waterproof. Finally, they put on a half-face mask in order to prevent their inhaling airborne radioactive elements.

This cartoon is from *Earth Island Journal* (San Francisco), Vol. 2, No. 2 (Spring 1987), 14. Cartoon by and courtesy of Gar Smith.

When working in highly contaminated areas such as in the pedestal directly under the nuclear reactor (see illustration 3) or in other parts of the dry well, a full mask or oxygen mask is worn. In order to enter Area C, workers then pass through an air-locked double steel door. The corridor before this door is called Matsuno Roka (Pine Corridor) by the workers. This name comes from the traditional Kabuki story *Chushingura*[18] and indicates that once you enter this corridor, you are in an area of great danger.[19] (See illustrations 4, 5, and 6.)

Illustration 2. **Area C Uniform**   Illustration 3. **Concrete Shield Building**

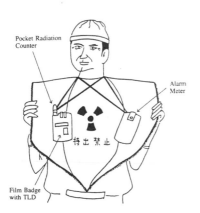

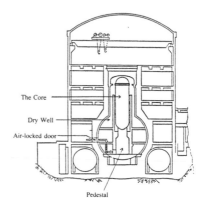

Illustration 4. **Area C Uniform**

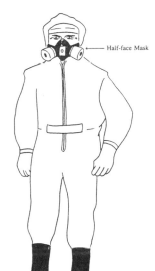

←— Half-face Mask

Illustration 5. **Area C Uniform**

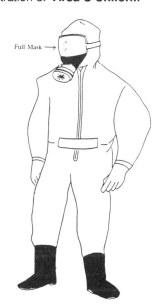

Full Mask —→

Illustration 6

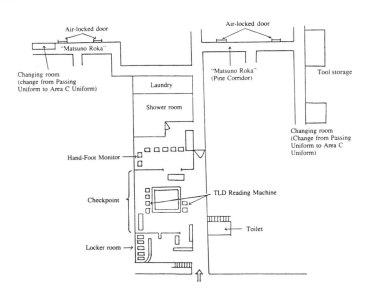

Working Conditions

Subcontracted workers in nuclear power plants are usually allocated the most dangerous work in the most contaminated areas. They are required to perform such tasks as pouring high-level liquid waste into drums, decontaminating nuclear waste tanks, changing waste collector filters, washing sludge from contaminated filter elements, cutting and changing pipes near the core vessel, removing radioactive dust from various parts of the pump, mopping up radioactive water, and washing work uniforms and underwear. All these jobs involve a high risk of exposure to excessive levels of radiation. Particularly during the regular inspection, the work carried out inside the dry well close to the core subjects workers to high levels of irradiation within a short time. In such cases, a worker's operation time is restricted to a few minutes or even a few seconds, so that even small jobs are done by rotating a few dozen workers. The workers refer to the teams of subcontracted workers involved in such operations as *tokko-tai* (suicide squads).

Theoretically, an alarm meter should warn workers of high levels of radiation, although in reality the system is far from perfect. There are various types of alarm meters, some with a set warning level and others with an adjustable warning level. These meters are distributed according to the danger levels at the site of each operation. When working in a high-contamination area, workers are given alarm meters set with a higher warning level. However, if a worker does not specify a particular warning level when collecting the alarm meter at the checkpoint, he may be given the highest level one. A careless worker may not even be aware of the warning level on the alarm meter he is carrying.[20] But no matter what the warning level, if the meter battery is not properly charged, the alarm will not sound. Apparently inadequate charging is a frequent problem.[21]

Another problem arises when warnings sound in the middle of tasks and workers are instructed by their foremen to reset their meters so they may continue to work.[22] Similarly, when alarm meters sound it often happens that workers are unable to stop owing to the nature of the operation in which they are engaged. The maximum warning level on alarm meters is usually 80 millirems. But in certain operations the radiation dosage is far beyond this maximum level. For example, there is an area called the Torus sump-pit which contains highly irradiated sea water. Periodically, this area is cleaned thoroughly. First the surface fluid is removed, after which the remaining water is pumped out. Then the radioactive sludge at the bottom of the pit is scooped out and the pit itself is jet-washed. During this operation it is quite usual for workers to receive between 60–80 millirems of radiation and sometimes they are exposed to 110 millirems within a few minutes.[23] Carrying an alarm meter in such areas is no more than a formal gesture since the alarms are typically ignored.

In an attempt to maintain minimum irradiation dosages there are set levels of irradiation for each operation within the plants. It is assumed that when the total irradiation dosage to all the workers involved in a particular operation surpasses the set levels for that particular operation, the task will be temporarily stopped. However, in reality, the set levels of irradiation are often raised as the dosage to which workers are exposed increases.[24]

When workers return to the checkpoint after working in Area C, they themselves read the levels on the pocket radiation counters and record these in note-books. However, because electric power companies officially permit exposure amounting to only 100 millirems per worker per day, workers are often forced by their foremen to record false figures of around 70–80 millirems, even if the true reading is well over 100 millirems.[25] The main reason that workers readily obey the foremen's instructions is that if the irradiation dosage exceeds 300 millirems within one week, they will be prevented from working for the next few days. Because they are paid on a daily basis, their income diminishes according to the days they take off. Thus, although they are well aware of the danger, workers try to continue working at the nuclear power plants by forging records in this way.

As the figures recorded by the workers from the pocket radiation counters are frequently adjusted for the records, this tally naturally comes to differ consider-ably from the figures shown on the film badges that they wear. The latter are totaled every few weeks or monthly, and in some cases there is a difference of as much as 400 millirems in a single month.[26] In order to disguise this discrepancy so that they may continue to work, workers often borrow film badges from others working in less dangerous areas. In extreme cases, they work in Area C without wearing their film badges.[27]

It is obvious that as far as dosages of irradiation are concerned, there is deliberate discrimination against subcontracted workers in order to protect the employees of the electric power companies and the prime contracting compa-nies. By law, no worker may be exposed to more than 5,000 millirems (5 rems) per year, although the electric power companies and prime contracting compa-nies stipulate that their employees (i.e., non-subcontracted workers) should not be irradiated over 1,500 millirems (1.5 rems) per year.[28] Moreover, while the irradiation dosage records of subcontractors are frequently and easily tampered with, relatively stringent checks on irradiation dosages are made on other em-ployees. A further example of this is the routine undergone when workers leave Area C. It is standard practice for all workers to have a shower and receive an irradiation check. At the Fukushima plant of the Tokyo Electric Power Company there was, until recently, a discrepancy in the instruments used for monitoring irradiation. While subcontracted workers used only hand-foot monitors and a simple small Geiger counter for the rest of the body, employees of the Tokyo EPC used the "gate monitor," which checks the entire body surface at once.[29]

In each nuclear power plant there are several workers called radiation control officers who are regarded as specialists on radiation. These people are usually employees of one of the prime contracting or subcontracting companies. Offi-cially, it is their responsibility to monitor radiation levels in various areas within the plants and to control labor distribution in order to avoid irradiation of work-ers beyond the levels set by regulations. But this is nothing but an official policy, as the authority of these radiation control officers within labor management is virtually nonexistent. For example, these officers are never called to help plan operations within Area C. Typically, an operation in Area C is almost complete by the time they are told of it.[30] Indeed, monitoring radiation levels is often an extra task for these officers, who are normally expected to help subcontractors in various ways and to work with them.

If the radiation control officers are too strict in carrying out their radiation monitoring checks, they become disliked, not only by the electric power companies, but also by the subcontracted workers. It is the latter who suffer if officers claim that radiation levels in a particular area are excessive, for they are required to carry out the decontamination work. Thus, here too, a deceptive method is often adopted. If after repeated decontamination treatment of a particular area it is impossible to reduce the level of radiation to that set by regulations, an officer generally asks subcontracted workers to clean only a small portion of the area requiring decontamination. When the radiation level of this small portion falls below the required level, decontamination work is officially declared complete.[31]

Internal Irradiation

Nuclear power plant workers face not only the physical danger of external irradiation, but also that of internal (inhaled or ingested) irradiation. Regulations demand that a half-face mask or full mask be worn in areas of high-level radiation and in dusty areas. However, those operations where masks are required are usually in areas close to the core—such as inside the dry well—where the temperature is very high. Because workers wear so much protective clothing, within a few minutes of beginning work they start to perspire profusely, have difficulty in breathing, and often experience severe headaches. In addition, steamy moisture builds up inside the full masks and makes it difficult to see one's work. Consequently, many workers simply remove their masks, hang them around their necks, and continue their task, simultaneously inhaling radioactive gas.[32] It seems that the workers are more concerned with escaping from the immediate physical discomfort than they are worried about internal irradiation.

The danger of internal irradiation is exceedingly high among subcontracted workers who are engaged in laundry work, that is, the washing and drying of the uniforms, underwear, gloves, masks, and the like which are worn by workers assigned to dangerous areas. The workers collect the garments from special dumping bins, put them into plastic bags, and take them back to the laundry where they wash and dry them. Because uniforms are easily contaminated, workers have to change garments every time they change working areas. Each worker changes at least twice a day, once in the morning and once in the afternoon. In extreme cases, workers change four or five times a day. During regular inspections, in particular, the number of garments requiring washing increases greatly. At each barrier in Area C there are special bins designated for each item to be washed. Every time subcontracted workers from the laundry collect them (at least a few times a day) there is a danger of inhaling radioactive dust from the used garments. Normally, these workers do not wear a solid mask, but at best wear only a gauze mask to prevent inhaling dust. Of course, this does not adequately protect them from internal irradiation. Even washed garments sometimes retain radiation, so that there is still a possibility of suffering internal radiation when removing the garments from the dryer and putting them away.[33]

Internal irradiation is checked by a machine called a whole-body counter. Each worker's internal irradiation dosage is checked prior to taking up employment at a nuclear power plant, at the end of the contract, and once every three months in between. However, with this monitoring machine it is difficult to detect types of radiation from sources other than Manganese 54 and Cobalt 60. Alpha-rays and beta-rays, in particular, are impossible to monitor on this machine. Moreover, although electric power companies conduct checks with whole-body counters, they simply hand the detected counts of radioactivity to subcontractors and do not convert the results into irradiation dosages. Therefore, if no one in a subcontracting company knows how to convert the given data into irradiation dosages, the checks remain meaningless.[34]

Consequently, accurate figures of internal irradiation of nuclear power plant workers do not appear in official statistics. Once radioactive material is taken into the body, there is virtually no way to extract it. Thus it is almost impossible to estimate the quantities of irradiation to which these subcontracted workers are exposed, as they are constantly subjected to the danger of both internal and external irradiation. The only assumption one can make is that the official statistical data published by the Bureau of Radiation Control is not at all reliable. It is probably fair to assume that the true amount of irradiation subcontracted workers receive in any given period is several times greater than the amount recorded in the official statistics.

Irradiation and Cancer

It is not surprising, therefore, that the rate of cancer and leukemia occurring among subcontracted workers at nuclear power stations is extraordinarily high. In March 1977, Yanosuke Narazaki, a member of the lower house of the Japanese parliament, released the results of his own research into the causes of death of nuclear power plant workers.[35] (See Table 10.4). According to this survey, 106 subcontracted workers died during the ten years between July 1966 and March 1977, and seventy-five of these were due to some kind of illness. Of these seventy-five, thirty-two died from cancer or brain tumors and three deaths were due to leukemia. In other words, 46.6 percent of the workers died from diseases related to either cancer, brain tumors, or leukemia. This percentage is 2.3 times that for cancer and leukemia among the population at large. It should also be noted that this survey dealt only with already deceased workers, and that no investigation has ever been carried out into the large number of workers who are currently suffering from these types of diseases.

According to an internal report compiled in August 1984 by the nuclear

Table 10.4

Subcontracted Worker Deaths Related to Nuclear Power Plants
(July 1966–March 1977)

Nuclear Power Plant (Year operations began)	Accidental Deaths at Nuclear Power Plants		Deaths Resulting from Irradiation	
Japan Atomic Power Company Tokai Plant (1966)	Deaths from Falls	2	Deaths from Cancer	8
	Other	2	Deaths from Brain Damage	6
			Deaths from Heart Disease	1
			Other	3
Japan Atomic Power Company Tsuruga Plant (1970)	Deaths from Falls	1	Deaths from Cancer	4
	Other	2	Deaths from Brain Damage	2
			Deaths from Leukemia	1
Tokyo Electric Power Company Fukushima Plant (1971)	Deaths from Falls	2	Deaths from Cancer	8
	Other	2	Deaths from Brain Damage	12
			Deaths from Heart Disease	7
			Deaths from Leukemia	2
Chubu Electric Power Company Hamaoka Plant (1976)		0	Deaths from Cancer	3
Chugoku Electric Power Company Shimane Plant (1974)	Deaths from Falls	1	Deaths from Cancer	2
			Other	2
Kansai Electric Power Company Mihama Plant (1970)	Deaths from Falls	7	Deaths from Cancer	7
	Other	2	Deaths from Brain Damage	3
			Deaths from Heart Disease	4
Kansai Electric Power Company Takahama Plant (1974)	Deaths from Falls	2		0
	Other	3		
Subtotals	Deaths from Falls	15	Deaths from:	
	Other	16	Cancer	32
			Brain Damage	23
			Heart Disease	12
			Leukemia	3
			Other	5
Total		31		75

Source: Based on the survey conducted by Y. Narazaki, published in *Asahi Shimbun* 17 March 1977.

Table 10.5

A. Deaths of Kansai EPC Employees (1985–1984)

Name	Age	Date of Death	Disease	Position
Mr. Shinzo Ishida	56	July 1984	Cancer of the Pancreas	Chief of the Repairs Section at Mihama Plant
Mr. A.	49	9 Dec. 1983	Acute Cardiac Insufficiency	Health Officer
Mr. Tsutomu Takagi	22	2 Dec. 1983	Leukemia	Operator at Mihama Plant
Mr. Takashi Yuhara	55	27 Sept. 1984	Leukemia	Chief of the Repairs Section in Ohi Plant
Mr. Kiyoshi Ito	40	23 Oct. 1979	Leukemia	Irradiation Control Officer at Mihama Plant

B. Kansai EPC Employees Currently Suffering from Cancer-related Diseases (August 1984)

Mr. B.	20s	Brain tumor
Mr. C.	50s	Cancer of the bladder
Mr. D.	30s	Leukemia
Mr. E.	20s	Leukemia

C. Deaths of Subcontracted Workers Who Worked at Kansai EPC Power Plants (August 1978–October 1983)

Name	Age	Date of Death	Disease	Power Plant
Mr. Noboru Shimizu	54	7 Jan. 1982	Cancer of the Esophagus	Mihama
Mr. Nobutada Kitagawa	56	Oct. 1983	Stomach Cancer	Mihama
Mr. Ryosuke Suzuki	56	1982	Liver Cancer	Mihama and other
Mr. Sakae Morimoto	58	10 Oct. 1978	Liver Cancer	Tsuruga and other
Mr. Takashi Yamazaki	38	1982	Liver Cancer	Tsuruga and other
Mr. Kenzo Nakajima	60	1 Aug. 1980	Stomach Cancer	Tsuruga and other

Source: Internal reports compiled in August 1984 by the nuclear power section of the Kansai Electric Power Company.

power section of the Kansai Electric Power Company (which has nine nuclear reactors in Fukui Prefecture), between September 1983 and August 1984 three company employees died of cancer or leukemia, four employees are presently suffering from cancer or leukemia, and between 1978 and 1983 six subcontracted workers died of cancer. (See Table 10.5.) According to one source, the death rate from cancer-related diseases among these subcontracted workers is six times that of the general population.[36] It should be noted that the Kansai EPC internal report does not include any investigation of how many subcontracted workers are currently suffering from this type of illness.

In 1984 Gempatsu Bunkai, the union organization for subcontracted workers at nuclear power plants, revealed the contents of this secret report to the public and criticized the abnormally high rate of cancer/leukemia patients among nuclear power plant workers.[37] In self-defense, the Kansai EPC claimed that the total irradiation dosage of an employee who died of cancer was between 200 and 1,300 millirems, and that of a subcontracted worker who had similarly died of cancer was between 20 and 4,050 millirems. The company further claimed that these figures were below the regulation permissible level of 5,000 millirems per year and 3,000 millirems for three months.[38] The company thereby denied any causal relationship between cancer-related diseases and irradiation. However, as has already been explained, the official records of irradiation dosages to which nuclear power plant workers are exposed are extremely unreliable.

It is also said that there are many cases of suicide among young workers at nuclear power plants. There is no statistical record of this problem, but most instances seem to be of unmarried or newly married young men. It is believed that they are driven to this action by either the psychological pressure associated with difficulty in finding a marriage partner or the fear of producing a handicapped child because of exposure to radiation.

The wage that subcontracted workers at nuclear power plants receive is far from a reward for work, but could be called a special danger allowance. Because it is easy for subcontracted workers to gain relatively high wages for short working hours, they tend to spend their money gambling. In addition, in order to escape the psychological fears associated with irradiation, they tend to use drugs. Thus, Yakuza organizations further extend their control over subcontracted workers by lending money and selling drugs to them. In a vicious circle, the subcontracted workers are trapped into continuing to work at the nuclear power plants in order to pay back their debts. For subcontracted workers at nuclear power plants it is impossible to gain pleasure from work by learning new things and developing new skills. It is an anomaly that such premodern and unscientific modes of labor exist in the so-called high-tech industry of nuclear power. This situation vividly exposes the various contradictions of nuclear power technology.

Notes

1. S. Nishikawa, "Sangyō Kōzō no Henbō" (Changes in Industrial Structure), in *Kigyō to Rōdō* (Industry and Labor) *(Juristo Sōgō Tokushu,* No. 14, Yūhikaku, 1979), 66. "Temporary workers" are people under contract of less than one year and "day laborers" are people employed on a daily basis for the duration of several months. "Seasonal workers" are categorized, therefore, as "temporary workers."

2. Ibid., p. 69. The average age of the Japanese work force in 1985 is estimated at 41.3 years for males and 40.6 years for females.

3. H. Senda, *Enerugii Sangyōkai* (The Energy Industry World) (Tokyo: Kyōiku-sha, 1984), pp. 202–205; K. Higuchi, *Yami ni Kesareru Gempatsu Hibakusha* (Irradiated Nuclear Power Plant Workers Who Fade into Oblivion) (Tokyo: Sanichi Shobō, 1984), pp. 210–214.

4. This diagram is based on the case of a labor supplier, Takeshi Umeda, who in 1979 was exposed to a large dose of radiation while working at the Tsuruga Plant. The information is from T. Shibano, *Gempatsu no Aru Fūkei* (A View of Nuclear Power Plants), vol. 1 (Tokyo: Mirai, 1983), p. 66. See also Brett de Bary's chapter in this volume, "Sanya: Japan's Internal Colony."

5. It is widely believed that in addition to the percentages withheld by prime contractors, subcontracting companies take percentages amounting to about 10,000 yen per worker per day. This information is from Gempatsu Bunkai, *Gempatsu Nyusu* (Nuclear Power Plant News) no. 1 (1981) and was mentioned by S. Saito, chairman of Gempatsu Bunkai, during an interview conducted by the author in 1985 in Tsuruga, Japan.

6. S. Morie, *Gempatsu Hibaku Nikki* (The Diary of an Irradiated Nuclear Power Plant Worker) (Tokyo: Gijutsu to Ningen, 1982), pp. 158–160.

7. K. Horie, *Gempatsu Jipushii* (Nuclear Power Plant Gypsies) (Tokyo: Gendai Shokan, 1984), 107; *Shūkan Posto*, 17 November 1978.

8. T. Shibano, *Gempatsu no Aru Fūkei*, p. 160.

9. *Fukui Shimbun*, 1 February 1980.

10. For an earlier article on this same subject that includes a detailed presentation of the opinions of subcontracted workers, see Junko Yamaka, "The Hidden Foundations of Nuclear Power: Radiation and Discontent for Subcontracted Workers," *AMPO*, Vol. 13, No. 4 (1981), pp. 46–52. See also "Voices from the Darkness: Books on Work Inside Nuclear Power Plants," *AMPO*, vol. 12, no. 1 (1980).—Ed.

11. J.W. Gofman and A.R. Tamplin, *Poisoned Power: The Case Against Nuclear Power Plants Before and After Three Mile Island* (Emmaus, PA: Rodale Press, 1979), pp. 78–79.

12. Ibid., 74–75. Regarding the debate about setting a permissible level of irradiation dosage, see Chap. 2 in *Nuclear Power: Both Sides—The Best Arguments for and Against the Most Controversial Technology*, ed. M. Kaku and J. Trainer (New York: W.W. Norton and Company, 1982), pp. 27–79. The critical views of Japanese scientists on this issue can be found in the following works: S. Ichikawa, *Idengaku to Kakujidai* (Genetics and the Nuclear Age) (Tokyo: Shakai Shisō-sha, 1984); M. Taketani (ed.) *Genshiryoku Hatsuden* (Nuclear Power) (Tokyo: Iwanami, 1976); and S. Nakajima and I. Anzai, *Genshiryoku o Kangaeru* (On Nuclear Power) (Tokyo: Shin Nippon Shuppan, 1983).

13. Obtained during an interview conducted by the author with subcontracted workers in Tsuruga in January 1985.

14. S. Morie, *Gempatsu Hibaku Nikki*, p. 44; and K. Horie, *Gempatsu Jipushii*, pp. 250–252.

15. K. Horie, *Gempatsu Jipashii*, p. 250.

16. Ibid., pp. 148–152.

17. S. Morie, *Gempatsu Hibaku Nikki*, p. 124.

18. In this famous story, two fighting warlords met in the Pine Corridor of Edo Castle. During the ensuing encounter, one was injured. This event has brought about the association of dangerous places with the Pine Corridor.

19. K. Horie, *Gempatsu Jipushii*, pp. 152–155.

20. Ibid., p. 95.

21. S. Morie, *Gempatsu Hibaku Nikki*, p. 102.

22. Ibid., p. 102; Shibano, *Gempatsu no Aru Fūkei*, 25–26; and also mentioned by S. Saito during an interview conducted by the author in Tsuruga in January 1985.

23. Morie, *Gempatsu Hibaku Nikki*, pp. 118–120.

24. Horie, *Gempatsu Jipushii*, 107; Han Genshiryoku Jiten Henshū Kai, *Han Gempatsu Jiten* (The Anti-Nuclear Encyclopedia) vol. 1 (Tokyo: Gendai Shokan, 1978), p. 25.

25. Morie, *Gempatsu Hibaku Nikki*, p. 117, and also mentioned by S. Saito during an interview conducted by the author in Tsuruga in January 1985.

26. Ibid., p. 134.

27. Ibid., pp. 120–121; Shibano, *Gempatsu no Aru Fūkei*, pp. 64–65; Han Genshiryoku Hatsuden Jiten Henshū Kai, vol. 1, p. 261.

28. Morie, *Gempatsu Hibaku Nikki*, p. 148.

29. Horie, *Gempatsu Jipushii*, pp. 156–157, and his "Gempatsu no Uchi to Soto" (Inside and Outside Nuclear Power Plants) in *Rōdōsha no Sabaku* (Labourers in the Desert), ed. by E. Watanabe (Tokyo: Tsuge Shoso, 1982), pp. 154–155.

30. Morie, *Gempatsu Hibaku Nikki*, p. 129 and pp. 154–155.

31. Ibid., pp. 31, 89, and 223–234.

32. Ibid., pp. 183–184; K. Horie, *Gempatsu Jipushii*, pp. 183 and 278–283; Higuchi *Gempatsu Hibakusha*, pp. 126–127.

33. Morie, *Gempatsu Hibaku Nikki*, pp. 49 and 53–55.

34. Ibid., pp. 79–81, 207–209. For a more detailed scientific analysis of the effects of internal irradiation, see I. Anzai, *Karadano Nakano Hoshano* (Radiation in the Human Body) (Tokyo: Gōdō Shuppan, 1979).

35. *Asahi Shimbun*, 17 March 1984.

36. *Fukui Minshu Shimbun*, 25 August 1984.

37. Document obtained by the author from S. Saito in January 1985; *Fukui Shimbun*, 30 and 31 August 1984; *Asahi Shimbun*, 27 October 1984. For further details regarding subcontracted workers suffering from cancer, see Higuchi, *op. cit.*, *Gempatsu Hibakusha*, pp. 7–143, and his *Photo Document: Japan's Nuclear Power Plant's Photo* (Tokyo: Origin Shuppan, 1979), pp. 11–49.

38. *Fukui Shimbun*, 31 August 1984.

11

Dilemmas and Accommodations of Married Japanese Women in White-Collar Employment

Atsumi Reiko*

Introduction

In the 1970s much of the literature on the role of married Japanese women presented a picture that roles should be clearly demarcated and segregated by gender.[1] According to this ideal a man's main role is to earn a living, whereas a married woman's primary role is to run the household, manage the family finances, and look after the welfare of the family. Fundamental to this gender role segregation was the notion that women had a natural aptitude for matters relating to the home and to the family, and that a woman's most important and rewarding role was that of nurturing her family. This view lies behind the complete interdependence and role complementarity that characterize the Japanese husband-wife relationship.

Seemingly in contrast to these ideals, recent labor statistics show that in Japan over 60 percent of women between thirty-five and fifty-four are now in the labor force. Furthermore, the proportion of married female employees to all female employees has drastically increased during the last twenty years. In 1984 nearly 60 percent of female employees were married, whereas female employees who had never been married constituted only 32 percent of the total.[2] Table 11.1 shows that between 1962 and 1984 the ratio of married to unmarried females at work has nearly reversed. This increase in the proportion of married female employees may be interpreted as a result of a change in the attitudes of the Japanese toward married women working outside the home.

Other data, however, indicate that a large proportion of married female employees are part-time workers. Tanaka and Azuma report that the proportion is 41 percent.[3] Another survey of married female employees between twenty-five and forty-nine indicates that 52 percent are part-time workers, an increase for

*I wish to express my sincere thanks to all of my informants, who kindly spared their valuable time for this research. I am also grateful to reviewers who read an earlier version of this chapter and made very useful comments, and to Michelle Jibson for her comments on the style and wording of my chapter.

Table 11.1

Percentages of Female Employees by Marital Status

Year	Unmarried	Married	Widowed/Divorced
1962	55.2	32.7	12.0
1965	50.3	38.6	11.0
1970	48.3	41.4	10.3
1975	38.0	51.3	10.8
1980	32.5	57.4	10.0
1984	31.5	59.2	9.3

Source: Taken from the Rōdōshō Fujinkyoku, *Fujin rōdō no jitsujō* (Tokyo: Okurasho, 1985), p. 23 of appendices.

those thirty-five and over.[4] A survey undertaken by the Federation of the Private Broadcasting Workers' Union in 1974 showed that regular full-time female employees amounted to only 35.5 percent of all working women; the other 64.5 percent were employed on a part-time or contract basis.[5] Considering that married women constitute the greater proportion of part-time workers,[6] the aforementioned increase in the proportion of married women in employment may not mean a change in attitudes or values in any fundamental way. On the contrary, it may well mean that married women themselves prefer to work part time because they believe that part-time employment does not interfere with the satisfactory performance of their role as domestic nurturers.

As a preliminary project a small number of full-time housewives were interviewed in the metropolitan Tokyo area in 1982. These housewives did not fully approve of a married woman working outside the home unless there was a dire economic need or the outside job was socially important. They thought that the amount of money they might earn was minimal and the contribution they might make to society through such outside employment was insignificant and therefore did not justify the kind of sacrifice it would entail at home. This perception is often blamed on Japanese employment practices. In fact, such practices have acted against and effectively discouraged women from desiring to remain as full-time employees. The starting salary for young female employees in the private sector, for example, averaged 5 to 10 percent less than that of their male counterparts (see Table 11.2). This initial gap widened as long as male and female colleagues continued their employment with the same company.

Japanese managers explained the existence of an initial gap by pointing out that men and women were hired to perform different functions.[7] A gap in later years was mainly due to the fact that most Japanese companies have not offered career-track positions to female employees.[8] This has not been seriously questioned until very recently, and most company managers and the women themselves believed that the major role of women was in the home. It has simply been assumed and expected that female employees would normally resign from their

Table 11.2

The Average Starting Salary of Female Employees as a Percentage of the Average Starting Salary of Male Employees (in all Industries)

Newly graduated from:	1976	1980	1984
Junior High School	90.9	90.3	94.8
Senior High School	95.4	95.2	94.7
Junior College	98.5	96.7	94.2
University (Non-Technical)	92.9	94.9	94.8

Source: Taken from the Rōdōshō Fujinkyoku, *Fujin rōdō no jitsujō* (Tokyo: Okurasho, 1985), p. 53 of appendices.

jobs in their middle to late twenties to get married and raise families.[9] Such resignations normally took place before a woman reached an age for the first promotion. It has been commonly accepted that a woman who stayed in the company beyond this "marriageable age" would not be very well respected unless she has a special skill or qualification.[10] Knowing all this, and having been socialized into the belief that a woman's deepest reward comes from fulfilling the traditional role of wife and mother, the majority of women have found marriage and child-rearing the most natural option.

After the adoption of the Equal Employment Opportunity Law in April 1986, such discriminatory employment practices theoretically ought to disappear. Concerns, however, have already been expressed that this law may worsen the working conditions of women. Further, the effectiveness of the Equal Employment Opportunity Law is questioned since it has no provisions for punishing offenders. It is also feared that discrimination may exist in a different guise.[11] In any case, it is too early to assess the real impact of the law. I will argue in this article that unequal job opportunities for women are only one and not necessarily the major contributing factor to the majority of women discontinuing their employment after marriage and childbirth. Many other conditions and complex circumstances are involved in a married woman's decision to continue her full-time employment through her child-rearing years.

This article is concerned with the following sorts of questions: If the ideal of gender role segregation is still widely practiced, how do married women who are fully employed cope with the situation? Are they carrying a double workload, or are they different and free from the gender-role-segregation model? If not, what are the conditions and circumstances that allow them to carry out the dual role?

To explore these questions, fieldwork was carried out in the metropolitan Tokyo area in 1985. Eighteen women (fourteen full-time and four part-time employees) were successfully interviewed. Each woman was individually interviewed three or four times at her place of work, her home, and/or an office provided by Sophia University in Tokyo. The interviews and the research project generally had three main objectives: One was to assess the degree of persistence of the gender role segregation among Japanese women who were employed outside the home. Another was to identify the conditions and circumstances that enabled them to continue full-time employment. The third was to find some explanations for the findings. This chapter is based on an analysis of the data primarily derived from these intensive interviews with eighteen women and secondarily from related materials collected in the field.

Characteristics of the Informants

All of the women agreed to cooperate in the research after being personally introduced to me by my friends, relatives, and acquaintances. To be considered an appropriate informant, a woman must have been married, had one or more children, and have worked outside the home more or less continuously through her child-rearing years. Women whose upbringing or educational background seemed to be special or unusual, such as those with a postgraduate education or those who had studied and/or lived abroad, were excluded from the analysis.

Except for two full-time workers, all of the women interviewed were in their thirties and forties at the time of the interview. One of the two exceptions was in her mid-twenties and the other in her mid-fifties. Their level of education, particularly that of the full-time workers, was much higher than that of women of comparable age in the general population (see Table 11.3). Seven of my informants (six full-time workers) were university graduates and another seven (six full-time workers) were either junior college graduates or had had some postsecondary education. Only four had not gone beyond high school.

Interestingly, three women with full-time employment earned their university degrees by attending night courses while concurrently maintaining full-time jobs—not a popular course of action in Japan, especially for women. In 1974 only 5 percent of all female university students in Japan attended night courses. The comparable figure for male students was 9 percent.[12]

The jobs these eighteen women held at the time do not represent the full range of jobs most commonly held by female employees in Japan. In 1980 one-half of the total number of female employees were engaged in production, service, and sales work.[13] None of my informants, however, was employed in any of these occupations, as this study focuses on the white-collar workers. Although seven informants (six full-time workers) held clerical-secretarial positions, none worked for Japanese manufacturing or commercial companies. Two worked for the local government, and one each for a research institute, a welfare organization, a religious organization, and a foreign government. Three were school teachers and four were in child-care services, both professions well established as suitable occupations for women.

The sample has some other peculiarities. For example, looking at the occupations of the full-time employees' husbands, the majority did not work for manufacturing or commercial firms. Two were schoolteachers; two were civil

Table 11.3

Percentages of Female Students Who Advanced to Upper Secondary and Tertiary Levels of Education after Graduating from the Preceding Level

Year	High School	Junior College	University
1955	47.4	2.6	2.4
1960	55.9	3.0	2.5
1965	69.9	6.7	4.6
1970	82.7	11.2	6.5
1975	93.0	19.9	12.5
1980	95.4	21.0	12.3
1985	94.9	20.8	13.7
Percentage of all interviewees to graduate at these levels	22.2	38.9	38.9

Source: Taken from the Rōdōshō Fujinkyoku, *Fujin rōdō no jitsujō* (Tokyo: Ōkurashō, 1985), p. 34 of appendices.

servants; two were in counseling and community service; one was in law practice; one was in a labor union organization; one was a researcher; one was a newspaper reporter; one was an editor in a publishing company; and one was self-employed. Only two were employed in small companies.

My informants who worked full time could be divided into two categories. One consisted of those who had stayed in the same profession (three teachers and one nurse) or with the same employer (two in local government and one at a research institute). The other category was comprised of those who had changed jobs two or more times, reflecting their search and struggle for more satisfying positions that would accommodate their personal and family requirements.

The above peculiarities are not accidental. They are the inevitable, and hence meaningful, consequence of selecting informants on the basis of the aforementioned criteria. The peculiarities indicate the distinctive nature of the full-time married female white-collar employee in Japan. The over-representation of those with tertiary education among my informants with full-time employment implies that these women are equipped with a special skill and/or qualification and have entered a profession or an occupation that is interesting and rewarding. The very nature of such work most likely sustained these women in their jobs even through their child-rearing years.

Not represented in my sample are women holding clerk-secretary positions in Japanese companies. This clearly indicates that it is difficult for women to remain employed as full-time white-collar workers in Japanese companies after marriage and the birth of a child. According to one informant, Naomi (a thirty-seven-year-old part-time employee at a bank), all married female employees at her branch were part-time workers. Numerous episodes during my fieldwork confirmed that many young women who were employed as white-collar workers by a Japanese commercial or manufacturing firm chose (or were induced) to resign in their mid-twenties, or at the latest when they were expecting a baby. Another informant, Junko (a forty-year-old secretary at a research institute), related that the majority of her junior college classmates took jobs with trading companies as such jobs appeared ideal to them at the time. None of those women remained employed by the same company through their child-rearing years. Ironically, Junko took a position at a research institute since she was not living with her parents and hence did not satisfy a condition of employment with those trading companies. The positions that my informants in full-time employment held, on the other hand, were more favorably defined in this regard.

The fact that the majority of the husbands of these women were not company employees indicates that their working conditions and the ideological orientation associated with their occupations (for example, teaching, community service, law practice, etc.) may well have lent support to their wives continuing their full-time employment. A similar result is also reported by E. Mouer. In her study only 15.9 percent of the professional women were married to company employees, whereas 53 percent of the housewives with a similar level of education were married to businessmen or company employees, whose life styles tend to require the support of full-time housewives.[14]

Findings Derived from the Interviews

A great majority of the working women interviewed in this study seemed to be fundamentally similar to nonworking women or full-time housewives in two respects. First, they did not share domestic activities and family responsibilities (other than those related to child rearing) with their husbands. Second, they expressed more concern about their children than about their husbands or their conjugal relationships.

As expected, the women in part-time employment faithfully fulfilled the traditionally prescribed woman's role, not challenging the ideal that gender roles should be segregated. Of course, the major reason for their not holding full-time jobs was their realization that they would be unable to carry out the prescribed woman's role properly if they did. Although two of the full-time workers also approximated the ideal on their own (although only with considerable effort), the other full-time workers fulfilled the prescribed role by depending on help provided by a close relative, such as their mother or mother-in-law. A similar proportion of professional women studied by Osako also enjoyed this arrangement.[15] The close relative lived in the same household or very close to their home. The extent of help rendered by such a person varied from individual to individual and according to the woman's stage of life. The most important help given by such a person was in the area of child care. For example, Kayoko (a thirty-eight-year-old prefectural government employee) and her husband moved into the upstairs rooms of her parents' house when she was expecting her first child. They have remained there ever since. Her mother looked after her first son at home for a year and a half until he was old enough to be placed in a nursery school in the neighborhood. Her mother subsequently took care of Kayoko's second son at home for a year and seven months before he was put in the nursery. Kayoko took her sons to the nursery school on the way to work in the morning as her workplace was relatively close to her house, but she had to depend on her mother to pick them up in the afternoon before the nursery school closed at five. The availability of such help was crucial to the woman concerned, and it would have been impossible for her to continue full-time employment without it. As shown above, even if a woman is fortunate enough to be able to place her child in a conveniently located public child-care center, she will not be able to take her child to the center or pick him or her up because the normal operating hours of such a center are from 8 A.M. to 5 P.M.

In relying on a close relative, these women were unwittingly perpetuating traditional patterns of family life. In the traditional family household the younger couple were both engaged in productive activities, while the older woman looked after small children. The present situation differs in that the young wife controls the household finances and family affairs. This arrangement, however, seems to reinforce the lineal relationship rather than the conjugal relationship as the two women work together in the domestic arena, exchanging information on children and household matters. It also appears to discourage the husband's participation in domestic activities. A few informants explicitly said that their husbands did not like to do domestic chores because of the presence of either the husband's own mother or his mother-in-law in the household.

Nonetheless, a few husbands participated in domestic activities and shared family responsibilities with their wives. For example, Akiko's husband (a forty-two-year-old lawyer) usually prepared breakfast for the family and made lunches for the children to take to school, and Atsuko's husband (a thirty-seven-year-old local government employee) did the vacuuming and occasionally some cooking. The extent of these husbands' participation in domestic duties was far from equal sharing, but what mattered most to these working women was not the amount of actual practical help rendered by her husband, but the expression of his psychological and ideological support through appropriate gestures and words. In this regard, most of my informants with full-time employment acknowledged that they were receiving some sort of emotional and psychological support from their husbands.

My informants showed little concern about the fact that their husbands did not bear an equal share of the domestic workload. Most women already had other persons they could rely on. A few women admitted that jobs around the house could be done much faster and more efficiently by themselves than by their husbands. If they were asked, most husbands were willing to help their wives in the domestic arena, but few would initiate domestic work on their own. The wives also acknowledged that the current situation was, in a way, their own fault because the women themselves did not encourage their husbands when they did try. Accordingly these husbands saw little reason to give domestic chores a high priority.

With the help of a trusted family member and the emotional and ideological support of the husband, the women working full time managed to fulfill both the domestic role and the role of a full-time employee. In addition to these two essential requirements, several other considerations seem to relate to a woman's decision to continue her full-time employment after having children.

One is access to reliable child-care facilities in the vicinity of her home. The number of child-care facilities has grown rapidly in recent years. As of 1980 there were 21,960 child-care facilities in Japan. This is an increase of 20 percent since 1975.[16] However, the majority of these facilities cater to older children, with children three years old and older constituting 80 percent of the total children cared for in such facilities.[17] As mentioned earlier, operating hours of these facilities present a problem since most working women leave home before the opening hour of the child-care center and remain in the workplace until after the closing hour.

Another factor is a favorable work environment, which includes the established practice of taking full maternity leave and nursing hours, the strong support and understanding of her immediate colleagues, and relatively easy working hours (for example, almost no overtime work, complete two-day weekends, etc.). Where there are strong labor unions in the workplace, female employees are in a much better position because both male and female colleagues support a woman taking full maternity leave and nursing hours. Nursing leave without pay (up to the first birthday of the child) has been available since 1976, but at present the practice is limited to women employed in the areas of teaching, nursing, social work, and the like in public institutions.[18] The majority of my informants did not benefit from this nursing leave without pay. Other desirable conditions include a relatively short commuting time,[19] jobs with low levels of gender-based discrimination, and jobs that are perceived as being "socially meaningful," such as teaching, child care, health and medical work, social work, counseling, research, etc.

If a family is having a hard time economically, a married woman has no other choice but to work full time, regardless of whether she has a small child or not. Akiko (a forty-two-year-old ward assembly member) and her husband married against their parents' advice when they were both university students. Akiko withdrew from her university studies and began working full time, first in a wholesale store, and next in a public corporation. After two years the first child was born, but she continued her full-time work in the public corporation, leaving the baby in care of a "nursing mama," because her husband was studying for a bar examination at the time. In contemporary Japan, however, where 80 to 90 percent of the population regard themselves as belonging to the middle stratum of society,[20] economic necessity in a majority of cases does not mean need for survival but need for meeting the rising costs of education and housing. Michiko (a forty-year-old editor in a religious organization), for instance, worked part time until a year before I interviewed her, but since a full extra income was needed to send her son to the university, she started to work on a full-time basis. When the economic circumstances of a family permit, Japanese women who do not hold "socially meaningful" jobs normally cease full-time employment upon pregnancy or sometimes even before, knowing that their positions will not lead to a rewarding future. Bamba cites the results of a survey of unmarried female workers. To the question "How long do you want to work in your present office?" the majority (74 percent) answered until marriage or childbirth; an additional 20 percent said that they would leave as soon as possible.[21] A more recent survey by the prime minister's office also provides a similar picture. Marriage and domestic and family responsibilities constitute the primary reasons (70 percent) for women quitting work.[22]

Even when a woman wants to continue to work through her child-rearing years, she may be "compelled" to resign against her wishes as she sees no other way out at the time. Such a woman reluctantly resigns from her work, wishing to return to the labor force after several years of child rearing. A few of my informants witnessed this at their workplace. The probability of such a woman returning to full-time employment *several* years afterwards, however, is rather slim, because by then the full-time employment market is practically closed to her unless she has a special skill or qualification. Thus she joins the future reservoir of Japan's part-time workers. Only a small minority of women with a firm ideological commitment are able to return to work under these difficult or nearly impossible conditions. One of my informants, Yoshiko (a forty-six-year-old nursery school teacher) who had no close relatives to rely on, was compelled to resign from her first job at a publishing company when she became pregnant. No child-care facilities were available in her area in the mid-1960s. She overcame the hurdle by acquiring qualifications as a nursery school teacher through extension studies while she stayed home to take care of the baby. This was a timely choice since qualified workers were in demand at a newly formed child-care service in her housing complex a year later. This opened a completely new path in her working career.

Although none of the women who had chosen to continue their full-time employment expressed regret at their choice, some did admit that they felt sorry for their children. They were extremely sensitive to criticism aimed at working mothers who could not perform their roles as mothers properly. My informants were very much concerned about their performance of that role. They sometimes felt that the long working hours and work commitments made them inadequate in this respect. The feelings of inadequacy were at times expressed as "guilt feelings." The following episode, related by Yoshiko, demonstrates how much a Japanese working mother is sensitive to the critical eyes of others when it comes to her role as a mother, and how easily she is hurt when she is made aware that she is not fulfilling her role of an attentive and nurturing mother. When Yoshiko's first child reached school age, there was no after-school day-care service for school-age children *(gakudō-hoiku)* in their school district. Yoshiko and her husband decided to sent their son to the school in the next school district where such service was available for a few hours after school for children in first to third grade. Unfortunately it was a little far and it took half an hour for the first-grader to walk home late in the afternoon. One evening when Yoshiko came home from work, one of her neighbors asked her if she was aware that her son often came home alone in the dark crying. This seemingly harmless remark of a neighbor obviously hurt Yoshiko a great deal, as she began to cry when she recalled the episode. She felt so sorry for her son, she said, but she could not resign from her job as a nursery school teacher for she considered it a worthwhile occupation. Yoshiko's husband supported her, and they coped with the situation by buying a car and both acquiring driver's licenses. This shortened her commuting time and enabled her to pick up her son on the way home. A woman's employment outside the home could only be justified, in their minds, if she were engaged in the kind of work considered to be "socially meaningful."

Conclusions

The findings of this study have revealed that gender role segregation was evidently practiced by my informants who had been employed full time in white-collar occupations through their child-rearing years. In order to satisfy the requirements of the traditional role of wife and mother, and the economic role of an employee, most of the women depended on the help of a close relative such as a mother or a mother-in-law. In addition, the findings have shown that various other conditions had to be met for a married woman to be able to remain in full-time employment in Japan through her child-rearing years. These working women often experienced physical as well as psychological hardship. Why did my informants who were full-time employees accept the traditional role of women and try hard to perform a dual role? Why weren't there more men who would share domestic duties and family responsibilities with their wives? Why did most of these working women show little concern about their husbands not becoming involved in domestic activities and family responsibilities? After all, why does gender role segregation persist in contemporary urban Japan?

Some might argue that unequal employment opportunities for women have discouraged Japanese women from continuing full-time employment beyond marriage or childbirth, and hence contributed to the perpetuation of the traditional gender role segregation. Although this argument fits well with the case of full-time housewives and wives with part-time employment, it does not account for the attitudes or behavior of my informants who had held full-time jobs through their child-rearing years. Nor does it explain the variation among husbands in terms of the degree of their involvement in domestic matters. Above all the argument does not really explain the persistence of the idea of the separation of gender roles. Essentially circular in logic, the argument would be that gender role segregation persists because of discriminatory employment practices resulting from the gender role ideal.

A more viable explanation, I would propose, is that the model of segregated gender roles has been promoted and reinforced by Japanese industrialists to achieve and maintain a high economic growth rate. The idea has provided a good excuse for leading Japanese companies to exploit their male employees as extensively and thoroughly as possible. It is internationally recognized that Japanese employees work much longer and take fewer days of vacation than their counterparts in comparably developed Western societies. In 1978 Japanese workers in all industries worked an average of 2,114 hours a year. This is about 200 hours longer than the average American or English worker in that year, and 400 hours longer than the average worker in West Germany and France. Owing to international criticism that Japanese workers are overworked, the Japanese government has tried over a five-year period to reduce the total annual working hours per worker to 2,000 hours by promoting two-day weekends and more holidays and reducing overtime work hours. No success has been reported. The total annual working hours for the average worker in 1984 was 2,115.[23]

Japanese workers have been imbued with an idea that working hard and long is necessary for Japan's survival. A nationwide survey of workers (both male and female) employed in establishments with 100 or more employees revealed that 47 percent of those surveyed considered it proper to sacrifice one's private life for the sake of the company's work. The percentage was much higher for those workers in management (73 percent).[24] In my previous research the belief that "the country depends on our hard work" was strongest among the elite company employees interviewed, and this was the source of their energy and pride.[25] Most of the male Japanese company employees have been compelled to conform to this norm, even though they may not totally subscribe to it. It is hard to be a nonconformist in a large Japanese company, as work assignments are allocated to a group rather than to an individual. No Japanese company man wants to be alienated from his peers. Those who cannot bear that kind of pressure would not choose to be company employees in the first place, let alone be an elite employee in a large company. Those who want to succeed in the system often have to sacrifice home and family life for the sake of the company.[26]

Such a high degree of commitment to work by male company employees is only possible when their private lives are taken care of by their wives. The fact that the proportion of working women's husbands who are company employees is low also supports this contention. It is interesting to note that none of the wives of the nineteen company employees in my previous research held a full-time job outside the home.[27]

As the norm prescribes that women bear responsibility for domestic matters, it has been hard, if not impossible, for a company man to excuse himself from work or take a half day off for domestic or family reasons. Married women, on the other hand, have been reminded that their full support is required in the home if their husbands are to devote time and energy to their work. This was evident with my informants with part-time jobs and those full-time housewives I interviewed previously. This ideology is so pervasive that even many of my informants whose husbands were not of this sort tried to manage domestic work without their husbands' assistance. Sometimes an employee of a large company or the government may have to take a post in a faraway place for a few years. If an employee wants to stay in the system and succeed, he must take it, although such a transfer is most likely to force a married man to be separated from his family *(tanshin funin)*. Nearly half of the male employees surveyed nationwide in 1985–86 considered *tanshin funin* necessary and unavoidable for the sake of the company. The percentage of those who support such a practice is much higher for the middle-aged men among whom *tanshin funin* is most prevalent.[28]

On the other side of the coin, management in many Japanese companies quite openly discouraged women employees from continuing to work after marriage. In many ways they communicated their ideology that a woman's main responsibility lies in the home, caring for her family. One reason for taking this position is obvious. Women cannot be exploited as much as their male counterparts. Until April 1986 the protective Labor Standards Law had "protected" women employees from engaging in certain jobs, such as late night work. There are also, of course, maternity leaves and other related provisions. By highlighting the utmost importance of the mother's role, the model of segregated gender roles has furnished Japanese companies with an excellent ideology to justify their discouraging women from remaining in the labor force as full-time employees after marriage and particularly after childbirth. This very model has at the same time facilitated the exploitation of married women as part-time employees. Part-time employees receive low pay, little job security, and none of the regular promotions or benefits that full-time regular employees may enjoy in a Japanese company. Nevertheless, such employment allows a woman to earn her own income and to carry out the prescribed role satisfactorily. In this way, Japanese companies have not only avoided dealing with the problems associated with maternity leave, nursing hours, and child-care arrangements of the average working woman, but they have also profited from hiring married women as a part-time labor force that can be used as a buffer to adjust personnel levels as changing economic circumstances may require.[29]

The political elite of the country have similarly used the idea of segregated gender roles to shift the governmental responsibility for meeting the basic social and welfare needs of the people to individual citizens, in particular to women. Japanese women are repeatedly socialized into a belief that mothers are the best caretakers of small children, that the mother's physical presence at home when school-age children return from school is essential for their healthy emotional development, and that the elderly are happiest when a family member takes care

Some large companies have educational courses for their employees' wives to train them to always smile—"a backup for the fighting forces." In this cartoon, the sign on the wall says "Always smiling, smiling for husbands," and at the lower right a dissenter is carrying a sign saying "Smiling lectures on divorce!" This cartoon is from *AMPO: Japan-Asia Quarterly Review*, vol. 18, no. 2–3 (1986), p. 69.

of them.[30] This shift of responsibility has retarded the development of public social-welfare programs, services, and facilities. The number of public child-care facilities did increase in the 1970s, but in order to place a child in such a facility, proof is required that no one can look after the child at home. A nationwide investigation into the conditions of child-care facilities in 1980 revealed that 94.2 percent of the children who were enrolled in the facilities were from families where the mother worked full time.[31]

"A Prospectus for Strengthening the Family Base" issued in 1979 reveals that the Japanese government intends to protect and further reinforce traditional gender role segregation by stressing the responsibility of the home in the care of children and aging parents.[32] If this is how the government plans to cope with the problems of a rapidly aging country, it will serve to present yet another difficulty for working women. None of my informants has yet encountered the problem involved in caring for an ailing parent or parent-in-law, but some expressed concern about this issue, saying that should anything happen to their aging parents or parents-in-law, they may have to give up their present jobs as they must fulfill the prescribed role of being the dutiful caretaker and nurturer. They have the mixed feeling of wanting to care for their elderly but also feeling obliged to do so at the same time. It is only natural for those who had been helped greatly by a particular relative while their children were small to try to return the debt when they see no other acceptable alternative in the foreseeable future.

I postulate here that the mass media and school curricula, especially textbooks, have also played profound roles in propagating gender role segregation as a dominant ideology. This problem has been investigated by a number of scholars and groups since 1975, and will be pursued by me in a forthcoming research project.

Possible Implications

Gender role segregation is an important norm in contemporary Japan, believed by the majority of Japanese people to be both natural and desirable. Women fulfilling the prescribed domestic and nurturing role seem to enjoy a high degree of emotional reward. The small sampling I studied in 1985 and have presented in this article supports the generalization that in Japan gender role segregation is so pervasive that even those who hold full-time jobs outside the home are not excluded from the practice. Thus, if a married woman wants to continue in full-time employment, she has to find a trusted family member to help her in domestic and child-care duties, as she could not hope to count on her husband in this respect. Without any appropriate arrangement of this sort it is not only impossible for a married woman to continue full-time employment, but it is also likely that she would be bitterly criticized by the people with whom she has close contact. Even when a working mother somehow endures such criticism, she may still experience inner doubts that lead to a feeling of inadequacy as a mother. Favorable circumstances, including subtle supports and encouragements, are necessary for a married woman to be able to continue in full-time employment through the child-rearing years. Only with an extraordinary commitment to her profession and the firm emotional and ideological support of her husband and her colleagues can a woman manage to continue full-time employment.

The model of segregated gender roles has effectively contributed to the "economic miracle" of Japan, but the "miracle" has been accomplished at a severe cost to the humanity of those involved. In a society where economic values are overstressed, those who are weaker, less efficient, and less economically productive tend to be ignored and oppressed. In such a society intrinsic human values and individual dignity are apt to be slighted. Some of the problems now occurring among schoolchildren (for example, bullying) are just the tip of the iceberg of this grave problem. Problems that children exhibit are alarming symptoms reflecting the ills produced by the dominant values of the society. Japanese women have undergone discrimination of various kinds in employment since the outset of Japan's industrialization. In recent decades these discriminatory practices have often been attributed to the idea of gender role segregation. In this article I have attempted to show that the idea of segregated gender roles is not the villain but a scapegoat, and that women are not the only victims in this whole enterprise.

286 THE OTHER JAPAN

Notes

1. For example, see Kunitachi-shi, ed., *Shufu to onna* (Housewives and women) (Tokyo: Mirai-sha, 1973); Takie S. Lebra, "Sex Equality for Japanese Women," *The Japan Interpreter*, vol. 10, no. 3–4 (1975), pp. 284–295; Susan J. Pharr, "The Japanese Women: Evolving Views of Life and Role," in L. Austin, ed., *Japan—The Paradox of Progress* (New Haven: Yale University Press, 1976), pp. 301–327; M.M. Osako, "Dilemmas of Japanese Professional Women," *Social Problems*, vol. 26 (1978), pp. 15–25; Susanne H. Vogel, "Professional Housewife: The Career of Urban Middle Class Japanese Women," *The Japan Interpreter*, vol. 12, no. 1 (1978), pp. 17–43; Fukaya Masashi, "Socialization and Sex Roles of Housewives," in M. White and B. Molony, eds., *Proceedings of the Tokyo Symposium on Women* (Tokyo: The International Group for the Study of Women), pp. 133–149; and Kokusai Josei Gakkai, ed., *Gendai Nihon no shufu* (Contemporary Japanese housewives) (Tokyo: Nihon Hōsō Shuppan Kyōkai, 1980).

2. Rōdōshō Fujin-Kyoku, *Fujin rōdō no jitsujō* (Facts on women's labor) (Tokyo: Okurasho Insatsu-Kyoku, 1985), appendix, p. 23.

3. K. Tanaka and Y. Azuma, *Shin gendai fujin no ishiki* (New consciousness of contemporary women) (Tokyo: Gyosei, 1985), p. 157.

4. Nakano-ku jidō seishōnen-bu, *Koyōsarete hataraku kikon josei no shokugyō to seikatsu* (The occupation and life of married women in employment) (Tokyo: Nakano-ku, 1983).

5. Bamba Tomoko, "The 'Office Ladies' Paradise: Inside and Out," *Japan Quarterly*, vol. 26, no. 2 (1979), p. 246.

6. Tanaka and Azuma, *Fujin no ishiki.*

7. Takeuchi Hiroshi, "Working Women in Business Corporations—The Management Viewpoint," *Japan Quarterly*, vol. 29, no. 3 (1982); Dorothy Robins-Mowry, *The Hidden Sun* (Boulder: Westview Press, 1983), p. 172; and Jon Woronoff, *Japan's Wasted Workers* (Totowa, NJ: Allanheld, Osmum & Co., 1983), pp. 111–147.

8. Ibid., and Takeuchi, "Working Women."

9. Woronoff, *Japan's Wasted Workers*, p. 132; and Thomas P. Rohlen, *For Harmony and Strength* (Berkeley: University of California Press, 1974), p. 48.

10. Bamba, " 'Office Ladies' Paradise," pp. 241–247.

11. Inoue Shigeko, "Danjo Koyō Kikai Kinto-hō, Kaisei Rōdō Kijun-hō no shikō ni atari ni-san no mondaiten o miru" (Examining a few problems in the enforcement of the Equal Employment Opportunity Law and the Revised Labor Standards Law), *Fujin Rōdō* no. 11 (1986), pp. 7–13; Tada Toyoko, "Danjo Koyō Kikai Kinto-hō wa shokuba ni dō eikyō suruka" (What impacts the Equal Employment Opportunity Law has on the workplace), *Fujin Rōdō*, no. 11 (1986), pp. 25–32; Ōba Ayako, "Danjo koyō kikai kinto to rōdōjikan tanshuku ni tsuite no gimon" (Doubts concerning equal employment opportunity and the reduction of working hours), *Fujin Rōdō* no. 11 (1986), pp. 33–40; and Takenaka Emiko, " 'Kinto-hō' go no joshi koyō" (Employment of women since the Equal Opportunity Law), *Fujin Kyōiku Jōhō*, no. 15 (1987), pp. 2–9.

12. Mary Jean Bowman, *Educational Choice and Labor Markets in Japan* (Chicago: The University of Chicago Press, 1981), p. 162.

13. Rōdōshō Fujin-Kyoku, *Fujin rōdō no jitsujō*, appendices, pp. 16–17.

14. Elizabeth J. Mouer, "Gender Role Socialization, Achievement Motivation and Occupational Choice among Professional Women and Housewives in Japan" (Ph.D. diss., Griffith University, 1984), pp. 278, 282.

15. M.M. Osako, "Dilemmas of Japanese Professional Women," *Social Problems*, vol. 26 (1978), pp. 15–25.

16. Gyōseikanri-chō, *Hoiku-jo no genjō to mondaiten* (Conditions and problems of child care facilities) (Tokyo: Okurasho Insatsukyoku, 1982), p. 42.

17. Ibid., p. 14.

18. Higuchi Keiko, "Ikuji Kyūhyō-hō" in Jiyū Kokumin-sha, ed., *Gendaiyōgo no kisochishiki* (Fundamental knowledge of contemporary words) (Tokyo: Jiyū Kokuminsha, 1986), p. 472.

19. It is not unusual for a salary earner in Tokyo to spend more than an hour one way in commuting to work. Commuting by car is unusual for the majority of salary earners in the Tokyo metropolitan area where the public transport system is well developed and extremely reliable.

20. Kimindo Kusaka, "What Is the Japanese Middle Class?"

21. Bamba, " 'Office Ladies' Paradise," p. 24.

22. Sorifu Kōhōshitsu, "Fujin no shūgyō" (Women's work), *Yoron Chōsa* vol. 16, no. 4 (1984), pp. 2–56.

23. S. Akita, "Rōdō-jikan tanshuku mondai" (Problems of reducing working hours), in Jiyū Kokumin-sha, ed., *Gendaiyōgo no kisochishiki*, p. 430.

24. Rōdō Daijin Kambō Seisaku Chōsa-bu, *Nihonteki koyō kankō no henka to tembō* (Change and prospects in Japanese employment practices) (Tokyo: Okurasho Insatsu-kyoku, 1987), p. 56.

25. Atsumi Reiko, "Personal Relationships of Japanese White-Collar Company Employees" (Ph.D. diss., University of Pittsburgh, 1975).

26. Ronald Dore, *British Factory—Japanese Factory* (Berkeley: University of California Press, 1974), pp. 248–251.

27. Atsumi, "Personal Relationships of Japanese White-Collar Company Employees," p. 149.

28. Rōdō Daijin Kambō Seisaku Chōsa-bu, *Henka no tembō*, p. 56.

29. Thomas P. Rohlen, " 'Permanent Employment' Faces Recession, Slow Growth and Aging Work Force," *The Journal of Japanese Studies*, vol. 5 (1979), pp. 235–272.

30. This belief was very common among the full-time housewives interviewed in 1982 and my informants with part-time jobs; also see Kunitachi-shi, *Shufu to onna*.

31. Gyōseikanri-chō, *Genjō to mondaiten*, p. 8.

32. Nihon Kodomo o Mamoru Kai, ed., *Kodomo hakusho* (White paper on children) (Tokyo: Sōdo Bunka, 1980), pp. 222–225.

12

The "Problem" of Foreign Workers in Contemporary Japan

*John Lie**

The rapid mobility of labor and capital across national boundaries is a critical feature of the contemporary capitalist world-economy.[1] Japan is no exception, and the influx of foreign workers *(gaikokujin rodosha)* became perhaps the most discussed social problem in the late 1980s and early 1990s. While the Japanese mass media was rife with sensationalist coverage, a heated public debate raged on whether Japan should be "open" or "closed" to foreign workers.[2]

In this essay I focus on a paradox. On the one hand, there were intense and protracted discussions of the "problem" of foreign workers. On the other hand, there were no obvious causes for alarm. In spite of the growing presence of foreign workers, their estimated number was under 500,000, or .5 percent of the total population of Japan in 1990. The vast majority of them, moreover, performed tasks that most Japanese shunned. Why were there, then, intense and acrimonious debates on the problem of foreign workers in Japan? While conservatives stressed their threat to Japanese society, liberals spoke of exploitation and human rights abuses. More significantly, however, the presence of foreign workers challenged the prevailing preconception of the racial and cultural homogeneity of Japan. In so doing, it also threatened to resurrect Japan's unresolved colonial legacy, including the discriminated-against Korean minority.

Foreign Workers in Japan

The "foreign workers" in the dominant Japanese discussion referred neither to the existing Korean and Chinese minorities nor to Europeans and North Americans in Japan, but rather to the manual and service workers mainly from Asian

*An earlier version of this chapter was presented at the American Sociological Association annual meeting in Pittsburgh, PA, in August 1992. I acknowledge the financial assistance provided by the Japan Foundation and the Research Board of the University of Illinois at Urbana-Champaign. I wish to thank Nancy Abelmann and Hiroshi Ishida for their thoughtful comments. Thanks also to Bill Doub and the anonymous *BCAS* reviewers for their helpful suggestions.

Table 12.1

Registered Foreigners in Japan, 1992

Residence Status	1990	1992
Work Visa (Entertainers)	67,983 (21,138)	85,487 (22,750)
Temporary Visitors	16,467	33,333
Students	84,310	102,953
Trainees	13,249	19,237
Dependents of Japanese	130,218	209,269
Long-Term Residents	54,359	122,814
Total	1,075,317	1,281,444

Source: Homusho Nyukoku Kanrikyoku (Ministry of Justice, Immigration Control Bureau), *Shutsu-nyukoku kanri kankei tokei gaiyo* (Statistical abstract of administering people entering and departing Japan) (Tokyo: Nyukan Kyokai, 1991, 1993).

countries other than Korea and China. In short, the "problem" of foreign workers in Japan referred primarily to illegal workers from underdeveloped countries.

By 1992 there were 1.28 million registered foreigners living in Japan, which was about 1 percent of the total Japanese population.[3] (All non-Japanese citizens who live in Japan for over three months must register with the local political authorities.) The largest nationalities were 688,000 Koreans and 195,000 Chinese, who accounted for about 70 percent of all the registered foreigners in Japan in 1992. Their absolute number has not significantly fluctuated over the post–World War II period, and they have not been considered part of the problem of foreign workers. Neither have the 85,000 foreigners with work visas, the largest group of whom were 22,000 people on "entertainment" visas. Fewer people with work visas were in Japan on commercial, professorial, religious, and other professional visas, most of which were held by North Americans and Europeans (see Table 12.1).

There were, however, illegal workers. Surrounded by water with a comprehensive system of surveillance, Japan is a difficult country to enter without a visa. Hence the number of illegal workers could not be much higher than the sum of visa "overstays" and those on nonwork visas. In 1992, there were nearly 68,000 deportees and over 290,000 visa overstays. In addition, many people on student visas (113,000) and trainee visas (19,000) worked illegally. In 1990 the Ministry of Labor estimated that there were 280,000 "illegal disguised foreign employees" and 500,000 foreign workers overall.[4]

Where did these illegal workers come from? In 1990 the highest numbers were from the Philippines, South Korea, Thailand, China, Pakistan, Malaysia, and Bangladesh. By 1992 Thai, Malaysians, Filipinos, and Iranians were the largest nationalities. Particularly after 1990 *nikkeijin* (Japanese émigrés and their descendants) became increasingly prominent. The March 1989 changes in immigration law—which became effective in June 1990—restricted the influx of foreign workers. In response, labor brokers and employers targeted alternative means to "import" workers, especially ethnic Japanese from South America.[5] In 1987 Brazilian citizens in Japan amounted to little more than 2,000; by 1992 their total skyrocketed to nearly 148,000. Similarly, the number of Peruvians jumped from just over 600 to over 31,000 in the same time period.[6]

In the 1980s the Japanese mass media referred to the new migrant workers as *japayukisan*. The term *japayukisan* derives from *karayukisan*, who were Japanese prostitutes who worked overseas in the late nineteenth century. *Japayukisan* thus implies sexual workers, engaged in what the Japanese call the "water trade" *(mizushobai)*. Until 1988 the vast majority (80–90 percent) of workers deported from Japan were women working in the water trade as bar hostesses and prostitutes.[7] Although men accounted for only 7 percent of deportees in 1984, their share increased to over 80 percent by 1990.[8] In part because of the shifting gender composition of foreign workers, by the early 1990s the term *japayukisan* became less frequently used in the media. Men tended to work in manual labor, mostly in construction (50 percent) and manufacturing (28 percent), while women worked as "hostesses" (34 percent), industrial workers (17 percent), and prostitutes (11 percent).[9] Migrant workers thus labored in the worst jobs that Japanese society offered. In this regard, they were no different from the majority of migrant workers in the world.[10]

The Social Origins of Migrant Labor

The rise of new foreign workers in Japan can be traced to structural factors as well as to concrete organizations that have facilitated people's movement across national boundaries. The foremost structural source was the inequality between nations. Around 1900 the Japanese gross national product (GNP) per capita was 30 times that of the Philippines and 125 times that of Bangladesh (see Table 12.2). A Bangladeshi worker could earn in a day in Japan what she or he would take months to earn back home.

Underlying the cross-national economic inequality were more specific conditions conducive to labor flow from underdeveloped Asian countries to Japan. The Japanese demand for low-paid manual and service labor became pressing by the late 1980s. Why didn't the inflow of foreign workers begin earlier in Japan? In West Germany, for example, the influx of foreign workers *(Gästarbeiter)* began in the 1950s. The West German government concluded a series of treaties with foreign governments—beginning with Italy in 1955 and then with Greece and Spain in 1960—to "import" foreigners to work in low-paid manual and service jobs. Already by 1960 the total had reached 280,000.[11] In postwar Japan, however, internal rural migration and women's entrance into the labor force filled the jobs that foreigners had assumed in West Germany by 1960. *Dekasegi* (migrant) workers from rural areas labored in the off-farm season in construction and other manual work, while female part-time workers were employed as low-paid labor.[12] There were 549,000 *dekasegi* workers in 1972, but the figure thereafter declined steadily: 365,000 in 1976, 288,000 in 1981, and 216,000 in 1986.[13]

Table 12.2

Per Capita GNP Comparison

Country	Per capita GNP*	Index (Japan = 100)
Japan	$23,810	100.0
United States	$20,910	87.8
Malaysia	$2,160	9.0
Thailand	$1,220	5.1
Philippines	$710	3.0
Sri Lanka	$430	1.8
Pakistan	$370	1.6
China	$350	1.5
India	$340	1.4
Bangladesh	$180	0.8

Source: World Bank (1991).
*In 1989 U.S. dollars.

Economic growth and the associated urbanization and economic enrichment had dried up the domestic sources of cheap labor by the 1980s, when labor shortages became increasingly acute. In 1989 the Ministry of Labor reported that the ratio of advertised employment to job seekers was 1.35, indicating a serious labor shortage, particularly in smaller firms and construction and manufacturing.[14] The Japanese media referred to these jobs as 3K *(kitsui, kitanai,* and *kiken)*, which might be rendered in English as 3D: difficult, dirty, and dangerous. The new foreigners thus assumed the jobs that rural or female Japanese workers had done before. Some low-cost housing for Japanese *dekasegi* workers has simply been converted into foreign workers' residences.[15]

These structural conditions created a situation ripe for labor migration from poorer Asian countries to Japan.[16] Yet how did this potential turn into concrete reality? Individual migrant workers by and large do not move from one country to another even if information is available about labor shortages and high wages. This is especially critical in the case of Japan, where the political and cultural barriers are enormous. Hence formal organizations and social networks are critical in the migration process.[17] Indeed, labor brokers played a crucial role in the early stages in recruiting foreign workers and finding them employment. Brokers served as the conduit in the transnational labor market: locating potential workers, issuing fake passports or visas, arranging for plane flights, having agents receive workers at the airport and transport them to their places of work.[18] Over time, the social networks of foreign workers have come to provide new migrant workers with employment and other information and support.

The *yakuza* (Japanese mafia) and the *boryokudan* (organized gangs) have been important actors in the international trafficking of human labor. The two major occupations of foreign workers—construction for men and sexual work for women—are enterprises closely associated with the *yakuza*.[19] The *yakuza* engagement in business is similar to the mafia organization of cheap, immigrant labor for burgeoning industries in the late nineteenth-century United States. Just as members of a discriminated-against minority became the mafia in the United States, members of discriminated-against minorities are overrepresented in the Japanese counterpart. Many *yakuza* members are *burakumin* (outcasts) and Korean residents in Japan.[20]

One of the most publicized media stories on the international traffic of workers was the Rapan Incident trial (1988–89), which involved Filipina prostitutes. They came on fake passports and tourist visas that recruiters had provided. Forced into debt and dependence by a nightclub owner, they were raped, beaten, and confined to work as virtual sexual slaves. With the aid of Japanese activists they escaped and brought their case to the Japanese court. In the course of the trial, activists, journalists, and other investigators clarified the ties between the local *boryokudan* and labor brokers, as well as the complicity of the local police.[21]

As the Rapan Incident demonstrates, there are several causes for the new foreign workers' plight. They are often employed in low-paid and dangerous or undesirable jobs. The industries themselves tend to be illegal (for example, prostitution) or loosely regulated (for example, smaller construction firms). The workers are not unionized and face language and cultural barriers. Furthermore, without a proper visa they are under constant threat of deportation and are therefore easy prey to exploitative brokers and employers. The structure of exploitation inevitably revolves around the legal vulnerability of the new foreign workers and their informal dependence (for example, debt), vis-à-vis their brokers or employers.[22]

The growing awareness of foreign worker exploitation has generated myriad support groups. Some progressive unions, such as Zentoitsu, have been actively organizing foreign workers in construction and other industries. Support groups, such as HELP and Karabao no Kai, are actively assisting foreigners in a variety of ways, ranging from legal counsel to language training. Finally, some local political authorities, such as Kanagawa Prefecture, have set up agencies to disseminate useful information and to offer assistance to foreign residents.[23]

Japanese Debates on the "Problem" of Foreign Workers

The dominant Japanese debate in the late 1980s did not focus on foreign workers' conditions, but rather on their threat to Japanese society. The popular discussion, furthermore, neglected the obvious obverse of the influx of foreign workers: the significant economic expansion of Japanese corporations and the outflow of Japanese people to the rest of the world. From 1970 to 1988 there was a three-fold increase in the number of foreigners entering Japan, while the number of Japanese going abroad rose thirteen-fold.[24] The profound impact of Japanese corporations on the rest of Asia, ranging from worker exploitation to environmental degradation, has been amply documented.[25] Historically, Japanese have emigrated to other countries seeking better economic opportunities; as late as 1973, for example, ships carried Japanese emigrants to Brazil.[26]

These facts were, however, at best infrequently articulated in the late 1980s and early 1990s when Japanese responses to the new foreign workers were quite phenomenal; the mass media produced scores of documentaries, while pundits published countless books and articles on the topic.[27] The crystallization of disparate discourses pivoted around a practical policy issue: whether or not to allow them to work in Japan.[28] In other words, the question was whether Japan should be "open" or "closed" to foreign workers.

Opinion surveys were rather inconclusive. In the 1988 Sorifu (Prime Minister's Office) survey of 10,000 adult Japanese, 8.1 percent suggested that Japan not admit foreign workers, 26.1 percent advocated some restrictions, 35.1 percent favored open immigration, and 14.6 percent answered "don't know."[29] In a 1961 survey, "don't know"s numbered 51 percent. There was, however, a subtle shift in the Japanese opinion due to the growing recognition of the need for low-paid workers. A *Mainichi* newspaper survey in December 1988 reported 45 percent "for" as opposed to 48 percent "against" the influx of foreign workers. By January 1990 "for" had increased to 51 percent, while "against" had declined to 44 percent. According to the respondents, the primary rationale for the approval of foreign workers was the necessity of having workers do menial tasks that most Japanese are not interested in doing.[30]

The ongoing media debate over foreign workers has been a critical influence on the formation of public opinion. This debate has often been cast as the reprise of the question Japan faced in the mid–nineteenth century. According to the dominant Japanese historiography, Japan had been sequestered from foreign contact until the coming of Commodore Perry in 1853, when Japanese leaders were forced to decide whether to "open" the country *(kaikoku)* or to keep it "closed" *(sakoku)*.[31] It has been said that in the late twentieth century Japan faces a problem of comparable magnitude to the mid–nineteenth century turning point of modern Japanese history.

The *sakoku* (closing the country) faction has argued that the new foreign workers would undermine the uniqueness of Japan. Yano Toru, for example, wrote that the emperor system and Japanese world view are unique and should be protected from foreigners.[32] In a similar vein, Nishio Kanji warned that the non-Japanese population will cause the social disorganization that he observed in other countries.[33] Foreigners in Japan would threaten the well-functioning Japanese schools and other institutions and ultimately destroy social cohesion and order. As Nishio concluded: "This is not necessarily an economic problem. Frankly speaking, it is a problem of 'cultural defense.'"[34]

The *kaikoku* argument has advocated opening Japan on the humanitarian grounds that foreigners should be able to earn their livelihoods, and that Japan should fulfill its obligation as a wealthy country.[35] Onuma Yasuaki argued that

Japan would become a better member of the international community by "opening."[36] He added that "opening" the country will also "open" the "closed" spirit of Japan.

Both sides have largely agreed on the potential economic benefits (or, at least, neutral economic impact) of the new foreign workers, as well as the potential social costs of their continuous presence in Japan. The difference of opinion has stemmed from their relative calculations of costs and benefits to Japanese society.

Racial Ideology and the Colonial Legacy

What has been the point of the cantankerous and conflictual argument? Why should a small group of non-Japanese manual and service workers generate such an intense public debate? In short, the new foreign workers have been seen as a social problem because they challenge the ideology of racial and cultural homogeneity.

Quite often immigrant workers become a national policy issue as a result of interethnic conflict over resources. These conditions, however, do not exist in Japan. The number of foreign workers in Japan has been minuscule compared to that of most other wealthy nation-states. At the height of the influx of foreign workers in Germany or France the proportion of non-nationals in the total labor force was more than 20 times what it has been in Japan.[37]

In addition, elite, well-paying jobs in the government bureaucracy and large corporations have remained restricted to Japanese college graduates. Indeed, even the long-term residents of Japan, such as the Korean minority, have been barred from these jobs, which have been reserved for Japanese citizens (with citizenship based on "blood").[38] As the Japanese economy was doing extremely well in the late 1980s, many smaller manufacturing firms faced an acute shortage of workers, as did the sex industry and many demanding but low-paid jobs.[39] The small number of the new foreign workers and the absence of economic competition suggest that the problem of foreign workers has not been simply economic in nature.

The social problem is based not so much on an economic—but rather on the perceived symbolic—threat to Japanese society. The presence of *gaikokujin rodosha* has challenged the vision of the social integrity and solidarity of the Japanese body politic, which portrays Japan as a racially and culturally homogeneous country. Any influx of a "foreign" element is, therefore, a threat. This racial and nationalist ideology is at the core of Japanese conservative philosophy,[40] underlying disparate discourses in and on Japan.[41] Interestingly enough, even "racial Japanese," namely the descendants of earlier Japanese emigrants to South America who have returned to work in Japan, are often considered inappropriate for living and working in homogeneous Japan.[42]

The claim that Japan is a monoethnic society is, however, empirically false. Japan became a modern nation-state by incorporating diverse ethnic groups. The

Meiji state-making included the colonization of Ainu-*moshir* (Hokkaido) and Okinawa. The *burakumin* continue to be a discriminated-against minority group,[43] with an estimated 2 million *burakumin* in Japan in the 1960s.[44] In the course of Japanese imperialist expansion, many Koreans and Chinese entered Japan, and some remained after the Pacific War.[45]

The origins of the Korean and Chinese minorities point to a more obvious way in which the ideology of racial homogeneity is untenable. The debate over foreign workers has rarely mentioned the presence of other foreigners, especially the Korean and Chinese minorities.[46] The new foreign workers are racialized in the Japanese context as darker-skinned, low-paid manual and service workers from poorer Asian countries. Why should the focus be on the new immigrants? Why should the racial ideology bypass the larger and older groups of minority populations? To answer these questions, it is necessary to understand the living legacies of Japanese colonialism.

Public attention on the new foreign workers began in a period of great Japanese political and economic expansion. In the mid-1980s Prime Minister Nakasone's call for "internationalization" of Japan became a dominant political slogan.[47] The last great Japanese expansion ("internationalization") before and during World War II resulted in the enforced migration of Korean and Chinese workers into the Japanese archipelago. While the Japanese empire encompassed Korea, Taiwan, and Manchuria, many people from these areas entered Japan; the Korean migration into Japan alone totaled 2.3 million people in 1945.[48]

The ideology of monoethnic Japan is thus oblivious to prewar Japanese colonialism and capitalist development that led to the enforced migration of other nationalities into Japan. Utter ignorance or denial of this history has characterized much of the debate on foreign workers. It is not surprising that the *kaikoku-sakoku* debate has harked back to the nineteenth century, when Japan was "closed" from foreign contacts. The twentieth century—when Japan embarked on colonial expansion and forcefully brought over "foreign" workers—was conveniently bypassed. In point of fact, the continuity between the prewar and postwar periods is particularly striking in the government, where many politicians and officials who engineered the prewar colonial expansion have continued to lead the economic growth of the post-1945 period.[49]

The 1980s also witnessed vibrant social movements by minorities to fight their discriminated-against and oppressed conditions.[50] In the mid-1980s, for example, the movement to end fingerprinting *(shimon onatsu)* of resident foreigners became a celebrated cause. Led by resident Koreans in Japan, the movement mobilized a large number of people and became a major foreign policy issue between Japan and South Korea.[51] The "problem" of the new foreign workers arose precisely at the time minorities and other oppressed groups were no longer willing to work in the lowest rung of the Japanese employment hierarchy. The conservative racial ideology faced challenges from the politically organized communities of *burakumin*, Korean, Chinese, and others. Therefore, it became more palatable to argue this conservative ideology via the newcomers than via the longstanding, now well organized, ethnic communities. The spotlight on the new foreign workers effaced the history of various diaspora and oppressed communities in Japan.

The new immigrant workers have displaced earlier victims of capitalist exploitation and racial ideology. The amnesia of Japanese colonialism is critical in keeping buried the past atrocities as well as avoiding the problems raised by the earlier foreign workers. It is in this complex milieu that the new foreign workers have been judged a major problem because they directly threatened the dominant ideology of racial homogeneity and purity in Japan. The focus has elided the problems of the existing minority populations—the largest group of actually existing "foreign" workers—as well as the *burakumin* and other discriminated-against workers.

The exploitation generated by capitalist development and racial ideology overlaps in the problematic legacy of Japanese colonialism. Although neither colonies nor enforced labor migration exist in contemporary Japan, the origins of foreign workers in Japan lie in the economic inequality between Japan and the rest of Asia. In short, instead of formal colonialism, we have "internationalization"; instead of the Korean and Chinese minorities, there is the "problem" of the new foreign workers.

Conclusion

It is possible to view the debate over the new foreign workers in terms of "opening" or "closing" Japan, as many Japanese have been wont to do. In this view, the struggle is over different visions of Japan: liberal, tolerant, and diverse, as opposed to conservative, intolerant, and homogeneous. I have argued, however, that there have been distinct dimensions to the "problem" of racial ideology. The hegemonic conservative vision presents Japan as a racially homogeneous country, marginalizing the discriminated Korean and Chinese minority populations and ignoring the colonial legacy of prewar Japan. In bringing together the exploitation of workers, racial ideology, and the oppression of minorities with the Japanese colonial legacy, the "problem" of the new foreign workers refracts a longstanding ideological conflict in contemporary Japanese society.

Notes

1. See Saskia Sassen, *The Mobility of Labor and Capital: A Study in International Investment and Labor Flow* (Cambridge, UK: Cambridge University Press, 1988).

2. See, for example, Mainichi Shinbun Tokyo Honsha Shakaibu (MSTHS), ed., *Jipangu: Nihon wo mezasu gaikokujin rodosha* (Jipangu: foreign workers heading for Japan), rev. ed. (Tokyo: Mainichi Shinbunsha, 1990).

3. The statistics are drawn from Homusho Nyukoku Kanrikyoku (Ministry of Justice, Office of Immigration Control), various publications, various years. There is a convenient statistical portrait of foreign workers in Kunitomo Ryuichi, *Doko made susumu Nihon no*

naka no kokusaika chizu (Map of the extent of internationalization of Japan) (Tokyo: Nihon Jitsugyo Shuppansha, 1992), passim.

4. Ministry of Labour, "Foreign Workers and the Labour Market in Japan," in *Japan and International Migration: Challenges and Opportunities* (Tokyo: APIC, 1992), pp. 161–176.

5. Fujisaki Yasuo, *Dekasegi nikkei gaikokujin rodosha* (Ethnic Japanese foreign migrant workers) (Tokyo: Asahi Shoten, 1991). On Japan's new immigration policy, see Keiko Yamanaka, "New Immigration Policy and Unskilled Foreign Workers in Japan," *Pacific Affairs*, no. 66 (spring 1993), pp. 72–90.

6. Tanaka Hiroshi, "Foreigners in Japanese Society," *Japan Book News* (fall 1993), p. 4.

7. See, for example, Hama Natsuko, *Manira shofu monogatari* (Story of Filipina prostitutes) (Tokyo: San'ichi Shobo, 1988); and Mizumachi Ryosuke, *Okasareta Ajia: tai no japayukisan monogatari* (Violated Asia: the story of Thai *japayukisan*) (Tokyo: Buren Senta, 1988).

8. Inagami Takeshi, "Gästarbeiter in Japanese Small Firms," *Japan Labor Bulletin*, 1 Mar. 1992, p. 4.

9. Shimada Haruo, *Gaikokujin rodosha mondai no kaiketsusaku* (The solution for the foreign worker problem) (Tokyo: Toyo Keizai Shinposha, 1993), p. 32.

10. Michael J. Piore, *Birds of Passage: Migrant Labor and Industrial Societies* (Cambridge, UK: Cambridge University Press, 1979), pp. 50–51.

11. Klaus J. Bade, "Einheimische Ausländer: 'Gästarbeiter,' Dauergäste, Einwanderer" (Resident foreigners: guest workers, long-staying guests, and immigrants), in *Deutsche im Ausland: Fremde in Deutschland* (Germans in foreign countries: strangers in Germany) (München: Verlag C.H. Beck, 1992), pp. 392–401, p. 395. See also Tezuka Kazuaki, *Gaikokujin rodosha* (Foreign workers) (Tokyo: Chuo Koronsha, 1989), pp. 152–158.

12. See, respectively, Matsuzawa Tessei, "Street Labour Markets, Day Labourers, and the Structure of Oppression," in *The Japanese Trajectory: Modernization and Beyond*, ed. Gavan McCormack and Yoshio Sugimoto (Cambridge, UK: Cambridge University Press, 1988), pp. 147–164; and Kumitomo Fujiko, "Josei rodosha no byotoyokyu no hatten" (The development of female workers' demands for equality), in *Nihon josei seikatsushi* (The history of Japanese women's everyday life), vol. 5, ed. Joseishi sogo Kenkyukai (Tokyo: Tokyo Daigaku Shuppanakai, 1990), pp. 69–100. See in general Robert Miles, *Capitalism and Unfree Labour: Anomaly or Necessity?* (London: Tavistock, 1987), pp. 223–224.

13. Goto Jun'ichi, *Gaikokujin rodo no keizaigaku* (The economics of foreign labor) (Tokyo: Toyo Keizai Shinposha, 1990), p. 31.

14. See Kanto Bengoshi Rengokai (KBR), ed., *Gaikokujin rodosha no shuro to jinken* (Employment and human rights of foreign workers) (Tokyo: Akashi Shoten, 1989), pp. 178–80; and Umetani Shun'ichiro, "Fuho gaikokujin no jittai" (The reality of illegal foreigners), in *Asu no rinjin: gaikokujin rodosha* (Tomorrow's neighbors: foreign workers), ed. Hanami Tadashi and Kuwahara Yasuo (Tokyo: Toyo Keizai Shinposha, 1989), pp. 73–104, pp. 97–100.

15. Okuda Michihiro and Tajima Junko, eds., *Ikebukuro no Ajiakei gaikokujin* (Asian foreign workers in Ikebukuro) (Tokyo: Mekon, 1991), pp. 24–26.

16. See, for example, Keizai Kikakucho Sogo Keikakukyoku, *Gaikokujin rodosha to keizai shakai no shinro* (Foreign workers and the direction of the economy and society) (Tokyo: Okurasho Insatsukyoku, 1989), p. 22. See in general Manolo I. Abella, "Contemporary Labour Migration from Asia: Policies and Perspectives of Sending Countries," in *International Migration Systems: A Global Approach*, eds. Mary M. Kritz, Lin Lean Lim, and Hania Zlotnik (Oxford: Clarendon Press, 1992), pp. 263–278.

17. See, for example, Charles Tilly, "Transplanted Networks," in *Immigration Recon-*

sidered: History, Sociology, and Politics, ed. Virginia Yans-McLaughlin (New York: Oxford University Press, 1990), pp. 79–95. See also Yoko Sellek and Michael A. Weiner, "Migrant Workers: The Japanese Case in International Perspective," in *The Internationalization of Japan*, ed. Glenn D. Hook and Michael A. Weiner (London: Routledge, 1992), pp. 205–228.

18. See KBR, *Gaikokujin*, pp. 57–59, 63–65; Utsumi Aiko, "Aija no hitotachi to tomoni" (Together with the people of Asia), in *Ajia kara kita dekasegi rodoshatachi* (Migrant workers from Asia), ed. Utsumi Aiko and Matsui Yayori (Tokyo: Akashi Shoten, 1988), pp. 11–57; and Asano Kyohei, "Ryugakusei buroka wa kinman Nippon to kimagure nyukangyosei no adabana da!" (Foreign student brokers are the result of rich Japan and capricious immigration authorities), in *Nihon ga taminzoku kokka ni naru hi* (The day Japan will become a multiethnic nation), ed. Ishii Shinji (Tokyo: JICC, 1990), pp. 160–172.

19. See, for example, Asahi Shinbun Shakaibu (ASS), ed., *Chikakute chikai Ajia* (Near and nearby Asia) (Tokyo: Gakuyo Shobo, 1989), pp. 117–141.

20. Jacob Raz, "Self-Presentation and Performance in the *Yakuza* Way of Life: Fieldwork with a Japanese Underground Group," in *Ideology and Practice in Modern Japan*, eds., Roger Goodman and Kirsten Refsing (London: Routledge, 1992), pp. 210–234, p. 214.

21. See ASS, *Chikakute*, pp. 110–117; Arusu no Kai, ed., *Rapan jiken no kokuhatsu: tatakatta Firipin joseitachi* (The prosecution of the Rapan Incident: Filipina women who struggled) (Tokyo: Tsuge Shobo, 1990).

22. Ishiyama Eiichiro, *Firipin dekasegi rodosha: yume wo oi Nihon ni ikite* (Migrant Filipino workers: chasing the dream and living in Japan) (Tokyo: Shashiku Shobo, 1989), pp. 89–96.

23. On the role of support groups for foreign workers, see, for example, Ajiajin Rodosha Mondai Kondankai, ed., *Ajiajin dekasegi techo* (The handbook on Asian migrants) (Tokyo: Akashi Shoten, 1988); and two works cited by the Ajianjin Rodosha Mondai Kondankai, ed., *Okasareru jinken: gaikokujin rodosha* (Violated human rights: foreign workers) (Tokyo: Daisan Shokan, 1992). Ohara Shakai Mondai Kenkyusho offers a concise summary of the responses by the government, employers' associations, and labor unions to the "problem" of foreign workers in *Nihon rodo nenkan* (Japan labor yearbook), vol. 59 (Tokyo: Rodo Junposha, 1989). Furthermore, some Japanese authors have begun to address many of the issues discussed in this paper, including Komai Hiroshi, *Gaikokujin rodosha teiju e no michi* (The road to permanent settlement of foreign workers) (Tokyo: Akashi Shoten, 1993), ch. 6.

24. MSTHS, *Jipangu*, appendix 7.

25. See, for example, Shiosawa Miyoko, *Ajia no minshu vs. Nihon no kigyo* (The people of Asia vs. Japanese corporations) (Tokyo: Iwanami Shoten, 1986); and Rob Steven, *Japan's New Imperialism* (Armonk, NY: M.E. Sharpe, 1990).

26. Waldemar Valente, *O Japones no nordeste agrario* (The Japanese in the agrarian northeast) (Recife, Brazil: Instituto Joaquim Nabuco de Pesquisas, 1978), pp. 22–31; see in general Tanaki Hiroshi, *Zainichi gaikokujin: ho no kabe, kokoro no mizo* (Foreigners living in Japan: the wall of law, the gutter of heart) (Tokyo: Iwanami Shoten, 1991), pp. 188–193.

27. For overviews, see Tanaka, "Foreigners"; and John Lie, "Foreign Workers in Japan," *Monthly Review*, vol. 44, no. 1 (1992), pp. 35–42.

28. I should note, however, that by 1994 the terrain of the debate has shifted considerably. The inescapable presence of foreign workers makes the *sakoku* (closed) position increasingly untenable. The question is no longer whether to open or close Japan, but how to deal with the current presence and future influx of foreigners.

29. Nyukan Tokei Kenkyukai, *Waga kuni wo megaru kokusai jinryu no henbo* (The change in the international flow of people concerning our country) (Tokyo: Okurasho Insatsukyoku, 1990), p. 183.

30. MSTHS, *Jipangu*, p. 275.

31. The extent to which Japan was "closed" during the Tokugawa period has been exaggerated. See Ronald P. Toby, *State and Diplomacy in Early Modern Japan: Asia in the Development of the Tokugawa Bakufu* (Princeton: Princeton University Press, 1984); and Amino Yoshihiko, *Nihonron no shiza: retto no shakai to kokka* (The perspectives of Japanese historiography: society and state in the archipelago) (Tokyo: Shogakkan, 1990).

32. Yano Toru, *Nihon no kokusaika wo kangaeru* (Thinking about the international-ization of Japan) (Tokyo: Nikkan Kogyo Shinbunsha, 1988), pp. 46–49.

33. Nishio Kanji, *Senryakuteki "sakoku"ron* (Strategic "sakoku") (Tokyo: Kodansha, 1988).

34. Nishio Kanji, " 'Rodo kaikoku' wa do kentoshitemo fukano da" (No matter how you analyze it, opening up Japan to foreign workers is impossible), *Chuo Koron* (Sept. 1989), pp. 312–330, p. 330.

35. Miyajima Takashi, *Gaikokujin rodosha mukaeire no ronri: senshin shakai no jirenma no nakade* (The logic of welcoming foreign workers: within the dilemma of advanced societies) (Tokyo: Akashi Shoten, 1989), pp. 11–12.

36. Onuma Yasuaki, " 'Gaikokujin rodosha' donyu rongi ni kakerumono" (What is missing in the debate over the influx of foreign workers), *Chuo Koron* (May 1988), pp. 148–162.

37. See, for example, Denis Maillat, "The Long-Term Aspects of International Migra-tion Flows: The Experience of European Receiving Countries," in *The Future of Migra-tion*, ed., Organization for Economic Cooperation and Development (OECD) (Paris: OECD, 1987), pp. 38–63; and Zig Layton-Henry, "Citizenship and Migrant Workers in Western Europe," in *The Frontiers of Citizenship*, eds. Ursula Vogel and Michael Moran (New York: St. Martin's, 1991), pp. 107–124.

38. Yamamoto Fuyuhiko, "Nihon shakai koseiin to shite no gaikokujin" (Foreigners as members of Japanese society), in *Zainichi gaikokujin to Nihon shakai* (Resident for-eigners in Japan and Japanese society), eds., Yoshioka Masuo, Yamamoto Fuyuhiko, and Kim Yong Dal (Tokyo: Shakai Hyoronsha, 1984), pp. 13–56.

39. See Ishiyama, *Firipin*, pp. 18–22; and KBR, *Gaikokujin*, pp. 178–180.

40. See John Lie, "The Discriminated Fingers: The Korean Minority in Japan," *Monthly Review*, vol. 38, no. 8 (1987), pp. 17–23.

41. See, for example, Peter N. Dale, *The Myth of Japanese Uniqueness* (New York: St. Martin's, 1986); and Yoshino Kosaku, *Cultural Nationalism in Contemporary Japan: A Sociological Enquiry* (London: Routledge, 1992).

42. Hinago Akira, "Kaettekita nanbei imin" (Emigrants to South America who have returned), in *Nihon ga taminzoku kokka ni naru hi*, ed. Ishii Shinji, pp. 173–182. See also Fujisaki, *Dekasegi*.

43. See Jean-François Sabouret, *L'autre Japon: les burakumin* (The other Japan: the burakumin) (Paris: Maspero, 1983).

44. George De Vos and Wagatsuma Hiroshi, *Japan's Invisible Race* (Berkeley: Uni-versity of California Press, 1967), p. 116.

45. Irene B. Taeuber, *The Population of Japan* (Princeton: Princeton University Press, 1958), pp. 191–204.

46. The situation is, of course, not unique to Japan. For Britain and France, respec-tively, see Paul Gilroy, *There Ain't No Black in the Union Jack* (London: Hutchinson, 1987); and Sophie Body-Gendrot, "Migration and the Racialization of the Postmodern

City in France," in *Racism, the City, and the State*, ed., Malcolm Cross and Michael Keith (London: Routledge, 1993), pp. 77–92.

47. Kato Shuichi, "The Internationalization of Japan," in *The Internationalization of Japan*, ed., Hook and Weiner, pp. 31–316.

48. Tanaka, *Zainichi*, p. 194.

49. See, for example, John Lie, "War, Absolutism, and Amnesia: The Decline of War Responsibility in Postwar Japan," *Peace and Change*, no. 16 (1991), pp. 302–315.

50. See, for example, Yun Kon Ch'a, *Kozetsu no rekishi ishiki* (The historical consciousness of isolation) (Tokyo: Iwanami Shoten, 1987), ch. 1.

51. See Lie, "The Discriminated Fingers."

VI

Tarnished Miracles—Rising Hopes

In "Militarism, Colonialism, and the Trafficking of Women: 'Comfort Women' Forced into Sexual Labor for Japanese Soldiers" Watanabe Kazuko describes the nineties movement by former "comfort women" demanding acknowledgment and compensation from the government of Japan for the horrendous injuries inflicted on them by the Japanese military during World War II. These women were typically abducted and made to "serve" an average of thirty to forty men a day, with women who were not submissive brutally beaten and tortured. Li Bok-ngo, shown above, was a "comfort woman" for eight years after being kidnapped and brought to China from Korea. She was crippled by her captors to keep her from running away, and on one occasion she and others were forced to drink broth made from the severed heads of fellow "comfort women" who were murdered by the Japanese when they rebelled. This photo is by and courtesy of Ito Takashi, © 1993, and reprinted here with permission.

Although the citizens' struggle in Zushi City near Tokyo that Kenneth Ruoff discusses in "Mr. Tomino Goes to City Hall" was at a different level and on a much smaller scale than the international "comfort women" movement, Zushi City's grass-roots effort has similar wider implications for resistance in Japan. In the above photo Zushi City workers are taking direct action by making a disputed eleven-story condominium complex uninhabitable by sealing off its sewer connection on 1 June 1992 when the building was otherwise ready for occupancy. This photo is reprinted here courtesy of Kenneth Ruoff and Tomino Kiichiro.

Another powerful voice in Japan for change and expanded awareness is that of the poet Kurihara Sadako, whose poems are translated and introduced by Richard H. Minear in "Five Poems (1974–91) by the Hiroshima Poet Kurihara Sadako." Although herself a victim of the atomic bombing, Kurihara extends her concern to the need for the Japanese—particularly Emperor Hirohito—to accept responsibility for the fifteen-year Pacific War. In this picture Emperor Hirohito views firsthand the consequences of the war as he inspects bomb damage following the extremely destructive U.S. firebombing of Tokyo on 25–26 May 1945. This is an Imperial Household Agency photo.

13

Militarism, Colonialism, and the Trafficking of Women: "Comfort Women" Forced into Sexual Labor for Japanese Soldiers

*Watanabe Kazuko**

On 6 December 1991 Korean women who identified themselves as "military comfort women" filed a lawsuit against the Japanese government for violating their human rights. They demanded an official apology, some compensatory payment to survivors in lieu of full reparation, a thorough investigation of their cases, the revision of Japanese school textbooks identifying this issue as part of the colonial oppression of the Korean people, and the building of a memorial museum.[1] With this action these women finally started to break their silence and disclose the sexual war crimes committed by the Japanese Imperial Army almost fifty years ago.

The term *jugun ianfu*, "military comfort woman," is a euphemism for enforced military sex laborer or slave for the Japanese Imperial Army in the name of Emperor Hirohito. The term was coined by the Japanese government, military officials, and sexual industry agents, all hoping to obscure the dreadful reality behind the term.[2] The women were originally called *"teishintai,"* which means "voluntary corps," with the Confucian connotation of self-victimization. According to Yun Chung-ok, the founder of the Korean Council for the Women Drafted for Sexual Military Slavery by Japan, in this context the term also conveyed the more specific meanings of "drafting of women for sexual service to Japanese troops" and "patriotic voluntary military troops."[3] It was felt that Korean women would feel more obligated by the

*An earlier version of this article was read at the "Fifth International Interdisciplinary Congress on Women" held at the University of Costa Rica in February 1993. Since then it has been revised, and more information has been added to it. I wish to thank the Japanese and Japanese-Korean women's groups that provided me with information and stories about "comfort women," and E. Patricia Tsurumi and Edward Friedman of the *Bulletin of Concerned Asian Scholars* for their help with editing. We at the *Bulletin of Concerned Asian Scholars* also wish to thank Kevin Rooney, Kyung Menkick, and Alice Yun Chai for translating the caption information for us, and Ito Takashi, Yun Chung-ok, Shimada Yoshiko, E. Patricia Tsurumi, Alice Chai, Joan Ericson, Brenda Stoltzfus, and Saundra Sturdevant for helping us obtain graphics for this article.

connotations of self-sacrifice in the term *teishintai* because they were educated in the Confucian tradition. In reality the practice of "military comfort women" suggests not only the institutionalized, collective, systematic rape of Korean and other women by Japanese soldiers but also trafficking in women. Moreover, one person who witnessed what happened at the time, military doctor Aso Tetsuo, commented that Korean women were treated as if they were inhuman "female ammunition" and often referred to as "sanitary public toilets."[4]

War often violates human rights, but the case of the so-called military "comfort women" must be one of the cruelest of such violations. The historical example of "comfort women" teaches us how war perpetuates the exploitation of women and the violation of their human rights. The number of victims involved is estimated as nearly 200,000, although it is possible that the figures are even higher. It reminds us that systematic rape, institutionalized prostitution, and sexual slavery as well as war crimes were not only practiced in the past but can still be seen near military bases around the world such as those near Davao, Naha, and Phnom Penh. The collective rape in the former Yugoslavia is another form of war crime. Thus war and sexual exploitation are closely related in their violence against women that cuts across sex, gender, race, ethnic, and class lines.

The use of the term "comfort women" is obviously itself a travesty, and it would certainly be more accurate to refer to the women who did this work as "enforced military sex laborers or slaves," as Pak Fam (a Korean activist living in Japan) and the Association for Anti-Prostitution Activity suggest.[5] Nevertheless, I have used the term "comfort women" in this article because this remains the way they are most commonly referred to. I would prefer to at least encase the term in quotes to register my disapproval of it, but I have not done so because that would be cumbersome if it were done throughout the article.

Although Japanese, Chinese, Taiwanese, Filipina, Indonesian, as well as Dutch women also worked as "comfort women," the article focuses on Korean women, not only because they were the majority—80 percent—and have already formed a political movement, but also because the colonial and imperial system is more clearly evident in their case.[6] The article has, in fact, grown out of the actions of Japanese and Korean-Japanese women's groups concerned with the "comfort women" issue. I have been following their movements closely as a Japanese woman and thus as both a victim and a victimizer. I am indebted to members of these groups for helping me prepare the article by supplying me with their materials, ideas, and life stories.

Disclosures by Comfort Women

At the meetings and interviews organized by the Military Comfort Women Issue Uriyosong Network around the December 1991 lawsuit, Kim Hak-soon, sixty-eight, was the only plaintiff who revealed her name. In tears, she related her experiences as a comfort woman, explaining that her decision was prompted by the fact that since all had died she no longer had any close family members who would be ashamed of her past. Kim Hak-soon reported: "When I was seventeen years old, the Japanese soldiers came along in a truck, beat us, and then dragged us into the back. . . . I was told that if I were drafted I could earn lots of money at the textile company, and that it was also the emperor's order. I was taken to China to serve as a comfort woman for Japanese soldiers at military bases. I was raped on that first day, and it never stopped for a single day for the next three months."[7] Often forced to accommodate dozens of soldiers in a day, Kim tried to flee three times. Twice she was caught and severely beaten, and finally on the third attempt she escaped with the help of a Korean man. They later married, but she lost her husband and children during the Korean War.

In an interview Kim Hak-soon explained:

> I was born as a woman but never lived as a woman. . . . I suffer from a bitterness I do not know how to overcome. I only want to ask the Japanese government not to go to war again. I feel sick when I am close to a man. Not just Japanese men but all men—even my own husband, who saved me from the brothel—have made me feel this way. I shiver when I see the Japanese flag. Because it carried that flag, I hated the airplane I took to come to Japan. I've kept trying to disclose the facts. . . . Why should I feel ashamed? I don't have to feel ashamed.[8]

Since then significant political actions and campaigns around military comfort women have been on the increase, and hundreds of former comfort women have told similar stories. However, the Japanese government initially denied its involvement and rejected the survivors of sexual slavery, which infuriated the survivors of sexual slavery and motivated them to reveal their pasts and appeal through the courts.

On 13 April 1992 six more Korean women sued the Japanese government. One of them revealed how Korean women were captured and drafted from school. Shim Mija, a South Korean, was said to have rebelled against the Japanese armies by embroidering morning glories instead of the Japanese national flower, cherry blossoms, thus symbolizing that the Japanese government would wither in the evening. She was taken away from her school by the police, who then tortured and raped her. When she regained consciousness, she found herself already in a brothel in Japan. For the next six years she was forced to have sex with Japanese soldiers.[9]

In December 1992 a public hearing was held by a network of groups working on this issue in Tokyo.[10] Former comfort women from six countries testified before a panel that included Theo van Boven, an expert on international law and human rights and a special rapporteur for a United Nations subcommission on protecting minorities. One Chinese woman fainted, overcome by pain and anger, and South and North Korean women who once shared a brothel hugged each other on the stage. Jeanne O'Hearn, a Dutch woman and the first European woman to testify as a comfort woman, did so in front of her daughter. She calmly reported that two hundred Dutch women were forced to provide sex in Java. This event was broadcast on TV news programs in Japan. After this public hearing, the Filipina Comfort Women Core Group organized in the Philippines and filed a lawsuit against the Japanese government. Filipina women can locate brothels and have important documents to prove their claims because most of them were not destroyed after the war.

Supported by various human rights groups, on 5 April 1993 Song Siin-do, a seventy-one-year-old Korean living in Japan, filed a lawsuit against the government in the Tokyo District Court.[11] She gave birth in a brothel and her children were left behind in China when she fled to Japan after several years of forced sex labor in China. Her goal has been to change the perpetuation of sexual abuse of women, sexual exploitation, and war crimes under imperialism and colonialism; she has not asked for compensation.

Song Siin-do was also one of the survivors of violence against women who testified on 12 March 1994 at a public hearing of the Asian Tribunal on Women's Human Rights in Tokyo, organized by the Asian Women Human Rights Council and the Women's Human Rights Committee of Japan. Held after the women's human rights tribunal at the Vienna World Human Rights Conference in June 1993, this Asian tribunal brought female victims from other Asian countries to Japan to testify. These included survivors of the trafficking of women from the Philippines and Thailand who had worked as prostitutes in Japan, as well as sexual slaves for the Japanese military abroad and victims of war crimes. The "military comfort women" issue was gaining more international recognition as a violation of women's human rights.

History of Comfort Women

Many historians and activists in Korea and Japan have worked to reclaim these women's pasts, reconceptualizing this violation of human rights and historicizing the Japanese army's explicit military policy of wartime prostitution. Research shows that the modern Japanese system of prostitution for soldiers began as early as the turn of the century. In the invasion of Siberia starting in 1918 the Japanese military took Japanese prostitutes with them but then left them behind. Most of these women, daughters of poor farmers, had been sold into prostitution by their families and became prostitutes called *karayukisan*, foreign-bound (literally China-bound) women.[12]

In the 1920s, as part of Japan's imperial policies after the colonization of Korea in 1910, the Japanese Imperial Army began to mobilize Korean women as physical laborers or as enforced sex laborers. In particular, beginning with the Japanese invasion of China in 1932, the recruiting of Korean women as prostitutes was gradually institutionalized to arouse soldiers' fighting spirit, provide them with an outlet for the frustration and fear fostered by hierarchical military life, and, ostensibly, prevent random rapes. Since the official pretext of the war was that Japan was saving other Asian nations from colonization by Western countries, the Korean comfort women were needed to prevent Japanese soldiers from sexually abusing and collectively raping local Chinese women as they did during the Nanjing Massacre in 1937. The procurement of comfort women was institutionalized to avoid atrocities that would damage the reputation of the Japanese army.

At the beginning of World War II, the Japanese army brought Japanese prostitutes with them, but many of them were suffering from venereal diseases and infected the Japanese soldiers. So Japanese brokers recruited Korean village girls, seventeen to twenty years old, from poor families. Toward the end of the war, the supply of women was enlarged by more indiscriminate kidnapping of women aged fourteen to thirty, including married women. Under the enforcement of the Military Compulsory Draft Act in 1943, more women were taken by the Japanese Imperial Army; by then the number had reached approximately 200,000, among whom 70,000 to 80,000 were sent as comfort women to the front lines in Asia.[13]

At the end of World War II, most survivors of military sexual slavery were not informed of Japan's defeat. During Japan's retreat, some of them were deserted by the Japanese army, some were massacred, and others were driven into trenches or caves and either bombed or gunned down. Some of the women who returned home killed themselves when they were unable to overcome the bitter memories and shame; others survived in silence. Some of the former comfort women were obliged to support themselves by working as prostitutes in postwar Japan.[14]

Historically the emperor system and legal prostitution strengthened the double standard in Japan. The institution of prostitution was not legally prohibited until 1957. Enforcing respect for the emperor was used as part of the colonization of Asian people. Sixth-grade girls in Seoul's primary schools were drafted as *teishintai* laborers, called the emperor's children. A former Japanese teacher in Korea, Ikeda Masae, reported that "girls joined the 'comfort girls' corps of their own will by either persuading their parents or overcoming opposition from their family members."[15]

Comfort Women and the Trafficking of Women

The testimony of former comfort women and documents on them show how women were recruited by force, kidnapped from factories and farms, or taken away because of their rebellious attitude toward Japanese colonization. Each woman was made to serve an average of thirty to forty soldiers per day, with the soldiers waiting in line outside her small room. Women who were not submissive were brutally beaten and tortured, and escape was impossible due to strict surveillance.[16] Japanese soldiers were reminded that women were their common property.

Comfort women were usually placed in hierarchies according to class and nationality. Many Korean women seem to have come from lower-class worker and farmer families. Korean and other Asian women were assigned to lower-ranking soldiers, while Japanese and European women were for higher-ranking officers.

The institution of comfort women was a public practice. A document discovered in Washington, D.C. discloses how a civilian brothel owner who was captured in Burma applied to transport the comfort girls. He took Korean girls he purchased from Pusan to Burma with tickets provided by the Japanese army.[17] In another example, because of the shortage of comfort women toward the end of World War II, Korean village leaders were ordered to send young women to participate in "important business for the Imperial Army."[18]

Most of the Korean comfort women were forced to lose their own nationality, called by Japanese names, and forbidden to speak Korean.[19] A notice hanging at the entrance to a brothel on the outskirts of Shanghai stated: "We welcome courageous soldiers who are on duty for the holy war; Yamato *nadeshiko* [literally the flower called the "wild pinks of Yamato," meaning "our flowerlike women of Japan"] obediently dedicate their minds and bodies to you."[20] Those survivors, wherever they may be living, have been physically and emotionally battered. They suffer from physical health problems such as sterility, headaches, asthma, insomnia, and fears associated with their bitter experience. Nervous breakdowns are also common.

Why did it take fifty years to disclose this issue? Why have comfort women kept silent so long? These women's stories did not surface after the war in part because the Japanese government destroyed military documents and in part because many Korean women themselves tried not to face what happened to them. This may be a reaction in common with rape or sexual harassment cases where women often remain silent because of fear of further humiliation or being attacked again. A Korean-Japanese former comfort woman, Pe Bon-gi, isolated herself in Okinawa without any welfare support, rejecting attention. In 1991 she was found dead in her small cottage. Her story became known through a nonfiction work, *Akagawara no ie* (A house with a red roof), written by Kawada Ayako, who was one of the few who helped her during her life.[21]

Confucian taboos put a priority in Korea on women's chastity, thus inhibiting women from speaking about their own sexual terror.[22] Confucianism trapped women into perpetuating both the patriarchal system that created a double standard and the chastity myth. Moreover, Confucianism allowed men to continue to own women as private property. In the beginning women often had only two alternatives: either they could become comfort women or they could kill themselves to protect their own chastity—which Korean Confucianism taught them to consider more important than their lives. To live was to be guilty. They thought loss of chastity was shameful to their families. Some survivors committed suicide or stayed away from their families and led solitary lives. Thus these women suffered doubly and triply from sexual discrimination. "I was afraid to reveal my past for fifty years, but now I realize I've got only a short life left, and I will tell the whole world," said Kim Hak-soon, the first former comfort woman to reveal her name in court.[23]

In Japan women tend to be divided into two categories for men: mothers and prostitutes. Mothers produce soldiers as well as male children in the patriarchal institution of marriage and family, while prostitutes give the pleasure of sex in the equally patriarchal institution of prostitution. Women were, and continue to be, treated by men only as sex objects. Thus, the patriarchal, imperial, and legal prostitution system continued throughout Japan's period of modernization. The issue of comfort women as an integral part of Japanese patriarchy and imperialism cuts across divisions of state, class, gender, race, and ethnicity. Interwoven into all these divisions, the use of comfort women helped to institutionalize the trafficking of women.

Japanese Government Response to the Comfort Women Issue

On 16 January 1992, just before Japan's former prime minister Miyazawa visited South Korea, documents on "military comfort women" were discovered in the Self Defense Force Library in Tokyo by Yoshimi Yoshiaki, a professor of Japanese history at Chuo University.[24] Since then many documents on "military comfort women" have been found in Japan and Washington, D.C., and witnesses have come forward to disclose how institutionalized prostitution and sexual slavery were controlled and supervised by the Japanese Imperial Army.

Until Yoshimi's discoveries of incriminating documents, the Japanese government kept denying the compulsory drafting and recruiting of Korean women. During his visit to Korea on 17 January 1992, however, the Japanese prime minister apologized to the Korean people in a public speech in Parliament. Nevertheless, at that time he ruled out compensation for the military comfort women, suggesting that war compensation between Japan and Korea was settled in a 1965 agreement on war reparations. His comment disappointed the Korean and Japanese people committed to this issue.

In its second report on comfort women, the Cabinet Councilors' Office on External Affairs finally stated on 5 August 1993 that the "government admitted that Japanese military authorities were in constant control of women forced to provide sex for soldiers before and during WW II, and the government apologizes and expresses remorse over the issue." However, the Japanese government still did not bring up the issue of compensation.

After a year of further criticism and pressure, in November 1994 the Japanese government announced its plan to promote youth exchanges, create a center to support the financial independence of women, and establish a private-sector redress fund including a donation from the government to provide former comfort women with alternative compensation. However, former Korean comfort women and their supporters, primarily the Korean Council for the Women Drafted for Military Sexual Slavery by Japan, have rejected such donation or charity money as a token apology, demanding that the Japanese government provide compensation directly, along with an official letter of apology. The former comfort women and their supporters have been backed in this by a Geneva-based human rights group of legal experts from around the world, the

International Commission of Jurists (ICJ), which issued a 240-page report in late November 1994 urging the Japanese government to provide full rehabilitation and restitution, and as a purely interim measure the sum of U.S. $40,000 each to between 100,000 and 200,000 former comfort women.*

The Korean Council for the Women Drafted for Military Sexual Slavery by Japan also announced in July 1994 that it would file a complaint with the Permanent Court of Arbitration in The Hague to clarify whether Japan is obliged to compensate individual women who were forced to provide sex for Japanese soldiers before and during World War II. The Permanent Court of Arbitration requires agreement by both parties, however, and the Japanese government has repeatedly decided not to accept the request. There is a need for international pressure urging the Japanese government to voluntarily present itself at the international court.

Comfort Women as a Feminist Issue and Action

In Korea agitation by the women's movement as well as anger at the Japanese government's attitude has brought the comfort women issue into the spotlight. The revelation of the condition of comfort women triggered stormy national protests, fueling animosity in Korea and encouraging more disclosures and lawsuits. In both Korea and Japan, however, without the women's movement the disclosures about comfort women and their lawsuits may never have happened or perhaps would have taken much longer to surface.

The women's movement in Korea and Japan has started to encourage women to discuss their sexuality and control their own bodies. The most influential court case occurred in Korea in the late 1980s: a Korean woman for the first time talked publicly about being raped in prison by a policeman.[25] This case taught Korean women how important it was to protest all kinds of sexual abuse.

Both in Korea and Japan women have been discovering and renaming the violation of women's sexuality—including such sexual violence as sexual harassment, domestic violence, pornography, and stereotyped images of women and gender roles. Especially, women have come to notice that sexual violence, violation of women's human rights, and sex industries and prostitution in Asian

---

*The International Commission of Jurists (ICJ) is a nongovernmental organization in consultative status with the United Nations Economic and Social Council. The U.N. Human Rights Commission decided in August 1992 to look into the issue of compensation for comfort women, and the resulting ICJ report is the outcome of its mission to the Philippines, North and South Korea, and Japan in April 1993. The ICJ mission interviewed more than forty victims, three former soldiers, and government representatives, nongovernment organizations, lawyers, academics, and journalists. The report was then compiled by Ustina Dolopol of Flinders University in South Australia. The International Commission of Jurists, P.O. Box 160, 26 Chemin de Joinveille, CH-1216, Cointrin/Geneva, Switzerland. Telephone, (41 22) 788–47 47; fax (41 22) 788–488 80. —Ed., *BCAS.*

countries have worsened, and that women's bodies have been increasingly com-modified. Sensing this situation, in the mid-1970s feminist activists in Korea began actions against the sex industries. At the same time, the Asian Women's Association was organized in Japan and started to protest Japanese men's sex tourism, establishing connections between Korea and Japan. Trying to examine prostitution historically, these women discovered the issue of comfort women.

Thus women started to make the connection between comfort women and the Japanese cultural apparatus responsible for the current trafficking of women and sexual violence. Sexuality was and is used to control and rule both men and women. Created through legalized prostitution based on patriarchy, colonialism, and imperialism, the system of comfort women clearly demonstrates that capital-ism, sexism, and racism are linked and perpetuated both in the colonial and postcolonial eras.

Women's organizations and self-help groups were formed in Japan to politi-cize the issue. Through such groups women have been trying to bring about a revolution and liberation from patriarchy, militarism, and colonialism and to raise consciousness and establish their own autonomy. They have also been working to make this historic case of military slavery an international issue, utilizing international human rights laws that provide for an individual's right to compensation. This has become an urgent task, for it must be done before former comfort women are too old to be able to use compensation to improve their lives.

In August 1992 the Asian Women's Network of East Asian Countries was established in Seoul to exchange information, provide support, and nurture mu-tual empowerment.[26] The network sent a legal appeal to the U.N. Commission on Human Rights. This network has been creating a climate that will help survi-vors share their experiences.

To promote this network Yun Chung-ok, who is part of the same generation as the comfort women, has played a key role in the movement by conducting research on comfort women and helping establish the network of women's groups in Korea that are protesting the trafficking of women and sexual violence. This network has created a climate that has enabled women survivors to come forth to tell their experiences. In 1993 the second "Asian Solidarity Forum on Militarism and Sexual Slavery" was held in Tokyo with former comfort women and activists of eight Asian countries including South Korea, North Korea, China, Taiwan, the Philippines, Indonesia, Malaysia, and Japan. At the solidarity forum Yun Chung-ok's Seoul-based group, the Korean Council for the Women Drafted for Military Sexual Slavery by Japan, proposed as an additional new goal the prosecution of the persons responsible for the planning and execution of military sexual slavery.[27] Although the lawsuit by the Korean council was not accepted at the Tokyo district court, the council is moving ahead, as described in the previous section, by filing a complaint with the Permanent Court of Arbitra-tion in The Hague asking it to clarify whether Japan is obliged to compensate former comfort women.

Comfort women's hot lines have been installed by civic groups in both Korea and Japan. In the first three days the Japanese hot lines received 231 calls in Tokyo and 61 in Osaka. Most calls came from veterans over seventy years old, army doctors, and female nurses. There was one call from a former Japanese comfort woman included in the report published as *Jugun ianfu 110 ban* (Military comfort women hot lines). Nishino Rumiko, director of the Society Concerned with World War II, and the Group Supporting Comfort Women helped organize the hot lines. One former military man confessed: "I wanted to talk about these women for a long time, but I could not because it concerned my own sexuality. However, I felt relieved after telling you about my experience in the war."[28]

Three different types of action groups in Japan emphasize different aspects of the issues. The first type consists mostly of men such as the Karabao group, men's liberation groups, and imperialism. They see the Japanese armies using sexual enslavement to castrate Asian men and colonize Asian women as a way of controlling these countries. These male-dominated action groups note that the Japanese army enslaved *Korean* women's bodies to protect *Japanese* women's chastity. Korean men living in Japan also felt dehumanized by Japan's degradation of Korean women. Sexual debasement in wartime contributed to the inability of the colonized countries to struggle for independence and their own identity as human beings. They were deprived of their human rights.[29]

In contrast, Japanese feminist groups, which are broad and the members of which are from many different professions, emphasize sexism. Women like Suzuki Yuko and other historians see in the issue of comfort women the universality of sexual violence and discrimination practiced in such sex industries as sex tourism and trafficking in women. They feel that both developed and developing countries share the guilt of sexual exploitation by treating women as commodities and creating a sexist culture.

One of these feminists, Fukushima Mizuho, a Japanese woman lawyer who has been working on the lawsuits of migrant Asian women workers and comfort women, points out the similarity between comfort women during wartime and migrant women workers who work in the sex industries in present-day Japan: "There is a parallel between comfort women and Asian women today who are deceived into coming to Japan and are then forced to work as prostitutes against their wills. Both of these groups were and are deluded by the same seductive voice: if you come to Japan, you will easily find well-paid jobs."[30]

Similarly, historian Suzuki Yuko suggests, sex tourism by Japanese men in other Asian countries and trafficking in Asian women is a contemporary version of the Japanese Imperial Army's prior exploitation of Asian women as comfort women. The only difference lies in whether men are in military uniforms or in business suits. It is male degradation of women as commodities.[31] This analysis has been pointed out by many other feminists.

Many feminists also believe that men too are victims and are treated as commodities in militarist and capitalist societies.[32] As they see it, and I agree with their argument, male soldiers were regarded as animals in need of prostitutes because they were supposedly unable to control their own sexual impulses. Male soldiers were actually made inhumane in order to be "good" fighters. The military and colonial soldiers were stimulated by sexuality just like economic soldiers in the postcolonial era. Prostitution is the reward for businessmen who may suffer death from overwork *(karoshi)* for their companies, as it was for the Japanese Imperial Army soldiers who were forced to risk death for the emperor on the battlefield. In this way, women's sexuality has been used to expand the Japanese state's power in other Asian countries, and this continues today when migrant workers who come to Japan are forced into prostitution.

A third group, the Korean-Japanese women's groups such as the Military Comfort Women Issue Uriyosong Network based in Tokyo and the Group Considering the Korean Military Comfort Women Issue in Osaka, both of which were organized in 1991 to support former comfort women in Korea, tell us that the whole structure of sexism joined with racism allowed the Japanese army to institutionalize the comfort women system, and this combination continues today in sex industries that service Japanese men. The inhuman practice of comfort women is rooted in discrimination in gender, race, and ethnicity, and driven by the imbalance in the international economy and systematic commodifying of female bodies. Women's rights to control their own bodies were and are violated by a sexist and racist social structure both in the past and the present. Korean-Japanese women in Japan themselves have no civil rights so that they have experienced social as well as racial and gender discrimination. Korean-Japanese Hwangbou Kangja, a committed member of the Group Considering the Korean Military Comfort Women Issue, says that she first tried to avoid facing the issues of comfort women as a wartime tragedy. But when she realized the importance of these issues, she committed herself to them as a way of grasping her own identity and raising her consciousness.[33] Through protesting against the Japanese government and organizing international conferences together, Japanese and Korean-Japanese feminist groups have started a dialogue for working together for a better future.

Protest against a Condom Manufacturer

Women's action groups, such as Osaka Women against Sexual Assault, women teachers' unions, and the Group Considering the Korean Military Comfort Women Issue, have formed a coalition linking the issue of comfort women with sexual violence, postcolonial exploitation by Japanese corporations, and racism in our everyday lives. As a symbolic action they have undertaken actions against the Okamoto Rubber Manufacturing Company, the biggest condom maker in Japan. This company recently produced condoms with two names on the packages: "Rubber Man" and "Attack Champion" (Totsugeki Ichiban). The condom called Attack Champion suggests that the man's most important duty is to "charge" or "attack" enemies. In a sexual context this term is highly provocative, closely associated with collective rapes and pornographic cartoons such as *Reipu man* (Rape man).[34] The Japanese Imperial Army officially provided Japanese soldiers with the original condom called Attack Champion to use in brothels during World War II to protect the soldiers from venereal diseases. It is obvious that this reissued name is reminiscent of the comfort women and sex industries of earlier days.

The Okamato Manufacturing Company monopolized the condom business during World War II under the name Kokusai Rubber Company. During the present AIDS epidemic era, this company has expanded, building factories in Malaysia with the help of Japanese official development assistance money. Raw materials have been imported into Japan from the Asian countries the Japanese Imperial Army invaded, and the company's products have been sold in Asia as well as in the United States to help family planning, good contraception, and protection from AIDS. All this shows us how human-rights-violating sexism and racism are being perpetuated in the capitalist and postcolonial era.

Women's action groups have demanded that this company conduct research on its own company's past actions, take responsibility for its actions, publicly apologize for them, educate employees about human rights, acknowledge its part in the systematic rape of Asian women during World War II, and denounce violence against women. Also, these groups demand that each condom box have a label stating that "every sexual intercourse without the woman's consent is a rape."

Conclusion

So, what can we do now that we have learned about this brutal aspect of history? We need new strategies. Unless sexual violence and the commodification of women's bodies is eliminated, there will always be comfort women. Recently the world has seen additional offensive cases, such as a representative of the Japanese government suggesting providing Japanese Peace-Keeper Operation (PKO) soldiers with condoms when they were sent from Japan to Cambodia. This equipping of men to buy women in other Asian countries brings to mind the practice of comfort women.

We have to change the social structure as well as our consciousness, and acknowledge victims as courageous survivors. We have to keep re-creating a climate in which women will speak out against rape, sex tourism, prostitution, and the use of comfort women. Women must unite to fight against myths that obscure reality. A global women's movement has encouraged women to establish a network to halt the trafficking of women, unify the peace movement, and also form support groups for former military comfort women. Japanese women must establish close networks with Korean-Japanese women in Japan as well as with Korean women in Korea to change the social structures that allow men to exploit women's sexuality.

Global pressure is also needed to push the Japanese government to take full responsibility for what it has done in neighboring countries during war. The Japanese government is sensitive to international pressure. Women's collective voices must be a great force for change in the Japanese government's attitude regarding comfort women. By forcing the Japanese government to deal with the compensation issues, such pressure may help build closer relationships between Japan and other Asian nations.

We have to stop war; we have to monitor the new militarism in Japan— such as the bill attempting to allow the dispatch of Japanese Self-Defense Corps troops under the PKO and to change the constitution that prohibits any armaments. The United Nations Anti-Discrimination Act appropriately says that "without peace there would be no equality; without equality there would be no peace." I must add that there will be no human rights either. Hwangbou Kangja suggest that the Japanese government's treatment of the comfort women issue is a barometer of its sensitivity to human rights. Eight former comfort women have passed away in the last few years, three in 1993 alone. There is little time left.

Notes

1. Jugun Ianfu Mondai Uriyosong Nettowaku (Military Comfort Women Issue Uriyosong Network), ed., *Kono han o taku* (To liberate this bitterness) (Tokyo: Jugun Ianfu Mondai Uriyosong Nettowaku, 1992); and Kaiho Shuppansha, ed., *Kim Hak-soon-san no shogen* (The testimony of Kim Hak-soon) (Tokyo: Kaiho Shuppansha, 1993).

2. Kim Iryumiyon, *Tenno no guntai to Chosenjin ianfu* (The emperor's army and Korean comfort women) (Tokyo: Sanichi Shobo, 1976); Suzuki Yuko, *Jugun ianfu to Naisen kekkon* (Military comfort women and marriage between Japanese and Koreans) (Tokyo: Miraisha, 1992); Suzuki Yuko, *Chosenjin jugun ianfu* (Korean military comfort women) (Tokyo: Iwanami Shoten, 1991); and Suzuki Yuko, *"Jugun ianfu" mondai to sei boryoku* ("Military comfort women" issues and sexual violence) (Tokyo: Miraisha, 1994).

3. Yun Chung-ok, "Chosenjin jugun ianfu" (Korean military comfort women), in *Chosenjin jugun ianfu mondai shiryoshu* 3 (Chongshindae resource collection 3) (Tokyo: Chosenjin Jugun Ianfu Mondai o Kangaeru Kai). This collection is a Japanese version of Yun Chung-ok, *Chongshindae chaeryojip 3: chongshindae munje Ashia daehwee bokoso* (Chongshindae resource collection 3: report of the Asian conference on the "comfort women" issue) (Seoul: Hankuk Chongshindae Munje Daechaek Hyopwihwe [literally the Committee to Resolve the Comfort Women Issue, but the name used in English is the Korean Council for the Women Drafted for Military Sexual Slavery by Japan], July 1992).

4. Nishino Rumiko, *Jugun ianfu: moto heishitachi no shogen* (Military comfort women: testimony of former soldiers) (Tokyo: Akashi Shoten, 1991), pp. 42–43. Jugun Ianfu Mondai Kodo Nettowaku (Military Comfort Women Issue Action Network), *Jugun Ianfu Mondai Ajia Rentai Kaigi Hokokushu* (Report on the Asian Association Conference on the Comfort Women Issue) (Tokyo: Baibaishun Mondai to Torikumu Kai [Association of Anti-Prostitution Activity], 1993); and Kim Iryumiyon, *Tenno no guntai to Chosenjin ianfu*, p. 17.

5. National Christian Council, ed., *Report: The Asian Solidarity Forum on Militarism and Sexual Slavery* (Nishi-Waseda, Tokyo: National Christian Council, 1994).

6. Zainichi no Ianfu Saiban o Sasaeru Kai (Support Group for the Lawsuit of Korean Former Comfort Women Resident in Japan), ed., *Sojo* (Written complaints) (Tokyo: Zainichi no Ianfu Saiban o Sasaeru Kai, 1993).

7. Kaiho Shuppansha, ed., *Kim Hak-soon san no shogen*; and Jugun Ianfu Mondai Uriyosong Nettowaku, ed., *Kono han o koku.*

8. Ibid.

9. Hirabayashi Hisae, *Kyosei renko to jugun ianfu* (Forced recruits and military comfort women) (Tokyo: Nihon Tosho Centa, 1992), p. 189.

10. Executive Committee, International Public Hearing Concerning Post War Compensation by Japan, ed., *War Victimization and Japan: International Public Hearing Report* (Tokyo: Shuppan, 1993).

11. *Jugun Ianfu Mondai Uriyosong Nettowaku Nyusuretta* (The Military Comfort Women Issue Network newletter), no. 5 (April 1993); and the Zainichi no Ianfu Saiban o Sasaeru Kai, *Sojo.* This support group also published a booklet, *Zainichi moto jugun ianfu, Song Siin-do* (The story of Song Siin-do, Korean former "comfort woman" resident in Japan) (Tokyo: Zainichi no Ianfu Saiban of Sasaeru Kai, 1993).

12. Many books on Korean comfort women are available in Japanese. My report is based on Suzuki's three books (see n. 2) as well as her speeches.

13. Ibid.

14. Ibid.

15. Asahi Shinbun Sha, ed., *Onnatachi no Taiheiyo Senso* (Women's Pacific War) (Tokyo: Asahi Shinbun Sha, 1992).

16. Kankoku Teishintai Mondai Taisaku Kyogi Kai (The Japanese name for the Hankuk Chongshindae Munje Daechaek Hyopwihwe, in English the Korean Council for the Women Drafted for Sexual Slavery by Japan [see n. 3]), ed., *Shogen: Kyosei renko sareta Chosenjin gun ianfu tachi* (Testimony: kidnapped Korean military comfort women) (Tokyo: Akashi Shoten, 1993). This book was written in Korean and then translated into both Japanese and English.

17. Yun Chung-ok, *Chosenjin jugun ianfu mondai shiryoshu 2–3*, the Japanese version of Yun Chun-ok, *Chongshindae chaeryojip 2–3* (Chongshindae resource collection 2–3).

18. Ibid.

19. Zainippon Chosenminshu Josei Domei (People's Republic of Korea Resident in Japan Women's Association), ed., *Chosenjin "ianfu"* (Korean "comfort women") (Tokyo: Zainippon Chosenminshu Josei Domei, 1992).

20. Ibid.

21. Kawada Ayako, *Akagawara no ie* (A house with a red roof) (Tokyo: Chikuma Shobo, 1989). Also see Asahi Shinbun Sha, ed., *Onnatachi no Taiheiyo Senso.*

22. Kim Iryumiyon, *Jugun ianfu to Naisen kekkon*; and Yun Chung-ok, ed., *Chosenjin josei ga mita "ianfu mondai"* (Korean women's view of the comfort women issue) (Tokyo: Sanichi Shobo, 1992).

23. Jugun Ianfu Mondai Uriyosong Nettowaku, *Kono han o toku.*

24. Yoshimi Yoshiaki, ed., *Jugun ianfu shogen shu* (A collection of trial documents of military comfort women) (Tokyo: Otsuki Shoten, 1992).

25. Suzuki, *Chosenjin jugun ianfu.*

26. Jugun Ianfu Mondai Kodo Nettowaku, ed., *Jugun Ianfu Mondai Ajia Rentai Kaigi Hokokushu.*

27. National Christian Council, ed., *Report: The Asian Solidarity Forum on Militarism and Sexual Slavery.*

28. Jugun Ianfu 110 Henshu Iinkai (Military Comfort Women Hot Line Editorial Committee), ed., *Jugun ianfu 110 ban* (Military comfort women hot lines) (Tokyo Akashi Shoten, 1992).

29. Takagi Kenichi, *Jugun ianfu to sengo hosho* (Military comfort women and war compensation) (Tokyo: Sanichi Shobo, 1992).

30. Fukushima Mizuho, personal interview with the author, April 1992.

31. Suzuki, *"Jugun ianfu" mondai to sei boryoku.*

32. Ibid.

33. Hwangbou Kangja, "'Zaini' josei to Chosenjin jungun ianfu mondai" (The issue of forced military prostitution from the perspective of Korean women resident in Japan), *Joseigaku Nenpo* (Women's studies yearly report, vol. 13 (1992), pp. 36–45.

34. *Reipu man* (Rape man) is the title of a comic and the name of the central character, whose profession is to rape women.

14

Mr. Tomino Goes to City Hall:
Grass-Roots Democracy in Zushi City, Japan

*Kenneth J. Ruoff**

Introduction

On 31 July 1992 Mayor Tomino Kiichirō of the city of Zushi announced that he would not seek reelection in the November mayoral election. Since he was first elected mayor in November 1984, Tomino has been the most visible and blunt spokesman for a group of Zushi citizens seeking to halt the Japanese central government's plan to construct housing for U.S. navy personnel on the site of the former Ikego Ammunition Dump, a pristine tract of land in Zushi known to citizens there as the Ikego Forest. Zushi is about forty-five kilometers southwest of central Tokyo and six kilometers west of the massive U.S. naval base at Yokosuka. The Ikego Forest, 290 hectares of rolling hills, is one of the last patches of greenery in the urban sprawl around Tokyo. The citizens' movement to stop the Ikego Housing Project has attracted significant mass media attention since its inception in the fall of 1982 and has become one of the symbols of the growing environmental movement in Japan.

Tomino was elected mayor at the age of forty, and the young political ama-

*Although the first section of this article is for the most part the same as the 1993 article published in the *Bulletin of Concerned Asian Scholars*, it is followed by a seven-page update written in 1996. Robert Immerman of the East Asian Institute at Columbia University provided overall support for this project and made helpful comments on a draft of this chapter. Former mayor Tomino and Mayor Sawa were generous with their time, and I would like to thank them and the Zushi City civil servants, especially members of the Peaceful Relations Section, who answered numerous questions. John Urda also took the time to evaluate an earlier version of this article. When a shorter version was presented at the Columbia University Graduate Study Group in Modern Japanese History on 10 September 1992, Mark Jones, Ethan Mark, Matthew McKelway, Akitoshi Miyashita, Scott O'Bryan, Simon Partner, Franziska Seraphim, Sarah Thal, and Keith Vincent encouraged me to put it in manuscript form and submit it for review. Several suggestions of the anonymous *BCAS* reviewers were incorporated into the final article, and it is my pleasure to thank them as well.

teur not only attempted to rule for the people throughout his eight years in office but to reform the administrative structure of the city government to permit more citizen participation between elections. The mass media focused tremendous attention on the dynamic and telegenic young mayor, who was seen as a new breed of politician. Even as the mayor of a small city with a population of 57,000, Tomino had become renowned throughout Japan. Thus Tomino's announcement that he would not seek reelection was national news just as his election eight years earlier had been. It is rumored that Tomino will run for a seat in the Diet. The mayor, however, insists that his political career is over for now.

Mayor Tomino is a controversial figure in Japan. Along the same lines of Chibana Shoichi, Nakaya Yasuko, and Motoshima Hitoshi, voices of dissent chronicled by Norma Field in her *In the Realm of a Dying Emperor,*[1] Tomino has suffered the consequences of taking a firm political stand on volatile issues. Shortly after he was elected mayor on his pledge to halt the Ikego Housing Project, police authorities thought it necessary to station enough policemen to surround the mayor's home for three months to protect him and his family from possible attacks by members of right-wing groups.[2] Tomino was not especially frightened by the right-wing groups which vigorously protested his stance on the Ikego Housing Project. It was the support of right-wing groups such as the Issuikaithat that disturbed Tomino. Members of Issuikai insisted that it was outrageous for foreign troops to be stationed on the Emperor's land, and wished Tomino the best of luck in stopping the housing project. In 1988 Tomino participated in a televised debate with fifteen individuals, including right-wing activist Nomura Shūsuke, on the meaning of the Shōwa emperor. The two stand ideologically apart on the emperor system, but after the debate Nomura slapped Tomino on the back and encouraged him in his efforts to stop the housing project.[3] While sometimes drawing support from surprising and unwelcome quarters, Tomino's policies made him a figure of controversy throughout his eight years in office.

Purnendra Jain has traced the history of the citizens' movement in Zushi and the background of Tomino's election as mayor. However, Jain's hopeful prediction in his 1991 essay that "the Zushi movement should achieve its aim"[4] to halt construction of U.S. military housing in the Ikego Forest has not come true. The construction is under way, and the city as well as citizens' groups continue to lose every legal confrontation with the central government, which owns the Ikego Forest. The first U.S. Navy personnel could well move into the housing complex by the beginning of 1994.[5] While Mayor Tomino now accepts responsibility for failing to halt the Ikego Housing Project, he successfully instituted numerous other policies in the city of Zushi that became the subject of popular and scholarly debate in Japan.

The story of Tomino's administration is intricately linked with the Zushi citizens' movement. Although the movement's unifying goal has been halting the Ikego Housing Project, many of the citizens who were first politicized in opposition to the destruction of the Ikego Forest have extended their political commitment to comprehensive environmental protection and social issues, such as eliminating racial discrimination. By focusing on Tomino's final years in office, this article will trace how the Zushi experiment in grass-roots democracy greatly changed politics and administration in that city. During those last years the colorful mayor, responding to his constituency, continued to fight for the environment while pursuing controversial social policies.

On 14 November 1984 Tomino Kiichirō assumed his duties as mayor in a fashion that was to set the tone for his administration. In what from the view of the city bureaucrats was an outrageous invasion of the sanctity of city hall, Tomino invited the mass media to attend his first meeting with the bureau chiefs. He requested that the city civil servants open their hearts and city hall to the citizens. This meeting became the basis for a famous thirty-minute television program broadcast on NHK,[6] a Japanese network similar to the BBC. According to Tomino, the city bureaucrats initially seemed to perceive him as if he were an alien who had arrived in city hall via a UFO.[7]

Reexamining History

From the day that Tomino was elected, conservative members of the twenty-six-member city assembly seemed to wish that the UFO that had brought the young mayor to office would return to take him away. On 18 March 1992 the mayor once again infuriated conservative representatives when he proposed in his annual address to the city assembly that city funds be allocated to study how Koreans were used as forced laborers in Zushi during the Fifteen-Year War (1931–45). This came to be known in Zushi as the Korean problem (*Chōsenjin mondai*). Tomino believes that Japanese must accept war responsibility.[8] And so the mayor, with the support of progressive city assembly members, sought funding for a study that could be used to correct the official city history of the war era to include accounts of the brutalization of Korean laborers.

Tomino's proposal to rewrite the city's history was not the first time that he has sought to revise dominant interpretations of taboo areas of Japan's history. After several years in office, Tomino had become recognized as a social commentator,[9] and he proved willing to address even the most contentious topics. During a televised debate about the emperor system and the historical role of the Shōwa emperor when the emperor was on his deathbed, Tomino pushed fellow participants to explain why the Shōwa emperor is celebrated for individually having stopped the war but absolved of all responsibility for taking part in the decision to start the war.[10]

Zushi City was one of the few municipalities in Japan that did not issue an official get-well pronouncement for the Shōwa emperor during his illness.[11] Tomino supported Motoshima Hitoshi, mayor of Nagasaki, when he came under enormous pressure and threats for suggesting that the Shōwa emperor bore partial responsibility for the war. After Motoshima was nearly assassinated in January 1990, Tomino planned to visit him at the hospital. Motoshima insisted, not unreasonably, that Tomino stay away since he too could easily become a target of right-wing violence.

The death of the Shōwa emperor in 1989 seems to have resulted in somewhat of a new willingness among Japanese leaders to confront Japan's wartime past. Emperor Akihito acknowledged Japan's role as the aggressor against Korea with his statement of contrition to President Roh Tae-woo of South Korea in 1990. During the Fifteen-Year War, especially the period from the enactment of the National Conscription Law in 1939 until the end of the war, hundreds of thousands of Koreans were brought to work at the dirtiest and most dangerous jobs in Japan's wartime economy. In the area that is now the city of Zushi they were forced to build massive tunnels (seventy-three in Zushi and thousands in Kanagawa Prefecture), including those at the Ikego Ammunition Dump. Until the mayor's proposal, this historical fact remained unknown to or ignored by most citizens of Zushi, although not forgotten by some old-timers, including the mayor's uncle. The mayor's uncle also remembered that when the American military took over the Ammunition Dump black soldiers were given the duty of working in the tunnels. Zushi's lapse in memory simply reflected the central government's assiduous avoidance of the question of the imperial Japanese military's pitiless treatment of Koreans and other Asians.

In the same year that Emperor Akihito apologized to President Roh, Mayor Tomino undertook a trip to Germany, both former East and West Germany. The Berlin Wall had just come down as a result of citizens' movements—something close to the mayor's heart—and he wanted to see post–Cold War Europe in its nascent stage. While in Germany he visited numerous monuments that record the infamous era of the Nazis. He learned that many of the monuments to Germany's ugliest era had in fact been preserved because individual citizens had stepped in to stop their decay or demolition.[12] This made a deep impression on him. It also jarred his own memory of history.

When Tomino was a small boy in Zushi he befriended a Korean boy. At the time there were three Korean communities in Zushi. These communities were largely isolated, and the Koreans were treated as outcasts. But Tomino accepted invitations to go to his Korean friend's home on several occasions. He was always received with great courtesy by the boy's parents. Reflecting on this treatment today, Tomino wonders if it meant a great deal to the Korean parents, isolated as they were from the larger Japanese community, to see a Japanese boy willing to come to their home. Later he learned from his relatives how Koreans were treated during the war. But the Korean communities in Zushi largely disintegrated during the time that Mayor Tomino went to Kyoto University and then took over the family business manufacturing machines to draw the water out of garbage to allow for efficient burning. Most of the Koreans in Zushi moved to other parts of Japan. There was nothing in the official city history to suggest the origins of these communities or the discrimination suffered by the Koreans. This local history came flooding back to Tomino during his stay in Germany.

During his tenure as mayor, Tomino was sensitive to the concerns of those who suffer from discrimination. He refused to report to the central government the names of Korean residents who violated the law by refusing to be finger-printed.[13] In fact, in 1988 Tomino considered stopping the fingerprinting process in Zushi altogether. The civil servants working under him advised him that if he ordered the process stopped, not only would he be breaking the law, but he would be forcing the bureaucrats under him to do so as well. The mayor reluc-tantly continued to administer the fingerprinting procedure, which he considers to be a human rights violation.[14] However, a mayor has the power to change the city's employment policies by administrative fiat, and in 1991 Tomino changed them in order to allow Korean residents of Japan to seek employment in Zushi as civil servants. In April 1992 one Korean began working as a regular employee in city hall. It was the first time that a public corporation in eastern Japan had hired a Korean as a regular civil servant.

Following the historian Yoshimi Yoshiaki's disclosure of overwhelming evi-dence proving the Japanese military's role in the recruitment, or kidnapping, of Korean women to serve as prostitutes for Japanese soldiers during the Fifteen-Year War,[15] Prime Minister Miyazawa Kiichi issued yet another official apology during a January 1992 visit to South Korea. While at the national level the prime minister and the foreign ministry attempted to limit the damage caused by Yoshimi's disclosure, Tomino hoped to sponsor an investigation of his city's own history that would lead local citizens to reflect seriously on Japan's past treatment of Koreans and other Asians. The debate his proposal ignited in Zushi is representative of different Japanese views about how to best deal with a past that neighboring countries refuse to simply forget.

Conservative representatives made racial slurs during and after the meeting at which Tomino introduced the proposal.[16] The mayor was jeered by some city assembly members during his speech. Representative Kojima Saburō remarked that the treatment of Koreans was no different from that of Japanese. He empha-sized that "under the emperor's everlasting rule, Koreans were treated equally to Japanese."[17] Socially progressive members of the assembly were appalled by their conservative colleagues' statements and willingness to gloss over the past. But enough representatives wanted to "let sleeping dogs lie" *(neta ko o okosu koto wa nai)*, or did not feel that city funds should be spent on such a project, to give the victory initially to the conservatives: the proposal was rejected by a margin of one vote.

Both Mayor Tomino's proposal and what came to be known as the discrimi-natory statements *(sabetsu hatsugen)* of some of the city assembly members received significant coverage in the national press.[18] Letters of protest from fourteen human rights and historical associations were sent to the city assembly. Saitō Tadashi of the Kanagawa Prefectural Fact Finding Organization Regarding the Forced Labor of Koreans (Kanagawa-ken Chōsenjin kyōsei renkō shinsō chōsadan [KPFORFLK]) admonished Hirai Yoshio, the conservative chairman of the assembly who had cast the deciding vote, for the assembly's denial of historical facts and demanded an apology.[19] Hidaka Rokurō of the Kanagawa Human Rights Center (Kanagawa jinken sentaa) also wrote to Hirai to blast the city assembly for its loss of memory of history as well as to insist upon an apology.[20] Significant attention came to be focused on those city assembly members who had belittled the mayor's proposal. On 17 April Hirai and four other representatives who had made objectionable statements retracted their outspoken words and offered apologies. Mayor Tomino vowed to reintroduce the proposal at the June session of the city assembly in order to gain special budgetary approval.

On 7 June, shortly before the city assembly reopened on 16 June, KPFORFLK conducted an initial field investigation of the tunnels built in Zushi by Korean laborers during the war.[21] One aged Korean man recounted the horrible conditions under which he and others had worked in Zushi. Yi Yong-jin, seventy, remembered how there were numerous cave-ins that resulted in many grave injuries. He further noted that the injured were not provided with any medical care.[22] On 24 June the city assembly voted to fund a three-year study. Officials in the Peaceful Relations Section (Heiwatoshi suishinkai) of Zushi city hall will work with scholars to compile a report that will serve as a basis for rewriting the official city history.

Although Zushi has clearly set an example for local governments and communities to address unpleasant historical questions, Tomino adamantly insists upon the independence of Zushi's study from outside organizations and political parties. The goal of the study is limited to setting the local record straight, to making local citizens reflect on the city's dirty laundry. Nor is Zushi's study a substitute for an official study carried out by the central government.

The Environmental Movement

The "Korean problem" was not the only issue during 1992 that made Zushi the object of national and even international media attention. The so-called Concrete Incident (Konkuriito jiken) also attracted national media attention beginning in June, though in fact its history began several years earlier. The city had long been at odds with the Makkuhomuzu Construction Company, which had defied the city's zoning policies in building an eleven-story condominium complex along Zushi's seashore. Since local governments had yet to win legal authority to enforce strict local zoning laws, the Makkuhomuzu Construction Company thought little of ignoring the wishes of the mayor and his staff in planning and then undertaking construction of a building that was to be thirty-two meters high. The prefecture had approved the company's application without taking into consideration the changes desired by the city. The building, now completed, is a complex of eighteen condominiums, and it is twice as tall as any other building along Zushi's seashore. In the view of the mayor and most citizens of Zushi, the eleven-story building—visible from most spots in the city—is a ghastly addition that mars the skyline of a city renowned for its scenic views.

Tomino has come to be considered a leading spokesman of the environmental movement. He argues that in Japan environmental destruction has progressed to the point that most individuals live in surroundings so spiritually empty that they bring about a slow death. To reverse this trend at the local level, from his earliest days in office Tomino has sought to freeze development in the city of Zushi. But the mayor was long frustrated by the city's lack of legal power to control what he and many citizens of Zushi had come to see as runaway development in their city. The fact that the condominium complex was built in the first place suggests the former powerlessness of city governments to limit development in the face of laws greatly favoring private property rights and reserving the authority to approve construction plans to the prefectural governments. But the results of the Concrete Incident may serve to empower city governments in the future regarding questions of development.

A mayor has final decision-making power regarding the use of city sewers. Although the city of Zushi had long refused to grant the Makkuhomuzu Construction Company a sewer permit for the condominium complex, the company went ahead with construction. In May 1992, just before the time when several tenants hoped to move into the new condominiums, the Makkuhomuzu Construction Company connected the building to the Zushi City sewer line. Mayor Tomino promptly declared the connection to be a violation. On 1 June, under the direction of the mayor, city workers blocked the sewer connection with concrete, returning the building to an uninhabitable state.

It should have come as no surprise to the Makkuhomuzu Construction Company that Mayor Tomino ordered his staff to block the sewer connection. In his book published the previous year Tomino had suggested that he might not permit the building, once finished, to be connected to the city's sewer system.[23] The national newspapers carried pictures of the city workers pouring concrete to seal the connection, so it is clear that the city had alerted the mass media in advance of the event.[24] News of the Concrete Incident spread throughout the country as proponents of the environment and development took sides to debate the issue. On 15 June the Makkuhomuzu Construction Company filed suit against the city of Zushi in the Yokohama District Court.[25]

Mayor Tomino had prepared well in advance for the lawsuit that was sure to come. His legal advisors had informed him that the city had a pretty good chance of successfully defending its action. But even if the city lost the suit, Tomino believed that the lengthy legal process—conceivably as long as ten years— would inflict terrible monetary damages on the construction company (the city had no intention of allowing the building to be connected to the sewer system until all legal options were exhausted). In contrast, the worst the city could expect was to be fined about $1,000. Tomino's goal was to send a message by making an example of this company that had so casually flouted the desires of the city in constructing a building completely inharmonious with Zushi's cityscape. Construction companies and their financiers refusing to abide by Zushi's zoning administrative guidance risked economic disaster.

The Yokohama District Court returned a verdict unusually rapidly. Although the judges did not order the building to be demolished—an option that neither the mayor nor citizens of Zushi had considered even remotely possible—the court's decision can only be viewed as a victory for the city. In ordering that the city and the construction company reach a compromise *(wakai)*, the court permitted the city to demand conditions that will inflict significant economic damages on the construction company.

In order to ensure that its message gets across, Zushi has been permitted to insert a clause requiring that the three top condominiums—the ones with spectacular views of Mount Fuji on a clear day—remain empty for three years.[26] Thus until 1995 the construction company will not receive one penny of payment for the three best condominiums, each of which would sell for at least one million dollars. In sending a message about the nature of future development in Zushi, Mayor Tomino has won a significant victory that may have important ramifications for local autonomy if questions of the environment become increasingly important political issues both at the national and local levels. If this case becomes a precedent, local governments will have gained more power to direct development. Extending local autonomy has long been one of Tomino's overriding goals.

Expanding Democracy

The mass media's focus on Tomino's politics has made the mayor a spokesman for democracy as well as for the environment. In his *Guriin demokurashii: ima Ikego kara uttaeru,* Tomino argued why the Zushi citizens' movement was the first example in Japan of Green Democracy, which he characterized as follows: (1) nature conservation has become a vote-getter; (2) there is a new tendency by citizens to question how security needs can be balanced with protecting the environment; (3) there is a new consciousness on the part of citizens of the relationship between the central and local governments, with a growing movement for more local autonomy; (4) there is a growing realization by citizens that "textbook democracy," or politics carried out by amateurs, is effective; and (5) there is a growing sentiment among the postwar generations that democracy is proving to be effective and successful.[27]

Tomino considers his personal history to embody the potential strength of Japan's postwar democracy. Before the central government announced its plans to build housing for U.S. soldiers in the virgin Ikego Forest situated next to his home, Tomino had little interest in politics. He was running the family business and his thoughts were also on the stars—he has long been fervently interested in astronomy. But when the Ikego controversy arose, principles of grass-roots democracy that he had learned in the immediate postwar era—Tomino was born in 1944—bubbled to the surface. "I belong to a generation that was physically nourished by U.S. food aid," Tomino likes to tell American visitors to his city, "and spiritually nourished on American principles of democracy."

Overnight Tomino became involved in the grass-roots movement to stop the Defense Facilities Administration Agency from carrying out its plan to build approximately 1,000 units of housing on the site of the former Ikego Ammunition Dump. Urged by citizens' groups to run for mayor, Tomino presented himself as an independent candidate. He was elected over Mishima Torayasu, an incumbent mayor who, although he had years of political experience and was supported by the powerful and monied Liberal Democratic Party (LDP), had betrayed the wishes of the majority of Zushi citizens in secretly negotiating a deal with the central government in the spring of 1984 that ended the city's official opposition to the housing development plan.[28] At the age of forty, Tomino became one of the youngest mayors in Japan, and proof that nature conservation does win votes, at least at the local level.

From his first day in office Tomino's primary goal was to reverse the central government's decision to sacrifice the Ikego Forest. The mayor and the majority of Zushi citizens rejected the central government's insistence that the destruction of the Ikego Forest was justified because security needs, as dictated by the U.S.–Japan Security Treaty, outweighed environmental concerns. The mayor's opposition to the plan drew him into bitter conflict with the conservative pro-development majority in the city assembly, which thought it had put the Ikego issue to rest on 10 April 1984. On that day the city assembly had passed a resolution supporting Mayor Mishima's plan to accept the development of Ikego Forest in return for plums from the central government such as land for building a city hospital. In his first speech to the city assembly on 5 December 1984, Tomino rejected the validity of this decision:

> Although I appreciate the efforts made by former mayor Mishima and members of the assembly, I interpret the last election results as evidence that the citizens choose to oppose the construction of U.S. military housing in order to protect the environment, and that this nullifies previous decisions made by the city before the election.[29]

In an attempt to browbeat and humiliate the young mayor, who was a political amateur and at least twenty years younger than many of the city assembly representatives, the chairman of the city assembly at that time found various pretenses to declare that the mayor had insulted the city assembly. Mayor Tomino is a humorous man who loves a joke. When first elected, he would sometimes smile when speaking at city assembly meetings. The chairman of the city assembly would say that by smiling the mayor was insulting the city assembly and demand an apology. If Mayor Tomino did not apologize, the chairman promptly declared the city assembly in recess until the mayor was willing to make amends. In this manner city business was repeatedly paralyzed.[30]

It is no wonder that Mayor Tomino has referred to the city assembly of his early years in office as "something like a hellish otherworld" (*jigoku no yō na bessekai*).[31] The mayor was not the only individual to suffer the unusual democratic practices of the city assembly dominated by conservatives. One reason that the Zushi citizens' movement is distinct is that housewives have been at the forefront of the movement from its inception. It was mostly women of the city who first gathered in front of the gate to the Ikego Ammunition Dump in 1982 to protest the planned housing project and these same women formed the core of citizens' groups such as the Citizens' Association for the Protection of Nature and Children (Midori to kodomo o mamoru shimin no kai) created to unify citizen protest against the development. Five women eventually won election to the city assembly where they came to form the core of the Green faction (*midori-ha*). Sawa Mitsuyo, one such housewife, endured the taunts of conservative male city assembly members when she first entered the man's world of politics after being elected in 1986:

> They told me to act like a woman, to be more meek (*otonashii*). If they could somehow claim that I insulted the assembly, they would demand a recess until I apologized. When I apologized they would say it was insufficient and demand a written apology. It was distasteful, but I fought them. Through my publicity organs I leaked to the citizens how they were tormenting me, and I learned to go to the press as well. When they learned I wouldn't play the weak role, they stopped bothering me.[32]

On 8 November 1992 Sawa was elected mayor of Zushi, a significant step for a housewife who wanted nothing to do with politics before the Ikego Housing Project became an issue. She defeated her closest opponent, Hirai Yoshio, the conservative city assembly chairman who was supported by the LDP, by more than 4,000 votes.[33] Hirai was one of five candidates who expressed their willingness to discontinue Tomino's policy of opposing the Ikego Housing Project, while Sawa ran as an independent with a platform that included continued opposition to the central government's development of the Ikego Forest. The total votes of the five candidates who favored ending the city's opposition to the housing project considerably exceeded Sawa's vote total, however, suggesting declining support for the city's uncompromising stance.

Sawa is the second woman in Japan ever to be elected to the position of city mayor.[34] It is doubtful that Sawa will succeed in stopping the Ikego Housing Project. The leveling of some of the hills in the forest has already disheartened many citizens. But the new mayor is committed to trying all the same. During Tomino's administration, the city established ties with several international environmental organizations, such as the Sierra Club, National Wildlife Federation. Audubon Society, and Environmental Defense Fund. Mayor Sawa has asked these organizations to lobby President Bill Clinton, and especially Vice President Al Gore, who is known for his pro-environmental stance, in a final attempt to save the Ikego Forest. Although it is the Japanese government, under a cost-sharing agreement, that is undertaking the construction of housing in the Ikego Forest for U.S. military personnel, Mayor Sawa and many citizens in Zushi believe that if the U.S. government pressured the Japanese government to halt the Ikego Housing Project, it would do so. Correctly or incorrectly, some Japanese see outside pressure (*gaiatsu*) from the United States as the only means to make the Japanese government act on a variety of fronts. In addition to working through international environmental organizations, Mayor Sawa plans to travel to the United States in 1993 to draw attention to environmental importance of the Ikego Forest.

While whatever the result of Mayor Sawa's international lobbying, she does have one advantage in administering the city of Zushi that Tomino enjoyed only during his last two years in office: the conservative majority in the city assembly has been voted into the minority because of having paid insufficient attention to the environmental concerns of the citizens. Mayor Sawa can expect support for many of her proposals from what is known as the citizens' faction (*shimin-ha*), a majority coalition that includes not only all the members of the Green faction, but representatives from the Japan Socialist Party, the Japan Communist Party, and the Clean Government Party (Kōmeitō). Long one of Tomino's most devout supporters, Mayor Sawa can be expected to continue many of his innovative policies, such as the completion and institution of a city charter (*kenshō*) by 1994.

While many cities in Japan have adopted city charters, they rarely do more than pithily call for "world peace and a beautiful environment." Should Zushi adopt the city charter now being written, it would become the first city in Japan with a city charter that defined how citizens had decided the city should be administered. This would be the city's most concrete step in extending its autonomy from the central government provided, of course, that the city charter withstands whatever legal challenges it may face. Tomino clearly intended the city charter to be more than a symbolic act when he commissioned a group of scholars to study the issue in 1991.[35] The charter would be partially a protest against the central government. For example, by giving all residents of Zushi regardless of their nationality the right to vote in city elections, a proposal that is under consideration, Zushi would raise the question of why second- and third-generation Korean residents of Japan are denied the right to vote.

Although Tomino was unsuccessful in convincing the central government to halt the Ikego Housing Project, he remained popular throughout his eight years in office and was expected to win reelection should he have chosen to run. There were two reasons for this. First, citizens understood that the odds were stacked against their movement succeeding in convincing the central government to find another location for the housing. Second, Mayor Tomino has managed to introduce a high level of citizen participation in city decisions. Maximizing citizen participation in government is what Tomino, who continues to refer to himself as a citizen and not a politician, calls textbook democracy.

In Zushi and other municipalities citizens have long had the option of voicing their concerns directly to the mayor and his bureau chiefs at ward meetings. Although ward meetings antedated Tomino's administration, by all accounts their atmosphere has undergone a significant change since Tomino was elected. Citizens have become much more vocal in voicing their opinions and requesting better service. At the Hisagi Ward meeting on 30 May 1992, citizens were unrelenting in their demands on Mayor Tomino and his bureau chiefs. Several senior citizens berated the assistant fire chief for poor ambulance service. One citizen demanded that action be taken to stop caterpillars from devouring the cherry trees in a park near his house. And to strengthen his case, the man had brought evidence, a jar of the caterpillars, which he presented to the mayor. After examining the living evidence with a look of concern, Tomino turned the caterpillars over to the chief of the environmental bureau, who promised to investigate the matter promptly.

Today citizens of Zushi also have several new mechanisms to ensure that the city bureaucrats are responsive to their demands. One of Mayor Tomino's first actions was to institute a "letter to the mayor" system. Citizens can write their concerns on preprinted postcards that are delivered straight to the mayor. Or citizens can serve on any one of the numerous citizens' advisory committees that have been established since Tomino took office to offer input on, for example, improving parks. In order to keep citizens informed of city affairs, the city has significantly increased the number of information pamphlets and newsletters it distributes.

Tomino has even instituted a program based on the U.S. Freedom of Information Act to open the business of city hall to citizens who are not satisfied with the information they receive through official newsletters. Before Tomino became mayor, the city of Zushi, like many government agencies in Japan, was not hospitable to citizens' demands for information. Today at the Information Access Section (Jōhō kōkaika), however, citizens can request information on most details of city business (the details of sensitive land negotiations between the city and private individuals would be one exception). Ironically, it is a local flake[37] who has made most use of the Information Access Section—he comes virtually every day to demand news for his crude, muckraking weekly tabloid, the *Kanagawa janaru*. The Information Access Section, in addition to keeping a local eccentric busy trying to prove that Mayor Tomino was enjoying expensive French meals with taxpayers' money, has been used by citizens to gain information about a teacher who was said to have disciplined a student physically.[37]

Bureaucrats, sometimes not without approval, and citizens, almost always with approval, agree that the business of city hall is now carried out under the glare of the public eye. Some bureaucrats grumble that citizens complain too much (*monku ga ōi*). In contrast, citizens now remember how city officials used to be unhelpful. Hanada Masamichi, a retired judge and longtime resident of Zushi, spoke of Tomino's influence in making city hall more responsive to citizens' concerns:

It would be an exaggeration to say that the roads have greatly improved since Tomino was elected, although they have improved a bit. What has changed is that the city makes significant efforts to keep citizens informed about what is going on in city hall. Citizens are asked to take part in planning the city's future. And when one sends a letter of complaint, the reply is very quick.[38]

Although there was significant opposition among city bureaucrats to Mayor Tomino's proposal that city hall be opened to the citizens, the fact remains that the bureaucrats were in a poor position to resist the mayor's reforms, at least openly. And so the mayor, especially since the 1990 city assembly election that resulted in a generally pro-Tomino majority, was able to convince city bureaucrats to open city hall if not their hearts to the citizens. Some bureaucrats who initially thought Tomino was crazy admit to liking the new openness, although it can make their jobs more difficult. This trend toward openness should continue under Mayor Sawa's stewardship.

Conclusion

Most of the supporters of the ongoing Zushi citizens' movement are individuals younger than sixty who hold dear the principles of democracy emphasized in their postwar education. Tomino has high hopes for this generation, just as his supporters have equally high hopes that he will enter national politics. Tomino's success at reforming politics and administration in the city of Zushi resulted from the committed support of an intense and enduring local citizens' movement. The fact that the Zushi citizens' movement has thus far failed to halt the Ikego Housing Project could be interpreted as a sign of the weakness or ineffectiveness of grass-roots democracy in Japan. Although the citizens' movement succeeding in delaying the Ikego Housing Project several years, in the end the central government indeed proved impervious to the demands of the Zushi citizens. It is worth recalling, however, the most serious obstacle the citizens' movement faced: Zushi City did not own the Ikego Forest. The Ikego Forest was used for underground ammunition storage for nearly fifty years and the city was in the position of asking that the central government relinquish its ownership of the land, or at least make it into a national park. Moreover, while the movement to stop the Ikego Housing Project had support from some citizens throughout the nation, it did not have truly broad-based national support. Clearly there was an element of "not in my backyard" motivating the local citizens who formed the core of the movement to prevent the construction of housing for U.S. military personnel,[39] and the destruction of the Ikego Forest did not disturb large numbers of individuals throughout Japan. The results would have likely been different if the movement had been intense *and* national.

In Zushi, however, the grass-roots movement reshaped city politics and administration. Runaway development has been brought under control. Mayor Sawa is committed to protecting the environment, as are the majority of city assembly members. Today in Zushi virtually no decision, whether concerning school construction or river control, is implemented before city bureaucrats, often in consultation with citizens' committees, consider its environmental impact. And the city continues to pursue progressive social policies through its reformed employment practices, rewriting of history, and the compilation of a city charter.

During the last ten years, a thriving civil society comprised of overlapping citizens' groups has emerged in the small seaside city of Zushi. Citizens have tenaciously challenged a decision of the central government and also worked to make the city government more responsive to citizens. When the citizens in Zushi expressed their will through democratic means, city politicians responded or were voted out of office. While Zushi is only one community in Japan, the citizens' movement there provides evidence for the strength of democratic consciousness among the Japanese citizenry.

Notes

1. Norma Field, *In the Realm of a Dying Emperor* (New York: Pantheon Books, 1991).

2. Mayor Tomino Kiichirō, interview with the author, 27 June 1992.

3. In September 1993, Nomura committed suicide in the offices of the Asahi shinbun in Tokyo, apparently to protest a cartoon that had appeared the previous year in the *Shūkan asahi.* The cartoon mocked Nomura's election bid for a seat in the Lower House of the Diet. Nomura's suicide might be interpreted as an improvement in the tactics of the right-wing. Instead of violently attacking individuals with whom he disagreed, Nomura took his own life to make his statement.

4. Purnendra C. Jain, "Green Politics and Citizen Power in Japan: The Zushi Movement," *Asian Survey,* vol. 31, no. 6 (June 1991), p. 573.

5. Individuals interested in the city of Zushi's desperate last attempts to halt the construction of the housing can keep updated by means of an English-language newsletter published regularly by the city. Write to: the City of Zushi, 5–2–16, Zushi, Zushi-shi, Kanagawa-ken, 249 Japan, and ask to be put the mailing list for the "Ikego U.S. Naval Housing Newsletter."

6. The name of the program was "Toppu kōtai—Zushi shiyakusho de ima, nani ga?" (Change at the top—what now at Zushi City Hall?).

7. Tomino Kiichirō, *Guriin demokurashii: ima Ikego kara uttaeru* (Green Democracy: an appeal from Ikego) (Tokyo: Hakusuisha, 1991), p. 29.

8. Mayor Tomino, interview with the author, 22 May 1992.

9. Editorials by Tomino continue to appear regularly in the national newspapers. See, for example, "Rondan: Kokuren heiwa senryaku to Nihon no kōken (Opinion: U.N. peace strategies and Japan's contribution)," *Asahi shinbun,* 27 April 1993.

10. For a text of the debate, see "Gekiron: aizō no naka no Shōwa tennō" (Heated debate: admiration and rejection of the Showa emperor), *Bungei shunjū,* vol. 67. no. 4 (special issue, March 1989), pp. 220–235.

11. Murata Toshisuke, section chief, Jōhō Kōkaika (Information Access Section), Zushi City Hall, interview with the author, 19 June 1992.

12. Mayor Tomino, interview with the author, 22 May 1992. See also "Fureru zushi-shi gikai" (About the Zushi City Assembly), in *Konnichi no Kankoku,* vol. 17, no. 6 (June 1992), pp. 65–66.

13. See ibid., p. 65.

14. Furuno Yasuyo, correspondence with the author, 20 November 1992.

15. *New York Times,* 27 January 1992.

16. Some representatives referred to Koreans as "peninsula people" (*hantōjin*).

17. Kojima's exact words were *"Bansei ikkei no tennō no moto de wa Nihon kokumin to byōdō datta."* See *Zushi-shi gikai tayori* (News from the Zushi City Council), no. 26 (26 May 1992).

18. See *Yomiuri shinbun, Asahi shinbun,* 19 March 1992; and *Kanagawa shinbun,* 20 March 1992. The coverage continued for the next three months, until the city assembly eventually reversed its decision in late June.

19. Saitō to Hirai, 25 March 1992. On file in the Peaceful Relations Section of Zushi City Hall.

20. Hidaka to Hirai, 25 March 1992. On file in the Peaceful Relations Section of Zushi City Hall.

21. *Kanagawa shinbun,* 8 June 1992.

22. Ibid.

23. See Tomino, *Guriin demokurashii,* pp. 186–189.

24. See *Yomiuri shinbun, Asahi shinbun,* and *Tokyo shinbun,* 2 June 1992.

25. *Yomiuri shinbun,* 16 June 1992.

26. See *Yomiuri shinbun, Asahi shinbun, Tokyo shinbun, Kanagawa shinbun,* 15 July 1992.

27. Tomino, *Guriin demokurashii,* pp. 16–27. Mayor Tomino also outlined his interpretation of the significance of the Zushi Citizens' Movement in "Citizens' Movements and the Environment: A Mayor's Experiments and Achievements," a speech presented to the Japan Society of New York, 4 November 1991.

28. Before 1984, the city of Zushi had long been a stronghold of the LDP in both local and national elections.

29. Mayor Tomino Kiichirō, "Opening Address to the City Assembly," 5 December 1984 (Japanese text on file in the Office of the Mayor [Shichō kōshitsu], Zushi City Hall).

30. Sawa Mitsuyo, city assembly representative, Zushi City, in an interview with the author, 3 June 1992. As a result of her election victory on 8 November, Sawa is now the mayor of Zushi.

31. Tomino, *Guriin demokurashii,* p. 32.

32. Sawa, interview with the author, 3 June 1992.

33. Sawa received 11,942 votes, while Hirai received 7,810. Figures provided by the Zushi City Office.

34. No female city mayor had been elected in Japan until Kitamura Harue became the mayor of Ashiya City in Hyogo Prefecture in April 1991.

35. See "Fureru Zushi-shi gikai," p. 65.

36. The civil servants have coined a term for the few individuals who seem to devote their time to downright abuse of workers at city hall: *tokubetsu shimin* (special citizen). Requirements for awarding this euphemistic label have not been codified, but the most important qualification seems to be repeated incidents of yelling at city bureaucrats for several minutes with the apparent intention of humiliating them rather than seeking to have a problem solved. Consultations with bureaucrats in other cities such as nearby Kamakura have led some bureaucrats to devise a formula for calculating the expected number of special citizens according to the population of the city. While the bureaucrats admit that the formula remains highly unscientific, they have concluded that on average, for every 5,000 citizens there is one special citizen.

37. Murata, interview with the author (see n. 11).

38. Hanada Masamichi, interview with the author, 12 June 1992.

39. Citizens in Zushi opposed the housing project for a variety of reasons, but one reason that most citizens were hesitant to talk openly about was the fear that the housing project would bring the type of problems to Zushi that nearby Yokosuka has experienced in playing host to a large American naval base. It is no coincidence that the complete name of the main citizens' group leading the protests against the housing project is The Citizens' Association for the Protection of Nature and Children through Opposition to the Ikego American Military Housing Project.

Although the atmosphere in Yokosuka has changed considerably from the wild years of the Occupation and 1950s, the citizens there continue to complain about the prostitution that the base attracts as well as the unruly behavior of sailors on leave from their ships. There was a time when some bars in the neighborhood around the Yokosuka base were off-limits to Japanese nationals. Today, however, as a result of the weak dollar American soldiers have trouble affording the local bars. In June 1993 one bar near the base had a sign posted seeking to offset an apparent decline in American business by attracting Japanese customers. The sign read: "Japanese also especially welcome" (*Nihonjin mo daikangei*).

The Japanese government insists that the housing being built in the Ikego Forest will only be used for families. The trust between some citizens in Zushi and the government has been so poisoned, however, that some citizens envision another "betrayal" in the making.

UPDATE

The essay "Mr. Tomino Goes to City Hall: Grass-Roots Democracy in Zushi City, Japan" was originally published, in slightly shorter form, in the fall of 1993. The years since then in Zushi have resulted in what citizens who participated in the movement against the Ikego Housing Project call the "reverse course." This update will trace what became of the main characters in the movement, the innovative policies of former mayor Tomino, the citizens' movement, and the housing project.[1]

The Change from Tomino to Sawa

When Sawa Mitsuyo was elected mayor in November 1992, she was seen as Tomino's successor, a committed opponent of the Ikego Housing Project. It was clear at the time that her chances of convincing the government to halt the housing project were slim, and there was sympathy for her difficult position among observers of and participants in the citizens' movement. In some quarters, especially among supporters and observers from afar, there was criticism of Tomino's decision to step down as mayor. It seemed to some people that Tomino had withdrawn from the scene at an opportunistic moment, leaving his successor to take responsibility for not stopping the Ikego Housing Project.

Sawa faced the depressing chore of leading the final protest against the housing project even as the companies contracted by the government completed construction. Meanwhile Tomino accepted a position at Shimane University, a national university, as a professor of regional environmental policy. Tomino stresses that when he was first elected in 1984 he publicly stated that he would only serve four years but in the end served two four-year terms. Long-time participants in the movement remember his reluctance to run for a second term in 1988 and do not blame him for leaving office in 1992. Members of the Citizens' Association for the Protection of Nature and Children had long emphasized that their movement was a movement without leaders, only equal members. Tomino did not see himself as indispensable to the movement.

When I asked Tomino if he had any critical comments about the original essay, he questioned my stress on his leadership role and suggested that I could have better emphasized the influence of citizens' power in Zushi.[2] He insisted that he was only able to lead by drawing on the consensus of members of the citizens' movement. Tomino continued to be active in the movement after leaving office. The movement nonetheless seemed to sorely miss his leadership as mayor.

First, Tomino was respected for being very smart, not only by his supporters but by his opponents. Even his adversaries in Zushi marveled how Tomino, within six months of taking office, had mastered such fine details of city administration as why it was necessary for the city to charge such and such amount for the use of sewers. This made a deep impression on city bureaucrats who came to look at Tomino with respect and even a bit of fear. Tomino also displayed considerable talent in the art of performance. Arriving for meetings about ninety seconds late, Tomino would confidently stride through the door and take his seat. There never seemed to be a need for him to ask for quiet. Attention focused on him. He knew how to work the mass media, and the mass media made him into a star. Still a national figure today, Tomino answers questions about his political future in riddles stressing that under the *present* state of Japanese politics he can do more as a citizen than as an elected politician. More than one political party has asked him to run for national office under its banner.

As a professor, Tomino continues to be active on a variety of fronts beyond teaching at Shimane University. His schedule is filled with speaking engagements. He is an advisor to citizens' movements and mayors, and gives seminars to civil servants working in local governments about how to better serve citizens' needs. He is a research member of the International Union of Local Authorities based in Holland, and an active member in several Japanese scholarly associations including the Local Government Association and the Peace Association.

Mayor Sawa, for her part, was faced with succeeding someone who had developed a national stature. The challenge of taking over as mayor from Tomino was probably compounded by her sex. People familiar with the workings of Zushi City Hall agree that some senior bureaucrats in Zushi City Hall mocked Sawa from the moment she took office because she was a woman. Insiders say that she never gained the respect of certain city bureaucrats during the two years that she spent in office. Only Tomino's considerable charisma and authority had worked to push city bureaucrats, the majority of whom as a rule hate any deviation from the routine, to implement new policies. Sawa's consuming focus was the Ikego Housing Project and she came to be criticized even by supporters for neglecting other issues that the movement had come to embrace. Proposals put forth by Tomino but still under study when he left office were shelved. It should be remembered, however, that even if an uncompromising core remained active, the energy of the citizens' movement had flagged considerably before Sawa won election, so she had less citizens' power on which to draw.

The City Charter and Study of Korean Forced Laborers

The city charter was not presented to the city assembly for consideration during Sawa's administration and has now been abandoned. One of the intriguing aspects of Zushi's proposed city charter, giving foreigners the right to vote in local elections, has nonetheless become a national political issue. Zushi was not the first local municipality to raise this issue, but would have been the first to directly challenge the Election Law by providing foreigners with local suffrage. More than 400 municipalities have passed resolutions urging the Diet to amend the Election Law to give foreigners suffrage in local elections. It is unclear if the Diet will take action soon, but if it does this will be another example of a movement by local public corporations working its way upward to press the Diet into action.[3] In February 1995 the Supreme Court of Japan, while ruling that the Constitution did not provide foreigners with the right to vote in national elections, went out of its way to indicate that it saw no constitutional problems in providing foreigners with suffrage in local elections.[4] This decision, which surprised many legal scholars, removed legal questions that perhaps have served to delay the Diet from taking action.

Just as Zushi was at the forefront of the movement to extend democracy at the local level, it was one of the first municipalities to address the question of war responsibility. The Peaceful Relations Section recently completed its study of forced labor in Zushi during the war. In a result that surprised observers, since research began under the assumption that instances of forced labor had taken place, the study concluded that there was no clear evidence that the tunnels in the Ikego Ammunition Dump had been built by Korean forced laborers. While the report pointed out that working conditions in the tunnels had been horrible by present-day standards, it also concluded that the workers—both Koreans and Japanese—had received salaries and seemed to have had the right of mobility.

While the evidence indicated that forced labor had not taken place in Zushi, the report stressed that Asians were unquestionably used as forced laborers during the war in several places on the Japanese mainland, not to mention in territory held by the Japanese military.[5] The report also stressed that historically Koreans and other Asians suffered discrimination on a variety of fronts in Zushi as in the rest of Japan.[6]

When Tomino proposed the study in 1992, he was careful to stress that Zushi's study was no substitute for an investigation by the central government into issues of Japanese war responsibility. For the first six months of 1995, the question of how the government should phrase a resolution commemorating the fiftieth anniversary of the end of the war absorbed much public debate and nearly brought down the three-party coalition government headed by Prime Minister Murayama Tomiichi. While Murayama, head of the Social Democratic Party of Japan (SDPJ), serves as prime minister, the Liberal Democratic Party (LDP) is by far the most powerful of the three parties making up the coalition. The Japan Association of Bereaved Families of War Dead (Nihon izokukai), the Association of Shinto Shrines (Jinja honchō), and other right-leaning groups with considerable grass-roots networks pressured the rank and file of the LDP to keep an apology out of the resolution. The Association of Shinto Shrines spearheaded a petition movement against an apology that produced millions of signatures.[7] Largely as a result of the intransigence of LDP politicians who felt this pressure, the resolution passed by the Lower House of the Diet on 9 June was a watered-down statement that was widely criticized as failing to clearly define Japan's responsibility for its aggression during the war.

What was sometimes lost in the focus of the Diet resolution and the success of right-leaning groups in influencing its final wording, however, was a growing movement at the grass-roots level to forthrightly confront the issue of war responsibility. According to a public opinion poll conducted by the *Asahi shinbun* after the Lower House passed its resolution, only 14 percent of respondents felt that the wording of the resolution was sufficient, while 45 percent felt that it was insufficient (*fujūbun*).[8] Zushi was one early example of a grass-roots attempt to address unpleasant questions of war responsibility.[9] After the Lower House of the Diet passed the coalition government's resolution, several local government bodies, including the Kochi Prefectural Assembly, expressed their dissatisfaction at the Diet resolution by passing far more forthright statements of contrition about Japan's responsibility for the war, particularly the misery that Japan caused its neighbors in Asia.

The Final Stage of the Movement

While issues adopted by the Zushi citizens' movement became salient matters addressed at the national level in recent years, the core issue of the movement, the Ikego Housing Project, never came to be seen as more than a local problem. In 1994 the citizens' movement against the project entered the final stage that was to see the movement splinter and eventually collapse. With construction nearing completion and support for continued opposition to the project ebbing, Mayor Sawa decided to enter into negotiations with the central government to secure the best compromise possible under the circumstances.[10] She made her intention to negotiate a compromise with the central government public in late March 1994.

Nothing could have enraged the most committed members of the movement more than Sawa's decision to negotiate a compromise. Sawa kept secret the fact that she had been arranging to negotiate, and this secrecy reminded citizens of the actions of former mayor Mishima, who had secretly negotiated an agreement with the central government in 1984 to accept the housing project. This 1984 agreement was the catalyst for citizens to join together to drive Mishima from office and replace him with Tomino, who promised to oppose the housing project. When Sawa announced her intent to negotiate, many longtime members of the movement felt that they had been betrayed by one of their own. The faction of the movement most committed to opposing the housing project dates the reverse course in Zushi politics from Sawa's administration.

While the construction of the houses themselves was nearing completion when Sawa entered negotiations, the city of Zushi was still refusing to provide garbage or sewer services for the housing project once completed. Many supporters of the movement wanted the city to continue to express its outrage by refusing to provide such services, thus forcing the Defense Facilities Administration Agency to construct separate garbage and sewage processing facilities. During her 1992 campaign, Sawa had promised to oppose the housing project. At that time, she was seen as one of the most sincere members of the faction that refused to compromise on the question of the Ikego Housing Project.

After she entered into negotiations, however, Sawa was repeatedly asked to explain how she could justify having publicly promised to oppose the housing project only to later enter into negotiations. In June three city assembly members of the Green faction withdrew their support for Sawa.[11] One of the newsletters of the many overlapping citizens' groups that opposed the housing project included a cartoon lampooning Sawa. Sawa is shown matter-of-factly explaining to a disbelieving audience that "public promises and policies are different" (*kōyaku to seisaku wa chigaimasu*).[12] Some members of the movement demanded Sawa's resignation.

While Sawa infuriated many former supporters, public opinion polls of Zushi citizens showed support for a negotiated settlement. A poll conducted in July 1994 by the Prefectural and Local Government Research Center (Ken chihō jichi kenkyū sentaa) found that 73.2 percent of Zushi citizens supported a negotiated settlement if some of the greenery would be preserved.[13] On 17 November 1994, Mayor Sawa and a representative of the central government signed a compromise. The government agreed to leave 2.7 hectares originally slated for development undeveloped and gave strong assurances that the 200 hectares of the Ikego Forest never included in the housing project would be protected in the future. The city of Zushi agreed to provide garbage collection and sewer service as well as to officially end its opposition to the project. Many citizens of Zushi would have appreciated an apology from the central government, but none was forthcoming.[14] Former mayor Tomino denounced the agreement as being not a compromise but instead submission on the part of Zushi.[15]

The day after Sawa signed the compromise, she presented her resignation to the chairman of the city assembly and then announced her candidacy for mayor, hoping to make the election a referendum on the settlement. In the mayoral election that took place on 25 December, however, Sawa lost to LDP candidate Hirai Yoshio, one-time chairman of the city assembly and second-place finisher in the 1992 mayoral election. Hirai had long favored reaching a settlement with the central government regarding the Ikego Housing Project. Turnout in the election was low. Many members of the citizens' movement saw little difference between Hirai and Sawa and simply stayed home on election day. After the election, Sawa took up volunteer work, devoting herself to helping the elderly.

Conclusion

Now that the city no longer opposes the Ikego Housing Project, plans calling for the first American families to move into their houses in the fall of 1995 should proceed according to schedule. In March 1995, the main citizens' group, the Citizens' Association for the Protection of Nature and Children, disbanded. The remaining groups are hardly active. Like most citizens' movements, the Zushi citizens' movement rose and fell on one issue.

Mayor Hirai's campaign promise was to return Zushi to being a normal city. He is not inclined to experiment with new policies. Some legacies of the Tomino administration and the citizens' movement remain, however. Environmental consciousness remains high in Zushi, not only among the citizens but also among city bureaucrats and politicians. Development in Zushi has lessened, although some people feel that this decrease resulted more from the collapse of the so-called bubble economy than from policies of the city.

Administrative structures reformed when Tomino was mayor remain in place. The Environmental Bureau continues to closely study the environmental impact of city policies. The Information Access Section has become a model for public corporations throughout Japan. Numerous cities have sent delegations to study its operations. The Peaceful Relations Section, once charged with promoting the city's opposition to the Ikego Housing Project, remains in place but its duties have changed. Now it will be responsible for maintaining good relations with the American community that soon will take up residence in the Ikego Housing Project.

Notes to Update

1. Tomino Nanako, activist with her more famous husband in the movement against the Ikego Housing Project, lent me her collection of articles, newsletters, and pamphlets about the Zushi Citizens', Movement, which I used extensively in writing this update. I am grateful to her. Tomino Nanako has long been an active member of the Housewife Association (Shufuren) best known for its activities in promoting consumer protection.

2. Individuals interested in further details about the citizens' movement, especially its early history, should refer to: Jain's essay cited in the original essay; Chikaraishi Sadakazu, "The Zushi Alternative for U.S. Military Housing," *Japan Quarterly*, vol. 33, no. 3 (July–September 1986), pp. 257–263; Midori to Kodomo o Mamoru Shimin no Kai, ed., *Shimin kyōsōkyoku: Zushi shichōsen e no kiseki* (Mimizuku puresu, 1985) (This is the early history of the citizens' movement as written by members of the main citizens' group); and Zushi-shi, ed., *Ikego no mori: Ikego danyakugo henkan undō no kiroku* (Gyōsei, 1993).

3. In the 1960s, municipalities played an important role in pressuring the central government to make pollution control a priority. This pressure was felt by the predominant Liberal Democratic Party, which, reversing its stance, adopted pollution control as a policy beginning with the Pollution Diet of 1970. In the late 1970s, 46 of the 47 regional assemblies and hundreds of city, town, and village assemblies passed resolutions urging the Diet to pass the Era Name Law (*Genhōhō*). The Diet passed the law in 1979. The LDP was clearly inclined to pass the Era Name Law, but the overwhelming display of support by local assemblies helped lessen the influence of an intense minority opposed to the law and pushed the LDP to make passage of the law a priority. More recently municipalities played a role in pressuring the Diet to amend the Alien Registration Law. In 1992 the Diet changed the law to exempt permanent foreign residents of Japan, the majority of whom are Korean, from the fingerprinting requirement. Tomino was one of many mayors who had protested against this practice by, for example, not reporting the names of individuals who refused to be fingerprinted.

4. The date of the decision was 28 February 1995. For further information see Ichikawa Masato, "Teijū gaikokujin no chihō sanseiken," *Hōgaku semina,* no. 485 (1995.5), pp. 82–86. I would like to thank Professor Tsunemoto Teruki of Hokkaido University for directing me to this reference.

5. Perhaps the most famous instance of forced labor on the mainland was that of the Hanaoka Mine in Odate City in Akita Prefecture. About 1,000 Chinese forced laborers staged an uprising against the harsh labor conditions on 30 June 1945. The uprising was brutally suppressed and 113 laborers were tortured to death in retaliation for the killing of four employees of the Kajima Corporation, which operated the mine.

6. Tomino Kiichirō, interview with the author, 12 July 1995.

7. Sugitani Masao, section chief, outside affairs, Association of Shinto Shrines (Jinja Honchō), interview with the author, 22 March 1995. While many scholars and journalists insist that the Jinja honchō exaggerates its numbers, they also agree that it did collect mass numbers of signatures against an apology.

8. *Asahi shinbun*, 28 June 1995.

9. An earlier example, which perhaps marks the beginning of the grass-roots movement to confront questions of war responsibility, was the considerable display of grass-roots support for Mayor Motoshima of Nagasaki beginning in December 1988 in defiance of right-wing threats seeking to punish the mayor for his statement that the Shōwa emperor bore some war responsibility for the war. See *Nagasaki shichō e no 7300–tsū no tegami: tennō no sensō sekinin o megutte* (Komichi shobō, 1989).

10. In the fall of 1993, Sawa did travel to Washington to lobby against the Ikego Housing Project. Her efforts were met mostly with disinterest by American officials.

11. *Kanagawa shinbun,* 19 June 1995.

12. *Zushi netio nyūsu,* no. 8, 24 November 1994.

13. *Mainichi shinbun,* 22 July 1994. The poll nonetheless indicated that the support for a settlement had developed because of a growing feeling that this was the best result that the city could expect. The poll showed that many citizens remained angry at the central government's insistence at completing the housing project.

14. *Asahi shingun,* 18 November 1994.

15. *Kanagawa shinbun,* 18 November 1994.

15

Five Poems (1974–1991) by the Hiroshima Poet Kurihara Sadako

Translated and introduced by Richard H. Minear

In 1989, the *Bulletin of Concerned Asian Scholars* published my translations of four wartime poems by Kurihara Sadako (born 1913). The poems in this issue trace the evolution of Kurihara's thinking down to the present. Her conviction that the fifteen-year war was morally wrong has ensured that despite being a victim of Hiroshima, she has not locked herself into the role of atomic victim. She wrote "When We Say 'Hiroshima' " in 1974.

When We Say "Hiroshima"

When we say "Hiroshima,"
do people answer, gently,
"Ah, Hiroshima"?
Say "Hiroshima," and hear "Pearl Harbor."
Say "Hiroshima," and hear "Rape of Nanking."
Say "Hiroshima," and hear of women and children in Manila
thrown into trenches, doused with gasoline,
and burned alive.
Say "Hiroshima,"
and hear echoes of blood and fire.

Say "Hiroshima,"
and we don't hear, gently,
"Ah, Hiroshima."
In chorus, Asia's dead and her voiceless masses
spit out the anger
of all those we made victims.
That we may say "Hiroshima,"

and hear in reply, gently,
"Ah, Hiroshima,"
we must lay down in fact
the arms we were supposed to lay down.
We must get rid of all foreign bases.

Until that day Hiroshima
will be a city of cruelty and bitter bad faith.
And we will be pariahs
afire with remnant radioactivity.

That we may say "Hiroshima"
and hear in reply, gently,
"Ah, Hiroshima,"
we need first
to cleanse
our own filthy hands.

* * *

Like Ota Yoko, Toge Sankichi, and Maruki Iri and Maruki Toshi, Kurihara has paid particular attention to the plight of Korean victims of the bomb. She published "Out of the Very Stone" in 1979. The stone is a large monument to the Korean victims; it is located across the river just to the west—and outside the confines—of Peace Park. *Mul! Mul tal la!* (Kurihara gives it phonetically) is Korean for "Water! Water, please!"

Out of the Very Stone

Out of the very stone they sound,
the voices of the tens of thousands who burned to death;
charged with age-old bitter feelings,
they fill the night air:
Mul! Mul tal la! Mul tal la!
Water, please! Water, please!

From the riverbank monument
for which there was no room in Peace Park,
all night long, they come, the voices
    of the tens of thousands dead:
Mul! Mul tal la! Mul tal la!

Rounded up
as they tilled the soil in the fields of home,
rounded up

as they walked the streets of the towns and villages of home,
not allowed to say even a word of farewell
to wives and children, parents, brothers, sisters,
they were packed like livestock into transports
and shipped off, across the strait.

Forced to pray to foreign gods,
to swear allegiance to a foreign ruler,
in the end burned in that flash,
they were turned into black corpses
for swarms of crows to peck at.

Aigu! Mul! Mul tal la!
The homeland was torn in two,
and one torn half forced
to house thousands of atomic weapons.
Why should the atom be forced
on us and our half?
Leave, you foreign soldiers!
Take your atomic bombs, and leave!
The homeland is one.
O Wind, take the message—
that this torn half calls out to its own kind
out of the very stone.

* * *

    "Hiroshima and the Emperor's New Clothes" needs a word of explanation.
"The Emperor's New Clothes" is a story by Hans Christian Andersen about
an emperor who had been convinced by a pair of itinerant tailors that the
garment they had made him was so fine that people who were unfit for their
work or hopelessly stupid couldn't see it. Neither the emperor nor those
around him wanted to admit they couldn't see the garment, and so he ended
up parading in the streets nude. His loyal subjects watching the parade also
didn't want to say that they couldn't see any clothes on him, but finally a child
shouted out the truth—"But the emperor has nothing on at all!" When this
European tale is translated into Japanese, the term for emperor is *osama*, generic
prince, not reigning emperor. Hence the reference here is not to Hirohito but to
Suzuki Zenko, the prime minister in 1981 when Kurihara wrote the poem.

Hiroshima and the Emperor's New Clothes

Chubby,
glossy face shiny with sweat,

the emperor of the new clothes,
his (nuclear) bellybutton plain to see,
says he's coming to Hiroshima.
He says he'll pay his respects at the atomic cenotaph.
Can he really stand
bellybutton-bare before the monument
that says "the mistake shall not be repeated"?
The emperor of the new clothes,
who says black is white
and white is black
and makes lies and fraud the policy of the state,
says he's coming,
bare bellybutton and all.
In Hiroshima
not only the children
but also the old people, the men, the women
laugh, get angry
at the chubby emperor's
bellybutton antics.

In April he pays his respects at the shrine to war;
in August he pays his respects at the atomic cenotaph.
Repeating flat contradictions every day—
in the country across the sea
he says what they want him to say;
here at home, for domestic consumption,
he says black is white
and white is black.
But Hiroshima will not be fooled.
O, you 200,000 dead!
Come forth, all together,
from the grave, from underground.
Faces puffed up with burns,
black and festering,
lips torn,
say faintly, "We stand here in reproach."
Shuffle slowly forward,
both arms, shoulder high,
trailing peeled-off skin.
Tell them—
the emperor of the new clothes
and his entire party—
what day August 6 is.

* * *

"The Day the Showa Era Ends" is dated 8 December 1988. The emperor died (and the Showa era ended) one month later, in early January. This poem is Kurihara's contribution to an "anti-emperor anthology" (the words are from the jacket) of eighty-eight poems by eighty-eight poets to herald the passing of the Showa era; Kurihara herself was one of the organizers of the project.

The Day the Showa Era Ends

On the moat a swan drifts, oblivious;
deep within the Palace, the emperor lies ill,
now vomiting blood, now passing blood;
semiconscious,
does he think of them?

—the victims of the atomic bomb
lying on straw in those sheds and stables
of the farms to which they fled
that summer's day forty-three years ago,
afflicted by fevers, trembling from chills,
red spots breaking out all over,
hair falling out, receiving no medical treatment
    of any kind,
not knowing even the name of their disease,
who died with blood pouring from ears, mouths, noses;
—the victims of the atomic bomb who passed
    so much blood their bowels seemed to have melted,
who hadn't even rags to use for diapers,
who died drowning in blood.

Revived by transfusion after transfusion,
semiconscious,
does he mount his white horse
and roam distant battlefields?
The hell of starvation in the jungles on southern islands
and in the rocky mountains of the continent,
that made people eat snakes, frogs, even human flesh;
the soldiers wracked by malarial fevers
and shivering from chills
beneath the sizzling southern sun,
arms and legs blown away by naval artillery,
unable to move even an inch,
who breathed their last on foreign soil—
semiconscious,
does he pay them a call?

A single life counts the world;
one life counts as much
as any other.
Yet counting less than a feather,
husbands and sons went to their deaths singing,
"At sea be my corpse water-soaked;
   on land let grass grow over it.
Let me die beside my lord."
As he wanders the borderland between life and death,
does their one-time lord make his painful way
to Greater East Asian battlefields
to hand out Imperial gift cigarettes
and award Orders of the Golden Kite?

Even after the war ended
their one-time commander-in-chief
never expressed regret for his sin—the war.
The day the Showa era ends,
will the Greater East Asian war finally come to an end?
Or does Japan stand already
on the threshold of new war?
In August forty-three years ago
the cicadas cried bitterly throughout Japan;
their voices resound now,
deafeningly loud.

* * *

Kurihara wrote "Rather than Weapons, Roses" on 19 January 1991; it appeared in the *Asahi Shimbun* on 24 January. The *Hinomaru* is the Japanese flag.

Rather than Weapons, Roses

War: blood flows in rivers,
flows and is sucked into the sand—
a futile affair.

If war starts in the desert,
the desert will be red with blood,
corpses will lie exposed to the hot sun,
and the stench of rotten flesh
will flow out into the world.

Families in America
will pray for the safety of loved ones;

but fathers, children, husbands, lovers
will come back in body bags—
this when families are still crying Vietnam tears.

When the young people of America
come home in body bags,
America will ask that Japan, too, shed young blood,
show the *Hinomaru* in the Gulf,
give money, supplies, lives.
Setting Grenada and Panama to one side,
America confronts the Arabs:
the Palestinian problem is past, unreal,
but Kuwait is real.

In the Arabian sky, high-tech weapons
with their black fuselages intersecting,
black smoke billowing up;
sirens screaming—
forty-five years ago we too
lived in and out of air raid shelters, night and day.
Babies and the sick we took with us; fear immobilized us.
And at the end of it all,
Hiroshima was burned alive in the atomic flash.
We must not let the people of the desert
be wiped out by atomic and biochemical weapons.

Armed force won't bring about peace.
Stop the blasphemous broad-daylight carnage!
Japan, first country in the world
to renounce war for reasons of conscience:
the bellicose may criticize us
as unrealistic, one-country pacifists;
but let's stop them
from stuffing young people into body bags;
let's not let the *Hinomaru* wave again.

Rather than weapons, roses;
rather than sanctions, talks;
no side has hands
unstained by blood.

Conclusion

Sanrizuka farmers overwhelmed by the destruction of their land, livelihood, and homes by the forcible building of the New Tokyo International Airport (Narita) in 1978. As Joe Moore concludes in "Democracy and Capitalism in Postwar Japan," material prosperity for Japan has come at a heavy cost—the gradual dismantling of the postwar democratic revolution in the name of efficiency in pursuit of all-out growth. When, as at Narita, local people have placed a higher value on community, democracy, and a livable environment and attempted to stymie elite plans for "development," the state and private capital have not hesitated to use force to overcome resistance. At Narita this involved the mobilization of 14,000 riot troops! Since then the airport has been built and development has proceeded—along with public disillusionment with a style of elite rule that has become increasingly authoritarian and corrupt. This illustration is by Ishige Hiromichi of Nakago hamlet and appeared on the front cover of the March 1985 issue of *Mushiro-Bata: The Strawmat Banner,* a publication written by farmers and published periodically by the League of Shibayama and the Sanrizuka Farmers against the Sanrizuka Airport.

16

Democracy and Capitalism in Postwar Japan

Joe Moore

To speak of the "other Japan" as engaged in a struggle for democracy begs questions. Isn't democracy merely a "Western" concept? By using it, am I not imposing on Japan an alien cultural concept that is not universal but peculiar to the West in one historical epoch? Is it not true that the United States and other Western capitalist countries have been remaking themselves in Japan's image rather than the other way around? Isn't democracy relative to the level of economic prosperity anyway, meaningless to those without a high enough standard of living to make it a living reality? And could it not be just another word for liberal self-interestedness that has corroded modern society in the West? While these are too grand and sweeping questions to be dealt with here, any attempt at an answer requires that the questions be addressed both structurally and historically. It is my contention that democracy in the industrialized world is in fact in direct conflict with the need of capitalism to pursue efficiency in production. Contrary to the optimism of today's boosters of unfettered capitalist growth, democracy in the real sense of truly effective popular participation in political and economic decisions has not followed development.[1] Development has driven out democracy, both political and economic, as hindrances to national competitiveness.[2] Efficiency has been equated with top-down hierarchical control that speaks of democracy as mere mobilization of others for active participation in pursuit of goals decided upon and imposed from above.

Japan has led the way in the tailoring of democracy to suit the needs of corporate capitalism. Indeed, as long ago as the early 1970s Western scholars were writing in glowing terms of the Japanese corporation as the model for capitalism precisely because of its efficiency in mobilizing the work force behind the firm, seemingly unaware of or unworried about the implications for Japan's democratic institutions. This chapter takes a different view, namely that it is the very pursuit of efficiency within the corporation that has progressively corroded and eroded both political and economic democracy in society at large.

What follows is an attempt to provide a structure and brief history for this argument by laying out my view of the phases through which corporate capitalism and social movements have gone since World War II as they have engaged in the struggle over Japan's postwar democracy. These are hotly contested issues, and many scholars who would agree on the general point that capitalist development reinforces authoritarianism might disagree with the way that I have posed the issues below.[3]

One part of my concern will be to lay out the interlocking strategies—not only economic and political, but also social and cultural—that the elite of business, bureaucracy, and the conservative party has used in its restless search for efficiency, which has meant in practice achieving the highest possible rates of economic growth and undisputed political hegemony within Japan's democratic system. A primary battleground is the workplace, where managers seek to extend ever greater control over the minds and bodies of employees. Another is elections and government, where conservative politicians and bureaucrats have attempted to limit the meaning of democracy to the quest for the most effective strategies for stimulating national economic growth. Another is the marketplace, where business has campaigned to define the reproductive and social needs of family and community as mere satisfaction of individual consumer tastes. Yet another is the fractured family, where the enterprise has done its best to draw the salaryman/husband into the embrace of the male-dominated "enterprise family," which provides him with most of his needs—for food, sociability, and sex—and to subcontract the wife as unpaid provider of outside services essential for maintaining the salaryman's world.

Another part of my concern will be to clarify the role that Japan's social resistance movements have had in the fight to realize the postwar promise of political and economic democracy, most specifically movements aiming at attaining social equality and real popular participation in making the economic and political decisions that shape daily lives. That fight has encompassed tens of millions, most of whom have not participated directly in a political party or a social movement, but have been intimately touched by the issues raised. It includes women touched by the women's movement, because they know that they face, except for a decade or so of child-rearing, working for most of their life at menial jobs for perhaps half a man's pay while at the same time keeping the household together for the absent salaryman husband. And students repelled by pressure-cooker schooling designed to prepare them for the corporate salaryman ideal of total dedication to the enterprise. And foreign and Japanese workers who never become lifetime employees but do the dirty work of corporate Japan in the entertainment districts and on work sites. And countless others whose daily trials and frustrations periodically surface in resistance against "business" as usual. The broad scale and persistence of resistance consitutes a damning indictment of the failure of all-out capitalist development to make for a decent life for the ordinary people, for they show that even the

Japanese economic "miracle" cannot deliver the most essential goods of all—justice, equity, and dignity for all.

By the 1970s, the U.S. social science literature was dwelling on the failures of capitalist development in the so-called Third World, echoing the thinking of the conservative mainstream dating back to the turn of the century. Democratic "excesses" were singled out as to blame for faltering economic growth and political breakdown, not capitalism itself. In calling for a "politics of order,"[4] conservative academics argued that efficiency and democracy are fundamentally incompatible because democracy provides an opening for movements from below to achieve a redistribution of wealth and power to the injury of the capitalist class and therefore to economic growth. The proposition that authoritarianism is efficient was hardly new, nor the corollary that capitalism was the embodiment of efficiency. That had, in fact, been the perspective of Japan's capitalist elite since its coalescence in the World War I era. After a brief eclipse in the wake of World War II, when Japan underwent a democratic revolution, that same perspective reemerged in the late 1940s when U.S. and Japanese businessmen and politicians made common cause in attacking the postwar reforms and social movements for democratic "excesses" that purportedly undermined capitalist efficiency and rapid capitalist economic recovery. The same perspective still reigns in Japan, albeit suitably dressed up in the clothing of democracy and cooperation.

The counterposing of elites seeking authoritarian efficiency to bottom-up movements pursuing democracy, even when done from a self-interested capitalist and conservative perspective as above, has the unintended merit of highlighting the actual power that social resistance has had in constraining the elite's freedom of action in extending control over the enterprise and society at large. It serves as well to drive home the point that in Japan, too, the conflict between elite and social movements is a tale neither of passive victimization nor of inevitable defeat or victory. Rather, it is the tale of the shaping of postwar Japan as a process of conflict and compromise in a setting of high capitalism. The way stations in that tale are presented schematically in the outline below and subsequently developed in detail.

I. New Day (Sept. 1945–May 1946): Socialism or Capitalism—production control versus capitalist sabotage

II. Old Conflict (1946–1960): Confrontation over Capitalist Reconstruction—social democracy versus Taylorist efficiency

     1946–1948: The Search for Political and Economic Democracy—reforming Japanese capitalism

     1949–1960 Capitalist Efficiency Ascendant: reversing the democratic reforms

III. Historic Compromise (1960–1979): "Peace and Democracy" + Fordism = "Miraculous Growth"

   1960–1968 Paying the bills for high-speed economic growth

   1969–1975 Questioning the Fordist Compromise: resistance from outside and below

   1975–1979 Changing International Division of Labor: economic troubles and rationalization

IV. Conflict Renewed (1980–present): Restructuring for Capitalist Efficiency —grass-roots democracy versus global Taylorism

   1980–1989 Freeing the Corporation: internationalization and "administrative reform"

   1990–present Tarnished Miracles, Rising Hopes: after the bubble bursts

Evolution of Elite Strategies

Until the end of World War II, Japan's elites had few restraints from below on their zeal to bring about efficient development of the country's new capitalist order. They made no neat separation between economic efficiency in producing such things as textiles and steel and political efficiency in carrying out the authoritarian coordination of society from above, nor could they. They believed both to be necessary to make Japan's corporate giants (the zaibatsu) as profitable and productive as their international competition. There were two means available to resource-poor Japan for that task: adoption of modern technology and squeezing the highest possible productivity from labor, both of which required active state involvement.

In the first half of the twentieth century, the strategy of building a technologically efficient zaibatsu sector on the heights and using efficient cheap labor to underwrite the costs produced impressive results in industrial growth. As well, the policy of betting on the strong forced the great majority of the population to bear the costs—subsistence wages, city sweatshops, forced labor in unsafe mines, use of girls in grim textile mills, destruction of health and the environment through pollution, and subordination of agriculture and small business to zaibatsu interests. The endemic social misery of those decades fed resistance and a democratic movement that, by demanding a sharing of wealth and power, reinforced the elite's faith in the authoritarian road to capitalism. Movements for democratic reform like the labor unions, tenants' unions, and women's movement waxed and waned, sometimes gaining concessions. They were seldom able to consolidate their gains against two highly effective elite tactics—appeals to the values of familistic harmony and cooperation and straightforward use of suppression. The former resonated with the "traditional culture"[5] compounded to support the emperor system during the Meiji period, while the latter resonated with the authoritarian Taylorist scientific management that had gained currency throughout the industrialized world from around World War I.

It would be a stretch to call Japan's prewar management or "traditional culture" simply Taylorist—though Taylor's scientific principles of management were certainly discussed among businessmen.[6] The business elite loudly condemned the cold and conflict-filled class relations of the West that Taylorism symbolized, much preferring to praise themselves (and Japan) for maintaining warm and harmonious familial relations in the enterprise. Unique they were not, since a controlling and oppressive familism of a similar kind has had a similarly long existence in the West, too, for example at Pullman, National Cash Register, Ford, Kohler, and IBM. Nor were they warm and benevolent, for the authoritarian premises of Taylorism were not hard to find, for example, in the textile industry where enterprise familism for textile girls meant little more than closely supervised, jail-like dormitories to prevent runaways.[7] It would be quite accurate, therefore, to characterize both Taylorism and the "traditional culture" beloved of businessmen as authoritarian—the former openly so, the latter under the patina of patriarchal benevolence.

Taylorism as used here should be understood not solely in its narrow technical sense of a strategy for controlling labor minutely in order to extract from it the highest possible productivity—which it did through establishing a sharp divide between planning and execution, through managerial appropriation of worker knowledge, and a parallel "deskilling" of workers through a minute subdivision of labor designed to lower labor costs. Taylorism was far from being a mere technique of scientific management, as Taylor billed it. It was emblematic of the capitalism of its era in its idealization of technology and its insistence that scientific necessity demanded an authoritarian hierarchy in the firm for efficient economic organization,[8] complementing the idea that possession of private property conferred upon the owner unlimited power to dispose of the labor used in production. The political and bureaucratic allies of business readily applied the same rule to other areas of society, especially politics, where efficiency was similarly equated with authoritarian coordination from above. In sum, national Taylorism—to give it a name—should be seen as simultaneously a technique of labor control and a vision of society.

The authoritarian, hierarchical, and technocratic assumptions of Taylorism resonated with similarly authoritarian, hierarchical, and patriarchal assumptions of practical Japanese businessmen squaring off against labor-movement militance. They struck the same chord with the political and bureaucratic allies of business who were intent on imposing authority and order upon a potentially unruly civil society. The practice of national Taylorism, in short, meshed intricately with the familistic ideology and patriarchal practices of pre-surrender Japan, for the elite collectively feared and detested the democratic egalitarianism seeping into civil society from the pools of discontent accumulating in capitalist enterprise. The choice the elite posed for itself was between capitalist efficiency and order (i.e., national Taylorism) tempered by "traditional" values of familism, or the political strife of democracy and social and economic disorder.

Fordism, too, has the same two dimensions, referring originally to a technique of labor control suited to assembly-line production. As a method of controlling labor, Fordism took a step away from Taylorist coercion of low-paid, low-skilled labor as the primary means to increase production and cut costs. In perfecting the use of the assembly line to cope with problems of production (which was perfectly compatible with Taylorism in that it made compulsion look like a technical necessity), Henry Ford also brought about a tremendous leap in productivity and created a potentially serious problem. Now that a small number of assembly line workers could turn out an unending stream of cars, the problem shifted from production to consumption of the output. Fordism, however, wedded together two ideas that were incompatible with the original intent of Taylorism to create a possible solution: pay the male worker better, so that he and his family would be able to buy things as consumers; and rely upon better pay to motivate him to work more productively and with less compulsion. Fordism put an emphasis upon consent—which strongly appealed to Japan's elite—and upon creating a domestic consumer market through higher pay[9]—which did not.

Well before Fordism gained recognition as a larger system for capitalist accumulation, the Japanese business elite had already acted on an urge toward control of labor that went beyond the mechanistic scientific management of Taylorism. Rather than just relying on appropriating the skills and knowledge of workers for exclusive possession and use by management (which did take place to a substantial degree), the business exponents of enterprise familism came early to the realization that going a step further and appropriating the mind and total personality of workers was the best way to avoid the resistance and confrontation as seen in the West.[10] Consent was the goal, not mere control, because consent encompassed the will to work diligently and cooperatively for the goals of the enterprise out of identification of one's self and one's future with the fate of the enterprise family in the same manner that the wife supposedly puts her whole being into supporting the male-head-of-household family that represents her own future. The idea of obtaining willing consent through warmly paternalistic and cooperative familism was more honored in the breach than in practice, but it has run as a bright thread through the ideology of management for nearly a century.

Enterprise familism in theory but Taylorism in practice was the gist of the elite's approach in pre-1945 Japan, buttressed by nationalistic and racial appeals rooted in a Confucian natural hierarchy of merit and a Shinto mythology of national uniqueness. The ideology of the harmonious enterprise family was pervasive and powerful because it conformed to and supported patriarchal privilege in the conjugal family, bolstered the authoritarian elitism that permeated the Japanese leadership, and spoke to cultural values of harmony and consensus.

The people of Japan have been disparaged as collectively lacking the background to comprehend democracy truly and, more recently, as possessing a victim's mentality. This can only be seen as ludicrous, given the vitality of Japanese social movements in the twentieth century. To give but three examples, the women's, students', and labor movements have traditions going back at least to the World War I era and have since World War II posed fundamental challenges to elite dominance. Such movements may have been flawed and fallen short of the broad-ranging democratic transformation that seemed to be imminent in the first year or two following Japan's surrender, but that was not because of a failure of understanding, or a lack of conviction or tenacity. On the contrary, it was primarily due to resistance from movements from below during the 1940s, 1950s, and after, flawed as they were but each firmly rooted in the other Japan, that the key democratic gains were consolidated despite elite efforts to resurrect the prewar order.

The essential point is that while the surviving members of the old elite for the first fifteen years after the surrender (the "old guard," as it was called) attacked the democratization and tried to resurrect the authoritarian old order, they were unable to do so without the crutch of state power to enforce their paternalistic and patriarchal appeals to the "traditional culture." Worse yet from the elite's point of view, Japan's traditional culture was precisely what had been called into question by the disastrous war and the democratic opening after September 1945. Shorn of its fleece of traditional culture, the elite vision of the world stood revealed as nakedly Taylorist in practice.

To the old guard's horror, after Japan's defeat, workers and tenant farmers and many others defied their betters to organize politically against the authoritarian practices of the past under the banner of democracy, in rejection of the familiar old appeals to hierarchy, order, harmony, unity, and family. In fact, the labor movement fought for and got extensive control of such fundamental areas of enterprise policy as hiring and firing, decisions on what to produce and how to produce it, and discipline.

For the business elite, first things had to come first. Foremost in their minds in the late 1940s was how to recover the Taylorist ground lost to the leftist unions. In circumstances where labor had the upper hand, attempts to realize familistic harmony and cooperation could only lead to a further erosion of management's powers. Rolling back the union gains meant confrontation, even the use of force backed by state power, as was the case in reversing other of the democratic reforms as well. It was well understood by all that the authoritarian order in the enterprise and the authoritarian ordering of society went together. Thus, business rallied behind a determined campaign to restore the right to manage, the goal of which was to break the militant unions and regain absolute managerial authority at the point of production.

Although familism had been useful in the past and needed rehabilitation if it was to be so again in the future, that was not the immediate concern of business. Familism could come later (as indeed it did during the late 1950s along with higher wages and Fordism). Once business had the upper hand, it could selectively dole out *responsibility* for production, as opposed to *control* over production, through various top-down management schemes promoting "democratic" and familistic participation in meeting production goals set by management alone. The real question from the start was always participation for what—for achieving efficiencies for management's benefit or for improving the workers' lot through democratizing the workplace and recognizing workers' rights.

After the war, the problem for national Taylorism as a system was the same as it had been before—how to restrict democracy in the interests of promoting capitalist efficiency. This was a project that quickly went beyond the bounds of the enterprise into society at large where it led directly to political confrontation over restoration of the lineaments of the authoritarian order of the past. That confrontation began in the first bitter winter after Japan's defeat.

I. New Day (Sept. 1945–May 1946): Socialism or Capitalism— Production Control versus Capitalist Sabotage

Japan narrowly avoided mass starvation and total breakdown in the first winter after surrender. Seeking to escape the consequences of their actions, in the few weeks between surrender and the arrival of occupation forces, the Japanese civil bureaucracy and zaibatsu engaged in a joint plundering of the treasury and looting of government stockpiles. They destroyed records, shut down enterprises, cornered scarce goods, and profiteered and speculated on the black market. The result was devastating. In the winter of 1945–1946 industrial production plummeted to a low of 10 percent of what it had been in the mid-thirties, inflation destroyed the value of what little money people had, while unemployment reached an incredible thirteen million. The major cities were bombed out and villages were bursting with urban refugees that they could barely accomodate and feed.

The popular reaction to the economic collapse and the moral bankruptcy of the old guard began in late fall 1945 with worker seizure of mines and other enterprises and the arraigning of company executives before workers' courts reminiscent of the Russian October Revolution of 1917. Concurrently, the Supreme Command for the Allied Powers (SCAP), the Allied machinery for Japan's occupation) was dismantling the props of the authoritarian police state that dated back as far as Meiji.

The breaking down of barriers to democratic rights and economic justice produced a phenomenal burst of popular initiatives that found expression in organization of labor unions, tenant unions, and other movements whose object was a fundamental reshaping of Japan's economic and social institutions. Those movements momentarily threatened to run beyond the limits of liberal parliamentary politics and turn into a socialist revolution. One facet of that broad social movement is examined in the article by Joe Moore on production control and the struggle for political power in spring 1946.[11] SCAP policies at first reinforced the drive for a radical democratic reconstruction by policies aimed at bringing about Constitutional reform, breaking up the zaibatsu firms, clearing the way for land reform, and encouraging labor unions.

By spring 1946 takeovers of factories that the zaibatsu sit-down strike had idled, resistance to forced food requisitions in the countryside, citizen takeovers of food rationing depots, and a leftist political movement had come together in a mass movement in the streets that was bringing Japan close to political paralysis. When creation of a left-of-center people's government and a socialized economic system appeared really to be in the offing, SCAP stepped in with a threat to use U.S. troops to rescue the badly disorganized and demoralized old guard. The moment of danger passed.

Not even the most optimistic revolutionary was ready to risk a popular uprising that would bring confrontation with the U.S. Army. When Yoshida Shigeru, with open U.S. backing, formed a right-wing conservative government and turned to the attack, the movement in the streets lost its momentum. SCAP's intervention might have ended the crisis of power by foreclosing the possibility of revolutionary socialist government, but popular sentiment for root-and-branch democratization of Japanese society gathered force day by day.

Henceforth, the contest between the popular movement and the old guard was no longer to be whether there was to be a capitalist or socialist reconstruction, but what kind of a capitalist reconstruction—democratic or authoritarian. The contest settled into the more predictable form of electoral battles for control of the government and economic battles between labor and capital over control in the enterprise. Other popular movements lined up behind a leftist political movement—primarily the Socialist and Communist parties—pursuing power through the ballot box and drawing its main support from a labor movement trying to establish industrial unionism.

II. Old Conflict (1946–1960): Confrontation over Capitalist Reconstruction—Social Democracy versus Taylorist Efficiency

Democracy First—Reforming Japanese Capitalism

The popular movement for social democracy was grounded especially in the labor and tenant unions, and gained political expression in the parliamentary politics of the Japan Socialist Party (JSP) and the Japan Communist Party (JCP). In the fall of 1946 a labor-union offensive to secure recognition for industrial unionism and gain pay increases gave rise to a political campaign to topple the stridently anti-labor and anti-communist Yoshida cabinet and bring about the formation of a left-of-center coalition government in its place. SCAP intervened again at the last moment to prohibit the general strike scheduled for 1 February 1947 that seemed likely to bring Yoshida down. But when the elections in April gave the Socialist Party the most seats of any party in the Diet, the Yoshida conservatives on the far right were forced to step aside anyway for a coalition government headed by a socialist premier, Katayama Tetsu.

The conjuncture of many factors in 1947–1948 within Japan and abroad undermined the JSP during its moment in government, the most important being an inflation brought on by red-ink financing of economic recovery and the launching of the cold war. The economic problem was almost intractable and due above all to a continuing major cutback in production by the zaibatsu that was impossible to overcome short of nationalization of critical industries. In the end, the socialist government that had been the focus of so many hopes became the target of popular anger for its inability to overcome inflation and shortages, though in retrospect it is clear that the recovery plan was working. At the same time, the deteriorating situation of the Nationalist regime in China and the intensifying cold war in Europe stimulated a U.S. reassessment of its Asian policy. In the new grand design that was fleshed out in 1948, Japan was to assume China's role as the anti-communist bastion in Asia and to act as the lever for regional recovery by becoming the workshop of Asia.

Occupation priorities accordingly shifted toward economic reconstruction and attainment of political stability, meaning stable conservative rule. If the democratic reforms of the first two years got in the way, SCAP was ready to roll them back, the more so because influential circles in the United States were at this time rasing a hue and cry about breaking up the zaibatsu and giving encouragement to labor. Before the 1940s were out, Japanese figures purged for their complicity in military aggression and political suppression at home were being rehabilitated along with the zaibatsu, while suppression of labor and the left began in earnest.

Capitalist Efficiency First—Reversing the Democratic Reforms

The reverse course, as this is called, was premised on the belief within both U.S. and Japanese government and business circles that an excess of democracy was the cause of Japan's political and social instability, and had blocked economic recovery by allowing wage increases to price Japanese goods out of international markets. Democracy had, it was charged, proved itself to be inefficient economically. In an abrupt reversal, the labor movement was now identified as the root cause of the lagging economic recovery, not the zaibatsu sabotage or bureaucratic foot dragging that had intensified the economic crisis after Japan's surrender.

By the end of 1948, a conservative counterattack on the democratic reforms of the first period was well under way with SCAP's active cooperation. Yoshida was back in power with a directive from SCAP to enforce a plan for rigid economic austerity devised by a Detroit banker, the so-called Dodge Plan. In 1949, Yoshida worked closely with big business to reassert an absolute right to manage through a program of union busting, mass dismissals, red purges in public and private enterprises, and reactionary revision of Japan's new labor laws. The intent was to put the burden of austerity on the workforce and insofar as possible to destroy the basis for independent labor unions. Nikkeiren, the peak business federation established in early 1948 to combat the labor movement, spearheaded the Taylorist attack.

In 1949, the elite with SCAP backing imposed a radical "rationalization" of enterprises public and private that resulted in perhaps a million and a half sackings, destroyed the leftist and radical national union center Sanbetsu Kaigi (Japan Congress of Industrial Unions), and in cooperation with Sōdōmei (Japan Federation of Labor) established collaborative "second unions" at the level of the enterprise.[12] Nikkeiren went on in the 1950s to lead a business campaign to regain total managerial control over production from the shop-floor up. If unions could not be gotten rid of entirely due to guarantees of worker rights in the Constitution and the Trade Union Law, then at least workers could be driven back within enterprise walls into company-sponsored "second" unions. Although the drive to revive national Taylorism as an effective national strategy for renewed capitalist accumulation miscarried, the Nikkeiren campaign of union busting did clear the way for the birth of the cooperative enterprise union, Japan's much-celebrated "unique" contribution to labor-management harmony. The enterprise union would become a key part of Fordism when it transcended Taylorism at the end of the decade as the national strategy for continuing economic growth.[13]

Instead of political and social stability, the political reverse course and Taylorist economic offensive precipitated a confrontation with the defenders of the postwar democratization over what they saw as an attempt by the right to return to the authoritarian ways of the past. Instead of economic recovery, the reverse course, budgetary austerity, and Taylorist "rationalization" sackings brought on a slump so severe that in the spring of 1950 Japan was commonly thought to be heading into a full-scale depression.

The outbreak of the Korean War in June 1950 rescued the economy from collapse and provided the moment for a renewed bout of red purges and union busting that left the labor movement and the leftist parties battered. Nonetheless, the socialist and labor left, now organized in Sōhyō (General Council of Trade Unions of Japan), rallied in opposition to Japan's rearmament and to the Peace and Security Treaties negotiated with the United States in San Francisco in 1951. The Security Treaty bound Japan to U.S. cold-war foreign policy, exacting acceptance of U.S. military bases and Japan's rearmament as the price for regaining sovereignty. Japan's subordination to the United States became a barrier to accomodation with China, blocking negotiation of a peace treaty and reestablishment of economic relations, from which both had much to gain.

After Japan regained its independence in 1952, a succession of conservative governments undertook to roll back the democratic reforms even further. For example, there were attempts, with varying degrees of success, to recentralize and strengthen the police, revise the Constitution, rearm, enhance the emperor's status, and to use education to foster indoctrination of students with an official morality.

Japan's rearmament had begun even before the occupation was over. In 1950 after the Korean War broke out, SCAP told the Yoshida government to create a National Police Reserve, which became a body of 75,000 troops armed with machine guns, tanks, and mortars that was ostensibly to keep peace within Japan. Two years later, it was transformed, together with a "maritime police," into a Safety Agency. Then, under the U.S.–Japan Mutual Security Assistance Pact of 1954, the government forced through a bill creating the Ground, Sea, and Air Self-Defense Forces.

After the destruction of Sanbetsu Kaigi, the leftist majority in the labor movement reorganized in the new national center, Sōhyō, that initially adopted a much less confrontationist stance than its predecessor, Sanbetsu. As alarm over government intentions intensified in 1950 with the outbreak of the Korean War in June and a government crackdown on "reds" and union militants, Sōhyō followed the lead of the labor left back toward militant unionism under the leadership of the left socialist Takano Minoru. Sōhyō fought the continuing Nikkeiren-led attack on the independent unions and endorsed pacifist and socialist principles in the early 1950s in opposition to the Korean War and Japan's de facto military alliance with the United States. The feuding left and right wings of the Socialist Party eventually reunited in 1955, forming a bloc in the Diet large enough to prevent amendment of the Constitution and to make legislative dismantling of the democratic reforms more difficult and costly. In reaction, the conservatives promptly united in the Liberal-Democratic Party, which would go on to rule Japan for the next four decades.

The latter half of the 1950s saw intense and often violent conflict between the reconstituted conservative elite (of bureaucrats, businessmen, and LDP politicians) and a broad social movement focused on labor and the leftist parties. For a number of reasons, business began to regard the labor wars of the late 1940s and the 1950s as having outlived their usefulness. With few exceptions, the right to manage had been regained by the end of the decade and mass sackings had been carried out. Sōhyō had passed under new leadership in the mid-1950s and was being impelled toward grudging acceptance of enterprise unionism, which the more conservative unions outside Sōhyō had already embraced with enthusiasm, as the normal organizational structure for the Japanese labor movement.[14] The de facto defeat of militant industrial unionism in the late 1950s despite the efforts of

Sōhyō to defend the remarkable gains of the 1940s was sweetened with business and government toleration of national Sōhyō campaigns for wage rises through annual "spring struggles." That tactic had been arrived at as a means to overcome the "egoism" of enterprise unions (most striking in the Sōdōmei unions, but by no means absent in Sōhyō) in striking individual deals with employers for higher pay and job security in exchange for sweeping concessions on worker control within the enterprise. By the 1960s, the philosophy of putting the economic interests of the rank and file ahead of defending workers' demands for more control over the working lives was clearly dominant in the Japanese labor movement.

Well before Nikkeiren and its allies had broken the militant unions to the Taylorist halter, the more far-seeing business thinkers were abandoning Nikkeiren's hard-line Taylorism as unnecessarily confrontational. It led to endemic conflict with the labor movement, created a climate of distrust and resistance within the enterprise itself between workers and management, and, by that fact, hindered the attainment of complete control over the workforce and the labor process. Most important of all, the Taylorist reliance on coercion eroded the will to work enthusiastically and creatively to produce quality goods.

Dipping back into the past for ways to secure harmony and cooperation—for instance, reviving organic notions of familism and corporatism put forth by such institutions as the Kyōchōkai (Harmonization Society) in its search for industrial peace in the twenties and Sanpō (Industrial Patriotic Association) for mobilizing labor during the war—would not be enough. Despite the rhetoric, they had been ultimately Taylorist in seeking to justify the hard fact of reliance on a low-wage, low-skill, exploited labor force to produce low-cost goods. The old conditions simply could not be recreated, given the Constitutional recognition of labor and other rights. If a straightforward policy of coercion and indoctrination was not going to work, business began to see it would have to seek labor's cooperation and consent to make the most of technological advances and raise quality. The solution was found in the teachings of the Japan Productivity Center (JPC), an organization promoted by the United States initially and set up jointly by the United States and Japan in the mid-1950s to increase efficiency in production, raise standards of quality, and increase the productivity of labor.

As the JPC saw it, conventional rationalization as applied since the thirties had been based on Taylorism pure and simple. In neglect of "the human side of productivity," it had attempted to improve efficiency through "increased unemployment, decreased real salaries and wages, and intensified labour." That was exactly what Nikkeiren had been trying to do since 1948, at the cost of endemic industrial conflict. The JPC urged employers to go beyond the "classic way of thinking [that] holds that labor and management operate confrontationally." The overriding goal was increasing productivity, but it must be done in such a way as to "increase employment, salaries and wages, but decrease workloads (particularly in blue collar fields)."[15] Unions would have to be given a role in the productivity movement, if only to allay their suspicions; but this most emphatically did not mean the same kind of participation in management that the militant union movement had fought for in the 1940s. In May 1955 the JPC summarized its guiding principles as follows:

1) Maintenance and expansion of employment,

2) Cooperation and consultation between management and labor in increasing productivity,

3) Fair and equitable distribution of the fruits of improved productivity among management, labor, and the consumer.[16]

In a word, Fordism.[17]

The JPC defined labor-management cooperation as the "enhancement of communication" through consultation, which meant "discussing, studying and deliberating" on ways to increase productivity. But, "consultation between the two does not mean sharing management rights so far as final decision making" is concerned.[18] The JPC was no more ready to compromise on the right to manage than Nikkeiren. What it hoped to achieve by this new formulation was the ending of the confrontation between labor and business by elevating a bigger-pie approach to dividing up the benefits of economic growth to the level of national policy. It meant to seduce the rank and file of the local enterprise union in the big corporations with the dream of "participation" in management. In reality, the unions were to give over their right to have any say at all in how management used workers at the point of production in exchange for getting back in the rank-and-file's pay packets a fraction of the increased profits resulting from higher productivity. The JPC formulation did not of itself end the bitter conflicts between the elite and the social movements of the 1950s.

The climax to this period of national Taylorism came at the end of the decade during the government of Kishi Nobusuke (1957–1960). Kishi had been a notorious figure in Japan's exploitation of Manchuria in league with Tōjō Hideki, for which he was indicted and imprisoned as a Class-A war criminal during the occupation. He spent his years as prime minister trying to force through the right-wing political agenda; namely, increase the power of the police, put education under state control and reintroduce "ethics," enhance the political power of the emperor while restricting that of the Diet, get rid of Article 9 (the Peace Clause) to allow Japan's full rearmament, and drastically revise the Constitution to reverse Japan's democratization.

In 1960, Nikkeiren, big business, and the Kishi government backed Mitsui's decision to use massive force to break the strike by the coal miners' union at its Miike collieries. This action was the key to destroying the national miners' union, the last holdout of labor union militance. John Price's article on the Miike dispute describes the bitter struggle of the powerful and influential national miners' union to survive. It was the last act in the long battle that the militant wing of the labor movement had put up in the 1950s to maintain a substantial measure of worker autonomy against the business campaign to restore its unqualified right to manage. The miners fought for their jobs and their unions' survival in pitched battles that saw tens of thousands of company thugs and strikebreakers, armed police, and miners come to blows over possession of the mine facilities. At the same time, hundreds of thousands took to the streets in Tokyo to prevent renewal of the U.S.–Japan Security Treaty. In both cases, the government prevailed, at a high cost in life and injuries. Yet, the Kishi policy of confrontation was polarizing Japan and eroding electoral support for the LDP, an ominous trend for the LDP, which began to fear the election of a socialist government in the not-so-distant future.

In short, the powerful popular movement in support of the Miike strike and in opposition to the Security Treaty succeeded in forcing Kishi to resign and led to the Ikeda cabinet's strategic turn toward income doubling and a "low-posture" (*tei shisei*) policy in domestic politics and foreign affairs. Direct attacks on the postwar democratic gains and Constitutional protection of popular rights, parliamentary democracy, and pacifism did cease during the heyday of the high-speed economic growth. Concentration on a national policy of all-out economic growth and acceptance of the democratic political status quo promised to be the best way to secure the elite's hold on power. The outcome of the confrontations arising from the revival of national Taylorism, then, was a compromise between the embattled social movements and the elite, a compromise that took the particular form of "peace and democracy" and Fordism.[19]

A few basic points need to be underscored about the lasting importance of the first fifteen years after surrender. First, the democratic reforms embedded in the Constitution foreclosed the straightforward use of coercion that had underlain the pre-1945 order and forced the elite to adjust to the necessity of eliciting consent to their actions all the way from the shop floor to national politics. That is, a determined opposition could hold the elite accountable for its policies and actions in thousands of new ways and places. Above all, this was happening through the ballot box since leftist parties had solidly established themselves and in the workplace since militant unions had made substantial and in some cases radical inroads on management control.

Second, Japan's business elite faced an immediate crisis of control in the enterprise, which the Taylorist mainstream planned to overcome by restoring its unquestioned "right to manage." Reestablishing control was imperative for the success of the top-down retrenchment and rationalization that the elite required for a capitalist-led industrial revival, be it Taylorist or Fordist in national strategy.

Third, there was a real alternative to the elite's strategy. The JSP had put forward a policy of nationalization and social democracy in which labor unions and other mass organizations would be a constituent part of a national economic revival led by a social-democratic government.

Fourth, the Taylorist efforts to break labor's control in the workplace and gut the democratic reforms were guaranteed to produce a political backlash. That had to be reckoned with by building an efficient conservative political machine, lest a united opposition gain an electoral majority and topple the conservatives from power.

Fifth, U.S. intervention from 1948 onward on the side of an elite-led capitalist reconstruction prevented this explosive mixture of economics and politics from blowing the old order apart. The Taylorist counterattack could not have been sustained politically had not the United States thrown its support behind that strategy for capitalist revival. First, in what is accurately called the reverse course, the United States in the late forties began the attack on the key democratic reforms of the first phase of the postwar occupation. Second, the United States provided Japan with the economic wherewithal to reinvigorate Japanese capitalism after the outbreak of the Korean War in June 1950 through spending vast sums for military procurements during the Korean War and through favorable trade policies afterwards.

Sixth, despite the formal establishment of sexual equality during the first flush of democratization and the fall into disrepute of familism as a general concept for organizing society, the reign of familism and patriarchy would prove to be far more tenacious than foreseen. It would reemerge as enterprise familism in the late 1950s and become a key part of the dominant ideology of Fordism from the 1960s onwards.

III. Historic Compromise (1960–1979): "Peace and Democracy" + Fordism = "Miraculous Growth"

Peace and Democracy

Fordism came to Japan in 1960, out of necessity as much as out of farsightedness. As 1960 approached, the elite faced a number of troublesome problems. Business had failed to penetrate foreign markets outside of the United States; and the U.S. military procurements that had brought about the 1950s boom had been shrinking. The government had aroused a powerful opposition movement that peaked with the Miike miners' struggle and the Anti-Security Treaty demonstrations before the Diet in Tokyo. The LDP had to deal with a reunified Socialist Party and a solidification of popular support for the the basic democratic reforms.

The political strategy of the elite after 1960 was, after pulling back from confrontation with the popular movement, to use the machinery of government to build a political machine capable of turning out an LDP vote. Elections became a matter of corrupt "money politics" where business supplied unlimited campaign funds in exchange for political favors, much like the pattern in other industrialized countries. It was a system that ensured LDP control of the Diet through a combination of a rural gerrymander, pork-barrel politics in the Diet, and a multi-member constituency system that favors incumbents. The system exaggerated LDP seats in the Diet, allowing it to rule uninterruptedly for four decades, much of that time with less than a majority of the popular vote (the LDP popular vote in elections for the House of Representatives dropped below 50 percent in 1967 never to rise above half again), and to evade its Constitutional accountability to the Diet or the electorate. In an echo of the past, power came to reside in the corridors of the government ministries and in the boardrooms of big business, with the LDP brokering differences in strategy and policy.

Thus, "peace and democracy" was far from being democratic in the Constitutional sense of being based on the direct responsibility of elected leaders to a sovereign citizenry. The elite was nonetheless forced to be "responsible" in the sense of having to take heed of the social movements' power to resist further direct attacks on the democratic rights protected in the Constitution and to press for minimal social welfare reforms. A phrase coined in the 1980s, "soft" authoritarianism, captures the elite's mode of operation very well indeed.

Despite the success of the conservative elite in entrenching itself in power in the late 1950s, a large bloc of voters (35–40 percent) continued to support the leftist opposition. The Sōhyō union rank and file ensured the JSP nearly 28–29 percent of the vote until the late 1960s, despite the defection of the right wing from the JSP in 1960 to form the Democratic Socialist Party in alliance with the right wing of the labor movement. In 1964 the Buddhist sect Sōka Gakkai gave birth to yet another party, the Kōmeitō or Clean Government Party, that was attuned to those who had not done well from the economic miracle and vacillated between wanting to join the ranks of business and wanting to support the reformist policies of the left. The combined power of these three together has left the LDP little choice but to continue courting the votes it needed through economic policies focused on rapid growth and expanding consumerism. The two-thirds majority in the Diet necessary for amending the Constitution and reordering Japan's national priorities was simply unattainable.

Sato Eisaku, who became prime minister in 1964, continued the low-posture policies of Ikeda. Elections settled into ritualized contests for power that turned on LDP claims of success in delivering the economic goods. This was the classic period of peace and democracy, when the illusion prevailed that all-out economic growth would make Japan uniformly prosperous, peaceful, and democratic. The factional struggle for power within the LDP, where victory (and the premiership) went to the best practitioners of money politics, ensured that the big-business suppliers of money would have the leading voice in determining national policies. Business acted in tandem with the bureaucrats in MITI and other ministries in hammering out policies for growth, unfettered by concerns over pollution and other social costs. Before the 1960s were out, the immense and accumulating costs of unregulated growth could no longer be ignored, since social movements were arising that questioned the premises of "peace and democracy" and Fordism.

The high-speed economic growth of the 1950s and 1960s literally transformed Japan. From a small-scale producer of textiles, light manufactured goods,
traditional products, and agricultural products in the early postwar period, Japan
became by 1970 the third-ranked economic power in the world and a major
producer of chemicals, steel, ships, cars, machinery, and a tremendous array of
consumer goods like cameras, TVs, and household appliances. The countryside
emptied as the young went to the cities in search of jobs and a new life. A new
"middle class" of salaried white- and blue-collar workers incorporated into
Japan's largest enterprises came into being. Their urban way of life was set forth
as the model for all Japan—giving rise to the "traditional" postwar family made
up of salaryman husband devoted to the company and housewife devoted to
being a good wife and wise mother.

The primary stimulus for high-speed growth was not foreign trade, but domestic spending. Business spent lavishly on new factories in the so-called scrap-
and-build policy, government built new roads and public projects for business
needs, and consumers pursued the latest gadgets up an escalator that by the
1970s would create a market for millions of cars, and in the 1980s a flaunting of
wealth through conspicuous consumption on a grand scale. The privileged economic relationship with the United States continued, with the Vietnam War
providing another tremendous shot in the arm in the form of demand for muni-
tions, supplies, repairs, and "rest and recuperation" for the U.S. military—until
the war bankrupted the U.S. government both morally and financially.

Agriculture did not fare so well. From the early 1950s, small farm villages
and towns sent a swelling stream of men and women workers to the cities to fill
non-regular jobs in big business and small. Because these workers provided a
source of cheap labor that could be hired and fired at will, they became the
mainstay through the 1960s of the part-time/temporary workforce in large and
small firms, especially in the subcontracting firms that relied upon cheap labor to
supply the large firms with the low-cost items they demanded. The massive
movement of rural men and women into wage work in the cities dovetailed with
a strategy for economic growth that was primarily focused on and driven by an
expanding domestic market, since their wages, too, fed an expanding consumer
market.

The forcible housebreaking of labor in the private sector in the late 1950s
allowed the elite to pursue a Fordist strategy with minimal danger by virtue of
the cooperative, even collaborative relationships with the now cautious and often
conservative leadership of most of the enterprise unions in Japan's largest private
and some of the public enterprises. The Fordist regime generated growth rates
and profits high enough for big business to extend guaranteed employment and
real wages to its male core workers. In exchange, management in private industry in particular gained a free hand to mobilize the active cooperation in the
workplace that was the key to obtaining the large increases in productivity that
contributed so much to economic growth. There was resistance, of course, both

passive and active,[20] but not widespread enough in the private sector to threaten the employment system overall. The public sector was another matter; it took another two decades to crush labor militance there.[21] This civilized relationship within the enterprise could work so long as a large, not so well paid, and insecure workforce existed outside the large firms to serve as a warning of the penalties for dissent and to underwrite the profits of big business through subcontracting. The dual economy that developed in the era of high-speed growth was not incidental but essential to the existence of the privileges extended to male elite workers.

In the 1960s, the Japan Productivity Center continued promoting its ideology of management that stressed labor-management cooperation in increasing productivity linked to a "fair and equitable" distribution of the fruits of productivity increases among management, labor, and the consumer. The means for proper worker participation in management was to be joint labor-management councils dedicated solely to raising productivity. Some unions in large enterprises did intend to make the labor-management councils avenues for participation in management, but basically failed. Over the years management devised various small-group participation schemes—QC (quality control) groups and the like—designed to increase worker motivation and strengthen work group solidarity.[22] The public-sector unions like Jichirō (the All-Japan Prefectural and Municipal Workers' union), Kokurō (the National Railway Workers' Union, and Nikkyōsō (the Japan Teachers' Union) did better at protecting worker interests than the more supine unions affiliated with Sōdōmei and its eventual successor Dōmei. But in any case it was difficult to withstand sustained employer pressure to use such means to increase productivity. From the start, participation was a one-way street, never intended to extend to such vital worker interests as lowering the intensity of the work pace, or to betterment of working conditions, or to worker protection unrelated to increasing efficiency. Management-initiated schemes for eliciting this type of one-sided worker "participation" have proliferated like rabbits since the 1960s—and have been very successful in pushing productivity up and undermining the unions.[23]

Ten-percent-plus growth rates brought both jobs and a measure of prosperity to others who did not benefit directly from the privileges extended to core employees in large enterprises, that is, those rural people who went to the city to find work and those urban males who held the better paid and more secure positions/jobs in medium- and small-sized businesses. The gap between the elite workers and mass workers narrowed during the 1960s, in part owing to Sōhyō's annual spring struggle for wage hikes (which set the standard for wage increases throughout the economy) and in part owing to business competition for younger workers. But it did not close. Nonetheless, the rapid overall rise in real wages in the 1960s and early 1970s did indeed provide a major stimulus to personal consumption and was a major contributor to the legitimization of the LDP's claim to power as the architect of postwar prosperity.

Paying the Bills for High-Speed Economic Growth

It was also in this period that the patriarchal contours of postwar Japanese society hardened into the familiar mold that has largely remained until today. In the past, women had been routinely barred from regular jobs for wages capable of supporting a family, until the wartime labor shortage compelled a reluctant mobilization of women. After the fighting ended and the soldiers returned, business sacked en masse those women who had held industrial and other "men's" jobs in industrial work, transportation, and the like.

They had few choices: return to their home villages, try to make a go of it in petty businesses, or take up marginal jobs for wages in the city as waitresses, textile workers, day laborers, prostitutes, and so forth. In any case, many simply could not leave the work force. Those early days after the war were hard and most women had to work without ceasing at home and outside just to survive. A large number did go back to the village and agriculture, which in 1950 still accounted for 38.6 percent of all workers and 61.3 percent of women workers.[24] With the sudden revival of industry with the Korean War procurements came an increased need for labor, which was primarily men and some women from the countryside. As a result of the movement of women out of agriculture over the two decades from 1955 to 1975, the participation rate for women in the overall labor force (paid and unpaid) dropped from 56.7 percent to 45.7 percent. These figures hid a dramatic increase in percentage of paid female employees. Women who worked for wages went from 31.2 percent to 59.8 percent over the same period.[25] Women left the village and farm work in droves, but did not go to work for wages in nearly the same numbers as they had worked on the farm. There were plenty of men from the countryside available to fill city jobs and supply an income adequate for supporting a household.[26]

The idea that women ought to stay within the household and be "good wives and wise mothers" in service to the husband and his employer's needs was a "tradition" partly revived and partly invented in this very period.[27] It went hand in hand with the ideology of a "uniquely Japanese" employment system first popularized in English by James Abegglen's 1958 book, *The Japanese Factory*. The supposedly all-embracing lifetime employment system that was then evolving would in many large firms produce a supremely flexible, cooperative, and productive male work force dedicated to promoting the fortunes of the enterprise family; but it simultaneously removed the male employee from his own family.

Few of the devotees of the Japanese employment system made the connection at the time, but it is now clear that the "housewifization" of middle-class women (to borrow Maria Mies's term)[28] corresponded to the need of business to incorporate the male workers almost entirely into the enterprise family and simultaneously encourage consumerism on a scale sufficient to absorb the rapidly increasing output of goods. Henceforth, it became expected that young women, after an early stint at work from the late teens to the mid twenties, would marry and settle down as a good wife and wise mother whose job was to run the household in its entirety for a period of about thirty years while the salaried employee husband's life was consumed by the demands of the enterprise family. Her responsibilities would be great—bearing and raising and educating the next generation, caring for the older generation (the husband's parents), serving her husband's needs for clean clothes, bath, and bedding, managing the household and its finances, and, of course, purchasing and consuming. The purchase and consumption of food, household appliances, TVs, clothes, and eventually a car— these were two of the housewife's major contributions to high-speed economic growth. Advertising became skilled at instilling the desire to keep up consumption standards appropriate to the husband's employment, standards that eventually had little to do with actual utility and much to do with status. The radical splitting of the family in two in the 1960s (which sharply segregated production on the one side, from reproduction and consumption on the other) came to be seen as traditional, but was in fact new in its thoroughness. Furthermore, it applied with greatest force to the families of a minority, of that one-third of male workers who held core jobs in large enterprises.

For most of the 1960s, thanks to housewifization and a rapid growth in jobs and real pay, the growth in purchasing power was in rough balance with the proliferation of consumer products. Even so, cracks persisted in Japanese society into the late 1960s, although this was the classic period of Fordist growth. It is not well understood just how lopsided the benefits of Fordism were. Business took the first cut out of the profits created by productivity increases, while the second cut went to that 35 percent or so of the work force in the unions. Business concessions to these core workers were offset by the low wages, lack of benefits, and absence of job security for the mostly un-unionized workers in the millions of small- and medium-sized businesses.[29] Agricultural families benefited little despite a rise in productivity due to mechanization and use of chemical fertilizers, pesticides, and the like, because industrial agriculture itself was problematic. Farm families and their offspring found it more and more difficult to stay in agriculture and gain a reasonable living from small-scale holdings. Outright poverty in certain parts of the country was substantial. According to Kōji Taira,[30] as late as 1968 14.5 percent of families or 7.8 percent of individuals had incomes below the official poverty line. Other estimates range upwards to 20 percent or more. Without question much of the poverty was concentrated in those parts of the population least able to defend themselves, that is, among those most discriminated against in education and employment—*burakumin*, Koreans, Ainu, and women who had to support themselves.

Among these who suffered from the economic "miracle" sweeping Japan were the day laborers described by Brett de Bary, the disappearing farmers discussed in Ohno Kazuoki's article, the fisherfolk of Minamata poisoned by mercury pollution who appear in Christopher Stevens's contribution, and the office woman depicted in Tamae Prindle's translation of Shimizu Ikko's business novel. There were many other costs. "Development" projects destroyed local communities for the sake of big business interests, as at Sanrizuka where the government used police force to remove the farmers and get the airport built. Many among that great majority of employees who worked hard and long in the countless struggling businesses at the base of the dual economy lived close to the margins in densely packed high-rise concrete housing blocks. Women found themselves slotted into the restricted role of housewife and mother. Burakumin, Koreans, and Ainu were the targets of systematic and often overtly hostile discrimination in virtually any activity undertaken outside of the segregated communities to which they were largely confined.

Ohno traces the decay of Japanese agriculture back to the 1950s and 1960s when there was U.S. pressure on Japan to become a market for U.S. agricultural commodities, to expand its military budget and armaments, and to become dependent on food imports in order to lessen the potential danger of full-scale rearmament. Ohno notes the importance of the 1961 Fundamentals of Agriculture Law, which brought agricultural policy into line with the switch to high-speed economic growth based on industry. By encouraging mechanization and use of new techniques of cultivation using chemicals and by stimulating a reorientation of food production toward a Western model, the law had the effect of reducing the number of farm households. The effect was startling. In the single decade 1960–1970, the proportion of the working population that was in agriculture fell from 26.8 percent to 15.9 percent, only to drop to 9.1 percent in 1980 and to 6.2 percent in 1990. Over the same period the farm population dropped over the 1960s from almost 12 million to 8.1 million, and to less than 4 million in 1990.[31]

As Ishimure Michiko reminds us through Christopher Stevens's translation from *Bitter Sea, Pure Land*, more than anyone else, the fishing people of Minamata felt the full consequences of all-out development. Their way of life and their very lives were destroyed by the symbol of development that had been in their midst since the first decade of the twentieth century, the Chisso Corporation. Despite clear evidence obtained in the late 1950s in its own labs that mercury from its effluent was the cause of the terrible disease spreading through the community, the Chisso Corporation, in connivance with the Ministry of International Trade and Industry (MITI) and other pro-development ministries, deliberately suppressed the evidence and continued the systematic pollution of the seas around Minamata with mercury. The Minamata sufferers' tenacious fight for recognition of the cause of their illness and for redress from Chisso inspired other social movements to come and forced the government to enact pollution control measures in the 1970 Diet session. Yet, Chisso never made adequate compensation for the human cost, as comes through with terrible clarity in Ishimure's section on the boy Yamanaka Kuhei. Chisso fought bitterly against making even the paltry payments the individual sufferers eventually received.

Brett de Bary's picture of Sanya deals with that most vulnerable group of workers—the day laborers who, organized in labor gangs controlled by gang-sters, do the hard and dangerous work of development on construction sites. The horrendous living conditions for the day laborers who are concentrated in urban slums like Tokyo's Sanya and Osaka's Kamagasaki are just as much the product of Fordism as the lifetime employment, automatic pay increases, and benefits extended to the core workers. They, too, are part of the floating work force that provides a buffer to insulate the core workers from the periodic bouts of jobless-ness that accompany the ups and downs of the business cycle.

In Brian (Daizan)Victoria's article on corporate zen, the reader meets up with one of the most contradictory images of Japan—the salaryman as corporate warrior selflessly Zen-like in his egoless sincerity of purpose—dedicated to the cause of his corporate master, even at the cost of his personal life. Yet the cause of his corporate master is crassly materialistic, namely to sell products for a profit. More tellingly, if the corporate warrior is asked, he is likely to say that he doesn't like his job and would do something else, if only he could.[32] Here, too, social costs are systematically ignored or discounted.

The success of the Fordist regime in Japan has depended in the last instance upon constant reinforcement of a cultural hegemony focused on the familistic enterprise. In this view of the world, the corporate enterprise family becomes the keeper of the cooperative ideal in society that was in essence the family writ large. The image that the enterprise has fostered of itself as the repository of the Japanese cultural tradition—loyalty, warm personal relations, benevolence, sin-cerity, guardian of social and economic progress—coincided with the 1950s vision of the Japan Productivity Center and reached back to the World War I era amalgam of familism and Taylorism. A positive image of the corporation did begin to attain hegemony in Japanese society in the 1960s. Certainly, the steadily rising wages and benefits under the productivity deal of the late 1950s fostered a high degree of enterprise egoism among the privileged blue- and white-collar workers in the large enterprises. Despite the vocal militance of the left-of-center Sōhyō Federation and the public-sector unions, the unionized core of factory labor was effectively incorporated at the level of the large private enterprise along with the office workers, a process that has fittingly been called white-collarization.

Shimizu's novel illustrates the difficult situation women found themselves in if for any reason—staying single or getting divorced—they departed from the "traditional" woman's path. This was the age of the good wife and wise mother when the women who did not marry and leave the enterprise at the proper time could expect little better treatment for her efforts than the woman cast aside in "Silver Sanctuary." The corporation endorsed and promoted this role for women. Business coveted the ability to cast aside women workers when it suited them, since this provided yet another layer of insulation between the core male worker and the buffeting of the labor market.

To some, it seemed that society as a whole was being reconstructed in the corporation's image. The schools were turning into ladders for students to climb on their way to enter corporate service—albeit for male students given a substantial shove from "education mamas." The national unions broke apart at the base, with each enterprise unit becoming more and more narrow and isolated—and closely identified with its own particular corporate enterprise. Service as union officials became a preferred route to a high post later in enterprise personnel management.

Questioning the Fordist Compromise—
Resistance from Outside and Below

In spite of it all, the image of a warmhearted, paternalistic, and, in the rosiest portraits, democratic corporation did not become so pervasive and deeply rooted as to be unchallengeable. The rising costs of all-out growth could not be ignored. The deadly conformity of the corporate world, among other things, stimulated enough resistance that the image was vulnerable, surprisingly vulnerable. When in the late 1960s and early 1970s the corporation came under fierce attack, it was badly shaken. Although the social movements of the 1970s could be said with some accuracy to have originated in the highly political groups that constituted the student and antiwar movements of the late 1960s and early 1970s, it was not politics on a grand revolutionary scale that carried the resistance forward. Rather, it was the convergence of environmental, social, and local political concerns that energized dissent in the 1970s.

Japan's involvement as a staging area for the Vietnam War brought social conflict at home as a student and young workers' movement arose that not only went into the streets in the name of peace and democracy to force Japan to cease supporting the war effort, but also to repudiate the postwar materialism that had reigned since Ikeda and had reduced education to vocational training. That was why the elite found the defection of the students in the late 1960s so threatening—for the youth being groomed to enter the factories and offices found that prospect intolerable. Thus, the rise of the New Left, the antiwar movement, the student movement, a young workers' movement, progressive local governments, and other dissident groups represented a double break. It was a break with the growth-at-all-costs corporate ideology behind Fordism, which they attacked as both hollow and oppressive. It was a break with the limited elite vision of "peace and democracy," to which they counterposed egalitarian, participatory democracy as an antidote to corrupt, LDP money politics.

When the neo-Marxist vision of popular democracy put forth by the New Left and the antiwar and student movements broke apart in the early 1970s along with the movements themselves, the fragments that went out into the community each inherited a piece of the democratic vision. The women's movement was perhaps the most important inheritor in that it addressed the totality of the capitalist system as it had developed by the 1970s. It raised questions not only about female sexuality, motherhood, and family, but also about the intimate interrelationship of the women's sphere to such fundamental issues as the enterprise "family" that turned men into "corporate warriors" severed from the biological family, the developmentalism that despoiled both nature and neighborhoods, and the corporate world-view that conceived of all before it as commodities, above all women. The concerns of the women's movement of the 1970s are too broad and disparate to encapsulate easily, but the section on the women's movement by Muto Ichiyo[33] shows how feminist thinkers like Tanaka Mitsu addressed what seemed to be the crucial issues at the moment that the Fordist compromise was fraying. Many of the concrete issues to be taken up in the 1970s had already surfaced in the 1960s, only to be swept up in the wider antiwar movement, but they now came to the fore. Two key institutions would come under particularly harsh attack—"development" that was in fact destructive of the local community and the gendered division of labor that reinforced the rule of patriarchy.[34] Despite the severity of the critique of developmentalism and sexism that targeted the corporate society and patriarchy[35] that had consolidated under Fordism in the late 1960s and early 1970s, the historic compromise that underlay Fordism and peace and democracy held until economic and political events in the early 1970s undermined the elite's ability to deliver the economic goods by putting an end to the high growth rates.

Changing International Division of Labor— Economic Troubles and Rationalization

Until the early 1970s, Japan's high-speed growth had depended primarily upon capital spending by business and government and upon growing consumerism. Exports were driven primarily by the need to import the resources essential for domestic industry, not by a necessity to find markets and profits for industries with goods that could not be sold at home. That was to change, as high-speed growth had laid a broad base for expansion of output. When all manner of goods from steel, ships, chemicals, radios, motorcycles, cameras, color TVs, cars, and machinery to sophisticated electronics came into mass production, large-scale exports became imperative; and other countries began to see Japan as a threat, particularly the United States.

By the end of the 1960s, the immense cost of the Vietnam War was already undermining the U.S. economy, which prompted the U.S. government to take actions that shocked Japan's leaders. In quick succession the Nixon administration announced a new military doctrine of military disengagement in Asia, abandoned the gold standard, attacked the yen and Japanese trade policies, and made an accomodation with China without even notifying Japan beforehand, its most faithful ally in enforcing the hostile containment policy for twenty years. All this called into question the U.S. alliance and trade relationship that had been the bedrock of Japan's foreign policy since 1950. After Tanaka Kakuei became the new Japanese prime minister in July 1972, he promptly went to Beijing in a blaze of publicity to meet with the leadership of the People's Republic of China, in part to signal the end of passive acceptance of the U.S. lead in foreign policy.

Tanaka brought into office with him a grandiose plan for rebuilding Japan that was intended to continue Fordist high-speed economic growth by dispersing industry throughout the country. Despite the U.S. economic measures, Japan's growth held up well until 1973, when the quadrupling of the price for crude oil after the Arab-Israeli war in October ended the 10 percent growth rates of the 1960s overnight. Tanaka's plan fell apart in an atmosphere of intense speculation in land, inflation (reaching almost 25 percent in 1974),[36] and deep recession. Momentarily in 1974 the Japanese economy contracted, bringing unemployment and a sense of crisis in its wake. To combat the increased costs of energy and transport, government and business initiated a policy of promoting high-technology manufactures over heavy industry, which began to move overseas. This, in combination with energy conservation, a shift toward nuclear power from oil, and a trend away from manufacturing to services, enabled the economy to weather the second oil shock of 1979 with relative ease.

Tanaka's resignation in December 1974 over the Lockheed scandal marked the beginning of the end for the Fordist compromise, since business and government took up two interrelated strategies with profoundly anti-Fordist implications. On the one hand, there was an immediate return to Taylorist policies of extreme rationalization; on the other, there was a decisive shift toward exports.

The Taylorist rationalization aimed at pruning the expensive core male workers who had been at the center of the Fordist compromise—by subcontracting out less essential operations, by intensification of labor and resistance to wage increases, by replacing labor with new technologies (such as microelectronics, computerized production, and robots), or simply by hiring low-paid, part-time women, especially married women, in their place. Employers looked to women to fill the gap because the countryside had been drained of most of its labor by this time. Employment of married women began to rise in 1975. The employment curve for women took on an M-shape that reflected the changing situation for women. The old pattern was work until marriage, then leaving the workforce entirely to raise children and run the household. Now women were returning to work in their forties to fill business needs for part-timers. But they did so because of economic pressure to contribute to the expense of the children's education, the cost of housing, and saving for retirement.[37]

The Taylorist rationalization policies taken toward the core workforce in the 1970s brought, as might be expected, greater reliance upon coercion within the enterprise to deal with resistance to the intensification of labor. At Toshiba Electric an informal organization called the Ohgikai (the Fan Society) became a key factor in controlling the workers after its companywide organization in 1973. Its purpose was to combat dissent by collecting intelligence on the political attitudes and activities of workers, to work with management and the police to drive leftists out, and generally to assist management in carrying out policies like rationalization, i.e., dismissals and speed-ups.[38] The ideologists of Japanese management in Japan and abroad largely ignored the bedrock of coercion behind Japanese-style industrial relations that the Ohgikai laid bare. It was ironic that Western writers like Ezra Vogel and Ronald Dore were at that very time writing books that idealized Japanese management methods and urged them upon the West.

The decisive shift toward exports to absorb the immense outpouring of goods that the domestic market was less and less capable of consuming brought recovery to moderate rates of growth by the end of the decade. Exports of machinery and equipment (especially cars and electrical equipment) sustained the expansion of the 1980s, but intensified the conflict with the United States over ballooning Japanese trade surpluses.[39] The turn to exports also put pressure on living standards, since the elite's view was that high wages and state social spending were responsible for inflation and for making industry less competitive. The collaborative unions in the export industries agreed in the mid-1970s to go along with the business demand that wage increases be held well below increases in productivity. In return, business and government held out the promise of union participation with the elite in devising economic policy, with the implicit understanding that collaboration would secure the position of the cooperative unions in export industries against the continuing wave of rationalization.

The new policy had a parallel track that the right-wing unions welcomed: a sustained government attack on the rival leftist national union center, Sōhyō. Sohyo had resisted the new policy on wages; and its more militant public sector unions had gone out in 1975 on a "strike for the right to strike." The strike was broken largely because the private sector unions refused their support, setting an ominous precedent for the 1980s when the government destroyed Sōhyō by privatizing public enterprises, thereby completing the incorporation of labor in a new national center led by the right-wing unions. As a result of worsening economic conditions for industrial workers and anti-labor policies of business and government, the proportion of the work force belonging to unions went into a long-term decline that has not yet ended, from about 35 percent in the 1970s to less than 25 percent in the 1990s.[40] It had been a long fall for labor from the heady days of the late 1940s when it was the leading edge of a mass progressive social movement.

In contrast to the elite's ability to devise an effective strategy of exports and rationalization in the 1970s, its political troubles worsened. At the very time that growth was faltering, the costs of decades of social and environmental exploitation were coming due. Furthermore, the Lockheed revelations about structural corruption in the LDP and intimacy with *yakuza* and the radical right led to demands from within the LDP for reform and the splitting off of a small reform party, the New Liberal Club. More importantly, a challenge from below to the LDP had been building for some time with the election of leftist mayors and governors in the largest cities—Tokyo, Osaka, Kyoto, and Yokohama had leftist administrations by 1973. By 1975, progressives held two-thirds of the mayors of the big cities and had made significant advances in prefectural and local politics. Then came a near defeat in the 1976 elections to the House of Representatives when the LDP received only 41.8 percent of the popular vote,[41] managing to stay in power because of the rural gerrymander and by recruitment of a number of independents.

It was hardly the case that Japanese society was as harmonious and united socially and politically as outsiders believed during the era of high-speed economic growth, much less during the 1970s. Nor did the cooptation and gradual incorporation of the labor movement spell the end of social protest. The student revolt, the antiwar movement, the Narita and Minamata struggles had all tapped into the accumulating discontents of unfettered capitalist growth. Then, in the 1970s a great variety of other social movements, many locally based, appeared that wanted action to redress the balance between economic growth and the popular welfare. Movements for citizens' rights, environmental protection, women's rights, and better treatment for the aged undermined the basis for LDP rule in the 1970s at both the local and national level.

The swing of the electorate to the left forced the LDP to at least start addressing long-standing issues like corruption, remilitarization, pollution, the aged, social security, and medical care. One measure of the climate of the 1970s was the laughter and ridicule that greeted Mishima Yukio's suicide before the Self Defence Forces in 1970 that the writer had intended to arouse Japan to cast off the postwar democratic legacy. In spite of Mishima's melodramatic act, throughout the decade the elite kept well clear of issues like Constitutional revision that the right wing so passionately wanted. In 1976 the government felt compelled to set an informal limit of 1 percent of GNP for military spending. Furthermore, the LDP oversaw the introduction of social welfare measures, albeit belatedly and partially, through such things as the pollution laws of 1970 and subsequent legislation to increase pensions and coverage under national health insurance. Although these actions probably saved the LDP from being ejected from office, they in no way implied a desire to restore Fordism to vitality through a Keynesian-style state redistribution of wealth. To the contrary, the shift toward exports undermined the very premises of Fordism by calling forth a neo-Taylorist rationalization of labor that reached beyond Japan's borders.

IV. Conflict Renewed (1980–present):
Restructuring for Capitalist Efficiency—
Grass-Roots Democracy Versus Global Taylorism

Freeing the Corporation—Internationalization and "Administrative Reform"

The 1980s ushered in a change in elite strategy from domestic Fordism to global Taylorism. The focus changed to the export of goods, production processes, and capital. This was not a reversion to the national Taylorism of the 1940s and 1950s; nor was it a total repudiation of the Fordism of the 1960s and 1970s. The global or neo-Taylorism of the 1980s (often called flexible production or lean production by its fans) attempted to reconcile the two: (1) by the export of dis-integrated fragments of production processes to cheap-labor locations abroad that replicated the patron-subcontractor relationship that had already existed in Japan for nearly three decades; and (2) by shrinking but not eliminating the privileged and expensive core workforce of lifetime employees. Business valued their loyalty and example too highly for that, and in any case could offset their cost by Taylorist rationalization for everyone else, at home or abroad. The use of sophisticated Taylorist techniques to cut costs by decentralizing production within Japan and outside was a development made possible by technological changes in transport and manufacturing in the 1970s. The essential point is not the "flexibility" business gained through technological sophistication in production and marketing, but the worsening conditions of employment and cuts in the social programs that accompanied the global export blitz.

It could not be taken for granted that the sacrifices the elite demanded at home to realize the globalization of Taylorism would be gladly borne. On the contrary, repudiating the Fordist compromise through Thatcherite or Reaganite attacks on labor and the Keynesian state might bring on troubles that the LDP could not handle—unless the country could be moved away from peace and democracy back toward the authoritarian past. The political counterpart to global Taylorism, then, was not to be Fordist peace and democracy that had at least provided minimal recognition of democratic rights, but "corporate democracy." This was an elite conception of rule that would bypass the Constitutional order of parliamentary democracy by creating means for the leaders of unionized labor to represent the corporate interests of the core workers at the top in private consultation with the business, bureaucratic, and political members of the elite.

The wave of neo-Taylorist rationalization carried out so successfully by Japanese enterprises in the name of internationalization from the late 1970s onward was the leading edge of the industrialized world's race for the bottom in cutting labor costs in order to export competitively. The effects have been felt painfully in cuts in real wages and rising unemployment everywhere, but especially in the industrialized north.

In the early 1980s the Japanese elite did seem to be rising to the economic challenge of overproduction and stagnation. The elite strategy since the mid-1970s had been for the big corporations to concentrate on high-tech, knowledge-intensive goods and services, and to allow dirty, energy-hungry heavy industry to move overseas, much of it to ASEAN countries, as Rob Steven points out, so that shipping costs could be reduced and conflict over pollution could be avoided. Despite a partial "hollowing out" of heavy industry, Japan continued to import vast amounts of natural resources and semi-finished goods to process for re-export as cars, machinery, stereos, TVs, and the like, thereby accumulating huge surpluses. These were in turn invested abroad, increasingly in Asia. Steven details the process where, by the 1990s, Japanese economic interests became dominant in Southeast Asia, anticipating the possible creation of a large Asian Yen bloc.

Although the return to moderate rates of growth in the 1980s produced full employment and an expansion of the consumer market, the benefits were ever more unevenly spread. The workplace restructuring begun in the late 1970s was far reaching and initiated the decline of the unionized, highly trained and well-paid male lifetime employees as a proportion of the work force. Their place was taken by non-union low-paid workers of either sex, such as female part-time production workers, day-laborers controlled by *yakuza* labor contractors, and female office-temporaries supplied by private employment agencies. In addition, more and more tasks were being subcontracted out to smaller dependent companies employing non-unionized, low-paid male and female workers without job security. Research on the differences between the union leadership at Toyota and Nissan illustrates how management saw even the limited amount of power labor bosses like the head of the Nissan union had as a major impediment to competing with Toyota. Thus Nissan's new president set himself the task in the early 1980s to smash any vestiges of union power on the shop floor and create a company union—with complete success.[42]

Subcontracting has a long history in Japan as a way to reduce labor costs and evade expensive legal and contractual responsibilities to regular employees. It assumed even greater prominence in the late 1970s and 1980s because of the intensification of work and cost cutting in the workplace that management gurus have given such trendy names as lean production, just-in-time production, flexible production, and continuous improvement (*kaizen*), more notoriously known as management by stress. The hallmark of this trend has been the shedding of core workers accompanied by speed-up and the shedding of less profitable processes and labor by subcontracting. The prime example is the car industry, where as much as three-quarters of the parts that go into a car are produced by subcontractors.[43] Through just-in-time (JIT) manufacturing methods, the core company becomes little more than an assembly plant—highly automated and lightly staffed—at the top of a pyramid of highly dependent and less-and-less profitable sub-sub-contractors running sweatshops in order to produce parts at cut-rate prices "just on time" for delivery to the large plant where final assembly takes place. For the small sub-contractor, it is either cut costs or go out of business. Accordingly, marginal businesses started hiring illegal workers from abroad in the late 1980s and 1990s in order to meet the big business buyers' constant demands for lower and lower prices. Others, no longer profitable in Japan, have gone abroad to countries where repressive governments see to it that labor is cheaper yet and unprotected by unions or labor laws.

Since the move toward global Taylorism, a rift has opened between the core workers whose skills and allegiance were and are still crucial to the legendary productivity of big business and the "other" workers outside the enterprise. Labor's share of total income in Japan has long been lower than other industrialized countries; and it dropped further in the mid-1970s.[44] One result was a worrisome widening of the gap between the wealthy and the poor—which had not been as wide in Japan as in other countries— that has put in question Japan's reputation as a "middle-mass" society. Furthermore, the dual structure of the economy that appeared to be closing in the 1960s not only has not gone away, it has deepened and taken on troubling sexual and international dimensions.[45] The practical meaning of the global Taylorism of the 1980s for the women and men outside the umbrella of the large enterprises was harder times, justified by the elite as necessary to make the economy more competitive for export.

The LDP recovered control of the Diet in the 1980 elections; and rightist politicians began to press for rewriting the Constitution and reorienting Japanese society in conformity with "traditional" cultural values. Once again, laments about the postwar moral vacuum of youth got louder. The LDP blamed it for the new generation's wavering politics; and business complained that the younger generation of "new people" lacked the self-sacrificing work ethic so central to enterprise familism. When Nakasone Yasuhiro became prime minister in November 1982, he took it as his mission to put the political fortunes of the LDP on firm ground by moving the national center of gravity away from peace and democracy and economism and toward the emperor-centered nationalism espoused by the right wing. He envisaged the rehabilitation of the military as an offensive fighting force, raising the emperor to transcendant religious and political status, and enforcement through the education system of the moral certainties of the old, prewar order—patriarchal familism, respect for authority, consciousness of Japan's racial distinctiveness, and self-sacrifice for the nation. It seemed as if Mishima Yukio had slit his belly a decade too soon.

Taking a cue from the Thatcher-Reagan agenda, Nakasone attacked state regulation and spending on social programs by means of so-called administrative reform and began privatizing public enterprises like the national railways. Nakasone and his successors in the LDP had some success in dismantling state regulations, cutting social welfare provisions, privatizing state enterprises, and enhancing the emperor's political stature, but the goal of Constitutional revision eluded them. One significant victory was the privatization policy that fatally weakened the progressive wing of the labor movement by destroying public-sector unions, undoubtedly one of the policy's major purposes, since they were the backbone of Sōhyō and the heart of the JSP electoral base. Another was the incremental strengthening of the Japanese military, which by the early 1990s had had its mission expanded yet again, this time to include operations abroad in peace-keeping operations of the United Nations. Yet another was the government's twisting of the Equal Employment Opportunity Law that defeated its ostensible purpose of providing equity in employment and ended up providing a fig leaf for a rewriting of Japan's labor laws that further undermined the position of women in the work force.

The 1980s had begun rather well for the elite with a return both to respectable growth rates and respectable LDP votes in elections. Cost cutting and rationalization continued, and the scramble to make money seemingly fit well with the rightist politics of a postwar settling of accounts and a return to traditional values. As the decade wore on, the export-led recovery begun in 1980 merged into a real estate and investment boom in the late 1980s, the infamous "bubble economy" of feverish speculation, conspicuous consumption, and mass consumerism.

Right-wing intellectuals like Shimizu Ikutarō and Etō Jun and jingoistic politicians like Ishihara Shintarō had joined Nakasone in picking up the banner of nationalism and authoritarianism, calling variously for Japan to stand up as a sovereign state, carry out a massive military strengthening complete with nuclear weapons, cast off the impaired cultural and political structure imposed by the United States, and learn to say no to U.S. demands. Far from arousing popular enthusiasm for a rightist cultural and political renovation, their calls were drowned out in a decade of yuppie excess. In the end, the rightist ideology sat uneasily with the rampant materialism and individualism that Fordism had encouraged.

Worse yet, the LDP's share of the vote dropped at the end of the decade when the conservative elite was wracked by recurring revelations about the network of big-business, underworld, and right-wing corruption and influence peddling that underlay the bubble economy and had tarred, apparently, everyone up to and including prime ministers. Popular disillusionment with politics spread. Even though the policy of growth first had catapulted Japan into first place as a world economic power and created a consumer paradise at home, it had at the same time depleted the LDP's most potent source of appeal to Japanese voters since 1960—that it was best at producing the economic goods.

The leftist parties tried to survive the debacle of the 1980s by distancing themselves yet further from their Marxist roots and by capitalizing on public disillusionment with LDP money politics. Beyond that, they offered nothing compelling enough to stave off their seemingly terminal decline except for a brief period in the late 1980s when Doi Takako was chair of the JSP. Even as the investment speculation boom was reaching its peak, Doi momentarily got through by focusing attention on issues that mattered to many Japanese—the environment, greater participation for women, and making national politics relevant to the concerns of grass-roots groups. While the Doi vision for the JSP was not particularly socialist, it did produce a major defeat for the LDP in the upper-house elections of 1989. The JSP did less well in the 1990 lower-house elections and badly in local elections after that, whereupon Doi resigned. The right socialists who replaced her moved the party even further from identification with a socialist or even a social agenda. They even abandoned the name "socialist" in 1991, renaming the JSP the Social-Democratic Party of Japan (SDPJ). The collapse of the bubble economy that began in 1990, therefore, did not result in a renewal of the socialist left, although its social policies had momentarily touched deep concerns that had animated the social movements of the 1980s.

The 1980s saw a twofold change in the ideological context for the political compromise of peace and democracy that had accompanied Fordism, a change toward "corporate democracy." First, the familist ideology of management elaborated in the large enterprises was generalized and projected upon Japan as a whole by popularizers in the government, the media, and academia after the Tanaka cabinet fell in the mid-1970s.[46] Japanese society, it was argued by reference to Nakane Chie, Murakami Yasusuke, Ezra Vogel, and the like, had become a middle-class or new "middle-mass" consensus society based upon group values. The new middle mass was, in fact, neither new, nor middle, nor mass. It was a muddled construct that excluded only the very wealthy and the very poor from an ill-defined "middle" in which everyone from factory workers and farmers, mom and pop shop owners and doctors, to managers and engineers was lumped together. But it was no less useful to the maintenance of corporate hegemony for all that.

Second, the nationally organized opponents of corporate supremacy—the once-militant labor unions and the leftist parties—were themselves fading. By 1991, union membership had dropped below a quarter of the paid workforce, a new low, and continued heading downward. Battered by business and government attacks on the one hand, and having bought into a narrow economistic version of material prosperity on the other, the JSP/SDPJ and organized labor were only too easily seduced by the elite's offers of political and economic incorporation in the 1980s through formation of a new tripartite labor-business-government relationship. The denouement for labor would come in 1989 when the ghost of Sōhyō dissolved itself, most of its member unions joining Rengō (the National Council of Labor Unions), the conciliatory and compromising national labor front promoted by the export-industry unions and Dōmei that organized in 1987. The SDPJ would reach a similar low point in the mid-1990s with the formation of a SDPJ-headed coalition cabinet with the LDP in June 1994, perhaps foreshadowing its own dissolution and absorption by one of the parties to its right that has formed out of the LDP.

Business and government leaders viewed Rengō positively as a vehicle for bringing a unified labor movement into the circle of policy making as a junior partner. Rengō has not succeeded in bringing all of the labor movement under its umbrella and accounts for only about three-fifths of all unionized workers. Other, more militant, even radical national centers continue to exist and carry on the legacy of Sōhyō and Sanbetsu. Nonetheless, a labor policy group composed of Nikkeiren, Ministry of Labor bureaucrats, party politicians, scholars, and journalists did come into being, which in corporatist style set about forging a broad area of agreement at the top on a variety of issues.[47] In short, Nikkeiren was to represent capital, Rengō labor, and the Ministry of Labor the public interest in establishing labor policies. Once established, such policies would no longer be regarded as issues to be debated and decided upon by the public through democratic processes, but as policy decisions to be implemented from the top down by business and union executives and bureaucrats.

The vision of corporate society sprang from the actual penetration of corporate values into Japan's economic, political, social, and cultural life. By the 1980s, corporate supremacy had gone so far that the national agenda did look to be identical with the business agenda. Certainly, there were strong forces within the elite other than business that had long wanted to move the country towards a corporate order, above all the career bureaucrats at the top. No less than the imperial bureaucracy before World War II, the postwar bureaucracy has seen its primary goal to be the regulation of Japan as a well-ordered society—by means of the family register, tight central regulation of education, and intrusive local police surveillance (the police box system). In this, it parallels the intense drive of the capitalist enterprise to achieve total hegemony over its work force. The "administrative reform" pressed by the LDP was similarly infused with the premise of hierarchical control, as can be seen most clearly in proposals for reform of education and Constitutional revision. Indeed, a common drive for hierarchical control and cultural hegemony has helped weld together the business and bureaucratic leaders with the LDP into an elite.

Yet, all is not well for Toyotism,[48] the epitome in the 1980s of the intense and exploitative system of labor control that has underlain the competitive strength of the Japanese enterprise. Management by stress (*kaizen*) has itself reached the breaking point with each additional gain in productivity coming only through ever greater pressure on both blue- and white-collar workers that is putting their famed loyalty to the enterprise at risk. What the result will be—"humanization" of management, shorter working hours, the end of lifetime employment, more automation, greater reliance on cheap labor at home and abroad—is not clear. But the future of the Japanese employment system may well be decided in the workplace, not by management, as worker resistance to the attempts at total incorporation of their personal lives undermines the premises of enterprise familism.

The articles in section 5 all speak to the complex inter-relationship of capitalist economic strategies to gender, culture, politics, and ideology in the realm of everyday life. Tanaka Yuki's careful analysis of the exploitation of temporary and day laborers in the nuclear power industry gives an example of how Fordism for the few and neo-Taylorism for the many came to be practiced in the 1980s. The power companies' response to the harder economic times was to increase its already heavy reliance upon transient temporary and day laborers provided by *yakuza*-dominated labor contractors to do virtually all the dangerous and unpleasant maintenance and repair work the plants constantly need. Major reasons for this were cutting labor costs and avoiding liability for radiation-induced discases. The "gypsy" work force the contractors provide is too fragmented and transient to organize to protect itself in the present to obtain job security, better wages, health care and benefits—or to organize later on to demand compensation for radiation-induced illness.

Atsumi Reiko's article on the difficulties faced by employed married women highlights one of the most important strategies business has followed in its neo-Taylorist restructuring—discrimination against women workers to fill the business need for a flexible pool of low-paid floating labor that could be hired and fired at will. As Atsumi notes, the great majority of the millions of additional women entering the work force from 1975 onwards were married (by the mid-1980s over half of married women held jobs). Furthermore, the overwhelming majority of these women could only find part-time or temporary work in factories, offices, and service jobs like supermarket, janitorial, and cleaning work. Whether or not the feminization of the part-time workforce represents conscious business policy, patriarchal attitudes, women's preferences, or is a result of constant ideological conditioning about the primacy of the women's domestic roles, the outcome is the same—overwork. In fact, women did not passively accept their exclusion from the better jobs assigned to men. They fought for equal opportunity for women in the workplace. Although the legislative battle for an effective equal employment opportunity law was lost and women are still excluded from the secure and well-paid regular jobs available to men,[49] the issue itself is still very much alive in the 1990s.

Another result of men's absence and women having to carry a double burden has been the rapid commodification of many aspects of family and social life. All manner of things become items for sale on the market—instant foods, cleaning services, child care, wedding parties, funeral ceremonies, and, of course, personal companionship and sexual intercourse. In extreme cases, companionship and sex may virtually disappear between husband and wife, filled for the husband by male co-workers in the same enterprise "family," paid bar hostesses, and prostitutes,[50] and for the wife by neighbors, TV, and frustration or a lover.

For the elite, there is an obvious parallel between housewife and prostitute in that both fill service roles for corporate warriors. The housewife serves the enterprise in her role of wife and mother that dignifies her as essential in managing the household, raising and educating the children, taking care of the aging parents of her absent husband, and ultimately caring for the ex-warrior from retirement until his death. The hostess or prostitute (often supplied by *yakuza*) serves the enterprise as an object for the rest and recuperation seen to be essential for intensifying the solidarity among the corporate warriors within the enterprise by encouraging the belief that even while away from office they are still on enterprise duty.[51] The ideal of patriarchal familism that business incessantly preaches in fact represents the splitting of the family into two nearly separate spheres and socializes men into a world where women are objectified as either "mother" or "prostitute." Evidence of the elite's deep-seated identification of patriarchy and capitalist social relations of production[52] can nowhere be seen more clearly than in the global Taylorism of the 1980s.

The systematic mobilization of foreign workers that started with the importation of women sex-workers and quickly extended to male laborers was yet another facet of the globalization of capitalist relations of production in the 1980s. It represents the deepening of the neo-Taylorist urge towards cost cutting and intensified social control, for there can be no more vulnerable, and therefore exploitable, workforce than the *yakuza*-controlled foreign workers John Lie describes, especially those who overstay their visas or in some other way become "illegals." They are all too easy to portray in the media as being responsible for any outbreak of criminal behavior, such as robbing convenience stores or dealing in drugs, because they are highly visible as a cultural "other." Reputed to eat strange foods, dress differently, and cause trouble simply by not conforming to Japanese ways like the daily hot bath, illegal workers have captured much attention despite their small numbers. Yet all has not been bleak. Foreign workers have stood up in resistance and Japanese supporters in the 1980s and 1990s have publicized the injustice being done and provided practical help to many. As Lie points out, if the Japanese economy resumes moderate rates of growth in the 1990s, labor shortages brought on by a combination of low birth rates, exhaustion of the rural labor pool, and limitations on mobilizing women yet further will intensify pressure to bring in foreign workers in even greater numbers.

The system of peace and democracy had been badly damaged by the turn to global Taylorism from the end of the 1970s. It rested upon a political balance between parties of the left and right that produced a tacit understanding that the state would pursue the corporate agenda in economic matters, but not attempt to enforce the same style of authoritarian rule on the political structure. In the 1980s, the pursuit of administrative and electoral reform, union busting, and constitutional revision provided clear evidence that for the LDP and its bureaucratic and corporate counterparts at least, the institutions of peace and democracy were now fair game. Henceforth, the theme would be the political incorporation of Rengō as a halter-broken national center for labor into LDP politics and the use of demagogic electoral appeals to the so-called new middle mass of salaried blue- and white-collar employees lacking deep political convictions, but motivated by a cynical distrust of party politics and a fear of a descent in status. The essentially apolitical salaried middle was viewed, in short, as prime material for ideological manipulation that would play upon its yearnings for belief and economic security in an age when neither seemed possible. Of such stuff was corporate democracy to be made.

Tarnished Miracles, Rising Hopes—After the Bubble Bursts

The situation was far more complex than the theorists of corporate democracy and middle-mass society would have it. Corporate democracy did not in fact sweep all before it on a tide of complacent mass consumerism. On the contrary, the "miracle" looked badly tarnished in the mid-1990s,[53] since the bursting of the bubble economy in 1991 ushered in economic stagnation and the highest levels of unemployment since the 1950s (officially 3–4 percent, but in actuality twice that or more). Overseas production of goods in many industries increased rapidly, rising to 40–50 percent in the auto and electronics industries. At the same time, large enterprises within Japan were cutting their workforce through early retirements, transfers, and dismissals that in some firms reached 10–15 percent in 1994 alone. Nikkeiren called for accelerating the move toward "flexible employment," meaning taking on more female part-time, temporary, and dispatched workers who could easily be fired.[54] Yet, there were hopeful trends to be seen in the search for democratic ways of cooperative working and living that unite global and local concerns of ecological, feminist, labor, and political movements at the grass roots. The "other Japan" was not acquiescent, despite the demoralization of leftist intellectuals following the collapse of the Soviet Union and other nominally socialist or communist regimes.

The grass-roots movement in Zushi City analyzed in Kenneth Ruoff's article may have turned away from active involvement in the old-style national politics of the left. But they nonetheless retained their vitality and their commitment to the democratic ideal of building equitable social and economic relations. Their concerns went beyond the not-in-my-back-yard egoism so often attributed to environmentalists to encompass the pursuit of racial justice and other social goals. Nor have the elite's attempts to evade the question of war responsibility been successful, most obviously in the case of the "comfort women" discussed in Watanabe Kazuko's article. No one can miss the parallel between the elite's treatment of the "comfort women" and the sex tourism and importation of foreign women to be sex workers for the corporate world. Furthermore, the movement for redress for the "comfort women" has put the issue of fairness and justice before the public by calling into question the conservative attempt to whitewash Japan's culpability in World War II and return to the values of imperial Japan. The poems of Kurihara Sadako speak of hope, for all their anger. They are reminders that there is resistance to the elite's efforts to exalt the emperor and place full-blown military forces at the disposal of the state. The day laborers living in urban ghettoes like Sanya and Kamagasaki have been far from reconciled to their fate, though unable to do much about it. Over the past two decades they have made repeated protests and demonstrations, including a six-day "riot" in Kamagasaki in 1990 that made world news.[55]

In contrast to the decline of organized labor and the leftist parties, the multitude of groups working for specific goals, such as cooperative production and distribution of organic food, opposition to nuclear power, support of women's rights, and protection of the natural environment have deepened their influence, at times notching up some victories. Ordinary workers in enterprises of all sizes have fought for better treatment both inside and outside the framework of organized labor, often in small second unions that have exhibited extraordinary tenacity.[56] Women have gone to college and university, traveled, and taken jobs in greater numbers than ever before, some achieving careers outside the home, others chafing against the many restrictions that remain. There is talk of a de-facto "marriage strike" arising from the reluctance of many young women to commit any sooner than absolutely necessary (and perhaps never) to the restraints of life as a salaryman's wife. Business complaints about the lack of dedication of the new generation suggest the existence of a subterranean revolt against the corporate warrior ideal and the prospect of death-from-overwork (*karōshi*). It may well be that peace and democracy and Fordism have had the unintended result of legitimizing the individual search for a meaningful life. They have, without question, blunted the appeal of the right with its message of nationalism and sacrifice for nation, enterprise, and family.

The social movements may have lost the theoretical moorings they once shared with the leftist parties in Marxism, which, some would argue, has itself disintegrated as a comprehensive world view before the challenge of postmodernism. But they have not lost their compass, which even in the climate of yuppie indulgence in the 1980s and 1990s continues to point toward freedom from oppression and democratic participation. The situation is far from hopeless. The neo-nationalist nostrums proffered by Nakasone, Ishihara, and Ozawa have not been up to the task of rehabilitating the pre-Fordist past, despite the intoxicating visions of "re-Asianization,"[57] and calls coming from business and government figures in the 1990s for Japan to throw off its subordination to the West and assume its rightful place at the head of a greater Asian cultural family. Calls for sacrifice for nation, emperor, and family run up against the deep died scepticism revealed by the public indifference to Hirohito's death and a willingness to question his role in the wars of his reign.[58] The economic treadmill of constant growth in production and increased consumption for their own sake is losing its appeal. Concern over reclaiming the environment, over reconstructing community life, and over developing humane social relations quietly continues to spread. There is hope, though not certainty, that a way will be found out of the morass to which the elite's policies of economism have led.

Notes

1. The direct linking of democracy to capitalist development was put with the same kind of simplistic clarity in W.W. Rostow's *The Stages of Economic Growth* (Cambridge: Cambridge University Press, 1960).

2. Indeed, James Fallows makes a similar point in *Looking at the Sun* (New York: Random House, 1994), in which he characterizes the "Asian system" as a type of "corporatism." By this he seems to mean that economics becomes a tool of power, a means for nations to achieve "political and historical purposes" that quite consciously exclude "Western" individual freedoms and human rights (see chaps. 2–4 especially).

3. I would like to acknowledge my debt to John Price, whose critique of this piece pointed out difficulties with my treatment of the union movement, and to Paddy Tsurumi for her perceptive comments. Of course, I alone am responsible for any errors and shortcomings.

4. For a clear statement, see Samuel Huntington, *Political Order in Changing Societies* (New Haven: Yale, 1968). Chalmers Johnson is a lineal descendant of this stream.

5. Both "tradition" and "culture" must be used with the utmost care, because, in the Japanese case, they are highly selective constructions of the past deeply colored by the contemporary interests of the Japanese elite. See, for example, Peter Dale, *The Myth of Japanese Uniqueness* (New York: St. Martin's, 1986) and Ross Mouer and Yoshio Sugimoto, *Images of Japanese Society* (London: Kegan Paul International, 1986), pioneers in this subject that has attracted immense attention since as a prime topic of postmodernist analysis.

6. Craig R. Littler, *The Development of the Labour Process in Capitalist Societies: A Comparative Study of the Transformation of Work Organization in Britain, Japan, and the USA* (London: Heinemann, 1982), pp. 157–158. Littler's discussion of Taylorism is especially useful in coming to grips with its overall meaning from the workshop to the level of ideology.

7. E. P. Tsurumi, *Factory Girls: Women in the Thread Mills of Meiji Japan* (Princeton: Princeton University Press, 1990).

8. David F. Noble, *America by Design: Science, Technology, and the Rise of Corporate Capitalism* (New York: Alfred A. Knopf, 1977).

9. Quinton Hoare and G. N. Smith, eds. and trans., *Selections from the Prison Notebooks of Antonio Gramsci* (New York: International Publishers, 1971), pp. 277–318.

10. Byron Marshall, *Capitalism and Nationalism in Prewar Japan: The Ideology of the Business Elite, 1868–1941* (Stanford: Stanford University Press, 1967). Others have made this point since, but none so elegantly as Marshall. See, for example, Katō Tetsurō and Rob Steven, "Is Japanese Capitalism 'Post-Fordist?' " paper presented to the 8th New Zealand Asian Studies Association Conference, August 17–19, 1989.

11. For a more comprehensive treatment, see Joe B. Moore, *Japanese Workers and the Struggle for Power, 1945–1947* (Madison: University of Wisconsin, 1983).

12. Sanbetsu was already under attack from within the labor movement by the so-called democratization movement *(mindō)*, itself riven by left-right splits. The left wing of the mindō opposed the right wing's tactic of setting up collaborationist second unions as much as it opposed the Leninist style of some leaders and unions in the Sanbetsu. See John Price, "Valery Burati and the Formation of Sōhyō during the U.S. Occupation of Japan," *Pacific Affairs*, vol. 64, no. 2 (summer 1991), pp. 208–225.

13. Joe B. Moore, "Nikkeiren and Restoration of the Right to Manage in Postwar Japan," *Labour and Industry* 3:2–3 (June/Oct. 1990): 286–291; see also Joe B. Moore, "Purging Tōhō Cinema of the 'Two Reds': A Case Study of the Reverse Course in the Japanese Labour Movement, 1947–1948," *Canadian Journal of History*, no. 26 (Dec. 1991); and Joe B. Moore, "The Toshiba Dispute of 1949: The 'Rationalization' of Labor Relations," *Labour, Capital and Society*, vol. 23, no. 1 (Apr. 1990).

14. Kawanishi Hirosuke, *Enterprise Unionism in Japan* (London: Kegan Paul, 1992), pp. 144–174.

15. Moore, "Nikkeiren," p. 296.

16. Ibid., pp. 296–297.

17. William K. Tabb, *The Postwar Japanese System: Cultural Economy and Economic Transformation* (New York: Oxford, 1995), pp. 32–38, 288. Tabb argues that "the Japanese system replaces Taylorism and Fordism with flexible production" (p. 37). But his explanation of Fordism is simplistic in viewing it primarily as a production technique. Tabb's great debt to Chalmers Johnson's conception of "developmental-state capitalism" (p. 35) colors the entire book and, to my mind at least, is the most unsatisfactory part of what is otherwise the best all-around analysis of Japanese capitalism in English.

18. Moore, "Nikkeiren," p. 297.

19. The debate over how to characterize Japanese capitalism became intense in the

1980s and 1990s, with most arguing that the Japanese system was somehow very different either from Taylorism or Fordism because "flexible accumulation" had overcome the rigidities of the assembly lines and the trade unions of Fordist production. Two recent works—David Harvey's *The Condition of Postmodernity* (London: Basil Blackwell, 1989) p. 191f especially; and Alain Lipietz's *Towards a New Economic Order: Postfordism, Ecology and Democracy* (New York: Oxford, 1992), pp. 36–42—offer a healthy measure of scepticism regarding the extravagant claims for Japanese capitalism as a new economic system offering a way out of the looming problems of under-consumption and environmental destruction.

20. Kawanish Hirosuke, *Enterprise Unionism in Japan* (London: Kegan Paul, 1992), Part Three especially.

21. Ben Watanabe, "Difference: Union Leadership between Toyota and Nissan," unpublished paper (Sept. 1992), 11 pp.

22. Nomura Masami, "The Myth of the Toyota System," *AMPO*, vol. 25, no. 1 (1994), pp. 18–25 provides a recent look at the Toyota system in operation.

23. Totsuka Hideo, "Building Japan's Corporate Society," *AMPO*, vol. 25, no. 1 (1994), pp. 14–16.

24. Mary C. Brinton, *Gender and Work in Postwar Japan* (Berkeley: University of California, 1993), p. 26.

25. Larry S. Carney and Charlotte G. O'Kelley, in Kathryn Ward, ed., *Women Workers and Global Restructuring* (Ithaca: ILR Press, 1990), p. 127; and Brinton, p. 33.

26. Brinton, *Women and the Economic Miracle,* pp. 26–28.

27. Osawa Mari, "Corporate-Centered Society and Women's Labor in Japan Today," *U.S.-Japan Women's Journal* 3 (Sept. 1992): pp. 25–33; and Niwa Akiko, "The Formation of the Myth of Motherhood in Japan," *U.S.-Japan Women's Journal* 4 (Feb. 1993): pp. 80–81.

28. Maria Mies, *Patriarchy and Accumulation on a World Scale* (London: Zed, 1986).

29. Kobayashi Ken'ichi, "Japanese Style Labor-Management Relations and Employment and Industrial Relations in Small and Medium Enterprises," *Journal of International Economic Studies* 1 (March 1985): pp. 53–71.

30. Koji Taira, "Dialectics of Economic Growth, National Power, and Distributive Struggles," in Andrew Gordon, ed., *Postwar Japan as History* (Berkeley: University of California, 1993) pp. 178–79.

31. *Asahi Shimbun Japan Almanac 1993,* 1993 ed., s.v. "Relative Importance of Agriculture," p. 110.

32. Yoshio Sugimoto, "The Manipulative Bases of 'Consensus' in Japan," in Gavan McCormack and Yoshio Sugimoto, eds., *Democracy in Contemporary Japan* (Armonk: M.E. Sharpe, 1986), p. 66.

33. The section included here is part of a book-length work on Japanese social movements that the author, Muto Ichiyo, is preparing for publication. The editor would like to thank the author for permission to use this extract.

34. Ehara Yumiko, "Japanese Feminism in the 1970s and 1980s," *U.S.-Japan Women's Journal*, no. 4 (Feb. 1993), p. 56ff.

35. Osawa Mari, "Corporate-Centered Society and Women's Labor in Japan Today," *U.S.-Japan Women's Journal*, no. 3 (Sept. 1992), pp. 25–33 esp.

36. Takafusa Nakamura, *Lectures on Modern Japanese Economic History, 1926–1994* (Tokyo: LTCB International Library Foundation, 1994), p. 253.

37. Osawa, "Corporate-Centered Society," pp. 9–24; Carney and O'Kelly, pp. 128–129; and Nakamura, *Lectures on Modern Japanese Economic History,* p. 240.

38. Yamamoto Kiyoshi, "The 'Japanese-Style Industrial Relations' and an 'Informal' Employee Organization: A Case Study of the Ohgi-kai at T Electric," *Annals of the Institute of Social Science*, no. 32 (1990), p. 192ff. See also Totsuka Hideo, "Building Japan's Corporate Society," *AMPO*, vol. 25, no. 1 (1994), p. 13.

39. Keizai Koho Center, *Japan 1985: An International Comparison*, 1985 ed., s.v. "Japan's Exports by Commodity (1968–1984)," p. 42; Nakamura, *Lectures on Modern Japanese Economic History*, pp. 268–269, 278–279.

40. *Asahi Shimbun Japan Almanac* 1993, p. 87.

41. J.A.A. Stockwin, *Japan: Divided Politics in a Growth Economy* (2nd ed). (New York: W.W. Norton, 1982), p. 112.

42. Watanabe "Difference: Union Leadership between Toyota and Nissan."

43. Norma J. Chalmers, *Industrial Relations in Japan: The Peripheral Workforce* (London: Routledge, 1989), p. 256.

44. *Asahi Shimbun Japan Almanac 1993*, p. 86.

45. Brinton, *Women and the Economic Miracle*, pp. 133, 136; Carney and O'Kelly, "Women's Work and Women's Place in the Japanese Economic Miracle," passim.

46. Koji Taira, "Dialectics of Economic Growth, p. 181.

47. Ehud Harari, "Japanese Labor Organization and Public Policy," *Social Science Japan*, no. 6 (Feb. 1996), pp. 22–25.

48. Nomura Masami, "The End of 'Toyotism'? Recent Trends in a Japanese Automobile Company," paper presented at the Lean Workplace Conference, Centre for Research on Work and Society, Sept. 30–Oct. 3, 1993, 32 pp., see esp. pp. 13–20.

49. Joyce Gelb, "Tradition and Change in Japan," *U.S.-Japan Women's Journal*, no. 1 (Aug. 1991); and Takenaka Emiko, *U.S.-Japan Women's Journal*, no. 2 (Jan. 1992).

50. Anne Allison, *Nightwork: Sexuality, Pleasure, and Corporate Masculinity in a Tokyo Hostess Club* (Chicago: University of Chicago, 1994).

51. Ibid.

52. Osawa, "Corporate-Centered Society," pp. 30–33; Takenaka, "The Restructuring of the Femal Labor Force in Japan in the 1980s," pp. 4–11.

53. Gavan McCormack, *The Emptiness of Japanese Affluence* (Armonk: M.E. Sharpe, 1996), pp. 288–289 and chap. 2.

54. Hasegawa Minoru, "After the 'Bubble Economy': A Storm of Dismissals—Workers Becoming Vulnerable," *APWSL Japan*, vol. 6, no. 21 (Mar. 1996), pp. 2–3.

55. Edward Fowler, "Minorities in a 'Homogeneous' State: The Case of Japan," in Arif Dirlik, ed., *What Is in a Rim?: Critical Perspectives on the Pacific Region Idea* (Boulder: Westview Press, 1993), p. 225.

56. Kawanishi Hirosuke, *Enterprise Unionism in Japan* (London: Kegan Paul, 1992).

57. Laura Hein and Ellen H. Hammond, "Homing in on Asia: Identity in Contemporary Japan," *Bulletin of Concerned Asian Scholars*, vol. 27, no. 3 (July–Sept. 1995), pp. 3–17 passim.

58. Norma Field, *In the Realm of a Dying Emperor* (New York: Pantheon, 1991).

About the Contributors

Atsumi Reiko teaches cultural anthropology and social psychology in the Faculty of Letters (Behavioral Sciences) at Okayama University in Okayama, Japan.

Brett de Bary teaches Japanese literature and Japanese film at Cornell University in Ithaca, New York, U.S.A. She has published translations of modern Japanese literature and critical articles on modern Japanese literature, postmodern theory, and feminism.

John Lie teaches sociology at the University of Illinois in Urbana, Illinois, U.S.A. His publications include *Blue Dreams* (with Nancy Abelmann, 1995), *Sociology of Contemporary Japan* (1996), and *Political Economy of South Korean Development* (1997).

Richard H. Minear teaches history at the University of Massachusetts, Amherst, Massachusetts, U.S.A. He is the author of *Japanese Tradition and Western Law* (1970) and *Victors' Justice: The Tokyo War Crimes Trial* (1971) and editor and translator of Yoshida Mitsuru, *Requiem for Battleship Yamato* (1985), *Hiroshima: Three Witnesses* (1990), and Kurihara Sadako, *Black Eggs* (1994).

Joe Moore teaches history in the Department of Pacific and Asian Studies at the University of Victoria in Victoria, British Columbia, Canada. He is coeditor of *The Japan Reader,* author of *Japanese Workers and the Struggle for Power, 1945–1947,* and former managing editor of the *Bulletin of Concerned Asian Scholars.*

Muto Ichiyo teaches in the sociology department at the State University of New York in Binghamton, New York, U.S.A. An activist, he helped found the Pacific-Asia Resource Center and the English quarterly *AMPO: Japan-Asia Quarterly Review,* as well as being one of the initiators of the People's Plan for the

21st Century (PP21), an Asian-Pacific program for the formation of people's alliances for an alternative future. He has also written books on Japanese politics, social movements, and culture, including *Seijiteki sozoryoku no fukken* (Restoring political imagination).

Ohno Kazuoki is an independent journalist who lives in Tokyo, Japan, and writes about agriculture and rural development. He has served as secretary-general of the Research Council on Agricultural Problems and has worked to promote a program for Asian farmers to exchange information about farmers' movements and agricultural situations in other countries.

John Price is a research associate at the Institute of Asian Research at the University of British Columbia in Vancouver, British Columbia, Canada. He is the author of *Japan Works: Power and Paradox in Postwar Industrial Relations* (1996).

Tamae Prindle teaches Japanese language and literature at Colby College in Waterville, Maine. Her major publications include the translations *Made in Japan and Other "Business Novels"* (1989), *Labor Relations: Japanese Business Novel* (1994, by Watanabe Kazuo), and *The Dark Side of Japanese Business: Three "Industry Novels"—Silver Sanctuary, The Ibis Cage, Keiretsu* (1996, by Shimizu Ikkō).

Kenneth Ruoff is a doctoral candidate in the Department of History at Columbia University in New York, U.S.A. During the time that he prepared his chapter for this book he was a lecturer in political history in the Faculty of Law at Hokkaido University. He is completing a dissertation, "Symbol Monarchy in Japan's Postwar Democracy, 1945–1995," and he is the coauthor of a forthcoming book about Hara Kazuo's 1987 documentary *Yukiyukite shingun* (The Emperor's naked army marches on).

Rob Steven teaches political science at the University of New South Wales in Sydney, Australia. His recent publications include *Japan's New Imperialism* (1990) and *Japan and the New World Order: Global Investments, Trade, and Finance* (1996).

Christopher Stevens did graduate work in Japanese language at Cornell University in Ithaca, New York, U.S.A. He later lived in Tokyo and worked as a freelance professional translator.

Yuki Tanaka is a visiting research fellow at Australian National University in Canberra, Australia. His books include *Hidden Horrors: Japanese War Crimes in World War II* (1996), which deals mainly with war crimes committed against

Australians, and *Shiraresaru senso hanzai* (Unknown war crimes), published in 1993. His current research is mostly on the international effects of Japan's nuclear power program and the influence of the Pacific War on Australian-Japanese relations.

Brian (Daizen) Victoria teaches Japanese language and culture at the University of Auckland in Auckland, New Zealand. He is a fully ordained Soto Zen priest who lived and trained in Japan for more than fifteen years, having first gone there in 1961 as a missionary for the Methodist Church. He holds an M.S. in Buddhist Studies from the Soto Zen-affiliated Komazawa University in Tokyo and a Ph.D. from Temple University.

Watanabe Kazuko teaches U.S. literature and culture as well as human rights courses at Kyoto Sangyo University in Kyoto, Japan. Active in women's issues, particularly violence against women and women's human rights, she edited *Josei boryoku jinken* (Women, violence, and human rights) (1994) and wrote *Feminizumu shosetsu ron: joseisakka no jibun sagashi* (The theory of feminist fiction: women writers' search for self) (1993). She is currently studying nineteenth-century U.S. women writers.

Index

A

Abeggeln, James
    The Japanese Factory, 372
Abortion, 159–60
Agricultural Trade and Development Act
    (PL480), 181
Agriculture
    abandoned farmland and, 195
    Agricultural Trade and Development Act
        (PL480), 181
    capitalist control over, 193–94
    costliness of, 193
    dairy products and, 178–79
    economic growth and, 181–86
    environment and, 192–93
    farm depletion, 189–91
    farmer depletion, 195
    fruits, 177
    Fundamentals of Agricultural Law and,
        184, 185, 192
    GATT and, 178
    health and safety issues, 194–95
    mandarin oranges, 177
    modernization of, 191–92
    monoculture and, 193
    Mutual Security Act (MSA), 180–81
    postwar decline of, 370, 373, 374
    price drops and, 179
    productivity decline, 195–96
    rice, 177
    selective expansion and, 192
    self-sufficiency decline, 195–97

Agriculture *(continued)*
    and supplemental outside jobs, 192, 193
    world markets, 179–88
Akagawara no ie (Kawada Ayaka), 310
Akira Iwai, 60
Aki Shobo, 155
Anesaki Masaharu
    History of Japanese Religion, 119
Aoi-Shiba-no-Kai (Blue Law
    Association), 160
Arai Construction Company, 93
Asahi Shimbun, 54
"Asian Solidarity Forum on Militarism
    and Sexual Slavery," 313
Asian Women's Network of East Asian
    Countries, 313
Aso Tetsuo, 305–6
Atcheson, George, 36
Atsumi Reiko, essay by, 272–85

B

Baba Tsunego, 18
Bary, Brett de, essay by, 80–95
Bitter Sea, Pure Land (Ishimure Michiko,
    trans. Stevens), 374
Blue Law Association
    (Aoi-Shiba-no-Kai), 160
Boryokudan, 291
Boven, Theo van, 307
"Boy Yamanaka Kuhei, The" (Ishimure
    Michiko), 132–44
Buraku, 84